1997 Food & Wine

AN ENTIRE YEAR'S RECIPES FROM AMERICA'S FAVORITE FOOD MAGAZINE

Farfalle with Morels and Fresh Pea Sauce (p. 94)

1997 Food & Wine

AN ENTIRE YEAR'S RECIPES FROM AMERICA'S FAVORITE FOOD MAGAZINE

American Express Publishing Corporation
New York

FOOD & WINE MAGAZINE
EDITOR IN CHIEF: Dana Cowin
FOOD EDITOR: Tina Ujlaki
CREATIVE DIRECTOR: Steven Scoble

FOOD & WINE BOOKS
EDITOR IN CHIEF: Judith Hill
ART DIRECTOR: Nina Scerbo
MANAGING EDITOR: Terri Mauro
EDITORIAL ASSISTANT: Evette Manners
COPY EDITOR: Barbara A. Mateer
ART ASSISTANT: Leslie Andersen
PRODUCTION MANAGER: Yvette Williams-Braxton

VICE PRESIDENT, BOOKS AND INFORMATION SERVICES: John Stoops
MARKETING DIRECTOR: Mary V. Cooney
MARKETING / PROMOTION MANAGER: Roni Stein
OPERATIONS MANAGER: Doreen Camardi
BUSINESS MANAGER: Joanne Ragazzo

COVER PHOTO: Quentin Bacon (Curried Pumpkin Soup with a Spicy Lentil Crisp, p. 77)
BACK PHOTO: Michael McLaughlin (Ginger Star Shortcakes with Summer Berries, p. 383)

AMERICAN EXPRESS PUBLISHING CORPORATION
©1998 American Express Publishing Corporation

ISBN 0-916103-43-9 (hardcover)   ISSN 1097-1564

Published by American Express Publishing Corporation
1120 Avenue of the Americas, New York, New York 10036

Manufactured in the United States of America

contents

page 10   chapter 1 • **hors d'oeuvres**

26   chapter 2 • **first courses**

48   chapter 3 • **salads**

68   chapter 4 • **soups**

86   chapter 5 • **pasta**

110   chapter 6 • **shellfish**

128   chapter 7 • **fish**

162   chapter 8 • **chicken**

194   chapter 9 • **other birds**

212   chapter 10 • **pork veal**

234   chapter 11 • **beef lamb game**

262   chapter 12 • **other main dishes**

284   chapter 13 • **bread pizza sandwiches**

302   chapter 14 • **rice potatoes**

314   chapter 15 • **vegetables**

328   chapter 16 • **condiments dips sauces syrups**

338   chapter 17 • **cakes cookies**

358   chapter 18 • **tarts pies**

374   chapter 19 • **fruit desserts**

390   chapter 20 • **other desserts**

406   chapter 21 • **beverages**

416   index

p. 399

p. 23

Swordfish with Oregano and Lemon (p. 146)

foreword

1997

1997 will remain in my memory as the year that chefs as celebrities broke into the mainstream, from TV to best-seller lists. FOOD & WINE led the way among epicurean magazines with a multitude of stories about

our readers' favorite cooks across the country, including Jean-Georges Vongerichten from Jean Georges in New York City, Joachim Splichal from Patina in Los Angeles and Robert Del Grande from Cafe Annie in Houston. For home cooks yearning to re-create some of the complex flavors of restaurant dishes, we translated the chefs' complicated, multistep recipes into doable delights. (Who knew that you, too, could cook like Jean-Georges!) We helped readers understand how to use such unfamiliar ingredients as yuca, black Thai sticky rice and wasabi. Some of my favorite recipes from the year are Shrimp with Yarrow and Baked Lemon (p. 31), Saigon Salad (p. 67), Seared Lamb alla Romana (p. 256) and Ginger Star Shortcakes with Summer Berries (p. 383). The 1997 FOOD & WINE annual encapsulates what's new, bringing you simple explanations of great food with fresh flavors.

Dana Cowin

EDITOR IN CHIEF
FOOD & WINE MAGAZINE

Citrus Custard Tarts with Caramalized Figs (p. 369)

For your convenience, recipes that have appeared in columns or articles specifically dealing with low-fat or quick cooking have been marked:

L for low-fat   **Q** for quick

CHAPTER 1 hors d'oeuvres

Roasted-Vegetable and Fontina Tart (p. 19)

13	Skillet-Toasted Almonds
13	Potent Garlic Dip
13	Smoky Guacamole
13	Smoky Eggplant Dip
13	Green-Olive Tapenade
14	Smoked-Trout Spread
14	Chive-Spiked Smoked Salmon on Chips
14	Catalan Tomato Bread
14	Roasted-Vegetable Bruschetta
15	Grilled-Asparagus Bruschetta
16	Goat-Cheese, Tomato and Red-Onion Bruschetta
16	White-Bean and Swiss-Chard Bruschetta
17	Porcini Crostini
17	Chicken-Liver Crostini
17	Tall Tim's Texas Toasts
18	Sweet-Onion and Toasted-Walnut Rounds
18	Japanese Eel Canapés with Horseradish Crème Fraîche
19	Minted Zucchini Patties
19	Roasted-Vegetable and Fontina Tarts
21	Individual Spinach-and-Cheese Phyllo Pies
21	Three-Cheese-Stuffed Phyllo Triangles
22	Malanga Fritters
22	Sake-Glazed Sea Bass
23	Garlic Shrimp
23	Shrimp Purses
24	Smoked Shrimp
24	Smoked Chicken Breast
25	Smoked Molasses-Cured Duck Breasts
25	Smoked Italian Sausages
25	Smoked Cheese

Skillet-Toasted Almonds

Skillet-Toasted Almonds

8 SERVINGS

This addictive, lightly spiced snack is best when the nuts are freshly toasted.

- ½ pound whole blanched almonds (about 1½ cups)
- ¼ cup extra-virgin olive oil
- 1 small dried red chile
- 1 teaspoon fine sea salt

In a heavy medium skillet, combine the almonds, oil and chile. Cook over moderately low heat, stirring constantly, until the almonds are golden, about 5 minutes. Discard the chile. Using a slotted spoon, transfer the almonds to paper towels and pat dry, and then put them in a bowl and toss with the salt. Serve warm or at room temperature. –*Diana Sturgis*

Potent Garlic Dip

MAKES ABOUT 2½ CUPS

There are many versions of Greek garlic dip, some thickened with bread, others with potatoes. This version uses both—and almonds, too. It's great spread on bread or toast, and is a vibrant sauce for grilled, roasted or fried fish.

- ½ small Idaho potato, cut into 2-inch chunks
- 5 ounces stale peasant bread (about one-quarter of a large loaf), crusts removed, bread sliced 1 inch thick
- ½ cup blanched whole almonds (about 3 ounces)
- 5 large garlic cloves, pureed
- 2 tablespoons fresh lemon juice
- 2 tablespoons white-wine vinegar
- ¾ teaspoon sugar

Salt and freshly ground white pepper
- ¼ cup extra-virgin olive oil

Minced flat-leaf parsley, for garnish (optional)

1. In a small saucepan of boiling salted water, cook the potato until tender, about 15 minutes. Drain, let cool and then peel the chunks and cut them into ½-inch cubes. In a bowl, cover the bread with water and let soak until completely saturated, about 2 minutes. Transfer the bread to a plate.

2. In a food processor, pulse the almonds until very finely ground. Add the garlic, lemon juice, vinegar and sugar, season with salt and pepper and process until smooth. Lightly squeeze some of the water from the bread and add half the slices to the food processor. Puree until incorporated. The mixture should be very thick but pourable, like thick pancake batter: If it's too thick, add a bit of the water; if it's too runny, squeeze more water from the remaining bread. Add the remaining slices to the processor and puree, and then check the consistency again.

3. Add the potato and process the mixture until smooth. With the machine on, add the oil in a steady stream until incorporated. Transfer the dip to a bowl and refrigerate until chilled, about 1 hour. Season with salt and pepper, garnish with parsley and serve. –*Nicola Kotsoni*
MAKE AHEAD The dip can be refrigerated overnight, but wait to add the parsley until just before serving.

Smoky Guacamole

8 SERVINGS

The best guacamole is made with ripe avocados, which have a naturally smoky taste. For an extra hit of that charcoal flavor, use a chipotle-chile hot sauce. Serve the guacamole with tortilla chips.

- 6 large ripe avocados, halved and pitted
- 6 tablespoons fresh lemon juice
- 1 garlic clove, minced
- 1 small onion, finely chopped

Hot sauce
Salt

In a large bowl, using a fork, coarsely mash the avocados. Add the lemon juice, garlic and onion. Mix again, lifting the fork occasionally to make the guacamole fluffy. Season with hot sauce and salt. Serve at once. –*John Hopkins*

Smoky Eggplant Dip

MAKES ABOUT 4 CUPS

- 5 pounds medium eggplants
- ½ medium red onion, minced
- 2 medium garlic cloves, crushed to a paste
- 2 tablespoons fresh lemon juice, plus more if needed
- 2 tablespoons vegetable oil
- 2 tablespoons extra-virgin olive oil
- 2 teaspoons white-wine vinegar
- 1½ teaspoons sugar

Salt and freshly ground white pepper
- ¼ cup finely chopped flat-leaf parsley

Toasted peasant bread, for serving

1. Light a grill or preheat the broiler. Grill or broil the eggplants about 8 inches from the heat for about 30 minutes, turning occasionally, until charred all over and softened. Let the eggplants cool slightly, and then peel them, keeping them as intact as possible. Transfer the peeled eggplants to a colander set over a bowl, cover with plastic wrap and let drain in the refrigerator for at least 4 hours or overnight.

2. Halve the eggplants lengthwise and remove as many seeds as possible. Finely chop the eggplants so that they are nearly pureed, but with some texture. Transfer to a bowl and stir in the onion, garlic, lemon juice, vegetable and olive oils, vinegar and sugar. Refrigerate the dip for at least 1 hour or overnight. Season with salt and pepper and more lemon juice, if necessary. Stir in the parsley and serve with the toast. –*Charles Bowman*

Green-Olive Tapenade

MAKES ABOUT ¾ CUP

Serve this salty, intensely flavorful relish on toast rounds, or toss it with pasta.

- 1 cup green brine-cured olives, such as Sicilian or picholine (about 5 ounces), pitted and coarsely chopped
- 3 anchovy fillets, drained and coarsely chopped

2 tablespoons drained capers

2 tablespoons coarsely chopped flat-leaf parsley

3 tablespoons extra-virgin olive oil

2 teaspoons cognac

In a food processor, combine the olives, anchovies, capers and parsley and process to a paste. Scrape the paste into a small bowl and then stir in the oil and cognac. —*Marcia Kiesel*

MAKE AHEAD The tapenade can be refrigerated for up to two days; let return to room temperature before serving.

BELOW: **Chive-Spiked Smoked Salmon.** BOTTOM: **Ingredients for Catalan Tomato Bread.**

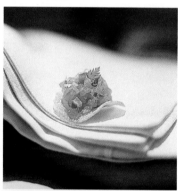

Smoked-Trout Spread

MAKES ABOUT ²/₃ CUP

Put together this buttery spread, flavored with lemon and dill, in a matter of minutes. Serve with sesame crackers, toast or bagel chips.

One 4-ounce smoked trout fillet, skin and any stray bones removed, flesh flaked

1 stick (4 ounces) unsalted butter, at room temperature

1 tablespoon chopped dill

1 teaspoon grated lemon zest

Combine all the ingredients in a food processor. Process until smooth, scraping down the sides once or twice. Transfer the mixture to a crock. —*Diana Sturgis*

MAKE AHEAD The spread can be refrigerated, covered, for up to one day.

WINE A crisp, aromatic Sauvignon Blanc: Turley's 1995 J. Fritz Sauvignon Blanc, Rochioli from California or Didier Dagueneau from France

Chive-Spiked Smoked Salmon on Chips

MAKES 30 HORS D'OEUVRES

At the Wine Center at Meadowood, a Napa Valley resort, deep-fried potato chips serve as the base for the salmon. Store-bought thick-cut potato chips save the time of deep-frying.

½ pound smoked salmon, minced

3 tablespoons finely chopped chives

1 small shallot, finely chopped

1 teaspoon extra-virgin olive oil

¼ teaspoon finely grated lemon zest

30 thick-cut potato chips

30 chervil sprigs, for garnish (optional)

In a bowl, combine the salmon, chives, shallot, oil and lemon zest. Mound about ½ tablespoon of the mixture on each chip; garnish with chervil. —*Pilar Sanchez*

WINE The combination of fish with Chardonnay is wonderful. The acid cuts through the fish's oils and the fruit accents its flavors. Try the 1992 Barnett Vineyards Chardonnay, 1994 Elkhorn Peak Winery Chardonnnay or 1995 Kent Rasmussen Winery Chardonnay.

Catalan Tomato Bread

4 SERVINGS

Pa amb tomàquet, as this appetizer is known in Spain, offers irrefutable proof that the best dishes are often the simplest. There are two ways to serve it: The first is to provide guests with garlic cloves, halved tomatoes, a cruet of oil and a bowl of salt and let them do the work. The second is for the cook to do the rubbing and drizzling.

8 large slices country-style bread, about ½ inch thick

4 garlic cloves (optional)

2 very ripe tomatoes, halved crosswise

Spanish extra-virgin olive oil

Coarse sea salt

Freshly ground pepper

1. Light a grill. When the fire is medium hot, grill the bread for 2 minutes per side, or until nicely browned and crisp.

2. Serve each diner a garlic clove and half a tomato. Have them rub their toast with the garlic, and then with the cut tomato. (The idea is to apply a thin film of tomato to the bread.) Then they can drizzle the toast with oil, sprinkle on salt and pepper and eat. —*Steven Raichlen*

BEER Choose a light-bodied Trappist ale, such as Orval from Belgium, to balance the sweet tomato flavor.

Roasted-Vegetable Bruschetta

8 SERVINGS

This earthy appetizer features a trio of roasted root vegetables (plus little red potatoes) tossed with a mustard vinaigrette. Cutting the vegetables into half-inch pieces gives the bruschetta a homey feel; you can vary the size of the pieces, but don't dice the vegetables too finely or they will lose their texture.

1 pound medium beets
1 tablespoon water
1¼ pounds medium carrots,
     cut into ½-inch pieces
1 pound turnips, trimmed and
     cut into ½-inch pieces
1 pound small red potatoes,
     cut into ½-inch pieces
¼ cup extra-virgin olive oil
Kosher salt
Freshly ground pepper
Sixteen ½-inch-thick slices of Italian
     bread
2 large garlic cloves, halved
2 tablespoons Dijon mustard
2 teaspoons fresh lemon juice
2 tablespoons coarsely chopped
     mint

1. Preheat the oven to 400°. Put the beets on a large piece of aluminum foil; sprinkle with the water. Wrap the beets in the foil and roast for about 1 hour, or until tender when pierced with a knife. Let cool slightly in the foil, peel and cut into ½-inch pieces. Leave the oven on.

2. Meanwhile, in a large bowl, combine the carrots, turnips and potatoes. Add 1 tablespoon of the oil, season with salt and pepper and toss well to coat. Spread the vegetables in an even layer on a large rimmed baking sheet. Roast, stirring occasionally, for about 45 minutes, or until tender and lightly browned.

3. Preheat the broiler. Rub the bread on both sides with the garlic halves and, using 1 tablespoon of the oil, brush one side of each bread slice. Arrange the bread, oiled-side up, on a large baking sheet and toast for about 1 minute, or until lightly browned.

4. In a large bowl, combine the remaining 2 tablespoons oil with the mustard and lemon juice and season with salt and pepper. Add the roasted beets, carrots, turnips and potatoes to the dressing and toss to coat. Season the vegetables again with salt and pepper. Top each garlic toast with a heaping ½ cup

Roasted-Vegetable Bruschetta

of the roasted vegetables and garnish with the mint. *–Rori Spinelli*

Grilled-Asparagus Bruschetta

10 SERVINGS
Savory prosciutto, mild ricotta cheese and grilled asparagus make a simple but delicious bruschetta. If you can find Teleme, a quintessential California soft cheese, so much the better.

10 medium asparagus spears,
     trimmed to 6-inch lengths
Extra-virgin olive oil, for brushing
Salt and freshly ground pepper
Ten ½-inch-thick slices cut diagonally
     from a large baguette
¾ cup fresh ricotta or
     5 ounces Teleme cheese
10 thin slices of prosciutto

1. Heat a grill pan or cast-iron skillet. Brush the asparagus with oil; season with salt and pepper. Grill over moderate heat, turning occasionally, until crisp-tender and blackened in spots, about 8 minutes. Transfer the asparagus spears to a work surface and halve them crosswise.

2. Brush the bread slices on both sides with the oil. Grill over moderate heat until golden, about 1 minute per side.

3. Spread the cheese on the toasts and cover with the prosciutto. Cross two asparagus halves on top of each bruschetta and season with pepper. Serve the bruschetta immediately. *–Reed Hearon*
MAKE AHEAD The grilled toasts and asparagus can stand separately at room temperature for up to eight hours. Rewarm the toasts before proceeding.

Goat-Cheese, Tomato and Red-Onion Bruschetta

4 SERVINGS

Assemble the bruschetta just before serving, or set out the prepared ingredients and let guests make their own.

Sixteen ½-inch-thick slices cut
    diagonally from a baguette
  8 ounces goat cheese, at room
    temperature
  3 medium tomatoes, finely chopped
  1 small red onion, minced

Toast the baguette slices to warm them. Spread each slice with 1 tablespoon of goat cheese and top with 1 tablespoon of tomato and 1 teaspoon onion. Serve immediately.   *−Georgeanne Brennan*

WINE The tanginess of goat cheese makes it a classic pairing with the tart herbaceousness of Sauvignon Blanc, and the sharpness added here by the tomatoes and the onions clinches the choice. Look for the 1996 Buena Vista or the 1995 Quivira Reserve, both from California.

White-Bean and Swiss-Chard Bruschetta

MAKES 20 HORS D'OEUVRES

Wilted Swiss chard makes an authentic topping for this truffle-scented bruschetta, but you can substitute large spinach leaves.

Twenty ¼-inch-thick slices cut
    diagonally from a baguette
  ½ cup olive oil
  1 small onion, finely chopped
  6 garlic cloves, minced
  2 cups cooked white beans, such
    as cannellini, rinsed if canned
  2 teaspoons minced thyme
Salt and freshly ground pepper
  1 pound Swiss chard, leaves only,
    coarsely chopped and rinsed but
    not dried
  1½ tablespoons white truffle oil

1. Preheat the oven to 400°. Arrange the baguette slices on a baking sheet and brush lightly on both sides with 3 tablespoons of the olive oil. Bake for about 8 minutes, or until the bread is lightly browned.

2. Heat 2 tablespoons of the olive oil in a large skillet. Add the onion and garlic and cook over low heat, stirring, until the onion softens, about 5 minutes. Add the beans and cook, stirring, until heated through, about 3 minutes. Scrape the mixture into a food processor or blender and puree until smooth. With the machine on, add 2 tablespoons of the olive oil. Transfer the bean puree to a bowl, stir in the thyme and season with salt and pepper; keep warm.

3. Wipe out the skillet and set it over moderately high heat. Add the Swiss chard and stir until wilted. Transfer the Swiss chard to a colander, let cool slightly and then squeeze out the excess liquid.

4. Heat the remaining 1 tablespoon of olive oil in the skillet. Add the Swiss chard and season with salt and pepper. Cook over moderately high heat, stirring, until heated through.

5. Spread each toast with about 1 tablespoon of the bean puree and top with some of the Swiss chard. Drizzle lightly with some of the truffle oil. Serve warm or at room temperature.   *−Maria Helm*

MAKE AHEAD The recipe can be made through Step 2 the day before. Refrigerate the bean puree overnight and rewarm before serving. Store the toasts at room temperature.

WINE A soft, toasty Champagne that is balanced by crisp acidity, such as the

Goat-Cheese, Tomato and Red-Onion Bruschetta

nonvintage Champagne de Venoge, is ideal with the earthiness of the white beans, the richness of the truffle oil and the sweetness of the onion.

Porcini Crostini

8 SERVINGS

If fresh porcini are unavailable, you can replace them with other meaty wild mushrooms.

- ½ cup olive oil
- 1 pound fresh porcini mushrooms, thinly sliced
- 2 large garlic cloves, minced
- 2 teaspoons tomato paste
- ¼ cup dry white wine
- ¼ cup water

Chopped flat-leaf parsley

Salt and freshly ground pepper

- 8 large thick slices of Tuscan bread, cut into thirds and toasted

Heat the oil in a large stainless-steel skillet. Add the mushrooms and garlic and sauté over moderately high heat until the mushrooms are beginning to brown, about 10 minutes. Meanwhile, in a small bowl, dilute the tomato paste with the wine and stir in the water. Stir the wine mixture into the mushrooms and cook until absorbed, about 2 minutes. Add parsley and season with salt and pepper. Spoon the mushrooms onto the toasts and serve at once.   *–Egi Maccioni*

Chicken-Liver Crostini

8 SERVINGS

- ¼ cup plus 2 tablespoons olive oil
- 1 cup finely chopped onion
- 1 tablespoon finely chopped sage, plus more for garnish
- 1 garlic clove, minced
- 1½ pounds chicken livers, trimmed and cut into ½-inch pieces
- 2 tablespoons dry white wine
- 1 teaspoon tomato paste dissolved in ½ cup warm water
- ¼ cup chopped capers

One 2-ounce can flat anchovy fillets, drained and minced
- 2 tablespoons unsalted butter, cut into ½-inch pieces

Salt and freshly ground pepper

Tabasco or crushed red pepper (optional)
- 8 thick slices of Tuscan bread, halved and toasted lightly

Heat the oil in a large stainless-steel skillet. When the oil is hot, add the onion, sage and garlic and cook over moderate heat, stirring occasionally, until softened, about 4 minutes. Add the chicken livers and cook for 2 minutes, stirring occasionally. Add the wine and the diluted tomato paste and simmer over high heat until the liquid has evaporated and the livers are thoroughly cooked, about 6 minutes. Remove from the heat and stir in the capers, anchovies and butter. Season with salt, pepper and Tabasco. Serve warm on the toasted bread, sprinkled with sage.   *–Egi Maccioni*

MAKE AHEAD The liver mixture can be refrigerated overnight. Bring to room temperature and then reheat gently.

Tall Tim's Texas Toasts

16 SERVINGS

This delicious appetizer combines grilled slices of home-style corn bread with piquant onion marmalade and tangy cheese.

- 1 large red bell pepper
- 1 large poblano chile

Sixteen ½-inch-thick slices of Jalapeño Corn Bread (p. 288)
- ½ pound soft mild goat cheese
- 3 tablespoons Red-Onion Marmalade (recipe follows)
- ½ cup freshly grated cotija or Parmesan cheese

1. Light a grill, preferably charcoal. Grill the red pepper and the poblano over a medium-hot fire, turning often, until charred all over. Transfer to a bowl, cover with plastic wrap and let steam for

ABOVE: **Porcini Crostini.**

TOP: **Chicken-Liver Crostini.**

5 minutes. Discard the charred skin, stems and seeds and cut the red pepper and the poblano into thin strips.

2. Grill the corn-bread slices, turning once, until nicely toasted. Spread each toast with goat cheese and top with about ½ teaspoon of the marmalade, a few red-pepper and poblano strips and ½ tablespoon of the grated cheese. Cut each toast in half diagonally and serve.

RED-ONION MARMALADE

MAKES ABOUT 1 CUP

- ¼ teaspoon cumin seeds
- ¼ teaspoon coriander seeds

4 tablespoons unsalted butter

3 medium red onions, thinly sliced

1 garlic clove, minced

1 teaspoon kosher salt

1 teaspoon freshly ground pepper

⅓ cup water

1 tablespoon currant jelly

1. In a large skillet, toast the cumin and coriander seeds over high heat, shaking the pan, until fragrant and lightly toasted, about 10 seconds. Transfer the seeds to a plate to cool, then grind in a mortar or spice grinder.

BELOW: **Japanese Eel Canapés.**
BOTTOM: **Sweet-Onion and Toasted-Walnut Rounds.**

2. Melt the butter in the skillet. Add the onions, garlic, salt and pepper and cook over moderate heat, stirring, until the onions are wilted, about 5 minutes. Reduce the heat to low and cook, stirring occasionally, until the onions are very soft and caramelized, about 15 minutes. Add the toasted spices and cook for 1 minute. Add the water and simmer until the mixture is thick and jammy, about 5 minutes. Stir in the currant jelly and let cool to room temperature.   *–Tim Keating*

MAKE AHEAD The marmalade can be refrigerated for up to five days. Return to room temperature before using.

Sweet-Onion and Toasted-Walnut Rounds

This is the perfect starter for a meal that ends with Banana Tarts with Bittersweet Chocolate Sauce (p. 370); together, they use a full recipe of Pâte Brisée.

MAKES 25 HORS D'OEUVRES

2 tablespoons olive oil

4 large onions, thinly sliced

2 teaspoons sugar

Salt and freshly ground pepper

⅓ recipe Pâte Brisée (p. 370)

25 walnut halves

1. Heat the oil in a large saucepan. Add the onions and cook over moderately low heat, stirring, until softened, about 15 minutes. Add the sugar and cook, stirring frequently, until the onions are golden, about 30 minutes longer. Season with salt and pepper and let cool to room temperature.

2. Preheat the oven to 375°. On a lightly floured surface, roll out the Pâte Brisée to a ¼-inch thickness. Using a 2-inch biscuit cutter, cut out twenty-five rounds and arrange them on a large baking sheet. Mound about 1 tablespoon of the onion mixture on each pastry round and top with a walnut half. Bake for about 30 minutes, or until the pastry is golden brown. Transfer the rounds to a large platter. Serve warm or at room temperature.   *–Maria Helm*

MAKE AHEAD The finished rounds can stand at room temperature up to four hours. Rewarm in a 400° oven.

Japanese Eel Canapés with Horseradish Crème Fraîche

MAKES 40 HORS D'OEUVRES

The eel called for in these unusual canapés is available at Japanese markets. The recipe is also delicious made with smoked salmon or smoked trout.

2 tablespoons well-drained prepared horseradish

1 cup crème fraîche

1 loaf of Gingerbread (recipe follows)

14 ounces Japanese seasoned broiled eel or ¼-inch-thick slices of smoked salmon

1½ tablespoons soy sauce

3 tablespoons melted unsalted butter

½ cup finely diced red onion

¼ cup snipped chives

1 small bunch chervil

1. In a small bowl, stir the horseradish into the crème fraîche and refrigerate for at least 20 minutes.

2. Preheat the broiler. Cut the loaf of gingerbread into twenty ¼-inch-thick slices and halve each slice. Arrange the slices on two large baking sheets and broil, one pan at a time, for about 25 seconds to crisp the gingerbread edges. Let cool.

3. Cut the fish into forty ¾-inch-wide diagonal strips. Arrange the strips on a baking sheet and brush them with the soy sauce and 1 tablespoon of the melted butter. Broil for 1 to 2 minutes, or until crisp.

4. Lightly brush the gingerbread with the remaining 2 tablespoons of butter. Top each piece with ½ teaspoon of the horseradish cream and a piece of broiled fish. Garnish with a dab of horseradish cream, a sprinkling of red onion and chives and a small chervil sprig.

GINGERBREAD

MAKES TWO 8-BY-3-INCH LOAVES

This recipe makes twice as much gingerbread as you'll need for the eel canapés, but you'll be happy to have a mild, not-too-sweet loaf around the house for snacks.

- 2 large eggs, at room temperature
- ½ cup molasses
- ½ cup brown sugar
- 6 tablespoons unsalted butter, softened
- 6 tablespoons vegetable shortening
- 2½ cups all-purpose flour
- 2 teaspoons baking soda
- ¾ teaspoon ground ginger
- ½ teaspoon ground cinnamon
- ½ teaspoon freshly grated nutmeg
- ½ teaspoon baking powder
- ¼ teaspoon ground cloves
- 1 cup boiling water

1. Preheat the oven to 350°. Grease and flour two 8-by-3-inch loaf pans. In a large bowl, beat the eggs with an electric mixer until foamy. Beat in the molasses, brown sugar, butter and shortening. Sift in all of the dry ingredients and stir with a wooden spoon until incorporated. Stir in the boiling water until the batter is smooth.

2. Pour the batter into the prepared pans. Bake for 35 to 40 minutes, or until a toothpick inserted in the center comes out clean. Let the loaves cool slightly in the pans, then turn out onto a rack to cool completely. –*Susan Regis*

MAKE AHEAD The gingerbread can be well-wrapped and refrigerated up to one week or frozen up to one month.

Minted Zucchini Patties

MAKES ABOUT 5 DOZEN

Bread crumbs and a little Parmesan cheese bind these golden zucchini cakes. They are best served warm but are still delicious at room temperature.

- 6 medium zucchini (about 3 pounds), coarsely grated
Salt
- ½ medium white onion, minced
- ½ cup freshly grated Parmesan (about 1½ ounces)
- ¼ cup all-purpose flour, plus more for coating
- ¼ cup plain dry bread crumbs
- 2 teaspoons mint
- 1 large egg, lightly beaten
Vegetable oil, for cooking

1. In a colander set over a bowl, toss the zucchini with 1 tablespoon of salt. Set a plate directly on the zucchini and weigh it down with a heavy can. Let the zucchini drain for at least 4 hours at room temperature or overnight in the refrigerator. Remove any excess liquid by squeezing handfuls of the zucchini in a kitchen towel.

2. Transfer the zucchini to a bowl and stir in the onion, Parmesan, flour, bread crumbs, mint and egg. Using slightly moistened hands, roll scant tablespoons of the batter into about sixty balls. Flatten the balls to form 1½-inch patties about ⅓ inch thick and coat them lightly with flour.

3. Heat ½ inch of vegetable oil in a large skillet until shimmering. Working in batches, fry the patties over moderately high heat, turning once, until golden and crisp, about 1½ minutes per side; lower the heat if necessary. Transfer the patties to paper towels to drain and keep warm while you cook the remaining patties. Sprinkle the patties with salt and serve. –*Charles Bowman*

Roasted-Vegetable and Fontina Tarts

8 SERVINGS

These puff-pastry tarts are best made with small purple Italian eggplants or pinkish Rosa Bianca eggplants, both of which tend to be less bitter and have fewer seeds than larger ones. With Tomatoes with Pesto Oil (p. 29) and Wilted Arugula and Prosciutto Frittata (p. 31), the tart slices make a handsome antipasti platter (see photo, p. 28).

- 3 tablespoons extra-virgin olive oil
- 1 garlic clove, minced and then mashed with the side of a knife
- ¾ pound eggplants, peeled and sliced crosswise ⅓ inch thick
Salt and freshly ground pepper
- 2 medium yellow summer squash or zucchini, sliced lengthwise ¼ inch thick
- ½ pound fresh shiitake mushrooms, stemmed
- 1 medium red bell pepper, quartered
One 9-ounce sheet puff pastry, preferably all butter
- 4 ounces Italian fontina, thinly sliced

1. Preheat the broiler and position a rack 8 inches from the heat. In a bowl, combine the oil and garlic. Brush the eggplant slices with 1½ tablespoons of the garlic oil, arrange on a broiler pan and season lightly with salt and pepper. Broil the eggplants for about 8 minutes, turning once, until tender and deep golden. Transfer to a platter to cool. Repeat the process with the summer squash, using ½ tablespoon of the garlic oil and broiling for about 6 minutes.

2. In a medium bowl, toss the shiitakes and red pepper with the remaining 1 tablespoon of garlic oil and season with salt and pepper. Arrange the red pepper, skin-side up, on the broiler pan and add the shiitakes. Broil for about 6 minutes, turning the shiitakes once, until the mushrooms are tender and golden and the red-pepper skin is charred. Add the shiitakes to the platter. Transfer the red pepper to a small bowl, cover with plastic wrap and let steam for 15 minutes. Peel and cut into thin strips. ➤

Roasted-Vegetable and Fontina Tart

3. Line a large sturdy baking sheet with parchment paper. Cut the puff-pastry sheet in half to form two 10-by-4-inch rectangles. On a lightly floured surface, roll out the pastry to form two 14-by-5-inch rectangles, about ⅛ inch thick. Set the pastry rectangles on the prepared baking sheet and refrigerate until firm.

4. Preheat the oven to 375°. Arrange the cheese on the pastry, leaving a 1-inch border. Arrange the eggplants, shiitakes and squash on the cheese and crisscross the pepper strips on top. Fold the pastry sides up and pinch the corners. Refrigerate until the pastry is firm, about 10 minutes.

5. Bake the tarts for about 40 minutes, or until they are puffed and golden and the bottoms are cooked. Let cool slightly on the baking sheet, then transfer to a rack. Cut the tarts crosswise into 2-inch slices and serve warm or at room temperature.

MAKE AHEAD The tarts can stand at room temperature for up to two hours.

Individual Spinach-and-Cheese Phyllo Pies

MAKES ABOUT 50 PIES

Packed with spinach and savory feta, these pies can also be made into triangles; follow the instructions for Three-Cheese-Stuffed Phyllo Triangles (right).

- ¼ cup plus 2 tablespoons extra-virgin olive oil
- 1 small white onion, minced
- 1 small leek, white and tender green, finely chopped
- Three 10-ounce packages thawed frozen chopped spinach, squeezed dry
- ¼ cup minced fresh dill
- ½ cup whole-milk cottage cheese
- 3 ounces feta, finely chopped
- 2 tablespoons freshly grated Parmesan
- 1 tablespoon plain dry bread crumbs

- 1 teaspoon salt
- ¼ teaspoon freshly ground white pepper
- 1 large egg, lightly beaten
- One 1-pound package phyllo dough
- 2 sticks (½ pound) unsalted butter, clarified (see box, next page)

1. Heat the oil in a large skillet. Add the onion and leek and cook over moderately high heat, stirring, until just golden, about 5 minutes. Add the spinach and dill and cook, stirring, for 2 minutes. Let cool slightly.

2. In a bowl, combine the cottage cheese, feta, Parmesan and bread crumbs. Add the spinach mixture and season with the salt and pepper. Stir in the egg.

3. Line two baking sheets with parchment paper. Stack thirteen sheets of phyllo on a work surface, short end toward you. (Keep the remaining phyllo covered with plastic wrap and a damp towel.) Cut the phyllo lengthwise into quarters, so that each sheet yields four 17-inch-long strips; keep the strips covered separately.

4. Set another sheet of phyllo on the work surface, long end toward you, and brush lightly with some of the butter. Lay one long phyllo strip along the bottom edge of the buttered phyllo and lightly butter it. Cut the phyllo into thirds the short way so that you have three 12-inch-long strips with a double thickness at the bottom. Mound a scant tablespoon of the spinach filling in the center of the bottom of each strip and shape the filling into a 1½-inch log. Fold the sides of the phyllo in, overlapping them slightly, and gently press down to seal. Brush the inside of the phyllo strip with butter and roll up tightly from the bottom to form a cigar. Set the pastry on a prepared baking sheet, seam-side down, and brush the top lightly with butter. Continue making the rolls with the remaining phyllo dough and filling.

instant meze

A meze table is a Greek buffet of appetizerlike dishes, such as Minted Zucchini Patties (p. 19), Individual Spinach-and-Cheese Phyllo Pies and Three-Cheese-Stuffed Phyllo Triangles. Meze tables are best when there's lots of variety, with contrasting textures and a range of flavors, from salty to sweet to tangy. Here are several items you can pick up at the supermarket.

Olives More than one type—perhaps classic Kalamatas and cracked green olives.

Pickled Vegetables Mild or spicy pickled peppers or pickled beets.

Marinated Peppers Green bell peppers—the usual Greek choice—or red ones.

Bread Crusty white or whole-wheat peasant loaves, a necessity for meze; or pita bread, though it's not traditional.

5. Preheat the oven to 400° and position two racks in the upper and lower thirds of the oven. Bake the pastries for about 20 minutes, or until they are golden and crisp, switching the pans halfway through baking. Let cool slightly, then serve warm. —*Charles Bowman*

MAKE AHEAD The pastries can be made through Step 4, wrapped well and frozen for up to one week.

Three-Cheese-Stuffed Phyllo Triangles

MAKES ABOUT 42 TRIANGLES

A combination of feta, Parmesan and cottage cheese makes a tasty filling for phyllo dough.

- ½ pound feta, finely chopped
- 1 cup plus 1 tablespoon whole-milk cottage cheese
- ⅓ cup freshly grated Parmesan
- ¼ cup all-purpose flour
- 2 large eggs, lightly beaten

¼ teaspoon freshly ground white pepper

One 1-pound package phyllo dough

2 sticks (½ pound) unsalted butter, clarified (see box, right)

1. In a medium bowl, combine the feta, cottage cheese and Parmesan. Stir in the flour, eggs and pepper.

2. Line two baking sheets with parchment paper. Lay one sheet of phyllo on a work surface with the long side facing you. (Keep the remaining phyllo covered with plastic wrap and a damp towel.) Brush the phyllo lightly with some of the butter; top with a second sheet and brush with more butter. Cut the pastry lengthwise into four 12-inch-long strips.

---

meze table

Classic Greek Salad (p. 57)

Black-Eyed-Pea Salad (p. 65)

Minted Zucchini Patties (p. 19)

Nicola's Stuffed
Artichokes (p. 317)

Stuffed Tomatoes with
Vegetables and Pine Nuts (p. 320)

Cool Cucumber Yogurt
Dip (p. 332)

Potent Garlic Dip (p. 13)

Smoky Eggplant Dip (p. 13)

Three-Cheese-Stuffed
Phyllo Triangles (p. 21)

Individual Spinach-and-Cheese
Phyllo Pies (p. 21)

WINE Accompany this buffet of Greek appetizers with a Greek wine. For a red, choose the 1993 Boutari Xinomavro Merlot or the 1994 Hatzimichalis Merlot; for a white, the slightly dry 1994 Boutari Kallisti, the fruitier 1994 Strofilia or the 1995 Amethystos Fumé. If you can't find Greek wines, try a Chablis and a Beaujolais from France.

Mound a scant tablespoon of the filling in the center of the end of each strip. Working with one strip at a time, fold the bottom edge up to meet the left edge and form a triangle. Fold the triangle up, then over to meet the right edge, keeping its triangular shape. Continue folding up the length of the phyllo, folding the triangle lightly. Brush the top with butter. Set the triangle on one of the baking sheets. Continue making triangles with the remaining phyllo dough and filling.

3. Preheat the oven to 400°. Position two racks in the upper and lower thirds of the oven. Bake the triangles for about 16 minutes, or until golden and crisp, switching the pans halfway through cooking. Let the triangles cool briefly and serve warm. —*Charles Bowman*

MAKE AHEAD The phyllo triangles can be wrapped well after Step 2 and frozen for up to one week.

Malanga Fritters

MAKES ABOUT 2 DOZEN

2 pounds malanga (see box, opposite page), peeled and cut into 1-inch chunks

1 cup grated Mexican cotija, Nicaraguan Chontaleño or Pecorino Romano cheese (4 ounces)

2 tablespoons all-purpose flour

Salt and freshly ground pepper

Peanut oil, for frying

1. In a large saucepan, cover the malanga with 2 inches of water and bring to a boil. Reduce the heat and simmer until tender, about 15 minutes. Drain well and let cool, then refrigerate until very cold, at least 4 hours.

2. In a food processor, combine the malanga with the cheese, flour, ½ teaspoon of salt and ¼ teaspoon of pepper. Process until smooth.

3. In a medium saucepan, heat 4 inches of peanut oil to 375°. Meanwhile, quickly form the malanga mixture into 1½-inch

---

clarified butter

Clarifying separates the butter from the milk solids, which can scorch during baking. To clarify butter, warm it over low heat just until melted, and then let stand for five minutes. Skim the solids off the top, and then pour the clear butter into a bowl. Clarified butter can be refrigerated for up to two months and frozen for up to three months.

---

balls. Working in batches, fry the balls until golden, about 3 minutes. Drain on paper towels, season with salt and pepper and serve hot. —*Michael Cordúa*

WINE 1995 Barone Fini Pinot Grigio

Sake-Glazed Sea Bass

4 SERVINGS L

2 tablespoons soy sauce

2 tablespoons mirin, or dry sherry mixed with a pinch of sugar

2 tablespoons sugar

1 tablespoon sake

1 teaspoon peanut oil

One 6-ounce sea-bass fillet with skin, cut into 4 equal pieces

4 Scallion Pancakes (recipe follows)

½ cup finely julienned carrot

½ cup finely julienned daikon

1. In a stainless-steel saucepan, cook the soy sauce, mirin, sugar and sake over low heat, stirring until the sugar dissolves.

2. Heat the oil in a medium nonstick skillet. Add the sea bass, skin-side down, and cook over high heat, turning once, until lightly browned, about 1 minute per side. Pour off any oil and add the soy-sauce glaze to the pan. Cook the fish, basting and turning, until just translucent, about 2 minutes.

3. Lay a pancake on each of four small plates; set the sea bass on top. Garnish with the carrot and daikon and serve.

SCALLION PANCAKES

MAKES 5 PANCAKES

- 2 teaspoons black sesame seeds
- ½ cup low-fat (1%) milk
- ¼ cup all-purpose flour
- 1 large egg, lightly beaten

Pinch of salt

- 2 tablespoons thinly sliced scallion
- ½ teaspoon Asian sesame oil

Vegetable-oil cooking spray

1. In a small dry skillet, toast the sesame seeds over moderate heat until fragrant, about 1 minute. Transfer the seeds to a plate to cool.

2. In a bowl, whisk the milk, flour, egg and salt until smooth. Cover and let stand at room temperature for 30 minutes. Stir in the scallion, sesame oil and sesame seeds.

3. Coat a 6- or 7-inch nonstick skillet with vegetable-oil cooking spray and warm over moderately high heat. Add 2 tablespoons of the batter and gently swirl to coat the bottom of the pan. Cook until the pancake is golden around the edges, about 45 seconds. Flip carefully and cook until set, about

malanga

Malanga (ma-LAHN-ga), a root used in Latin American cooking, has flesh that's creamy beige to pinkish violet, a texture that's crisp but slippery and a taste that's reminiscent of nuts, especially black walnuts. The roots weigh from eight ounces to two pounds and look like yams or cavemen's clubs, depending upon their size. They have thin, brown skin covered with shaggy hairs.

How to buy Select very firm, light-colored, unblemished roots. Available year-round.

How to store Keep in a cool, dry area for up to five days.

How to use Peel and cut into pieces.

30 seconds longer. Transfer the pancake to a plate and repeat with the remaining batter. —*Tylun Pang*

MAKE AHEAD The pancakes can stand at room temperature for four hours. Rewarm them over high heat.

Garlic Shrimp

8 SERVINGS

For a more casual appetizer, cook the shrimp in their shells, leaving guests the fun of peeling them; before cooking, cut each shell down the back and remove the vein with a toothpick.

- ¼ cup extra-virgin olive oil
- 5 garlic cloves, smashed
- 1 pound medium shrimp, shelled and deveined
- 1 teaspoon fine sea salt

1. In a large resealable plastic bag, combine the olive oil and garlic. Add the shrimp and let marinate at room temperature for 30 minutes, turning occasionally, or refrigerate for up to 4 hours for a stronger garlic flavor.

2. Heat a heavy broiler pan or two large heavy skillets over two burners. Add the shrimp in a single layer and cook over moderate heat until browned on the bottom and pink around the edges, about 1 minute. Quickly turn the shrimp and cook until just opaque throughout, about 1 minute more. Transfer the shrimp to a medium bowl, toss with the salt and serve. —*Diana Sturgis*

Shrimp Purses

MAKES 2 DOZEN PURSES **L**

- 1¼ pounds raw medium shrimp
- ½ cup finely chopped fresh or drained canned water chestnuts
- 3 tablespoons finely chopped cilantro
- 2 teaspoons cornstarch
- 1½ teaspoons sake or vodka
- 1½ teaspoons Asian sesame oil
- 1 teaspoon sugar
- 1¼ teaspoons salt

ABOVE: **Sake-Glazed Sea Bass.**
TOP: **Malanga Fritters.**

- ¼ teaspoon white pepper
- 48 gyoza skins or wonton wrappers
- ½ cup soy sauce
- ¼ teaspoon Asian chili-garlic paste

1. Shell and devein the shrimp, leaving the tails on twenty-four of them. Mince the rest and transfer to a bowl. Stir in the water chestnuts, cilantro, cornstarch, sake, oil, sugar, salt and pepper.

2. Lay six of the gyoza skins on a work surface. Mound a scant tablespoon of shrimp filling in the center of each. Top with a whole shrimp, allowing the tail to stick out. Brush six more gyozas lightly with water and set one, moistened-side down, on each shrimp. Press the edges gently to seal. Lightly brush the tops with water and bring the edges into the middle to form a purse, pressing down lightly. Continue with the remaining gyozas, filling and shrimp.

BELOW: Smoked Shrimp.
BOTTOM: Shrimp Purses.

3. Arrange the purses in a steamer basket, seam-side down. Set the basket in a pot over 1 inch of boiling water, cover and steam until the purses feel firm, 8 to 10 minutes.

4. Meanwhile, in a small bowl, combine the soy sauce and chili-garlic paste. Transfer the purses to a platter and serve with the sauce. —*Tylun Pang*

Smoked Shrimp

4 SERVINGS

One bite of these shrimp and a gulp of vodka will transport you to Scandinavia.

  2 teaspoons sugar
  2 teaspoons caraway seeds
  1 teaspoon salt
  1 cup water
  ¾ pound large shrimp, shelled and deveined
  5 fresh red chile peppers (optional)

Light Tea-Smoking Mixture
  (opposite page)
Spicy Rémoulade Sauce (recipe follows)
  or sweet-and-hot mustard

1. In a large bowl, combine the sugar, seeds and salt with 1 cup of water. Stir to dissolve the sugar. Add the shrimp, cover and refrigerate for 30 minutes; drain.

2. Add the chiles, if using, to the tea-smoking mixture. Smoke the shrimp according to the Basic Wok-Smoking Method (opposite page) until they are just cooked through and have a burnished look, 7 to 8 minutes. Serve with the rémoulade sauce.

SPICY RÉMOULADE SAUCE

MAKES ABOUT ½ CUP

  ½ cup mayonnaise
  2 tablespoons chopped pickled gherkins
  2 tablespoons chopped onion
  2 teaspoons fresh lemon juice
  1 teaspoon mustard, preferably Creole
  ½ teaspoon finely grated lemon zest
Salt and freshly ground pepper
Hot-pepper sauce, to taste

In a small bowl, combine all of the ingredients and serve. —*Marcia Kiesel*

MAKE AHEAD The sauce can be refrigerated, covered, for up to three days.

Smoked Chicken Breast

4 TO 6 SERVINGS

  1 tablespoon light brown sugar
  1 teaspoon salt
Two 10-ounce whole boneless chicken breasts with skin
Strong Tea-Smoking Mixture (opposite page)
Spicy Rémoulade Sauce (above) or sweet-and-hot mustard, for serving

1. In a small bowl, combine the brown sugar and salt. Put the chicken breasts in a large shallow dish and rub them on both sides with the brown-sugar mixture. Cover and refrigerate overnight.

wok smoking

I use two smoking mixtures. Quick-burning yet fragrant, the light mixture gives a smoky flavor to ingredients that don't need to be cooked through. The strong mixture, which lasts up to thirty minutes, smokes and cooks foods. Make the appropriate mixture and then proceed with the Basic Wok-Smoking Method.

Light Tea-Smoking Mixture: Combine one-third cup long-grain rice, two tablespoons loose black tea and two tablespoons light brown sugar.

Strong Tea-Smoking Mixture: Combine one-half cup long-grain rice, a quarter cup of loose black tea and three tablespoons light brown sugar.

Basic Wok-Smoking Method: Line the inside and the lid of a twelve- to fourteen-inch wok with aluminum foil, allowing about four inches of overhang. Put the smoking mixture in the bottom of the wok. Set a ten-inch cake rack

Line a wok, ABOVE, with foil and add the tea-smoking mixture, RIGHT.

about three inches above the smoking mixture, pinching the foil around the rack if necessary to secure it. Set the wok over moderate heat, on a wok ring if using a gas stove, until thin streams of smoke begin to rise, eight to ten minutes. Arrange the food to be smoked in a single layer on the rack; quickly cover with the

lid. Wearing oven mitts, crimp the foil all around the lid to completely seal the wok. Keep the burner on moderate heat; smoke the food according to the instructions in the recipe. *–Marcia Kiesel*

---

2. Smoke the chicken with the tea-smoking mixture according to the Basic Wok-Smoking Method (above) until it is golden brown and just cooked through, about 30 minutes. Let rest for 5 minutes before slicing. Serve warm or cold, with the rémoulade sauce. *–Marcia Kiesel*

Smoked Molasses-Cured Duck Breasts

4 TO 6 SERVINGS

- 2 tablespoons unsulphured molasses
- 2 teaspoons Dijon mustard
- 1 teaspoon salt
- ½ teaspoon freshly ground pepper
- 4 small skinless duck-breast halves (about 5 ounces each)

Strong Tea-Smoking Mixture (above)

ı. In a large shallow dish, combine the molasses, mustard, salt and pepper. Add the duck breasts and coat them all

over with the mixture. Cover the duck breasts and refrigerate overnight.

2. Smoke the duck breasts with the tea-smoking mixture according to the Basic Wok-Smoking Method (above) until they are medium rare, about 15 minutes. Let the duck breasts rest for about 5 minutes before slicing. Serve warm or cold. *–Marcia Kiesel*

Smoked Italian Sausages

4 TO 6 SERVINGS

- 1 pound sweet or hot Italian sausages, pricked with a fork

Strong Tea-Smoking Mixture (above)

Slices of crusty bread, for serving

Pickles, for serving

Sweet-and-hot mustard, for serving

In a large saucepan, cover the sausages with cold water and bring to a boil over high heat; boil the sausages 5 minutes and drain. Smoke with the tea-smoking mixture according to the Basic Wok-

Smoking Method (above) over moderately low heat for 20 minutes. Serve sliced, warm or cold, with the bread, pickles and mustard. *–Marcia Kiesel*

Smoked Cheese

4 TO 6 SERVINGS

- ½ pound soft cheese, such as Italian fontina, Bel Paese or Bulgarian feta, or firm cheese, such as cheddar or Monterey jack

Light Tea-Smoking Mixture (above)

Toasted baguette slices or crackers, for serving

Place the cheese in a shallow heatproof dish small enough to hold it snugly; smoke with the tea-smoking mixture according to the Basic Wok-Smoking Method (above), 8 to 10 minutes for soft cheeses, 12 to 15 minutes for firm. The cheese should be very soft to almost completely melted. Serve warm, still in the dish, with the toasts or crackers. *–Marcia Kiesel*

CHAPTER 2 first courses

Bay Scallops in Wood-Sorrel Butter Sauce (p. 36)

29 Tomatoes with Pesto Oil

29 Chilled Leek Terrine with Caviar

30 Fried Yuca Turnovers with Black Beans and Chorizo

30 Savory Eggplant and Dill Frittata

31 Wilted Arugula and Prosciutto Frittata

31 Shrimp and Avocado in Mustard Vinaigrette

31 Shrimp with Yarrow and Baked Lemon

32 Green Parsley Risotto with Sautéed Shrimp

32 Shrimp in Rich Curried Pea Broth

34 Crepas Cariocas

34 Dilled Shrimp Vol-au-Vents

36 Bay Scallops in Wood-Sorrel Butter Sauce

36 Potato-Chip Tower with Scallops and Caviar

38 Seared Sea Scallops

39 Soft-Shell Crabs with Nasturtiums

39 Bambou Crab Cakes

40 Crab Ravioli with Shallot Cream

42 Lobster Salad with Curried Vinaigrette

42 Lobster with Nutmeg Vinaigrette and Chestnut Puree

42 Garlicky Steamer Clams in Ale

43 Clams à la Marinière

43 Jicama Cannelloni with Snapper Seviche

43 Hot-Smoked Salmon with Green-Apple Slaw

44 Sweet Corn Pancakes with Smoked Salmon

45 Cured Salmon with Peppercorns

45 Salmon with Ginger and Lime

45 Spicy Tuna Tartare

47 Pan-Flashed Ahi

47 Saigon Wings

FROM LEFT: Tomatoes with Pesto Oil, Roasted-Vegetable and Fontina Tarts (p. 19) and Wilted Arugula and Prosciutto Frittata (p. 31).

Tomatoes with Pesto Oil

8 SERVINGS

Ripe tomatoes drizzled with fragrant basil oil and topped with crisp Parmesan-accented bread crumbs make a simple and refreshing first course.

½ cup light olive oil

¾ cup coarse stale bread crumbs

1½ tablespoons freshly grated Parmesan

Salt and freshly ground pepper

⅓ cup packed basil leaves

1 pound medium tomatoes, sliced crosswise ⅓ inch thick

I. Heat 1 tablespoon of the oil in a medium skillet. Add the bread crumbs and cook over moderately high heat, stirring, until crisp and deep golden, about 5 minutes. Immediately transfer the bread crumbs to a plate and stir in the cheese. Season with salt and pepper.

2. In a blender or mini-processor, puree the basil leaves with the remaining 7 tablespoons of oil and a pinch of salt until smooth.

3. Arrange the tomatoes on a platter or eight plates. Drizzle the pesto oil over and around the tomatoes and sprinkle with the Parmesan crumbs.

MAKE AHEAD The Parmesan crumbs and pesto oil can be refrigerated separately for up to one day. Let return to room temperature before serving.

Chilled Leek Terrine with Caviar

8 SERVINGS

Assembling this cool-looking first course is easy, but slicing the terrine can be tricky; be sure to hold it firmly while gently sawing with a serrated knife.

6 pounds medium leeks, white and tender green trimmed to 5-inch lengths, halved lengthwise

Salt and freshly ground white pepper

½ cup crème fraîche or sour cream

Fresh lemon juice, to taste

About 2 ounces caviar

Chilled Leek Terrine with Caviar

I. Bring a large pot of salted water to a boil. Tie the leeks together with kitchen string, using six halves per bundle. Add the bundles to the boiling water; cook until just tender throughout, 10 to 15 minutes. Drain and transfer to a large bowl of ice water to cool completely. Drain again and pat dry; cut the strings.

2. Line an 8-by-4-inch loaf pan with plastic wrap, allowing several inches of overhang on each side. Arrange the leeks in the pan, cut-side up, overlapping slightly; season each layer with salt and pepper. Cover with the overhanging plastic wrap. Set another small loaf pan on top; weigh it down with cans. Refrigerate overnight.

3. In a bowl, mix the crème fraîche with the lemon juice until smooth. Spoon the mixture onto eight small plates and mound a little caviar alongside. Uncover the leek terrine and pour off any liquid. Carefully turn the terrine out onto a cutting board and discard the plastic wrap. Using a serrated knife, cut the terrine into 1-inch slices. Set each slice on a plate and serve.   *—Pilar Sanchez*

MAKE AHEAD The terrine can be refrigerated up to two days before slicing.

WINE 1995 Elkhorn Peak Winery Pinot Noir. Its fruit is a gentle counterpart to the vegetable character of the leeks; the wine brightens the flavor of the terrine.

Fried Yuca Turnovers with Black Beans and Chorizo

4 TO 6 SERVINGS

Yuca, a root used in Latin American cooking, is boiled and mixed with cheese to form the "dough" for these turnovers.

SAUCE

- 2 cups mayonnaise
- ½ cup finely chopped cilantro
- 3 tablespoons fresh lime juice
- 1 small jalapeño pepper, minced
- 1 garlic clove, minced
- ¼ cup warm water

Salt and freshly ground pepper

BELOW AND BOTTOM: Fried Yuca Turnovers with Black Beans and Chorizo

TURNOVERS

- 2 pounds fresh yuca (see box, p. 35), peeled and cut into 1-inch chunks, or 1½ pounds frozen yuca
- 2 cups cooked black beans, rinsed and drained if canned
- 2 cups grated Mexican cotija, Nicaraguan Chontaleño or Pecorino Romano cheese (½ pound)
- 4 ounces Spanish chorizo, casings removed, sausage finely chopped
- 2 medium onions, finely chopped
- 1 teaspoon crushed red pepper

Salt

- 1 teaspoon freshly ground black pepper

Peanut oil, for frying

1. MAKE THE SAUCE: Combine the mayonnaise, cilantro, lime juice, jalapeño and garlic in a blender. Add the water and blend until smooth. Season with salt and pepper and refrigerate.

2. MAKE THE TURNOVERS: In a large saucepan, cover the yuca with 2 inches of water and bring to a boil. Simmer until tender, 15 to 20 minutes. Drain well and let cool, then refrigerate until cold, at least 4 hours.

3. In a medium bowl, mash the black beans to a fine paste. Mix in 1 cup of the cheese and the chorizo, onions and red pepper. Transfer the mixture to a medium saucepan; cook over moderately high heat, stirring often, until thick and smooth, 8 to 10 minutes. Let cool.

4. In a food processor, combine the cold yuca with the remaining 1 cup of cheese; season with salt and the black pepper and process until smooth. Divide the yuca dough into twelve equal pieces. Line a tortilla press with waxed paper and flatten each piece of yuca dough into a ¼-inch-thick round. Alternatively, on a lightly floured surface, roll each piece of the yuca dough into a 4-inch round.

5. Place 1½ tablespoons of the bean filling in the center of each round. Fold the dough to form half-moons; pinch the edges to seal.

6. In a medium saucepan, heat 4 inches of peanut oil to 375°. Fry the turnovers in batches until just beginning to turn golden, about 3 minutes per side. Serve the turnovers hot, with the sauce on the side. —*Michael Cordúa*

WINE 1994 Bodegas Montecillio Viña Cumbrero Blanco

Savory Eggplant and Dill Frittata

12 SERVINGS

- 2 small eggplants (about 7 ounces each), peeled and cut into ¼-inch dice

Kosher salt

- ¼ cup olive oil
- 2 medium onions, thinly sliced
- 1 dozen large eggs

Freshly ground pepper

- 2 tablespoons coarsely chopped dill

1. Preheat the oven to 350°. Put the eggplants in a colander and toss with 1 teaspoon of kosher salt. Place a small plate on top of the eggplants and weight it down with canned goods. Set the colander in the sink until the eggplants release their liquid, about 30 minutes. Gently squeeze the eggplants to remove additional moisture.

2. In a large ovenproof skillet, preferably nonstick, heat 2 tablespoons of the oil. Add half the eggplant and cook over moderately high heat, stirring occasionally, until browned, about 4 minutes. Transfer the eggplant to a large plate and repeat with the remaining oil and eggplant. Reduce the heat to low. Add the onions; cook until tender, about 6 minutes. Return the eggplant to the skillet.

3. Meanwhile, in a large bowl, whisk the eggs with a pinch each of salt and pepper. Add the eggs to the eggplant-and-onion mixture in the skillet and increase the heat to moderate. Use a spatula to pull the cooked egg into the center, allowing the uncooked egg to fill the bottom of the skillet. When the frittata is mostly set, gently stir in the dill. Put the skillet in the oven and cook the frittata until it is just set, about 5 minutes.

4. Shake the skillet to loosen the frittata and run a spatula around it if necessary. Carefully slide the frittata onto a platter and let cool slightly. Cut the frittata into twelve wedges and serve warm or at room temperature.   *–Peter Hoffman*

MAKE AHEAD The frittata can be made up to two hours ahead. Cover but do not refrigerate.

Wilted Arugula and Prosciutto Frittata

8 SERVINGS

Salty prosciutto and peppery arugula are the key ingredients in this light frittata. If your nonstick skillet has a plastic handle, wrap it in aluminum foil before broiling.

- 6 large eggs, lightly beaten
- 2 tablespoons freshly grated Parmesan

Salt and freshly ground pepper

- 2 tablespoons extra-virgin olive oil

One ¼-inch-thick slice of prosciutto (about 2 ounces), cut into ¼-inch dice

- 1 large bunch of arugula, stems trimmed, leaves sliced ½ inch thick

1. Preheat the broiler and position a rack near the heat. In a bowl, gently beat the eggs with the Parmesan and a generous pinch each of salt and pepper.

2. Heat 1 tablespoon of the oil in a large ovenproof nonstick skillet. Add the prosciutto and cook over moderately high heat, stirring frequently, until it is barely browned, 1 to 2 minutes. Add the arugula and cook, stirring, until wilted, about 1 minute. Drizzle the remaining 1 tablespoon of oil around the outer edge of

foraging facts

As foraging for plants like the wild yarrow in Shrimp with Yarrow and Baked Lemon becomes more popular, ethnobotany classes are cropping up all over the country. For foraging activities in your area, send a SASE to: Dr. Suzan Donleavy-Johnston, Coordinator of Botany Education, Department of Continuing Education, The New York Botanical Garden, Bronx, NY 10458.

When cooking with wild plants–as with any food–keep in mind that some people can eat anything, but others can't. "Even wild foods and herbs that are perfectly safe for most people can cause unpredicted allergic reactions," says Donleavy-Johnston.

the skillet. Pour the eggs into the skillet; stir to distribute the prosciutto and arugula evenly. Cook without stirring until the edges and bottom are set but the top is still soft and runny, about 6 minutes.

3. Place the frittata under the broiler. Cook for about 1 minute, or just until golden and set. Invert the frittata onto a cutting board, cut into eight wedges and serve warm or at room temperature.

Shrimp and Avocado in Mustard Vinaigrette

2 SERVINGS **Q**

- 1½ tablespoons red-wine vinegar
- 1½ tablespoons Dijon mustard
- ¼ cup olive oil

Salt and freshly ground pepper

- ½ pound medium shrimp, shelled and deveined
- 1 ripe Hass avocado, halved lengthwise, pitted and peeled
- 2 tablespoons diced plum tomato
- 2 tablespoons minced chives

1. In a small bowl, whisk together the vinegar and mustard. Slowly whisk in the oil. Season with salt and pepper.

Shrimp and Avocado in Mustard Vinaigrette

2. In a small saucepan of boiling water, cook the shrimp until just opaque, about 1 minute. Drain.

3. Set the avocado halves on plates and spoon in the shrimp. Drizzle with the dressing. Garnish with the diced tomato and the chives.   *–Amy Farges*

Shrimp with Yarrow and Baked Lemon

6 SERVINGS

These butterflied shrimp look attractive when cooked, and they taste sublime. Baking the lemon is a nice technique that sweetens as well as warms it. You can buy dried yarrow in health-food stores, but the flavor is very strong; stick with fresh yarrow, or substitute dill or bronze fennel leaves.

- 3 tablespoons extra-virgin olive oil
- 1 tablespoon minced garlic
- 3 lemons
- 6 tablespoons sugar
- 2 tablespoons chopped yarrow leaves, plus a few sprigs for garnish
- 24 large shrimp–shelled, deveined and cut almost in half lengthwise down the back

Salt

Cayenne pepper

1. Preheat the oven to 450° and light the grill, if you're using one. In a small bowl, stir together the oil and garlic. ➤

2. Cut the pointed ends from the lemons so they'll sit flat; halve crosswise. Set flesh-side up in a glass or ceramic baking dish and spoon 1 tablespoon of the sugar on each half. Bake for 10 to 15

BELOW: **Shrimp in Rich Curried Pea Broth.** BOTTOM: **Shrimp with Yarrow and Baked Lemon.**

minutes, or until the sugar is melted and the pulp soft. Preheat the broiler, if using.
3. Sprinkle the chopped yarrow inside the shrimp and pinch closed. Brush with the garlic oil and season with salt and cayenne. Grill or broil 2 to 3 minutes per side, or until opaque. Squeeze some of the lemon juice over the shrimp; garnish with the yarrow sprigs. Serve with the lemons. *–Jean-Georges Vongerichten*
WINE 1995 Andrew Murray Roussanne. Its exotic aromas of peach, apricot and jasmine along with its lush texture should complement the layers of flavors here.

Green Parsley Risotto with Sautéed Shrimp

8 SERVINGS

1 large bunch flat-leaf parsley (about 2 ounces), tough stems removed

2 tablespoons ice water
Salt and freshly ground pepper
About 7 cups chicken stock or canned low-sodium broth
¼ cup plus 2 tablespoons olive oil
2 cups arborio rice (about 14 ounces)
1½ pounds large shrimp, shelled and deveined
1 cup freshly grated Parmesan (about 3 ounces)

1. In a saucepan of boiling salted water, cook the parsley for 10 seconds. Drain and refresh in a bowl of ice water; drain again. Transfer to a blender, add the 2 tablespoons ice water and season with salt and pepper. Process until smooth.
2. In a saucepan, bring the stock to a boil. In another saucepan, heat the ¼ cup oil. Add the rice and cook over moderately high heat, stirring, until translucent, about 5 minutes. Add 1 cup of the stock and stir until almost absorbed. Continue adding the stock, 1 cup at a time, stirring constantly until the liquid is absorbed before adding more. The rice is done when it's tender and creamy but still firm to the bite, 20 to 25 minutes. Season with salt and pepper; keep warm.
3. Heat the remaining 2 tablespoons of oil in a large skillet. Add the shrimp, season with salt and pepper and cook over moderate heat, stirring often, until pink and firm to the touch, about 5 minutes.
4. Add the Parmesan to the risotto and then stir in the parsley puree. Spoon the risotto into bowls and garnish with the shrimp. *–Pilar Sanchez*
WINE 1995 Kent Rasmussen Winery Pinot Noir. The intense black-cherry and raspberry flavors of this earthy Pinot play nicely off the parsley in the risotto.

Shrimp in Rich Curried Pea Broth

4 SERVINGS

6 thin asparagus stalks, cut into 1-inch pieces
1 small zucchini, cut into ½-inch dice

Green Parsley Risotto with Sautéed Shrimp

1 small yellow summer squash,
cut into ½-inch dice

1 cup fresh or thawed frozen peas

12 pearl onions, peeled

2 medium purple or Yukon Gold
potatoes, peeled and cut into
½-inch dice

1 small carrot, cut into ¼-inch dice

4 tablespoons unsalted butter

Salt

¾ cup water

Freshly ground pepper

2 slices lean bacon, cut into ½-inch
dice

1 medium leek, white and tender
green, minced

1 garlic clove, minced

¾ teaspoon curry powder

2 cups chicken stock or canned
low-sodium broth

⅔ cup heavy cream

1 tablespoon olive oil

1 pound medium shrimp, shelled
and deveined

1. In a medium saucepan of boiling salted water, cook the asparagus until just
tender, about 3 minutes. Using a slotted
spoon, transfer the asparagus to a colander, rinse with cold water and drain.
Put the asparagus in a bowl. Add the

33

zucchini and yellow squash to the boiling water, cook until just tender, then transfer to the colander to drain; add to the asparagus. Add ½ cup of the peas to the boiling water and cook until tender. Drain and add to the other vegetables.

2. In a large skillet, combine the onions, potatoes and carrot. Add 1 tablespoon of the butter, ¼ teaspoon of salt and ½ cup of the water. Bring to a simmer over moderate heat; cook until the vegetables are tender and glazed, about 10 minutes. Add the blanched vegetables and season with salt and pepper.

3. Melt 2 tablespoons of the butter in a medium saucepan. Add the bacon and cook over moderately low heat until most of the fat is rendered, about 4 minutes. Stir in the leek and garlic. Cook until wilted, about 2 minutes. Add the remaining ½ cup of peas and the curry powder. Cook, stirring, until fragrant, about 1 minute. Add the stock and bring to a simmer. Pour in the heavy cream; simmer over low heat until slightly reduced and flavorful, about 20 minutes.

4. Pour the mixture into a blender; puree until smooth. Pass through a fine sieve and return to the saucepan. Simmer over low heat until reduced to 2½ cups, about 5 minutes; the broth should have the consistency of light cream. Season with salt and pepper and keep warm.

5. Heat the oil in a large skillet until shimmering. Add the shrimp, season with salt and pepper and cook over moderate heat, stirring, until pink, about 3 minutes. Add the reserved vegetables and the remaining ¼ cup of water and cook until warmed through. Remove the skillet from the heat and stir in the remaining 1 tablespoon of butter. Season with salt and pepper.

6. Mound the shrimp and the vegetables in four shallow bowls. Ladle the broth into the bowls; serve at once. –*Tony Clark*
WINE 1995 Robert Mondavi Fumé Blanc from California

Crepas Cariocas
6 SERVINGS

Two Latin American staples, boniato and plantain, fill these unusual crêpes. They're named for the pretty girls in Rio de Janeiro.

CRÊPES
- 3 large eggs
- 2 tablespoons all-purpose flour
- 1 tablespoon cold water
- 1 tablespoon milk

Pinch of salt

FILLING
- 1 boniato (1 pound), scrubbed and patted dry (see box, opposite page)
- 1 ripe medium plantain
- 1 tablespoon heavy cream

SAUCE
- 2 tablespoons unsalted butter
- 1 tablespoon minced garlic
- ¼ cup sherry
- 1 chicken bouillon cube
- 2 cups heavy cream
- 18 small shrimp (about ¾ pound), shelled and deveined
- 3 canned hearts of palm, drained and sliced ½ inch thick on the diagonal

1. MAKE THE CRÊPES: In a medium bowl, whisk together the eggs, flour, water, milk and salt. Heat a 7-inch non-stick crêpe pan or skillet over moderately high heat. Pour 2 tablespoons of the batter into the pan, tilting the pan quickly to coat the bottom evenly. Cook the crêpe until lightly browned on the bottom, about 45 seconds. Turn the crêpe and cook until lightly browned on the other side, about 30 seconds. Transfer the crêpe to a plate and cover it with a sheet of waxed paper. Continue with the remaining crêpe batter, layering the crêpes between sheets of waxed paper.

2. MAKE THE FILLING: Preheat the oven to 400°. Place the boniato in a baking dish and bake for about 30 minutes, or until it is brown and tender. Let

the boniato cool slightly. Turn the oven down to 350°.

3. Meanwhile, bring a large pot of water to a boil. Trim ½ inch from each end of the plantain and plunge it into the boiling water. Boil the plantain until tender when pierced at the thickest part, 5 to 7 minutes. Drain well and let the plantain cool. Peel the plantain and cut it into 1-inch pieces.

4. Halve the boniato and scoop out the flesh. In a food processor, combine the plantain and boniato with the cream. Puree until smooth.

5. MAKE THE SAUCE: In a saucepan, melt the butter over moderately high heat. Add the garlic and cook, stirring often, until softened. Add the sherry and bouillon cube and simmer until reduced by half. Add the cream and boil until thickened and reduced to 1 cup. Remove from the heat and add the shrimp and the hearts of palm. Cover and set aside for 10 minutes.

6. Mound 2 tablespoons of the filling in the center of each crêpe and carefully roll into a cylinder. Arrange the filled crêpes in a shallow baking dish and sprinkle them with 2 tablespoons of water. Cover with aluminum foil and bake for about 20 minutes, or until the crêpes are heated through. Rewarm the sauce. Set one crêpe on each plate and spoon the sauce on top, making sure to distribute the shrimp and the hearts of palm evenly.   –*Michael Cordúa*
WINE 1995 Clos Du Val Chardonnay

Dilled Shrimp Vol-au-Vents
12 SERVINGS

A vol-au-vent, the classic French puff-pastry shell, can feature a variety of fillings; here individual shells hold shrimp in a creamy dill sauce.

- 3 cups fish stock or bottled clam juice

Small pinch of saffron threads
- 2 sticks (½ pound) unsalted butter

yuca

Also known as cassava or manioc, yuca (YOO-ka) is fibrous, with dense bone-white flesh; the processed form is tapioca. The roots measure from one-and-a-half to four inches in diameter, weigh from eight ounces to five pounds and look like long sweet potatoes with thick woody brown skin. They're usually sold waxed.

How to buy Look for firm unblemished roots. Available year-round, fresh and frozen.

How to store In the refrigerator for up to four days, but best used soon after purchase.

How to use To peel, cut into large pieces, slit lengthwise, insert a paring knife beneath the bark and underlayer, and unwrap. Halve lengthwise and remove the fibrous core.

Jicama, LEFT; boniato, TOP; yuca, RIGHT; and malanga, CENTER.

¼ cup plus 2 tablespoons
   all-purpose flour
1 cup heavy cream
Salt and freshly ground pepper
Twelve 3-inch frozen puff-pastry
   shells
1 large egg, lightly beaten with
   1 teaspoon of water
2 garlic cloves, crushed
¼ cup minced dill, plus dill sprigs
¾ cup dry white wine
1½ pounds medium shrimp, shelled
   and deveined

1. In a medium saucepan, bring the fish stock to a boil over moderately high heat. Remove from the heat and stir in the saffron. Cover and set aside for 10 minutes.

2. Melt 1 stick of the butter in another medium saucepan. Add the flour and whisk over moderately high heat until smooth and bubbling, about 3 minutes. Add the fish-stock mixture and boil, whisking often, until thickened, 3 to 5 minutes. Stir in the cream, season the sauce with salt and pepper and remove from the heat.

3. Preheat the oven to 400°. Arrange the pastry shells on two baking sheets and brush the tops with the beaten egg. Bake for about 25 minutes, or until the pastry shells are golden brown and cooked through. Scoop out and discard the doughy center from the shells. Turn the oven off and keep the pastry shells warm inside.

4. In a large skillet, melt the remaining stick of butter. Add the garlic and the minced dill and cook over moderately high heat, stirring often, until fragrant, about 2 minutes. Add the wine and boil for 6 minutes; discard the garlic. Add the shrimp and cook, turning often, until pink and firm, about 5 minutes. ➤

boniato

A tropical sweet potato also known as batata, boniato (bou-nee-AH-tou) has a chestnutlike flavor and dry, white flesh. It's not as sweet as a sweet potato.

How to buy Pick hard tubers with pink, purplish, reddish or cream-colored skin with no soft spots. Ignore uneven color and rough skin. Though available year-round, boniato is scarce during February and March.

How to store Keep at cool room temperature for a few days.

How to use Cook with the skin on. If peeled, cover with water immediately to prevent discoloration.

5. Rewarm the cream sauce over low heat. Divide the cooked shrimp among the pastry shells and spoon the warm cream sauce on top. Garnish the shrimp-filled vol-au-vents with sprigs of dill and serve. *–The Frescobaldi family*

MAKE AHEAD The cream sauce and cooked shrimp can be prepared and then refrigerated separately overnight. Rewarm the sauce and the shrimp gently in separate pans over low heat before proceeding.

WINE 1996 Frescobaldi Pomino Bianco. The blend of Pinot Bianco and Chardonnay grapes in this wine creates a delicate balance of acidity and vibrant fruit flavors that will pair wonderfully with the richness of the vol-au-vents and the shrimp.

Dilled Shrimp Vol-au-Vent

Bay Scallops in Wood-Sorrel Butter Sauce

4 SERVINGS

The sauce, which is akin to beurre blanc, contains just enough butter to make it taste rich. If you can't find wood sorrel, try sheep sorrel or cultivated sorrel. You can also use basil; the dish will taste completely different but be delicious nonetheless.

- 4 tablespoons cold unsalted butter, cut into tablespoons
- 1 medium shallot, minced
- Salt
- ½ cup Champagne vinegar
- ¼ cup heavy cream
- Cayenne pepper
- 1 pound bay scallops, membranes removed
- 2 medium tomatoes—peeled, seeded and cut into ⅓-inch dice
- ½ cup tightly packed wood sorrel leaves, finely shredded

I. In a large stainless-steel skillet, melt 1 tablespoon of the butter over moderate heat. Add the shallot and season with salt. Cook, stirring, until the shallot is just beginning to brown, about 1 minute. Add the vinegar and cook, shaking the skillet, until reduced to about 1 tablespoon. Add the cream and bring just to a boil. Add the remaining 3 tablespoons of butter, one piece at a time, swirling the pan to incorporate; the sauce will be quite thick. Season the sauce with salt and cayenne.

2. Add the scallops and tomatoes. Cook, stirring constantly, until the scallops are just opaque, about 3 minutes. Stir in three-quarters of the sorrel; cook for 30 seconds. Transfer to a platter. Garnish with the remaining sorrel and serve immediately. *–Jean-Georges Vongerichten*

WINE 1995 Günter Wittmann Westhofener Steingrube Albalonga Auslese. Wildly aromatic, this wine is sweet enough to match the scallops and temper the cayenne, and acid enough to counter the buttery sauce.

Potato-Chip Tower with Scallops and Caviar

6 SERVINGS

- 2 tablespoons unsalted butter, melted
- 1 large Idaho potato, peeled
- Salt and freshly ground pepper
- 4 teaspoons finely chopped chives
- ⅓ cup crème fraîche
- 6 large sea scallops (about 4½ ounces), halved horizontally
- 1 ounce sevruga caviar (3 tablespoons)
- 1 small head frisée, leaves separated

I. Preheat the oven to 375°. Line a large heavy baking sheet with parchment paper and lightly brush the parchment

Bay Scallops in Wood-Sorrel Butter Sauce

with some of the butter. Using a mandoline, cut the potato crosswise into paper-thin slices. Spread about twenty-four of the potato slices (to get eighteen perfect chips for assembling the towers) in a single layer on the parchment. Brush the potato slices with the remaining butter and season them with salt and pepper.

2. Cover the potato slices with another piece of parchment and top with a second baking sheet. Bake the potato slices for 25 to 30 minutes, or until evenly golden; rotate the baking sheet once during baking so the slices brown evenly. Transfer the chips to a tray lined with paper towels. Reduce the oven temperature to 300°.

3. In a small bowl, stir the chives into the crème fraîche and set it aside.

Spread the scallop halves on a baking sheet and bake for 1 to 2 minutes, or just until they lose their transparency; the scallops should still be rare.

4. To assemble the potato-chip towers, place one potato chip in the center of each plate. Top the potato chip with ¾ teaspoon caviar, a scallop half and a dab of the chive crème fraîche. Repeat the layering once and top with a potato chip. Garnish the potato-chip towers with a large pinch of frisée and serve at once. –*Joachim Splichal*

MAKE AHEAD The baked potato chips can stand at room temperature for up to two hours.

WINE This rich and earthy dish is particularly well-suited to a classic Chardonnay. Try the 1992 Raveneau Valmur Chablis.

Potato-Chip Tower with Scallops and Caviar

Seared Sea Scallops
6 SERVINGS
- ½ cup hazelnuts (about 2½ ounces)
- 1½ tablespoons clarified unsalted butter (see box, p. 22)
- 5 small Belgian endives, quartered lengthwise through the cores
- Salt and freshly ground pepper
- 2 cups stemmed fresh spinach (about 3 ounces)
- 6 large sea scallops
- Citrus Vinaigrette (recipe follows)
- 1 tablespoon mixed chopped herbs, such as flat-leaf parsley and chives

1. Preheat the oven to 350°. Spread the hazelnuts on a pie plate. Toast in the oven until fragrant, about 10 minutes. Wrap the nuts in a kitchen towel; rub them against each other to remove the skins. Let cool completely, then coarsely chop the nuts.

2. In a large heavy nonstick skillet, heat 1 tablespoon of the butter. Fit the endives in the skillet, season with salt and pepper and cook over moderate heat, turning, until lightly browned and tender, about 12 minutes; remove to a plate. Add the spinach to the skillet, season with salt and pepper and cook, stirring, until just wilted, about 1 minute; remove to another plate.

3. Wipe out the skillet and add the remaining ½ tablespoon of butter. Add the scallops, season with salt and pepper and cook over moderately high heat until browned, about 1½ minutes per side.

4. Add half of the vinaigrette to the endives and half to the spinach and toss both gently. Arrange the spinach on six warmed plates. Set three endive quarters on top of each serving with the endive bases touching. Place a scallop at the base of the endives; sprinkle the hazelnuts and herbs over all. Serve at once.

CITRUS VINAIGRETTE
MAKES ABOUT ⅔ CUP
- 5 tablespoons extra-virgin olive oil
- 3 tablespoons fresh lemon juice

3 tablespoons finely chopped chives

3 tablespoons finely chopped
flat-leaf parsley

2 tablespoons finely chopped
shallots

Salt and freshly ground pepper

In a small bowl, whisk the oil with the lemon juice, chives, parsley and shallots. Season the vinaigrette with salt and pepper. *–Joachim Splichal*

MAKE AHEAD The dressing can stand for up to four hours; whisk before using.

WINE 1995 Spottswoode Sauvignon Blanc. The ripe fig, melon and herbal flavors of this white match the sweet scallops and grassy endive, while the fresh acidity of the wine keeps it from overwhelming the dish.

Soft-Shell Crabs with Nasturtiums

4 SERVINGS

1 tablespoon unsalted butter

3 tablespoons grapeseed or other
mild vegetable oil

4 medium soft-shell crabs, cleaned
and patted dry

Salt and freshly ground pepper

8 loosely packed cups nasturtium
flowers and leaves, or watercress

2 teaspoons Champagne vinegar

1. In a large skillet, melt the butter in 2 tablespoons of the oil until the foam subsides. Season the crabs with salt and pepper and add them, top-side down, to the skillet. Cook over high heat until crisp and browned, about 3 minutes. Turn and fry until the crabs are golden and cooked through, about 2 minutes longer.

2. Meanwhile, in a large bowl, toss the nasturtiums with the remaining 1 tablespoon of oil. Add the vinegar and a generous pinch each of salt and pepper. Toss again, arrange on four plates, set a crab on each and serve. *–John Cochran*

WINE 1995 Clos de la Poussie Sancerre from France

Bambou Crab Cakes

8 SERVINGS

These crab cakes are best-sellers at Bambou in Manhattan. They're served with a drizzle of molasses glaze for a lightly sweet Caribbean flavor.

1½ pounds fresh lump crabmeat,
picked over

¾ cup mayonnaise

⅓ cup chopped red bell pepper

⅓ cup finely chopped red onion

1½ teaspoons Old Bay Seasoning

1½ teaspoons kosher salt

¼ teaspoon freshly ground pepper

2 cups fresh bread crumbs

3 tablespoons unsalted butter

¼ cup vegetable oil

¼ cup balsamic vinegar

¼ cup unsulphured molasses

3 medium tomatoes, sliced
crosswise ¼ inch thick

ABOVE: **Soft-Shell Crabs with Nasturtiums.**

TOP: **Seared Sea Scallops.**

8 basil sprigs

1 tablespoon plus 1 teaspoon
Chive Oil (recipe follows)

1. In a large bowl, gently mix the crabmeat, mayonnaise, red pepper, onion, Old Bay Seasoning, salt and pepper. Stir in 1 cup of the bread crumbs and shape the mixture into eight 4-inch crab cakes. Spread the remaining 1 cup of crumbs on a plate and coat each cake with the crumbs. Set the crab cakes on a baking sheet, cover and refrigerate for at least 20 minutes or up to 4 hours.

2. In a large skillet, melt 1½ tablespoons of the butter in 2 tablespoons of the oil. Add four of the crab cakes to the skillet and cook over moderate heat, turning once, until crusty, golden brown and heated through, about 10 minutes. Transfer to a baking sheet and keep warm in a low oven while you cook the remaining crab cakes in the remaining butter and oil.

3. Meanwhile, in a small stainless-steel skillet, combine the vinegar and molasses and simmer over low heat until slightly thickened, about 2 minutes.

Bambou Crab Cakes

4. Arrange the tomato slices in the center of eight plates and set the crab cakes on top. Garnish with a basil sprig. Drizzle 2 teaspoons of the molasses glaze and ½ teaspoon of the Chive Oil around each serving.

CHIVE OIL

MAKES ABOUT ¼ CUP

1½ cups coarsely chopped chives

½ cup extra-virgin olive oil

1 teaspoon fresh lemon juice

½ teaspoon kosher salt

Combine all of the ingredients in a blender and puree. Pass the mixture through a fine strainer without pressing down on the solids. *—Herb Wilson*

MAKE AHEAD The Chive Oil can be refrigerated overnight.

WINE These sweet and salty appetizers are perfect foils for effusively fruity, off-dry California Johannisberg Rieslings, such as the 1996 Firestone and the 1996 Jekel.

Crab Ravioli with Shallot Cream

8 SERVINGS

The cream, shallot and touch of mustard in the sauce match the simple elegance of the crab. Chinese wonton skins, available in most supermarkets, make an instant and delicate wrapping.

½ tablespoon unsalted butter

½ tablespoon all-purpose flour, plus more for dusting

¼ cup half-and-half or whole milk

½ pound lump crabmeat, picked over

1 large scallion, white part only, minced

1 teaspoon minced tarragon

½ teaspoon Dijon mustard

Salt and freshly ground white pepper

48 wonton wrappers

SHALLOT CREAM

2 tablespoons unsalted butter

1 large shallot, minced

1 cup heavy cream

⅓ cup clam broth

2 teaspoons Dijon mustard

1 tablespoon minced flat-leaf parsley

Salt and freshly ground white pepper

1. Melt the butter in a medium stainless-steel saucepan over moderate heat. Add the flour and cook, whisking, for 30 seconds. Add the half-and-half and cook, whisking constantly, until very thick, about 1 minute. Remove from the heat and let cool. Fold in the crabmeat, scallion, tarragon and mustard; season with salt and pepper. Divide the filling into twenty-four equal portions.

2. On a work surface, lightly brush 3 wonton wrappers with water. Place one portion of the crab filling in the center of each. Cover with a second wonton wrapper, press out any air pockets and seal. Using a 2½-inch round or fluted biscuit cutter, trim the excess dough. Transfer the ravioli in a single layer to a baking sheet lined with plastic wrap. Repeat with the remaining wrappers and filling.

3. MAKE THE SHALLOT CREAM: Melt the butter in a large stainless-steel skillet. Add the shallot and cook over low heat, stirring, until softened but not browned, about 4 minutes. Add the cream and clam broth and bring to a boil over high heat. Off the heat, whisk in the mustard and parsley and season with salt and white pepper. Cover and set aside.

4. Cook the ravioli in a large pot of boiling salted water, stirring occasionally, until they rise to the surface, about 3 minutes. Using a slotted spoon, transfer the ravioli to a colander to drain. Add the drained ravioli to the shallot cream and toss gently over low heat. Serve immediately. *—Grace Parisi*

MAKE AHEAD The uncooked ravioli can be dusted with flour and refrigerated for up to one day.

WINE Turley's 1995 Landmark Overlook Chardonnay

Crab Ravioli with Shallot Cream

Lobster Salad with Curried Vinaigrette

Lobster Salad with Curried Vinaigrette

2 SERVINGS

This refreshing appetizer is just as good with lump crabmeat or cooked shrimp.

- ⅓ cup extra-virgin olive oil
- 3 tablespoons sherry vinegar
- 1 teaspoon fresh lemon juice
- 1 teaspoon sweet paprika
- ½ teaspoon Madras curry powder
- ½ teaspoon pure chile powder, such as ancho
- ½ teaspoon salt
- ½ cup finely diced unpeeled European cucumber
- ½ cup finely diced red bell pepper
- 2 scallions, finely chopped
- ½ pound cooked lobster meat, cut into 1-inch chunks
- ½ cup finely diced mango
- ½ cup frisée
- 4 Belgian endive spears
- 4 chives

1. In a medium bowl, whisk together the oil, vinegar, lemon juice, paprika, curry powder, chile powder and salt. Stir in the cucumber, red pepper and scallions; let marinate for 10 minutes.

2. Fold in the lobster, mango and frisée and spoon into two martini glasses or goblets or onto two small plates. Garnish each with two endive spears and two chives and serve. *–Jonathan Eismann*

Lobster with Nutmeg Vinaigrette and Chestnut Puree

20 SERVINGS

The flavors of nutmeg and chestnut are deliciously paired with simple steamed lobster served in its shell.

- 2 cups chicken stock or canned low-sodium broth
- 2 cups apple cider
- 6 shallots, minced
- 3 bay leaves
- 2 tablespoons sherry vinegar
- ½ cup heavy cream
- 1½ teaspoons freshly grated nutmeg
- 1 tablespoon vegetable oil
- 1 medium onion, chopped

Two 15-ounce cans whole chestnuts packed in water, drained

- 3 tablespoons pure maple syrup
- 2 tablespoons unsalted butter
- ½ cup crème fraîche or sour cream

Salt and freshly ground pepper

- 4 large scallions, chopped
- 2 tablespoons chopped parsley

Ten 1¼-pound boiled lobsters, halved

- ¼ pound mixed young salad greens

1. In a large saucepan, combine 1 cup of the stock with the cider, shallots, bay leaves and sherry vinegar. Boil over high heat until reduced by half, about 25 minutes. Add the heavy cream and nutmeg and simmer over moderate heat until slightly thickened, about 5 minutes. Remove from the heat.

2. In a medium saucepan, heat the oil. Add the onion and cook over moderate heat until softened. Add the remaining 1 cup of stock and the chestnuts and simmer until the liquid reduces by a third, about 4 minutes. Remove from the heat and add the maple syrup and butter. Transfer the contents of the saucepan to a blender and puree until smooth. Blend in the crème fraîche. Transfer the puree to a clean saucepan and season with salt and pepper. Cover and keep warm.

3. Gently reheat the nutmeg vinaigrette. Add the scallions and parsley and season with salt and pepper.

4. Cut the lobster tail meat into 1-inch chunks and replace it in the tail sections of the lobsters. Divide the chestnut puree between two large platters, spooning it into the center of each. Arrange the lobster halves around the puree. Spoon the warm vinaigrette over the lobsters, garnish the platters with the greens and serve at once. *–Todd English*

MAKE AHEAD The recipe can be prepared through Step 2 and refrigerated overnight. Finish the nutmeg vinaigrette and rewarm the chestnut puree before serving.

Garlicky Steamer Clams in Ale

20 SERVINGS

Clams and beer are synonymous with summer. This recipe, which includes both, is best prepared in three batches.

- 9 pounds steamer clams
- ⅓ cup cornmeal
- 1 stick plus 1 tablespoon (4½ ounces) unsalted butter
- 6 tablespoons minced garlic

Three 12-ounce bottles pale ale

- 3 tablespoons fresh lemon juice
- ½ cup plus 1 tablespoon coarsely chopped parsley

Freshly ground pepper

1. In a large sinkful of cold water, rub the clams together to remove grit. Drain the sink and repeat the process four or five times until the water is clear. Add the clams to a fresh sinkful of water, sprinkle the cornmeal over them and let soak for 20 minutes. Drain and rinse the clams thoroughly.

2. In a large stainless-steel saucepan, melt 3 tablespoons of the butter over moderate heat. Add 2 tablespoons of the garlic and cook until softened, about 2 minutes. Add 1 bottle of ale and bring to a boil. Add one-third of the

clams, cover tightly and cook over high heat, shaking the pan frequently, until all of the clams are open, 3 to 4 minutes. Add 1 tablespoon of the lemon juice and 3 tablespoons of the parsley and season with pepper. Transfer the clams and their cooking juices to a large bowl and serve. Repeat with the remaining ingredients in two batches. —*David Page*

Clams à la Marinière

4 SERVINGS **Q**

- ½ cup chicken stock or canned low-sodium broth
- ¼ cup plus 2 tablespoons dry white wine
- 2 tablespoons finely chopped garlic
- 2 tablespoons extra-virgin olive oil
- 1 tablespoon unsalted butter
- 4 dozen littleneck clams (about 3½ pounds), as small as possible, well scrubbed
- 2 tablespoons finely chopped flat-leaf parsley

Freshly ground pepper

Crusty French bread, for serving

In a large stainless-steel saucepan, combine the stock, wine, garlic, oil and butter; bring to a boil. Add the clams, cover and cook over high heat until they open, 5 to 8 minutes; remove them as they open. (Discard any that do not open.) Stir in the parsley and a generous pinch of pepper. Serve in deep bowls with plenty of bread to sop up the juices. —*Jocelyn Bulow*

jicama

A native of Mexico, jicama (HEE-ka-ma) is a round or turnip-shaped root with apple-like cream-colored flesh.

How to buy Look for firm, smooth, unblemished roots with thin tan skin. Jicama is available year-round.

How to store Refrigerate for up to three weeks.

How to use Serve raw to show off its juicy crunch and delicate sweetness.

Jicama Cannelloni with Snapper Seviche

8 SERVINGS

Use a very sharp mandoline to slice the jicama. Buy a root large enough to make slices that are four by six inches and trim the root to fit the mandoline.

- 1 cup fresh lemon juice (from 4 lemons)
- ¾ cup fresh lime juice (from 4 limes)
- 1 small jalapeño pepper, seeded and minced
- 1 pound skinless red-snapper fillets, cut into 1-by-⅛-inch strips
- 16 small shrimp (about ¾ pound), shelled and deveined
- ½ cup finely chopped red onion
- ¼ cup finely chopped cilantro
- 1 mango, peeled and cut into thin strips
- 16 paper-thin slices of peeled jicama (see box, left)
- 1 cup guacamole

1. In a large glass bowl, combine the lemon juice, lime juice and jalapeño. Pour ⅓ cup of this marinade into a small glass bowl and set aside. Add the snapper to the large bowl and mix well; cover and refrigerate for 2 to 4 hours, stirring occasionally.

2. Meanwhile, bring a large pot of salted water to a boil. Add the shrimp and cook just until pink and firm, about 2½ minutes. Drain and let cool. Add the shrimp to the marinade in the small bowl and toss well. Cover and refrigerate 2 to 4 hours, stirring occasionally.

3. Drain the snapper. Transfer to a medium bowl; mix in the onion and cilantro.

4. To assemble the cannelloni, arrange two mango strips on a slice of jicama. Top with 1 tablespoon each of the guacamole and the snapper seviche. Roll the jicama around the filling to form a tight cylinder and garnish with a shrimp. Repeat with the remaining ingredients and serve at once. —*Michael Cordúa*

WINE 1995 Château d'Arricaud Graves

ABOVE: **Jicama Cannelloni with Snapper Seviche.** TOP: **Garlicky Steamer Clams in Ale.**

Hot-Smoked Salmon with Green-Apple Slaw

10 SERVINGS

Savory salmon is glazed with a spicy molasses sauce and flavored with just the right amount of smoke. It's delicious with or without the slaw. If you have a home smoker, use wood chips in place of the tea-and-sugar mixture.

GLAZE

- 2 tablespoons peanut oil
- ½ cup finely chopped onion
- ½ cup unsweetened apple juice
- 1 cup unsulphured molasses

ABOVE: **Salmon with Ginger and Lime.**
TOP: **Sweet Corn Pancake with Salmon.**

½ cup soy sauce
⅓ cup apple cider vinegar
¼ cup honey
2 teaspoons crushed red pepper
2 teaspoons curry powder
1 teaspoon sweet paprika
½ teaspoon ground coriander
½ teaspoon Old Bay Seasoning
½ teaspoon black peppercorns
SMOKED SALMON
1 skinless, boneless side of salmon (about 3 pounds)
½ cup long-grain white rice
¼ cup loose black tea
3 tablespoons light brown sugar
Green-Apple Slaw (recipe follows), optional

I. MAKE THE GLAZE: Heat the peanut oil in a medium saucepan. Add the onion and cook over moderately high heat, stirring frequently, until softened, about 5 minutes. Add the apple juice and bring to a boil. Cook until the juice is reduced and the onion is browned, about 5 minutes. Add the remaining glaze ingredients. Lower the heat to moderate and simmer until the mixture is thick and syrupy, about 30 minutes. Strain the glaze and let cool.

2. MAKE THE SMOKED SALMON: Using sturdy tweezers or small pliers, remove the pin bones from the salmon. Trim away the thin line of fatty flesh that runs the length of the fillet, then halve the fish lengthwise, cutting along the central line. Cut each half into five equal pieces.

3. In a small bowl, combine the rice, tea and brown sugar. Line a large wok with aluminum foil, allowing about 4 inches of overhang all around, and spread the rice mixture in the foil. Set a 10-inch round wire rack in the wok 3 inches above the smoking mixture. Set the wok over moderate heat (on a wok ring if you are using a gas stove) and heat until thin streams of smoke begin to rise, 8 to 10 minutes.

4. Brush the salmon all over with some of the molasses glaze. Arrange the salmon on the cake rack and quickly cover the wok with the lid. Wearing oven mitts, crimp the overhanging foil all around the lid to completely seal the wok. Cook over moderately high heat just until the fish flakes, about 12 minutes.

5. Preheat the oven to 400°. Arrange the salmon on a baking sheet and brush with additional molasses glaze. Bake the salmon for about 3 minutes, or until just warmed through. Arrange the salmon on a platter with the slaw. Serve hot or at room temperature.

GREEN-APPLE SLAW
MAKES ABOUT 2 QUARTS
1 cup pecan halves (about 4 ounces)
½ cup mayonnaise
2 tablespoons honey
1 tablespoon fresh lime juice
1½ teaspoons yellow mustard
1½ teaspoons kosher salt
½ teaspoon freshly ground pepper
4 cups finely shredded cabbage
3 medium Granny Smith apples, coarsely shredded
3 medium carrots, coarsely shredded
2 medium red bell peppers, thinly sliced
½ cup 2-inch pieces of chives

I. Preheat the oven to 400°. Toast the pecans for about 5 minutes, or until fragrant. Let cool.

2. In a small bowl, combine the mayonnaise, honey, lime juice, mustard, salt and pepper. In a large bowl, combine the cabbage, apples, carrots and red peppers. Just before serving, add the dressing, the pecans and the chives and toss well.   *—George Mahaffey*

MAKE AHEAD The smoked salmon can be refrigerated overnight before baking. The glaze for the salmon can be refrigerated for up to two weeks. The dressing for the slaw can be refrigerated for up to two days. Let the toasted pecans stand at room temperature.

WINE Cru Beaujolais or light California Red. While many people love Beaujolais Nouveau, a cru Beaujolais, such as the 1995 Château Thivin Côte de Brouilly, has more stuffing and a juiciness that suits this smoked salmon.

Sweet Corn Pancakes with Smoked Salmon
8 SERVINGS
2 teaspoons olive oil
1 cup fresh corn kernels
Kosher salt and freshly ground pepper
1 cup all-purpose flour
1½ teaspoons baking powder
½ teaspoon table salt
2 large eggs, lightly beaten
1 cup milk

2 tablespoons unsalted butter, melted

2 teaspoons vegetable oil

Eight 7-inch-long strips of smoked salmon (about ½ pound)

1 small head of oak leaf lettuce, separated into leaves

2 tablespoons plus 2 teaspoons Chive Oil (p. 40)

1. Heat the olive oil in a medium skillet. Add the corn kernels and cook over moderate heat, stirring, until almost tender, about 2 minutes. Season the corn with kosher salt and pepper and transfer to a plate to cool completely.

2. In a medium bowl, sift together the flour, baking powder and table salt. Gently stir in the eggs and milk. Add the melted butter and the corn kernels and stir to make a smooth batter; don't overmix.

3. Warm 1 teaspoon of the vegetable oil in a large nonstick skillet. For each pancake, drop ¼ cup of batter into the skillet and spread to make a 4-inch round. Form four pancakes and cook over moderate heat, turning once, until the pancakes are golden brown, about 5 minutes. Transfer to a baking sheet and keep warm in a low oven. Repeat the process with the remaining vegetable oil and batter to make a total of eight pancakes.

4. Lay the smoked-salmon slices out on a work surface. Place two or three lettuce leaves at one end of each slice so that the tops of the leaves protrude, and then roll up the salmon slices around the lettuce leaves.

5. To serve, place a warm corn pancake in the center of each plate. Stand a salmon roll, with the leaves sticking up, in the center of each pancake and drizzle each of the plates with 1 teaspoon of the Chive Oil. *—Herb Wilson*

MAKE AHEAD The batter for the pancakes can be refrigerated for up to four hours.

Cured Salmon with Peppercorns

10 SERVINGS

Cured fish is a typical Ligurian antipasto; this version gets its tang from lemon juice and white wine. Use the freshest, best-quality salmon here.

1½ pounds skinless center-cut salmon fillet

⅔ cup fresh lemon juice

⅓ cup dry white wine

3 tablespoons extra-virgin olive oil (optional)

½ to 1 tablespoon brined green or pink peppercorns

Fine sea salt

1. Using a very sharp thin-bladed knife, cut the salmon fillet straight down across the grain into ⅓-inch-thick slices.

2. In a small bowl, combine the lemon juice and the wine. Arrange the salmon slices on a glass or ceramic platter and pour the lemon mixture on top. Refrigerate for 45 minutes. Pour off the liquid and pat the salmon dry. Drizzle with the oil, scatter the peppercorns on top and season with salt. *—Reed Hearon*

Salmon with Ginger and Lime

8 SERVINGS

Thin slices of salmon are made into little rosettes and briefly baked. If you prefer, you can arrange and cook the rosettes on individual ovenproof plates instead of on a baking sheet as called for here.

1 pound trimmed skinless center-cut salmon fillet

Olive oil

1½ tablespoons fresh lime juice

1 tablespoon minced fresh ginger

1½ teaspoons finely grated lime zest

Fine sea salt

1. Using a very sharp thin-bladed knife, cut the salmon fillet straight down across the grain into delicate ⅛-inch-thick slices; you should have at least thirty-two slices. (Alternatively, ask your fishmonger to do this for you.) Lightly oil a baking sheet, set a salmon slice on it and bring the ends together to form a loop. Repeat with three more slices, arranging the rounded sides out like the petals of a flower and bunching the ends together in the center; try not to overwork the slices. Repeat with the remaining salmon slices to make a total of eight rosettes.

2. Preheat the oven to 350°. In a bowl, combine the lime juice, ginger and lime zest. Sprinkle about ½ teaspoon evenly over each rosette and season with salt. Bake in the center of the oven for about 3 minutes, or until the salmon is opaque around the outside and still bright pink inside. Using a spatula, transfer the salmon rosettes to small warmed plates and serve. *—Mireille Guiliano*

MAKE AHEAD The rosettes can be refrigerated on the baking sheet for up to one day before baking.

WINE A full-bodied Champagne like the Veuve Cliquot 1988 Rosé Réserve works particularly well with citrus and offers a nice counterpoint to the rich salmon.

Spicy Tuna Tartare

8 SERVINGS

¼ cup soy sauce

3 tablespoons mirin, or dry sherry mixed with a pinch of sugar

1 tablespoon sake or vodka

¼ cup Asian sesame oil

1 tablespoon plus 1 teaspoon extra-virgin olive oil

1 teaspoon finely grated fresh ginger

1 teaspoon minced garlic

1 teaspoon cayenne pepper

½ teaspoon freshly ground black pepper

1½ pounds chilled sushi-quality tuna steaks

⅓ cup pine nuts

2½ tablespoons sesame seeds

Saigon Wings

½ medium Golden Delicious apple

¼ European cucumber, peeled and finely diced

2 large scallions, white and tender green, minced

1 medium Hass avocado, cut into ¼-inch dice

1 sheet of nori, cut into thin strips (optional)

8 quail-egg yolks (optional)

1. In a small stainless-steel saucepan, bring the soy sauce, mirin and sake to a boil over moderately high heat. Cook until reduced to ⅓ cup, about 4 minutes. Transfer to a bowl and let cool completely, then add the sesame oil, the 1 tablespoon olive oil, the ginger, garlic, cayenne and black pepper. Let the sauce stand at room temperature for at least 2 hours or refrigerate overnight.

2. Using a very sharp knife, slice the tuna ⅓ inch thick. Cut each slice into ⅓-inch-thick matchsticks and then finely chop the tuna; work quickly so that the tuna stays cold. Transfer the tuna to a bowl and refrigerate.

3. Heat the remaining 1 teaspoon olive oil in a small skillet. Add the pine nuts and stir over moderately high heat until lightly toasted, 4 to 5 minutes. Transfer to a paper-towel-lined plate and rub to remove the oil. Coarsely chop the pine nuts and put them in a small bowl. Add the sesame seeds to the skillet and toast over moderately high heat, stirring constantly, until golden, 2 to 3 minutes. Add to the pine nuts.

4. Peel and finely dice the apple. In a bowl, combine the tuna, pine nuts, sesame seeds, apple, cucumber and scallions. Stir the sauce and add ½ cup to the tuna mixture. Toss quickly and thoroughly. Spoon the tartare onto eight chilled plates and sprinkle with the avocado and nori. Set a quail-egg yolk in the center of each serving and drizzle a little of the sauce around the plates. Serve immediately. *–Sotohiro Kosugi*

WINE 1994 Trefethen Vineyards Chardonnay or 1995 Cakebread Cellars Chardonnay, both from California

Pan-Flashed Ahi

4 SERVINGS **L**

This dish calls for the best-quality tuna you can find. Miso paste is available at health-food stores.

¼ cup cider vinegar

2 tablespoons white miso paste

1 tablespoon honey

1 tablespoon minced scallion

1 teaspoon Asian chili-garlic paste

1 teaspoon minced fresh ginger

1 teaspoon Asian sesame oil

½ teaspoon vegetable oil

6 ounces yellowfin (ahi) tuna steak, at least 1 inch thick

Salt and freshly ground pepper

1 cup finely julienned daikon

6 basil leaves

1. In a bowl, combine the vinegar, miso, honey, scallion, chili-garlic paste, ginger and sesame oil.

2. Heat the vegetable oil in a nonstick skillet until almost smoking. Add the tuna, season with salt and pepper and sear over high heat until well browned, about 2 minutes per side. Transfer to a plate and refrigerate until chilled.

3. Spoon the vinaigrette onto a small platter. Cut the tuna into eight even slices and arrange the slices in the vinaigrette. Garnish with the daikon and basil and serve. *–Tylun Pang*

Saigon Wings

4 SERVINGS

The best window onto a nation's cuisine is its food markets. This is one Vietnamese vendor's version of chicken wings; it's as easy to make as it is flavorful. To increase the exposed surface area of meat, the wings are spread open and skewered. To be authentic, you'll need lemongrass and fish sauce for the marinade, both of which are available at Asian markets and specialty shops. In a pinch, substitute four strips of lemon zest for the lemongrass and soy sauce for the fish sauce.

4 garlic cloves, chopped

2 medium shallots, chopped

2 stalks lemongrass, tender white inner bulbs only, chopped

One 1-inch piece fresh ginger, peeled and chopped

2 tablespoons sugar

⅓ cup Asian fish sauce

3 tablespoons fresh lemon juice

1 tablespoon vegetable oil, plus more for basting

12 whole chicken wings (2½ to 3 pounds)

¼ cup finely chopped unsalted dry-roasted peanuts

1. In a mortar, pound the garlic, shallots, lemongrass, ginger and sugar to a paste. Stir in the fish sauce, the lemon juice and the 1 tablespoon oil. Alternatively, puree the ingredients in a mini-processor. Transfer to a large bowl.

2. Make three deep slashes in the meaty part of each chicken wing. Add the wings to the bowl, stir to coat and marinate for 4 hours at room temperature, or preferably overnight in the refrigerator.

3. Light a grill. Thread the chicken wings on bamboo skewers, splaying each wing as widely as possible; reserve the marinade. Brush the chicken wings with vegetable oil and grill over a medium-hot fire for 6 to 8 minutes per side, basting them once or twice with the reserved marinade, until crusty. Do not baste the wings during the last 5 minutes. Transfer the chicken wings to a platter and sprinkle with the peanuts. Serve the wings at once. *–Steven Raichlen*

BEER The floral, heavy-hop bouquet and moderate maltiness of a dry American pale ale will enhance the wings' sweet-salty, aromatic flavors. Sierra Nevada Pale Ale, from California, is the best choice.

CHAPTER 3 salads

Summer Bean and Radish Salad (p. 58)

51 Autumn Salad with Radicchio, Apples and Grapes

51 Avocado Grapefruit Salad with Pomegranate Dressing

52 Fennel and Watercress Salad with Cranberries and Pecans

52 Parsley and Endive Salad

52 Watercress Salad

53 Green Salad with Lemon Vinaigrette

53 Baby-Green Salad with Chive Blossoms

53 Chickweed Salad

53 Romaine Leaves with Honey Mustard Dressing

53 Toasted Goat Cheese with Mesclun

54 Endive and Roquefort Salad

54 Dead-Simple Balsamic Vinaigrette

54 Creamy Parmesan, Basil and Pine-Nut Dressing

55 No-Fat Ginger Soy Dressing

55 Sweet Peanut Dressing

55 Green-Olive Orange Dressing

55 Greek-Style Feta Dressing

56 Mango Black-Pepper Dressing

56 Spicy Coleslaw

56 Apple Carrot Slaw

57 Red and Yellow Tomato Salad

57 Classic Greek Salad

58 Roast Carrot Salad with Muscadine Vinaigrette

58 Summer Bean and Radish Salad

60 Bean Salad with Lime Vinaigrette

60 Wax-Bean Salad with Toasted Hazelnuts

60 Roasted Beets with Arugula

61 Pickled-Beet Salad with Amaranth and Hazelnuts

62 Thai Mushroom Salad

62 Shaved-Artichoke Salad

62 Spring Asparagus Salad with Quail-Egg Toasts

63 Leeks with Miso Vinaigrette

64 New-Potato Salad with Grilled Red Onions

64 Elizabeth's Potato Salad

64 Panzanella

65 Tabbouleh-Style Three-Grain Salad

65 Black-Eyed-Pea Salad

65 Coconut Shrimp with Tamarind Vinaigrette

66 Casablanca Salad

66 Sara's Lobster and Mango Salad

67 Tuna and Potato Salad

67 Saigon Salad

Autumn Salad with Radicchio, Apples and Grapes

Autumn Salad with Radicchio, Apples and Grapes

12 SERVINGS

This colorful salad features a sweet and tart dressing made with fresh grape juice; to make the juice, squeeze several seedless grapes over a bowl.

1½ cups coarsely chopped walnuts (about 6 ounces)
¼ cup plus 2 tablespoons fresh lemon juice
2 tablespoons balsamic vinegar
2 tablespoons fresh grape juice (see above)
½ cup olive oil
¼ cup plus 2 tablespoons walnut oil
Salt and freshly ground pepper
1 tablespoon finely chopped mint
4 medium heads of radicchio (about 2 pounds), torn into large pieces
4 Belgian endives, cored and torn into large pieces
2 Granny Smith apples—halved, cored and thinly sliced
2 cups seedless red or purple grapes (about ½ pound)

1. Preheat the oven to 350°. Toast the nuts on a baking sheet for about 7 minutes, or until fragrant; let cool completely.
2. In a small glass or stainless-steel bowl, combine the lemon juice, vinegar and grape juice. Stir in the oils. Season with salt and pepper and stir in the mint.
3. In a large serving bowl, toss the radicchio with the endives, apples, grapes and walnuts. Add the dressing and toss to coat. —*The Frescobaldi family*
MAKE AHEAD The toasted walnuts can be kept at room temperature for up to four days.

Avocado Grapefruit Salad with Pomegranate Dressing

10 SERVINGS

Tart, lightly perfumed pomegranate molasses is available from Middle Eastern grocery stores and by mail order from Kalustyan (212-685-3451).

Avocado Grapefruit Salad with Pomegranate Dressing

1 quart vegetable oil, for frying
20 medium shallots (1½ pounds), thinly sliced
½ cup all-purpose flour
3 ruby red grapefruits
¼ cup extra-virgin olive oil
¼ cup pomegranate molasses, plus more for drizzling
1 tablespoon red-wine vinegar
Salt and freshly ground pepper
16 cups loosely packed baby lettuces, such as arugula, frisée and radicchio
2 Hass avocados, each cut into 15 wedges
3 tablespoons pomegranate seeds, for garnish (optional)

1. In a large saucepan, heat the vegetable oil to 300° over moderately high heat; alternatively, test the oil by adding a small bread cube—the bread should turn light brown in 1 minute. Toss the shallots with the flour until they are completely coated, shaking off the excess. Fry the shallots in batches until they are golden and crisp, about 5 minutes. Using a slotted spoon, transfer the shallots to paper towels to drain.
2. Using a sharp knife, peel the grapefruits, removing all the bitter white pith. Cut between the membranes to release the sections. In a small glass or stainless-steel bowl, combine the olive oil with the ¼ cup of pomegranate molasses, the vinegar, ½ teaspoon of salt and ¼ teaspoon of pepper.
3. In a large glass or stainless-steel bowl, toss the lettuces with ⅓ cup of the

pomegranate dressing and mound them on a large serving platter. Put the avocado wedges and the grapefruit sections in the bowl, season with a pinch of salt and a pinch of pepper and toss with the remaining pomegranate dressing. Arrange the avocado-and-grapefruit mixture over the lettuces and garnish the salad with the pomegranate seeds. Drizzle a little pomegranate molasses around the edge of the serving platter and then top the salad with the fried shallots.   *–George Mahaffey*
MAKE AHEAD The fried shallots can be kept in an airtight container at room temperature for up to two days.

Fennel and Watercress Salad with Cranberries and Pecans
20 SERVINGS
- 1 cup pecan halves
- ½ cup dried cranberries, chopped
- ¼ cup red-wine vinegar
- ¼ cup balsamic vinegar
- 1 tablespoon minced garlic
- 1¼ teaspoons salt
- 1 cup extra-virgin olive oil
- 6 bunches watercress, large stems removed
- 3 fennel bulbs–trimmed, cored and thinly sliced lengthwise
- 3 small heads radicchio, cored and torn into bite-size pieces

I. Preheat the oven to 400°. Spread the pecans on a baking sheet; toast in the oven for about 7 minutes, or until fragrant and lightly browned. Set aside to cool.

2. In a glass or stainless-steel bowl, combine the cranberries, vinegars, garlic and salt. Whisk in the oil. Set the vinaigrette aside for at least 20 minutes.

3. In a large salad bowl, toss the watercress, fennel, radicchio and pecans. Stir the dressing; pour over the salad. Toss well. Serve at once. *–Chris Schlesinger*

Parsley and Endive Salad
8 SERVINGS **Q**
- 2 tablespoons sherry vinegar
- ½ teaspoon salt
- ¼ teaspoon freshly ground pepper
- 2 teaspoons Dijon mustard
- ¾ cup extra-virgin olive oil
- 3 large bunches flat-leaf parsley (about ¾ pound), torn into small sprigs, large stems discarded
- 3 medium heads Belgian endive (about 1½ pounds), cored and thinly sliced crosswise

One 4-ounce piece of prosciutto, coarsely chopped

In a large glass or stainless-steel bowl, combine the vinegar, salt and pepper; whisk until the salt dissolves. Stir in the mustard. Gradually whisk in the oil in a thin steady stream until the mixture emulsifies. Add the parsley, endive and prosciutto and toss to coat. *–Jan Newberry*
MAKE AHEAD The dressing can be refrigerated for up to two days.

Watercress Salad
4 SERVINGS **Q**
- 1 tablespoon fresh lemon juice
- 3 tablespoons olive oil

Salt and freshly ground pepper
- 1 large bunch of watercress

Whisk together the lemon juice, oil, and salt and pepper to taste. Just before serving, whisk the dressing again, add the watercress and toss. *–Diana Sturgis*

Parsley and Endive Salad, with Savory Artichoke Bread Pudding (p. 275)

Green Salad with Lemon Vinaigrette

8 SERVINGS

- 1 teaspoon caraway seeds (optional)
- ¼ cup extra-virgin olive oil
- 2 tablespoons fresh lemon juice

Salt and freshly ground pepper

- 1 pound spinach, tough stems removed
- 1 large head of red oak leaf lettuce

1. In a small skillet, toast the caraway seeds over moderate heat, stirring, until fragrant, about 3 minutes. Let cool, and then crush with the side of a heavy knife.

2. In a large glass or stainless-steel bowl, combine the olive oil with the lemon juice and the caraway. Season the vinaigrette with salt and pepper. Add the spinach and lettuce, toss well and serve. —*Rori Spinelli*

Baby-Green Salad with Chive Blossoms

4 SERVINGS

When chives are allowed to flower, they produce purple blossoms that make an unusual onion-flavored addition to salads. Garlic flowers and nasturtiums are good alternatives. You can find wasabi powder at specialty-food stores, Asian markets and many supermarkets.

- 1½ teaspoons wasabi powder
- 1 tablespoon rice-wine vinegar or 1 tablespoon white-wine vinegar mixed with a pinch of sugar
- 2 tablespoons peanut oil

Salt

- ½ teaspoon minced chives

Vegetable oil, for frying

- ½ cup all-purpose flour
- ½ cup ice water
- 1 large egg yolk
- 1 cup chive flowers with 1 inch of stem attached (about 2 ounces)
- 6 cups baby greens

Freshly ground pepper

1. In a small bowl, whisk the wasabi powder with the vinegar and 1½ teaspoons

of water. Whisk in the peanut oil until emulsified and season with salt. Stir in the minced chives.

2. Heat ¾ inch of vegetable oil in a small saucepan. In a medium bowl, combine the flour, ice water and egg yolk; the batter will be a little lumpy. Working in batches, dip one-third of the chive flowers in the batter and add them to the oil. Cook over moderately high heat, stirring occasionally, until lightly golden and crisp, about 2 minutes. Transfer the chive flowers to a rack to drain and season them with salt. Repeat with the remaining chive flowers.

3. In a large bowl, toss the greens with the dressing. Season the salad with salt and pepper and mound on four plates. Top with the fried chive blossoms and serve immediately. —*Grace Parisi*

Chickweed Salad

4 SERVINGS

Chickweed is the flavor of summer; it tastes the way freshly shucked corn smells—raw and haylike. If it's not available, any mild green, such as lamb's lettuce, will do.

- 4 teaspoons fresh lemon juice
- 4 teaspoons walnut oil

Salt and freshly ground pepper

- 6 cups chickweed leaves and tender stems (about 6 ounces)

Pour the lemon juice into a large salad bowl. Gradually whisk in the oil. Season with salt and pepper. Add the chickweed, toss until evenly dressed and serve at once. —*Jean-Georges Vongerichten*

WINE 1995 Cave de Maltaverne Sancerre Rouge, a light, snappy red with a peppery quality and oak-free finish

Romaine Leaves with Honey Mustard Dressing

6 SERVINGS

- 6 hearts of romaine lettuce, separated into leaves
- ¼ cup extra-virgin olive oil

- 2 tablespoons fresh lemon juice
- 2 tablespoons Dijon mustard
- 1 tablespoon grainy mustard
- 1 tablespoon honey
- 1 tablespoon prepared horseradish

Salt and freshly ground pepper

Wash the lettuce and pat dry. Cover and refrigerate to crisp for up to 3 hours. In a small glass or stainless-steel bowl, whisk together the oil, lemon juice, Dijon mustard, grainy mustard, honey and horseradish. Dress the lettuce just before serving. —*Joachim Splichal*

Toasted Goat Cheese with Mesclun

6 SERVINGS

- 2 teaspoons fresh lemon juice
- 2 teaspoons malt vinegar
- 1 teaspoon finely chopped basil
- ½ teaspoon minced garlic
- 2 tablespoons finely chopped flat-leaf parsley

Salt and freshly ground pepper

- ¼ cup extra-virgin olive oil
- ¼ cup plus 2 tablespoons homemade dry bread crumbs
- 1½ teaspoons finely chopped mixed herbs, such as thyme, rosemary and dill
- 2 tablespoons unsalted butter— 1 tablespoon melted

One 11-ounce log of fresh goat cheese, cut crosswise into 6 disks and chilled

- ½ pound mesclun

1. In a large glass or stainless-steel bowl, combine the lemon juice, vinegar, basil, ¼ teaspoon of the garlic, 1 tablespoon of the parsley and a pinch each of salt and pepper. Whisk in the oil in a thin stream until emulsified.

2. In a shallow bowl, toss the bread crumbs with the remaining ¼ teaspoon garlic and 1 tablespoon parsley, the mixed herbs and the 1 tablespoon melted butter. Press the crumbs onto both sides of the goat-cheese disks. ➤

BELOW: **Toasted Goat Cheese with Mesclun.** BOTTOM: **Endive and Roquefort Salad, with Roast Pork with Balsamic Onion Marmalade (p. 218).**

3. Melt the remaining 1 tablespoon butter in a large nonstick skillet. Add the goat cheese; cook over high heat until the disks are toasted on the bottom, about 1 minute. Carefully turn and cook until toasted, about 30 seconds more.

4. Add the mesclun to the dressing and toss. Mound the salad on six plates, set a warm goat-cheese disk on each and serve at once.   *—James Henahan*

Endive and Roquefort Salad

4 SERVINGS **Q**

- 2   tablespoons balsamic vinegar
- ¼   cup extra-virgin olive oil
- 2   tablespoons walnut oil
- 1   tablespoon finely chopped chives
- Salt and freshly ground pepper
- 4   medium endives, cored and cut crosswise into 1-inch pieces
- 2   ounces Roquefort, crumbled (about ⅔ cup)
- ¼   cup chopped walnuts

Pour the vinegar into a salad bowl. Whisk in the olive oil in a thin stream, then whisk in the walnut oil. Stir in the chives. Season the dressing with salt and pepper, add the endives and toss. Garnish with the cheese and walnuts and serve.   *—Jocelyn Bulow*

Dead-Simple Balsamic Vinaigrette

MAKES ABOUT 1 CUP

Use this vinaigrette to dress any kind of salad greens.

- ¾   cup extra-virgin olive oil
- ¼   cup balsamic vinegar
- 1   tablespoon minced oregano
- 1   teaspoon minced garlic
- Salt and freshly ground pepper

In a glass or stainless-steel bowl, combine the oil, vinegar, oregano and garlic. Season the dressing with salt and pepper; whisk to blend. *—Chris Schlesinger and John Willoughby*

Creamy Parmesan, Basil and Pine-Nut Dressing

MAKES ABOUT ½ CUP

Spicy greens, especially arugula and radicchio, will go well with this creamy dressing.

- 2   tablespoons grated Parmesan
- 2   tablespoons basil leaves
- 1   tablespoon toasted pine nuts
- ½   teaspoon minced garlic
- ⅓   cup olive oil
- 2½ tablespoons balsamic vinegar

In a food processor or blender, puree the Parmesan, basil, pine nuts and garlic. Slowly add the oil, processing continuously. Add the vinegar and pulse to combine. *—Chris Schlesinger and John Willoughby*

No-Fat Ginger Soy Dressing

MAKES ABOUT ²/₃ CUP

This is best with in-between or spicy greens, such as napa or red cabbage or any Asian greens.

- ¼ cup fresh lime juice
- 2 tablespoons soy sauce
- 2 tablespoons fish sauce
- 1 tablespoon minced mint
- 1 tablespoon minced cilantro
- 2 teaspoons minced fresh ginger
- 1½ teaspoons sugar
- ¼ teaspoon crushed red pepper
- Salt and freshly ground black pepper

In a glass or stainless-steel bowl, combine the lime juice, soy sauce, fish sauce, mint, cilantro, ginger, sugar and red pepper. Season with salt and black pepper and whisk to blend. –*Chris Schlesinger and John Willoughby*

Sweet Peanut Dressing

MAKES ABOUT 1½ CUPS

Toss this with in-between greens, such as green cabbage.

- ²/₃ cup peanut oil
- ¼ cup chopped roasted peanuts
- ⅓ cup rice-wine vinegar
- 2 tablespoons minced ginger
- 2 tablespoons unsulphured molasses
- 2 tablespoons sesame oil
- Salt and freshly ground pepper

In a glass or stainless-steel bowl, combine the peanut oil, peanuts, vinegar, ginger, molasses and sesame oil. Season the dressing with salt and pepper and whisk to blend. –*Chris Schlesinger and John Willoughby*

Green-Olive Orange Dressing

MAKES ABOUT 1½ CUPS

This bold dressing is best with spicy greens like chicory.

- 1 cup fresh orange juice
- ¾ cup olive oil
- 6 tablespoons finely chopped green olives

ABOVE: **Green-Olive Orange Dressing.**
RIGHT: **Greek-Style Feta Dressing.**

- ¼ cup red-wine vinegar
- 1 teaspoon fennel seeds, ground
- Salt and freshly ground pepper

In a stainless-steel saucepan, simmer the orange juice over moderate heat until reduced to ¼ cup, about 20 minutes. Remove the pan from the heat and let cool to room temperature. Add the oil, olives, vinegar and fennel seeds. Season the dressing with salt and pepper; whisk to blend. –*Chris Schlesinger and John Willoughby*

Greek-Style Feta Dressing

MAKES ABOUT ²/₃ CUP

Romaine is this dressing's classic partner, but other subtle greens like butterhead will work well.

- 6 tablespoons olive oil
- 2 tablespoons fresh lemon juice
- 2 tablespoons crumbled feta
- 1 tablespoon finely chopped oregano
- ½ teaspoon minced garlic
- Pinch of cinnamon (optional)
- Salt and freshly ground pepper

In a glass or stainless-steel bowl, combine the oil, lemon juice, feta, oregano, garlic and cinnamon, if using. Season the dressing with salt and pepper and whisk to blend. –*Chris Schlesinger and John Willoughby*

Mango Black-Pepper Dressing

MAKES ABOUT ¾ CUP

Try this spicy dressing with spicy greens like mizuna.

- ⅓ cup olive oil
- 2½ tablespoons balsamic vinegar
- 2 teaspoons cracked black pepper
- 1 teaspoon kosher salt
- ½ teaspoon sugar
- ½ teaspoon crushed red pepper
- ¼ cup finely chopped fresh mango

In a glass or stainless-steel bowl, combine the oil, vinegar, black pepper, salt, sugar and red pepper and whisk to blend. Add the mango and whisk the dressing again. –*Chris Schlesinger and John Willoughby*

shades of greens

When you can't find a good bunch of a particular leafy green, just substitute another in the same flavor family. We divide the categories this way: **Subtle** Butterhead lettuces, such as Boston and Bibb. Loose-leaf lettuces, such as red leaf, green leaf and oak leaf. Cos lettuces, such as romaine. Crisp head lettuces, such as iceberg. **Spicy** Asian greens, such as tatsoi, mizuna and komatsuna. Baby cooking greens, such as turnip, kale and mustard greens. Peppery European greens, such as arugula, chicory, endive, escarole, dandelion greens, radicchio and watercress. **In-Between** Cabbages, such as red, green, napa, Savoy and Chinese. –*Chris Schlesinger and John Willoughby*

Spicy Coleslaw

16 SERVINGS

- 1 teaspoon cumin seeds
- 1 teaspoon coriander seeds
- 1 cup mayonnaise
- 4 small shallots, coarsely chopped
- 1 to 2 jalapeño peppers, finely chopped with their seeds
- 3 tablespoons finely chopped canned green chiles
- 2 garlic cloves, finely chopped
- 2 tablespoons finely chopped cilantro
- 2 tablespoons pure maple syrup
- 1 tablespoon Worcestershire sauce
- 1 tablespoon Dijon mustard
- 1 tablespoon malt vinegar

Salt

- 2 to 3 tablespoons fresh lime juice
- 6 cups shredded green cabbage
- 3 cups shredded red cabbage
- 1 large red bell pepper, cut into matchstick strips
- 1 large yellow bell pepper, cut into matchstick strips
- 1 large green bell pepper, cut into matchstick strips
- 2 medium carrots, coarsely shredded

1. In a small dry skillet, toast the cumin seeds and the coriander seeds over moderate heat, stirring, until fragrant, about 2 minutes. Let cool, then grind the seeds to a powder in a mortar or spice grinder.

2. In a blender or food processor, combine the mayonnaise, shallots, jalapeño peppers, canned chiles, garlic, cilantro, maple syrup, Worcestershire, mustard, vinegar and the ground cumin and coriander seeds and process until smooth. Season the dressing with salt and the lime juice.

3. In a large salad bowl, mix the green and red cabbage with the bell peppers and carrots. Add the dressing and toss well to coat. Refrigerate until slightly chilled or for up to 3 hours. Season with salt before serving.   –*Dean Fearing*

MAKE AHEAD The dressing for the coleslaw can be made up to one day ahead and refrigerated.

Apple Carrot Slaw

20 SERVINGS (ABOUT 16 CUPS)

This is a light, tangy, highly seasoned slaw made with cabbage and a home-made spice blend.

- 3 large Granny Smith apples
- ¼ cup plus 2 tablespoons fresh lemon juice
- One 2-pound head Savoy cabbage— halved, cored and shredded
- 6 large carrots, cut into thin matchstick strips
- 12 large scallions, minced
- ½ cup chopped parsley
- ½ cup plus 1 tablespoon apple juice
- ½ cup plus 1 tablespoon cider vinegar
- ¼ cup plus 2 tablespoons olive oil
- 3 tablespoons Home Spice Mix (recipe follows)
- 2 teaspoons salt
- 1 teaspoon freshly ground pepper

1. Thinly slice the apples. Cut the apple slices into matchstick strips and transfer them to a glass or stainless-steel bowl. Add the lemon juice to the apples and toss well. Add the cabbage, carrots, scallions and parsley.

2. In a medium glass or stainless-steel bowl, whisk together the apple juice, vinegar, oil, spice mix, salt and pepper. Pour the dressing over the apple slaw and toss well. Serve the slaw at room temperature or chilled.

HOME SPICE MIX

MAKES ¾ CUP

- ¼ cup coriander seeds
- ¼ cup cumin seeds
- ¼ cup mustard seeds

1. In a small skillet, combine the coriander seeds, cumin seeds and 2 tablespoons of the mustard seeds. Toast over moderately high heat, shaking the pan, until the seeds are fragrant and lightly colored, about 2 minutes. Transfer the seeds to a plate.

2. When the toasted seeds have cooled, transfer them to a spice grinder and grind to a coarse powder, and then stir in the remaining 2 tablespoons of whole mustard seeds.   *–David Page*

MAKE AHEAD The slaw can be refrigerated for up to one day. The spice mix can be stored in an airtight glass jar for up to one week.

Red and Yellow Tomato Salad

20 SERVINGS

If you can't find the small pear-shaped tomatoes called for below, use any sweet and delicious red, yellow or orange cherry tomatoes instead.

- ¼ cup plus 2 tablespoons red-wine vinegar
- 2 red onions, thinly sliced
- 4 large garlic cloves, thinly sliced
- 2 pounds red pear-shaped tomatoes, halved lengthwise
- 2 pounds yellow pear-shaped tomatoes, halved lengthwise
- ½ cup chopped basil
- ¼ cup plus 2 tablespoons olive oil
- 1 tablespoon Home Spice Mix (above)

Salt and freshly ground pepper

1. In a medium stainless-steel saucepan, bring the red-wine vinegar to a simmer over moderate heat. Add the onions and garlic, cover and simmer until the onions begin to soften, about 5 minutes. Transfer the mixture to a bowl to cool.

2. In a large salad bowl, toss the tomatoes with the onion mixture, basil, oil and spice mix. Season the salad with salt and pepper and serve at room temperature.   *–David Page*

Classic Greek Salad

Classic Greek Salad

12 SERVINGS

- 1½ pounds ripe tomatoes, cut into ½-inch chunks
- 1 pound feta, cut into ⅓-inch dice
- 2 seedless cucumbers, peeled and cut into ½-inch dice
- 1 large red onion, thinly sliced
- ½ cup extra-virgin olive oil
- ¼ cup red wine vinegar
- 2 tablespoons minced oregano
- 2 tablespoons minced flat-leaf parsley
- 2½ teaspoons salt
- ¼ teaspoon freshly ground white pepper
- 12 anchovy fillets

Pitted Kalamata and cracked green olives (optional)

1. In a large salad bowl, combine the tomato chunks, the diced feta, the diced cucumbers and the sliced onion.

2. In a small glass or stainless-steel bowl, combine the olive oil, the red-wine vinegar, the minced oregano and parsley, and the salt and pepper.

3. Pour the dressing over the tomato mixture and toss the salad gently, being careful not to break up the feta. Mound the salad on a serving platter. Scatter the anchovy fillets and the Kalamata and cracked green olives all around the salad and serve.   *–Charles Bowman*

Roast Carrot Salad with Muscadine Vinaigrette

8 SERVINGS

Muscadine, the traditional sweet Southern wine, makes a great base for this vinaigrette because it balances the bitterness of the greens. If dandelion greens are unavailable, use all watercress. To use regular carrots instead of baby, peel and cut into slender three-inch pieces.

VINAIGRETTE

- 1 cup muscadine or other sweet wine, such as sweet Riesling
- 1 teaspoon Dijon mustard
- 1 teaspoon salt
- ¾ teaspoon freshly ground pepper
- ½ teaspoon fresh lemon juice
- ¼ cup plus 2 tablespoons vegetable oil

SALAD

- 2 pounds baby carrots, green tops trimmed to ½ inch
- 1½ tablespoons olive oil
- 4 cups packed dandelion greens, torn into bite-size pieces (about ¾ pound)
- 2 bunches of watercress, large stems trimmed
- ½ cup Pickled Pepper Relish (recipe follows)

Roast Carrot Salad with Muscadine Vinaigrette

1. MAKE THE VINAIGRETTE: In a small stainless-steel saucepan, boil the wine over moderate heat until reduced to ⅓ cup, about 9 minutes; let cool. Stir in the mustard, salt, pepper and lemon juice, then whisk in the vegetable oil.

2. MAKE THE SALAD: Preheat the oven to 400°. Toss the carrots with the olive oil and spread them on a large, heavy baking sheet. Roast the carrots for about 20 minutes, or until tender and lightly browned; let cool.

3. In a large salad bowl, toss the dandelion greens and watercress with half of the dressing. Mound the greens on eight plates. Toss the carrots in the remaining dressing and arrange them on the greens. Scatter 1 tablespoon of the relish over each salad and serve at once.

PICKLED-PEPPER RELISH

MAKES 1 PINT

- ¼ cup cider vinegar
- 3 tablespoons sugar
- ¼ teaspoon mustard seeds

---

salad tips

Salads are one of the highlights of summer dining—easy to make and light to eat, they're a great way to take advantage of the season's fresh greens. But even the spiciest arugula can get boring if you use the same old dressings. Here are some tips:

An equal partnership of greens and dressing is what makes a proper salad.

Make dressings quite strong, so that even a thin coating on greens will be tasty. Don't taste test by the spoonful; just dip a piece of the green into the dressing.

Use only enough dressing to coat the greens lightly. You can always add more dressing, but you can't take it away. *–Chris Schlesinger and John Willoughby*

- ¼ teaspoon celery seeds
- ¼ teaspoon salt

Pinch of turmeric

- 1 medium red bell pepper, cut into ⅓-inch dice
- 1 medium green bell pepper, cut into ⅓-inch dice
- 1 large Vidalia or other sweet onion, cut into ⅓-inch dice

In a medium stainless-steel saucepan, combine the vinegar, sugar, mustard seeds, celery seeds, salt and turmeric and bring to a boil over moderately high heat. Stir in the red and green bell peppers and the onion and simmer over moderately low heat, stirring occasionally, until the peppers are tender and most of the liquid has evaporated, about 15 minutes. Let the pepper relish cool before serving. *–John Fleer*

MAKE AHEAD The carrot salad can stand at room temperature for up to four hours. The Pickled-Pepper Relish can be made up to a week ahead and refrigerated.

Summer Bean and Radish Salad

20 SERVINGS

- ¼ cup red-wine vinegar
- 1 tablespoon Dijon mustard
- 1 tablespoon coarsely ground mustard seeds
- 1 tablespoon finely chopped shallots
- ¾ cup extra-virgin olive oil
- 2 teaspoons thyme leaves

Salt and freshly ground pepper

- 1 pound Romano beans, cut on the diagonal into 1½-inch lengths
- 1 pound yellow wax beans, cut on the diagonal into 2- to 3-inch lengths
- 1 pound green beans, cut on the diagonal into 2- to 3-inch lengths
- ½ pound radishes, sliced into thin rounds

Summer Bean and Radish Salad

1. In a medium bowl, whisk together the vinegar, mustard, mustard seeds and shallots. Whisk in the olive oil in a slow steady stream. Add the thyme and then season the dressing with salt and pepper.

2. In a large pot of boiling salted water, cook the Romano beans, yellow wax beans and green beans together until just tender, about 8 minutes. Drain the beans, rinse with cold water, and then drain again and pat thoroughly dry with paper towels.

3. In a salad bowl, toss the cooked beans and the radishes with the dressing. Season the salad with salt and pepper and serve. *–David Page*

MAKE AHEAD The dressing and the beans can be refrigerated separately for up to one day.

Bean Salad with Lime Vinaigrette

12 SERVINGS

- 3 pounds green beans, trimmed
- 3½ tablespoons fresh lime juice
- 3½ tablespoons extra-virgin olive oil
- 1 teaspoon finely grated lime zest
- 1 teaspoon salt
- 1 small red onion, thinly sliced

1. In a large saucepan of boiling salted water, cook the green beans, stirring a few times, until just tender, about 5 minutes. Drain the beans, rinse with cold water, and then drain the beans again and pat them thoroughly dry with paper towels.

2. In a large salad bowl, whisk the lime juice with the oil, lime zest and salt. Add the beans to the dressing and toss. Add the onion and toss again. Serve the salad at once. *–Marcia Kiesel*

MAKE AHEAD The cooked beans can be refrigerated overnight. Dress just before serving.

Wax-Bean Salad with Toasted Hazelnuts

8 SERVINGS

- ½ cup hazelnuts (about 2½ ounces)
- 1 large garlic clove, lightly smashed

Salt

- 1¾ pounds yellow wax beans, trimmed
- 2 tablespoons fresh lemon juice
- ¼ cup plus 1 tablespoon extra-virgin olive oil

Freshly ground pepper

- 2 medium heads of radicchio— halved, cored and finely shredded
- 2 tablespoons finely chopped flat-leaf parsley

1. Preheat the oven to 350°. Toast the hazelnuts in a small pan for about 15 minutes, or until they are fragrant and the skins blister. Transfer the nuts to a dish towel and rub them together to remove the skins. Let cool, and then coarsely chop the hazelnuts.

2. Bring a large pot of water to a boil. Add the garlic, 2 tablespoons of salt and the beans and boil until the beans are tender, about 7 minutes. Drain the beans and garlic, rinse with cold water, and then drain again and pat thoroughly dry with paper towels. Cut the beans into 2-inch lengths.

3. Mash the cooked garlic to a paste and transfer to a small glass or stainless-steel bowl. Stir in the lemon juice and then the oil and season with salt and pepper.

4. In a large salad bowl, toss the beans with the radicchio, the parsley and the garlic dressing. Season the salad with salt and pepper, sprinkle it with the hazelnuts and serve.

MAKE AHEAD The cooked beans and the garlic dressing can be refrigerated separately overnight. The toasted hazelnuts can stand overnight at room temperature.

Roasted Beets with Arugula

8 TO 10 SERVINGS

Citrus-roasted beets are mixed with arugula and salty ricotta salata to make a refreshing salad. You can use baby beets, either red or golden, instead of the medium beets; just reduce the cooking time.

- 2 pounds medium beets
- 10 thyme sprigs, plus 1 teaspoon minced thyme
- 5 garlic cloves, lightly crushed
- ½ cup dry white wine
- ½ cup fresh orange juice

Salt

- ¼ cup plus 2 tablespoons extra-virgin olive oil
- 2 tablespoons red-wine vinegar
- 1 teaspoon finely grated orange zest

Freshly ground pepper

- 1 large bunch of arugula, torn into bite-size pieces
- 5 ounces ricotta salata or feta, diced or crumbled

1. Preheat the oven to 400°. In a stainless-steel 13-by-9-inch baking dish, combine the beets, thyme sprigs, garlic, wine, orange juice and a pinch of salt. Cover the dish with aluminum foil and bake the beets for about 1¼ hours, or until they are tender. Let the beets cool slightly, then peel them and cut them into wedges. Discard the beet-cooking liquid.

2. In a large glass or stainless-steel bowl, combine the oil, vinegar, orange zest and minced thyme. Add the beet wedges, season with salt and pepper and toss the beets with the dressing. Then toss the dressed beets with the arugula. Transfer the beet salad to a platter and sprinkle the ricotta salata on top. *–Reed Hearon*

MAKE AHEAD The dressed beets can be refrigerated overnight. Let return to room temperature before tossing the beets with the arugula.

Pickled-Beet Salad with Amaranth and Hazelnuts

4 SERVINGS

- 1 cup nonfat plain yogurt
- Salt and freshly ground pepper
- 2 medium beets (about 7 ounces total), peeled and coarsely grated
- ½ cup dry red wine
- 2 tablespoons red-wine vinegar
- 1 teaspoon light brown sugar
- 1 jalapeño pepper—halved lengthwise, seeded and minced
- ½ cup hazelnuts (about 2½ ounces)
- 2 cups water
- 1 cup amaranth or quinoa (about 6 ounces)
- 2 medium Bosc pears
- 2 tablespoons extra-virgin olive oil
- 2 teaspoons fresh lemon juice
- 2 tablespoons minced chives
- 1 large Belgian endive, cored and sliced crosswise 1 inch thick
- 2 teaspoons hazelnut oil

1. Put the yogurt in a strainer set over a medium bowl and let drain in the refrigerator overnight or for up to 2 days. Transfer the yogurt cheese to a bowl and season with salt and pepper.

2. In a small stainless-steel saucepan, combine the beets, wine, vinegar, brown sugar and jalapeño. Simmer over low heat until the liquid is slightly reduced, about 10 minutes. Season with salt and pepper.

3. Preheat the oven to 350°. Toast the hazelnuts on a baking sheet for about 8 minutes, or until golden brown. Transfer the nuts to a kitchen towel and rub them together to remove the skins. Coarsely chop the nuts.

4. In a small saucepan, bring the water to a boil. Add a pinch of salt and the amaranth, stir well and cover. Simmer over low heat, stirring occasionally, until the amaranth is tender and the water has evaporated, about 15 minutes. Season the amaranth with salt and pepper and let cool, stirring once or twice.

Roasted Beets with Arugula

5. Light a charcoal grill or preheat a grill pan. Peel, quarter and core the pears. Coat them with 2 teaspoons of the olive oil and season with salt and pepper. Grill or pan-sear the pears over moderate heat until lightly charred, about 3 minutes per side. Let cool, then cut the pears into 1-inch pieces.

6. In a large glass or stainless-steel bowl, combine the lemon juice, the chives and the remaining 1 tablespoon plus 1 teaspoon olive oil. Add the endive, the pears and ¼ cup of the toasted hazelnuts. Toss well and season with salt and pepper.

7. Set four 3½- to 4-inch ring molds or four 4-ounce cans that are open at both ends on a baking sheet. Drain the pickled beets, reserving the liquid. Spoon the endive salad into the molds, pressing gently to form the bottom layer. Spread the yogurt cheese over the salad in each of the molds and top with a heaping tablespoon of the pickled beets and ⅓ cup of the amaranth. Cover the molded salads with plastic wrap and refrigerate until completely chilled, about 30 minutes.

8. Slide a metal spatula underneath one of the molded salads and transfer it to a plate. Pressing gently on the center of the salad, lift the mold up and off the salad. Repeat the procedure with the remaining salads. Garnish each plate with little mounds of the remaining pickled beets and scatter the remaining toasted hazelnuts around. Drizzle the reserved beet liquid and the hazelnut oil around the salads, top with the crispy leeks and serve.   *–Keith Luce*

MAKE AHEAD The recipe can be made through Step 2 up to five days ahead. Refrigerate the beets and the drained yogurt separately.

WINE 1996 Geyser Peak Johannisberg Riesling or 1996 Gundlach-Bundschu Gewürztraminer, both from California.

Thai Mushroom Salad

4 SERVINGS

If oyster and portobello mushrooms are not available, use white mushrooms. Serve the salad with rice.

  ½ **pound portobello mushrooms, stemmed, caps coarsely chopped**

  ½ **pound oyster mushrooms, stemmed, caps coarsely chopped**

  1 **garlic clove**

  ½ **teaspoon sugar**

1 to 2 **teaspoons crumbled dried red chile or crushed red pepper**

  3 **tablespoons fresh lime juice**

  2 **tablespoons Thai fish sauce (nam pla)**

  2 **tablespoons thinly sliced shallots**

1½ **cups mint leaves**

Tender Bibb or Boston lettuce leaves

1. In a large saucepan, bring 2 inches of water to a boil. Add the mushrooms, cover partially and cook until tender, about 4 minutes. Drain the mushrooms.

2. In a mortar, pound the garlic and sugar to a paste. Add the chile and pound to blend. Add the lime juice and fish sauce and mix well.

3. Transfer the mushrooms to a bowl. Add the shallots and dressing. Toss gently to coat, add the mint and toss again. Line a platter with lettuce leaves; mound the salad on top. Serve at room temperature. *–Jeffrey Alford and Naomi Duguid*

Shaved-Artichoke Salad

10 SERVINGS

  ¼ **cup plus 1 tablespoon fresh lemon juice**

2½ **pounds smallest baby artichokes (about 35)**

  1 **medium shallot, finely chopped**

  ½ **cup extra-virgin olive oil**

Salt and freshly ground pepper

  2 **cups shaved Parmesan (about 2 ounces)**

1. Stir 3 tablespoons of the lemon juice into a bowl of water. Working with one artichoke at a time, pull off the dark outer leaves and trim ½ inch off the top. Peel the stem. Halve the artichoke, slice thinly lengthwise and add to the water.

2. In a large salad bowl, whisk the shallot into the remaining 2 tablespoons of lemon juice. Whisk in the olive oil in a thin stream and season with salt and pepper.

3. Drain the artichokes well and toss them with the dressing. Refrigerate for at least 1 hour or overnight. Season with salt and pepper and garnish with the Parmesan.   *–Reed Hearon*

Spring Asparagus Salad with Quail-Egg Toasts

10 SERVINGS

You can buy quail eggs in specialty-food stores and some supermarkets, or omit the eggs and serve the toasted brioche alongside the salad.

  3 **pounds large asparagus spears, peeled and trimmed**

Ice water

  3 **large leeks, white and tender green, sliced crosswise ½ inch thick**

Thai Mushroom Salad

¼ cup Champagne vinegar
1 tablespoon fresh lemon juice
1 small shallot, minced
½ teaspoon sugar
¼ cup plus 2 tablespoons extra-virgin olive oil
¼ cup pure olive oil
Salt and freshly ground pepper
Ten ½-inch-thick brioche slices, about 3-by-2 inches
2 teaspoons vegetable oil
10 quail eggs
5 cups frisée, torn into bite-size pieces
2 tablespoons minced chives

1. Bring a large saucepan of salted water to a boil. Add the asparagus spears and cook over high heat until they are just tender, about 4 minutes. Using a slotted spoon, transfer the asparagus spears to a large bowl of ice water, then drain them on paper towels. Add the leeks to the saucepan of boiling water and boil until just tender, about 3 minutes. Drain the leeks, refresh them in the ice water and pat them dry with paper towels.

2. In a small glass or stainless-steel bowl, combine the vinegar, lemon juice, shallot and sugar. Whisk in the extra-virgin and pure olive oils and season the vinaigrette with salt and pepper. In a medium glass or stainless-steel bowl, toss the leeks with ⅓ cup of the vinaigrette and let marinate at room temperature for 20 minutes.

3. Preheat the oven to 400°. Bake the brioche slices on a baking sheet for about 5 minutes, or until lightly crisp. Set the toasts aside on the sheet and leave the oven on.

4. Heat the vegetable oil in a large non-stick skillet. Crack the quail eggs into the skillet and cook them over moderately high heat, without turning, until the whites are lightly browned and the yolks are bright yellow and slightly runny, about 2 minutes. Set a sunny-side-up egg on top of each toasted piece of brioche.

5. Put the asparagus on a large plate. Add ½ cup of the marinated leeks, season the asparagus with salt and pepper and toss gently. In a bowl, toss the frisée with 3 tablespoons of the remaining vinaigrette. Rewarm the quail-egg toasts in the oven.

6. Arrange the dressed asparagus on ten plates. Scatter the remaining leeks on top. Mound a little frisée alongside the asparagus and set a warm quail-egg toast on top. Sprinkle with the chives and pass the remaining vinaigrette separately at the table. *–Maria Helm*

MAKE AHEAD The vegetables can be refrigerated separately overnight. Let them return to room temperature before proceeding with Step 2.

WINE Asparagus is a difficult vegetable to pair with wines. This dish needs a crisp white with a touch of sweetness, such as the 1995 Buttonwood Farm Santa Ynez Valley Marsanne, with its delicate melon and green-peach aromas and flavors.

Leeks with Miso Vinaigrette

2 SERVINGS

Japanese light miso paste flavors the vinaigrette here. It's available at Asian markets and health-food stores.

4 medium or 8 small leeks, white and tender green
3 tablespoons rice vinegar
1 tablespoon fresh lemon juice
2½ teaspoons Japanese light miso paste
½ teaspoon Dijon mustard
½ teaspoon mayonnaise
½ teaspoon minced fresh ginger
⅛ teaspoon cayenne pepper
Pinch of salt
2 tablespoons extra-virgin olive oil
¼ cup peanut oil
2 tablespoons thinly sliced red bell pepper

Spring Asparagus Salad with Quail-Egg Toasts

1. In a medium saucepan of boiling salted water, cook the leeks over moderately high heat until tender when pierced with a knife, about 12 minutes for medium leeks and 8 minutes for small ones. Refresh the leeks in a bowl of cold water for 1 minute, then drain and pat dry. Halve the leeks lengthwise.

2. In a blender or food processor, combine the vinegar, lemon juice, miso, mustard, mayonnaise, ginger, cayenne and salt and mix for 30 seconds. With the machine on, gradually add the olive oil, and then the peanut oil, and mix until completely smooth. Scrape the vinaigrette into a bowl.

3. Spread the cut-side of the leeks with about 2 tablespoons of the miso vinaigrette so it permeates the layers. Cover and refrigerate until ready to serve.

4. To serve, drizzle the leeks with the remaining miso vinaigrette and garnish them with the sliced red bell pepper. Serve the salad chilled or at room temperature. *–Jonathan Eismann*

MAKE AHEAD After Step 3, the leeks and the remaining vinaigrette can be refrigerated separately overnight.

New-Potato Salad with Grilled Red Onions

16 SERVINGS

- 5 pounds medium red potatoes

Coarse salt

- 8 poblano chiles
- 1 pound medium red onions, sliced ½ inch thick
- ⅓ cup plus 1 tablespoon extra-virgin olive oil
- 2 tablespoons oregano leaves
- 1 tablespoon coriander seeds
- ¼ teaspoon cumin seeds
- 6 thick slices of bacon
- 2 tablespoons red-wine vinegar
- 1 cup chopped cilantro
- 3 jalapeño peppers, seeded and minced

Freshly ground pepper

1. In a large saucepan, cover the potatoes with water, add 1 tablespoon of salt and bring to a boil. Simmer over moderate heat until tender, about 20 minutes. Drain and let cool. Quarter the potatoes and put them in a large glass or stainless-steel bowl.

2. Meanwhile, light a grill or preheat the broiler. Grill or broil the poblanos until charred all over. Transfer to a bowl, cover with plastic wrap and let steam for 5 minutes. Discard the charred skin, stems and seeds and cut the chiles into thick rounds.

3. Brush the onion slices with the 1 tablespoon oil and grill or broil them until tender and lightly caramelized on both sides, about 10 minutes.

4. In a medium skillet, toast the oregano leaves over low heat until just fragrant, about 10 seconds. Transfer the oregano to a plate. Add the coriander and cumin seeds to the skillet and cook, stirring, until fragrant, about 1 minute. Mince the seeds with a knife or grind in a mortar. Add the bacon to the skillet and cook over moderate heat until crisp, about 6 minutes. Let cool, then coarsely chop the bacon.

5. In a small glass or stainless-steel bowl, stir the remaining ⅓ cup of oil with the vinegar, cilantro, oregano and toasted spices. Add the jalapeños, bacon, grilled onions and dressing to the potatoes and toss the salad gently. Season with salt and pepper.   –Robert Del Grande

MAKE AHEAD The salad can stand at room temperature up to four hours.

Elizabeth's Potato Salad

20 SERVINGS

- 1 dozen large eggs
- 7 pounds large baking potatoes, washed but not peeled

Salt

- 2 cups mayonnaise
- ¼ cup evaporated milk
- 3 tablespoons Dijon mustard
- 2 tablespoons cider vinegar
- 2 tablespoons sugar

Freshly ground pepper

- 1 large onion, finely chopped
- 3 celery ribs, cut into ⅓-inch dice
- 1 tablespoon paprika
- 2 tablespoons chopped chives

1. In a large saucepan, cover the eggs with lukewarm water and bring to a boil over high heat. Boil vigorously for 2 minutes. Cover, remove from the heat and let stand for 12 minutes. Drain the eggs and cool under running water, shaking the pan to crack the shells. When the eggs are cool enough to handle, peel them. Refrigerate until cold.

2. Put the potatoes in a large pot and add lukewarm water to cover. Add 3 tablespoons of salt and bring to a boil over high heat. Cook until the potatoes are completely tender but not falling apart, about 25 minutes. Drain the potatoes and spread out on a large baking sheet to cool slightly. Peel the potatoes while they are still warm; let cool.

3. In a medium glass or stainless-steel bowl, whisk the mayonnaise with the evaporated milk, mustard, vinegar, sugar and a generous pinch each salt and pepper.

4. Thinly slice the eggs crosswise and transfer to a large bowl. Cut the potatoes into 1-inch chunks. In a large bowl, gently mix one-third of the eggs, potatoes, onion and celery with one-third of the dressing. Season with salt and pepper and transfer to a serving bowl. Repeat with the remaining ingredients in two more batches. Sprinkle with the paprika and chives.   –David Page

MAKE AHEAD The eggs, potatoes and dressing can be refrigerated separately for up to two days. Bring to room temperature before proceeding with Step 4. The completed potato salad can be refrigerated for up to one day. Remove from the refrigerator one hour before serving; sprinkle with the paprika and chives at the last minute.

Panzanella

8 SERVINGS

If you have time, toss the cucumbers with salt and drain them for thirty minutes before assembling the salad.

- 4 thick slices of stale coarse peasant bread (about ½ pound)
- ⅓ cup extra-virgin olive oil
- 2 tablespoons red-wine vinegar
- 2 garlic cloves, minced
- ½ teaspoon crushed red pepper
- ½ teaspoon salt
- ¼ teaspoon freshly ground black pepper
- 6 cups lightly packed salad greens
- 4 large tomatoes, cut into 1-inch dice
- 2 medium cucumbers—peeled, halved lengthwise, seeded and thinly sliced crosswise
- 1 medium red onion, thinly sliced
- ½ cup coarsely chopped basil

1. In a large bowl, cover the bread with cold water and let soak for 10 minutes. Squeeze out the excess water. In a small glass or stainless-steel bowl, whisk the oil with the vinegar, garlic, red pepper, salt and black pepper.

2. In a large salad bowl, toss the salad greens with the tomatoes, cucumbers, onion and basil. Crumble in the soaked bread with your hands. Add the dressing and toss well. Refrigerate the salad for up to 4 hours and serve it well chilled.   *–Egi Maccioni*

Tabbouleh-Style Three-Grain Salad
20 SERVINGS

This salad was inspired by *With the Grain* (Knopf), by Raymond Sokolov.

  1   cup (6 ounces) Wehani rice, rinsed
Salt
  1   cup (7 ounces) pearl barley
  1   cup (6 ounces) coarse grade cracked wheat (bulgur)
  4   tomatoes, cut into ½-inch dice
  2   European cucumbers—peeled, seeded and cut into ½-inch dice
  1   cup chopped parsley
1½   cups olive oil
  ½   cup fresh lemon juice
Freshly ground pepper

1. In a medium saucepan, cover the rice with 4 cups of cold water, add a large pinch of salt and bring to a boil. Cover partially and simmer over low heat, stirring occasionally, until the grains of rice are just tender, about 45 minutes. Drain the rice and rinse it under cold water; drain well. Spread the rice out on a baking sheet and let cool completely.

2. Meanwhile, in a medium saucepan, cover the barley with 4 cups of water, add a large pinch of salt and bring to a boil. Cover partially and simmer over low heat, stirring occasionally, until just tender, about 40 minutes. Drain well. Spread the barley on a baking sheet and let cool completely.

3. In a medium saucepan, bring 3 cups of water to a boil. Add a large pinch of salt and the cracked wheat, stir well and simmer over low heat for 10 minutes. Remove the pan from the heat,

cover and set aside for 15 minutes. Drain off any excess water, transfer the cracked wheat to a platter and let cool completely.

4. In a large glass or stainless-steel bowl, toss the cooled grains with the tomatoes, cucumbers and parsley. Add the olive oil and the lemon juice and toss well. Season with salt and pepper. Serve the salad at room temperature or chilled.   *–David Page*

MAKE AHEAD Once the grains have all cooled completely, they can be combined and refrigerated for up to three days. Bring to room temperature before proceeding with Step 4. The finished salad can be refrigerated for one day.

Black-Eyed-Pea Salad
12 SERVINGS

This earthy salad makes a lovely counterpoint to Potent Garlic Dip (p. 13).

  1   pound dried black-eyed peas, picked over and rinsed
  1   small red onion, finely chopped
  ¼   cup plus 2 tablespoons extra-virgin olive oil
  ¼   cup red-wine vinegar
  ¼   cup finely chopped flat-leaf parsley
Salt and freshly ground white pepper

In a large bowl, cover the black-eyed peas with cold water and let soak overnight. Drain and rinse the peas; transfer to a large saucepan. Add 3 quarts of water and bring to a boil over high heat. Lower the heat to moderate and cook until tender, 30 to 35 minutes. Drain the peas, rinse with cold water and drain again. Transfer the peas to a large salad bowl and add the onion, oil and vinegar. Toss the black-eyed peas with the parsley, season with salt and white pepper and serve.   *–Nicola Kotsoni*

MAKE AHEAD The dressed peas can stand at room temperature for up to four hours. Add the parsley, salt and pepper just before serving.

Coconut Shrimp with Tamarind Vinaigrette
8 SERVINGS

Caribbean tamarind syrup, the key to the sweet-tart salad dressing, is available at specialty-food stores and Latin American markets.

About 1 cup all-purpose flour, for dredging
  6   large eggs, lightly beaten
  3   cups shredded sweetened coconut (about 9 ounces)
 16   jumbo shrimp—shelled, deveined and cut almost in half lengthwise down the back
  1   quart vegetable oil, for frying
  2   tablespoons tamarind syrup
  2   tablespoons balsamic vinegar
  2   tablespoons extra-virgin olive oil
  1   teaspoon kosher salt
  ¼   teaspoon freshly ground pepper
  8   cups mixed salad greens, torn into bite-size pieces

1. Put the flour, eggs and coconut in separate shallow bowls. Dredge each of the shrimp first in the flour, then in the eggs and then in the coconut; be sure to press the coconut firmly onto the shrimp. Arrange the coconut-coated shrimp on a baking sheet. Cover the shrimp and refrigerate them for at least 1 hour or overnight.

2. In a medium saucepan, heat the vegetable oil over moderate heat to 350°. Working with two at a time, fry the shrimp until golden brown, about 4 minutes. Drain the shrimp on a rack set over a baking sheet. Keep the fried shrimp warm in a low oven.

3. In a blender, process the tamarind syrup, vinegar, oil, salt and pepper. Put the greens in a bowl, add the dressing and toss to coat. Mound the salad on eight small plates. Set two of the fried shrimp beside each of the salads and serve.   *–Herb Wilson*

Casablanca Salad

10 SERVINGS

Mint adds a refreshing punch to this warm shrimp salad.

- ½ cup plus 1 tablespoon extra-virgin olive oil

- 2½ tablespoons sherry vinegar
- Salt and freshly ground pepper
- 1 medium onion, finely chopped
- 1½ pounds medium shrimp, shelled and deveined
- ¼ cup mint leaves, torn in half
- 3 tablespoons golden raisins (optional)
- ¼ teaspoon ground cumin
- 1 pound mesclun

1. In a small bowl, whisk 7½ tablespoons of the oil with the sherry vinegar. Season with salt and pepper.

2. Heat the remaining 1½ tablespoons of oil in a large skillet. Add the onion and cook over moderate heat, stirring, until softened and just beginning to brown, about 7 minutes. Add the shrimp,

LEFT: **Saigon Salad.**
BELOW: **Casablanca Salad.**

mint, raisins, cumin and a pinch each of salt and pepper and cook, stirring, until the shrimp are pink, about 7 minutes.

3. In a large bowl, toss the mesclun with the dressing. Mound the salad on ten plates. Scatter the shrimp over the salads. —*Michel Benasra*

WINE Open a crisp lean white, such as a Pinot Grigio. Try the 1995 Doro Princic or the 1995 Santa Margherita.

Sara's Lobster and Mango Salad

4 SERVINGS

My daughter, Sara, recently returned from Cambodia filled with admiration for the region's light, robustly flavored salads based on shredded green mangoes with bean sprouts, peanuts, fresh green chiles, cilantro and Asian fish sauce. Maine lobster seemed like a natural addition.

- 2 cooked 1½-pound lobsters
- 2 teaspoons chopped fresh ginger
- 2 teaspoons sugar
- 1 garlic clove, halved
- 1 small Thai chile, minced
- 3 tablespoons fresh lime juice
- 1 tablespoon Asian fish sauce
- 1 teaspoon Asian sesame oil
- 2 cups green (unripe) mango or papaya, peeled and julienned
- 1 European cucumber—halved lengthwise, seeded and julienned
- ¼ cup small basil leaves or 2 tablespoons chopped basil
- ¼ cup small mint leaves or 2 tablespoons chopped mint
- ¼ cup cilantro leaves or 2 tablespoons chopped cilantro
- ¼ cup coarsely chopped unsalted peanuts

1. Remove the meat from the lobster knuckles and claws. Twist the tails off the bodies. Split the tails lengthwise and remove the tail meat. Pull out and discard the black intestinal vein. Cut all the lobster into bite-size chunks.

2. In a mortar, pound the ginger with the sugar, garlic and chile to make a paste. Alternatively, chop the ingredients in a mini-processor. Stir in the lime juice, fish sauce and sesame oil.

3. In a salad bowl, toss the mango, cucumber, basil, mint and cilantro. Add the dressing and toss well. Arrange the lobster on top and sprinkle with the peanuts. Serve at room temperature or slightly chilled. –*Nancy Harmon Jenkins*

WINE 1996 Bonny Doon Ca' del Solo Big House White or 1994 San Pietro Gavi

Tuna and Potato Salad

6 SERVINGS

12 small new potatoes, scrubbed but not peeled (about 1½ pounds)

Two 6-ounce cans tuna in olive oil

2 tablespoons white-wine vinegar

1 teaspoon salt

¼ teaspoon freshly ground pepper

2 celery ribs, strings removed, celery finely chopped (½ cup)

2 scallions, thinly sliced

¼ cup chopped flat-leaf parsley

Romaine lettuce leaves or watercress

1. In a medium saucepan, cover the potatoes with cold water, bring to a boil and cook until tender, about 17 minutes. Drain the potatoes and let them cool slightly, then quarter them or cut into 1-inch chunks.

2. Drain the oil from the tuna into a glass or stainless-steel bowl and whisk in the vinegar, salt and pepper. Add the potatoes, tuna, celery, scallions and parsley and toss well. Serve the salad on the lettuce leaves. –*Diana Sturgis*

Saigon Salad

12 SERVINGS

¼ cup soy sauce

2 tablespoons vegetable oil, plus 1 cup for frying

7 garlic cloves, coarsely chopped

Two 2½-pound sirloin steaks

8 shallots, thinly sliced

One 2-inch piece of fresh ginger, peeled and coarsely chopped

2 tablespoons sugar

1 large jalapeño pepper, coarsely chopped

½ cup fresh lime juice

⅓ cup Asian fish sauce

Salt and freshly ground pepper

3 pounds cabbage, cored and shredded

1 cup coarsely chopped mint leaves

1 cup coarsely chopped cilantro

4 cups mung bean sprouts

1½ cups chopped unsalted peanuts

1. In a shallow dish, combine the soy sauce with the 2 tablespoons of oil and four of the garlic cloves. Coat the steaks with the marinade and refrigerate for at least 1 hour or overnight.

2. In a saucepan, heat the remaining 1 cup of oil until shimmering. Working in three batches, fry the shallots over moderately high heat, stirring, until browned, about 4 minutes; lower the heat if necessary. Drain on paper towels.

3. In a mini-processor, combine the remaining 3 garlic cloves with the ginger, sugar and jalapeño; process to a paste. Blend in the lime juice and fish sauce.

4. Light a grill or preheat the broiler. Season the steaks with salt and pepper and grill or broil over moderately high heat for about 5 minutes per side, or until nicely browned and medium rare. Let rest for 10 minutes. Slice the steaks ¼ inch thick. Stack the slices and cut them lengthwise into ¼-inch-thick strips. In a very large bowl, combine the steak, cabbage, mint and cilantro. Toss the salad with the dressing and sprinkle with the bean sprouts, peanuts and fried shallots. –*Marcia Kiesel*

WINE Although beef might make you think red—the 1994 Steele Wines Du Pratt Vineyard Zinfandel would work well—the Asian spices here suggest a fruity white, such as the 1995 Dopff Au Moulin Riesling.

CHAPTER 4 soups

Curried Pumpkin Soup with a Spicy Lentil Crisp (p. 77)

71 Yellow-Tomato Gazpacho with Olivata Croutons

71 Parsnip and Carrot Soup

71 Chilled Carrot Ginger Soup

72 Sweet Pea Soup with Chive Oil

73 Corn Chowder with Spicy Red-Pepper Cream

74 Spinach and Parsley Soup with Lemon

75 Creamy Root-Vegetable Soup

75 Roasted-Vegetable Soup

77 Butternut-Squash Soup with Scallion Cream

77 Curried Pumpkin Soup with Spicy Lentil Crisps

79 Sicilian Potato and Pasta Soup

79 Risi e Bisi

80 Mid-Winter Soup

81 Smoky Escarole and Carrot Soup

81 Cannellini and Escarole Soup with Garlic Oil

81 Spinach and Crabmeat Soup with Country-Ham Croutons

82 Sam Hayward's Lobster and Sweet-Corn Soup

83 Spanish Mussel and Chorizo Soup

83 Smoked-Fish Chowder

84 Minestra Maritata

85 Tortilla Soup

85 Thai Chicken and Coconut Soup

Yellow-Tomato Gazpacho

Yellow-Tomato Gazpacho with Olivata Croutons

8 SERVINGS

Yellow tomatoes give this "summer in a cup" soup a pleasant sweetness. Freeze leftovers in an ice-cube tray and add them to Bloody Marys.

3½ pounds yellow tomatoes, cored and halved crosswise
¼ cup dry white wine
¼ cup rice-wine vinegar
1 tablespoon Worcestershire sauce
2 medium cucumbers—peeled, seeded and coarsely chopped
1 medium yellow bell pepper, coarsely chopped
½ cup coarsely chopped Vidalia or other sweet onion
½ teaspoon minced garlic
2 to 3 tablespoons fresh lime juice
1 teaspoon Tabasco sauce
Salt and freshly ground pepper
½ cup thinly sliced scallion greens, for garnish
Olivata Croutons (recipe follows)

1. Working over a fine sieve set over a bowl, remove the seeds from the tomatoes. Strain the juices. Pour ½ cup of the tomato juices into a small glass measure and add the wine, vinegar and Worcestershire sauce.

2. Working in batches, puree the tomatoes with the cucumbers, bell pepper, onion and garlic in a blender until smooth, adding a little of the tomato-juice mixture to each batch. Pass the gazpacho through a fine sieve and season with lime juice, Tabasco sauce, salt and pepper. Refrigerate until chilled. Garnish the gazpacho with the scallions and serve with the Olivata Croutons.

OLIVATA CROUTONS

8 SERVINGS

Olive-oil cooking spray
Eight ¼-inch-thick baguette slices
¼ cup sun-dried tomatoes (not oil-packed)

Boiling water
½ cup pitted Kalamata olives (about 5 ounces)
1 tablespoon finely chopped basil
1 teaspoon extra-virgin olive oil
½ teaspoon finely chopped garlic
Salt and freshly ground pepper

1. Preheat the oven to 400°. Lightly coat a baking sheet with olive-oil cooking spray. Arrange the baguette slices on the baking sheet, lightly coat them with olive-oil cooking spray and bake for about 7 minutes, or until the toasts are golden and crisp. Let the toasts cool completely on the baking sheet.

2. In a small bowl, soak the sun-dried tomatoes in the boiling water until they are plump, about 10 minutes; drain well. In a mini-processor, combine the sun-dried tomatoes with the olives, basil, oil and garlic and pulse until finely chopped but not pureed. Transfer the mixture to a small bowl and season with salt and pepper. Spread each crouton with 1 tablespoon of the olivata mixture and serve. —John Fleer

MAKE AHEAD The yellow-tomato gazpacho is best made a day ahead and refrigerated. The olivata mixture can be refrigerated for up to three days. The croutons can be kept in an airtight container at room temperature, also for three days.

WINE An aromatic Sauvignon Blanc with hints of spice and citrus will complement the gazpacho. Two options to consider: the 1995 Matanzas Creek Sauvignon Blanc or the 1995 Chateau Potelle Sauvignon Blanc.

Parsnip and Carrot Soup

4 SERVINGS Q

While parsnips are available year round, they're at their best during the cold months when they're just harvested.

12 thin slices from a baguette
2 tablespoons unsalted butter, melted
1 small garlic clove, peeled

2 tablespoons vegetable oil
4 medium parsnips (about 1 pound), peeled and diced
4 medium carrots (about 1 pound), diced
1 medium leek, white and tender green, thinly sliced
5 cups chicken stock or canned low-sodium broth
1 bay leaf
Salt and freshly ground pepper
½ cup tubetti or other small pasta
1 tablespoon chopped parsley

1. Brush the bread slices on both sides with the butter and toast until golden. Lightly rub one side of the croutons with the garlic clove.

2. Heat the oil in a large saucepan. Add the parsnips and the carrots and cook over moderately high heat until the vegetables are golden, about 10 minutes. Stir in the leek, then add the stock and bay leaf. Season with salt and pepper, cover and bring to a boil. Cook over low heat until the vegetables are soft, about 13 minutes.

3. Meanwhile, cook the pasta in boiling salted water until not quite al dente, about 8 minutes; drain. Add the pasta to the soup, cover and cook until al dente, about 3 minutes. Discard the bay leaf. Stir in the parsley and serve with the garlic croutons. —Grace Parisi

Chilled Carrot Ginger Soup

6 SERVINGS

1 tablespoon canola oil
1 medium onion, chopped
2 pounds carrots, sliced
4 quarter-size slices of peeled fresh ginger, lightly smashed
2½ cups chicken stock or canned low-sodium broth
Salt and freshly ground white pepper
2 to 3 teaspoons fresh lemon juice
1 teaspoon honey
Dash of hot sauce (optional)
Cilantro leaves, for garnish

Chilled Carrot Ginger Soup

1. Heat the oil in a large saucepan. Add the onion and cook over moderately low heat, stirring occasionally, until softened, about 5 minutes. Add the carrots and ginger and cook for 5 minutes, stirring occasionally. Add 2 cups of the stock, season with salt and pepper and bring to a boil. Cover and simmer over low heat until the carrots are tender, about 25 minutes.

2. Strain the cooking liquid into a heat-proof bowl and discard the ginger. In a blender, puree the vegetables with 1 cup of the cooking liquid until smooth. Stir the puree into the vegetable-cooking liquid in the bowl and add the lemon juice, the honey and the remaining ½ cup of stock. Refrigerate the soup until it is chilled or for up to 1 day. Season the soup with salt, pepper and hot sauce, and serve garnished with cilantro leaves.   *–Katrin Theodoli*

Sweet Pea Soup with Chive Oil

8 SERVINGS **Q**

Vibrant green in color and tasting of baby peas, this soup is like a whiff of spring. The quick, easy chive oil adds a fresh herbal note.

- 6 slices of bacon, cut into ½-inch pieces (optional)
- 2 tablespoons unsalted butter
- 4 medium leeks, white parts only, coarsely chopped
- 5 cups chicken stock or canned low-sodium broth

Two 10-ounce packages frozen baby peas (4 cups)

- 1 small Idaho potato, peeled and coarsely grated

Salt and freshly ground white pepper

- ¼ cup chopped chives
- ⅓ cup canola oil

1. Cook the bacon in a small skillet over moderate heat, stirring, until browned and crisp, about 6 minutes. Drain and set aside.

2. Melt the butter in a large saucepan. Add the leeks and cook over low heat, stirring occasionally, until they are barely softened, about 5 minutes. Add the chicken stock, baby peas and grated potato and bring to a boil over high heat. Cover partially and cook until the vegetables are tender but still bright, about 10 minutes.

3. In a blender, puree the soup in batches until very smooth. Season with salt and pepper. Return to the pan; keep warm over low heat.

4. Rinse the blender. Add the chives and the canola oil to the blender and puree until smooth, about 4 minutes; scrape down the sides as necessary. Transfer the chive oil to a small bowl and season with salt.

5. Ladle the soup into shallow soup plates, drizzle with the chive oil and sprinkle with the bacon. *–Grace Parisi*

WINE A Gewürztraminer: Turley's 1995 Martinelli Dry Select; Zind Humbrecht from Alsace

MAKE AHEAD The soup and chive oil can be refrigerated separately for up to two days. Reheat the soup gently before serving.

Corn Chowder with Spicy Red-Pepper Cream

4 SERVINGS

A spoonful of Spicy Red-Pepper Cream added to the bowls of chowder at serving time brightens the taste of the corn without overwhelming the vegetable's fresh flavor.

- 4 ears of corn, shucked
- 1 slice of bacon, chopped
- ¼ cup plus 2 tablespoons finely chopped onion
- 3 tablespoons finely chopped celery

- 3 small red potatoes, cut into ½-inch dice (½ pound)
- 1½ cups chicken stock or canned low-sodium broth
- 1 teaspoon thyme leaves
- 1 bay leaf
- Salt and freshly ground pepper
- 1½ cups milk
- Spicy Red-Pepper Cream (recipe follows)

1. Using a sharp knife, cut the corn kernels from the cobs. In a heavy casserole, cook the bacon over moderately low heat until slightly crisp, 3 to 4 minutes. Add the onion and the celery and cook until they are softened, about 4 minutes. Add the potatoes, the chicken stock, the thyme and the bay leaf. Season with salt and pepper and bring to a boil. Cover and simmer over low heat until the potatoes are just tender, about 10 minutes. Add the milk and simmer for 5 minutes. Add the corn kernels and simmer until they are tender, 3 to 4 minutes. Remove the bay leaf and then season the corn chowder with salt and pepper.

2. Ladle the corn chowder into soup bowls and top each serving with a spoonful of the red-pepper cream. ➤

Sweet Pea Soup with Chive Oil

Spinach and Parsley Soup with Lemon

SPICY RED-PEPPER CREAM

MAKES ABOUT ½ CUP

- 1 large or 2 small red bell peppers
- 2 teaspoons medium-hot chile powder or ¼ teaspoon cayenne pepper
- 1½ teaspoons oregano leaves
- ½ tablespoon olive oil
- ¼ teaspoon salt
- 1 tablespoon heavy cream

I. Roast the pepper over a gas flame or under the broiler, turning, until charred all over. Transfer the pepper to a bowl, cover with plastic and let steam for 20 minutes. Peel the pepper and discard the core, ribs and seeds. Coarsely chop the pepper.

2. In a blender or mini-processor, puree the pepper with the chile powder, oregano, oil and salt. Transfer the puree to a small bowl and then stir in the heavy cream.   *—Georgeanne Brennan*

MAKE AHEAD The corn chowder can be refrigerated for up to four hours and reheated. The Spicy Red-Pepper Cream can be made up to a day ahead and refrigerated.

Spinach and Parsley Soup with Lemon

10 SERVINGS

To preserve the fresh flavor of this creamy-but-light spinach soup, don't add the crème fraîche until just before serving.

- 2 tablespoons unsalted butter
- 1 medium onion, coarsely chopped
- 1 tablespoon plus 1 teaspoon honey
- 5⅓ cups chicken stock or 3⅓ cups canned low-sodium broth plus 2 cups water

2 pounds fresh spinach, tough stems discarded and leaves rinsed

1 cup tightly packed flat-leaf parsley leaves, plus 2 tablespoons finely chopped parsley for garnish

2 cups crème fraîche or sour cream

2 tablespoons plus 2 teaspoons fresh lemon juice

Salt and freshly ground pepper

Julienned lemon zest, for garnish

1. Melt the butter in a large stainless-steel saucepan. Add the onion and cook over moderately high heat, stirring, until it is softened and lightly browned, about 6 minutes. Add the honey and cook, stirring, for 1 minute. Add the chicken stock and raise the heat to high; boil for 5 minutes. Stir in the spinach and the whole parsley leaves. Bring the soup to a boil and cook until the spinach is tender but still bright green, about 3 minutes. Working in batches, puree the soup in a blender until it is smooth. Return the soup to the saucepan.

2. Stir 1½ cups of the crème fraîche into the soup and gently reheat; don't allow the soup to boil. Stir in the lemon juice and then season the soup with salt and pepper. Ladle the soup into shallow soup plates, add a dollop of crème fraîche to each serving and garnish the soup with the chopped parsley and the julienned lemon zest. Serve the soup at once.   *–Maria Helm*

MAKE AHEAD The soup can be made through Step 1 and refrigerated for up to six hours. Reheat the soup before proceeding.

WINE The 1994 Trefethen Napa Valley Chardonnay, with its crisp, non-malolactic acidity, will contrast with the richness of the spinach soup and bring out the tanginess of the crème fraîche and the lemon.

Creamy Root-Vegetable Soup

4 SERVINGS **L**

2 teaspoons olive oil

1 pound parsnips, peeled and coarsely chopped

1 small celery root, peeled and sliced ⅓ inch thick

2 medium carrots, thinly sliced

1 medium red potato, cut into 1-inch dice

1 large leek, white and tender green, thinly sliced

2 garlic cloves, minced

3 thyme sprigs

Salt

½ cup water

1 quart chicken stock or canned low-sodium broth, defatted

Freshly ground pepper

1 tablespoon minced rosemary

1. Heat the oil in a large saucepan. Add the parsnips, celery root, carrots, potato, leek, garlic, thyme, ½ teaspoon of salt and the water. Cook over moderately high heat, stirring, until the liquid has evaporated and the vegetables start to brown, about 10 minutes. Add the stock, cover the pan and reduce the heat to moderately low. Cook until the vegetables are very tender, about 30 minutes.

2. Transfer the vegetable soup to a blender and puree until smooth. Season with salt and pepper. Ladle the soup into bowls, sprinkle with the rosemary and serve.   *–Amanda Cushman*

MAKE AHEAD The soup can be refrigerated for up to one day.

Roasted-Vegetable Soup

8 SERVINGS

Roasted beets add sweetness and a rich red color to this satisfying autumn soup. If you like, you can reserve the beet greens for making Sautéed Fall Greens with Caraway (p. 323). The texture of the soup should be thick and slightly rough.

1½ pounds medium beets

1 head of garlic, top sliced off to expose the cloves

1 tablespoon water

1 pound carrots, cut into 1-inch pieces

1 pound turnips, cut into 1-inch wedges

2 medium onions, quartered

¼ cup plus 1 tablespoon extra-virgin olive oil

Coarse salt and freshly ground pepper

16 thin slices baguette

7 cups chicken stock or canned low-sodium broth

1 cup finely chopped mint

1. Preheat the oven to 400°. Put the beets and the garlic on a large piece of aluminum foil and sprinkle them with the water. Wrap the beets and the garlic in the foil and roast for about 1 hour, or until the beets are tender when pierced with a knife and the garlic feels soft when pressed. Let the beets and garlic cool slightly. Peel and quarter the beets and put them in a large bowl. Squeeze the soft garlic cloves from their skins onto the beets.

2. Meanwhile, on a large rimmed baking sheet, toss the carrots, turnips and onions with the 1 tablespoon oil and season the vegetables with salt and pepper. Spread the vegetables in a single layer and roast for about 1 hour, stirring occasionally, until tender and browned. Add the roasted vegetables to the beets.

3. Arrange the baguette slices on another baking sheet and bake for about 3 minutes, or until toasted.

4. Working in batches, coarsely puree all of the roasted vegetables in a food processor, adding enough chicken stock to moisten the mixture. Transfer the puree to a saucepan, add the remaining chicken stock and bring to a simmer over moderate heat. Season the soup with salt and pepper. ➤

Roasted-Vegetable Soup

5. In a small bowl, stir the remaining ¼ cup of oil into the mint and season with salt and pepper. Spoon the mint onto the toasts. Ladle the soup into bowls and serve with the toasted baguette slices. —*Rori Spinelli*

MAKE AHEAD The soup can be refrigerated overnight and the toasts can be stored in an airtight container.

Butternut-Squash Soup with Scallion Cream

6 TO 8 SERVINGS

Two 2-pound butternut squash, peeled and cut into 2-inch cubes
1 stick (4 ounces) unsalted butter– 4 tablespoons melted
Salt and freshly ground pepper
1 medium onion, coarsely chopped
2 medium celery ribs, cut into 1-inch pieces
1 medium leek, white and tender green, coarsely chopped
1 large carrot, cut into 1-inch pieces
1 tablespoon finely chopped fresh ginger
1 tablespoon thyme leaves
2 quarts chicken or vegetable stock or canned low-sodium chicken broth
½ cup cold heavy cream
2 medium scallions, minced
2 chives, chopped

1. Preheat the oven to 375°. In a large roasting pan, toss the squash with the 4 tablespoons melted butter and a pinch each of salt and pepper. Roast for about 40 minutes, stirring occasionally, until the squash is tender.

2. Meanwhile, melt the remaining 4 tablespoons butter in a large saucepan. Add the onion, celery, leek and carrot and cook over moderate heat, stirring occasionally, until the vegetables are barely softened, about 8 minutes. Stir in the ginger, thyme and roasted squash. Add the stock and bring to a boil over high heat. Partially cover, reduce the heat to moderately low and simmer the soup until the vegetables are very tender, about 20 minutes.

3. Working in batches, puree the soup in a blender. Return the soup to the saucepan; season with salt and pepper.

4. Reheat the soup. In a medium bowl, whip the heavy cream until soft peaks form. Add the scallions and a pinch of salt and whip to firm peaks.

5. Ladle the soup into bowls or shallow soup plates and garnish with a dollop of the scallion cream and a sprinkling of the chives. Serve at once. —*James Henahan*

MAKE AHEAD The soup can be prepared through Step 3 and refrigerated for up to one day.

WINE Look for a white with lively acidity but some depth of flavor, such as a Pinot Blanc. The 1994 Trimbach or the 1994 Hugel, both from Alsace, are refreshingly crisp but have enough flavor to balance the soup.

Curried Pumpkin Soup with Spicy Lentil Crisps

20 SERVINGS

What makes this lightly spiced, slightly fruity soup so simple is the fact that the pumpkins are roasted before they are peeled rather than after.

9 pounds sugar pumpkins or butternut squash, halved lengthwise
1 cup water
2 tablespoons vegetable oil
5 pears—peeled, cored and cut into 2-inch chunks
3 large Spanish onions, sliced
10 garlic cloves, chopped
3½ tablespoons curry powder
Salt and freshly ground pepper
4 quarts chicken stock or canned low-sodium broth
1½ cups dry white wine
1 cup crème fraîche or heavy cream
Lentil Crisps (recipe follows)

Butternut-Squash Soup with Scallion Cream

1. Preheat the oven to 350°. Place the halved pumpkins on two large rimmed baking sheets and add ½ cup of water to each sheet. Bake the pumpkins for about 1½ hours, or until tender. When the pumpkins are cool enough to handle, discard the seeds and peel the pumpkins.

2. Heat the oil in a large heavy casserole. Add the pears, onions, garlic, curry powder and a large pinch each of salt and pepper. Cook over moderate heat, stirring occasionally, until the onions are tender, about 15 minutes.

3. Add the cooked pumpkins, chicken stock and wine and bring to a boil over high heat. Stir well, reduce the heat to moderate and simmer for 45 minutes. Remove from the heat and let cool for 5 minutes.

4. Working in batches, puree the soup in a blender or food processor until smooth; transfer to a clean saucepan and season with salt and pepper.

5. To serve, reheat the soup, ladle it into shallow bowls or cups and swirl in the crème fraîche. Garnish with the Lentil Crisps. ➤

Curried Pumpkin Soup with a Spicy Lentil Crisp

LENTIL CRISPS

MAKES 20 CRISPS

Lentil flour is available at Indian markets and some specialty-food stores. To make your own, finely grind three-quarters of a cup of green lentils in a coffee mill or spice grinder.

- ¾ cup lentil flour
- ¾ cup all-purpose flour
- ¾ cup semolina
- 1 tablespoon plus 1 teaspoon curry powder

Salt

- 1 teaspoon freshly ground pepper
- 1 cup warm water

Olive oil, for brushing

1. Preheat the oven to 425°. In a bowl, combine the lentil and all-purpose flours with the semolina, curry powder, 1 teaspoon salt and the pepper. Add the water and mix until a smooth dough forms.

2. Transfer the dough to a well-floured work surface and knead for 2 minutes. Form the dough into a disk and quarter it.

3. Brush a baking sheet with oil. On a generously floured work surface, roll one piece of the dough into a 14-by-7½-inch rectangle. With a pizza cutter or sharp knife, cut the dough into five 14-inch-long strips. Transfer the strips to the baking sheet and brush lightly with oil. Sprinkle with salt and bake until browned and crisp, about 10 minutes. Transfer to a rack to cool and repeat with the remaining dough.   –Gordon Hamersley

MAKE AHEAD The soup can be refrigerated for up to three days. Reheat and season with salt and pepper before serving. The crisps can be stored overnight in an airtight container and recrisped briefly in a 400° oven.

Sicilian Potato and Pasta Soup

4 SERVINGS **Q**

- 1 medium onion, finely chopped
- 1 tablespoon extra-virgin olive oil
- 2 tablespoons tomato paste
- 1 pound Yukon Gold or other waxy potatoes, cut into ¾-inch cubes
- 3 good-quality vegetable bouillon cubes, dissolved in 1 cup of boiling water
- ¼ teaspoon crushed red pepper
- 5 cups water
- 1 cup tubetti or other small pasta
- 1 large tomato, cut into ¾-inch dice
- 3 tablespoons finely chopped mixed herbs, such as flat-leaf parsley, basil and sage

Salt

- ½ cup mascarpone or sour cream

In a saucepan, cook the onion in the oil over moderate heat, stirring, until just softened, about 5 minutes. Stir in the tomato paste and cook for 1 minute. Add the potatoes, bouillon, crushed pepper and water. Cover and bring to a boil. Stir in the pasta and cook until al dente, about 10 minutes. Stir in the tomato and herbs and cook for 1 minute longer. Season the soup with salt and serve with the mascarpone.   –Grace Parisi

WINE 1995 Corvo Bianco or 1995 Regaleali Bianco, both from Sicily

Risi e Bisi

8 SERVINGS

This green-pea and rice soup, an Italian favorite, is more like a risotto than a soup, thanks to the starchy arborio rice. Fresh peas are strongly recommended; use frozen only as a last resort. To enhance the color, add half of the pea pods (strings and inner membranes removed) with the whole peas and mint; the pods dissolve into the soup.

About 7 cups Chicken Stock (recipe follows) or canned low-sodium broth

- 4 cups fresh young peas (about 4 pounds in the pod) or thawed frozen peas
- ¼ cup finely chopped mint
- 4 tablespoons unsalted butter
- 1 tablespoon extra-virgin olive oil

ABOVE: **Risi e Bisi.** TOP: **Sicilian Potato and Pasta Soup.**

- 1 small red onion, finely chopped
- 1½ cups Arborio rice (about 10 ounces)
- ¼ cup finely chopped flat-leaf parsley
- 1½ cups freshly grated Parmesan (about 5 ounces)

Salt and freshly ground pepper

1. In a medium saucepan, bring the stock to a simmer. Add 2 cups of the peas and 3 tablespoons of the mint and blanch over low heat for 1 minute. Using

a slotted spoon, transfer the peas to a food processor and add ½ cup of the stock. Pulse the peas to a coarse puree. Keep the remaining stock warm.

2. In a large heavy saucepan, melt the butter in the oil. Add the onion and cook over moderate heat until softened and lightly colored, about 4 minutes. Add the rice and stir for 3 minutes.

3. Add the remaining 2 cups of un-cooked peas and 1 tablespoon of mint to the rice and stir-fry over moderate heat for 1 minute. Add the hot stock, 1 cup at a time, and stir constantly until it is partially absorbed before adding more (as for risotto), 20 to 25 minutes. The texture should be soupy; if necessary, add more stock. Just before the rice is al dente, stir in the pureed peas.

Smoky Escarole and Carrot Soup

4. Rewarm the soup over moderate heat. Stir in the parsley and half of the Parmesan and season with salt and pepper. Serve at once, sprinkling with the remaining cheese at the table.

CHICKEN STOCK

MAKES ABOUT 8 CUPS

- 4 pounds chicken legs, wings or backs
- 1 medium red onion, coarsely chopped
- 1 large carrot, coarsely chopped
- 1 large celery rib, coarsely chopped
- 1 unpeeled head of garlic
- 1 large thyme sprig
- 1 bay leaf
- 4 quarts water

In a large pot, combine all the ingredients. Bring the stock to a simmer over moderate heat. Cook gently, skimming occasionally, for 1½ hours; strain the stock. *—Ruth Rogers and Rose Gray*

MAKE AHEAD The stock can be cooled and then refrigerated for up to three days or frozen for up to one month.

WINE 1995 Pieropan Soave Classico Superiore. Unlike most neutral Soaves, it's bone dry, crisp and citrusy. It works well as an aperitif, but the acidity means it's also a brilliant match with this spring soup. Other quality Soave Classicos to look for are Anselmi and Gini.

Mid-Winter Soup

8 SERVINGS

This vegetarian soup is a stew-thick, satisfying comfort food for winter. If you like, you could use three cups of left-over cooked Wehani Rice (p. 306), Black Thai Sticky Rice (p. 307) or brown rice instead of the raw rice in this soup. In that case, add the cooked rice shortly before serving—just long enough to heat it through.

- ½ cup dried porcini mushrooms
- 2 cups boiling water
- 2 tablespoons olive oil
- 1 medium onion, diced
- 1 cup raw Wehani rice, rinsed
- 2 bay leaves
- ¼ teaspoon freshly ground pepper
- 4 cups homemade vegetable stock or water
- 1 pound waxy potatoes, such as red bliss or Yukon Gold, cut into 1-inch dice
- ½ pound carrots, cut into 1-inch dice
- 1½ teaspoons salt

Freshly grated Parmesan or Pecorino, for serving

Chopped flat-leaf parsley, for serving

I. Soak the porcini in the boiling water until softened. Drain, reserving the liquid, and chop.

2. Heat the oil in a large saucepan. Add the onion and cook over moderately high heat until slightly softened, 2 to 3 minutes. Add the porcini and stir briefly. Add the rice, bay leaves, pepper, stock and the reserved porcini-soaking liquid and bring to a boil. Reduce the heat to low, cover partially and simmer for 10 minutes.

3. Add the potatoes and the carrots and bring to a boil. Cover partially and simmer over moderately low heat until the rice and the vegetables are tender, about 30 minutes. Add the salt and simmer the soup for a few minutes more. Ladle the soup into bowls and pass the grated cheese and the parsley at the table. *–Jeffrey Alford and Naomi Duguid*
WINE 1994 Sanford Pinot Noir

Smoky Escarole and Carrot Soup

8 SERVINGS

- ½ cup dried pinto beans (about 3½ ounces)
- 1 bay leaf
- 2 thyme sprigs
- 4 cups cold water

Salt

- 4 ounces smoked bacon, cut into ½-inch dice
- 3 medium carrots, cut into ½-inch dice
- 1 large onion, coarsely chopped
- 6 cups chicken stock or canned low-sodium broth
- 1 pound escarole, tough stems discarded, leaves cut into 2-inch pieces

Freshly ground pepper

- 1 large garlic clove, minced
- ¼ cup coarsely chopped flat-leaf parsley
- 2 tablespoons extra-virgin olive oil

1. In a medium bowl, cover the beans with cold water and let soak overnight. Drain and rinse the beans. Alternatively, cover the beans with cold water and

bring to a boil. Remove from the heat and let stand for 1 hour, and then drain and rinse the beans.

2. In a medium saucepan, combine the beans with the bay leaf and the thyme sprigs, cover with the water and bring to a boil over moderately high heat. Reduce the heat to low and simmer, stirring occasionally, until the beans are tender, about 1 hour. Discard the bay leaf and thyme, season the beans with salt and let them stand in their cooking liquid.

3. In a large saucepan, cook the bacon over moderate heat, stirring occasionally, until crisp, about 5 minutes. Add the carrots and onion and cook, stirring, for 1 minute. Add the stock and bring to a boil. Stir in the escarole, cover and reduce the heat to low. Simmer the soup until the escarole is just tender, about 10 minutes. Add the beans and their cooking liquid and season with salt and pepper. Cook the soup until the beans are heated through.

4. In a small bowl, combine the garlic, parsley and oil. Stir into the soup just before serving. *–Marcia Kiesel*
MAKE AHEAD The soup can be made through Step 3 and refrigerated up to one day. Rewarm gently before serving.
WINE 1995 Georges Duboeuf Chiroubles, or Livio Felluga Tocai Friulano.

Cannellini and Escarole Soup with Garlic Oil

4 SERVINGS **Q**

- 4 thick slices of bacon, cut crosswise into ½-inch strips
- 1 small head of escarole, coarsely chopped
- 4 garlic cloves—1 minced, 3 crushed
- ¼ teaspoon crushed red pepper

Salt and freshly ground black pepper

Three 15-ounce cans cannellini beans, drained and rinsed

- 2 cups chicken stock or canned low-sodium broth
- 1½ cups water

- 2 tablespoons extra-virgin olive oil
- 2 tablespoons freshly grated Parmesan

1. In a large saucepan, cook the bacon over moderately high heat until crisp, about 6 minutes. Using a slotted spoon, transfer the bacon to a plate. Pour off all but 2 tablespoons of the fat and return the saucepan to moderately high heat. Add the escarole, minced garlic and crushed red pepper and season with salt and black pepper. Cook, stirring, until the escarole wilts, about 2 minutes.

2. Meanwhile, in a blender or food processor, puree half of the cannellini beans with the stock until smooth. Add the pureed and whole beans, bacon and water to the saucepan and bring to a boil. Reduce the heat to moderately low and cook until the escarole is tender, about 10 minutes.

3. Meanwhile, in a small skillet, cook the crushed garlic in the oil over moderate heat until it is golden, and then discard the garlic. Drizzle the soup with the garlic oil and sprinkle with the grated Parmesan. *–Grace Parisi*
WINE 1995 Long Vineyards Sauvignon Blanc or 1995 Silverado Vineyards Sauvignon Blanc

Spinach and Crabmeat Soup with Country-Ham Croutons

10 SERVINGS

- 1 large Idaho potato
- 3 tablespoons peanut oil
- ½ cup coarsely chopped onion
- ½ cup coarsely chopped celery
- ½ cup coarsely chopped green bell pepper
- ¼ cup coarsely chopped carrot
- 3 tablespoons finely chopped country ham or prosciutto
- 1 pound small shrimp, unpeeled
- 3 tablespoons coarsely chopped unsalted roasted peanuts
- 3 tablespoons chopped parsley

1 tablespoon chopped garlic
1 tablespoon kosher salt
2½ teaspoons Old Bay Seasoning
1 bay leaf
2 quarts fish stock, chicken stock or canned low-sodium chicken broth
1½ quarts milk
¼ cup cornstarch mixed with ¼ cup water
1 pound fresh spinach, large stems discarded, leaves finely chopped
1 pound lump crabmeat, picked over
10 Country-Ham Croutons (recipe follows)

ι. Preheat the oven to 400°. Prick the potato all over and bake for about 40 minutes, or until tender. Let the potato cool slightly, then peel and coarsely grate enough to yield 1 cup.

2. Heat the oil in a large stockpot. Add the onion, celery, green bell pepper, carrot and ham and sauté over moderately high heat until the vegetables are wilted, 4 to 5 minutes. Add the shrimp, peanuts, parsley, garlic, salt, Old Bay Seasoning and bay leaf and sauté for 3 minutes

Sam Hayward's Lobster and Sweet-Corn Soup

more. Add the potato, fish stock and milk and bring just to a boil. Whisk in the cornstarch mixture and return to a boil. Lower the heat and simmer the soup for 40 minutes. Discard the bay leaf and let the soup cool for 20 minutes.

3. Working in batches, puree the soup with the spinach leaves in a blender or food processor until smooth. Strain the pureed soup into a large saucepan.

4. To serve, gently reheat the soup over moderate heat. Add the crabmeat and warm for 1 minute. Ladle the soup into shallow bowls and garnish each serving with a Country-Ham Crouton.

COUNTRY-HAM CROUTONS
MAKES 10 CROUTONS

Country ham, cold-cured in salt and sugar and then aged, is available at specialty-food stores and most supermarkets throughout the South.

Ten ⅜-inch-thick slices of French or Italian bread
¼ cup extra-virgin olive oil
One ½-pound piece of country ham or prosciutto
3 tablespoons mayonnaise
2 tablespoons finely chopped parsley

ι. Preheat the oven to 450°. Brush the bread slices on both sides with the oil. Bake for about 3 minutes per side, or until golden brown. Let cool.

2. Put the ham in a small saucepan and cover it with cold water. Simmer over moderate heat for 5 minutes. Drain the ham and let cool completely.

3. Finely chop the ham and put it in a small bowl. Stir in the mayonnaise and parsley. Mound the ham generously on the toasts and serve. *–George Mahaffey*

MAKE AHEAD The soup can be prepared through Step 3 and refrigerated for up to two days. Keep the croutons in an airtight container. The ham topping can be refrigerated overnight.

WINE The best match here is a German Riesling. The crabmeat in the soup

is sweetly plump and a bit salty, and those flavors are nicely balanced by the 1992 Joh. Jos. Prüm Wehlener Sonnenuhr Auslese, from the middle Mosel. Another fine choice is the 1992 Egon Müller Scharzhofberger Auslese, a relatively round vintage from the Saar, which tends to produce steely wines.

Sam Hayward's Lobster and Sweet-Corn Soup
6 TO 8 SERVINGS
1½ teaspoons fine sea salt
Four 1- to 1¼-pound live lobsters
5 tablespoons unsalted butter
2 ounces pancetta, sliced ¼ inch thick and cut into small dice
½ cup finely diced fennel
2 medium leeks, white part only, cut into small dice
1 cup dry white wine
½ cup heavy cream
1 jalapeño pepper, seeded and cut into small dice
4 cups corn kernels (from 6 ears)
Freshly ground pepper
¼ cup chopped chervil or parsley

ι. Fill a large stockpot with 2 inches of water, add 1 teaspoon of the salt and bring to a boil over high heat. Put the lobsters in the boiling water, head first, and cook until they start to turn red, about 4 minutes. With tongs, transfer the lobsters to a bowl to cool; reserve the cooking water.

2. Remove the meat from the lobster knuckles and claws. Twist the tails off the bodies. Split the tails lengthwise and remove the tail meat. Pull out and discard the black intestinal vein, then cut the tail into large pieces. Cover and refrigerate the lobster meat.

3. Return the lobster shells to the liquid in the stockpot; simmer over moderate heat for 20 minutes. Strain the broth into a bowl and let stand for 10 minutes. Pour off and reserve 6 cups of the broth, leaving behind any grit at the bottom.

4. In a large saucepan, melt 2 tablespoons of the butter. Add the pancetta and cook over moderately low heat until lightly browned, about 5 minutes. Add the fennel and cook, stirring, until it is wilted, about 3 minutes; transfer the pancetta and fennel to a plate. Add the leeks to the pan and cook until translucent, about 5 minutes. Add the wine and boil until reduced by one-third, about 4 minutes. Add the reserved lobster broth, the cream, the jalapeño and the remaining ½ teaspoon of the salt. Bring to a boil over moderately high heat. Add the corn and simmer until tender, about 10 minutes.

5. Remove the soup from the heat and let cool for 5 minutes. Working in batches, coarsely puree the soup in a blender. Return the soup to the pan and add the pancetta and fennel. Season with salt and pepper and keep warm.

6. In a grill pan or skillet, melt the remaining 3 tablespoons of butter over moderately high heat. Add the lobster meat and cook until lightly seared and heated through. Season the lobster with salt and pepper.

7. Ladle the soup into shallow bowls, garnish with the lobster and the chervil and serve.   *—Nancy Harmon Jenkins*
WINE 1995 Jekel or Chateau Ste. Michelle Johannisberg Riesling

Smoked-Fish Chowder

Spanish Mussel and Chorizo Soup

4 SERVINGS **Q**

If you have trouble finding chorizo, use hot Italian sausage or spicy kielbasa instead.

- 1 tablespoon extra-virgin olive oil
- 2 chorizo sausages (6 ounces), halved lengthwise and sliced ¼ inch thick
- 1 shallot, finely chopped
- 1 large garlic clove, lightly crushed
- ¼ teaspoon whole fennel seeds, bruised with the side of a knife

Two 3-inch strips of orange zest
Two 8-ounce bottles clam juice
One 14-ounce can diced tomatoes, with their juices

- 1⅓ cups water
- ½ cup orzo
- 2 pounds mussels, scrubbed and debearded

Crusty Italian or French bread

Heat the oil in a large saucepan. Add the chorizo sausages, shallot, garlic, fennel seeds and orange zest and stir over moderate heat until just beginning to brown, about 5 minutes. Add the clam juice, tomatoes and water. Cover and bring to a boil. Stir in the orzo, cover and cook until it is barely al dente, about 8 minutes. Add the mussels, cover and cook until they open, 4 to 5 minutes. Discard any unopened mussels and the orange zest. Serve the soup with the bread.   *—Grace Parisi*
WINE 1995 Morgan Malvasia Bianca from California or 1994 CUNE Blanco Seco from Rioja, Spain

Smoked-Fish Chowder

4 SERVINGS **Q**

- 2 tablespoons unsalted butter
- 1 large onion, finely chopped
- 2 celery ribs, thinly sliced
- ¾ pound red-skinned potatoes, cut into ¾-inch chunks
- ¼ teaspoon dried thyme

Two 8-ounce bottles clam juice

- 1½ cups hot water
- ½ pound smoked trout fillets, skinned and flaked
- 1 cup fresh or frozen corn kernels
- 1 cup heavy cream

2 tablespoons minced flat-leaf
   parsley

Salt and freshly ground pepper

Melt the butter in a large heavy sauce-pan. Add the onion and celery; stir over moderately high heat for about 5 minutes. Add the potatoes and thyme. Cook until just heated through, about 1 minute. Add the clam juice and water; bring to a boil. Reduce the heat to moderately low, cover and cook until the potatoes are just tender, about 7 minutes. Add the trout, corn and cream. Cover and cook over low heat until the vegetables are tender, about 5 minutes. Add the parsley. Season with salt and pepper. *–Grace Parisi*

WINE 1996 Trefethen Dry Riesling from California or 1995 Delas Frères Viognier from France

Minestra Maritata

Minestra Maritata

10 TO 12 SERVINGS

This is the dish that opens the great Christmas Day feast in Neapolitan households. *Minestra maritata* means married soup, presumably because of the highly successful pairing of rich meat stock and slightly bitter greens. It's a beautiful dish–dark winter greens and clear amber broth–with origins that go back to the sixteenth century. In days of yore, all sorts of animal parts were used to add substance to the broth, including pig's ears (lots of cartilage there to give body to the soup) and guanciale, or cured pork cheeks. The Italian modern version is simpler, with more familiar meats and a variety of greens not generally available in America–borage and chicory shoots, for instance. If you happen to have such things in your garden, by all means include them.

1 stewing hen or regular chicken
   (3 to 4 pounds)
1 pound veal or beef shank
1 pound country-style pork ribs
2 celery ribs, including the leafy
   tops, coarsely chopped
2 medium carrots, coarsely chopped
2 garlic cloves, crushed
1 to 2 small dried red chiles
About 6 quarts cold water
Salt and freshly ground pepper
6 pounds fresh greens, cored and
   stemmed as necessary, including
   any or all of the following:
   escarole, dandelion, broccoli rabe
   and chicory
Freshly grated Parmigiano-Reggiano,
   for serving

1. In a very large stockpot, combine the hen, veal shank, pork ribs, celery, carrots, garlic and dried chiles. Add enough of the water to just cover the meats and bring to a simmer over moderately low heat. Add a large pinch of salt and pepper and reduce the heat to low. Cover partially and cook until the broth is very flavorful, about 3 hours.

2. Meanwhile, in a large pot of boiling salted water, cook the greens in two or three batches until just tender, 5 to 8 minutes; if you are using a combination of greens, cook each variety separately. Drain the greens and when they're cool enough to handle, squeeze them dry and coarsely chop.

3. When the broth is done, remove the meats. Strain the broth through a fine sieve into a large bowl. Remove all the meat from the hen, veal shank and pork ribs. Cut the meat into bite-size pieces.

4. Skim the fat from the surface of the broth and pour it into a clean stockpot, stopping when you reach the solids at the bottom. Add the meats and greens to the broth and bring just to a simmer.

Season the soup with salt and pepper and serve piping hot in soup plates. Pass the grated Parmigiano-Reggiano at the table. —*Nancy Harmon Jenkins*

MAKE AHEAD The soup can be refrigerated for up to two days.

WINE Serve an Italian sparkling wine–perhaps a nonvintage Zardetto Prosecco–or a fruity, dry regional white such as the 1995 Regaleali Nozze d'Oro, to offset the bitter greens.

Tortilla Soup

4 SERVINGS Q

Ancho chiles are actually dried poblanos. Choose anchos that are still pliable, or soften them by warming them in a 350° oven for a minute or so.

Four 6-inch corn tortillas
1 to 2 tablespoons vegetable oil
8 cups chicken stock or canned low-sodium broth
4 fresh or canned plum tomatoes, coarsely chopped, with their juices
1 medium all-purpose potato, peeled and cut into 1/3-inch dice
1 ancho chile—stemmed, seeded and cut into thin strips
1 medium onion, thinly sliced
2 garlic cloves, coarsely chopped
1/2 teaspoon dried marjoram
Salt
1 small zucchini, cut into 1/2-inch dice
1 small yellow squash, cut into 1/2-inch dice
1 pound small skinless, boneless chicken-breast halves, cut crosswise into 1/2-inch strips
Cilantro sprigs, for garnish
1 lime, quartered, for garnish
Sour cream, for garnish

1. Preheat the oven to 425°. Brush both sides of the tortillas with the vegetable oil. Cut the tortillas into 1/2-inch-wide strips and spread them in a single layer on a large baking sheet. Bake the tortilla strips for about 5 minutes, or until they are golden.

2. In a large stainless-steel saucepan, combine the stock, tomatoes, potato, ancho, onion, garlic, marjoram and 1 teaspoon of salt; bring to a boil. Reduce the heat to moderate and simmer until the vegetables are almost tender, about 15 minutes. Add the zucchini and yellow squash and cook for 1 minute longer. Add the chicken and simmer until just cooked through, about 5 minutes. Season with salt.

3. Ladle the soup into warmed soup plates or bowls. Float a few of the tortilla strips on top of each serving. Garnish each serving with several cilantro sprigs, a lime quarter and a dollop of sour cream. Serve the remaining tortilla strips on the side. Enjoy the soup right away, before the baked tortilla strips become soggy. —*Victoria Wise*

WINE The spiciness of the soup suggests an off-dry, fruity white to balance the heat. Try the 1995 Dry Creek Dry Chenin Blanc from California.

Thai Chicken and Coconut Soup

4 SERVINGS Q

To make the soup more substantial, add about two cups of steamed jasmine rice or cooked rice noodles before serving. Coconut milk, Asian curry paste and fish sauce are available at most supermarkets.

One 13.5-ounce can unsweetened coconut milk
1 1/2 to 2 teaspoons green curry paste
Four 2-inch strips of lime zest
2 quarter-size pieces of fresh ginger, lightly crushed
1/2 teaspoon sugar
3 cups chicken stock or canned low-sodium broth
2 medium skinless, boneless chicken-breast halves, cut into 3/4-inch pieces
3 tablespoons Asian fish sauce
1/4 cup cilantro leaves, coarsely chopped
6 basil leaves, coarsely chopped
1 tablespoon fresh lime juice

In a large saucepan, combine the coconut milk, curry paste, lime zest, ginger and sugar and bring to a simmer over moderate heat. Add the chicken stock, cover and simmer over moderately low heat for 8 minutes. Raise the heat to moderate and bring the soup to a boil. Add the chicken-breast pieces, the fish sauce, 3 tablespoons of the cilantro and the basil. Stir and simmer the soup until the chicken-breast pieces are cooked through, about 4 minutes. Discard the ginger and the lime zest. Add the remaining 1 tablespoon of cilantro to the soup and stir in the lime juice. Serve the soup hot. —*Grace Parisi*

WINE 1995 Carl Graff Urziger Schwarzlay Riesling Spätlese or 1996 Henry Estate Müller-Thurgau from Oregon

quick soup tips

1. **Give canned broth extra flavor** by simmering reserved chicken or meat bones in the broth for fifteen minutes; strain the liquid and use for soup.

2. **Check out salad bars for ready-to-use ingredients,** such as precut vegetables or cooked shrimp, chicken and meat.

3. **Add leftover cooked pasta, meat and vegetables** for instant substance. Most cooked vegetables can also be pureed and then stirred in to thicken soups.

4. **Use frozen vegetables,** such as peas, spinach or corn, to cut prep time. Add them to chunky soups or puree them with broth, cream and sautéed onion and then simmer to make a smooth soup.

CHAPTER 5 pasta

Wild-Mushroom Fettuccine (p. 92)

89 Penne Rigate with Fresh Herbs

89 Pasta with Olive Oil, Garlic and Parsley

89 Mushroom Sauté

89 Tomato Sauce

90 Pasta with Nut Pesto

90 Summer Pasta

90 Penne with Ricotta and Tomato Sauce

91 Pasta alla Norma

91 Penne with Sautéed Zucchini and Ricotta

92 Wild-Mushroom Fettuccine

94 Farfalle with Morels and Fresh Pea Sauce

94 Pasta with Cannellini Spinach Pesto

94 Pasta Shells Stuffed with Grilled Radicchio

97 Pasta and Chickpeas

98 Spinach-Filled Crespelle with Lemon Sauce

98 Mara's Pasta with Broccoli and Scallop Sauce

99 Farfalle with Crabmeat and Oregano Butter

100 Linguine with Clams, Bacon and Hot Red Pepper

101 Spaghetti alla Siracusana

102 Pasta with Sardines

102 Christmas Spaghetti with Walnuts

102 Fusilli with Oven-Roasted Tomatoes and Chicken

104 Perciatelli alla Gricia

105 Rigatoni Timbale alla Gangivecchio

105 Pasta with Rabbit and Fava Beans

106 Pasta with Abruzzi-Style Lamb Sauce

106 Baked Pasta with Ragù and Ricotta

108 Italian Couscous with Parmesan and Herbs

108 Moroccan-Style Couscous

109 Vegetable-Studded Couscous

Penne Rigate with Fresh Herbs

Penne Rigate with Fresh Herbs

4 SERVINGS

I may have been inspired to make this recipe by the food of southern Italy, but the dish fits right in with the cooking of the American South, which is enjoying a revival of kitchen gardens. When making your own herb mixture, start with basil and parsley as a base and add the more fragrant herbs as accents.

- 1 pound penne rigate
- ¼ cup plus 2 tablespoons extra-virgin olive oil
- 4 garlic cloves, minced
- 2 cups loosely packed herb leaves, finely chopped
- ½ cup freshly grated Pecorino or Parmigiano-Reggiano, plus more for serving

Salt and freshly ground pepper

1. Cook the pasta in a large pot of boiling salted water until al dente. Drain the pasta and return it to the pot.
2. Meanwhile, in a medium skillet, heat the oil. Add the garlic and cook over moderately high heat until softened but not browned, about 30 seconds. Add the herbs and cook until just wilted, about 1 minute. Stir the contents of the skillet into the pasta with the ½ cup cheese. Season with salt and pepper and toss. Serve immediately; pass the additional cheese separately. –*John Martin Taylor*

WINE The generous amount of herbs and garlic make this pasta a natural for the 1994 Columbia Crest Merlot from Washington State or the 1995 St. Supéry Sauvignon Blanc from California.

Pasta with Olive Oil, Garlic and Parsley

4 SERVINGS

Serve this simple pasta alone or top it with either–or both–the Mushroom Sauté or the Tomato Sauce that follow. For a hearty entrée, serve all three with Braised Lamb Shanks (p. 255)

- 1 pound rigatoni or other tubular pasta
- ½ cup extra-virgin olive oil
- 4 tablespoons unsalted butter
- 3 medium garlic cloves, minced
- 1½ teaspoons salt

Freshly ground pepper

- ¼ cup chopped flat-leaf parsley

1. Boil the rigatoni in a large pot of salted water until al dente; drain and return the rigatoni to the pot.
2. Meanwhile, in a small saucepan, combine the oil, butter, garlic, salt and a few grinds of pepper. Cook over moderately high heat, stirring often, until the garlic is softened, 1 to 2 minutes.
3. Toss the pasta with the olive-oil sauce and parsley and serve. –*Joshua Eisen*

MAKE AHEAD The olive-oil sauce can stand, covered, at room temperature for up to one day.

Mushroom Sauté

4 SERVINGS

High heat and an uncrowded pan ensure that the mushrooms caramelize. This sauté will dress a pound of pasta.

- ¼ cup extra-virgin olive oil
- 1½ pounds portobello mushrooms, stems removed, caps thickly sliced
- ½ pound white mushrooms, stems removed, caps thickly sliced

Salt and freshly ground pepper

- 2 tablespoons unsalted butter
- 4 garlic cloves, chopped
- ¼ cup freshly grated Parmigiano-Reggiano
- 3 tablespoons white wine or water
- ¼ cup chopped flat-leaf parsley

1. Working in batches, in a large heavy skillet, heat some of the oil and add some of the mushrooms. Cook over high heat, without stirring, until the mushrooms are lightly browned, about 4 minutes. Season with salt and pepper, turn and cook until tender, about 4 minutes. Transfer to a bowl.

CLOCKWISE FROM TOP LEFT: **Mushroom Sauté; Pasta with Olive Oil, Garlic and Parsley; Tomato Sauce; and Braised Lamb Shanks (p. 255).**

2. In the same skillet, melt the butter. Add the garlic and cook, stirring, until it is softened, 1 to 2 minutes. Stir in the Parmigiano-Reggiano, the wine and the sautéed mushrooms. Stir in the parsley and serve. –*Joshua Eisen*

Tomato Sauce

4 SERVINGS

If you can't find porcini powder, pulverize dried sliced porcini in a coffee grinder. This sauce will dress a pound of pasta.

- ½ cup olive oil
- 1 medium onion, finely chopped

One 16-ounce can peeled Italian tomatoes, chopped, with their liquid

- 1 tablespoon porcini powder (about ⅛ ounce)

Salt and freshly ground pepper

- ⅓ cup chopped flat-leaf parsley

1. In a large heavy skillet, heat the oil. Add the onion, cover and cook over low heat, stirring often, until softened but not browned, about 20 minutes. ➤

2. Add the tomatoes. Cook over moderately high heat, stirring often, until thickened, about 10 minutes. Stir in the porcini powder; simmer for 2 minutes more. Season with salt and pepper, stir in the parsley and serve. *–Joshua Eisen*

MAKE AHEAD The sauce can be refrigerated for two days, but don't add the parsley until ready to serve.

Pasta with Nut Pesto

12 SERVINGS

This version of Arab-inspired *casareccia con la frutta secca* is adapted from *La Cucina Siciliana di Gangivecchio* (Knopf).

- ½ cup hazelnuts
- 2 cups lightly packed basil
- ½ cup blanched whole almonds
- ½ cup walnut pieces
- ½ cup shelled unsalted pistachios
- ½ cup pine nuts
- ½ cup freshly grated Parmigiano-Reggiano
- ½ cup freshly grated Pecorino Romano
- ⅓ cup chopped flat-leaf parsley
- 6 medium garlic cloves

Salt and freshly ground pepper

- ¾ cup extra-virgin olive oil
- 2 tablespoons unsalted butter, softened
- 2 pounds casareccia or penne

Summer Pasta

1. Preheat the oven to 350°. Toast the hazelnuts in a small baking pan until fragrant, about 12 minutes. Transfer the nuts to a clean kitchen towel and rub them against each other to remove the skins. Let cool completely.

2. In a food processor, combine the basil, hazelnuts, almonds, walnuts, pistachios, pine nuts, the cheeses, parsley, garlic and a pinch each of salt and pepper. With the machine on, pour in the oil in a thin stream and process until the nuts are finely chopped. Add the butter and process until blended but still grainy.

3. Fill a large pot with water, cover and bring to a boil. Add salt and the pasta. Cover partially until the water just returns to a boil, then uncover, stir the pasta and cook until al dente. Drain the pasta, reserving 1 cup of the cooking water. Transfer the pasta to a warmed large serving bowl. Add the nut pesto and toss to combine. Add 2 to 3 tablespoons of the reserved pasta-cooking water if the sauce is too thick. Serve immediately.   *–Giovanna Tornabene*

MAKE AHEAD After Step 2, transfer the pesto to a large jar, tap out any air bubbles and press a piece of plastic wrap directly on the surface. Cover and refrigerate for up to one week. Bring to room temperature before proceeding.

Summer Pasta

8 SERVINGS

This is a summertime best-seller at Circo in New York City, and it's very easy to make. Serve it with plenty of Italian bread to mop up the delicious juices.

- 1 pound fresh mozzarella, cut into small dice
- 8 medium tomatoes, cut into small dice
- 4 garlic cloves, finely chopped
- 1 cup olive oil
- 1 cup coarsely chopped basil
- 1 tablespoon plus 1 teaspoon kosher salt

Freshly ground black pepper
Crushed red pepper

- 1½ pounds spaghetti or penne rigate

1. In a bowl, toss the mozzarella with the tomatoes, garlic, oil, basil and salt. Season generously with black pepper and crushed red pepper. Let stand for 30 minutes.

2. Meanwhile, bring a stockpot of water to a boil. Salt the water and stir in the pasta. Boil, stirring occasionally, until al dente, about 12 minutes; drain well. Return the pasta to the pot, add the sauce and toss very well. Serve hot or at room temperature.   *–Egi Maccioni*

Penne with Ricotta and Tomato Sauce

4 SERVINGS **Q**

Try fresh sheep's-milk ricotta if it's available; it has a delicate flavor and a light texture. For a richer topping, whisk one tablespoon of mascarpone into the ricotta in Step 1.

- 1 cup fresh whole-milk ricotta (about ½ pound)
- ¼ cup extra-virgin olive oil

Kosher salt
Freshly ground pepper

- 3 pounds ripe tomatoes, cored and chopped
- ½ cup diced onion
- 1 garlic clove, minced
- 2 tablespoons chopped basil
- 2 tablespoons freshly grated Parmigiano-Reggiano
- ¾ pound penne

1. In a small bowl, whisk the ricotta with 2 tablespoons of the oil, ½ teaspoon of salt and ¼ teaspoon of pepper. Cover and set aside at room temperature for up to 4 hours.

2. In a large stainless-steel saucepan, simmer the tomatoes over moderate heat until very soft, about 10 minutes. Pass them through the medium disk of a food mill or use a rubber spatula to push them through a coarse strainer.

3. Wipe out the saucepan and heat the remaining 2 tablespoons of oil in it. Add the onion and garlic and cook over low heat until softened but not browned, about 4 minutes. Add the tomato sauce and 1 tablespoon of the basil and simmer over moderately low heat until the sauce thickens, about 20 minutes. Stir in the Parmigiano-Reggiano and season with salt and pepper.

4. Fill a large pot with water, cover and bring to a boil. Add salt and the penne. Cover partially until the water just returns to a boil, then uncover, stir the pasta and cook until al dente. Drain the pasta and add it to the sauce; toss to coat the pasta well. Serve immediately in warmed bowls, topped with a dollop of the ricotta mixture and a sprinkling of the remaining basil. *–Michael Romano*

MAKE AHEAD The sauce can be refrigerated for up to three days. Reheat before stirring in the cheese, salt and pepper and proceeding with Step 4.

WINE 1993 Avignonesi Vino Nobile de Montepulciano. Made mostly from Sangiovese grapes, this is a hefty, juicy wine that will wrap itself around the ricotta and tomato sauce.

Pasta alla Norma

4 SERVINGS

This peasant dish from La Minosse in Siracusa, Italy, is like Sicily in a bowl.

- 1 pound ripe plum tomatoes, halved crosswise
- ¼ cup extra-virgin olive oil
- 1 small eggplant, cut into 2-by-½-inch sticks

Salt and freshly ground pepper

- 1 small onion, finely chopped
- ½ cup water
- 2 tablespoons finely shredded basil
- ¾ pound penne rigate
- 1 cup crumbled ricotta salata or mild feta (5 ounces)

I. Working over a strainer set over a bowl, seed the tomatoes; press on the seeds and pulp to extract as much of the juice as possible. Cut the tomatoes into ½-inch chunks and transfer them to the bowl with the tomato juice.

2. In a medium nonstick skillet, heat 3 tablespoons of the oil. Add the eggplant and season with salt and pepper. Cook over moderately high heat, stirring occasionally, until the eggplant is tender and just beginning to brown, about 5 minutes. Transfer to a medium bowl.

3. Add the remaining 1 tablespoon of oil to the skillet, add the onion and cook over moderate heat until softened, about 4 minutes. Add the water, the salt and pepper and all but 2 tablespoons of the tomatoes. Cover and cook over low heat until the tomatoes are very soft, about 15 minutes. Transfer the sauce to a food mill and puree to remove the skins. Alternatively, press through a sieve with a rubber spatula. Return the sauce to the skillet, add the basil and all but 2 tablespoons of the eggplant and cook over low heat until warmed through.

4. Meanwhile, fill a large pot with water, cover and bring to a boil. Add salt and the pasta. Cover partially until the water just returns to a boil, then uncover, stir the pasta and cook until al dente. Drain well, reserving ½ cup of the cooking water, and transfer the pasta to a warmed large serving bowl. Add the sauce, three-quarters of the ricotta salata and a good grinding of pepper; toss well. Add some of the reserved pasta-cooking water if the pasta is dry. Garnish the pasta with the reserved tomatoes, eggplant and ricotta salata and serve immediately. *–Antonio Visetti*

Penne with Sautéed Zucchini and Ricotta

8 SERVINGS

- 2½ pounds small zucchini
- 1½ pounds penne
- 3 tablespoons extra-virgin olive oil, plus more for drizzling

ABOVE: **Pasta alla Norma.**

TOP: **Penne with Ricotta and Tomato Sauce.**

- 5 medium garlic cloves, minced

Salt and freshly ground pepper

- 1 cup finely shredded basil
- 1 pound ricotta
- ¾ cup freshly grated Parmesan (about 3 ounces)

I. Bring a large pot of salted water to a boil. Add the zucchini and blanch for 2 minutes; they should still be crisp. Using

Penne with Sautéed Zucchini and Ricotta

a slotted spoon, transfer the zucchini to a work surface and slice crosswise about ⅓ inch thick.

2. Bring the water back to a boil, add the pasta and cook until al dente, about 11 minutes. Drain the pasta and return it to the pot.

3. Meanwhile, heat the 3 tablespoons of oil in a large saucepan. Add the garlic and cook over moderately high heat, stirring, until soft but not brown, about 1 minute. Add the zucchini slices; season with salt and pepper. Cook, stirring often, until the zucchini is very tender but not falling apart, about 12 minutes. Fold the zucchini into the pasta along with the basil, ricotta and ½ cup of the Parmesan. Season the pasta with salt and pepper and toss to combine. Drizzle

in olive oil to taste. Transfer the pasta to shallow soup plates, sprinkle with the remaining ¼ cup of the Parmesan and serve.   *–Ruth Rogers and Rose Gray*
WINE 1995 Allegrini Valpolicella Classico. Valpolicellas are red wines that can be drunk slightly chilled. This version has enough acidity to cut the richness of the ricotta without overpowering it or the zucchini. Also try the 1994 Masi Valpolicella Classico.

Wild-Mushroom Fettuccine

12 SERVINGS

Porcini and chanterelles are especially good mushrooms to use in this pasta because they stay firm when they are tossed with the fettuccine. You'll want to avoid oyster mushrooms, however,

since they have a tendency to become too flabby during cooking.

- 1 stick (4 ounces) unsalted butter
- ¾ cup finely chopped shallots
- 4 garlic cloves, minced
- 2 pounds assorted fresh wild mushrooms, cleaned and thickly sliced if large

Salt and freshly ground pepper
- 1½ cups dry white wine
- 3 cups chicken stock or canned low-sodium broth
- 2½ pounds good-quality fresh or dried fettuccine
- ¼ cup finely chopped parsley
- 1½ cups Parmesan shavings (about 1½ ounces)

I. Divide the butter between two large skillets and melt until foaming. Add half of the shallots to each skillet and cook them over moderately high heat, stirring, until slightly softened, about 2 minutes. Add half of the garlic to each skillet and cook, stirring, for 1 minute longer. Add half of the mushrooms to each skillet, season with salt and pepper and raise the heat to high. Cook the mushrooms, stirring, until they have exuded their liquid and are lightly browned, 7 to 10 minutes. Using a slotted spoon, transfer the mushrooms to a large bowl.

2. Pour the wine into one of the skillets and boil it over high heat, stirring, until it is reduced to about 2 tablespoons, about 10 minutes. Add the stock and boil until reduced by half, about 20 minutes. Return the mushrooms to the skillet, season with salt and pepper and keep warm.

3. Meanwhile, bring a very large pot of water to a boil. Add salt, and then add the fettuccine and cook until al dente. Drain the fettuccine and then toss it with the mushrooms and the sauce. Sprinkle the pasta with the chopped parsley and garnish with the shaved Parmesan.   *–The Mondavi family*

Wild-Mushroom Fettuccine

Pasta with Cannellini Spinach Pesto

Farfalle with Morels and Fresh Pea Sauce

4 SERVINGS

If you buy shelled peas, you'll need about six ounces for this delicious, earthy, morel-studded pasta.

- 1¾ cups chicken stock or canned low-sodium broth
- ¾ pound fresh peas, shelled
- ¾ pound farfalle
- 4 ounces thick-sliced bacon, cut crosswise into ½-inch strips
- 6 ounces small fresh morels— rinsed, drained and halved lengthwise
- ½ cup heavy cream

Salt and freshly ground pepper

- 2 tablespoons finely chopped garlic chives or 2 scallions, minced

I. Bring a large pot of salted water to a boil. In a medium saucepan, bring the chicken stock to a boil. Add the peas to the stock and cook over moderately high heat until just tender, about 10 minutes. Transfer the stock and all but a small handful of the peas to a blender and puree until smooth.

2. Cook the farfalle in the pot of boiling water until al dente, about 15 minutes; drain and return to the pot.

3. Meanwhile, heat a medium skillet. Add the bacon and cook over moderately high heat, stirring frequently, until browned and crisp, about 7 minutes. Transfer to a paper-towel-lined plate. Pour off all but 1 tablespoon of the bacon fat from the skillet. Add the morels and cook until they release their liquid, about 4 minutes. Raise the heat to high, add the cream and season with salt and pepper. Cook until slightly reduced, about 2 minutes. Stir in the pea puree and whole peas and cook until just heated through.

4. Add the pea sauce, bacon and chives to the pasta. Toss well, then transfer to plates and serve at once. –*Grace Parisi*

WINE Smoky bacon, sautéed morels, cream, garlic—the ingredients in this rich pasta dish point directly to a flavorful but balanced red as the ideal match. A Rioja from Spain would fit the requirements perfectly. Look for the 1991 Marqués de Riscal or the 1991 Conde de Valdemar.

Pasta with Cannellini Spinach Pesto

4 SERVINGS **L**

This lean, protein-rich pesto is packed with spinach and thickened with white beans. If you don't have orecchiette, serve the pesto with ziti or penne.

- ½ pound fresh spinach, large stems discarded and leaves rinsed
- 1½ cups cooked cannellini beans, drained and any liquid reserved
- 2 large garlic cloves, minced
- 1 medium scallion, minced
- ¾ cup packed coarsely chopped basil leaves
- 1 tablespoon fresh lemon juice
- 1 tablespoon extra-virgin olive oil

Salt and freshly ground pepper

- ¾ pound orecchiette

- ½ cup crumbled feta (about 3 ounces)
- 2 tomatoes, chopped

I. Bring a large pot of salted water to a boil. Meanwhile, heat a large skillet; add the spinach with the water that clings to the leaves and cook over high heat, stirring, until wilted, about 2 minutes. Put the spinach in a colander and press out the excess liquid. Chop the spinach and transfer it to a food processor. Add 1¼ cups of the cannellini beans, the garlic, scallion, basil, lemon juice, oil, a pinch each of salt and pepper and a few tablespoons of the reserved bean liquid or water. Puree the mixture until smooth.

2. Add the pasta to the boiling water and cook until al dente. Drain, leaving enough water to keep the pasta moist. Transfer the pasta to four bowls; top with the pesto, feta, tomatoes and the reserved ¼ cup beans. Grind fresh pepper over the pasta and serve. –*David Hirsch, Linda Dickinson and Susan Harville*

WINE This dish has enough richness to work with a bright, up-front red, such as the 1995 Guigal Côtes du Rhône from France or the 1995 Cline Côtes d'Oakley Rouge from California.

Pasta Shells Stuffed with Grilled Radicchio

10 SERVINGS

Packed with three cheeses and shredded radicchio, these pasta shells are set off by a roasted tomato and fennel sauce. The quantities here make two shells per person for a first course. To serve the dish as a main course, allow three or four for each diner.

SAUCE

- ¼ cup extra-virgin olive oil
- 1 medium fennel bulb—halved, cored and thinly sliced crosswise
- 1 small onion, thinly sliced
- 2 pounds ripe plum tomatoes, peeled and seeded
- 3 medium garlic cloves, lightly smashed

Farfalle with Morels and Fresh Pea Sauce

Pasta Shells Stuffed with Grilled Radicchio

2 teaspoons finely chopped
flat-leaf parsley

½ teaspoon fennel seeds (optional)

¼ teaspoon dried thyme

½ cup red wine

2 cups chicken stock or canned
low-sodium broth

Salt and freshly ground pepper

STUFFED SHELLS

¾ pound radicchio, halved
lengthwise and cored

Olive oil, for brushing

Salt and freshly ground pepper

1¾ cups fresh ricotta (about ¾ pound)

4 ounces mozzarella, cut into
⅓-inch dice

½ cup freshly grated Parmesan
(about 1½ ounces)

1 large egg, lightly beaten

1 medium shallot, minced

1 garlic clove, minced

2 tablespoons finely chopped
flat-leaf parsley

¼ teaspoon dried thyme

Small pinch freshly grated nutmeg

12 ounces dried jumbo pasta shells

I. MAKE THE SAUCE: Preheat the oven to 450°. Heat the oil in a large stainless-steel ovenproof skillet. Add the fennel and onion and cook over moderately high heat, stirring occasionally, until wilted and browned, about 10 minutes. Add the tomatoes, garlic, parsley, fennel seeds and thyme and roast in the oven for about 45 minutes, or until the tomatoes are just beginning to brown. Transfer the roasted vegetables to a blender or food processor and pulse until coarsely chopped.

2. Set the skillet over high heat and add the wine. Cook, scraping up any brown bits, until reduced by half. Add the wine to the vegetables in the blender and puree until almost smooth. Transfer to a medium stainless-steel saucepan, add the stock and cook over moderate heat until thickened, about 20 minutes. Season with salt and pepper.

3. MAKE THE STUFFED SHELLS: Light a grill or preheat the broiler. Brush the radicchio with oil and season with salt and pepper. Grill or broil for about 4 minutes, turning frequently, until browned. Let cool slightly, then thinly slice the radicchio. Transfer to a medium bowl and add the ricotta, mozzarella, ¼ cup of the Parmesan, the egg, shallot, garlic, 1 tablespoon of the parsley, the thyme, nutmeg, ½ teaspoon of salt and ¼ teaspoon of pepper.

4. Bring a large pot of salted water to a boil. Add the pasta shells and cook until just tender, 8 to 10 minutes. Drain, rinse with cold water and drain again.

5. Spread half of the tomato sauce in a 13-by-9-inch stainless-steel baking dish. Choose the twenty best shells; reserve the rest for another use. Transfer the radicchio mixture to a large pastry bag without a tip or a plastic bag with a large corner snipped off and pipe the stuffing into the shells. Arrange the filled shells open-side up in the baking dish and sprinkle them with the remaining ¼ cup of Parmesan and 1 tablespoon of parsley.

6. Preheat the oven to 375°. Bake the stuffed shells for about 20 minutes, or until the shells are heated through and the sauce is bubbling. Preheat the broiler and broil the shells for about 2 minutes, or until golden on top. Rewarm the remaining tomato sauce and serve with the shells.   —Maria Helm

MAKE AHEAD The stuffed shells can be refrigerated overnight; allow an extra five minutes for baking. Refrigerate the remaining tomato sauce separately.

WINE The best choice is the 1994 Badia a Coltibuono Chianti Classico, a velvety and voluptuous wine with light oak, berry-cherry flavors and soft tannins. The oak goes well with the grilled flavor of the radicchio, while the fruit balances its slight bitterness and echoes the soft fruitiness of the fennel and tomato.

wines of sicily

The bold, assertive flavors of Sicilian food call for wines that are equally upfront: Sicily's own fresh, bone-dry whites and robust, ripe reds. Sicilian dishes like Pasta and Chickpeas, Pasta alla Norma (p. 91), Spaghetti alla Siracusana (p. 101) and Pasta with Sardines (p. 102) would go equally well with a red, such as the 1992 Regaleali Cabernet Sauvignon or the 1993 Corvo Rosso, or a white, such as the 1994 Rapitalia Alcamo, the 1994 Regaleali Nozze d'Oro or the 1994 Corvo Bianco. Rigatoni Timbale alla Gangivecchio (p. 105) is best with a red; Pasta with Nut Pesto (p. 90), with a white. For a non-Sicilian white, consider a Pinot Grigio, a Soave or a Rioja; for a red, try a hearty Rhône or a California Cabernet Sauvignon or Zinfandel.

Pasta and Chickpeas

4 SERVINGS

For this bean-soup-like *pasta e ceci*, adapted from *The Flavors of Sicily* (Clarkson Potter), soaked dried chickpeas are cooked with garlic, celery, onion, carrot and rosemary. Canned chickpeas are just as good and much quicker.

4 cups drained canned chickpeas

1 cup chicken stock or canned
low-sodium broth

2 cups water

Salt and freshly ground pepper

1 pound red Swiss chard, stems
sliced ¼ inch thick, leaves cut
into 1-inch ribbons

¼ pound spaghetti, broken into
1-inch pieces (about 1½ cups)

¼ cup extra-virgin olive oil

2 tablespoons finely chopped
flat-leaf parsley

I. In a food processor, puree 3 cups of the chickpeas with the stock and the water. Transfer the chickpea puree to a large saucepan, add the remaining chickpeas and season with salt and pepper. Add the chard stems and cook over low heat until tender, about 15 minutes. Stir in the leaves and simmer until wilted, about 5 minutes.

2. Meanwhile, fill a medium pot with water, cover and bring to a boil. Add salt and the spaghetti. Cover partially until the water just returns to a boil, then uncover, stir the spaghetti and cook until al dente. Drain, reserving some of the cooking liquid, and add the pasta to the chickpeas. Add some of the reserved cooking liquid if the mixture is too thick. Serve in shallow soup plates, drizzled with the oil and sprinkled with the parsley.   *–Anna Tasca Lanza*

Spinach-Filled Crespelle with Lemon Sauce

4 SERVINGS

Cannelloni are usually dressed with a béchamel, but here I've chosen a pungent lemon sauce to brighten up this sometimes heavy dish. To save time I've used crespelle, a delicate pasta made in a frying pan like crêpes, instead of rolled pasta. The first few have a tendency to stick and tear until the pan is well seasoned and the heat is regulated. In any case, there's plenty of batter.

Spinach-Filled Crespelle with Lemon Sauce

CRESPELLE

1 cup all-purpose flour
3 large eggs
1½ cups whole milk
3 tablespoons olive oil, plus more for cooking the crespelle
Salt

FILLING AND SAUCE

1½ pounds spinach, stemmed and washed but not dried
1 cup plus 2 tablespoons freshly grated Parmigiano-Reggiano (about 3 ounces)
½ cup ricotta
1 large egg, lightly beaten
Pinch of freshly grated nutmeg
Salt and freshly ground pepper
1 cup heavy cream
3 tablespoons unsalted butter
1½ tablespoons fresh lemon juice
1 tablespoon minced lemon zest
½ teaspoon dried thyme

I. MAKE THE CRESPELLE: Combine the flour, eggs, milk, the 3 tablespoons of oil and a pinch of salt in a food processor and blend until smooth. Transfer the batter to a pitcher and let rest at room temperature for about 30 minutes.

2. Lightly oil a 7- or 8-inch nonstick skillet or crêpe pan and set it over moderately high heat. Pour in 3 tablespoons of the batter and quickly tilt the skillet in a circular motion to spread the batter evenly over the bottom. Cook the crespelle for about 45 seconds on one side, then flip it and cook for about 20 seconds on the other side. Continue making the crespelle, stacking them as you go. Add more oil to the pan as needed.

3. MAKE THE FILLING AND THE SAUCE: Preheat the oven to 425°. Set a large skillet over high heat. Add the spinach and cook, stirring, until just wilted. Transfer the spinach to a colander; let cool and squeeze out as much

water as possible. Chop the spinach and transfer it to a bowl. Beat in ½ cup of the Parmigiano-Reggiano, the ricotta, egg, nutmeg and a pinch each of salt and pepper.

4. In a small stainless-steel saucepan, bring the heavy cream and the butter to a boil. Add the lemon juice, lemon zest and thyme and cook over moderate heat, stirring occasionally, until the sauce is slightly reduced and beginning to thicken, about 5 minutes. Remove the saucepan from the heat and stir in ½ cup more of the Parmigiano-Reggiano. Spread a thin layer of the sauce in the bottom of a 13-by-9-inch (3-quart) baking dish.

5. Spread twelve of the crespelle with a thin layer of the spinach filling. Loosely roll up the crespelle and place them, seam-side down, on top of the sauce in the baking dish. Pour the remaining sauce over the top of the crespelle and sprinkle with the remaining 2 tablespoons of Parmigiano-Reggiano. Bake for 15 to 20 minutes, or until lightly browned and bubbling. Serve the crespelle immediately.   *–Erica De Mane*

MAKE AHEAD The crespelle can be cooled completely, wrapped tightly in aluminum foil and refrigerated for up to three days or frozen for up to three weeks. Bring to room temperature before proceeding with Step 3.

WINE The creamy lemon sauce makes these crespelle an ideal showcase for a fine, fragrant white. Look for the 1995 Bruno Giacosa Arneis or the 1994 La Scolca Black Label Gavi.

Mara's Pasta with Broccoli and Scallop Sauce

4 TO 6 SERVINGS

Mara Martin, owner of Da Fiore in Venice, is one of the most precious friends I have gained through cooking. Her dishes are rigorously based on the superb local seafood and the preparations are by and large those of the understated, light-handed Venetian tradition. She doesn't shrink from updating them, however, when she finds a promising new union of ingredients, as in this combination of scallops and broccoli from the south of Italy. Mara has a generous hand with butter, which may distress those who think olive oil is the only cooking medium for Italian seafood. But it is butter that does what needs to be done here, tenderly reconciling the reticent mildness of the thin scallop slices with the sourish, vegetal quality of the broccoli. It is impossible to imagine a seafood sauce with a blend of flavors more smooth or ravishing.

1 pound broccoli
Coarse salt
½ pound scallops, preferably bay
1 stick (4 ounces) butter
½ cup finely chopped onion
1 pound pennini or maccheroncini
2 teaspoons thyme leaves
⅛ teaspoon finely chopped fresh chile, or more to taste
½ cup freshly grated Parmigiano-Reggiano

I. Peel the broccoli stems, removing all of the tough, dark green skin and any stringy parts. Separate the broccoli florets from the stems and wash the florets and stems.

2. Bring a large pot of water to a boil and add 2 tablespoons of salt. Add the thick broccoli stems and cook them for 7 minutes, and then add the broccoli florets. When the water returns to a boil, cook the broccoli for 12 minutes longer. Drain well.

3. Wash and drain the scallops. Trim off the small beige filament from the side of each of the scallops. Slice the scallops crosswise into thin rounds and pat them dry.

4. Separate the larger broccoli florets into smaller ones and slice all of the stems into thin rounds.

5. Put 6 tablespoons of the butter and the onion in a large skillet. Turn the heat to moderately high and cook, stirring often, until the onion is softened but not browned, 3 to 5 minutes. Add all of the broccoli and stir gently to coat. Reduce the heat to moderate and cook the broccoli for 6 minutes, stirring occasionally; set aside.

6. Fill a large pot with 4 quarts of water and bring to a boil. Add 1½ tablespoons of salt, cover and return to a boil. Add the pasta to the pot and stir rapidly with a wooden spoon. Cover the pot and bring the water back to a boil, then uncover and cook the pasta, stirring frequently, until it is al dente.

7. Meanwhile, add the sliced scallops, thyme leaves and fresh chile to the broccoli and season with salt. Cook briefly until the scallops turn white, 2 to 3 minutes. Remove from the heat and stir in the cheese.

8. When the pasta is nearly done, add the remaining 2 tablespoons of butter to the scallops and broccoli. Return the pan to moderate heat and stir gently. Drain the pasta and add it to the skillet. Toss thoroughly for no more than 20 seconds, then transfer to a warm bowl and serve at once. —*Marcella Hazan*
MAKE AHEAD The broccoli can be boiled and drained a few hours in advance, but do not refrigerate it.

Farfalle with Crabmeat and Oregano Butter

6 SERVINGS **Q**

For a more intense tomato flavor, reconstitute the sun-dried tomatoes in the white wine that's called for in the recipe. Just bring the tomatoes and wine to a simmer in a small stainless-steel saucepan, and then remove the saucepan from the heat to steep until the tomatoes are plumped. Chop the tomatoes and add them with the wine to the saucepan in Step 2.

8 sun-dried-tomato halves
1 cup boiling water
2 tablespoons olive oil
1 large shallot, minced
2 garlic cloves, minced
½ cup dry white wine
¼ cup chicken stock or canned low-sodium broth
½ pound fresh Dungeness or lump crabmeat, carefully picked over
2 teaspoons chopped oregano or marjoram
1½ sticks (6 ounces) unsalted butter, cut into tablespoons
Kosher salt
Freshly ground pepper
1 pound farfalle
1 tablespoon coarsely chopped flat-leaf parsley

I. In a small stainless-steel heatproof bowl, cover the sun-dried-tomato halves with the boiling water. Set the sun-dried-tomato halves aside until they are softened, about 20 minutes. Drain the reconstituted sun-dried tomatoes and chop them coarsely.

2. Fill a large pot with water, cover and bring to a boil. Meanwhile, in a large stainless-steel saucepan, heat the oil. Add the shallot and garlic and cook over moderate heat until softened but not browned, about 5 minutes. Add the sun-dried tomatoes and cook for 1 minute. Add the wine and boil over high heat until almost evaporated, 2 to 3 minutes. Add the stock and bring to a boil. Gently stir in the crabmeat and oregano and cook until heated through, about 2 minutes. Remove the pan from the heat and add the butter; stir until smooth. Season the crab sauce with salt and pepper.

3. Add salt and the farfalle to the pot of boiling water. Cover the pot partially until the water just returns to a boil, then uncover, stir the pasta and cook until al dente. ➤

4. Drain the pasta; transfer to a large warmed serving bowl. Pour the sauce over the pasta, add the parsley and toss well. Serve at once. *–Michael Romano*
WINE 1995 Ronco del Gnemiz Tocai Friulano. The crisp and flowery flavors of this wine highlight the delicate sweetness of the crab.

Farfalle with Crabmeat and Oregano Butter

Linguine with Clams, Bacon and Hot Red Pepper

4 SERVINGS

I love to sneak American ingredients into Italian dishes. Here's a favorite adaptation, the traditional southern Italian white clam sauce with my own smoky and spicy touches.

2½ pounds small clams, scrubbed
 1 cup dry white wine
Salt
 1 pound linguine
Two ⅛-inch-thick slices slab bacon, cut into ⅛-inch dice
 1 small fresh hot red chile, seeded and minced

5 garlic cloves, minced

⅓ cup extra-virgin olive oil

2 teaspoons minced lemon zest

½ cup chopped parsley

1 teaspoon minced oregano

1. Bring a large pot of water to a boil. Meanwhile, in a large deep stainless-steel skillet, combine the clams and wine. Cook over high heat, partially covered, until all the clams are opened, 5 to 8 minutes. Using a slotted spoon, transfer the clams to a large bowl. Return the skillet to high heat and boil until the liquid is reduced to ¾ cup. Strain the liquid into a heatproof measuring cup and set aside.

2. Add salt and the pasta to the boiling water in the pot and cook, stirring often, until al dente. Meanwhile, wipe out the skillet and set it over moderate heat. Add the bacon and cook, stirring occasionally, until crisp, about 4 minutes. Add the chile and garlic and cook over low heat, stirring, until the garlic is just golden, about 1 minute. Add the reserved clam-cooking liquid, the oil and the lemon zest and simmer for 1 minute. Add the clams, parsley and oregano and cook until just heated through. Remove from the heat.

3. Drain the pasta well, shaking out any excess water, and transfer it to a large deep platter. Add the sauce; toss to combine. Season with salt. –*Erica De Mane*

W I N E The role of wine here is to provide a pleasingly sharp but fruity contrast. Consider the 1995 Plozner Tocai Friulano or the 1995 Trimbach Sylvaner.

Spaghetti alla Siracusana

4 SERVINGS

It's the crisp bread crumbs that make this simple dish special. For more sardine flavor, use two cans.

Salt

¾ pound spaghetti

½ cup olive oil

1 cup fresh bread crumbs

½ cup freshly grated Pecorino Romano

One 3.75-ounce can oil-packed sardines, preferably imported, drained

2 garlic cloves, minced

2 tablespoons tomato paste dissolved in ¼ cup water

Freshly ground pepper

1. Fill a large pot with water, cover and bring to a boil. Add salt and the spaghetti. Cover partially until the water just returns to a boil, then uncover, stir, and cook until al dente. Drain and transfer to a warmed large serving bowl, cover and keep warm.

2. Meanwhile, in a large skillet, heat ¼ cup of the oil. Add the bread crumbs and cook over moderately high heat, stirring constantly, until golden and crisp, about 4 minutes. Transfer to a bowl and stir in the cheese. ➤

ABOVE: **Spaghetti alla Sircusana.** TOP: **Linguine with Clams, Bacon and Hot Red Pepper.**

3. Wipe out the skillet. Add the remaining ¼ cup of oil, the sardines and garlic and cook over moderate heat, stirring, until the sardines break up, about 2 minutes. Remove from the heat and stir in the dissolved tomato paste. Pour over the pasta and toss. Season with pepper. Stir in 3 tablespoons of the bread crumbs. Sprinkle half the remaining bread crumbs on top and serve. Pass the remaining bread crumbs at the table.   *–Antonio Visetti*

Pasta with Sardines

6 SERVINGS

This surprisingly unfishy version of *pasta con le sarde* is adapted from *The Flavors of Sicily* (Clarkson Potter).

Salt

- 1   fennel bulb (about 1 pound), tops trimmed, bulb quartered
- ¾   cup extra-virgin olive oil
- 1   pound fresh sardines, filleted
- 1   medium onion, chopped
- 4   anchovy fillets, chopped
- 2   tablespoons pine nuts
- 2   tablespoons currants
- 4   cups tomato sauce, preferably homemade

Freshly ground pepper

- ¾   cup fresh bread crumbs
- 1   pound perciatelli or spaghetti

1. Fill a large pot with water, cover and bring to a boil. Add salt and the fennel. Cook until tender, about 8 minutes. Remove the fennel with a slotted spoon and finely chop, discarding the core. Reserve the water for cooking the pasta.

salted anchovies

To prepare the salted anchovies called for in the recipe for Christmas Spaghetti with Walnuts, rinse them under running water. Strip the fillets away from the bones; discard the bones and tails. Don't worry about getting every tiny bone out of the fillets—most will dissolve in the sauce anyway.

2. In a large stainless-steel saucepan, heat ½ cup of the oil. Add the sardines, onion and anchovies and cook over moderately high heat, stirring, until the onion begins to brown, about 5 minutes. Add the fennel, pine nuts and currants and cook for 3 minutes. Add all but 3 tablespoons of the tomato sauce, cover partially and cook over moderately low heat until thick, about 25 minutes. Season with salt and pepper and keep warm.

3. Meanwhile, heat the remaining ¼ cup of oil in a medium stainless-steel skillet. Add the reserved 3 tablespoons of tomato sauce and the bread crumbs and cook over moderately high heat, stirring, until golden and crisp, about 4 minutes. Transfer to a plate.

4. Return the pot of water to a boil, add the pasta and cook until al dente; drain well. Return the pasta to the pot, add the sauce and toss over low heat for 1 minute. Transfer the pasta to a warmed platter and top it with ¼ cup of the bread crumbs. Serve the pasta immediately. Pass the remaining bread crumbs at the table.   *–Anna Tasca Lanza*

Christmas Spaghetti with Walnuts

4 TO 6 SERVINGS

Despite its rich flavors, *u spaghett' anatalina*, a meatless pasta for Christmas Eve, is poor-folk food, a dish for those who can't afford to have more than a few anchovies in the festive sauce. The importance of using extremely fresh nuts in this dish cannot be overstressed.

- 1   cup walnuts
- ½   cup extra-virgin olive oil
- 6   garlic cloves, finely chopped
- 4   whole salted anchovies (see box, left) or 10 oil-packed anchovy fillets, coarsely chopped
- 1   pound spaghetti

Sea salt

- ½   cup minced flat-leaf parsley

1. Preheat the oven to 400°. Spread the walnuts in a pie pan and toast in the oven for 4 minutes, or until fragrant. Transfer the nuts to a kitchen towel and rub together to flake away as much of the skin as possible. Coarsely chop the nuts.

2. In a large saucepan, warm the oil. Add the garlic and cook over moderately low heat, stirring occasionally, until softened. Add the anchovies and cook, stirring and pressing them into the oil with the back of a fork until almost dissolved. Stir in the walnuts and keep warm.

3. Cook the pasta in a large pot of boiling salted water until almost al dente. Add ½ cup of the cooking water to the sauce; bring to a simmer. Drain the pasta; add it to the sauce. Turn and stir to coat with the sauce as it finishes cooking, 1½ to 2 minutes. Season with salt. Transfer to a warmed bowl; garnish with the parsley. Serve at once.   *–Nancy Harmon Jenkins*

WINE Garlic, anchovies and walnuts need a fragrant white to bridge their flavors. Try a 1995 Fiano di Avellino from Mastroberardino or Feudi di San Gregorio.

Fusilli with Oven-Roasted Tomatoes and Chicken

4 SERVINGS **L**

If you have leftover cooked skinless chicken breasts, use them instead of poaching the meat in Step 2; you'll need about one pound. Chicken broth or water is fine in place of the cooking liquid.

- 2   pounds plum tomatoes, halved lengthwise
- 2   teaspoons olive oil

Salt and freshly ground pepper

- 1   pound skinless, boneless chicken breasts, trimmed of fat
- 3   cups water
- 1   small head of escarole, coarsely chopped
- ¾   pound dried fusilli
- 3   garlic cloves, finely chopped
- 1   teaspoon finely chopped rosemary
- ⅓   cup finely shredded basil

2 tablespoons freshly grated
Parmesan

1. Preheat the oven to 400°. Set the tomatoes, cut-side up, on a large baking sheet. Drizzle with the oil and season with salt and pepper. Bake about 45 minutes, or until very soft and lightly browned. Peel and transfer to a medium bowl.

2. In a medium saucepan, cover the chicken breasts with the water and bring to a simmer over moderate heat. Cover partially and simmer over low heat until the chicken breasts are just cooked through, about 15 minutes. Cut the chicken breasts into thin slices and cover with plastic wrap to keep the

meat moist. Reserve ¼ cup of the cooking broth.

3. Meanwhile, bring a large pot of salted water to a boil. Add the escarole and cook over high heat until just tender, about 4 minutes. Using a slotted spoon, transfer the escarole to a colander. Bring the water back to a boil and add

Pasta with Sardines

the fusilli. Cook until al dente, about 8 minutes. Drain the fusilli, leaving a little cooking water to keep the pasta moist, and return it to the saucepan; keep warm.

---

menu

Creamy Root-Vegetable Soup (p. 75)

Fusilli with Oven-Roasted Tomatoes and Chicken (p. 102)

Shiitake-Mushroom Sauté with Watercress (p. 322)

1996 TALTARNI FROM AUSTRALIA OR 1995 CAIN MUSQUÉ FROM CALIFORNIA

Fusilli with Oven-Roasted Tomatoes and Chicken

4. Pour the reserved cooking broth into a large skillet. Add the garlic; cook over moderately high heat for 30 seconds. Add the escarole and stir to blend. Season the escarole with salt and pepper. Add the roasted tomatoes with their accumulated juices and the chicken and cook until heated through. Stir in the rosemary. Add the mixture to the fusilli and toss well, then season with salt and pepper. Transfer to a large platter and sprinkle with the basil and Parmesan. Serve at once. *—Amanda Cushman*

WINE A Sauvignon Blanc from the New World, such as the 1996 Taltarni from Australia or the 1995 Cain Musqué from California, has enough of an herbal edge to set off the bitter notes of the escarole in this pasta dish.

Perciatelli alla Gricia

4 SERVINGS **Q**

This dish is actually the base recipe for a trilogy of classic Roman pastas. Add some beaten egg to the steaming hot pasta and pancetta and you have *alla carbonara*. Add fresh chiles, white wine and tomatoes and you have *all'amatriciana*. For this recipe, use the rendered fat from the pancetta and resist the temptation to add chopped parsley to the finished dish for color; it just confuses the flavors. Serve the pasta with grilled marinated vegetables.

- **2 tablespoons extra-virgin olive oil**
- **½ pound pancetta or guanciale, thinly sliced and cut into long thin strips**

Kosher salt

- **1 pound perciatelli or spaghetti**
- **½ cup freshly grated Pecorino Romano, plus more for serving**

Freshly ground pepper

1. Fill a large pot with water, cover and bring to a boil. Meanwhile, in a large heavy saucepan, heat the oil. Add the pancetta. Cook over moderate heat, stirring occasionally, until crisp, about 10 minutes. Remove from the heat.

2. Add salt and the perciatelli to the boiling water. Cover partially until the water just returns to a boil, then uncover, stir the pasta and cook until al dente.

3. Drain the pasta, reserving 1 cup of the cooking water. Add the pasta, the pasta-cooking water and the ½ cup of grated cheese to the saucepan with the pancetta and set over moderate heat. Season with six to eight turns of a pepper mill; toss well. Serve in warmed bowls. Pass additional cheese and pepper separately. *—Michael Romano*

WINE 1990 Rocca di Castagnoli Chianti Classico Riserva Poggio a' Frati. This Chianti makes a great combination with the sharp Pecorino flavors and it stands up to the peppery bacon.

Rigatoni Timbale alla Gangivecchio

8 SERVINGS

This recipe, adapted from *La Cucina Siciliana di Gangivecchio* (Knopf), represents a more refined style of Sicilian cooking. Pasta, sausage, ground veal, fennel, tomato sauce and cheese are baked in a mold, then turned out for serving.

- ½ cup plus 1 tablespoon extra-virgin olive oil
- 2 medium onions, finely chopped
- 1¼ pounds Italian sausage, removed from the casings and crumbled
- 2¾ cups Concentrated Tomato Sauce (recipe follows)
- 6 cups water

Salt and freshly ground pepper

- 1¼ pounds ground veal

Pinch of sugar

- 2 medium fennel bulbs, fronds chopped, bulbs quartered
- 1½ pounds rigatoni
- ½ cup fine dried bread crumbs

Unsalted butter, softened

- ⅓ cup freshly grated Parmigiano-Reggiano
- ⅓ cup freshly grated Pecorino Romano

1. In a large stainless-steel saucepan, combine ¼ cup of the oil with half the onions, the sausage meat and 2 cups of the Concentrated Tomato Sauce. Cook over moderately high heat, stirring often, until bubbling. Stir in 2 cups of the water, cover partially and cook until thick, about 1 hour. Season with salt and pepper.

2. Meanwhile in a large deep skillet, heat ¼ cup of the oil. Add the remaining onion and cook over moderately high heat until softened. Add the veal and cook over high heat, stirring to break the meat apart, until it just begins to brown, about 10 minutes. Add the remaining ¾ cup of Concentrated Tomato Sauce, the sugar and the remaining

4 cups water and bring to a boil. Cover partially and cook over moderately low heat until thick, about 1 hour.

3. Preheat the oven to 375°. In a large pot of boiling salted water, cook the fennel bulbs until tender, about 8 minutes. Using a slotted spoon, transfer the fennel to a work surface. Cut out the cores and discard; cut the bulbs into ¼-inch dice and transfer to a large bowl. Bring the water back to a rapid boil. Add the pasta. Cover partially until the water just returns to a boil, then uncover, stir and cook until al dente. Drain the pasta and add it to the bowl with the fennel.

4. In a small bowl, toss the bread crumbs with the remaining 1 tablespoon oil. Generously butter two 2-quart soufflé dishes. Coat the dishes with the crumbs, tap out any excess and reserve.

5. Add both of the sauces to the rigatoni along with the grated cheeses and the fennel fronds; stir well and season with salt and pepper. Spoon into the soufflé dishes and pack down lightly. Sprinkle the remaining crumbs on top and bake for about 30 minutes, or until golden and the sauce is bubbling. Transfer the dishes to a rack and let rest for 15 minutes. To unmold, place a large plate over each soufflé dish and invert; remove the soufflé dish. Serve the timbale immediately, cut in wedges.

CONCENTRATED TOMATO SAUCE

MAKES ABOUT 4 CUPS

- 1 cup extra-virgin olive oil
- 1 medium onion, finely chopped
- 3 cups tomato paste
- 1 teaspoon sugar

Salt and freshly ground pepper

Heat the oil in a large heavy stainless-steel saucepan. Add the onion and cook over moderate heat, stirring often, until golden. Stir in the tomato paste, sugar and a pinch each of salt and pepper. Reduce the heat to low. Cook the sauce for 1 hour, stirring often; the oil

will remain partially separate throughout cooking. *–Giovanna Tornabene*

MAKE AHEAD The timbale can be made through Step 2 and the sauces refrigerated for up to three days. Bring to room temperature before proceeding. The Concentrated Tomato Sauce can be made in advance and refrigerated for five days.

Pasta with Rabbit and Fava Beans

4 SERVINGS

- 1 rabbit (about 2¾ pounds), trimmed of fat

Salt and freshly ground pepper

A handful of savory, oregano and thyme sprigs

- ½ pound thickly sliced pancetta or bacon
- 2 tablespoons dry white wine
- 1 pound fresh fava beans, shelled
- ½ pound dried penne
- 2 tablespoons unsalted butter
- ½ cup chicken stock, or 1 cup canned low-sodium broth boiled down to ½ cup
- ¼ cup mascarpone or heavy cream

1. Preheat the oven to 350°. Season the rabbit inside and out with salt and pepper and stuff the cavity with two-thirds of the herb sprigs. Arrange the remaining sprigs on top. Wrap the rabbit in the pancetta strips, making sure the loin and legs are covered. Using cotton string, tie the rabbit at 2-inch intervals to secure the pancetta. Set the rabbit in a roasting pan and roast for 30 minutes. Turn, baste with the wine and cook for about 30 minutes more, or until the juices run clear when a thigh is pierced; the meat will be pink around the joints. Let cool.

2. Finely chop enough of the cooked pancetta to equal ⅓ cup. Discard the remaining pancetta and the herbs. Remove the rabbit meat from the bones and cut it into ¾-inch pieces. ➤

3. In a small saucepan of boiling salted water, blanch the fava beans for 1 minute. Drain the beans and rinse with cold water. Peel off and discard the tough bean skins.

4. In a medium saucepan of boiling salted water, cook the penne until it is al dente, about 11 minutes. Drain the pasta and toss it with 1 tablespoon of the butter.

5. Meanwhile, in another large saucepan, bring the chicken stock to a boil. Add the fava beans and simmer over moderately low heat until they are tender, about 3 minutes. Add the reserved pancetta and the rabbit and cook over moderately high heat, stirring, until the stock is almost completely absorbed, about 2 minutes. Remove from the heat and stir in the pasta, the mascarpone and the remaining 1 tablespoon of butter. Season with salt and pepper and serve at once. —*Tim McKee*

WINE 1995 Alderbrook Chardonnay from California

Pasta with Abruzzi-Style Lamb Sauce

4 TO 6 SERVINGS

The deep, intense flavor of lamb sets this apart from other classic meat sauces. So does the fact that the meat is not ground, but cut into small pieces and cooked as though it were a stew. You can use any cut of lamb for this sauce, as long as it is not too lean.

- 1 tablespoon extra-virgin olive oil
- ¼ cup chopped onion
- 2 ounces thinly sliced pancetta, finely chopped
- 1 tablespoon chopped rosemary
- ½ pound boneless lamb, cut into very fine dice

Coarse salt and freshly ground pepper
- ½ cup dry white wine
- 1 large can (28 ounces) Italian plum tomatoes with their juices, coarsely chopped

- 1 pound penne or maccheroncini
- ⅓ cup freshly grated Romano

I. Put the oil and onion in a large skillet and cook over moderately high heat, stirring frequently, until the onion is pale gold. Add the pancetta and rosemary and cook, stirring occasionally, until the pancetta fat is rendered; the pancetta should remain soft.

2. Add the lamb and cook until browned, about 5 minutes. Season with salt and pepper and stir. Add the wine and simmer until evaporated, about 10 minutes.

3. Put in the tomatoes and simmer gently, stirring from time to time, until the fat begins to separate from the sauce, about 15 minutes.

4. Meanwhile, fill a large pot with 4 quarts of water and bring to a boil. Add 1½ tablespoons salt, cover and return to a boil. Add the pasta and stir rapidly with a wooden spoon. Cover, bring back to a boil and then uncover and cook the pasta, stirring frequently, until al dente.

5. Drain the pasta and immediately transfer it to a warmed bowl. Toss with the lamb sauce and the cheese. Serve at once; pass additional cheese at the table. —*Marcella Hazan*

MAKE AHEAD The sauce can be refrigerated for up to two days.

Baked Pasta with Ragù and Ricotta

8 TO 10 SERVINGS

This time-consuming preparation is usually made with ziti—in Italy, the dish is called *ziti alerti*, which translates as alert bachelors, or *ziti in piedi*, bachelors on their feet. But ziti as we know them in this country are too small for this treatment so I've made the dish with manicotti, first cooking the pasta partially, then cutting the tubes in half to make them stubby and relatively easy to fill. Of course, you could also make this as a conventional oven-baked pasta, mixing the barely cooked

pasta with the ragù and the ricotta and then topping it with ragù and Parmigiano-Reggiano and baking until the top is nicely browned. But here's how to make the dish in the old-fashioned Neapolitan way.

- ¼ cup extra-virgin olive oil
- 2 medium onions, finely chopped
- 2 garlic cloves, thinly sliced
- 1 very green celery rib, finely chopped
- 1 medium carrot, finely chopped
- 2 pounds meaty country-style pork ribs
- 1 pound beef shank, in one piece

Salt and freshly ground black pepper
- 1 cup red wine

One 28-ounce can crushed tomatoes
Freshly grated nutmeg
Crushed red pepper
- ¼ cup plus 2 tablespoons minced flat-leaf parsley
- 2 tablespoons minced basil

Three 8-ounce packages of manicotti
- 2½ cups ricotta (1¼ pounds)
- ½ cup freshly grated Parmigiano-Reggiano

I. Heat the oil in a large enameled cast-iron casserole. Add the onions, garlic, celery and carrot and cook over low heat, stirring frequently, until softened but not browned, about 8 minutes.

2. Push the vegetables to the edge of the casserole and add the pork ribs and beef shank. Season the meats with salt and black pepper, increase the heat to moderate and cook, turning, until nicely browned on all sides. Add the wine and cook until reduced by half, about 4 minutes. Stir in the tomatoes, nutmeg and crushed red pepper and mix well with the vegetables. Season with salt and pepper and bring to a simmer. Cover, reduce the heat to very low and cook at a bare simmer for 3 hours, stirring occasionally; check from time to time to make sure the sauce doesn't scorch. If it becomes very thick, add a tablespoon or two of water. ➤

Pasta with Rabbit and Fava Beans

3. Remove the meats from the pan, scraping off the sauce. Shred the meats with a fork, discarding all the bones and fat. Return the meats to the sauce; stir in 2 tablespoons of the parsley and the basil. Season the sauce with salt and black pepper. You should have about 8 cups of meaty ragù.

4. Preheat the oven to 375°. Cook the manicotti in a large pot of boiling salted water until it is half-cooked, about 5 minutes. Drain the manicotti immediately and rinse under cool water to stop the cooking. Cut each of the manicotti in half crosswise.

BELOW: **Making couscous.**
BOTTOM: **Moroccan-Style Couscous.**

5. Lightly oil the bottom and sides of a 12-inch baking dish. Spread 1½ cups of the ragù over the bottom of the dish and stand the halved manicotti upright in the ragù, wedging the tubes in closely together; some of the pasta tubes will split, but you should have about forty standing when you're done.

6. In a medium bowl, mix 2 cups of the ragù with 2 cups of the ricotta and season with salt. Carefully spoon the ricotta-ragù mixture into each tube, filling it two-thirds of the way. Dollop a bit of the remaining plain ricotta on top of each tube. Spoon the remaining ragù over the stuffed manicotti and top with the grated Parmigiano-Reggiano and the remaining ¼ cup parsley.

7. Place the baking dish in a larger roasting pan. Cover the baking dish lightly with aluminum foil, sealing the edges of the foil around the dish but tenting the foil over the manicotti. Carefully pour ⅛ inch of very hot water into the roasting pan. Bake the manicotti for 15 minutes. Remove the foil, increase the oven temperature to 400° and bake for 5 to 10 minutes longer, or until lightly browned on top. Remove from the oven and let rest for 10 minutes before serving.   *–Nancy Harmon Jenkins*

MAKE AHEAD The ragù can be refrigerated for up to four days.

WINE This hearty meat-ragù-and-ricotta pasta dish is definitely red-wine territory. Choose a full-flavored southern Italian wine such as the 1993 Mastroberardino Radici Taurasi or the 1994 Regaleali Cabernet Sauvignon.

Italian Couscous with Parmesan and Herbs

8 SERVINGS

Chewy Italian couscous, also called freula, is a Sardinian-style toasted semolina pasta. It comes in small, medium and large grains and is available at specialty-food stores. Any small pasta, such as ditalini, orzo or acini de pepe, makes a good alternative to medium-grain freula.

> 1   pound medium-grain Italian couscous (about 2½ cups)
> 4   tablespoons unsalted butter, cut into ½-inch pieces
> ¼   cup freshly grated Parmesan
> 2   tablespoons finely chopped flat-leaf parsley
> Salt and freshly ground pepper

Bring a large pot of salted water to a boil. Add the couscous and cook over moderately high heat, stirring occasionally, until tender but still chewy, about 20 minutes. Drain well and return the couscous to the pot. Add the butter and Parmesan and stir over low heat until melted. Add the parsley, season with salt and pepper and serve.

Moroccan-Style Couscous

10 SERVINGS

> Three 10-ounce packages couscous (about 4¼ cups)
> 3¾   cups chicken stock or canned low-sodium broth
> ⅓   cup vegetable oil
> 2   teaspoons salt
> ½   teaspoon white pepper
> ¼   teaspoon ground cumin
> ¼   teaspoon freshly grated nutmeg
> Pinch of crumbled saffron threads

1. Pour the couscous into a large bowl. In a medium saucepan, combine the stock with the oil, salt, pepper, cumin, nutmeg and saffron. Bring to a boil over moderate heat. Slowly pour the stock mixture over the couscous and stir gently to moisten the grains. Cover the bowl with a clean dish towel and let stand for 10 minutes.

2. Gently rub the couscous between lightly oiled hands to aerate and separate the grains. Cover again and let stand, rubbing occasionally to break up any lumps, until the couscous has doubled in volume and the grains are light and fluffy, about 30 minutes. Rewarm in the bowl over a saucepan of steaming water before serving. *–Michel Benasra*

MAKE AHEAD The cooked couscous can be refrigerated overnight. Rub the couscous to break up any clumps and transfer to a steamer basket lined with a double layer of cheesecloth. Steam over one inch of boiling water in a large saucepan until heated through.

Vegetable-Studded Couscous

6 SERVINGS **L**

Red and yellow bell peppers, zucchini, red onion and parsley make for a particularly colorful couscous. Accompany this low-fat grain dish with small amounts of meat, poultry or fish for a well-rounded meal; grilled catfish would go especially well.

1½ cups couscous (about 10 ounces)
1 medium red onion, finely chopped
⅓ cup finely chopped celery
⅓ cup finely chopped red bell pepper
⅓ cup finely chopped yellow bell pepper
⅓ cup finely chopped zucchini
⅓ cup dried currants
½ cup finely chopped flat-leaf parsley
2½ cups Vegetable Stock (p. 312) or chicken stock, or 2 cups canned chicken broth mixed with ½ cup water

Salt and freshly ground pepper

1. In a large bowl, toss together the couscous, red onion, celery, red and yellow bell peppers, zucchini, currants and parsley.

2. In a small saucepan, bring the stock to a boil. Pour it over the couscous, tossing with a spatula to evenly combine. Cover and let stand until the liquid is absorbed, about 10 minutes. Season with salt and pepper; serve warm or at room temperature. *–Cary Neff*

CHAPTER 6 shellfish

Mussel and Potato Stew (p. 126)

113 Spicy Steamed Crabs

113 Lobster Pad Thai

114 Mediterranean Baked Lobster with Olive Crumbs

114 Lobster-Stuffed Cabbage Rolls

115 Sherry-Creamed Lobster with Biscuits

116 Lobster Fisherman's Stew

116 Spicy Goan Shrimp

117 Shrimp with Tomato and Chile Pepper

117 Sichuan Shrimp in Lettuce Leaves

118 Chile Shrimp and Grits

118 Garlic Cheese Grits with Shrimp

119 Tandoori Prawns

119 Shellfish Stew with Chorizo and Rouille

120 Sautéed Scallops with Rosemary and Lemon

121 Bay Scallops with Sautéed Chanterelles

121 Scallops in Zucchini Nests

121 Scallops with Cider, Gewürztraminer and Sage

123 Olive-Oil and Pinot Blanc Squid with Peppers

123 Cioppino

125 Clams with Saffron, Tomato and Garlic

125 Oyster and Potato Stew with Crisp Bacon

126 Mussel and Potato Stew

127 Thai Red Curry with Mussels

Spicy Steamed Crabs

Spicy Steamed Crabs

12 SERVINGS

Use your fingers to spread the flavor of the spicy paste from the shells to the meat and to get at every delectable morsel. Be sure to supply everyone with wooden mallets, nutcrackers and picks. To make handling easier, refrigerate the crabs for at least one hour or overnight before preparing them.

⅓ cup plus 2 tablespoons cumin seeds (about 1½ ounces)

45 garlic cloves (about 2 heads), peeled and smashed

⅔ cup fresh lemon juice

30 bay leaves, broken

½ cup sweet paprika, preferably Hungarian

¼ cup pure hot chile powder

¼ cup vegetable oil

Kosher salt

20 live crabs (about 1½ pounds each)

3 sticks (¾ pound) unsalted butter

3 large scallions, finely chopped

3 tablespoons finely chopped cilantro

1½ teaspoons finely grated lemon zest

I. In a small skillet, toast the cumin seeds over moderate heat until they are fragrant, about 1 minute. Let cool, then transfer the seeds to a mini-processor or mortar. Add the garlic cloves and process or crush to a coarse paste. Scrape the mixture into a bowl and stir in ⅓ cup of the lemon juice, the bay leaves, paprika, chile powder, oil and 1 tablespoon of salt.

2. Pour 1 inch of water into two very large stockpots. In each pot, arrange a round rack or steamer basket; it should just fit inside. Cover and bring to a boil over high heat. Spread about 2 tablespoons of the paste over the back and on the front claws of each crab. Set the crabs on the racks in the pots, cover and steam until the crabs are bright pink, about 15 minutes.

3. Meanwhile, in a small saucepan, melt the butter over low heat. Remove from the heat and stir in the scallions, cilantro, lemon zest and the remaining ⅓ cup of lemon juice. Season the mixture with salt and keep warm.

4. Pour the butter mixture into small dipping bowls. Using tongs, transfer the crabs to the table. To eat, begin by pulling off a crab's top shell. Break off the claws and gently tap them with the mallet to crack the shells without crushing the meat. Remove the meat from the shells with your fingers. Break the body into sections and remove the meat with your fingers. –Marcia Kiesel

WINE Try a lively, spicy dry white wine, such as an Oregon Pinot Gris. Go for the 1996 Ponzi or the 1996 Sokol Blosser. Or serve the obvious choice: your favorite beer.

Lobster Pad Thai

6 SERVINGS

Jerry Clare, chef and co-owner of The Belmont in Camden, Maine, learned to make pad thai while studying in Thailand and adapted the dish for lobster when he returned to New England.

2 tablespoons fine sea salt

Two 1½-pound live lobsters

1 pound dried rice vermicelli

1 large stalk fresh lemongrass, tender bulb only, minced

2 tablespoons sugar

1 tablespoon Asian shrimp paste or anchovy paste

1 tablespoon chili paste

3 tablespoons peanut oil

½ pound medium shrimp, shelled and deveined

2 tablespoons minced fresh ginger

¼ cup fresh lime juice

¼ cup fresh lemon juice

1 tablespoon fish sauce

6 large scallions, chopped

1 large egg, beaten with 2 tablespoons of water

3 tablespoons chopped cilantro

1 cup (4 ounces) dry-roasted peanuts, coarsely ground

2 cups bean sprouts

Lime wedges, for serving

I. Fill a large stockpot with 2 inches of water, add the salt and bring to a boil over high heat. Put the lobsters in the boiling water, head first, and cook until they start to turn red, about 4 minutes. With tongs, transfer the lobsters to a bowl to cool.

2. Meanwhile, put the vermicelli in a large bowl, cover with warm water and let soak until pliable, about 20 minutes. Drain in a colander and set aside.

3. Remove the meat from the lobster knuckles and claws. Twist the tails off the bodies. Split the tails lengthwise and remove the tail meat. Pull out and discard the black intestinal vein. Cut all of the lobster meat into 1-inch chunks and place in a bowl. Add any accumulated lobster juices, cover and refrigerate until needed.

4. In a mini-processor, combine the lemongrass and 1 tablespoon of the sugar and process to a coarse paste. Scrape into a bowl. In another small bowl, combine the remaining 1 tablespoon of sugar with the shrimp paste and chili paste.

5. Heat a wok or a large wide skillet over high heat. Add the oil and when it is almost smoking, add the lobster and shrimp and stir-fry until the shrimp are barely pink throughout, about 2 minutes. Add the lemongrass paste and ginger and stir-fry until fragrant, about 1 minute. Add the shrimp-paste mixture and stir-fry for 1 minute longer. Add the drained rice noodles, lime juice, lemon

menu

Spicy Steamed Crabs (p. 113)

Bean Salad with
Lime Vinaigrette (p. 60)

Crispy Corn Bread (p. 288)

1996 PONZI PINOT GRIS

Lobster Pad Thai

juice and fish sauce and stir-fry until the noodles are translucent and pleasantly chewy, about 3 minutes. Add the scallions and egg and stir-fry until the egg is almost set, about 2 minutes.

6. Remove the pad thai from the heat and mound on a large platter. Sprinkle the cilantro, peanuts and bean sprouts over the top and serve at once with lime wedges.   *–Nancy Harmon Jenkins*
WINE 1994 Torres Viña Sol from Spain or a Japanese beer, such as Asahi

Mediterranean Baked Lobster with Olive Crumbs

2 SERVINGS

The stale bread is an important ingredient here; it should be from a country-style loaf, not overly sour and with no added flavorings. Have the fishmonger split and clean the lobsters for you shortly before you plan to cook them.

Two 2-pound live lobsters, split
    lengthwise, head sacs and intestinal
    veins removed, tomalley reserved
  ¼ cup plus 1 tablespoon extra-virgin
    olive oil
1½ cups finely diced stale
    coarse-textured bread
  ½ cup finely chopped parsley
  ¼ cup coarsely chopped Niçoise or
    Gaeta olives
  2 tablespoons fresh lemon juice
  1 teaspoon balsamic or
    aged-red-wine vinegar
  ½ teaspoon finely grated lemon zest
Salt and freshly ground pepper
Lemon wedges, for serving

I. Preheat the oven to 450°. With the back of a large knife or with a mallet, crack the lobster claws and knuckles all over. Rub the exposed lobster meat with the 1 tablespoon oil.

2. In a medium bowl, toss the bread with the parsley, olives, lemon juice, vinegar, lemon zest, the reserved tomalley and the remaining ¼ cup of oil.

3. Set the split lobsters, cut-side up, on a large baking sheet. Season the lobsters with salt and pepper and spread the stuffing over the bodies and tails, mounding it generously. Bake the lobsters in the upper third of the oven for about 15 minutes, or until the stuffing is crusty and the meat pulls away from the shell. Serve the lobsters at once with lemon wedges. *–Nancy Harmon Jenkins*
WINE 1995 Columbia Crest or Raymond Amberhill Chardonnay

Lobster-Stuffed Cabbage Rolls

8 SERVINGS

These elegant rolls can also be prepared using one-half pound of already cooked lobster meat in place of the live lobster and shrimp.

Fine sea salt
One 1½-pound live lobster
  1 stick (4 ounces) cold unsalted
    butter
  ⅓ cup finely diced red bell pepper
  ¼ cup finely diced celery
  ¾ cup finely diced carrots
  ¼ pound shelled medium shrimp or
    scallops, coarsely chopped
  1 large egg white
  ¼ cup plus 2 tablespoons fresh
    bread crumbs
  3 tablespoons minced chives
Freshly ground black pepper
Cayenne pepper
  1 head Savoy cabbage (1 pound)
  1 small onion, thinly sliced
  6 ounces shiitake mushrooms,
    stems discarded, caps thinly
    sliced
  2 shallots, minced

1 cup chicken stock or canned low-sodium broth

2 tablespoons chopped chervil or parsley

1. Fill a large stockpot with 2 inches of water, add 2 tablespoons of salt and bring to a boil over high heat. Put the lobster in the boiling water, head first, and cook until it turns red, about 12 minutes. With tongs, transfer the lobster to a bowl to cool.

2. Remove the meat from the lobster knuckles and claws. Twist the tail off the body; reserve the greenish tomalley and any red roe. Split the tail lengthwise and remove the tail meat. Pull out and discard the black intestinal vein. Cut all the lobster meat and the roe into ½-inch dice and place in a bowl. Add the tomalley.

3. In a small saucepan, melt 4 tablespoons of the butter over moderately low heat. Add the red pepper, celery and ¼ cup of the carrots and cook, stirring, until the vegetables are almost tender, about 5 minutes. Let cool to room temperature.

4. In a food processor, combine the shrimp and egg white and puree until very smooth. Scrape the puree into a bowl and fold in all the lobster meat, cooked vegetables, bread crumbs, chives, ½ teaspoon of salt, ¼ teaspoon black pepper and a pinch of cayenne. Cover and refrigerate until chilled.

5. Remove ten large intact outer leaves from the head of cabbage and set aside. Cut the remaining cabbage in half; core and shred it.

6. In a large saucepan of boiling salted water, blanch the whole cabbage leaves, two or three at a time, until they are just tender, about 3 minutes. Drain the cabbage leaves and let cool. Add the shredded cabbage to the boiling water and cook for 1 minute. Drain the cabbage in a colander and refresh under cold running water; drain again.

7. In a large skillet, melt 1 tablespoon of the butter. Add the onion and sauté over moderately high heat until browned, about 4 minutes. Add the shredded cabbage and cook for 2 minutes. Season with salt and pepper; let cool completely.

8. Preheat the oven to 350°. Butter an 11-by-9-inch glass baking dish. Select the eight best-looking cabbage leaves and pare down the thick central ribs so that they are flush with the leaves. Spread the leaves on a work surface and form one-eighth of the lobster filling into a 3-inch log across the center of each leaf. Top with one-eighth of the shredded cabbage mixture. Fold the two sides of each cabbage leaf in toward the center, then snugly roll up the leaf; use the two extra cabbage leaves to patch any tears. Arrange the cabbage rolls, seam-side down, in the prepared baking dish, leaving a little bit of space between the rolls.

9. In a large skillet, melt 1 tablespoon of the butter over moderate heat. Add the mushrooms, shallots and the remaining ½ cup of diced carrots. Cook, stirring, until the vegetables begin to brown, about 6 minutes. Add the stock and bring to a simmer. Season with salt and pepper and pour over the cabbage rolls. Cover the dish with aluminum foil and bake for about 25 minutes, or until the rolls are firm and heated through.

10. Transfer the rolls to a warmed platter; cover loosely with aluminum foil. Pour the juices from the baking dish into a small saucepan and bring to a boil. Off the heat, whisk in the remaining 2 tablespoons butter, 1 tablespoon at a time. Add the chopped herbs, season with salt and pepper and pour over the cabbage rolls. Serve at once.   *—Jasper White*

MAKE AHEAD The assembled cabbage rolls can be refrigerated overnight; bring to room temperature before baking.

WINE 1995 Rutz Cellars Dutton Ranch or Beaulieu Vineyard Carneros Chardonnay

wine with lobster

On its own, lobster is sweet, which is why steamed lobster mates perfectly with fruity but dry wines with enveloping flavors, such as Alsace Rieslings or low-oak Chardonnays (plain lobster makes woody wines taste harsh). Richer dishes, such as Mediterranean Baked Lobster with Olive Crumbs, call for a deeper flavored Chardonnay, and sweeter ones, such as Sam Hayward's Lobster and Sweet-Corn Soup (p. 82), less-dry Rieslings. Spicy, fruity flavors, such as Sara's Lobster and Mango Salad (p. 66), are best paired with simple dry whites.

Sherry-Creamed Lobster with Biscuits

4 SERVINGS

2 tablespoons fine sea salt

Two 1½-pound live lobsters

3 tablespoons unsalted butter

¼ cup medium-dry sherry, such as amontillado or oloroso

1 tablespoon all-purpose flour

1 cup whole milk

½ cup light cream

Freshly ground pepper

Hot Biscuits, for serving (recipe follows)

1. Fill a large stockpot with 2 inches of water, add the salt and bring to a boil over high heat. Put the lobsters in the boiling water, head first, and cook until they start to turn red, about 4 minutes. With tongs, transfer the lobsters to a bowl to cool.

2. Remove the meat from the knuckles and claws. Twist the tails off the bodies; reserve the greenish tomalley and any blackish roe (the roe doesn't turn red until it's fully cooked). Split the tails lengthwise and remove the meat. Pull out and discard the black intestinal vein. Cut the lobster meat into 1-inch chunks and transfer to a bowl. ➤

115

3. In a small saucepan, melt 2 tablespoons of the butter with the sherry. Pour the sherry butter over the lobster and set aside.

4. In a medium saucepan, melt the remaining 1 tablespoon of butter over moderately high heat. Stir in the flour to make a paste. Gradually whisk in the milk until smooth, then bring to a boil, whisking constantly. Simmer over low heat, whisking often, until the sauce is glossy and no floury taste remains, about 5 minutes. Add the cream and simmer for 2 minutes more. Fold in the lobster meat and sherry butter and season with pepper. Blend in the reserved tomalley and roe and simmer until the lobster is cooked through, about 2 minutes longer. Serve with the biscuits on the side.

WINE 1995 Signorello Sémillon or 1994 Robert Mondavi Stags Leap District Sauvignon Blanc

HOT BISCUITS

MAKES 8 BISCUITS

- 2 cups all-purpose flour
- 2 teaspoons baking powder
- ½ teaspoon salt
- 6 tablespoons unsalted butter, cut into small pieces and chilled
- ½ cup plus 1 tablespoon cold milk, plus more for brushing

1. Preheat the oven to 450°. Sift the flour, baking powder and salt into a large bowl. Cut in the butter until the mixture resembles coarse meal. Pour in the milk and stir gently with a wooden spoon until the biscuit dough just comes together.

2. On a floured surface, pat the dough into a ½-inch-thick round. Using a 2½-inch biscuit cutter, stamp out eight biscuits. Place the biscuits on a baking sheet and brush the tops with milk. Bake for 10 minutes, or until golden. Serve hot.   —Nancy Harmon Jenkins

Lobster Fisherman's Stew

4 SERVINGS

Once the lobster and crackers are added in Step 4, this stew can simmer gently for hours before adding the tomalley and roe. In fact, Maine cooks say, the longer it "sets," the better. The crackers should dissolve and thicken the stew.

- 2 tablespoons fine sea salt
- Two 1¼-pound live lobsters
- 6 cups water
- 3 cups whole milk
- 1 cup light cream
- 4 tablespoons unsalted butter
- 1 cup coarsely crushed oyster crackers or common crackers, plus additional crackers for serving
- Freshly ground pepper
- Cayenne pepper

1. Fill a large stockpot with 2 inches of water, add the salt and bring to a boil over high heat. Put the lobsters in the boiling water, head first, and cook until they start to turn red, about 4 minutes. With tongs, transfer the lobsters to a bowl to cool.

2. Remove the meat from the lobster knuckles and claws. Twist the tails off the bodies; reserve the greenish tomalley and any blackish roe (the roe doesn't turn red until it's fully cooked). Split the tails lengthwise and remove the tail meat. Pull out and discard the black intestinal vein. Cut the tail meat into 1-inch chunks. Cover and refrigerate the lobster, tomalley and roe.

3. Crush all of the lobster shells and place them in a large saucepan. Add the water and simmer over moderate heat for 20 minutes. Strain the broth through a fine sieve, pressing hard on the lobster shells to extract as much flavor from them as possible. Return the broth to the saucepan. Add the milk and the cream and simmer over low heat for 5 minutes.

4. In a large skillet, melt the butter over moderate heat. Add the crushed crackers and stir until lightly toasted, about 2 minutes. Stir the crackers and the lobster meat into the soup and simmer very gently—the stew must never come near a boil—over low heat for 1 hour, stirring occasionally. Gently whisk in the reserved tomalley and roe. Season with salt and pepper and a pinch of cayenne. Serve the stew with additional oyster crackers.   —Nancy Harmon Jenkins

WINE 1993 Hugel Gewürztraminer or 1995 Muré Gewürztraminer

Spicy Goan Shrimp

4 SERVINGS Q

If you buy shrimp in the shell and peel them yourself, you'll need two pounds. Note that the shrimp can be marinated for several hours if time permits. Serve the shrimp with a basmati rice pilaf and sautéed spinach.

- 6 dried red Thai chiles
- 12 whole black peppercorns
- 8 whole cloves
- One 1-inch piece of cinnamon stick
- ½ teaspoon cumin seeds
- One 1-inch piece of fresh ginger, peeled
- 6 garlic cloves
- 2 tablespoons wine vinegar
- 1 teaspoon brown sugar
- Sea salt
- 1½ pounds shelled and deveined raw medium shrimp
- 3 tablespoons vegetable oil
- Lime wedges, for serving

1. Grind the chiles, peppercorns, cloves, cinnamon and cumin in a spice grinder or in a mortar with a pestle. Pulse the ginger, garlic and vinegar in a blender until smooth, scraping down the sides of the blender often. In a small bowl, combine the ground spices and garlic paste with the brown sugar and a generous pinch of salt. Rub this paste over the shrimp; let marinate for 30 minutes.

2. Heat 1½ tablespoons of the oil in each of two large skillets. Add half of the shrimp to each pan in a single layer and sauté over high heat until golden and just opaque throughout, about 1½ minutes per side. Transfer the shrimp to a platter, garnish with lime wedges and serve. —*Michael Romano*

WINE 1995 Selbach-Oster Zeltinger Schlossberg Riesling Spätlese. This is a delightfully aromatic and thirst-quenching foil to the rich shrimp.

Shrimp with Tomato and Chile Pepper

6 SERVINGS

If the shrimp release a lot of liquid during cooking, transfer them to a warmed plate with a slotted spoon and boil the sauce until it is thickened. Any leftovers can be chopped in a food processor and used as a pasta sauce or added to risotto.

- 3 tablespoons finely chopped onion
- ¼ cup extra-virgin olive oil
- 2 teaspoons minced garlic
- 1 large jalapeño pepper, seeded and minced
- 3 tablespoons finely chopped flat-leaf parsley
- 1⅔ cups finely diced peeled ripe plum tomatoes or imported canned plum tomatoes, with their juices

Salt

- 2 pounds medium shrimp—shelled, deveined, washed and dried

Grilled or toasted crusty bread, for serving

I. In a large stainless-steel skillet, cook the onion in the oil over moderate heat, stirring occasionally, until it is translucent, about 5 minutes. Add the garlic and the jalapeño and cook until the garlic becomes a pale gold. Stir in the parsley, then add the tomatoes with their juices and a liberal sprinkling of salt. Reduce the heat and cook at a steady simmer, stirring occasionally, until the tomatoes cook down and the oil begins to separate from the sauce, about 20 minutes.

2. Add the shrimp to the skillet and stir to coat with the sauce. Cover and simmer until the shrimp are just cooked through, 2 to 3 minutes. Season with additional salt and serve immediately with the grilled bread. —*Marcella Hazan*

MAKE AHEAD The sauce can be refrigerated for up to one day. Bring the sauce back to a simmer before adding the shrimp.

WINE The delicate flavor of shrimp calls for white wine—unless the dish has the assertive ingredients this one does. The tanginess of the tomatoes and the heat of the jalapeño point to a flavorful red with some acidity. A Barbera from Italy, such as the 1990 Prunotto Barbera d'Alba Romualdo or the 1991 Pio Cesare Barbera d'Alba, would fill the bill perfectly.

Shrimp with Tomato and Chile Pepper

Sichuan Shrimp in Lettuce Leaves

4 SERVINGS **L**

Wrapping foods in lettuce leaves is popular throughout China. The most commonly used type of lettuce has fragile leaves that snap easily and have a texture quite similar to that of iceberg.

SAUCE

- 1 tablespoon ketchup
- 2 teaspoons oyster sauce
- 1 tablespoon Shao-Hsing wine or dry sherry
- ¾ teaspoon sugar

Salt and freshly ground white pepper

- 2 teaspoons cornstarch dissolved in 2 teaspoons cold water

SHRIMP

- 2 teaspoons Shallot Oil (p. 336)
- 2 teaspoons minced fresh ginger
- ½ tablespoon bean sauce
- ¾ pound shrimp—shelled, deveined and cut into ½-inch pieces

1 small red bell pepper, cut into
¼-inch dice

1 small green bell pepper, cut into
¼-inch dice

¼ cup finely diced water chestnuts

1 jalapeño pepper, minced (with
seeds)

3 tablespoons Crisp Shallots
(p. 336)

12 iceberg lettuce leaves

I. MAKE THE SAUCE: Combine all of the ingredients in a small bowl.

2. MAKE THE SHRIMP: Set a wok over high heat for 30 seconds. Add the Shallot Oil and stir to coat the wok. When a wisp of white smoke appears, stir in the ginger and the bean sauce. Add the shrimp and stir, and then add the red and green bell peppers, the water chestnuts and the jalapeño and stir-fry until the vegetables are crisp-tender, about 3 minutes.

3. Make a well in the center of the wok, pushing everything up the side slightly; stir the sauce and add it to the well. Stir in the shrimp and vegetables and stir-fry until heated through, about 2 minutes. Stir in the shallots; serve with the lettuce leaves. —*Eileen Yin-Fei Lo*

WINE The sweet spiciness of this shrimp dish rules out an overly subtle wine. Stick with modest, crisp whites, such as the 1995 Louis Martini Folle Blanche from California or the 1995 Sauvion et Fils Château du Cleray Muscadet from France.

Chile Shrimp and Grits

4 SERVINGS

This dish takes its inspiration from Cajun cuisine. A trio of chiles–árbol, ancho and jalapeño–gives the shrimp and grits a powerful kick. If you like your shrimp extra hot, double the amounts of the spices. Better still, buy small shrimp in their shells and toss them with quadruple the spices; just take care licking your fingers when you peel and eat the shrimp. If you don't have time to chill and fry the grits, you can certainly serve them straight from the pot.

3¾ cups water

1 cup quick (not instant) grits

Coarse salt

6 bacon slices

2 tablespoons olive oil

½ tablespoon ground cumin

¾ teaspoon pure ancho chile
powder or hot paprika

¼ teaspoon ground árbol chiles or
cayenne pepper

¼ teaspoon freshly ground black
pepper

1 pound medium shrimp, shelled
and deveined

4 garlic cloves, thinly sliced

2 to 3 green or red jalapeño peppers–
stemmed, seeded and thinly
sliced lengthwise

8 small scallions, thinly sliced
diagonally

1½ tablespoons fresh lime juice

½ cup chicken stock or canned
low-sodium broth

I. Generously butter an 8- or 9-inch square baking dish. In a medium saucepan, bring the water to a boil. Stir in the grits and ½ teaspoon salt and bring to a simmer over low heat. Cook, stirring occasionally, until all the liquid is absorbed, about 10 minutes. Pour into the baking dish and chill until firm, at least 1 hour. Invert the grits onto a work surface and cut into quarters, then halve diagonally to make eight triangles.

2. In a large heavy stainless-steel skillet, cook the bacon over moderate heat until crisp. Transfer the bacon to paper towels to drain, and then crumble it.

3. Reheat the bacon fat in the pan. Add the grits triangles and cook over high heat until golden, about 4 minutes per side. Transfer the triangles to a platter and keep warm.

4. Wipe out the skillet and heat the oil in it. In a large bowl, combine the cumin, chile powder, ground chiles, ¼ teaspoon salt and the black pepper. Add the shrimp and toss to coat.

5. Add the shrimp and garlic to the skillet and cook over high heat until the shrimp are just pink, about 2 minutes. Add the jalapeños and cook until they are crisp-tender, about 2 minutes. Add the scallions and bacon and cook for 1 minute more. Stir in the lime juice and stock and heat through. Spoon the shrimp and sauce over the grits cakes. —*Susan Feniger and Mary Sue Milliken*

BEER Samuel Adams Golden Pilsner

Garlic Cheese Grits with Shrimp

4 SERVINGS

Shrimp and grits is a famous low-country breakfast dish that has made its way onto menus across the country. Grits casseroles, rich with cheese, serve as side dishes throughout the South. In this updated main course, I've combined these two dishes and replaced the cheddar with goat cheese—some of the country's best producers of goat cheese are in the South.

4 tablespoons unsalted butter

1 garlic clove, minced

¾ cup coarse grits, preferably stone
ground

3 cups water

1 teaspoon salt

8 ounces soft goat cheese, at room
temperature

½ cup milk

3 large eggs, lightly beaten

1 tablespoon finely chopped
flat-leaf parsley

¼ teaspoon cayenne pepper

Freshly ground black pepper

½ pound medium shrimp, shelled
and deveined

I. Preheat the oven to 350° and lightly grease a 2-quart soufflé dish. Melt the butter in a medium saucepan over high heat. Add the garlic; cook until softened but not browned, about 30 seconds. Add the grits, water and salt and bring to a boil, stirring often to keep the grits from sticking. Cook over moderately low heat, stirring often, until the liquid is absorbed and the grits are barely tender, about 8 minutes.

2. Meanwhile, in a large bowl, combine the goat cheese, milk, eggs and parsley. Season with the cayenne and black pepper and stir until smooth. Add the hot grits and stir until the cheese is melted. Pour the grits mixture into the prepared soufflé dish, cover with aluminum foil and bake for 1 hour. Uncover and bake for about 30 minutes, or until the center is set and the top is golden.

3. When the grits are almost done, bring a pot of water to a boil. Add the shrimp and cook until just pink, about 1½ minutes. Drain the shrimp and pat them dry with paper towels.

4. Remove the grits from the oven; gently stir in the shrimp. Bake for 5 minutes. Serve immediately. –*John Martin Taylor*
WINE Together the goat cheese, garlic and sweet shrimp point to a savory California Sauvignon Blanc as the ideal partner. Look for the 1994 Grgich Hills Fumé Blanc or the 1995 Robert Pepi Two Heart Canopy Sauvignon Blanc.

Tandoori Prawns

4 SERVINGS

Tandoori (Indian barbecue) gets its name from the tandoor, a cross between a barbecue pit and an oven. The waist-high, urn-shaped clay vessel holds a charcoal fire in the bottom. Seafood, meats, even vegetables are roasted on vertical spits over the coals, while breads are baked directly on the walls of the tandoor. The oven's unique shape produces searing heat and concentrated smoky flavors. You can cook these prawns on a grill and will need one special ingredient: chickpea flour, also known as besan, which is available at Indian markets and some

health-food stores. In a pinch, you could replace the chickpea flour with whole-wheat flour.

- 6 garlic cloves, sliced
- 3 tablespoons coarsely chopped fresh ginger
- ½ teaspoon salt
- 2 tablespoons fresh lemon juice
- ⅔ cup whole-milk yogurt
- 1 large egg, lightly beaten
- ¼ cup chickpea flour or whole-wheat flour
- ½ teaspoon cayenne pepper
- ½ teaspoon turmeric
- ½ teaspoon ground cumin
- ½ teaspoon garam masala
- ½ teaspoon freshly ground white pepper
- 1½ pounds jumbo shrimp, shelled and deveined
- 3 tablespoons salted butter, melted
Lemon wedges, for serving

1. In a mortar, pound the garlic, ginger and salt to a paste; alternatively, puree in a mini-processor. Add the lemon juice and 2 tablespoons of the yogurt. Transfer the mixture to a large bowl. Whisk in the remaining yogurt along with the egg, chickpea flour, cayenne, turmeric, cumin, garam masala and white pepper. Stir in the shrimp and marinate for 2 hours.

2. Light a grill. Thread the shrimp onto skewers. To suspend the shrimp two to three inches above the grill, place rocks or bunched-up aluminum foil on either end of the grill. When the fire is hot, rest the skewers on the rocks and cover the grill. Cook for about 5 minutes, or until the marinade has formed a firm, crusty coating on the bottom of the shrimp. Baste the shrimp with the butter and turn the skewers. Cover and grill the shrimp until just cooked through, about 4 minutes longer. Transfer the shrimp to plates and serve at once, with lemon wedges. –*Steven Raichlen*
BEER The exotic flavors (clove, banana and bubble gum) and clean finish of

bottle-fermented German *hefe-weizen*, or wheat beers, suit the sweet prawns. Hacker-Pschorr Weisse is an example from a traditional producer.

Shellfish Stew with Chorizo and Rouille

6 SERVINGS

Rouille is a zesty garlic and red-pepper sauce that is usually served with bouillabaisse. Here it's stirred into the stew at the last minute to thicken and flavor it, and additional rouille is spread on the croutons that garnish the stew.

- 1½ teaspoons olive oil
- ¾ pound chorizo, casings removed, sausage sliced ¼ inch thick
- 1 medium onion, chopped
- ½ cup dry white wine
- 10 garlic cloves–4 minced, 6 smashed
- 3 cups bottled clam juice
One 15-ounce can crushed tomatoes
- ½ teaspoon dried thyme
- 1 medium baguette
- ½ cup mayonnaise
- ⅓ cup drained roasted red peppers from a jar
- ¼ teaspoon cayenne pepper
- ¾ pound large shrimp, shelled and deveined
- ¾ pound sea scallops, halved if very large
- ¼ teaspoon freshly ground black pepper
Salt

1. Heat the oil in a large skillet. Add the chorizo and cook over moderately high heat, stirring frequently, until browned, about 10 minutes. Transfer to a plate. Pour off all but 1 tablespoon of the fat.

2. Add the chopped onion to the skillet and cook over moderately low heat, stirring occasionally, until translucent, about 5 minutes. Add the wine and minced garlic and cook until the liquid is reduced to ¼ cup, about 3 minutes. Add the chorizo, clam juice, tomatoes

and thyme and bring to a simmer. Cover and cook for 20 minutes.

3. Meanwhile, cut a 3-inch piece from the baguette and cut off the crust. Soften the piece of crustless bread under running water and then squeeze the bread to remove the excess water. In a food processor, puree the softened bread with the mayonnaise, the red peppers, the smashed garlic cloves and the cayenne.

LEFT: **Bay Scallops with Sautéed Chanterelles.** BELOW: **Sautéed Scallops with Rosemary and Lemon.**

4. Preheat the broiler. Cut the remaining baguette into ¼-inch slices and arrange the slices on a baking sheet. Broil for about 3 minutes, turning once, until golden.

5. Add the shrimp and scallops to the skillet and bring to a simmer, by which time they should be just cooked through. Stir in ½ cup of the rouille and the black pepper. Season the stew and the remaining rouille with salt. Spread the rouille on the croutons. Serve the stew in shallow bowls, garnished with the croutons.   *—Susan Lantzius Rich*

WINE The rich, earthy rosés of Provence go particularly well with shellfish stews. Look for the 1996 Domaine Jean Bagnis l'Estandon Rosé.

Sautéed Scallops with Rosemary and Lemon

4 SERVINGS

If bay scallops are unavailable, use sea scallops that have been halved horizontally and then vertically.

1½ pounds bay scallops, rinsed and patted dry
¼ cup extra-virgin olive oil
2 medium garlic cloves, thinly sliced
1½ teaspoons whole rosemary leaves
Salt and freshly ground pepper
1½ tablespoons fresh lemon juice

1. Remove and discard the iridescent membrane on each scallop.

2. Warm the oil and garlic together in a large stainless-steel skillet over moderate heat. Cook, stirring occasionally, until the garlic is pale golden, about 4 minutes. Raise the heat to high and stir in the rosemary. Add the scallops in a single layer, season with salt and pepper and cook until opaque, 2 to 3 minutes. Using a slotted spoon, transfer the scallops to a bowl.

3. Add the lemon juice to the skillet and simmer until the liquid is reduced to a syrupy glaze. Return the scallops and any accumulated juices to the skillet. Toss to coat the scallops with the glaze. Cook until the scallops are just heated through. *–Marcella Hazan*

Bay Scallops with Sautéed Chanterelles

2 SERVINGS **Q**

- 1½ tablespoons unsalted butter
- ½ pound chanterelle mushrooms, trimmed, large ones quartered
- 1 tablespoon minced shallot

Salt and freshly ground pepper

- ½ pound bay scallops
- 1 cup packed small spinach leaves
- 2 tablespoons diced plum tomato
- 1 tablespoon minced chives

Steamed rice, for serving

1. In a large stainless-steel skillet, melt the butter over moderate heat. Add the chanterelles and shallot and cook, stirring, until wilted, about 3 minutes. Season with salt and pepper.

2. Add the scallops to the skillet and cook until they are opaque, about 2 minutes. Add the spinach and stir to wilt. Add the tomato and season again. Sprinkle on the minced chives and serve with the rice. *–Amy Farges*

WINE Scallops and chanterelles would harmonize with a round, ripe Chardonnay. Try the 1995 Meridian.

Scallops in Zucchini Nests

4 SERVINGS **Q**

To cut the squash into thin, even strips, use a mandoline–a French slicing tool– or one of the inexpensive German or Japanese versions.

- ¼ cup olive oil
- 2 medium zucchini (1 pound total), sliced lengthwise ⅛ inch thick
- 2 medium yellow squash (1 pound total), sliced lengthwise ⅛ inch thick
- 2 tablespoons dry white wine
- 2 tablespoons minced garlic

Kosher salt and freshly ground pepper

- 4 medium tomatoes–peeled, seeded and chopped
- 1 cup canned tomato puree
- ½ cup finely shredded basil
- 2 tablespoons heavy cream
- 1½ pounds large sea scallops

1. Heat 2 tablespoons of the oil in a large stainless-steel skillet. Add the zucchini and squash to the skillet, making sure the slices don't stick together, and cook over moderately high heat, stirring often, until barely softened, about 4 minutes. Add the wine and garlic and season with salt and pepper. Add the tomatoes, tomato puree, ¼ cup of the basil and the heavy cream and boil for 1 minute. Keep warm.

2. Season the scallops with salt and pepper. In a large heavy skillet, heat the remaining 2 tablespoons of oil. Add the scallops in a single layer and cook over high heat until they are golden on the bottom, about 3 minutes. Turn the scallops and cook just until white throughout, about 1 minute; transfer the scallops to a platter.

3. Using kitchen tongs, make a nest of the cooked zucchini and squash in the center of each of four heated plates. If the sauce seems to have thinned, simmer until it lightly coats a spoon. Arrange the scallops in the squash nests and spoon the sauce over all. Sprinkle

with the remaining basil and serve at once. *–Michael Romano*

WINE 1994 Alois Lageder Pinot Bianco Cru Haberlehof. Soft and creamy with floral nuances, this Italian white wine enhances the sweet scallops, zucchini and summer squash.

Scallops with Cider, Gewürztraminer and Sage

4 SERVINGS

Because of the sweetness of the cider, a dry Gewürztraminer will be best to use in this dish; don't use a late-harvest dessert wine.

- 1 cup apple cider
- ½ cup Gewürztraminer
- 6 tablespoons unsalted butter
- 1 pound sea scallops

Salt and freshly ground pepper

- 1 Granny Smith apple, unpeeled, cut into matchstick strips
- 16 small sage leaves
- 2 tablespoons fresh lemon juice

1. In a large heavy skillet, boil the cider and Gewürztraminer, skimming off the foam occasionally, until reduced to 3 tablespoons, about 10 minutes; pour into a small bowl.

2. Wipe out the skillet, add 2 tablespoons of the butter and melt over high heat. Season the scallops with salt and pepper and cook them until they are browned, about 2 minutes per side. Transfer the scallops to a warmed serving plate and cover loosely with aluminum foil. ➤

kitchen tip

Whenever something you are sautéing releases more liquid than you want– and it happens not infrequently with seafood that has been on ice too long– remove that something from the pan and boil the juices down to the consistency you desire. *–Marcella Hazan*

Scallops with Cider, Gewürztraminer and Sage

3. Add the remaining 4 tablespoons butter to the skillet and melt over high heat. Add the Gewürztraminer mixture, apple, sage and lemon juice and cook until the apple is tender and the sauce is slightly thickened, about 3 minutes. Season the sauce with salt and pepper. Spoon the sauce over the cooked scallops and serve. *—Cory Schreiber*

WINE 1996 Evesham Wood Vineyard Estate Willamette Valley Gewürztraminer. Consistently one of the finest Gewürztraminers in the state of Oregon, this is made in a richly textured Alsatian style that is perfect with the scallops. Exotic flavors of lychee, ripe apricot and peach are balanced with great acidity and a very clean, dry finish.

Olive-Oil and Pinot Blanc Squid with Peppers

4 SERVINGS

Pinot Blanc pairs well with olive oil and aromatics like fennel and coriander seeds. Save any leftover braising liquid for braising artichokes, tomatoes or red onions. Shelled shrimp could be substituted for the squid; braise them just until pink.

- 2 cups olive oil
- ⅓ cup Pinot Blanc
- ⅓ cup white-wine vinegar
- 1 medium onion, thinly sliced
- 1 head of garlic, separated into cloves and peeled
- 1 small bunch of parsley stems, tied with kitchen string
- 1 teaspoon fennel seeds, finely crushed
- 1 teaspoon coriander seeds, finely crushed
- 2 teaspoons salt
- 1 teaspoon freshly ground pepper
- 3 bell peppers—seeded, cored and cut into eighths
- 1 pound cleaned squid, sliced crosswise into ¼-inch rings

In a large stainless-steel saucepan, combine the oil, Pinot Blanc, vinegar, onion, garlic, parsley, fennel seeds, coriander seeds, salt and pepper. Bring to a simmer and add the bell peppers. Cook over moderately high heat, stirring, until the bell peppers are soft, about 20 minutes. Turn off the heat, add the squid and let it sit for 1 or 2 minutes. Using a slotted spoon, transfer the squid and the bell peppers to a platter and serve hot. *—Cory Schreiber*

MAKE AHEAD The bell peppers can be refrigerated in the braising liquid overnight. Rewarm and add the squid just before serving.

WINE 1996 Bethel Heights Vineyards, Willamette Valley, Pinot Blanc. Bright, floral and redolent of pear, citrus and honeydew melon, this is a fantastic wine. Its lean and fruit-forward style complements the herb and spice elements of the dish.

Cioppino

10 SERVINGS

This Ligurian fish stew is prepared with six different kinds of fish and shellfish. To make it more authentic, don't shell the shrimp and allow a little extra time for them to cook. Using water in which pasta has been cooked helps to lightly thicken the broth, but plain water will do.

- 8 garlic cloves—3 lightly crushed and 5 minced
- ¾ cup extra-virgin olive oil
- Two 35-ounce cans whole Italian peeled tomatoes, coarsely chopped, with their liquid
- Salt and freshly ground pepper
- 1 large onion, finely chopped
- 2 scallions, white and tender green, thinly sliced
- 1 tablespoon finely chopped marjoram
- 2 bay leaves
- ½ cup coarsely chopped flat-leaf parsley
- 4 anchovy fillets, coarsely chopped
- 3 tablespoons harissa
- 1½ cups dry white wine
- 2 cups water, preferably pasta-cooking water
- 1½ pounds firm-fleshed white-fish fillets, such as rockfish, halibut, scrod or tilefish
- 10 stone crab claws, cracked, or 3 live Dungeness crabs, cleaned and quartered
- 1¼ pounds small mussels, scrubbed and debearded
- 1 pound cleaned small squid, bodies cut into ½-inch rings, tentacles halved, or baby octopus
- ½ pound medium shrimp, shelled and deveined

Crusty bread, for serving

I. In a large stainless-steel pot, sauté the crushed garlic in ¼ cup of the oil over moderately high heat until golden, about 4 minutes. Add the tomatoes and their liquid and bring to a boil. Season with salt and pepper, reduce the heat to moderate and cook, stirring, until reduced to 5 cups, about 30 minutes. Mash in the sautéed garlic. Transfer the tomato sauce to a large bowl and wipe out the pot.

2. Return the pot to high heat and add the remaining ½ cup of oil. Add the onion, scallions, marjoram and bay leaves and cook, stirring, until softened, about 4 minutes. Add the parsley, anchovies, harissa and minced garlic and cook, stirring, until the anchovies break apart and the garlic is just turning golden, about 2 minutes.

3. Add the wine and cook over high heat until reduced by half, about 5 minutes. Add the water and tomato sauce and bring to a boil. Add the fish, crab, mussels, squid and shrimp, cover and cook until the seafood is cooked through and the mussels have opened, about 4 minutes. Discard the bay leaves

Cioppino

and any unopened mussels. Season the Cioppino with salt and pepper and serve with the bread.   *—Reed Hearon*

WINE Either the 1994 Ca' del Solo Charbono La Farfalla or the 1994 Michele Chiarlo Barbera d'Asti will meld with the Cioppino, since the acidic tomatoes blend nicely with the fruit in these red wines. The spice in the Charbono goes especially well with the rich crab here.

Clams with Saffron, Tomato and Garlic

4 SERVINGS

The sweetness of the Pinot Gris blends well with the briny-flavored shellfish and enhances the vinaigrette in this dish. You can easily prepare these clams on your kitchen stove or on an outdoor grill with wood chips added to the coals. If you prefer, mussels can be substituted for the clams.

Pinch of saffron threads
3 tablespoons white-wine vinegar
¼ cup olive oil
¼ cup vegetable oil
½ teaspoon freshly ground pepper
4 pounds clams, scrubbed and rinsed
1 cup cherry tomatoes, halved
2 shallots, thinly sliced
2 large garlic cloves, minced
½ cup Pinot Gris
½ cup flat-leaf parsley leaves

1. In a small stainless-steel saucepan, steep the saffron in the vinegar over low heat for 1 minute. Let cool, then whisk in the olive and vegetable oils and the pepper.
2. In a large stainless-steel skillet or saucepan, combine the vinaigrette with the clams, tomatoes, shallots, garlic and wine. Cover and cook over high heat for 5 minutes. Transfer any clams that have opened to a large bowl. Cover and continue to cook, removing the clams as they open. Pour the hot broth

over the clams, leaving behind any grit. Garnish the clams with the parsley and serve.   *—Cory Schreiber*

WINE 1996 Adelsheim Vineyard Oregon Pinot Gris. The bright citrus flavor in this wine, combined with its natural acidity, makes it a wonderful match for the clams. This is a very refreshing style of Pinot Gris that allows the fruit to shine and refresh the palate.

Oyster and Potato Stew with Crisp Bacon

8 SERVINGS

This creamy stew is made with half-and-half, so it's not too heavy.

2 tablespoons unsalted butter
2 medium onions, cut into ¼-inch dice
1 pound baking potatoes, peeled and cut into ¼-inch dice
1 medium fennel bulb—trimmed, halved, cored and cut into ¼-inch dice
1 medium carrot, cut into ¼-inch dice
3 cups fish stock or 1½ cups bottled clam juice mixed with 1½ cups water
2 cups half-and-half
½ pound slab bacon, cut into ¼-inch dice
2 dozen shucked oysters, with their liquor
Salt and freshly ground pepper
2 tablespoons finely chopped flat-leaf parsley

1. Melt the butter in a large stainless-steel saucepan. Add the onions and cook them over moderate heat, stirring occasionally, until they are softened, about 8 minutes. Add the potatoes, the fennel, the carrot, the fish stock and the half-and-half, reduce the heat to moderately low and simmer the vegetables gently until they are tender, about 15 minutes.

Clams with Saffron, Tomato and Garlic

2. Strain the stew into a bowl; set aside 1½ cups of the cooked vegetables. Transfer the remaining vegetables along with 2 cups of the cooking liquid to a blender or food processor and blend until smooth. Return the puree to the saucepan and stir in the reserved vegetables and liquid.
3. In a medium skillet, cook the bacon over moderately high heat until it is browned and crisp, about 8 minutes. Transfer to paper towels to drain.
4. Rewarm the stew over moderate heat. Add the oysters with their liquor and the bacon and cook until the oysters are just firm, 2 to 3 minutes. Season the oyster stew with salt and pepper and stir in the parsley. Transfer the stew to shallow soup plates and serve at once.   *—Mireille Guiliano*

MAKE AHEAD The oyster stew can be made through Step 2 and refrigerated for up to one day.

WINE This light shellfish stew, thickened with pureed vegetables and flavored with bacon, is especially good with the dry 1988 Veuve Clicquot La Grande Dame.

Mussel and Potato Stew

Mussel and Potato Stew

10 SERVINGS

Both mussels and potatoes are staples of Ligurian cooking. Here they are used with broccoli rabe to make a succulent light stew. Fruity olive oil contributes depth of flavor.

- **2 pounds Yukon gold potatoes, peeled and cut into 1½-inch cubes**
- **Salt**
- **½ pound broccoli rabe, thick stems peeled**
- **½ cup extra-virgin olive oil**
- **4 anchovy fillets, coarsely chopped**
- **4 garlic cloves, minced**
- **2½ pounds small mussels, scrubbed and debearded**
- **2 tablespoons coarsely chopped flat-leaf parsley**
- **½ cup water**
- **Freshly ground pepper**

1. In a medium saucepan, cover the potatoes with cold water. Add salt and bring to a boil over high heat. Cook the potatoes until they are tender, about 15 minutes. Drain the potatoes.

2. In a medium saucepan of boiling salted water, cook the broccoli rabe until crisp-tender and still bright green, about 5 minutes. Drain the broccoli rabe well and cut into 2-inch pieces.

3. In a deep 12-inch skillet, combine the oil, anchovies and garlic. Cook over high heat, mashing the anchovies, until fragrant, about 1 minute.

4. Spread the mussels in the skillet over the anchovy mixture and top them with the boiled potatoes and broccoli rabe and the chopped parsley. Add the water and season the stew with salt and pepper. Stir the stew several times, and then cover and cook until the mussels open and all of the vegetables are tender, about 8 minutes. Discard any mussels that do not open. Transfer the mussel and potato stew to soup plates and serve. *—Reed Hearon*

Thai Red Curry with Mussels

6 SERVINGS

The coconut milk, Thai red curry paste and Thai fish sauce can be found at Asian markets and many supermarkets

- ¼ cup dry white wine
- 2 bay leaves
- 1 teaspoon black peppercorns
- 3 pounds small mussels, scrubbed and debearded
- 1 tablespoon vegetable oil
- 3 medium shallots, thinly sliced
- 2 large garlic cloves, minced
- 2 teaspoons minced fresh ginger
- 1 to 3 tablespoons Thai red curry paste
- 1 cup unsweetened coconut milk
- 1 to 2 tablespoons light brown sugar
- 1 tablespoon Thai fish sauce (nam pla)
- 1 tablespoon fresh lime juice

Salt and freshly ground pepper

Steamed rice, for serving

- ½ cup cilantro leaves
- 2 scallions, thinly sliced crosswise

Diced lime sections, for garnish

Thai Red Curry with Mussels

1. In a large stainless-steel saucepan, bring the wine, bay leaves and peppercorns to a boil over moderately high heat. Add the mussels, cover tightly and steam, shaking the pan, until the mussels open, about 5 minutes. Using a slotted spoon, transfer the mussels to a large bowl and discard any that don't open. Strain the broth into a large measuring cup; you should have about 1¾ cups. Remove three-quarters of the mussels from their shells and reserve both the shelled and the unshelled mussels in a bowl.

2. Heat the oil in the saucepan. Add the shallots and cook over moderately high heat, stirring, until browned, about 7 minutes. Add the garlic and the ginger and cook, stirring, until fragrant, about 1 minute. Add the Thai red curry paste and cook, stirring, for 3 minutes. Pour in the mussel broth, stopping when you reach the grit, and simmer the sauce until it is slightly reduced and flavorful, about 4 minutes.

3. Add the coconut milk, brown sugar, fish sauce and lime juice to the sauce and simmer over moderate heat until the mixture is slightly thickened, about 4 minutes. Season the sauce with salt and pepper, add the mussels and simmer until they are heated through, about 2 minutes. Ladle the stew into a large bowl. Serve the stew at once on the rice, passing the cilantro leaves, sliced scallions and diced lime sections at the table. –*Susan Feniger and Mary Sue Milliken*

BEER Japanese Kirin lager

CHAPTER 7 fish

Chardonnay-Poached Salmon with Gamay Noir Vinaigrette (p. 157)

131   Shallot-Crusted Roast Halibut

131   Foil-Wrapped Halibut Fillets with Rosemary Butter

131   Coal-Roasted Halibut

133   Sea Bass Habanero

133   Mirin-Glazed Sea Bass with Bok Choy

134   Sesame-Coated Striped Bass

134   Grilled Wild Striped Bass

134   Black Bass with Burdock and Garlic Mustard

135   Pan-Roasted Red Snapper with Cilantro and Lime

137	Spicy Snapper
137	Fish in Crazy Water
137	Roasted Snapper with Peppers, Pine Nuts and Tomatoes
138	Christmas Eve Fish and Escarole Pie
139	Roasted Cod with Bacon-and-Spinach Stuffing
140	Fried Christmas Cod
141	Cod-and-Crab Cakes with Roasted-Pepper Coulis
143	Grilled Mahimahi and Green Tomatoes
143	Bahamian Grilled Fish
144	Gaspergou Courtbouillon
144	Bourride of Monkfish and Clams
145	Pan-Fried Catfish with Salmoriglio Sauce
146	Catfish Tacos with Tequila Cream Corn
146	Swordfish with Oregano and Lemon
147	Sweet-and-Sour Swordfish
148	Swordfish Kebabs with Coconut Milk
149	Pesto-Crusted Salmon
149	Cajun Salmon with Jicama-and-Melon Salad
149	Salmon Steaks with Grilled Salsa
150	Grilled Salmon with Sun-Dried-Tomato Sauce
153	Poached Salmon in Sorrel Sauce
153	Salmon with Curried Spinach
154	Cold Poached Salmon with Beets and Skordalia
155	Crispy Salmon with Balsamic Glaze
156	Salmon with Thai Rice Salad
157	Seared Salmon on Tartare Mashed Potatoes
157	Chardonnay-Poached Salmon with Gamay Noir Vinaigrette
159	Moroccan Spiced Salmon on Lentils
159	Marinated Poached Fresh Tuna with Caper and Anchovy Sauce

Shallot-Crusted Roast Halibut

Shallot-Crusted Roast Halibut

4 SERVINGS

A buttery topping keeps these halibut fillets moist as they roast in the dry heat of the oven.

1½ tablespoons olive oil
5 large shallots, minced
3 tablespoons unsalted butter
1 cup dried bread crumbs made from crusty Italian bread
2 tablespoons snipped chives
2 tablespoons minced flat-leaf parsley
2 teaspoons chopped thyme
2 teaspoons fresh lime juice
Salt and freshly ground pepper
Four 6-ounce skinless halibut fillets, 1 inch thick

1. Preheat the oven to 400°. Butter a baking sheet. In a heavy medium skillet, heat the oil. Add the shallots and cook over moderate heat, stirring, until softened but not browned, about 5 minutes. Transfer the shallots to a bowl and let cool.

2. In the same skillet, melt the butter over moderate heat. Add the bread crumbs and cook, stirring, until crisp and golden, about 5 minutes. Add the bread crumbs to the shallots along with the chives, parsley, thyme, lime juice, ½ teaspoon of salt and ¼ teaspoon of pepper. Toss the bread-crumb mixture with a fork.

3. Season the halibut fillets on both sides with salt and pepper. Put the fillets on the buttered baking sheet and thickly spread the bread-crumb mixture on top. Roast the halibut fillets for 18 to 20 minutes, or until the fish is just opaque throughout. Serve the fillets at once.   —Sarah Stegner

WINE 1994 Chalone Pinot Blanc. Here's a Pinot Blanc from an excellent producer out of Monterey. This medium-bodied wine will stand up to the shallot and bread-crumb crust and also enhance the halibut.

Foil-Wrapped Halibut Fillets with Rosemary Butter

4 SERVINGS

The fish emerges from the foil packets succulent, flaky and nicely infused with rosemary flavor. Try it with Roasted Tomato and Eggplant Tian (p. 321).

Four 6-ounce halibut fillets, about 1 inch thick
Salt and freshly ground pepper
4 teaspoons unsalted butter
Four 4-inch rosemary sprigs, plus longer sprigs for garnish

Preheat the oven to 450°. Cut four 12-inch sheets of heavy-duty aluminum foil. Season the fish with salt and pepper. Place ½ teaspoon of butter in the center of each foil sheet. Lay a halibut fillet on each sheet and top with ½ teaspoon of butter and one 4-inch sprig of rosemary. Enclose the fish in foil, crimping the edges to form a tight seal. Bake the fish for 10 minutes, or until it is opaque throughout. Transfer the fish to plates and garnish with the longer rosemary sprigs.   —Georgeanne Brennan

WINE Rosemary complements Chardonnay, and the herb's presence is a tipoff that a crisp California bottling—such as the 1995 Iron Horse or the 1995 Mirassou Family Selection—would be a fine choice.

Coal-Roasted Halibut

4 SERVINGS L

Cooking white-fleshed fish in foil protects it from the intense heat and allows its flavors to mingle with the leek mixture. Heavy-duty aluminum foil is a must here.

3 medium leeks, white part only, halved lengthwise and coarsely chopped
1 small celery rib, peeled and coarsely chopped
3 garlic cloves, finely chopped
2 cups basil leaves, plus 12 additional leaves

grilling tips

1. **Use bone-in fish** and chicken whenever possible; the bones add flavor and help keep the meat moist as it cooks.

2. **Make fires with different woods**—you'll find the fragrance perfumes whatever you're grilling. My favorite is apple wood; mesquite and hickory are great, too.

3. **Use roasted garlic and onions to add flavor to low-fat foods.** Wrap heads of garlic and halved onions in aluminum foil, place the package on the coals and cook until tender. Then rub the garlic over grilled vegetables, poultry or pork and serve the onions alongside.

4. **Make sure you're cooking over the right heat** so you don't dry out lean ingredients. In general, grill foods that are served rare over high heat so the outside sears while the inside stays juicy. For dishes that cook all the way through, the heat should be moderate to low. —Jim Cohen

1 cup parsley leaves
4 anchovy fillets
2 teaspoons olive oil
Four 6-ounce halibut steaks, about 1 inch thick
8 plum tomatoes, each cut into 6 wedges
4 small red potatoes, sliced ⅛ inch thick
Salt and freshly ground pepper
½ cup water

1. Light a charcoal grill. In a food processor, combine the leeks, celery, garlic, the 2 cups of basil, the parsley and anchovies and pulse until finely chopped. Spoon ½ teaspoon of oil in the center of each of four 18-inch aluminum-foil squares. Spread ½ cup of the leek mixture on the oiled foil squares. Set the halibut on top of the leeks and arrange

Sea Bass Habanero

the tomatoes, potatoes and the remaining 12 basil leaves around. Season the fish and vegetables with salt and pepper. Spoon 2 tablespoons of water around each fish steak. Bring the sides of the foil up and over the fish, sealing the edges together with short folds.

2. Spread the medium-hot coals out to an even layer and set the fish bundles in the coals, folded-side up. Cover the grill and cook until the bundles swell with steam and you can hear the liquid bubbling, about 30 minutes. Set a closed bundle on each plate and open them at the table. *—Jim Cohen*

WINE 1994 Chalone Estate Bottled Pinot Blanc The Pinnacles from California

Sea Bass Habanero

4 SERVINGS

Sea bass cooked in a flavorful broth emerges juicy as well as tasty. Browning the fish thoroughly helps to enrich the broth.

> 3 tablespoons extra-virgin olive oil
> Four 6-ounce sea-bass fillets, with skin if desired
> Salt and freshly ground pepper
> 1 small onion, thinly sliced
> 4 garlic cloves, thinly sliced
> 1 small mango, cut into ½-inch dice
> 1 large tomato, seeded and cut into thin strips
> 1 habanero chile, seeded and thinly sliced
> ½ cup dry white wine
> ¾ cup fish stock or ½ cup clam juice diluted with ¼ cup water
> 1 lime, cut into 8 wedges
> ¼ cup loosely packed cilantro leaves

1. Heat the oil in a large stainless-steel skillet until shimmering. Season the bass with salt and pepper and add to the skillet skin-side up. Cook over high heat until nicely browned but barely opaque throughout, about 1 minute per side. Transfer to a plate.

2. Add the onion to the skillet and cook over moderately high heat, stirring, until browned, about 3 minutes. Raise the heat to high. Add the garlic, mango, tomato, chile and a pinch each of salt and pepper. Cook until fragrant, about 2 minutes. Add the wine; cook until reduced by half, about 2 minutes. Add the stock and bring to a boil. Reduce the heat to moderately low. Simmer for 2 minutes.

3. Add the fish and the lime wedges to the skillet. Cover and cook until the fish is opaque throughout, 1 to 3 minutes. Season with salt and pepper. Transfer the fish and vegetables to four soup plates and spoon the broth over the top. Sprinkle with the cilantro and serve. *—Susan Feniger and Mary Sue Milliken*

WINE 1995 Washington State Chateau Ste. Michelle Johannisberg Riesling

Mirin-Glazed Sea Bass with Bok Choy

2 SERVINGS

For the subtly sweet, tangy sea bass, choose an unseasoned mirin or one that lists salt as the last ingredient.

> Four 3-ounce skinless sea-bass fillets, about 1 inch thick
> 1 cup mirin or ¼ cup sugar dissolved in 1 cup Chardonnay
> 3 garlic cloves
> ½ cup tomato juice
> 1 tablespoon plus 1 teaspoon sherry vinegar
> 2 teaspoons fresh lemon juice
> ¼ cup extra-virgin olive oil
> 2 cups coarsely chopped bok choy leaves, green part only
> 1½ teaspoons minced fresh ginger
> 2 tablespoons water
> 2 tablespoons unsalted butter
> Salt and freshly ground white pepper

1. In a resealable plastic bag, combine the sea-bass fillets and the mirin. Seal the bag and marinate in the refrigerator for 1 hour. Remove the sea-bass fillets from the marinade and pat dry.

Mirin-Glazed Sea Bass with Bok Choy

---

menu

Lobster Salad with Curried Vinaigrette (p. 42)

Mirin-Glazed Sea Bass with Bok Choy (p. 133)

Bittersweet Chocolate Bombes (p. 343)

WINE Champagne is the ideal choice for this romantic dinner for two. Given the spicy-sharp flavors in the lobster salad and the acidity in the bass, stick with nonvintage bottlings with a lighter, fruitier style, such as the Deutz Classic Brut, Lanson Black Label Brut or Pol Roger Brut Reserve.

---

2. Meanwhile, in a small saucepan of boiling water, simmer the garlic for 1 minute. Drain and let cool. Peel the garlic cloves and thinly slice them lengthwise. In a small glass or stainless-steel bowl, combine the tomato juice, vinegar and lemon juice. ➤

3. Heat 2 tablespoons of the oil in a medium stainless-steel skillet. Add the garlic and cook over low heat until golden, about 7 minutes. Using a slotted spoon, transfer the garlic to a bowl. Add the bok choy and ginger to the skillet and cook over moderately high heat for 30 seconds. Add 2 tablespoons of water and toss until the bok choy is wilted, about 1 minute. Add the tomato-juice mixture to the greens and cook for 1 minute more.

4. In a large heavy nonstick skillet, melt the butter in the remaining oil. Season the fish with salt and pepper and cook over moderate heat, turning once, until nicely browned on both sides and opaque throughout, about 3 minutes per side.

5. If necessary, rewarm the bok choy. Mound the warm bok choy on plates, spooning the sauce around it. Sprinkle the bok choy with the garlic slices and top each serving with a sea-bass fillet. Serve at once.   *−Jonathan Eismann*

Sesame-Coated Striped Bass

4 SERVINGS **L**

Sesame seeds, brought to America by African slaves, are known in the South as benne seeds. I use them to make a crisp, nutty coating for bass fillets.

  1 **large egg white**
Salt and freshly ground pepper

> ### menu
>
> **Sesame-Coated**
> **Striped Bass (p. 134)**
>
> **Summer Stew with**
> **Navy Beans and Okra (p. 325)**
>
> **Golden Rice Pilaf**
> **with Spices (p. 308)**
>
> 1995 SAUVION LA NOBLERAIE
> 1995 MARQUÉS DE
> CÁCERES BLANCO

  ¼ **cup plus ½ tablespoon sesame**
    seeds
Four 5-ounce striped bass fillets
    with skin
  2 **teaspoons vegetable oil**
  1 **large tomato, seeded and finely**
    chopped
Hot sauce (optional)

I. In a shallow bowl, season the egg white with salt and pepper and whisk lightly. Spread the sesame seeds on a large plate. Season the bass fillets with salt and pepper. Brush the flesh side of each bass fillet with the egg white and gently press the same side into the sesame seeds.

2. Heat the oil in a large nonstick skillet. Set the bass fillets in the skillet, seeded-side down, and cook them over moderate heat until the sesame seeds are golden, 2 to 3 minutes. Turn the fillets and continue cooking until they are just opaque throughout, about 3 minutes more. Top the bass fillets with the chopped tomato and serve with hot sauce.   *−Marvin Woods*

WINE Try a light, dry Muscadet from the Loire region of France, such as the 1995 Sauvion La Nobleraie, or a white Rioja from Spain, such as the 1995 Marqués de Cáceres Blanco.

Grilled Wild Striped Bass

20 SERVINGS

Wild striped bass make their home in the waters around Long Island.

  1 **cup olive oil**
  ½ **cup Home Spice Mix (p. 56)**
  ¼ **cup shredded mint leaves**
About 7 pounds wild striped bass
    fillets, sliced crosswise on the
    diagonal into twenty 6-ounce
    pieces (with skin)
Salt and freshly ground pepper

I. In a medium bowl, combine the oil, Home Spice Mix and mint leaves.

2. Light a charcoal grill. Season the fish with salt and pepper. Brush each fillet

---

> ### menu
>
> **Bambou Crab Cakes (p. 39)**
>
> **Sweet Corn Pancakes**
> **with Smoked Salmon (p. 44)**
>
> **Coconut Shrimp with**
> **Tamarind Vinaigrette (p. 65)**
>
> 1996 FIRESTONE
> JOHANNISBERG RIESLING
>
> ——
>
> **Pan-Roasted Red Snapper**
> **with Cilantro and Lime (p. 135)**
>
> **Caribbean-Spiced**
> **Grilled Pork Chops (p. 221)**
>
> 1996 BONNY DOON
> VIN GRIS DE CIGARE
>
> ——
>
> **Tropical Fruit Soup (p. 380)**

---

with the spiced oil, coating it well with the spices. Grill over a medium-hot fire, skin-side down, until deep brown and crusty, about 5 minutes. Turn; grill about 4 minutes longer or until just cooked through. Serve hot off the grill.   *−David Page*

Black Bass with Burdock and Garlic Mustard

4 SERVINGS

Salsify, or even carrots or parsnips, makes a good substitute for the earthy, nutty burdock, and any bitter green—dandelion, red mustard or radicchio—will work fine in place of the garlic mustard. For the fish, black bass, red snapper, rockfish or any firm-fleshed white fillet can be used; it's best if the skin is left on.

  3 **tablespoons canola oil**
  ¾ **pound burdock root, peeled and**
    sliced crosswise ⅛ inch thick
  1 **medium shallot, minced**
  1 **large garlic clove, minced**
  9 **tablespoons water**
  1 **tablespoon soy sauce**
Four 6-ounce black-bass fillets
Salt

Cayenne pepper

3 tablespoons unsalted butter

1 pound garlic mustard greens, tough stems removed, leaves finely shredded

1. In a medium stainless-steel skillet, heat 2 tablespoons of the oil. Add the burdock, shallot and garlic and cook over moderate heat, stirring often, until the burdock is golden and barely tender, about 15 minutes. Add 6 tablespoons of the water, one at a time. Cook until the liquid is nearly absorbed between additions. Add the soy sauce and remove from the heat. Cover and keep warm.

2. Make three small slashes about 2 inches long and ⅛ inch deep in the skin-side of the black-bass fillets and season both sides of the fillets with salt and cayenne.

3. In a large nonstick skillet, heat the remaining 1 tablespoon of oil. Add the black-bass fillets, skin-side down, and cook over high heat until the fish is opaque around the edges, about 6 minutes. Gently turn the black-bass fillets and cook them for 1 minute on the other side.

4. While the black-bass fillets are cooking, melt the butter in a medium saucepan over moderate heat. Swirl in the remaining 3 tablespoons of water, 1 tablespoon at a time. Add the garlic mustard greens and cook, stirring, until the greens are just wilted, about 1 minute.

5. Spoon the burdock mixture onto four plates and top each of the servings with a black-bass fillet, placed skin-side up. Then spoon the wilted garlic mustard greens around the black-bass fillets and serve. –*Jean-Georges Vongerichten*

W I N E 1994 Peter Michael Mon Plaisir Chardonnay. This is a big, bold, and rather creamy wine with nice mineral tones to match the earthiness of the burdock.

Pan-Roasted Red Snapper with Cilantro and Lime

8 SERVINGS

Quick-mixing flour, such as Wondra, creates the lightest coating for the fish.

2 teaspoons unsalted butter

2 tablespoons olive oil

Eight 5-ounce red-snapper fillets with skin

Quick-mixing flour, for dredging

Salt and freshly ground pepper

Lime wedges, for serving

Cilantro sprigs, for serving

1. Preheat the oven to 450°. In a large skillet, melt 1 teaspoon of the butter in 1 tablespoon of the oil. Dredge four fillets in the flour, skin-side only. Place in the skillet, skin-side down, and season with salt and pepper. Fry over moderately high heat until the skin is browned and crisp, about 4 minutes. Transfer to a baking sheet, skin-side up. Repeat with the remaining fillets, flour, butter and oil.

2. Bake the fish for about 4 minutes, or until just cooked through. Serve at once with the lime and cilantro. –*Herb Wilson*

W I N E The crisp fish needs a substantial wine that's also racy and refreshing. Try a dry rosé, such as the 1996 Bonny Doon Vin Gris de Cigare from California or the 1995 Domaines Ott Château de Selle Rosé Clair de Noirs from France.

Black Bass with Burdock and Garlic Mustard

Spicy Snapper

Spicy Snapper

20 SERVINGS

Here's a great make-ahead dish to prepare for a party—an escabèche with Caribbean flavors.

3¾ cups white-wine vinegar
¾ cup sugar
10 large sprigs thyme
3 tablespoons crushed allspice
5 medium carrots, thinly sliced
4 large garlic cloves, minced
4 to 6 Scotch bonnet chiles, halved
    and seeded
Kosher salt
¼ cup water
6 large celery ribs, peeled and
    sliced crosswise
2 red bell peppers, thinly sliced
2 red onions, thinly sliced
2 medium zucchini, halved
    lengthwise and sliced crosswise
Vegetable oil, for frying
Twenty 6-ounce firm white fish fillets
    with skin, such as Chilean sea
    bass or red snapper
Freshly ground pepper

1. In a large stainless-steel saucepan, simmer the vinegar, sugar, thyme, allspice, carrots, garlic and chiles with 6 tablespoons of salt and the water for 5 minutes. Cover, remove from the heat and let stand for 20 minutes. Add the celery, bell peppers, onions and zucchini.
2. Meanwhile, in each of two large skillets, heat ¼ inch of oil. Season the fish fillets with salt and pepper. Add the fillets in batches, skin-side down, and cook over high heat until browned on one side, about 8 minutes. Turn the fish and cook until done, about 4 minutes. Reduce the heat if the oil gets too hot.
3. Divide the marinade and the fillets, skin-side up, between two large deep platters. Scatter the vegetables around the fish. Set the fillets aside at room temperature to marinate for at least 1 hour and up to 6 hours. Serve at room temperature.   —Marcia Kiesel

Fish in Crazy Water

4 SERVINGS

Had it been up to me, I never would have sampled that Neapolitan creation Fish in Crazy Water. What's crazy water got to do with cooking and anyway, who wants to eat fish in water? Such were my thoughts until my friend from Amalfi, Pierino Jovine, one day simply brought the dish to the table without asking or telling. Now I am the one who goes crazy over it. Water is what brings together all the seasoning ingredients; the tomatoes, garlic, parsley, chile, olive oil and salt simmer in it for a full forty-five minutes, exchanging and compounding their flavors, producing a substance that is denser than a broth, looser, more vivacious and fresher in taste than any sauce, in which you then cook the fish.

1½ pounds ripe tomatoes, peeled and
    coarsely chopped, juices reserved
¼ cup extra-virgin olive oil
3 large garlic cloves, peeled and
    very thinly sliced
2 tablespoons minced parsley
⅛ teaspoon chopped fresh red
    chile, or more to taste
Salt
4 cups water
Four 6-ounce red-snapper fillets, skin on
4 slices of day-old or grilled
    sourdough bread

1. Choose a deep skillet in which the fillets will lie flat without overlapping. Put in the tomatoes, oil, garlic, parsley, chile, a large pinch of salt and the water. Cover the pan and bring the water to a steady simmer over moderate heat; simmer for 45 minutes. Uncover the pan and boil the liquid until it is reduced by half.
2. Add the fish, skin-side up; cook for 2 minutes. Using two spatulas, gently turn the fish. Season with salt. Simmer until cooked through, about 2 minutes more.
3. Put the bread in shallow bowls and place the fillets on top. Spoon the sauce all around and serve. —Marcella Hazan

Roasted Snapper with Peppers, Pine Nuts and Tomatoes

Roasted Snapper with Peppers, Pine Nuts and Tomatoes

4 SERVINGS

To get a crisp brown skin without overcooking the fish, sauté the snappers quickly before roasting.

¼ cup pine nuts
1 medium red bell pepper
1 medium green bell pepper
½ cup olive oil
4 large basil leaves, shredded
Salt and freshly ground black pepper
1 fennel bulb—halved, cored
    and cut lengthwise into thick
    sticks
2 garlic cloves, minced
2 cups canned crushed tomatoes
Pinch of crushed red pepper
2 pan-dressed 1½-pound red
    snappers

1. Preheat the oven to 400°. Toast the pine nuts in a pie pan for about 4 minutes, or until lightly browned. Rub the bell peppers with 1 tablespoon of the oil and place on a baking sheet. Roast for about 15 minutes, or until they are blistered and soft. When cool enough to

handle, remove the skins, stems and seeds. Cut the bell peppers into ½-inch strips and place in a bowl along with any juices. Add the pine nuts, basil and 2 tablespoons of the oil. Season with salt and pepper.

2. In a large skillet, heat 1 tablespoon of the oil. Add the fennel and garlic, cover partially and cook over moderately low heat, stirring occasionally, until the fennel is tender, about 10 minutes. Add the tomatoes and the crushed red pepper and simmer until thickened, about 8 minutes. Season the mixture with salt and pepper.

3. Increase the oven temperature to 500°. Heat two large ovenproof skillets over moderately high heat. Season the snappers inside and out with salt and pepper. Add 2 tablespoons of the oil to each skillet. When the oil is smoking, add a snapper to each skillet. Shake the skillets and cook the fish over moderately high heat until the skin is browned and crisp on the bottom, about 6 minutes. Using a metal spatula, turn the fish and cook for 1 minute. Transfer the skillets to the oven; roast the snappers for about 12 minutes, or until crisp on the bottom and just cooked through. Serve the roasted snappers with the

Christmas Eve Fish and Escarole Pie

bell peppers and tomato compote on the side. *–Steven Chiappetti*

MAKE AHEAD The roasted bell peppers and the tomato compote can be refrigerated for up to one day.

WINE 1992 Michel Colin-Déleger Chassagne-Montrachet. This full-bodied Chardonnay is rich enough to handle the robust peppers and elegant enough to balance the fine texture of the fish.

Christmas Eve Fish and Escarole Pie

8 TO 10 SERVINGS
PASTRY

1 stick (4 ounces) unsalted butter, cut into small pieces and chilled
1¼ cups unbleached all-purpose flour
½ teaspoon salt
2 large egg yolks
3 to 4 tablespoons ice water

FILLING

1¼ cups dry white wine
1 cup water
6 or 8 whole peppercorns
2 thyme sprigs
1 bay leaf
2 pounds skinless haddock or red snapper fillets
2 tablespoons pine nuts
2 tablespoons golden raisins
1 medium onion, finely chopped
2 tablespoons extra-virgin olive oil
1 pound escarole, leaves rinsed but not dried
2 tablespoons coarsely chopped pitted Gaeta olives
1 tablespoon capers
Pinch of crushed red pepper
Salt and freshly ground black pepper
Egg wash made with 1 large egg yolk mixed with 1 tablespoon water

I. MAKE THE PASTRY: In a medium bowl, cut the butter into the flour until thoroughly combined. Add the salt. Mix in the egg yolks with a fork, adding enough of the ice water to make a cohesive dough. Transfer the dough to a

lightly floured work surface and knead very briefly. Gather the dough into a ball, wrap in plastic and refrigerate for at least 30 minutes.

2. MAKE THE FILLING: In a large saucepan, combine 1 cup of the wine with the water. Add the peppercorns, thyme and bay leaf and bring to a simmer over moderately low heat. Add the fish and poach gently until the fish is just firm, about 5 minutes; do not overcook as the fish will finish cooking in the pie. Transfer the fish to a plate to cool.

3. In a small skillet, toast the pine nuts over moderately low heat, stirring constantly, until golden. Transfer to a plate.

4. In a small saucepan, bring the remaining ¼ cup of wine just to a simmer. Add the raisins and set aside to steep.

5. In a medium saucepan, cook the onion in the oil over low heat until softened but not browned. Stir in the escarole and cook over moderately low heat until thoroughly wilted; add a tablespoon of water if necessary to prevent the escarole from burning. Drain the escarole and when it is cool enough to handle, squeeze it dry. Coarsely chop the escarole and place it in a bowl. Stir in the olives, capers and crushed red pepper.

6. Preheat the oven to 375°. If you have a baking stone or oven tiles, put them in the oven to preheat. Divide the chilled dough into two pieces, one a little larger than the other; keep the smaller piece chilled. On a very lightly floured work surface, roll out the larger piece of dough into a 13-inch round. Fit the dough into a 10-inch tart pan with a removable bottom, pressing it lightly into the side without stretching. Freeze the pie shell while you finish making the filling.

7. Drain the raisins and stir them into the escarole along with the pine nuts. Flake or cut the fish in large pieces and mix gently with the escarole, taking care not to break up the fish. Season generously with salt and black pepper.

Roasted Cod with Bacon-and-Spinach Stuffing

8. Roll out the remaining piece of dough into a 11-inch round. Remove the pie shell from the freezer and fill with the fish and escarole mixture, smoothing the surface. Cover with the dough round; crimp the edges to seal. If you have any leftover dough, make a pair of small fish cutouts, moisten lightly and set on top of the pie. Using a sharp knife, cut a few steam vents in the top crust. Lightly brush the pie with the egg wash. Bake on the bottom shelf of the oven for about 30 minutes, or until the top is golden brown. Let cool about 30 minutes before serving in wedges.   *–Tina Nicodemo*

MAKE AHEAD The recipe can be prepared through Step 5 up to a day ahead. Keep the pine nuts at room temperature. Refrigerate the fish, soaking raisins and escarole separately; bring to room temperature before assembling the pie.

WINE Escarole gives an attractive bitterness to this buttery pie. To balance the bite of the greens and contrast the richness of the fish, serve a refreshingly dry white from southern Italy, such as the 1995 Feu di San Gregorio Greco di Tufo or the 1995 Casa d'Ambra Biancolella Ischia.

Roasted Cod with Bacon-and-Spinach Stuffing

20 SERVINGS

This recipe will amply serve twenty as part of a larger menu. If it will be your only main course, however, double the recipe and make two fish.

- ½ **pound smoked bacon, cut into ½-inch dice**
- 3 **large celery ribs, cut into ½-inch dice**
- 1 **large onion, coarsely chopped**
- 3 **large garlic cloves, chopped**
- 1 **pound spinach, stemmed**

Salt and freshly ground pepper

- 2 **cups finely diced white bread, toasted**
- ¼ **cup chopped flat-leaf parsley**
- 1 **teaspoon chopped thyme**
- 1 **teaspoon chopped tarragon**

One 6-pound whole cod, boned, head off

- ¼ **cup extra-virgin olive oil**
- 2 **tablespoons fresh lemon juice**
- 3 **large leeks, white and tender green, sliced crosswise ½ inch thick**
- 2 **large fennel bulbs–halved, cored and thinly sliced**
- 1 **cup heavy cream**
- ¼ **cup freshly grated or drained prepared horseradish**
- 1 **cup dry white wine**
- ½ **teaspoon crushed red pepper**
- 2 **dozen littleneck clams, scrubbed and rinsed**

I. In a large skillet, cook the bacon over moderately low heat until it is lightly colored and most of the fat has been rendered, about 10 minutes. Using a slotted spoon, transfer the bacon to a plate. ➤

2. Pour off all but 2 tablespoons of the fat from the skillet. Add the celery and onion and cook over moderate heat until tender, about 8 minutes. Add the garlic and cook, stirring, until fragrant. Increase the heat to moderately high and add the spinach. Season with salt and pepper and cook, stirring, until the spinach has wilted and any excess liquid has evaporated, about 4 minutes.

3. Transfer the spinach mixture to a large bowl and add the bread, bacon, parsley, thyme and tarragon. Mix well and season with salt and pepper. Let the stuffing cool to room temperature.

4. Preheat the oven to 425°. Season the cod inside and out with salt and pepper and rub 2 tablespoons of the oil all over the outside of the fish. Open the fish and sprinkle the inside with the lemon juice, then fill with the stuffing and press gently to close. Using a sturdy needle and thread or toothpicks inserted vertically, loosely sew or pin the fish together. Transfer the cod to an oiled rack.

5. In a large roasting pan, toss the leeks and fennel with the remaining 2 tablespoons of oil; season with salt and pepper. Spread the vegetables in an even layer and set the cod on the rack on top. Roast in the center of the oven for 25 minutes.

6. Meanwhile, in a large bowl, whip the cream to soft peaks. Beat in the horseradish and season with salt and pepper; refrigerate.

7. Remove the roasting pan from the oven and pour the wine around the fish. Sprinkle with the crushed red pepper and arrange the clams around the cod, hinges down. Return to the oven and roast for about 15 minutes longer, or until the cod is just cooked through and the clams are open; check periodically, removing clams as they open. Cover the opened clams with aluminum foil to keep them warm.

8. When the cod is done, remove the pan from the oven and preheat the broiler. Remove all remaining open clams from the pan; discard any that have not opened. Broil the cod for about 2 minutes to crisp the skin, rotating the pan as necessary.

9. Cut the fish into serving pieces. Spoon the fennel and leeks onto plates and top with the cod and stuffing. Spoon any roasting juices over the top and garnish with the clams. Pass the horseradish cream at the table. *–Jody Adams*

MAKE AHEAD The prepared stuffing can be refrigerated for up to one day. The stuffed cod can be refrigerated for up to four hours before cooking.

Fried Christmas Cod

10 TO 12 SERVINGS

No true Neapolitan would dream of eating anything but fish on Christmas Eve, and salt cod is de rigueur. Throughout Italy, salt cod (baccalà) is bought presoaked and ready to cook from grocers and fishmongers. In this country, you'll have to soak the three pounds of boneless salt cod yourself for at least two days, changing the water four times daily, before it is plumped and ready to fry; look for boneless salt cod at fish shops in Italian, Greek and Portuguese neighborhoods. Be sure to soak it until it is tender and then dry it thoroughly before frying.The dish can also be made with fresh fish. Buy thick fillets of cod, haddock or a similar white fish.

1¼ cups plus 3 tablespoons warm
     water
½   teaspoon active dry yeast
1½ cups unbleached all-purpose
     flour, plus more for dredging
Large pinch of salt
 4   pounds fresh cod fillets or haddock
     or 3 pounds boneless salt cod (see
     above), cut into 2-inch strips
 1   quart extra-virgin olive oil,
     for frying

Finely chopped flat-leaf parsley
Tomato Sauce with Olives, Golden
     Raisins and Pine Nuts
     (recipe follows)
Lemon wedges

1. Pour ¼ cup of the water into a bowl, sprinkle the yeast on top and let stand until foamy, about 5 minutes. Add the 1½ cups of flour, 1 cup of the water and the salt. Beat the batter with a wooden spoon until it is thick, smooth and somewhat elastic. Cover and set aside to rise in a warm place for 30 minutes.

2. Meanwhile, arrange the fish on a rack set over a rimmed sheet pan. Season the fish with salt and refrigerate for 30 minutes.

3. In a medium saucepan, heat the oil over moderate heat until it reaches 360° on a deep-frying or candy thermometer. Beat the remaining 3 tablespoons of water into the batter to loosen it to the consistency of thick cream.

4. Pat the fish dry with paper towels. Dredge the pieces in flour, shaking off the excess. Working in batches, dip the fish in the batter and allow any excess to drip off. Fry the fish in the hot oil, turning the pieces once with tongs, until browned and crisp, about 6 minutes; adjust the heat as necessary to keep the temperature steady. Drain the fish on paper towels spread on a rack. Transfer to plates, sprinkle with parsley and serve at once with the sauce and lemon wedges.

TOMATO SAUCE WITH OLIVES,
GOLDEN RAISINS AND PINE NUTS
MAKES ABOUT 1¼ CUPS
 2   garlic cloves, chopped
 2   tablespoons extra-virgin
     olive oil
10   drained Italian canned tomatoes,
     coarsely chopped
 2   tablespoons pine nuts
 2   tablespoons golden raisins
 ¼   cup very hot water

menu

Butternut-Squash Soup
with Scallion Cream (p. 77)

Toasted Goat Cheese
with Mesclun (p. 53)

1994 TRIMBACH PINOT BLANC

———

Cod-and-Crab Cakes with
Roasted-Pepper Coulis (p. 141)

Two-Potato Pancakes (p. 313)

1995 MIRASSOU PINOT BLANC

———

Apple Pecan Crisp (p. 385)

EXTRA DRY MOËT & CHANDON
CHAMPAGNE

½   cup black Niçoise or Gaeta olives,
      pitted and coarsely chopped
2   tablespoons drained capers,
      chopped
Freshly ground black pepper

1. In a medium saucepan, cook the garlic in the oil over low heat until softened but not browned. Stir in the tomatoes and increase the heat to moderate. Cook, crushing the tomatoes occasionally with a fork, until the sauce is thick, about 15 minutes.

2. Meanwhile, toast the pine nuts in a dry skillet over moderate heat, stirring constantly, until golden brown, about 5 minutes. Transfer to a small plate. In a small bowl, plump the raisins in the water for 5 minutes and then drain.

3. Stir the pine nuts, raisins and olives into the sauce. Add the capers and season with pepper. Serve warm or at room temperature. *–Nancy Harmon Jenkins*

MAKE AHEAD The sauce can be refrigerated for up to two days.

WINE Fried fish and a sweet-savory sauce point to an assertive dry white as the best flavor foil. Try a straightforward Sicilian wine, such as the 1995 Corvo Bianco or the 1995 Regaleali Bianco.

Cod-and-Crab Cakes with Roasted-Pepper Coulis, with Two-Potato Pancakes (p. 313)

Cod-and-Crab Cakes with Roasted-Pepper Coulis

6 SERVINGS

Crisp fish cakes with a tangy roasted-red-pepper sauce make a satisfying main course for lunch or brunch.

COULIS
2   medium red bell peppers, cut into
      2-inch pieces
2   garlic cloves, peeled
½   small red onion, coarsely
      chopped
1   small jalapeño pepper, seeded
      and coarsely chopped
1   tablespoon extra-virgin olive oil
1   teaspoon red-wine vinegar
1   tablespoon finely chopped
      flat-leaf parsley
1   teaspoon kosher salt

COD-AND-CRAB CAKES
1   pound skinless cod fillets
Salt and freshly ground pepper
½   pound lump crabmeat, picked
      over
1½   cups fresh bread crumbs
2   tablespoons minced red bell pepper
2   tablespoons minced celery
2   tablespoons minced scallions
2   tablespoons fresh lemon juice
1   tablespoon Dijon mustard
3   tablespoons finely chopped
      flat-leaf parsley
1   cup plain dry bread crumbs
¼   cup plus 2 tablespoons olive oil
Lemon wedges, for serving

1. MAKE THE COULIS: Preheat the oven to 400°. Combine all the ingredients in a medium stainless-steel roasting

Grilled Mahimahi and Green Tomatoes

pan and cover tightly with aluminum foil. Bake for about 40 minutes, or until the vegetables are tender. Transfer the vegetables and any accumulated juices to a blender or food processor and puree the vegetable mixture until smooth. Leave the oven on.

2. Meanwhile, MAKE THE COD-AND-CRAB CAKES: Season the cod fillets with salt and pepper and arrange them on a lightly oiled nonstick baking sheet. Bake for about 10 minutes, or until the flesh flakes easily. Let cool.

3. Flake the cod into a large bowl and add the crabmeat, fresh bread crumbs, red bell pepper, celery, scallions, lemon juice, mustard and 2 tablespoons of the parsley. Season with salt and pepper.

4. On a plate, toss the dry bread crumbs with the remaining 1 tablespoon of parsley and season with salt and pepper. Divide the cod-and-crab mixture into twelve parts and shape each into a 1-inch-thick cake. Coat each cake well with the seasoned bread crumbs.

5. Rewarm the coulis in a stainless-steel saucepan. Heat 2 tablespoons of the oil in a large nonstick skillet. Add four of the cod-and-crab cakes and cook over moderately high heat until golden and crisp on the bottom, about 3 minutes. Gently turn the cakes and cook until golden on the other side, 2 to 3 minutes longer. Transfer to a platter and keep warm in a low oven. Fry the remaining cakes in two more batches, using 2 tablespoons of oil for each batch.

6. Spoon the red-pepper coulis onto six large plates. Set two cod-and-crab cakes on each plate and serve with lemon wedges. —*James Henahan*

MAKE AHEAD The cakes and coulis can be made through Step 4 and refrigerated separately for up to eight hours.

WINE Pinot Blanc will complement the codfish and crabmeat. You might try the 1995 Mirassou Pinot Blanc from California.

Grilled Mahimahi and Green Tomatoes

4 SERVINGS

I like to use mahimahi for this recipe because the firm, white flesh can be grilled without falling apart. Green tomatoes have certainly been fried by the truckload—in particular since the release of the popular film *Fried Green Tomatoes*—but I prefer them grilled. In the South we'll flout tradition if it means a way out of a hot kitchen, especially when the results are as delicious as they are here.

1½ pounds firm green tomatoes, sliced crosswise ¾ inch thick
¼ cup olive oil
Salt and freshly ground pepper
Four 6-ounce skinless mahimahi or tilefish fillets, about 1 inch thick

1. Light a charcoal grill or preheat a broiler with the rack placed 6 inches from the heat.

2. Place the green tomatoes on a baking sheet, drizzle the oil on top of them and season with salt and pepper. Lift the tomatoes off the baking sheet, allowing the oil to drain onto the sheet, and transfer the tomatoes to the grill or broiler pan. Cook until the tomatoes are charred and barely tender, 3 to 4 minutes per side, and then transfer them to a platter. Cover the tomatoes and keep warm.

3. Coat the mahimahi fillets on both sides with the oil from the baking sheet. Season the mahimahi with salt and pepper and grill or broil the fillets until they are cooked through, about 4 minutes per side. Serve the mahimahi fillets hot off the grill along with the grilled green tomatoes. —*John Martin Taylor*

WINE Light-fleshed fish and sharp tomatoes signal a light, simple, dry white. Consider an Alsace Pinot Blanc, such as the 1995 Hugel or the 1995 Lucien Albrecht.

Bahamian Grilled Fish

4 SERVINGS

This recipe typifies the way fish is cooked throughout the Caribbean. You start with fish so fresh it was swimming just a few hours earlier. You rub it with Bahamian goat peppers—similar in size and heat to the fiery Scotch bonnet—then marinate it in a mixture of garlic, ginger and fresh lime juice before grilling. You'll marvel at how something so simple can light up your mouth. I can't think of a more perfect dish for a Caribbean-style cookout.

2 tablespoons olive oil
2 large garlic cloves, minced
1½ tablespoons fresh lime juice
1 tablespoon minced fresh ginger
1 Scotch bonnet chile, seeded and thinly sliced
Four 6- to 8-ounce fish fillets, such as striped bass, sea bass, mahimahi or bluefish
Salt and freshly ground pepper
Lime wedges and hot sauce, for serving

1. In a large shallow glass or ceramic dish, combine the olive oil with the garlic, lime juice, ginger and Scotch bonnet chile. Add the fish fillets and turn to coat them well. Cover and refrigerate for 1 hour.

2. Light a grill. Remove the fish fillets from the marinade and scrape off most of the garlic and ginger pieces. Season the fish fillets with salt and pepper and grill them over a medium-hot fire for about 3 minutes per side or until nicely browned and barely cooked in the center. Serve the fillets with lime wedges and hot sauce. —*Steven Raichlen*

BEER Bière de garde, an amber-colored medium-bodied beer made during the winter in the north of France, is more fragrant than a lager and more musty and earthy than a pale ale. Jade is the most authentic and it is also organic.

Gaspergou Courtbouillon

12 SERVINGS

The thicker the fish fillets for this Louisiana stew, the better. Rice is the perfect accompaniment.

⅓ cup vegetable oil
2 large onions, coarsely chopped
1 green bell pepper, chopped
1 celery rib, coarsely chopped
4 garlic cloves, minced
Four 8-ounce cans tomato sauce
Salt and freshly ground black pepper
Cayenne pepper
5 pounds skinless firm white fish fillets, such as grouper, tilefish or halibut, cut into 4-inch chunks
1 cup chopped scallion greens

1. Heat the oil in a large enameled cast-iron casserole. Add the onions, green bell pepper, celery and garlic and cook over moderately high heat, stirring, until wilted, about 5 minutes. Add the tomato sauce and season lightly with salt, black pepper and cayenne. Simmer over moderately low heat for 30 minutes, stirring occasionally.

2. Generously season the fish with salt, black pepper and cayenne and add to the casserole. Pour in enough water to just cover the fish, stir gently and bring to a simmer. Reduce the heat to low and simmer gently until the fish is just cooked through, about 30 minutes; swirl the stew from time to time to mix the ingredients without breaking up the pieces of fish. Five minutes before the stew is done, add the scallion greens. –*Connie Serrette and Allen Zeringue*

WINE This tomatoey fish stew will go best with beer. Try a lager with character, such as Heineken or Carlsberg.

Gaspergou Courtbouillon

Bourride of Monkfish and Clams

6 SERVINGS

½ baguette, thinly sliced
¼ cup olive oil, plus more for brushing
1 garlic clove, peeled
2¼ pounds monkfish fillets, cut into 2-by-1-inch pieces
Freshly ground pepper
2 dozen small littleneck clams, scrubbed and rinsed
3 medium leeks, white and light green, sliced crosswise ¼ inch thick
1 teaspoon chopped thyme
¼ teaspoon crumbled saffron threads
Pinch of crushed red pepper
1½ cups dry white wine
1 cup Aioli (recipe follows)
1 teaspoon fresh lemon juice
Salt
1 tablespoon chopped parsley

1. Brush both sides of the bread with a little oil and toast until golden. Lightly rub each crouton with the garlic clove.

2. Heat the ¼ cup oil in a large stainless-steel skillet. Sprinkle the monkfish with pepper, add it to the pan in an even layer and cook over moderately high heat until browned on one side. Turn the monkfish and add the clams, leeks, thyme, saffron, crushed red pepper and wine. Cover the skillet and cook until the clams open, about 8 minutes.

3. Remove from the heat and add the Aioli. Gently shake the skillet and stir the sauce with a wooden spoon until it thickens and coats the fish and clams. Stir in the lemon juice. Season with salt.
4. Serve in warm shallow bowls, sprinkled with the parsley. Pass the garlic croutons separately.

AIOLI

MAKES ABOUT 1 CUP

- 4 garlic cloves, minced
- Kosher salt
- 2 egg yolks
- 1½ tablespoons fresh lemon juice
- Pinch of saffron threads (optional)
- 1 cup olive oil
- Cayenne pepper

Using the flat side of a chef's knife, crush the garlic and ½ teaspoon salt to a paste. Transfer to a bowl with the egg yolks, lemon juice and saffron and whisk to blend. Slowly whisk in the oil in a steady stream until a creamy sauce forms. Season with the salt and the cayenne.   *–Gordon Hamersley*

WINE Choose a good 1994 rosé from Provence, such as the Domaine Tempier Bandol, Château de Pibarnon Bandol or, if you're not feeling so flush, the Château Revelette Coteaux d'Aix en Provence. Any of these wines and this hearty seafood stew thickened with a garlicky mayonnaise will temporarily transport you to the south of France.

Bourride of Monkfish and Clams

Pan-Fried Catfish with Salmoriglio Sauce

4 SERVINGS

- ¼ cup plus 3 tablespoons extra-virgin olive oil
- 2 tablespoons capers, chopped
- 1 garlic clove, minced
- 1 tablespoon minced oregano
- 1 tablespoon minced mint
- Pinch of sugar
- Salt and freshly ground black pepper
- ¼ cup fresh lemon juice
- ½ cup all-purpose flour
- Cayenne pepper
- 4 skinless catfish fillets (about 7 ounces each)
- Lemon wedges, for garnish

1. In a bowl, combine the 3 tablespoons of oil with the capers, garlic, oregano, mint, sugar and a pinch each of salt and black pepper. In a small stainless-steel saucepan, heat the lemon juice, and then pour the hot juice over the caper mixture.

2. On a large plate, combine the flour with a pinch each of cayenne, salt and black pepper. In a large, heavy nonstick skillet, heat the remaining ¼ cup oil. Lightly coat the catfish fillets with the seasoned flour. Cook the catfish in batches over moderately high heat until the fillets are golden and cooked through, 7 to 9 minutes. ➤

3. Drain the catfish fillets briefly on paper towels and then transfer them to a platter. Pour the sauce on the catfish. Serve the catfish fillets with lemon wedges. —*Erica De Mane*

WINE Here's a classic American fish, paired with a classic Sicilian sauce. Pour a dry, tart Italian white, such as the 1994 Pieropan Soave.

Catfish Tacos with Tequila Cream Corn
8 SERVINGS
JALAPEÑO RÉMOULADE
- 1 small red bell pepper
- 4 medium jalapeño peppers
- ½ cup mayonnaise
- 1 tablespoon minced shallot
- 1 tablespoon finely chopped cilantro
- 1 tablespoon fresh lime juice
- Kosher salt
- Cayenne pepper

CATFISH TACOS
- 2½ pounds catfish fillets, cut lengthwise into 4-by-1-inch strips
- 2 cups buttermilk
- 8 flour tortillas
- ¾ cup masa harina or yellow cornmeal
- ⅓ cup yellow cornmeal
- 3 tablespoons cornstarch
- Kosher salt
- Canola oil, for frying

- ¼ head of iceberg lettuce, finely shredded
- 1 tablespoon fresh lime juice
- Kosher salt
- Tequila Cream Corn (recipe follows)
- 2 cups pico de gallo or good-quality tomato salsa
- ¼ cup grated cotija cheese or crumbled feta
- ¼ cup cilantro leaves
- ½ cup sour cream

I. MAKE THE JALAPEÑO RÉMOULADE: Preheat the broiler. Broil the red bell pepper and jalapeños until charred all over. Transfer to a bowl, cover with plastic wrap and let cool. Remove the skin, cores and seeds and finely dice. Transfer to a bowl and stir in the mayonnaise, shallot, cilantro and lime juice. Season the rémoulade with salt and cayenne and refrigerate for at least 1 hour or overnight.

2. MAKE THE CATFISH TACOS: In a large bowl, cover the catfish with the buttermilk and refrigerate for 1 hour. Heat a large cast-iron skillet. One at a time, cook the tortillas over moderate heat until warmed through, about 15 seconds per side. Stack the tortillas, wrap in aluminum foil and keep warm. On a large plate, combine the masa harina, cornmeal, cornstarch and ¼ teaspoon salt. Remove the catfish strips from the buttermilk, shaking off any excess, and coat them with the cornmeal mixture.

3. Heat ½ inch of canola oil in the large skillet. Working in batches, fry the catfish over moderate heat, turning occasionally, until golden brown and cooked through, about 4 minutes. Transfer the catfish to a wire rack set over a baking sheet to drain.

4. In a medium bowl, toss the lettuce with the lime juice and ¼ teaspoon of salt. Spread a generous tablespoon of the jalapeño rémoulade on half of each tortilla and top with the catfish and lettuce. Fold the tortillas. Spoon the cream corn onto eight large plates and set a taco on top of each. Garnish with the pico de gallo, cheese, cilantro and sour cream; serve at once.

TEQUILA CREAM CORN
ABOUT 2 CUPS
- 1 tablespoon unsalted butter
- 1 tablespoon minced shallot
- 1 tablespoon minced garlic
- 2½ cups fresh or frozen corn kernels
- ½ small red bell pepper, finely chopped
- ¾ cup heavy cream
- 2 tablespoons tequila
- ½ cup thinly sliced scallions
- ¼ cup finely chopped cilantro
- 1 tablespoon fresh lime juice
- Kosher salt

Melt the butter in a large skillet. Add the shallot and garlic and cook over moderate heat, stirring, until softened, about 1 minute. Add the corn and red bell pepper and cook over moderately high heat just until tender, about 4 minutes. Add the cream and tequila and cook, stirring, until slightly thickened, 3 to 4 minutes. Just before serving, reheat the corn and stir in the scallions, cilantro and lime juice. Season the corn with salt. —*George W. Brown, Jr.*

WINE 1995 Dry Creek Dry Chenin Blanc from California

Swordfish with Oregano and Lemon
4 SERVINGS **L**
- 1 tablespoon olive oil
- 2 teaspoons fresh lemon juice
- 2 tablespoons coarsely chopped oregano
- Four 5-ounce swordfish steaks, about 1 inch thick
- Kosher salt and freshly ground pepper

I. Light a grill. In a large stainless-steel baking dish, combine 2 teaspoons of the oil with the lemon juice and oregano. Add the swordfish, turn to coat and let marinate for 5 minutes.

2. Using a damp paper towel, coat the grill with the remaining 1 teaspoon of oil. Remove the swordfish from the marinade and season with salt and pepper. Grill over a medium-hot fire, turning once, until browned and just cooked through, about 10 minutes. —*Jim Cohen*

WINE 1996 Iron Horse Vineyards Fumé Blanc from Sonoma, California

Swordfish with Oregano and Lemon

Sweet-and-Sour Swordfish

4 SERVINGS **L**

¼ cup ketchup

3 tablespoons white vinegar

3 tablespoons sugar

½ teaspoon dark soy sauce

⅓ cup cold water

3 tablespoons minced carrot

3 tablespoons minced green bell
  pepper

2 scallions, white part only,
  minced

2 teaspoons cornstarch
  dissolved in 2 teaspoons
  cold water

¼ teaspoon peanut oil

Four 4-ounce swordfish steaks, cut
  about 1 inch thick

Two ½-inch slices fresh ginger,
  lightly smashed

I. In a small stainless-steel saucepan,
combine the ketchup, vinegar, sugar,
soy sauce and water. Bring to a boil
over moderate heat, stirring. Add the
carrot, green pepper and scallions and
bring to a boil. Stir the cornstarch mixture and then add it to the pan; stir until
the sauce boils and thickens, about 30
seconds. Remove the sauce from the
heat and cover. ➤

Swordfish Kebabs with Coconut Milk

4 SERVINGS

This recipe comes from a most unlikely source, a Rio de Janeiro meat emporium called Porcao (Big Pig). Like most *churrascaria*s (barbecue restaurants), Porcao specializes in an astonishing assortment of grilled meats served on long spits and carved at the table. The following kebabs caught my eye because they weren't made with meat at all but with a sweet, mild freshwater fish. The closest equivalent in North America would be halibut, which isn't always readily available, so I usually use swordfish. Coconut milk is a traditional ingredient in Brazilian cooking. Its high fat content keeps the fish moist and flavorful. Be sure to use unsweetened, which is available at Asian groceries and most supermarkets.

- 2 medium onions, quartered
- 1 cup unsweetened coconut milk
- 6 garlic cloves, chopped
- ½ green bell pepper, chopped
- ¼ cup chopped parsley
- 2 tablespoons olive oil
- 1 teaspoon salt
- 1 teaspoon freshly ground black pepper
- 1½ pounds swordfish, cut into 2-inch cubes
- 1 large red bell pepper, cut into 1-inch squares

1. In a blender, combine one of the quartered onions with the coconut milk, garlic, green bell pepper, parsley, olive oil, salt and black pepper; puree until smooth. The mixture should be highly seasoned. Scrape the marinade into a large bowl. Add the swordfish cubes and toss to coat. Cover and refrigerate for 3 to 4 hours, stirring two or three times.

2. Light a grill. Separate the layers of the remaining onion quarters. Thread the fish onto four long, thick metal or bamboo skewers, alternating the fish

TOP: **Sweet-and-Sour Swordfish.** LEFT: **Swordfish Kebabs with Coconut Milk.**

2. Set a large skillet over high heat for 30 seconds. Add the peanut oil and when a wisp of white smoke appears, add the swordfish steaks and one slice of the ginger. Reduce the heat to moderate and cook the fish for 4 minutes. Turn the steaks, add the remaining slice of ginger and cook until the fish is just opaque, about 4 minutes longer. Transfer the swordfish to plates, spoon the sauce on top and serve.   *–Eileen Yin-Fei Lo*

WINE All this swordfish needs is a tart, refreshing white that can act as a flavor foil for the richness of the fish and the sweet yet tangy sauce. That's Sauvignon Blanc territory. Consider the 1996 Geoff Merrill from Australia or the 1995 Bernardus from California.

with the pieces of onion and the red-bell-pepper squares. Reserve the marinade.
3. Grill the kebabs over a hot fire for about 12 minutes, turning often and basting frequently with the reserved marinade; the kebabs are done when they are lightly browned all over and the fish and vegetables are just cooked through. Serve at once. —*Steven Raichlen*
BEER An English-style India pale ale, such as Samuel Smith's India Ale from England, is ideal; the bitterness will contrast with the coconut, while the maltiness will complement the meaty texture of the marinated fish.

Pesto-Crusted Salmon

6 SERVINGS

Serve this basil-infused fish with some steamed fresh spinach dressed with butter and lemon.

- 2 garlic cloves, finely chopped
- 2 tablespoons pine nuts
- 6 cups lightly packed basil leaves
- ½ cup plus 4 teaspoons olive oil
- 1½ cups fresh bread crumbs
- Salt and freshly ground pepper
- Six 6-ounce skinless salmon fillets
- 1 tablespoon unsalted butter, cut into 6 pieces

1. In a food processor, pulse the garlic and pine nuts to a paste. Add the basil leaves and process to a paste. With the machine on, slowly pour in the ½ cup oil, scraping down the sides once, to make a smooth pesto sauce. Scrape the pesto into a bowl and stir in 1 cup of the bread crumbs. Season the sauce with salt and pepper.
2. Preheat the oven to 350°. In a large skillet, warm 2 teaspoons of the oil over high heat. Season the salmon fillets on both sides with salt and pepper. When the oil is almost smoking, add three of the fillets and brown them quickly, turning once, about 1 minute per side. Repeat with the remaining fillets. Let the salmon cool to room temperature.

3. Spread 2 tablespoons of the pesto on one side of each fillet. Gently pack the remaining bread crumbs on top.
4. Warm 1 teaspoon of the olive oil in each of two large ovenproof skillets over moderate heat. When the pans are hot, carefully add the salmon fillets, pesto-side down. Put one piece of the butter next to each fillet to melt into the oil. Cook until the bread crumbs are toasted, about 3 minutes. Transfer the skillets to the oven without turning the fillets and bake for about 5 minutes, or until the salmon is just cooked through. Serve pesto-side up. —*Rick Moonen*
MAKE AHEAD The pesto can be refrigerated for up to two days. Pour a thin film of olive oil over the surface to prevent discoloration and cover tightly.
WINE A West Coast Pinot Noir, such as the 1993 Foris from Oregon or the 1994 Acacia Carneros from California

Cajun Salmon with Jicama-and-Melon Salad

4 SERVINGS

The sweet notes in the refreshing salad provide a cooling contrast to the spice-crusted fish. If you have a Cajun spice blend in your pantry, you can use it here instead of making your own.

- ¼ cup fresh orange juice
- 3 tablespoons chopped mint
- 3 tablespoons chopped cilantro
- 2 tablespoons fresh lemon juice
- 1 tablespoon extra-virgin olive oil
- 10 ounces jicama or bosc pear, peeled and cut into ½-inch dice
- 2 cups diced Galia or honeydew melon (½ inch)
- 1 teaspoon garlic powder
- 1 teaspoon onion powder
- 1 teaspoon oregano
- ¾ teaspoon cayenne pepper
- ½ tablespoon coarsely ground white pepper
- 1 tablespoon coarsely ground black pepper

- 1 tablespoon fennel seeds, crushed
- 2 tablespoons paprika
- Four 6-ounce salmon fillets with skin
- Salt
- 1 teaspoon vegetable oil
- 2 teaspoons unsalted butter

1. In a small bowl, combine the orange juice, mint, cilantro, lemon juice and olive oil. In a medium bowl, combine the jicama and melon. Keep both bowls in the refrigerator until ready to serve.
2. Preheat the oven to 450°. On a large plate, combine all of the spices. Season the salmon with salt and coat both sides of each fillet with the spice mixture.
3. Heat the vegetable oil in a large ovenproof skillet. When the oil is hot, add the salmon, skin-side down. Add the butter and shake the pan to incorporate the butter into the oil. Cook the salmon over high heat for 3 minutes, then transfer the skillet to the oven and roast for 2 minutes. Turn the fillets and roast them for about 3 minutes longer, depending on the thickness of the fish. Set the salmon on four large plates, skin-side up.
4. Toss the jicama and melon with the orange-juice dressing and season with a pinch of salt. Spoon the salad next to the fish; serve at once. —*Rick Moonen*
WINE An Alsace Pinot Blanc, such as the 1994 Marcel Deiss Bergheim or the 1994 Trimbach

Salmon Steaks with Grilled Salsa

4 SERVINGS **L**

This spicy salsa comes from my good friend Bob Bennett of Bennett's Bar & Grill in Duluth, Minnesota. Its sharp smoky flavors are the perfect contrast to the rich salmon.

- 4 fresh mild chiles, such as Anaheims or cubanelles
- 2 fresh moderately hot chiles, such as New Mexicos or poblanos
- 2 large jalapeño peppers

Salmon Steaks with Grilled Salsa

wine with salmon

With its meaty texture and strong flavor, salmon is one of the few fish that readily pairs with light red wines as well as whites.

Among reds, the low tannin levels of Pinot Noir and Gamay provide just enough astringency to balance the fish's oiliness.

For a white, look for bottlings with enough acidity to cut through the richness of the fish and fine-tune the choice by matching wine flavors with the dish's other ingredients—for example, try an herby Sauvignon Blanc with the Grilled Salmon with Sun-Dried-Tomato Sauce.

1 pound tomatillos—husked, rinsed, cored and halved lengthwise
1 pound plum tomatoes, halved lengthwise
1 medium red onion, sliced crosswise 1 inch thick
¼ cup coarsely chopped cilantro
2 tablespoons fresh lime juice
Salt and freshly ground pepper
1 teaspoon vegetable oil
Four 5-ounce salmon steaks or 14 ounces skinless salmon fillet
Lime wedges, for serving

1. Light a grill. When the coals are hot, grill the chiles and jalapeños, turning, until blistered and blackened, about 2 minutes per side; be careful not to burn. Discard the skins, stems and seeds and coarsely chop the chiles and jalapeños.

2. Over a medium-hot fire, grill the tomatillos and tomatoes, cut-side down, until lightly charred and tender, about 4 minutes. Turn and grill, skin-side down, for 1 minute. Grill the onion, turning, until lightly charred and tender, about 15 minutes. Coarsely chop the vegetables and put in a bowl. Add the chiles, jalapeños, cilantro and lime juice; season with salt and pepper.

3. With a damp paper towel, coat the grill with the oil. Season the fish with salt and pepper. Grill over a medium-low fire, turning once, until crusty brown and slightly rare, about 6 minutes per side. If using a fillet, cut it in four pieces. Serve with the salsa and lime wedges.   —*Jim Cohen*

WINE 1994 Sanford Winery Barrel Select Pinot Noir from California

Grilled Salmon with Sun-Dried-Tomato Sauce

4 SERVINGS

A crisp fresh fennel salad, tangy sun-dried tomatoes and a heady balsamic glaze complement the grilled salmon.

⅓ cup sun-dried tomatoes (not oil-packed)
¼ cup red wine
2 garlic cloves, sliced
1 shallot, sliced
Pinch of thyme
½ cup water
¼ cup vegetable oil
Salt and freshly ground pepper
1 cup balsamic vinegar
2 tablespoons extra-virgin olive oil
2 tablespoons minced chives
3 tablespoons fresh lemon juice
1½ pounds fennel bulbs—trimmed, halved, cored and very thinly sliced
Four 6-ounce skinless salmon fillets

1. In a medium stainless-steel saucepan, combine the sun-dried tomatoes, wine, garlic, shallot, thyme and water. Bring to a boil over moderately high heat. Reduce the heat to low, cover and

Grilled Salmon with Sun-Dried-Tomato Sauce

Poached Salmon in Sorrel Sauce

simmer for 5 minutes. Remove from the heat and let stand, covered, for 20 minutes. Transfer the mixture to a food processor and puree. With the machine on, add the vegetable oil in a slow, steady stream. Scrape the sauce into a bowl and season with salt and pepper.

2. In a medium stainless-steel saucepan, boil the vinegar over high heat until reduced to ¼ cup, about 10 minutes.

3. In a large bowl, combine 1 tablespoon of the olive oil with the chives and lemon juice. Season with salt and pepper. Add the fennel and toss well.

4. Light a grill or preheat a cast-iron grill pan. Brush the salmon fillets on both sides with the remaining 1 tablespoon of olive oil and season with salt and pepper. Grill the salmon over moderately high heat until nicely browned and just cooked through, about 4 minutes per side, depending on the thickness of the fillets.

5. Mound the fennel salad on dinner plates and set the salmon fillets on top. Spoon the sun-dried-tomato sauce around the fish; drizzle with the balsamic-vinegar glaze.   *–Rick Moonen*

MAKE AHEAD The sun-dried-tomato sauce and balsamic reduction can be cooled and refrigerated separately for up to one week.

WINE A California Sauvignon Blanc, such as the 1995 Cakebread Cellars or the 1995 Long Vineyards

Poached Salmon in Sorrel Sauce

4 SERVINGS

Be sure to add the sorrel to the sauce shortly before serving–its lovely green color fades quickly. Serve this elegant salmon dish with boiled or steamed new potatoes.

- 2 cups clam juice
- 2 cups dry white wine
- 1 large shallot, chopped
- 10 parsley stems
- 2 thyme sprigs
- 1 small bay leaf
- 1 cup water
- 1½ tablespoons unsalted butter
- 2 tablespoons all-purpose flour
- ½ cup heavy cream

Court Bouillon (recipe follows)

Four 6-ounce skinless salmon fillets

- 1 cup firmly packed finely shredded sorrel leaves (about 3 ounces)

Kosher salt

Freshly ground white pepper

Fresh lemon juice (optional)

1. In a medium stainless-steel saucepan, combine the clam juice, wine, shallot, parsley, thyme, bay leaf and water. Boil over high heat until reduced to 2 cups, about 25 minutes. Strain the reduction into a bowl.

2. Wipe out the pan. Add 1 tablespoon of the butter and melt over low heat. Stir in the flour to make a roux and cook, stirring, for 2 minutes. Remove from the heat and let the roux cool for 5 minutes.

3. Set the saucepan over moderate heat and gradually whisk the reduction into the roux to make a smooth sauce. Bring to a boil, whisking constantly. Reduce the heat to very low and simmer the sauce gently, whisking often, until no floury taste remains, about 10 minutes. Stir in the cream and simmer for 5 minutes longer. Remove from the heat.

4. Bring the Court Bouillon to a simmer. Add the salmon fillets and adjust the heat so that the liquid is barely simmering. Poach the salmon until just cooked through, about 6 minutes, depending on the thickness of the fish.

5. Meanwhile, bring the sauce to a simmer over moderate heat. Remove the pan from the heat and whisk in the remaining ½ tablespoon of butter. Stir in the sorrel to wilt it and season the sauce with salt, pepper and lemon juice, if using. If the sauce seems thick, thin it

with a little of the Court Bouillon; the sauce should have the consistency of light cream.

6. Using a slotted spoon or spatula, remove the salmon from the poaching liquid and drain briefly on paper towels. Set the salmon on warmed plates and spoon the sorrel sauce on top. Serve immediately.

COURT BOUILLON

MAKES ABOUT 6 CUPS

Court Bouillon is a classic French broth that can be made quickly and used for poaching fish and infusing it with flavor.

- 6 cups water
- 1½ cups dry white wine

Handful of parsley stems

- 1 medium onion, thinly sliced
- 1 large celery rib, thinly sliced

Large pinch of kosher salt

- ½ teaspoon whole black peppercorns

Combine all of the ingredients in a large stainless-steel saucepan and bring to a boil over high heat. Reduce the heat to moderate and simmer the broth for 10 minutes.   *–Rick Moonen*

MAKE AHEAD The sorrel sauce can be made through Step 3 and left at room temperature for up to one hour. Reheat gently before proceeding. The broth can stand at room temperature for up to five hours. Bring the unstrained broth to a simmer before using.

WINE A 1995 white Burgundy, such as the Roger Luquet Pouilly-Fuissé or the Colin-Deléger Chassagne-Montrachet Les Vergers

Salmon with Curried Spinach

12 SERVINGS

A good choice for a dinner party, this dish looks as if you've gone to some trouble when in fact it's really easy.

- 6 pounds fresh spinach, stemmed and washed but not dried, or four 10-ounce packages frozen leaf spinach, thawed

2 tablespoons vegetable oil

1 large Spanish onion, chopped

3 large garlic cloves, minced

2½ tablespoons curry powder

2 cups heavy cream

1 cup chicken stock or canned low-sodium broth

2 tablespoons Pernod or other anise liqueur

salmon: the basics

Here are some tips for buying and handling fresh salmon.

Today's chefs and home cooks rely on farm-raised salmon, since the wild fish is available only three to five months a year and is often in short supply. Certified Quality salmon from the Bay of Fundy in New Brunswick, Canada, is a reliable farm-raised fish that's sold nationwide.

To test for freshness, look for fish that appears moist and plump. Press a piece lightly: the flesh shouldn't separate, and your finger shouldn't leave an impression.

To ensure even cooking, buy fillets of equal thickness.

When you get the salmon home, unwrap it and put it in a sturdy resealable plastic bag. Close the bag, set it in a colander and cover it with ice cubes. Stand the colander in a deep dish to catch the drips and refrigerate. If the salmon is very fresh, it will keep for up to three days. Replenish the ice as necessary.

Before cooking salmon fillets, wipe down the skin-side to remove any scales. Run your hand over the fillets to locate any pin bones, which are most prevalent in the thicker part of the fish near the head. Hold the flesh surrounding the bones and pull them out with tweezers, pliers or a paper towel. Keep the fish chilled until you are ready to cook it.

4 teaspoons fresh lemon juice

Salt and freshly ground pepper

2 boneless sides of salmon, skinned (4½ to 5 pounds total)

2 tablespoons melted unsalted butter

1 large lemon, thinly sliced

1. If using fresh spinach, in a large Dutch oven, wilt it in batches over high heat, stirring with tongs. As each batch is done, transfer it to a colander set over a plate. When the spinach is cool enough to handle, gently squeeze it to remove some of the water but leave the spinach moist.

2. Coarsely chop the fresh or thawed spinach. Heat the oil in the Dutch oven, add the onion and cook over moderately-low heat, stirring occasionally, until softened but not browned, about 10 minutes. Add the garlic and curry powder and cook, stirring, until fragrant, about 5 minutes.

3. Preheat the oven to 500°. Stir the spinach into the Dutch oven along with the cream, stock and Pernod and simmer over low heat for 10 minutes. Add 2 teaspoons of the lemon juice and season with salt and pepper.

4. Generously butter two large shallow baking dishes. Divide the creamed spinach between the dishes. Place one side of salmon, skinned-side down, in each dish on top of the spinach, tucking the thin tail ends under the fillets if necessary. Rub each salmon fillet with 1 teaspoon of the lemon juice and brush with the melted butter. Season with salt and pepper.

5. Transfer the baking dishes to the oven and roast for about 20 minutes, or until the salmon is just cooked through and the spinach is bubbling. Remove from the oven and let stand for about 5 minutes.

6. Using a spatula, cut each fillet into six pieces. Spoon the spinach onto warmed plates, top with the salmon and garnish with lemon slices. –*Marcia Kiesel*

MAKE AHEAD The recipe can be prepared through Step 2 up to one day ahead.

WINE 1994 Louis Latour Corton-Charlemagne from France or 1994 Simi Reserve Chardonnay from California

Cold Poached Salmon with Beets and Skordalia

4 SERVINGS

Skordalia is a delicious potato sauce flavored with garlic and almonds. It's lovely with the pristine poached salmon, sweet beets and lively dressed greens.

Court Bouillon (p. 153)

Four 6-ounce skinless salmon fillets

6 small beets, tops trimmed

Kosher salt

½ cup plus 2 teaspoons red-wine vinegar

One 4-ounce all-purpose potato

3 large garlic cloves, chopped

2 tablespoons whole blanched almonds, lightly toasted

3 tablespoons white-wine vinegar

¼ cup seltzer

¾ cup corn oil

Freshly ground white pepper

2 cups lightly packed tender salad greens

2 tablespoons olive oil

1. Bring the Court Bouillon to a bare simmer. Add the salmon and poach until just cooked through, about 8 minutes, depending on the thickness of the fillets. Transfer the salmon to a platter and cover with damp paper towels. Refrigerate until ready to serve.

2. In a large stainless-steel saucepan, cover the beets with water and add 1 tablespoon of salt and the ½ cup red-wine vinegar. Boil over moderately high heat until tender when pierced, about 35 minutes. Drain the beets and when they are cool enough to handle, peel and cut them into ½-inch dice.

3. Meanwhile, in a small saucepan of boiling salted water, cook the potato until tender, about 8 minutes. Drain the potato and return it to the saucepan. Shake the pan over high heat for about 30 seconds to dry out the potato. Peel the potato and pass it through a ricer into a medium bowl.

4. In a mini-processor, pulse the garlic and almonds until fine. Add the garlic-and-almond mixture and the white-wine vinegar to the potato puree. Whisk in the seltzer and then the corn oil. Season with salt and pepper.

5. In a medium bowl, toss the salad greens with the remaining 2 teaspoons of red-wine vinegar and the oil. Season with salt and pepper. Mound the greens on four dinner plates. Scatter the beets over the greens. Place a salmon fillet on top of each salad. Spoon the skordalia around the fish and serve. *–Rick Moonen*

MAKE AHEAD The recipe can be prepared in advance through Step 4 up to one day ahead. Cover the poached salmon with plastic wrap and refrigerate.

WINE An Italian Pinot Grigio, such as the 1995 Tiefenbrunner or the 1995 Alois Lageder

Crispy Salmon with Balsamic Glaze

6 SERVINGS

1½ pounds sunchokes (Jerusalem artichokes), peeled

Salt

1 stick (4 ounces) unsalted butter

Freshly ground pepper

½ cup balsamic vinegar

2 tablespoons chicken stock or canned low-sodium broth

3 small fennel bulbs—trimmed, cored, feathery fronds reserved, each bulb cut into 6 wedges

2 tablespoons olive oil

Six 6-ounce salmon fillets with skin, preferably center-cut

All-purpose flour, for dredging

1. In a medium saucepan, cover the sunchokes with cold water and bring to a boil. Add salt and cook over moderately high heat until tender, 15 to 18 minutes. Drain, reserving ¼ cup of the cooking liquid. Transfer the sunchokes to a food processor and puree until smooth; if necessary, add a few tablespoons of the cooking liquid. Return the puree to the saucepan, stir in 2 tablespoons of the butter and season with salt and pepper.

2. In a medium stainless-steel saucepan, boil the vinegar over high heat until

reduced to 2 tablespoons, about 5 minutes. Add the stock.

3. In a second medium saucepan of boiling salted water, cook the fennel wedges over moderately high heat until just tender, about 15 minutes. Drain the fennel, reserving ½ cup of the cooking liquid. Rinse the fennel in cold water, then drain and transfer to a shallow baking dish with the reserved cooking liquid.

4. Preheat the oven to 450°. Cut 1 tablespoon of the butter into small bits and dot the fennel with them. Season

Salmon with Curried Spinach

Crispy Salmon with Balsamic Glaze

lightly with salt and pepper. Bake the fennel for about 10 minutes, or until tender and heated through; keep very warm. Leave the oven on.

5. Meanwhile, heat the oil in a large cast-iron skillet until shimmering. Dredge the skin-side of the salmon in flour, tapping off any excess. Add the salmon to the skillet, skin-side down, and season with salt and pepper. Cook over moderately low heat until the skin is just browned and the flesh near the skin turns opaque, about 5 minutes. Transfer the skillet to the oven and roast the salmon for about 4 minutes, or until barely cooked through. Transfer to a large plate, skin-side up, and let rest for about 5 minutes.

6. Gently rewarm the sunchoke puree over low heat. Rewarm the balsamic glaze over moderate heat. Whisk the remaining 5 tablespoons of butter into the glaze, 1 tablespoon at a time; don't let the sauce boil.

7. Spoon the sunchoke puree and the fennel onto six large plates. Set the salmon, skin-side up, on the puree. Spoon the balsamic sauce around the fish and garnish with the fennel fronds. —*Josiah Citrin and Raphael Lunetta*

MAKE AHEAD The sunchoke puree, balsamic glaze and fennel can be refrigerated separately for up to six hours.

WINE 1994 Chateau St. Jean Robert Young Vineyard Chardonnay from California

Salmon with Thai Rice Salad

4 SERVINGS Q

Rich broiled salmon is beautifully balanced by a light rice salad. The dressing's assertive flavors carry a big impact, so little oil is necessary.

1½ cups long-grain rice
2 tablespoons vegetable oil
3 tablespoons fresh lime juice
3 tablespoons Asian fish sauce
1 tablespoon plus ½ teaspoon sugar
Pinch of cayenne pepper
4 medium scallions, chopped
3 medium carrots, grated
1 cucumber—peeled, halved lengthwise, seeded and cut into ¼-inch dice
¼ cup plus 2 tablespoons chopped cilantro or parsley
Four 8-ounce skinless center-cut salmon fillets
¼ teaspoon salt
¼ teaspoon freshly ground black pepper

1. In a medium pot of boiling salted water, cook the rice until al dente, about 10 minutes. Drain, then rinse in cold water and drain again thoroughly.

2. In a large bowl, combine 1 tablespoon of the oil with the lime juice, fish sauce, sugar and cayenne. Let the dressing stand for 5 minutes, then stir in the rice, scallions, carrots, cucumber and cilantro.

3. Preheat the broiler. Oil a broiler pan or baking sheet. Arrange the salmon fillets on the pan and brush with the remaining 1 tablespoon of oil. Sprinkle with the salt and black pepper. Broil the fillets for about 5 minutes, or until they are just cooked through. Spoon the rice salad onto four plates and top with the salmon. —*Susan Lantzius Rich*

WINE Rieslings are among the most versatile of white wines and among the few that work well with salads. With this Thai-inspired dish, try the 1996 Selbach-Oster Riesling Kabinett from Germany.

Seared Salmon on Tartare Mashed Potatoes

4 SERVINGS

- 4 large Idaho potatoes, peeled and quartered
- 1¼ cups heavy cream
- 4 tablespoons plus 2 teaspoons unsalted butter
- ¾ cup coarsely chopped onions
- ½ cup coarsely chopped scallions
- ½ cup drained capers
- 2 tablespoons chopped dill
- Salt and freshly ground pepper
- 1 teaspoon olive oil
- Four 6-ounce salmon fillets with skin
- 2 tablespoons minced chives
- 2 tablespoons minced parsley

1. In large saucepan of boiling salted water, cook the potatoes until tender, about 15 minutes.

2. Meanwhile, combine the cream and the 4 tablespoons butter in a medium saucepan and simmer over low heat until reduced to 1 cup, about 15 minutes.

3. Drain the potatoes and return them to the saucepan. Shake the pan over high heat for about 30 seconds to dry out the potatoes. Remove from the heat and mash the potatoes with a potato masher. Add the reduced cream and stir in the onions, scallions, capers and dill. Season with salt and pepper, cover and keep warm.

4. Preheat the oven to 450°. In a large ovenproof skillet, warm the oil over high heat. Season the salmon with salt and pepper and when the oil is hot, add the fillets, skin-side down. Add the remaining 2 teaspoons of butter to the skillet, shaking the pan to incorporate the butter into the oil. Cook the salmon for 4 minutes, then transfer the skillet to the oven without turning the fillets. Roast for about 5 minutes, depending on the thickness of the fish.

5. Spoon the mashed potatoes onto warmed dinner plates and place the salmon fillets on top, skin-side up. Sprinkle with the chives and parsley and serve at once. —*Rick Moonen*

MAKE AHEAD The mashed potatoes can stand at room temperature for up to one hour. Reheat gently, stirring frequently, before serving.

WINE A 1994 California Chardonnay, such as the William Hill Reserve or the Robert Mondavi Carneros

Chardonnay-Poached Salmon with Gamay Noir Vinaigrette

4 SERVINGS

It's unusual to use both a white and a red wine in one dish, but here the robust Gamay Noir—a blend of Gamay and Pinot Noir grapes—in the vinaigrette balances the delicate Chardonnay in the court bouillon, a broth used for poaching the fish.

- 1 onion, coarsely chopped
- 1 carrot, coarsely chopped
- 1 celery rib, coarsely chopped
- 1 small leek, white and tender green, coarsely chopped
- 2 cups Chardonnay
- ½ cup coarsely chopped parsley stems
- 1 tablespoon fennel seeds, crushed
- 1 teaspoon coriander seeds, crushed
- 1 teaspoon peppercorns, cracked
- 1 bay leaf
- 3 cups water
- Salt
- Four 6-ounce skinless salmon fillets
- Warm Potato Salad with Gamay Noir Vinaigrette (recipe follows)
- Basil leaves (optional)

1. In a large skillet, combine the onion, carrot, celery, leek, Chardonnay, parsley, fennel seeds, coriander seeds, peppercorns, bay leaf and water and bring to a boil. Cover and simmer over low heat until the vegetables are tender, about 20 minutes. Strain the court bouillon into a heatproof bowl, pressing on the solids.

2. Wipe out the skillet. Add the court bouillon, bring to a simmer and season with salt. Add the salmon and cook over moderately low heat until almost opaque throughout, 6 to 8 minutes.

3. Meanwhile, layer the potato salad on four plates and garnish with basil leaves. Set a salmon fillet on each serving of potato salad, spoon some of the vinaigrette on top and serve.

WARM POTATO SALAD WITH GAMAY NOIR VINAIGRETTE

4 SERVINGS

There's enough vinaigrette here for the potato salad and the salmon. If you're not planning to make the fish, serve the extra vinaigrette over grilled steak, roast chicken or a sliced tomato salad.

- 1½ pounds baking potatoes
- Salt
- ½ cup Gamay Noir
- ½ cup extra-virgin olive oil
- ⅓ cup finely chopped red onion
- 3 tablespoons fresh orange juice
- 1½ teaspoons red-wine vinegar
- 1 teaspoon drained capers

Salmon with Thai Rice Salad

Chardonnay-Poached Salmon with Gamay Noir Vinaigrette

½ teaspoon Dijon mustard

½ teaspoon finely chopped basil

Freshly ground pepper

1. In a medium saucepan, cover the potatoes with cold water and bring to a boil. Add salt and simmer over moderately low heat until just tender, about 30 minutes.

2. Meanwhile, in a small saucepan, boil the Gamay Noir over high heat until reduced to 2 tablespoons, about 7 minutes. Transfer it to a medium heatproof bowl and let cool. Whisk in the remaining ingredients.

3. Drain the potatoes and let cool slightly; peel while still warm and slice crosswise ¼ inch thick. Put the potatoes in a large bowl and toss with ⅔ cup of the vinaigrette. Season with salt and pepper and serve warm or at room temperature. —Cory Schreiber

MAKE AHEAD The potatoes and vinaigrette can be refrigerated, separately, overnight. Bring both to room temperature before tossing together.

WINE 1994 Cameron Winery Reserve Willamette Valley Chardonnay. The reserve bottling from Cameron is a concentrated wine that tastes of Red Delicious apples, hazelnuts and creamy oak. Although it's a more substantial wine than you might normally pair with salmon, it works here because of the gutsy flavors in the vinaigrette.

Moroccan Spiced Salmon on Lentils

6 SERVINGS

The spicy condiment called harissa is available at specialty-food shops.

2 cups French green lentils (¾ pound), picked over and rinsed

6 cups water

Salt and freshly ground pepper

¼ cup coriander seeds

¼ cup fennel seeds

2 tablespoons cumin seeds

1 teaspoon cardamom seeds

2 teaspoons whole cloves

¼ cup plus 2 tablespoons olive oil

8 garlic cloves, minced

2 large shallots, minced

2 tablespoons harissa

One 35-ounce can Italian plum tomatoes, drained and chopped, juices reserved

Six 6-ounce salmon fillets with skin

1 tablespoon unsalted butter, cut into 6 pieces

1. In a medium saucepan, cover the lentils with the water and bring to a boil over high heat. Reduce the heat to low, cover and simmer, stirring occasionally, until the lentils are tender, about 25 minutes. Season with salt and pepper and set aside, covered.

2. In a medium skillet, combine the coriander, fennel, cumin and cardamom seeds with the cloves. Toast the spices over moderate heat, stirring, until fragrant, about 3 minutes. Transfer to a plate to cool. Finely grind the spices in a spice grinder or mortar.

3. In a medium stainless-steel saucepan, warm the ¼ cup oil over moderately low heat. Add the garlic and shallots and cook, stirring, until translucent, about 5 minutes. Add the harissa and 1 tablespoon of the spice mixture and cook, stirring, until fragrant, about 3 minutes. Add the tomatoes and their juices and increase the heat to moderate. Simmer the sauce, stirring occasionally, until the flavors are well blended, about 5 minutes. Season with salt and pepper.

4. Preheat the oven to 400°. Place two large ovenproof skillets over high heat. Add 1 tablespoon of the oil to each skillet. Season the salmon fillets with salt and pepper and coat them on both sides with the remaining spice mixture. When the oil is very hot, add three salmon fillets to each pan, skin-side down. Put one piece of the butter next

to each fillet and shake the pans to incorporate the butter into the oil. Sauté the salmon fillets for 3 minutes. Transfer the skillets to the oven without turning the fillets and roast the salmon for about 6 minutes, or until the skin is very crisp and the fish is just cooked through.

5. Meanwhile, reheat the lentils and the tomato sauce. Spoon the lentils into the center of warmed dinner plates and set the salmon fillets on top, skin-side up. Spoon the tomato sauce around the lentils and serve at once. —Rick Moonen

MAKE AHEAD The lentils and the tomato sauce can be refrigerated separately for three days. Store the spice mixture in a glass jar at room temperature.

WINE Try an Italian Merlot, such as the 1993 Mezzacorona or the 1993 Barone Fini.

Marinated Poached Fresh Tuna with Caper and Anchovy Sauce

4 SERVINGS

Are you familiar with what is easily the greatest of all Italian cold dishes, vitello tonnato? It is composed of cold poached veal sliced thin and layered lasagna-style with a sauce made of canned tuna packed in olive oil, mayonnaise, anchovies and capers. It must marinate for at least twenty-four hours, during which time the flavors of tuna and veal interpenetrate and produce something that is like no other dish of meat or fish in tenderness and sweetly piquant taste. Finding myself at John Haessler's splendid seafood shop in Wainscott on Long Island at the moment when a side of fresh yellowfin tuna was being sliced, I decided to use the principles of vitello tonnato to glorify not a piece of veal, but the tuna itself. At home, I cooked the tuna, then cut it into domino-shaped pieces, spread sauce over them, covered the dish tightly with plastic wrap

Marinated Poached Fresh Tuna with Caper and Anchovy Sauce

and left it out until dinner, eight hours later. The tuna was as I had hoped, nearly melting in tenderness and its taste breezily fresh, lightly piquant and appetizingly fragrant. Once we started nibbling, it was difficult to hold back. But hold back we did because I wanted to see if, like *vitello tonnato*, it would improve after a day or two in the refrigerator. In fact a similar exchange between the tuna and its condiments took place, and it became an even more perfectly integrated dish. Please don't eat the tuna icebox cold, but rather at the comfortable temperature of a not-too-warm dining room or a pleasantly ventilated patio.

 1 celery rib
 1 medium carrot
½ medium onion
¼ cup wine vinegar
Salt
 1 pound fresh yellowfin tuna, cut
    about 1 inch thick
 1 teaspoon finely chopped garlic
2 to 3 flat anchovy fillets, finely
    chopped
 2 tablespoons finely chopped
    capers
¼ cup fresh lemon juice
⅓ cup extra-virgin olive oil
 1 teaspoon mustard
Freshly ground pepper

I. In a deep-sided skillet, combine the celery, carrot, onion, vinegar, a pinch of salt and 1½ inches of water. Turn the heat to moderately high, cover and boil for 10 minutes.

2. Put in the tuna steak; when the water in the skillet returns to a boil, adjust the heat so that it simmers gently. Cover and cook the tuna until it is still pink in the center, 5 to 8 minutes.

3. Meanwhile, in a bowl, combine the garlic, anchovies and capers with the lemon juice, oil and mustard. Season with salt and pepper and beat with a fork to combine.

4. Remove the tuna from the skillet and pat dry. Slice it ½ inch thick.

5. Choose a deep glass or ceramic dish that can contain the tuna in a single layer. Lightly spread some of the sauce over the bottom of the dish. Put in the tuna slices, laying them flat, and cover with the remaining sauce, spreading it evenly. Cover the dish with plastic wrap. Let the tuna stand at room temperature for 6 to 8 hours.   —*Marcella Hazan*

MAKE AHEAD The tuna is even better if it is refrigerated for one or two days. Bring to room temperature before serving.

CHAPTER 8 chicken

Chicken with Mustard-Seed and Onion Sauce (p. 187)

165   Roasted Chicken with Garlic, Rosemary and Potatoes

165   My Favorite Roast Chicken

166   Roasted Chicken with Lemon and Parsley

168   Roast Chicken with Warm Potato Salad

168   Roast Chicken Stuffed with Tuscan Chard

169   Casserole Roast Chicken and Root Vegetables

171   Casserole Roast Chicken with Peas and Prosciutto

171   Casserole Roast Chicken with Garlic Cream

171   Deep-in-the-Heart-of-Texas Chicken

172   Dimples' Barbecued Chicken

173   Oven-Fried Chicken

173   Curried Chicken and Rice

175   Chicken with Fennel, Garlic and Currants

175   Sauté of Chicken and Shallots

176   Sautéed Chicken with Herbs and Vermouth

177   Braised Chicken Pizzaiola

177   Chicken Braised with Mission Figs

177   Braised Chicken in Arugula Cream

179   Chicken Smothered in Cream with Mushrooms

179   Coronation Chicken

179   Saucy Chicken and Arugula Meatballs

180   Soy-Sauce Chicken

181   Grilled Cured Chicken Breasts

181   Riesling-Marinated Chicken with Bacon-Wrapped Onions

182   Chicken and Red-Rice Curry

183   Grilled Chicken and Clam Paella

183   Roast Farm Chicken with Potatoes

185   Pan-Roasted Chicken Breasts with Mascarpone

185   Pan-Seared Chicken and Green-Olive Rollatini

187   Chicken Couscous Salad

187   Chicken with Mustard-Seed and Onion Sauce

189   Chicken with Olives, Raisins and Onions

190   Lemon Chicken with Golden Raisins

190   New Delhi Curried Chicken

192   Chicken Kebabs

192   Chicken Thighs with Malt Vinegar

192   Chicken Chili

Roasted Chicken with Garlic, Rosemary and Potatoes

Roasted Chicken with Garlic, Rosemary and Potatoes

4 SERVINGS

You don't need a needle and string to truss the bird. The simplest method is to tie the wings back with a piece of string and the legs together with another.

¼ cup olive oil

15 garlic cloves

1 tablespoon chopped rosemary leaves

Kosher salt and freshly ground pepper

One 4-pound chicken

3 cups chicken stock or canned low-sodium broth

3 tablespoons fresh lemon juice

2 pounds red potatoes, halved or quartered if large

2 tablespoons snipped chives, for garnish

1. Preheat the oven to 375°. In a large mortar or mini-processor, combine the oil, garlic and rosemary with 1 tablespoon of salt and 1 teaspoon of pepper and then pound or process to a paste. Rub the garlic paste under and over the skin of the chicken and in the cavity. Set the chicken on a rack in a large flameproof roasting pan and roast for 45 minutes.

2. Remove the rack with the chicken and discard the fat from the pan. Add the stock and lemon juice to the pan and bring to a boil over moderately high heat, scraping up any brown bits. Set the rack with the chicken in the pan. Place the potatoes around the chicken and roast for 30 to 40 minutes, basting often, until the juices run clear when a thigh is pierced.

3. Transfer the chicken to a carving board and cover it loosely with aluminum foil. Set the roasting pan over high heat and cook, stirring often, until the potatoes are very tender, 10 to 12 minutes. Season the potatoes with salt and pepper. Serve the roasted chicken on a large, warmed platter, surrounded

My Favorite Roast Chicken

with the roasted potatoes and sprinkled with the chives. Pass the pan juices separately. *–Steven Chiappetti*
WINE 1995 Georges Duboeuf Morgon. The lemon juice makes this dish challenging to match. Try a medium-bodied and fruity red instead of a white because of the assertive garlic and rosemary.

My Favorite Roast Chicken

4 SERVINGS

I adore roasting a chicken and taking my time over it. I've tried most methods as they have appeared through the years–the 250° slow roast, the 500° blast, the brown-bag method and so forth. I always return to the old-fashioned way that I learned in France, where I began to cook. My roast chicken starts with a butter massage and fifteen

minutes of high-heat roasting. It continues in a moderate oven with a handful of aromatic vegetables in the pan to flavor the juices. I enjoy attending to its progress, salting and basting as needed until I have a fine, fragrant, brown, perfectly roasted chicken.

2½ tablespoons unsalted butter

⅓ cup each chopped carrots, onion and celery

1 teaspoon dried thyme, savory or mixed herbs, or 2 thyme or savory sprigs

One 3½- to 4-pound chicken

Salt and freshly ground pepper

Parsley stems and celery leaves

Six ⅛-inch-thick lemon slices

½ cup each sliced onion and carrot

1 tablespoon fresh lemon juice

½ cup water

¾ cup chicken stock or broth

1. Melt 1 tablespoon of the butter in a skillet. Add the chopped carrots, onion and celery and cook over moderate heat until softened, about 5 minutes. Stir in the herbs.

2. Wash the chicken rapidly inside and out with hot water and pat thoroughly dry. For easier carving, cut out and discard the wishbone. Pull the neck skin up over the breast and secure it to the back with a toothpick. Salt and pepper the cavity and spoon in the cooked vegetables, a handful of parsley stems and celery leaves and the lemon slices. Massage the chicken all over with 1 tablespoon of the butter, then truss it (see box, below). Alternatively, tie the ends of the drumsticks together and tuck the wings under the body of the chicken.

3. Preheat the oven to 425°. Choose a flameproof roasting pan that is 1 inch

trussing

To truss with one piece of string, lay the chicken breast-down. Center a four-foot length of kitchen string under the middle of the breast. Draw the ends of the string around the shoulders, meeting at the backbone; tie securely, pinning the wings against the sides. Turn the bird breast up. Wrap the ends of the string around the ends of the drumsticks (above) to hold them close together. Tie securely.

larger than the chicken or a baking dish. Salt the bird all over and set it breast-up on a rack in the roasting pan. (Be sure to thoroughly wash all surfaces and utensils that have been in contact with the raw chicken.)

4. Roast the chicken in the oven for about 1½ hours, as follows:

At 15 minutes: Quickly brush the bird with the remaining ½ tablespoon of butter. Scatter the sliced onion and carrot around the bird. Reduce the oven temperature to 350°.

At 30 minutes: Baste the chicken with the pan drippings.

At 45 minutes: Brush the lemon juice over the chicken. Add the water to the pan to keep the vegetables from burning.

At 60 minutes: Baste the chicken with the pan drippings. Begin testing the chicken for doneness: the drumsticks should move fairly easily in their sockets and their flesh should feel somewhat soft. If not, continue roasting the chicken, basting and testing every 7 to 8 minutes.

5. Spear the chicken through the shoulders and lift it up to drain; if the last of the juices run clear yellow, the chicken is surely done. Set it on a carving board and discard the string. Let rest for 15 minutes.

6. Spoon all but 1 tablespoon of fat from the juices in the pan. Add the stock to the pan and boil rapidly until reduced and lightly syrupy. Strain the juices—you will have just enough to bathe each serving of chicken with a fragrant spoonful.   *–Julia Child*

WINE Roast chicken will be flattered by rich white wines and lighter red wines. Among the best bets are California Chardonnays, such as the 1995 Hahn and the 1994 Chateau St. Jean Belle Terre, and West Coast Pinot Noirs, such as the 1992 Amity Vineyards Willamette Valley and the 1993 Bouchaine Reserve.

Roasted Chicken with Lemon and Parsley

4 SERVINGS

- 2 tablespoons extra-virgin olive oil
- 2 medium onions, finely chopped
- 2 garlic cloves, finely chopped
- 1 cup finely chopped flat-leaf parsley
- 1 teaspoon finely chopped thyme

Salt and freshly ground pepper

- 4 tablespoons unsalted butter
- 2 tablespoons fresh lemon juice

One 4-pound chicken, rinsed and dried

1. Preheat the oven to 400°. In a large skillet, heat the oil. Add the onions and garlic and cook over moderate heat, stirring occasionally, until softened but not browned, about 5 minutes. Add the parsley and thyme, season with a generous pinch each of salt and pepper and cook until the herbs are barely wilted, about 1 minute. Stir in the butter and lemon juice and cook just until the butter melts. Scrape the herb stuffing onto a plate and let cool to room temperature.

2. Carefully loosen the chicken skin starting at the neck end, being careful not to tear it. Push about three-quarters of the herb mixture underneath the skin, working it over the breast and around the thighs and drumsticks. Stuff the remainder into the body cavity.

3. Tie the legs together and set the chicken on a rack in a roasting pan. Roast the chicken, basting occasionally, for about 1 hour and 25 minutes, or until the juices run clear when a thigh is pierced. Cover with aluminum foil after 45 minutes if the breast is browning too quickly.

4. Transfer the chicken to a cutting board and let rest for 10 minutes before carving.   *–Darra Goldstein*

WINE This heavily herbed, juicy, roasted preparation points to a dry, rich, herby white, perhaps California Fumé (Sauvignon) Blanc. Look for such examples as the 1995 Chateau St. Jean Sonoma County or the 1995 Benziger.

Roasted Chicken with Lemon and Parsley

Roast Chicken with Warm Potato Salad

Roast Chicken with Warm Potato Salad

4 SERVINGS

One 4-pound chicken

½ lemon

1 small head of garlic, halved crosswise

4 large thyme sprigs

3 bay leaves

Salt and freshly ground pepper

1 tablespoon olive oil

1½ pounds fingerlings or small red potatoes

1 pound haricots verts or thin green beans

1 tablespoon sherry vinegar

3 tablespoons coarsely chopped pitted Niçoise olives

1 tablespoon drained capers

¼ cup coarsely chopped mint

1. Preheat the oven to 425°. Set the chicken on a rack in a roasting pan and stuff the cavity with the lemon half, garlic, thyme, 1 bay leaf and a large pinch each of salt and pepper. Rub the chicken skin all over with the oil. Roast the chicken for about 1¼ hours, or until golden brown and just cooked through.

2. Meanwhile, bring a large saucepan of water to a boil. In a medium saucepan, cover the potatoes with cold water. Add the remaining 2 bay leaves to the potatoes and bring just to a simmer over moderately high heat. Reduce the heat to low and simmer until the potatoes are just tender, about 20 minutes. Drain and let cool slightly. Peel the potatoes and slice them ¼ inch thick, then transfer them to a bowl and keep warm.

3. Add salt to the large saucepan of boiling water, then add the haricots verts and cook, stirring often, until just tender, about 4 minutes. Drain and refresh with cold water. Pat thoroughly dry.

4. Discard the lemon, garlic and herbs from the chicken and tip the juices from the cavity into the roasting pan. Transfer the chicken to a carving board and let rest for 10 minutes. Discard about ¼ cup of rendered fat from the juices. Set the pan over two burners over moderate heat and bring to a boil. Add the vinegar, then add the sliced potatoes and the beans, tossing well to coat with the pan juices. Remove the pan from the heat and gently stir in the olives, capers and mint. Carve the chicken and add any accumulated juices to the salad. Season the salad with salt and pepper and serve at once with the chicken. —*Dan Silverman*

WINE 1995 Château de Pommard Burgundy from France, 1993 Henry Estate Barrel Select Umpqua Valley Pinot Noir from Oregon or 1995 Château de Pizay Morgon cru Beaujolais from France

Roast Chicken Stuffed with Tuscan Chard

12 SERVINGS

This succulent stuffed chicken is a Mondavi family specialty. The chard filling is piped under the skin to spread it evenly over the breasts.

4 tablespoons unsalted butter

2 small onions, finely chopped

4 garlic cloves, minced

1½ pounds Swiss chard, leaves only, coarsely shredded

½ cup coarsely chopped basil

Salt and freshly ground pepper

2 cups ricotta

3 large eggs, lightly beaten

3 chickens (3½ pounds each)

2 tablespoons olive oil

1. Melt the butter in a large skillet. Add the onions and cook over moderately high heat, stirring, until softened, about 5 minutes. Add the garlic and cook for 1 minute. Add the chard and basil and cook just until wilted, about 2 minutes. Season with salt and pepper; let cool.

2. In a large bowl, combine the ricotta and eggs. Stir in the chard mixture and season with salt and pepper.

3. Preheat the oven to 375°. Place a lightly oiled rack in a very large roasting pan. Using your fingers, gently loosen the chicken skin from the breast meat. Fit a large pastry bag with a ¾-inch

round tip and fill the bag with the ricotta stuffing. Pipe the stuffing under the breast skin of each bird. Brush the chickens with the oil and season inside and out with salt and pepper. Tie the legs together.

4. Arrange the chickens, breast-side up, in the roasting pan and roast for about 1½ hours, or until the skin is golden brown and the juices run clear when the thighs are pierced. Cover with aluminum foil and let rest for 15 minutes before carving. *–The Mondavi family*

MAKE AHEAD The cooked chard can be refrigerated overnight.

WINE 1993 and 1994 Luce, an unusual blend of Sangiovese and Merlot. Sangiovese's spicy flavors and firm tannins coupled with Merlot's silkiness and ripe fruit result in a wine that is the perfect match for this Tuscan-inspired chicken.

menu

Dilled Shrimp Vol-au-Vents (p. 34)

1996 FRESCOBALDI POMINO
BIANCO

Wild-Mushroom Fettuccine (p. 92)

1995 ROBERT MONDAVI FUME
BLANC RESERVE

**Roast Chicken Stuffed with
Tuscan Chard (p. 168)**

**Oven-Roasted Potatoes with
Orange Zest (p. 312)**

**Autumn Salad with Radicchio,
Apples and Grapes (p. 51)**

1993 AND 1994 LUCE

Caramel Apple Tart (p. 365)

1991 FRESCOBALDI POMINO
VIN SANTO

1995 LA FAMIGLIA DI ROBERT
MONDAVI MOSCATO BIANCO

Casserole Roast Chicken and Root Vegetables

Once you put the casserole in the oven, this one-pot meal can be left to cook virtually unattended. Roasting root vegetables concentrates their natural sugars, making them very sweet.

4 SERVINGS

1 tablespoon unsalted butter
1 tablespoon vegetable oil
One 4-pound chicken
Salt and freshly ground pepper
1 tablespoon dried rosemary
3 medium carrots, cut into ¾-inch dice
2 medium onions, diced
2 small white turnips, peeled and cut into ¾-inch dice
1 large Yukon Gold potato, peeled and cut into ¾-inch dice
1 cup peeled, diced banana squash or 1 large parsnip, peeled and cut into ¾-inch dice
½ medium celery root, peeled and cut into ¾-inch dice

1. Preheat the oven to 350°. In a large enameled cast-iron casserole, melt the butter in the oil over moderately high heat. Season the chicken inside and out with salt and pepper. Add the rosemary to the cavity and tie the legs together.

2. Set the chicken in the casserole on one breast and cook until browned, about 4 minutes. Carefully turn the chicken onto its other breast and cook until browned, about 4 minutes longer. Turn the bird on its back, scatter all the vegetables around it and season with salt and pepper. Cover and roast in the

Roast Chicken Stuffed with Tuscan Chard

Casserole Roast Chicken with Peas and Prosciutto

oven for about 1¼ hours, or until the juices run clear when a thigh is pierced; stir the vegetables every 20 minutes or so. Transfer the chicken and vegetables to a platter, cover and keep warm.

3. Skim the fat from the juices in the casserole. Boil, stirring, until reduced to ½ cup. Season with salt and pepper. Pour the sauce over the chicken and serve.   —*Michael Roberts*

W I N E 1994 Signorello Carneros Pinot Noir Las Amigas Vineyard

Casserole Roast Chicken with Peas and Prosciutto

Serve with bow-tie pasta tossed in extra-virgin olive oil and butter.

5 TO 6 SERVINGS

  2 tablespoons vegetable oil

One 5-pound chicken

Salt and freshly ground pepper

  1 large shallot, finely chopped

  ¾ cup dry vermouth

  3 ounces prosciutto, sliced ¼ inch thick and cut into ⅓-inch dice

One 10-ounce package frozen peas

  2 tablespoons unsalted butter

I. Preheat the oven to 475°. In a large enameled cast-iron casserole, heat the oil over moderately high heat. Season the chicken inside and out with salt and pepper and tie the legs together. Set the chicken in the casserole on one breast, cover and roast in the oven for 30 minutes. Carefully turn the chicken onto its other breast, cover and roast for 20 minutes. Turn the bird on its back, cover and roast for 20 minutes longer, or until the juices run clear when a thigh is pierced. Transfer the chicken to a platter, cover and keep warm.

2. Skim the fat from the juices in the casserole. Add the shallot and cook over low heat until soft, about 4 minutes. Add the vermouth and prosciutto and boil, stirring, until the sauce is reduced by half, about 4 minutes. Pour in any collected chicken juices. Add the peas

and simmer just to heat through. Remove from the heat and swirl in the butter until blended. Season the sauce with pepper, pour into a sauceboat and serve with the chicken.   —*Michael Roberts*

W I N E 1995 Bonverre Viognier Vin de Pays d'Oc

Casserole Roast Chicken with Garlic Cream

4 SERVINGS

Garlic and shallots cooked in wine and cream and poured over the bird infuse this dish with flavor. Serve it with roasted fingerling potatoes or the smallest white new potatoes you can find.

  2 tablespoons unsalted butter

  1 tablespoon vegetable oil

One 4-pound chicken

Salt and freshly ground pepper

  2 teaspoons dried rosemary

  8 medium garlic cloves, thinly sliced

  3 shallots, minced

  ¾ cup dry white wine

  ½ cup heavy cream

I. Preheat the oven to 475°. In a large enameled cast-iron casserole, melt 1 tablespoon of the butter in the oil over moderately high heat. Season the chicken inside and out with salt and pepper, add the rosemary to the cavity and tie the legs together. Set the chicken in the casserole on one breast. Cover and roast in the oven for 30 minutes. Carefully turn the chicken onto its other breast, cover and roast for 20 minutes. Turn the bird on its back and add the garlic and shallots. Cover and roast for 20 minutes longer, or until the juices run clear when a thigh is pierced. Transfer the chicken to a platter, cover and keep warm.

2. Skim the fat from the juices in the casserole. Add the wine and boil over high heat, stirring, until the sauce is reduced by half, about 5 minutes. Pour in any collected chicken juices. Add the cream and boil until the sauce is thick

three cooking techniques

1. **Casserole Roasting** A heavy, tightly lidded casserole traps moisture that's released from the roasting bird, so the juices baste the bird while it cooks. The moist heat inside the casserole cooks the chicken without drying it out the way a hot oven does.

2. **Brining** Soaking chicken in salt water gives you a juicier bird. This is why kosher chickens, which are brined before you buy them, often taste better than other chickens. Dissolve a quarter cup of kosher salt in one quart of water and brine your chicken in the refrigerator at least six hours or up to a day before cooking.

3. **Skillet Sautéing** Chicken pieces cooked without crowding in a skillet will render their own fat, forming a crusty surface that traps the juices inside.

enough to coat a wooden spoon, about 5 minutes more. Swirl in the remaining 1 tablespoon butter until blended and season with salt and pepper. Pour the sauce into a sauceboat and serve with the chicken.   —*Michael Roberts*

W I N E 1995 Gundlach-Bundschu Sonoma Valley Chardonnay

Deep-in-the-Heart-of-Texas Chicken

16 SERVINGS

For this succulent barbecued chicken, try adding a few water-soaked hickory chips to the fire right before you put the chicken on the grill.

Four 4-pound chickens, quartered

  ¼ cup vegetable oil

  4 teaspoons dried thyme

  2 teaspoons crushed red pepper

Salt and freshly ground black pepper

True Texas Barbecue Sauce (recipe follows)

Dimples' Barbecued Chicken

grilling basics

Direct Heat Most grilling is done over direct heat, with the food cooked right over the fire. Any recipes that call for grilling over direct heat can also be cooked under a broiler.

Indirect Heat When using indirect heat, food is cooked next to, rather than over, the fire, most often in a covered grill. The indirect method is used primarily for larger cuts of meat and whole fish or birds (as in Dimples' Barbecued Chicken) that would burn over direct heat before they could cook through. To set up a charcoal grill for indirect cooking, rake the lit coals to the periphery of the grill or place in the side baskets; cook the food in the center of the grill, away from the fire. To set up a gas grill, light the front and rear burners (or the burners on one side); cook in the center of the grill or on the side away from the fire. Any recipes that call for indirect grilling can also be cooked in the oven.

Light a grill, preferably charcoal. Rub the chicken with the oil and season with the thyme, crushed red pepper, salt and black pepper. When the fire is medium hot, arrange the chicken, skin-side down, on the grill. Cover and cook, rotating from time to time, so the fat is rendered, about 10 minutes. Turn the chicken, cover and continue cooking until almost cooked through, about 15 minutes longer. Uncover and generously spoon the barbecue sauce all over the skin. Turn the chicken skin-side down and grill, basting and turning so it doesn't burn, until the pieces are nicely glazed and slightly charred, about 10 minutes. Serve hot off the grill.

TRUE TEXAS BARBECUE SAUCE
MAKES ABOUT 3 CUPS

- 2 cups ketchup
- ½ medium onion, minced
- 2 garlic cloves, minced
- ½ cup Worcestershire sauce
- ⅓ cup fresh lemon juice
- 1 tablespoon unsulphured molasses
- 1 tablespoon malt vinegar
- 2 teaspoons kosher salt
- 2 teaspoons mustard, preferably Creole
- 1 teaspoon crushed red pepper
- 1 teaspoon Tabasco sauce
- ½ teaspoon dried thyme

Combine all of the ingredients in a medium stainless-steel saucepan and simmer over low heat for 10 minutes to blend the flavors. Remove from the heat and let cool.   *–Dean Fearing*

MAKE AHEAD The sauce can be refrigerated for up to one week.

Dimples' Barbecued Chicken
4 SERVINGS

Mention Jamaica and most people think of jerk, the spice-drenched, fiery, smoke-grilled pork or chicken that's considered Jamaica's national dish. Jerk has become so popular that it's easy to forget the island's other wonderful barbecued dishes, among them this incredibly flavorful, falling-off-the-bone tender chicken. I first savored it by flickering torchlight at a riverside eatery outside Kingston. The chef, although she'd blush to be identified as such, was a short, shy, warm-hearted woman named Fastina Sherman. When complimented on her cooking, or simply asked a question, she'd break into a deep-dimpled smile—no wonder everyone called her Dimples.

CHICKEN

- 8 medium scallions, finely chopped
- 2 garlic cloves, minced
- ½ to 1 Scotch bonnet chile, seeded and finely chopped, or ½ to 1 teaspoon Scotch-bonnet hot sauce
- 1½ tablespoons soy sauce
- 1 tablespoon vegetable oil
- 1 tablespoon sweet paprika
- 1 teaspoon thyme
- ½ teaspoon salt
- ½ teaspoon freshly ground pepper

One 4-pound chicken

BARBECUE SAUCE

- ½ cup ketchup
- 3 tablespoons soy sauce
- 2 scallions, minced
- 2 tablespoons dark brown sugar
- 2 tablespoons distilled vinegar
- 1 tablespoon minced fresh ginger
- 1 garlic clove, minced
- 1 tablespoon dark rum

GRILLING

- 2 cups wood chips, soaked in water for 1 hour and then drained

I. MARINATE THE CHICKEN: Combine the scallions, garlic, chile, soy sauce, oil, paprika, thyme, salt and pepper in a food processor and puree to a paste. Run your fingers under the breast skin of the chicken to loosen it. Spoon half of the marinade into the neck and central cavities of the chicken

barbecue tips

1. **Don't marinate your chicken or ribs in barbecue sauce** or oil before grilling; the second you put that sugary-sauced meat over heat you'll have a flare-up worthy of a flamethrower.

2. **Keep a plastic squirt bottle filled with water** for the flare-ups that do occur. But don't overdouse the flames or you'll have a cloud of steamy smoke cooking your food.

3. **Render nearly all the fat from the bird** when barbecuing chicken to get crisp skin. Do this by starting the chicken skin-side down over a moderate fire and cooking it slowly. Don't add the barbecue sauce too soon; the skin will turn black in a matter of seconds. Wait until the food's almost cooked through and then brush with the sauce and finish over low heat, turning and basting.

4. **Make sure you use enough barbecue sauce.** If it doesn't stick to your fingers when you eat your chicken or ribs, you didn't use enough sauce. *–Dean Fearing*

and rub the remaining marinade over the breast meat under the skin. Put the chicken in a sturdy plastic bag and marinate in the refrigerator for 12 to 24 hours, turning the bag a couple of times.

2. MAKE THE BARBECUE SAUCE: In a small saucepan, combine the ketchup, soy sauce, scallions, brown sugar, vinegar, ginger and garlic and bring the mixture to a boil. Simmer the sauce over low heat until it is thick, about 10 minutes; stir in the rum during the last 2 minutes.

3. GRILL THE CHICKEN: Light a grill for cooking over indirect heat (see box, opposite page) and set a drip pan in the center. When the temperature reaches 350°, toss the wood chips onto the

coals or add them to a smoker box. Remove the chicken from the bag of marinade and set it in the center of the grill, away from the flames. Cover the grill tightly and cook the chicken for 1 hour. Brush the chicken with the barbecue sauce and cook, covered, for about 45 minutes longer; baste the chicken with sauce from time to time. The chicken is done when it is deep brown and the juices run clear when the inner thigh is pierced. Let rest for about 15 minutes before carving. *–Steven Raichlen*

BEER A dry, crisp pilsner is perfect to balance the heat and the sweet in this barbecued chicken. One excellent choice would be the Paulaner Premium Pilsner from Germany.

Oven-Fried Chicken

20 SERVINGS

This method saves the cook from having to stand over a hot frying pan, and makes cleanup a whole lot easier.

- 6 cups fresh bread crumbs
- 2 cups freshly grated dry jack or Parmesan (8 ounces)
- 3 tablespoons thyme leaves
- 3 tablespoons coarsely chopped rosemary
- 1 tablespoon plus 1 teaspoon salt
- 1 tablespoon freshly ground pepper
- 1½ quarts buttermilk

Four 3½-pound chickens, each cut into 8 pieces

Preheat the oven to 400°. In a medium bowl, toss the bread crumbs with the cheese, thyme, rosemary, salt and pepper. Pour the buttermilk into a second bowl. Working in batches, soak the chicken in the buttermilk and then dredge in the seasoned bread crumbs. Arrange the chicken pieces on four large baking sheets and bake, two sheets at a time, for about 1 hour, or until the chicken is golden and cooked through. Serve the chicken hot or at room temperature. *–David Page*

Curried Chicken and Rice

4 SERVINGS

Sautéed chicken cooks with delicate basmati rice in this spicy pilaf. For the full Asian effect, serve it with a soothing raita (a yogurt condiment), chutney or pungent Indian pickle (lime pickle is nice) and a green vegetable like spinach or zucchini.

- 2 tablespoons vegetable oil

One 4-pound chicken, cut into 8 pieces

Salt and freshly ground pepper

- 1 medium onion, diced
- 1½ cups basmati or Texmati rice
- 3 tablespoons curry powder
- 1 teaspoon dried dill
- 1 teaspoon ground cumin

menu

FRESH LEMONADE (P. 415)

MARTINIS MADE WITH ROSE-HIP VODKA (P. 411)

Garlicky Steamer Clams in Ale (p. 42)

Homemade salami

TARGET ROCK ALE

1995 JAMESPORT VINEYARDS SAUVIGNON BLANC

Bratwurst

Oven-Fried Chicken (p. 173)

Barbecued Baked Beans (p. 327)

Elizabeth's Potato Salad (p. 64)

Apple Carrot Slaw (p. 56)

1994 BEDELL CELLARS MERLOT

Peach and Blueberry Crisp (p. 382)

1994 PAUMANOK VINEYARDS LATE HARVEST SAUVIGNON BLANC

1994 PELLEGRINI VINEYARDS FINALE

Sauté of Chicken and Shallots

½ to ¾ teaspoon crushed red pepper

2½ cups chicken stock or canned low-sodium broth

2 tablespoons finely chopped cilantro

1. Preheat the oven to 375°. In a large ovenproof skillet, heat the oil. Season the chicken pieces with salt and pepper. Add them to the skillet skin-side down and cook over moderately high heat, turning once, until browned, about 12 minutes; transfer to a plate.

2. Discard all but 2 tablespoons of the fat from the skillet. Add the onion and cook over moderate heat until barely soft, about 3 minutes. Stir in the rice, curry powder, dill, cumin, crushed red pepper and 1 teaspoon salt.

3. Return the chicken to the skillet and add the stock. Cover and bake in the oven for 20 minutes. Transfer the chicken breasts and wings to a plate, cover and keep warm. Cover the skillet and bake for about 20 minutes longer, or until the rice is tender. Spoon the rice onto a platter and set the chicken on top. Garnish with the cilantro and serve at once.   —*Michael Roberts*

WINE 1993 Zind-Humbrecht Muscat d'Alsace

Chicken with Fennel, Garlic and Currants

4 SERVINGS

½ cup red-wine vinegar

½ cup brown sugar

¼ cup extra-virgin olive oil

10 pitted green olives, crushed

3 garlic cloves, crushed, plus 2 heads of garlic, separated into unpeeled cloves

One 4-pound chicken, cut into 8 pieces

Salt and freshly ground pepper

½ cup dry white wine

½ cup water

4 small fennel bulbs, quartered lengthwise and cored

¼ cup dried currants

1 tablespoon soy sauce

Four 8-inch pitas, warmed

Oregano sprigs, for garnish

1. In a food processor, combine the vinegar, brown sugar, oil, olives and the three crushed garlic cloves; process to a coarse paste. Season the chicken with salt and pepper. Put the chicken in a bowl and pour the marinade over it. Add the wine and water and turn the chicken to coat. Cover and refrigerate for at least 2 hours or overnight.

2. Preheat the oven to 400°. Arrange the chicken pieces, skin-side up, in a large flameproof roasting pan. Scatter the fennel and unpeeled garlic around the chicken. Cover with aluminum foil and bake on the top shelf of the oven for 30 minutes. Turn the fennel and bake for 20 minutes. Uncover the pan, raise the oven temperature to 500° and bake for 20 minutes, or until the chicken is lightly browned and cooked through.

3. Transfer the chicken, fennel and garlic to a large bowl. Add the currants and soy sauce to the juices in the pan and cook over moderate heat until slightly reduced, about 5 minutes. Cover a platter with the pitas, top with the chicken, fennel and garlic and pour the sauce over all. Garnish with the oregano sprigs and serve.   —*Nira Rousso*

Sauté of Chicken and Shallots

4 SERVINGS

Serve this one-pot chicken dish with buckwheat groats, also known as kasha; use some of the rendered chicken fat to sauté the kasha before boiling it. Or serve couscous instead.

2 tablespoons olive oil

1 pound large shallots, peeled, root ends cut with an X

1 tablespoon unsalted butter

One 4-pound chicken, cut into 8 pieces

Salt and freshly ground pepper

Chicken with Fennel, Garlic and Currants

chicken tactics

1. **For best flavor,** buy a premium or a kosher chicken. In taste tests, both beat the supermarket variety.

2. **To make four servings,** buy one four-pound chicken or three-and-a-half pounds of chicken pieces.

3. **If a recipe calls for chicken pieces,** you can use only legs or only breasts if you prefer. Remember, white meat cooks faster than dark.

4. **Freeze wing tips, necks, backs and giblets** (except the liver) to make homemade broth.

5. **Never crowd the skillet** when sautéing chicken, or it won't brown. For most recipes, a heavy twelve-inch skillet or ten-inch sauté pan will do.

6. **If all the pieces don't fit** into the skillet, cut off the wing tips.

½ cup chicken stock or canned low-sodium broth

1 teaspoon dried thyme

1 tablespoon finely chopped flat-leaf parsley

1 lemon, cut into wedges

ABOVE: **Braised Chicken in Arugula Cream.**
TOP: **Chicken Braised with Mission Figs.**

1. In a large heavy skillet, heat the oil. Add the shallots and cook over moderately high heat, stirring, until browned, 8 to 10 minutes; transfer to a plate.

2. Melt the butter in the skillet. Season the chicken pieces with salt and pepper. Add them to the skillet skin-side down and cook, turning once, until browned, about 12 minutes; transfer the chicken to a plate. Discard the fat.

3. Return the chicken to the skillet with the shallots, stock and thyme. Cover and cook over moderately low heat for 20 minutes. Transfer the wings, drumsticks and any soft shallots to a platter. Cover and cook the rest of the sauté for another 5 minutes. Transfer the remaining chicken and shallots to the platter. Skim the fat from the pan juices, season with salt and pepper and pour the juices over the chicken. Sprinkle with the parsley, garnish with the lemon wedges and serve. *–Michael Roberts*

WINE 1995 Matanzas Creek Sauvignon Blanc

Sautéed Chicken with Herbs and Vermouth

4 SERVINGS

   1 tablespoon unsalted butter
   1 tablespoon vegetable oil
One 4-pound chicken, cut into 8 pieces
Salt and freshly ground pepper
   2 medium garlic cloves, finely chopped
   1 large shallot, finely chopped
   ½ teaspoon dried sage
   ½ teaspoon dried rosemary
   ¼ teaspoon dried thyme
   ¼ cup dry vermouth
   ½ cup chicken stock or canned low-sodium broth
   2 teaspoons chopped chives
   1 teaspoon finely chopped parsley

1. In a large heavy stainless-steel skillet, melt the butter in the oil. Season the chicken pieces with salt and pepper. Add them to the skillet skin-side down and cook over moderately low heat, turning once and shaking the skillet often, until cooked, about 30 minutes. Transfer the chicken to a platter.

2. Discard all but 1 tablespoon of the fat from the skillet. Add the garlic, shallot and dried herbs and cook, stirring, until barely soft, about 1 minute. Add the vermouth and boil, scraping up any brown bits from the bottom of the skillet, until reduced to a thick glaze. Add the stock and cook, stirring, to reduce slightly, 2 to 3 minutes. Add any accumulated chicken juices to the skillet, then strain the sauce. Stir in the chives and parsley and season with salt and pepper. Spoon the sauce over the chicken and serve. *–Michael Roberts*

WINE 1994 Murrieta's Well Livermore Valley Zinfandel

Braised Chicken Pizzaiola

4 SERVINGS

Pizzaiola in southern Italy refers to a dish, almost always beef, cooked with pizza flavorings, meaning canned plum tomatoes and dried oregano. The sauce is fine for everyday cooking, but see how different it can be when made with fresh ingredients.

2 tablespoons olive oil
One 3-pound chicken, cut into 8 pieces
Salt and freshly ground pepper
4 garlic cloves, thinly sliced
½ cup dry white wine
1 cup chicken stock or canned low-sodium broth
½ cup water
2 pounds ripe plum tomatoes— peeled, seeded and chopped
½ teaspoon chopped marjoram
½ teaspoon chopped oregano

1. Heat the oil in a large stainless-steel skillet. Season the chicken pieces with salt and pepper; add to the skillet and cook over moderate heat until brown and crusty, 6 to 8 minutes per side. Transfer the chicken to a platter and pour off the excess fat.

2. Add the garlic to the skillet and cook over low heat until lightly golden. Add the chicken and wine and cook over moderately high heat until it reduces to a thick glaze, about 2 minutes. Add the stock and water, partially cover and cook over low heat for about 30 minutes, turning the chicken once. Transfer the breast pieces to a platter and keep warm.

3. Add the tomatoes to the skillet. Cook until the dark meat of the chicken is tender, 10 to 15 minutes; transfer the dark meat to the platter. Add the marjoram and oregano to the sauce; cook over high heat until slightly thickened. Return all the chicken to the skillet. Cook until heated through, spooning the sauce over the pieces. Serve at once. *–Erica De Mane*
WINE Try a fruity red: the 1995 Dolcetto from Prunotto or Pio Cesare.

Chicken Braised with Mission Figs

Figs lend a fruity sweetness to the dish while absorbing the flavorful chicken-cooking liquid.

4 SERVINGS

2 tablespoons vegetable oil
One 4-pound chicken, cut into 8 pieces
Salt and freshly ground pepper
1 medium onion, finely diced
6 medium garlic cloves, finely chopped
1 tablespoon tomato paste
About 1⅔ cups chicken stock or canned low-sodium broth
16 plump dried black Mission figs or pitted prunes
2 tablespoons unsalted butter
2 tablespoons finely chopped flat-leaf parsley

1. Preheat the oven to 425°. In a large ovenproof skillet, heat the oil. Season the chicken pieces with salt and pepper. Add them to the skillet skin-side down and cook over moderately high heat, turning once, until browned, about 12 minutes; transfer to a plate.

2. Discard all but 2 tablespoons of fat from the skillet. Add the onion and garlic and cook, stirring, until barely soft, about 3 minutes. Stir in the tomato paste and 1⅓ cups of the stock. Return the thighs and drumsticks to the skillet, add the figs and bring to a boil. Transfer the skillet to the oven and braise the chicken, uncovered, for 20 minutes. Return the breasts and wings to the skillet and braise for 15 minutes longer. Transfer the chicken to a platter, cover and keep warm.

3. If the sauce seems too thick, stir in about ⅓ cup more stock over moderate heat. Swirl in the butter until blended; add the parsley. Season with salt and pepper. Spoon the sauce and the figs over the chicken and serve. *–Michael Roberts*
WINE 1994 Bruno Giacosa Piemonte Roero Arneis

Braised Chicken in Arugula Cream

4 SERVINGS

The blend of fresh and long-simmered ingredients is what makes this dish so special. Add the arugula at the last minute to keep its color and flavor vibrant.

2 tablespoons olive oil
One 4-pound chicken, cut into 8 pieces
Salt and freshly ground pepper
6 medium garlic cloves, finely chopped
1 large shallot, finely chopped
1 cup chicken stock or canned low-sodium broth
1 cup heavy cream
1 bunch arugula (about 5 ounces), coarsely chopped
2 tablespoons unsalted butter (optional)

1. Preheat the oven to 425°. In a large ovenproof skillet, heat the oil. Season the chicken with salt and pepper. Add to the skillet skin-side down and cook over moderately high heat, turning once, until browned, about 12 minutes; transfer to a plate. Discard the fat.

2. Add the garlic and shallot to the skillet and cook until fragrant, about 30 seconds. Return the thighs and drumsticks to the skillet, add the chicken stock and bring to a boil. Transfer the skillet to the oven and braise for 20 minutes. Add the cream and the chicken breasts and wings and braise for 15 minutes longer. Transfer the chicken to a platter, cover with aluminum foil and keep warm.

3. Set the skillet over high heat and boil until the sauce is reduced to 1 cup, about 7 minutes. Scrape into a blender or food processor, add the arugula and puree until smooth. If desired, add the butter and puree until blended. Season the sauce with salt and pepper, pour it over the chicken and serve. *–Michael Roberts*
WINE 1994 Beringer Napa Valley Chardonnay

Coronation Chicken

Chicken Smothered in Cream with Mushrooms

4 SERVINGS

The chicken becomes plump and flavorful as it cooks in cream and sherry. Serve with a simple rice pilaf to soak up the delicious sauce.

- 1 tablespoon unsalted butter
- 1 tablespoon olive oil
- One 4-pound chicken, cut into 8 pieces
- Salt and freshly ground pepper
- 1 pound small white mushrooms
- 1 medium shallot, finely chopped
- ¾ cup heavy cream
- ¼ cup sherry or Madeira
- 1 teaspoon dried tarragon
- 1 tablespoon truffle oil (optional)

1. In a large heavy skillet, melt the butter in the olive oil. Season the chicken with salt and pepper. Add to the skillet skin-side down. Cook over moderately high heat, turning once, until browned, about 12 minutes; transfer to a plate.

2. Discard all but 2 tablespoons of the fat from the skillet. Add the mushrooms and cook, stirring occasionally, until they release their liquid, about 5 minutes. Raise the heat to high and cook, stirring occasionally, until golden, about 5 minutes longer; transfer to a bowl.

3. Add the shallot to the skillet and cook over moderately high heat until barely soft, about 30 seconds. Return the thighs and drumsticks to the skillet. Add the cream, sherry and tarragon and bring to a boil. Cover and simmer over low heat for 20 minutes. Add the breasts, wings and mushrooms, cover and simmer for about 15 minutes longer. Transfer to a platter, cover and keep warm.

4. Increase the heat to high and boil the sauce, stirring, until thickened, about 5 minutes. Remove from the heat; whisk in the truffle oil, if using. Season with salt and pepper. Pour over the chicken and serve.   —*Michael Roberts*

WINE 1995 Sterling Vineyards Winery Lake Chardonnay

---

menu

Chilled Carrot Ginger Soup (p. 71)

—

Coronation Chicken (p. 179)
Herbed Rice Salad (p. 309)

1994 PIERRE SPARR CARTE D'OR GEWÜRZTRAMINER

—

Strawberry Tart (p. 361)

VEUVE CLICQUOT DEMI-SEC CHAMPAGNE

Coronation Chicken

6 SERVINGS

- 1 tablespoon canola oil
- 1 medium onion, chopped
- 1½ tablespoons curry powder
- ½ tablespoon tomato paste
- ½ cup red wine
- ½ cup water
- 1 bay leaf
- Pinch each of dried thyme and oregano
- 1 tablespoon fresh lemon juice
- ½ cup mayonnaise
- 1 tablespoon strained apricot jam
- 6 cups shredded cooked chicken
- ¼ cup currants (optional)
- Salt and freshly ground pepper
- 2 tablespoons chopped flat-leaf parsley

1. Heat the oil in a medium stainless-steel saucepan. Add the onion and cook over moderate heat, stirring occasionally, until softened, about 5 minutes. Add the curry powder and cook for 2 minutes. Stir in the tomato paste, then the wine, water and bay leaf and bring to a boil. Add the thyme, oregano and ½ tablespoon of the lemon juice and cook until thickened and reduced by three-quarters, about 6 minutes. Strain the sauce into a large bowl, pressing hard on the solids; let cool.

2. Add the mayonnaise, the jam and the remaining ½ tablespoon of lemon juice to the sauce. Fold in the chicken and currants, if using, and season with salt and pepper. Refrigerate until chilled or for up to 1 day. Sprinkle with the parsley and serve.   —*Katrin Theodoli*

WINE The sweet notes of apricot jam and currants point to a wine with some fruitiness and spice of its own. Best bet? A dry Alsace Gewürztraminer, such as the 1994 Pierre Sparr Carte d'Or or the 1992 Domaine Marcel Deiss Mittelwihr.

Saucy Chicken and Arugula Meatballs

4 SERVINGS

In Italy, meatballs are usually made with beef or veal, browned, simmered in a simple sauce, and then served with bread and a green salad. The ones here are made with chicken and arugula, a popular Italian combination, but not one generally used in meatballs. Making the meatballs small ensures that they cook quickly and that the sauce maintains its fresh taste.

MEATBALLS

- 2 tablespoons olive oil, plus more for sautéing the meatballs
- 3 thin slices pancetta or bacon (about 2 ounces), chopped
- 2 garlic cloves, minced
- 1 large bunch arugula (about 6 ounces), stemmed and finely chopped
- 1 pound ground chicken or turkey
- ½ cup plus 2 tablespoons plain dry bread crumbs
- ½ cup freshly grated Pecorino-Romano (about 1½ ounces)
- 2 tablespoons drained capers, chopped
- 1 large egg, lightly beaten
- ¾ teaspoon salt
- ⅛ teaspoon freshly ground pepper

SAUCE

- 3 tablespoons unsalted butter
- 2 large shallots, minced
- ¼ cup cognac or brandy

One 35-ounce can Italian peeled tomatoes with juice, coarsely chopped in a food processor

- 1 teaspoon finely chopped thyme

Salt and freshly ground pepper

I. MAKE THE MEATBALLS: In a large stainless-steel skillet, heat the 2 tablespoons of oil. Add the pancetta and cook over moderate heat until crisp, about 3 minutes. Add the garlic and cook, stirring, until fragrant, about 1 minute. Add the arugula and cook, stirring, until wilted, 1 to 2 minutes. Transfer to a plate and let cool.

Saucy Chicken and Arugula Meatballs

2. In a large bowl, combine the ground chicken, bread crumbs, cheese, capers, egg, salt and pepper. Add the arugula mixture and beat until well blended. Roll by teaspoonfuls into ¾-inch balls.

3. In a large skillet, heat ¼ inch of oil. Add half of the meatballs in a single layer and cook over moderate heat, turning, until browned all over, about 3 minutes. Using a slotted spoon, transfer the meatballs to a large plate. Discard the fat and wipe out the skillet. Repeat with the remaining meatballs.

4. MAKE THE SAUCE: In the same skillet, melt the butter over moderate heat. Add the shallots; cook until softened, about 3 minutes. Add the cognac, raise the heat to high and cook until

evaporated. Add the tomatoes and the thyme and season with salt and pepper. Bring to a simmer and cook until the sauce is thick, about 8 minutes.

5. Add the meatballs to the sauce and simmer over low heat just until heated through, about 3 minutes. Serve immediately.   —Erica De Mane

MAKE AHEAD The meatballs and sauce can be refrigerated separately for up to one day. Return to room temperature before proceeding with Step 5.

WINE The capers and pancetta in this dish call for a meaty, acidic Italian Cabernet Sauvignon–Sangiovese blend, such as the 1990 Capezzana Carmignano or the 1993 Castello dei Rampolla Sammarco.

Soy-Sauce Chicken

6 SERVINGS **L**

This is a festive chicken dish, one that was always made for the birthday of my *Ah Paw* (grandmother). We seldom prepared this at home, except for special occasions. Here I substitute chicken breasts for the more traditional whole chicken. The flavorful poaching liquid can be refrigerated and reused several times.

- 4 cups chicken stock

Three 3-inch-long cinnamon sticks

- 3 tablespoons brown sugar
- 4 star anise pods

One 2-inch piece fresh ginger, lightly smashed

- ¼ cup mushroom soy sauce
- ¼ cup Shao-Hsing wine or dry sherry
- 2 whole chicken breasts on the bone with the skin (about 2½ pounds in all)

I. In a large stainless-steel saucepan, combine the stock, cinnamon sticks, brown sugar, star anise and ginger and bring to a boil over high heat. Add the soy sauce and return to a boil. Reduce the heat to moderate and simmer for 20 minutes.

Riesling-Marinated Chicken with Bacon-Wrapped Onions

2. Add the wine and bring to a boil over high heat. Add the chicken, skin-side down, and return to a boil. Reduce the heat to low, cover and cook for 12 minutes. Turn the chicken, cover and cook for 12 minutes longer. Remove from the heat and let stand, covered, for 1 hour.
3. Remove the chicken from the liquid. Remove and discard the skin and bones. Cut the chicken crosswise into 1½-inch slices and serve.   *–Eileen Yin-Fei Lo*
WINE A fruity but dry Gewürztraminer, such as the 1995 Bouchaine from California or the 1995 Henry Estate from Oregon, would play off the spiciness of the poaching sauce.

Grilled Cured Chicken Breasts
8 SERVINGS **L**
This cure is also wonderful for butterflied quail; salt the birds for fifteen minutes.

- ¼ **cup kosher salt**
- 1 **tablespoon light brown sugar**
- 2 **teaspoons minced thyme**
- ½ **tablespoon freshly ground pepper**
- 1 **garlic clove, minced**

Eight 9-ounce bone-in chicken-breast halves with skin

- 1 **teaspoon vegetable oil**

I. In a small bowl, combine the salt, sugar, thyme, pepper and garlic. Arrange the chicken breasts in two large baking dishes and rub them all over with the salt mixture. Cover the chicken breasts and refrigerate for 20 minutes. Rinse the chicken breasts and pat dry with paper towels.
2. Light a grill. Using a damp paper towel, coat the grill with the oil. Grill the chicken breasts, skin-side down, over a medium-hot fire until the skin is crisp and browned, about 7 minutes. Turn and grill until just cooked through, about 9 minutes longer.   *–Jim Cohen*
WINE 1995 Charles Joguet Dioterie Chinon from Loire Valley, France

Riesling-Marinated Chicken with Bacon-Wrapped Onions
4 SERVINGS
A Late Harvest Riesling adds fruity flavor, and the sugar in the wine helps to caramelize the chicken skin. The salty bacon-wrapped red onion is an absolute delight paired with the Riesling, butternut squash and apple.

- ½ **cup Late Harvest Riesling**
- 1 **medium onion, coarsely chopped**
- 1 **head of garlic–1 small clove minced, the rest coarsely chopped**
- 4 **thyme sprigs**
- 6 **tablespoons extra-virgin olive oil**
- 4 **chicken-breast halves, on the bone with wings attached**
- 1 **tablespoon balsamic vinegar**
- 2 **teaspoons red-wine vinegar**
- ½ **tablespoon finely chopped basil**
- ¾ **teaspoon Dijon mustard**

Salt and freshly ground pepper

1 large red onion, cut lengthwise through the core into 8 wedges

One 1½-pound butternut squash—halved lengthwise, seeded and cut into 16 wedges

1 large apple—halved, cored and cut into 8 wedges

4 slices of bacon, halved crosswise

1. In a large resealable plastic bag, combine the Riesling, onion, chopped garlic, thyme and 2 tablespoons of the oil. Add the chicken, seal the bag and let the chicken marinate, refrigerated, for 2 hours, turning the bag occasionally.

2. Preheat the oven to 425°. In a small bowl, combine the balsamic and red-wine vinegars, the basil, mustard and minced garlic. Slowly whisk in 2 tablespoons of the oil and season with salt and pepper. Arrange the onion wedges on a rimmed baking sheet and drizzle with the dressing; toss to coat. On another rimmed baking sheet, toss the squash and apple wedges with 1 tablespoon of oil and season with salt and pepper. Roast the vegetables for about 30 minutes, or until the vegetables are tender and the onion has browned around the edges. Let cool.

3. Preheat the broiler and position a rack 8 inches from the heat. Wrap the onion wedges in the bacon and secure with toothpicks. Broil the onions for 3 minutes per side, or until crisp.

4. Turn the oven to 425°. Remove the chicken from the marinade. Scrape off the onions and garlic and pat dry with paper towels. Brush the chicken with the remaining 1 tablespoon of oil and season with salt and pepper. Transfer the chicken to an oiled baking pan and roast, skin-side up, until just cooked through, about 25 minutes. Reheat the onions, squash and apples while the chicken is cooking and serve.   *–Cory Schreiber*

WINE 1995 Argyle Dry Reserve Willamette Valley Riesling. This clean, lean Riesling is delicious on its own as a refreshing summer drink, but its flavors and aromas of peach, apricot and citrus peel also make it a fine complement to the fruity marinade.

Chicken and Red-Rice Curry
4 SERVINGS

This one-dish meal combines ingredients and cooking methods from Italy, India and our American South. Serve it with an assortment of condiments, such as flaked coconut, roasted almonds or peanuts, mango or peach chutney, and mixed pickles.

2 skinless chicken-breast halves on the bone

4 cups chicken stock or canned low-sodium broth

2 celery ribs, cut into 4-inch lengths

1 small onion, quartered

1 bay leaf

2 tablespoons olive oil

1 cup long-grain white rice

1 tablespoon curry powder

2 cups drained and chopped canned Italian plum tomatoes

2 teaspoons salt

¼ cup dried currants

1 tablespoon minced flat-leaf parsley

1. In a medium saucepan, combine the chicken with the stock, celery, onion and bay leaf and bring to a simmer.

Grilled Chicken and Clam Paella

Cook over moderately low heat until the chicken is just white throughout, about 18 minutes. Strain the liquid through a fine sieve and discard the onion and bay leaf; reserve 2 cups of the stock and the chicken and celery separately. Freeze the remaining stock for another use.

2. Wipe out the saucepan and add the oil and rice. Cook over moderate heat, stirring constantly, until the rice just begins to whiten, about 2 minutes. Stir in the curry powder and cook for 1 minute. Add the tomatoes and salt and cook until the liquid is almost absorbed, about 2 minutes. Add the 2 cups of reserved stock and bring to a boil. Cover and cook over low heat until the rice is tender, about 18 minutes. Remove the saucepan from the heat and fluff the rice with a fork; cover.

3. Meanwhile, remove the chicken from the bones and cut it into ¾-inch pieces. Finely chop the reserved celery. Add the chicken, celery, currants and parsley to the rice and toss gently. Cover and let stand for 5 minutes. Serve the dish hot. —*John Martin Taylor*

MAKE AHEAD Step 1 can be completed up to one day in advance.

WINE The spicy heat here is best balanced by a simple not-quite-dry white. Look for examples from California, such as the 1996 Alderbrook Gewürztraminer or the 1996 Pine Ridge Chenin Blanc.

Grilled Chicken and Clam Paella

8 SERVINGS **L**

This outdoor version of the Spanish classic is best made in a paella pan over a wood fire; the wide-open pan allows the fragrant smoke to roll over the food as it cooks. Make the fire with whatever wood you like. In Spain they use pine twigs; I prefer trimmings from my rose bushes.

- 1 tablespoon olive oil
- 1 medium leek, white and tender green, finely chopped
- 2 garlic cloves, minced
- 2 pounds skinless chicken breasts on the bone, cut crosswise into 2-inch pieces

Salt and freshly ground pepper

- 2 cups medium-grain rice, such as Valencia
- 1¼ cups fresh shelled fava beans (about 1½ pounds in the shell), peeled, or fresh or frozen lima beans
- 4½ cups hot chicken stock or canned low-sodium broth
- ¼ teaspoon saffron threads
- 2 large plum tomatoes, chopped
- 2 thyme sprigs
- 1 rosemary sprig
- 2 pounds littleneck clams, scrubbed

1. Light a grill. When the fire is hot, set a paella pan or medium roasting pan on the grill. Add the oil. Add the leek and garlic and cook, stirring, until wilted, about 2 minutes. Add the chicken breasts and season generously with salt and pepper. Cook, turning, until the chicken is beginning to brown, about 4 minutes.

2. Add the rice to the paella pan and stir to coat with oil. Add the fava beans and then the hot chicken stock and bring to a simmer. Stir in the saffron, shake the pan to loosen the rice and simmer for 4 minutes. Stir in the tomatoes, thyme and rosemary and season with salt and pepper. Spread the rice in an even layer and nestle the clams in the rice, hinges down. Cover the grill and cook until all the clams are open and the rice is tender, 15 to 20 minutes; rotate the pan halfway through cooking. Remove the paella pan from the grill, cover with a kitchen towel for 5 minutes to steam, and then serve the paella. —*Jim Cohen*

WINE Try the 1994 Domaine Weinbach Cuvée Théo Riesling from Alsace, France

---

menu

Seared Sea Scallops (p. 38)

1995 SPOTTSWOODE
SAUVIGNON BLANC

Roast Farm Chicken with Potatoes (p. 183)

Romaine Leaves with Honey Mustard Dressing (p. 53)

1994 ETUDE CARNEROS
PINOT NOIR

Summer Peach Clafoutis (p. 380)

1994 ARROWOOD PRESTON
RANCH LATE HARVEST
WHITE RIESLING

Roast Farm Chicken with Potatoes

6 SERVINGS

- ½ cup pure olive oil
- 12 medium Yukon Gold potatoes (about 3¾ pounds), peeled and sliced crosswise ½ inch thick

Salt and freshly ground pepper

- 4 tablespoons cold unsalted butter, cut into ¼-inch bits
- 3 garlic cloves, finely chopped
- 1 teaspoon finely chopped thyme
- 2 tablespoons extra-virgin olive oil
- 6 boneless chicken-breast halves with skin

1. Preheat the oven to 450°. Brush a large heavy rimmed baking sheet with some of the pure olive oil and arrange the potatoes on it in a single layer. Season the potatoes with salt and pepper, drizzle with the remaining pure olive oil and dot evenly with the butter. Bake in the middle of the oven for about 30 minutes, or until tender. Remove the baking sheet from the oven and turn the potatoes. Season them with salt and pepper and sprinkle with the chopped garlic and thyme. ➤

Roast Farm Chicken with Potatoes

2. Preheat the broiler. Broil the potatoes about 8 inches from the heat for about 10 minutes, or until browned; do not let the garlic burn. Using a spatula, transfer the potatoes to a rack.

3. Carefully position one rack in the upper third of the oven and another in the bottom third. Reduce the oven temperature to 400°. Heat 1 tablespoon of the extra-virgin olive oil in each of two large skillets. Season the chicken breasts with salt and pepper. Add the chicken to the skillets, skin-side down, and cook over moderately high heat until the skin is golden, about 5 minutes. Turn and cook for 1 minute. Transfer the chicken, skin-side up, to a baking sheet.

4. Arrange the potatoes on a baking sheet and set it on the lower rack in the oven. Set the chicken on the upper rack. Roast for 15 minutes, or until the chicken is cooked through and the potatoes are nicely crisped. Arrange on warmed plates and serve.   *–Joachim Splichal*

MAKE AHEAD After broiling, the potatoes can stand at room temperature for up to six hours.

WINE 1994 Etude Carneros Pinot Noir. With its bright red fruit and sweet spice components, this Pinot Noir nicely complements the smoky chicken and the thyme-flecked potatoes.

Pan-Roasted Chicken Breasts with Mascarpone

These savory chicken breasts are a simplified version of the whole birds that are boned and stuffed at The River Café in London. The prosciutto and mascarpone stuffing flavors the chicken, and the mascarpone also helps to thicken the lemony sauce.

8 SERVINGS

Eight 5- to 6-ounce boneless chicken
   breast halves with skin,
   preferably with wings attached
  8 thin slices of prosciutto (about
     1½ ounces)

  ½ cup plus 2 tablespoons
     mascarpone cheese (about
     5 ounces)
  1 tablespoon finely chopped thyme
  1 teaspoon finely grated lemon zest
Salt and freshly ground pepper
  2 tablespoons olive oil
  ⅓ cup fresh lemon juice

1. Gently run your fingers under the skin of each breast to form a small pocket. Fold the prosciutto slices and slip one under the skin of each breast.

2. In a small bowl, combine ½ cup of the mascarpone with the thyme, lemon zest, ¼ teaspoon of salt and a pinch of pepper. Carefully stuff 1 tablespoon of the mixture into each chicken-breast pocket, pressing lightly to form an even layer.

3. Preheat the oven to 450°. Heat 1 tablespoon of the oil in each of two large stainless-steel ovenproof skillets until almost smoking. Season the chicken with salt and pepper and add four breasts to each skillet, skin-side down. Cook over high heat until golden brown, about 3 minutes. Turn the breasts and cook for 2 minutes more. Transfer the skillets to the oven and roast for about 8 minutes, or until just cooked through. Transfer the chicken to a platter and keep warm.

4. Set each skillet over moderate heat. Add half of the lemon juice to each skillet and bring to a boil, scraping up the brown bits. Combine all the pan juices in one of the skillets. Add the remaining 2 tablespoons of mascarpone and simmer, stirring, until thickened and smooth, about 1 minute. Season the sauce with salt and pepper, pour it over the chicken and serve.   *–Ruth Rogers and Rose Gray*

MAKE AHEAD The chicken breasts can be stuffed a day ahead and refrigerated overnight.

WINE 1993 Isole e Olena Chianti Classico. It's a Chianti that's accessible at a young age, one of the best-quality simple Classicos on the market, from a producer who stresses the fruit more than

Pan-Roasted Chicken Breasts with Mascarpone, with Braised Spring Vegetables (p. 318).

the structure of the wine. It's lively and can cope with the zest and creaminess of the chicken. The 1994 Querciabella is another choice Chianti Classico.

Pan-Seared Chicken and Green-Olive Rollatini

8 SERVINGS

Piquant green olives make an invigorating contrast to the sweet caramelized-onion filling. You can use a large plastic bag that's been opened on two sides to cover the chicken before flattening it.

  4 whole boneless chicken breasts
     with skin (about 1¼ pounds each)
  1 tablespoon unsalted butter
  1 large onion, thinly sliced
  3 tablespoons coarsely chopped
     pitted green olives, such as Sicilian
  1 teaspoon finely chopped
     rosemary
Salt and freshly ground pepper
  1 tablespoon extra-virgin olive oil
  ½ tablespoon finely chopped
     shallots
  1½ pounds tomatoes—peeled, seeded
     and coarsely chopped

Pan-Seared Chicken and Green-Olive Rollatini, with Italian Couscous with Parmesan and Herbs (p. 108)

menu

Roasted-Vegetable and Fontina Tarts (p. 19)

Tomatoes with Pesto Oil (p. 29)

Wilted Arugula and Prosciutto Frittata (p. 31)

1996 ANSELMI SOAVE CLASSICO SUPERIORE SAN VINCENZO

Pan-Seared Chicken and Green-Olive Rollatini (p. 185)

Italian Couscous with Parmesan and Herbs (p. 108)

Wax-Bean Salad with Toasted Hazelnuts (p. 60)

1995 CASTELLO DI GABBIANO CHIANTI CLASSICO

Sweet Peaches with Creamy Zabaglione (p. 381)

1. Place each chicken breast between two layers of plastic and pound to a ½-inch thickness. Transfer to a large plate. Cover the chicken and refrigerate.

2. Melt the butter in a medium skillet. Add the onion and cook over moderately low heat, stirring, until softened and browned, about 20 minutes. Add a few tablespoons of water to the skillet to keep the onion from sticking. Transfer to a small bowl and add the olives, rosemary and a pinch each of salt and pepper. Let cool completely.

3. Lay the chicken, skin-side down, on a work surface and season with salt and pepper. Detach the skin from the meat but keep them together. Spread one-quarter of the filling on each breast, leaving a 1-inch border all around. Roll up the meat and wrap the skin around the meat to enclose it. Tie each roll in three places with cotton kitchen string.

4. Preheat the oven to 375°. Heat the oil in a large skillet until shimmering. Season the chicken with salt and cook over moderately high heat until browned all over, about 10 minutes. Transfer the chicken to a rimmed baking sheet and bake for about 10 minutes, or until an instant-read thermometer inserted in the center reaches 135°. Let the chicken rest for 5 minutes, then discard the string. Slice the chicken diagonally ½ inch thick.

5. Meanwhile, set the large skillet over high heat. Add the shallots and cook for 1 minute, scraping up any brown bits. Add the tomatoes and any accumulated chicken juices to the skillet and cook, stirring, just until heated through, about 4 minutes. Spoon the tomatoes onto individual plates and arrange the chicken on top.

MAKE AHEAD The rollatini can be prepared through Step 3 and refrigerated overnight. Let them return to room temperature before sautéing.

Chicken Couscous Salad

20 SERVINGS

- ¼ cup honey
- ¼ cup Dijon mustard
- ¾ cup plus 2 tablespoons olive oil
- 6 pounds skinless, boneless chicken-breast halves

Salt and freshly ground pepper

- 10 cups boiling water

Four 10-ounce boxes couscous

- ½ cup fresh lemon juice
- 1 tablespoon grated lemon zest
- 2 small onions, finely chopped
- 2 bunches watercress, chopped
- 1 cup shelled pistachios, toasted
- 1 cup sliced almonds, toasted
- 1 pound seedless grapes, halved

1. Preheat the oven to 450°. In a small bowl, combine the honey, mustard and the 2 tablespoons oil. Arrange the chicken on two large baking sheets and coat with the honey mustard. Season with salt and pepper. Bake for 20 minutes; remove from the oven. Baste with the juices and cover with aluminum foil.

2. In two large heatproof bowls, pour the boiling water over the couscous. Cover and let stand for 15 minutes. Transfer the couscous to a work surface and use two large forks to break it up; let cool. Gently rub the couscous into separate grains.

3. In a small bowl, combine the remaining ¾ cup of oil with the lemon juice, lemon zest, 2 tablespoons of salt and 2 teaspoons of pepper. Return the couscous to the two bowls and toss with the dressing. Add the remaining ingredients and toss well. Slice the chicken crosswise ½ inch thick. Serve the couscous on platters, topped with the chicken. *—Marcia Kiesel*

WINE 1995 Georges Duboeuf Vin de Pays de l'Ardèche Viognier from France

Chicken with Mustard-Seed and Onion Sauce

4 SERVINGS Q

Serve this speedy chicken dish with basmati rice and sautéed green beans.

- 5 tablespoons vegetable oil
- 2 tablespoons yellow mustard seeds
- 1 onion, thinly sliced
- 2 garlic cloves, minced
- 1½ teaspoons minced fresh ginger
- 1 teaspoon turmeric
- ½ teaspoon honey
- ⅛ teaspoon cayenne pepper
- 1 cup chicken stock or canned low-sodium broth
- ½ cup crème fraîche or heavy cream

Kosher salt and freshly ground black pepper

- 4 skinless, boneless chicken-breast halves

All-purpose flour, for dredging

- 1 tablespoon chopped flat-leaf parsley or cilantro

1. In a medium saucepan, warm 2 tablespoons of the oil over moderate heat. Add the mustard seeds and cover

Chicken with Mustard-Seed and Onion Sauce

the pan. When the seeds begin to pop, remove the pan from the heat and wait until the popping has stopped, about 30 seconds. Uncover the pan; the seeds will be dark gray.

2. Return the pan to the heat and add the onion. Cook the onion over moderate heat, stirring, until softened but not browned, about 5 minutes. Add the garlic, ginger, turmeric, honey and cayenne and cook, stirring, until fragrant, about 3 minutes. Add the chicken stock and boil over high heat until reduced by half, about 5 minutes. Add the crème fraîche and cook over moderately high heat, stirring occasionally, until the sauce lightly coats the back of a spoon, about

4 minutes. Season the sauce with salt and black pepper.

3. Remove the tender from each piece of chicken. Cut the breasts in half crosswise and lightly pound to an even thickness. Season them with salt and black pepper, then dredge lightly in flour, shaking off the excess.

4. In a large skillet, heat the remaining 3 tablespoons of oil. Add the chicken in batches and brown over moderately high heat, about 2 minutes per side. Arrange the chicken on plates or a platter. Spoon the sauce over the top of the chicken and sprinkle with the parsley. Serve at once.   *–Michael Romano*

MAKE AHEAD The sauce can be refrigerated for up to two days. Bring it to room temperature and reheat before serving.

WINE 1994 Charles Schleret Gewürztraminer Herrenweg. This refreshing white balances the creamy sauce while supporting the spicy cayenne and musky turmeric flavors.

Chicken with Olives, Raisins and Onions

12 SERVINGS

Mirroring the history of Spain, this dish shows Jewish, Arab and Spanish influences. Serve it with fried polenta or rice.

- 6 kosher chicken-breast halves on the bone
- 6 whole kosher chicken legs

Kosher salt and freshly ground pepper

- ⅓ cup pure olive oil
- 1½ cups dry kosher white wine
- ⅓ cup sherry vinegar
- 1½ pounds cippolini onions, peeled but with root ends kept intact
- 1¼ pounds green olives, preferably picholine, pitted
- 1½ cups golden raisins (about 7 ounces)
- 4 to 6 cups kosher chicken stock or canned low-sodium broth
- 4 whole cloves

ABOVE: **Chicken with Olives, Raisins and Onions, with Zucchini with Spicy Harissa (p. 319).**
TOP: **Chicken Couscous Salad (p. 187).**

- 4 imported bay leaves

Two 2½-inch-long cinnamon sticks

- ½ tablespoon whole black peppercorns
- ¾ cup pine nuts (4½ ounces)

1. Season the chicken pieces with salt and pepper. In a very large enameled cast-iron casserole, warm the oil. Add the chicken pieces to the casserole in batches and brown them over high heat, about 5 minutes per side. Remove the chicken pieces to a platter and discard the oil from the casserole. Add the wine and vinegar and boil over high heat, stirring, until reduced by half, about 6 minutes.

2. Return the chicken to the casserole and add the onions, olives, raisins and enough stock to cover the chicken by two-thirds. Tie the cloves, bay leaves, cinnamon sticks and peppercorns in cheesecloth and add them to the casserole. Bring to a simmer over moderately high heat and cover. Cook over very low heat until the chicken and onions are tender, 1 to 1½ hours. Skim off the fat. If the sauce seems thin, remove the solids and boil it down until it is full-flavored. Return the solids to the casserole and season the sauce with salt and pepper.

3. In a small skillet, toast the pine nuts over moderately low heat until they are lightly browned, 3 to 4 minutes.

---

menu

Casablanca Salad (p. 66)

1995 DORO PRINCIC
PINOT GRIGIO

———

Moroccan-Style Couscous (p. 108)

**Savory Vegetable and
Lamb Stew (p. 259)**

**Parsley and Garlic
Meatballs (p. 249)**

**Lemon Chicken with
Golden Raisins (p. 190)**

**Roasted Sweet Peppers in
Tomato Sauce (p. 320)**

1994 SHAFER MERLOT

———

**Oranges in Champagne
Syrup (p. 389)**

Sprinkle the chicken with the pine nuts and serve.   *–Peter Hoffman*
MAKE AHEAD Let the stew cool, then refrigerate overnight. Skim off the fat before bringing to room temperature and rewarming over low heat. Sprinkle with the pine nuts and serve.

Lemon Chicken with Golden Raisins

10 SERVINGS

This succulent chicken dish is best made with thin-skinned lemons, which have less bitter white pith than their thick-skinned counterparts. Thin-skinned lemons are smooth and soft; when you give them a light squeeze you should be able to feel the pulp inside.

- ½ **cup golden raisins**
- ½ **cup warm water**
- 2 **tablespoons vegetable oil**
- 6 **medium skinless, boneless chicken-breast halves**
- 6 **medium skinless chicken thighs**
- **Salt and freshly ground pepper**
- 1 **large white onion, halved lengthwise and thinly sliced crosswise**
- 1½ **small thin-skinned lemons, thinly sliced crosswise**
- ¼ **teaspoon ground cumin**
- 2 **cups chicken stock or canned low-sodium broth**

I. In a small bowl, soak the raisins in the water until softened, about 20 minutes; drain the raisins.

2. Heat 1 tablespoon of the oil in a large nonstick skillet. Season the chicken on both sides with salt and pepper and add the breasts to the skillet. Cook over moderately high heat until golden on the bottom, about 5 minutes. Turn the breasts and cook until golden on the other side, about 4 minutes longer; transfer to a plate. Heat ½ tablespoon of the oil in the skillet and repeat the process with the thighs.

3. Heat the remaining ½ tablespoon of oil in the skillet. Add the onion and sauté over moderately high heat until translucent, about 6 minutes. Transfer to a bowl.

4. Arrange the thighs in the middle of the skillet and the breasts around the side. Slip the lemon slices, sautéed onion and raisins between the chicken pieces and sprinkle with the cumin. Pour the chicken stock into the skillet and bring to a simmer over moderately high heat. Cover and simmer until the breasts are cooked through, about 10 minutes. Transfer the breasts to a large deep platter and cover with aluminum foil. Continue simmering the thighs, turning once, until cooked through, about 10 minutes longer. Add the thighs to the platter and surround the chicken with the lemon slices. Pour the sauce over the chicken and serve.   *–Michel Benasra*
MAKE AHEAD The cooked chicken can be refrigerated overnight. Rewarm in a 325° oven.

New Delhi Curried Chicken

6 SERVINGS

A lavish use of spices is the heart and soul of Indian cooking. This fragrant chicken dish is sweet, sour and spicy all at once. We always serve it with the zesty tomato relish.

- 2 **tablespoons unsalted butter**
- 6 **large mushrooms, thinly sliced**
- 6 **medium shallots, minced**
- ¾ **cup coarsely chopped cilantro stems and leaves plus ¼ cup leaves**
- 4 **jalapeño peppers, stemmed and coarsely chopped (with seeds)**
- 1 **tablespoon plus 1 teaspoon ground cumin**
- 2 **cups chicken stock or canned low-sodium broth**
- 1 **cup heavy cream**
- 2 **pounds boneless chicken breasts and thighs, with skin**

Salt and freshly ground pepper

2 tablespoons vegetable oil

1 tablespoon fresh lime juice

6 scallions

3 large egg yolks

3 tablespoons light brown sugar

¼ cup red-wine vinegar

Spicy Tomato Relish (recipe follows)

Plain yogurt, for serving

I. Melt the butter in a medium skillet. Add the mushrooms and shallots and cook over moderate heat until soft and lightly golden, about 8 minutes. Add the chopped cilantro, jalapeños and cumin, reduce the heat to moderately low and cook for 5 minutes. Add the stock, raise the heat to high and simmer until the liquid is reduced by half. Add the cream and bring to a boil. Remove from the heat and, working in batches, puree the sauce in a blender or food processor. Strain the sauce and return it to the skillet.

2. Light a grill or preheat the broiler. Season the chicken breasts and thighs lightly with salt and pepper. Mix the oil and lime juice in a small bowl and brush all over the chicken pieces and the scallions. Grill or broil the chicken pieces, skin-side down, until they are browned and cooked through, about 6 minutes per side for thighs and 5 minutes per side for breasts. During the last 2 minutes, grill or broil the scallions until tender and lightly charred. Transfer the chicken pieces and the scallions to a platter; keep warm.

3. Reheat the sauce. In a bowl, mix the egg yolks, sugar and vinegar. Gradually whisk 1 cup of the sauce into the egg mixture. Pour the egg mixture back into the skillet and stir over low heat until it is thickened and smooth, 2 to 3 minutes; don't let the sauce boil. Spoon the sauce over the chicken pieces and garnish with the scallions and cilantro leaves. Serve the chicken with the relish and yogurt.

SPICY TOMATO RELISH

MAKES ABOUT 3 CUPS

Use the leftovers of this vibrant relish on sandwiches or alongside roasted meat. A nicely wrapped jar also makes a great gift.

½ cup distilled white vinegar

2½ tablespoons light brown sugar

2¼ teaspoons kosher salt

1¼ pounds ripe plum tomatoes—peeled, seeded and cut into ¾-inch dice

12 scallions, white and tender green, thinly sliced diagonally

5 serrano chiles, stemmed and quartered lengthwise (with seeds)

New Delhi Curried Chicken

One 1½-inch piece of fresh ginger, finely julienned

3 garlic cloves, thinly sliced

1 tablespoon black or yellow mustard seeds

1 tablespoon cumin seeds

2 teaspoons cracked black peppercorns

1½ teaspoons crushed red pepper

½ teaspoon ground turmeric

½ cup olive oil

I. In a stainless-steel saucepan, heat the vinegar, sugar and salt, stirring constantly just until dissolved. Remove from

Spicy Tomato Relish

the heat. In a medium bowl, combine the tomatoes, scallions and serranos.

2. On a plate, arrange the ginger, garlic, mustard seeds, cumin, peppercorns, crushed red pepper and turmeric. In a medium saucepan, heat the oil until almost smoking. Add the ginger, garlic and spices all at once and stir over moderate heat until fragrant, about 1 minute. Remove from the heat and add the vinegar mixture. Add the dressing to the tomatoes and scallions and let cool. Cover with plastic wrap and refrigerate for at least 2 hours or up to 4 days. –*Susan Feniger and Mary Sue Milliken*

WINE 1994 Australian Shiraz, such as Lindemans or Penfolds

Chicken Kebabs

6 TO 8 SERVINGS

Serve these kebabs with Chelo (p. 307) or plain rice.

- 2 **pounds boneless chicken legs or breasts, well trimmed**
- 1 **cup plain yogurt**
- ⅛ **teaspoon saffron threads, crushed and dissolved in 2 tablespoons water (optional)**

---

heat relief

When your mouth is on fire, reach for neutral foods, such as corn tortillas or plainly prepared potatoes; cooling dips, such as cucumber raita; or a glass of milk. Cold beer or water lowers the surface temperature of your tongue but spreads the burning chile oil around your mouth.

- 1 **tablespoon minced garlic**
- 1 **tablespoon crushed dried mint**
- ½ **teaspoon freshly ground pepper**
- ½ **teaspoon salt**

1. Cut the chicken into 1-inch pieces. Combine all the remaining ingredients in a bowl. Add the chicken and stir to coat. Cover and refrigerate for 3 to 24 hours.

2. Light a charcoal grill or preheat the broiler. Loosely thread the chicken on metal skewers. Grill or broil 5 to 6 inches from the heat for about 10 minutes, turning as necessary for even cooking. Serve hot or room-temperature. –*Jeffrey Alford and Naomi Duguid*

Chicken Thighs with Malt Vinegar

Dark-meat chicken gains by being cooked with vinegar, which cuts some of the richness. I like to add strong aromatic elements—carrot, celery, onion and herbs—to keep the vinegar and wine in balance. Serve with fresh buttered noodles or steamed Yukon Gold potatoes.

4 SERVINGS

- 2 **tablespoons vegetable oil**
- 8 **chicken thighs (about 3 pounds)**
- **Salt and freshly ground pepper**
- 1 **carrot, cut into ¼-inch dice**
- 1 **celery rib, cut into ¼-inch dice**
- 1 **small onion, cut into ¼-inch dice**
- ⅓ **cup malt vinegar**
- ⅓ **cup dry white wine**
- 1 **cup chicken stock or canned low-sodium broth**
- 2 **teaspoons dried thyme**

- 2 **bay leaves**
- **Pinch of allspice**
- 2 **tablespoons unsalted butter**
- 2 **tablespoons finely chopped flat-leaf parsley**

1. In a large heavy stainless-steel skillet, heat the oil. Season the chicken thighs with salt and pepper. Add to the skillet skin-side down and cook over moderately high heat, turning once, until browned, about 15 minutes; transfer to a plate.

2. Add the carrot, celery and onion to the skillet and cook over moderate heat, stirring, until barely soft, about 3 minutes. Add the vinegar and wine and boil until nearly evaporated, scraping up the brown bits from the bottom of the skillet, about 1 minute. Return the chicken to the skillet and add the stock, thyme, bay leaves and allspice. Cover tightly and simmer gently over low heat until tender, about 30 minutes. Transfer the chicken and vegetables to a platter, cover and keep warm. Discard the bay leaves.

3. Skim the fat from the liquid in the skillet, then boil the juices until reduced to ½ cup. Remove the skillet from the heat and swirl in the butter until blended. Add the parsley and season with salt and pepper. Pour the sauce over the chicken and serve. –*Michael Roberts*

WINE 1995 Ruffino Orvieto Classico

Chicken Chili

4 SERVINGS **Q**

Wonderfully homey and flavorful, this chicken chili is lower in fat than the beef version and just as delicious.

- 2 **tablespoons canola oil**
- 1 **medium onion, chopped**
- 2 **large garlic cloves, minced**
- 1 **pound boneless, skinless chicken thighs, cut into thin strips**
- 4 **teaspoons pure chili powder**
- 1 **tablespoon ground cumin**
- 2 **teaspoons dried oregano**
- 3 **cups chicken stock or canned low-sodium broth**

Chicken Chili

1½ cups canned chopped tomatoes
  with their juice

2 jalapeño peppers, seeds and ribs
  removed, chopped

Salt and freshly ground pepper

One 15-ounce can pinto or red beans,
  drained and rinsed

One 15-ounce can black beans,
  drained and rinsed

⅓ cup chopped cilantro (optional)

Lime wedges, for serving

Hot sauce, for serving

I. In a large stainless-steel saucepan, heat the oil. Add the onion and garlic and cook over moderately low heat until barely tender. Add the chicken and cook over moderate heat until it is no longer pink, about 3 minutes. Stir in the chili powder, cumin and oregano. Add the stock, tomatoes with their juice and

jalapeños. Season with salt and pepper. Cover, bring to a boil and simmer over low heat for 15 minutes.

2. Stir in the beans. Simmer, uncovered, over moderately low heat until thickened, about 15 minutes longer. Serve with the cilantro; pass lime wedges and hot sauce on the side. *–Laura Byrne Russell*

WINE 1993 Ramsay Sangiovese or 1995 Vietti Dolcetto

CHAPTER 9 other birds

Hot and Tart Turkey (p. 204)

197 Cornish Hens with Nutty Brown-Rice Stuffing

197 Grilled Cornish Hens with Warm Potato-and-Portobello Salad

198 Roasted Guinea Hen with Red-Wine Thyme Sauce

198 Roasted Turkey with Figs and Muscat Gravy

203 Turkey and Mushroom Potpie

204 Turkey Chili Potpie with Corn-Bread Crust

204 Turkey and Oyster Potpie with Biscuit Topping

204 Hot and Tart Turkey

206 Pinot-Noir-Glazed Squabs with Roasted Vegetables

207 Spinach-Stuffed Quail with Apple Frisée Salad

207 Roast Quail with Hazelnuts and Port

209 White-Wing-Dove-Style Grilled Quail

210 Grilled Duck Breasts with Apricot Mustard

210 Pinot-Noir-Braised Duck Legs

210 Duck-Leg Stew with Lentils and Green Olives

Cornish Hens with Nutty Brown-Rice Stuffing

Cornish Hens with Nutty Brown-Rice Stuffing

8 SERVINGS

10 cups water

2⅔ cups converted brown rice (about 18 ounces)

Kosher salt

2 cups assorted unsalted nuts, such as walnuts, pine nuts and unskinned hazelnuts

1 cup raisins

3½ cups chicken stock or canned low-sodium broth

¼ cup finely chopped flat-leaf parsley

1 teaspoon dried thyme

½ teaspoon dried rosemary

Freshly ground pepper

Eight 1-pound Cornish hens, rinsed well and patted dry

1 stick (4 ounces) unsalted butter, melted

1. In a medium saucepan, bring 8 cups of the water to a boil. Stir in the rice and 1 teaspoon salt. Cook over moderately high heat, stirring occasionally, until tender but still slightly firm, about 25 minutes. Drain the rice; transfer to a large bowl.

2. Preheat the oven to 350°. Spread the nuts on a baking sheet and toast for about 7 minutes, or until lightly browned and fragrant. Transfer to a large plate to cool. If using hazelnuts, rub them vigorously in a kitchen towel to remove the skins. Coarsely chop large nuts, such as hazelnuts and walnuts. Add the nuts to the rice along with the raisins, 1½ cups of the stock, the parsley, thyme and rosemary. Season with salt and pepper.

3. Preheat the oven to 475°. Stuff each hen with 1 cup of the rice stuffing. Tie the legs together with cotton kitchen string. Wrap the remaining stuffing in aluminum foil. Set the hens on racks in two large roasting pans. Brush with the butter; season with salt and pepper. Roast in the upper and lower thirds of the oven for 10 minutes. Switch the pans. Baste the hens with ½ cup stock; roast 10 minutes more.

4. Reduce the oven temperature to 350°, baste the hens with another ½ cup of the stock and roast for about 25 minutes, until the birds are pale brown; baste occasionally. Raise the oven temperature to 400°. Switch the pans and baste the hens with the remaining 1 cup stock. Roast for about 30 more minutes, basting a few times, until the hens are richly browned and the temperature of the inner thighs registers 180° on an instant-read thermometer. Add water to the pans if the liquid evaporates during cooking. During the last 25 minutes of cooking, add the reserved stuffing to the oven and cook until heated through.

5. Transfer the hens to a large platter and cover loosely with aluminum foil. Spoon the reserved stuffing into a bowl and keep warm. Set each roasting pan over two burners over moderately high heat and add 1 cup of the remaining water to each. Boil the liquid, scraping up the brown bits, until flavorful, about 4 minutes. Strain the pan juices into a narrow measuring cup or bowl and skim the fat from the surface. Season with salt and pepper.

6. Pour the pan juices into a gravy boat. Cut the strings from the hens and serve, passing the pan juices and extra stuffing at the table. —Mireille Guiliano

WINE For contrasting fruitiness as well as harmony, try the 1985 Veuve Clicquot Rosé Réserve.

Grilled Cornish Hens with Warm Potato-and-Portobello Salad

4 SERVINGS Q

We prefer to use extra-virgin olive oil in the salad, but if the one on your shelf is so powerful that it would overwhelm the potatoes, mix it half and half with a less exalted olive oil.

1¾ pounds Yukon Gold potatoes

1½ pounds portobello mushrooms, stems removed

¼ cup vegetable oil

Salt and freshly ground pepper

2 Cornish hens (about 1¼ pounds each), halved lengthwise, backbones removed

½ cup chopped flat-leaf parsley

⅓ cup olive oil

2 garlic cloves, minced

1 tablespoon white-wine vinegar

1. Put the potatoes in a medium saucepan of salted water. Bring to a boil, reduce the heat and cook the potatoes until tender, 25 to 30 minutes. Drain the potatoes.

2. Meanwhile, light a grill or preheat the oven to 500°. Brush the portobello mushrooms with 2 tablespoons of the vegetable oil and sprinkle with ¼ teaspoon of salt and ¼ teaspoon of pepper. Grill the mushrooms or roast them

menu

Osetra caviar

Niçoise olives

Parmigiano-Reggiano

Oyster and Potato Stew with Crisp Bacon (p. 125)

1988 VEUVE CLICQUOT LA GRANDE DAME CHAMPAGNE

Salmon with Ginger and Lime (p. 45)

1988 VEUVE CLICQUOT ROSÉ RÉSERVE CHAMPAGNE

Cornish Hens with Nutty Brown-Rice Stuffing (p. 197)

1985 VEUVE CLICQUOT ROSÉ RÉSERVE CHAMPAGNE

Pear and Almond Tart (p. 364)

VEUVE CLICQUOT DEMI-SEC CHAMPAGNE

on a baking sheet, turning once, for about 15 minutes, or until they are browned and cooked through.

3. Brush the Cornish hens with the remaining 2 tablespoons of vegetable oil and sprinkle them with ½ teaspoon of salt and ¼ teaspoon of pepper. Grill the hens over moderate heat or roast them in the oven on a large rimmed baking sheet for 12 minutes. Turn and cook the hens for about 12 minutes longer, or until the juices run clear when a thigh is pierced.

4. Peel the potatoes. Slice the potatoes and mushrooms ¼ inch thick and transfer them to a large bowl. Add the parsley, olive oil, garlic and vinegar and season the mixture with salt and pepper. Toss gently but thoroughly. Mound the potato salad on plates and top each serving of potatoes with one of the grilled Cornish-hen halves. *–Susan Lantzius Rich*
WINE The clean taste of a Chardonnay-based Mâcon-Villages from Burgundy will highlight the grilled Cornish hens and potatoes. Try the 1996 from Louis Jadot.

Grilled Cornish Hens with Warm Potato-and-Portobello Salad

Roasted Guinea Hen with Red-Wine Thyme Sauce

10 SERVINGS

Succulent guinea-hen breasts are more flavorful than chicken. If you can't find them at a specialty-food store, mail-order them from D'Artagnan (800-327-8246)–or substitute chicken breasts.

- 3 tablespoons olive oil
- 10 guinea-hen breast halves, preferably with wings attached
- Salt and freshly ground pepper
- 10 thin pancetta slices, cut into ¼-inch strips
- 3 pounds small mushrooms, stemmed
- 2 large shallots, minced
- 2 cups red wine
- ⅔ pound baby carrots, trimmed
- 3 cups chicken stock or canned low-sodium broth
- 1 tablespoon finely chopped thyme
- 2 cups fresh or frozen peas
- 5 tablespoons unsalted butter

I. Divide the oil between two large stainless-steel skillets and heat. Season the guinea-hen breasts on both sides with salt and pepper. Add three breast halves to each skillet, skin-side down. Cook over high heat until browned, about 5 minutes. Turn and cook until the other side is browned, about 2 minutes; transfer to a platter. Brown the remaining breasts in the two skillets.

2. Add the pancetta to the skillets. Cook over low heat, stirring, until lightly browned, about 4 minutes. Using a slotted spoon, transfer the pancetta to a small plate. Divide the mushrooms between the skillets; season with salt and pepper. Raise the heat to moderately high and cook, stirring, until the mushrooms are browned and any exuded liquid has evaporated, about 8 minutes. Transfer to a large plate.

3. Return the pancetta to the skillets; add the shallots. Cook over moderately high heat, stirring, until the shallots are beginning to soften, about 3 minutes. Add 1 cup of wine to each skillet and boil until almost evaporated, about 8 minutes. Scrape the mixture from the skillets into a large, heavy roasting pan and add the mushrooms.

4. Preheat the oven to 450°. Set the roasting pan over two burners over moderately high heat. Add the carrots, chicken stock and thyme and bring to a simmer. Arrange the guinea hens on top, skin-side up. Transfer to the oven and roast for about 12 minutes, or until the breasts are just cooked through.

5. Transfer the breasts to the platter and cover with aluminum foil to keep warm. Set the roasting pan over two burners over high heat, add the peas and boil until the peas are tender and the cooking juices are reduced to 1½ cups, about 8 minutes. Pour in any accumulated juices from the hens. Remove the pan from the heat, stir in the butter and season with salt and pepper. To serve, set the guinea-hen breasts on large plates and spoon some of the sauce over and around each one. *–Maria Helm*
MAKE AHEAD The hens and mushrooms can be cooked through Step 3 and refrigerated separately overnight.
WINE This dish has its roots in classic Burgundian cuisine; thus it merits a Pinot Noir in the rich Burgundian style, such as the 1995 Robert Sinskey Vineyards Los Carneros of Napa Valley Pinot Noir.

Roasted Turkey with Figs and Muscat Gravy

20 SERVINGS

The turkey, stuffing and gravy all rely on the characteristic flavor of Muscat.

MUSCAT BUTTER

- 1 cup Muscat
- 2 sage leaves
- 1 Scotch bonnet chile, halved
- Salt
- 1 stick (4 ounces) unsalted butter, at room temperature

Roasted Guinea Hen with Red-Wine Thyme Sauce

Roasted Turkey with Figs and Muscat Gravy, with Brussels Sprouts with Walnuts, Balsamic Vinegar and Mint (p. 324).

TURKEY

One 20-pound turkey at room
    temperature, neck and giblets
    reserved for stock

Salt and freshly ground pepper

Anadama Bread and Fig Stuffing
    with Celery and Cracklings
    (recipe follows)

10 boiling onions, peeled and halved
    lengthwise

20 moist and plump dried black
    Mission figs, steeped in 2 cups of
    Muscat for 10 minutes

Thyme sprigs

Sage leaves

1 stick (4 ounces) unsalted butter,
    melted

4 fresh fig or grape leaves or rinsed
    brined grape leaves

¾ cup all-purpose flour

3 cups Rich Turkey Stock, plus
    reserved giblets (recipe follows)

1 tablespoon fresh lemon juice

I. MAKE THE MUSCAT BUTTER:
In a small saucepan, simmer the Muscat with the sage leaves, chile and a large pinch of salt until reduced to ⅓ cup, about 8 minutes. Remove from the heat and strain into a heatproof bowl. Let cool slightly, then whisk in the butter. Fill an injector with the Muscat butter.

2. MAKE THE TURKEY: Preheat the oven to 325°. Wipe the turkey completely dry and season it well inside and out with salt and pepper. Fill the central cavity with about 6 cups of the stuffing; seal the cavity with bamboo skewers. Fill the neck cavity with about 3 cups of the stuffing, cover with the skin and skewer shut. Put the remaining stuffing in a large baking dish and set aside.

3. Inject the Muscat butter deep into the thighs and breast of the turkey. Put the bird in a large roasting bag and set it in a large roasting pan. Scatter the onions around the turkey in the bag and add the steeped figs and their liquid, the thyme and sage. Pour 6 tablespoons

menu

Crystal-Coated Walnuts (p. 404)

Oysters and clams on the half-shell
with Mango Mignonette Sauce (p. 333)

Japanese Eel Canapés with
Horseradish Crème Fraîche (p. 18)

DOMAINE CARNEROS BRUT OR
MUMM CUVÉE NAPA

Lobster with Nutmeg Vinaigrette
and Chestnut Puree (p. 42)

Curried Pumpkin Soup
with Spicy Lentil Crisps (p. 77)

Roasted Turkey with Figs and
Muscat Gravy (p. 198)

Anadama Bread and Fig Stuffing
with Celery and Cracklings (p. 202)

Roasted Venison with
Beach-Plum Sauce (p. 260)

Roasted Cod with
Bacon-and-Spinach Stuffing (p. 139)

Brussels Sprouts with Walnuts,
Balsamic Vinegar and Mint (p. 324)

Mashed Turnips and Potatoes (p. 312)

Maple-Glazed Sweet Potatoes
and Apples (p. 313)

1997 GEORGES DUBOEUF
BEAUJOLAIS NOUVEAU OR
1997 BERINGER NOUVEAU GAMAY BEAUJOLAIS

Fennel and Watercress Salad with
Cranberries and Pecans (p. 52)

Pumpkin and Apple Tart
with Ginger (p. 366)

Pear and Hazelnut Tart (p. 364)

Pumpkin Caramel
Pudding Cakes (p. 349)

1995 WASHINGTON HILLS OR
1995 CHATEAU STE. MICHELLE HORSE HEAVEN VINEYARD
LATE-HARVEST RIESLING

of the melted butter over the turkey breast. Dip the fig leaves in the remaining 2 tablespoons melted butter and press them onto the bird. Seal the bag.

4. Roast the turkey for about 3 hours, or until it is just cooked through. About 25 minutes before the turkey is done, bake the dish of stuffing until heated through.

5. Remove the turkey from the oven. Open the bag carefully; there will be a lot of accumulated juices in it. Transfer the turkey, onions and figs to a platter, cover loosely with aluminum foil and keep warm.

6. Pour all of the pan juices into a large saucepan and skim off the fat. Bring to a boil over moderately high heat. Put the flour in a medium bowl and gradually whisk in the Rich Turkey Stock until smooth. Whisk this slurry into the juices in the saucepan and simmer, whisking frequently, until thickened. Reduce the heat to low and simmer the gravy until flavorful, about 10 minutes. Add the lemon juice and reserved giblets; season with salt and pepper. Carve the turkey at the table. Serve with the stuffing and gravy.

ANADAMA BREAD AND FIG STUFFING WITH CELERY AND CRACKLINGS

MAKES 24 CUPS

This hearty stuffing has a wonderful light molasses flavor with a little additional sweetness from the figs and the raisins in the bread. If you need to take a shortcut, you can use two pounds of cubed semolina bread, a cup of golden raisins and one-third cup of unsulphured molasses in place of the anadama bread.

- 2 loaves Corn and Semolina Anadama Bread (recipe follows), cut into ½-inch dice
- 3 pounds old-fashioned salt pork, sliced ½ inch thick
- 2 pounds onions, coarsely chopped
- 14 garlic cloves, chopped
- ¼ cup chopped herbs—a mix of thyme, rosemary and sage leaves
- 1½ pounds celery hearts, coarsely chopped
- ½ pound moist and plump dried black Mission figs
- 2 cups Muscat
- 2 tablespoons salt
- 1 tablespoon Bell's poultry seasoning
- 2 teaspoons freshly ground pepper
- 2 cups Rich Turkey Stock (recipe follows)
- 2 heaping cups chopped parsley

1. Preheat the oven to 375°. Spread the bread on two baking sheets. Toast in the oven for about 15 minutes, stirring occasionally, until dry. Transfer to a large bowl.

2. Rinse the salt pork and remove the rinds. Cut the salt pork into ½-inch dice and transfer to a large enameled cast-iron casserole. Cook over low heat until the fat has been rendered and the cracklings are golden and crisp, about 25 minutes. Drain the cracklings and add them to the bread in the bowl.

3. Pour off all but ⅔ cup of the fat from the casserole. Add the onions, garlic and herbs along with half of the celery hearts. Cook over moderately low heat, stirring occasionally, until the vegetables are softened, about 15 minutes. Add to the bread in the bowl.

4. In a medium saucepan, simmer the figs in the Muscat over low heat until softened, about 8 minutes. Pour the figs and Muscat over the bread and add the salt, poultry seasoning and pepper. Add the raw celery hearts, turkey stock and parsley and toss lightly until thoroughly mixed. Taste for seasoning.

CORN AND SEMOLINA ANADAMA BREAD

MAKES TWO 8½-BY-4½-INCH LOAVES

- 2 cups lukewarm water
- ⅔ cup molasses
- 2 packages active dry yeast
- 5 to 6 cups bread flour
- ½ cup cornmeal
- ½ cup semolina
- 1 tablespoon salt
- 1 cup golden raisins
- 4 tablespoons unsalted butter, softened

1. In a medium bowl, combine the water and molasses. Add the yeast and let stand until dissolved, about 10 minutes.

2. In a large bowl, sift 5 cups of the bread flour with the cornmeal, semolina and salt. Add the raisins and butter, then add the yeast mixture and blend well. Transfer the dough to a lightly floured surface and knead, adding up to one more cup of the bread flour to make a moist but not sticky dough. Continue kneading for a few minutes until the dough is smooth and elastic. Transfer the dough to a lightly buttered bowl, cover with plastic wrap and let rise until doubled in bulk, about 1¼ hours.

3. Punch the dough down and divide it in half. Form into two loose rectangular loaves and transfer to two buttered 8½-by-4½-inch loaf pans. Let rise until doubled in bulk, about 1 hour.

4. Preheat the oven to 375°. Bake the loaves for about 40 minutes, or until golden brown on top. Let cool in the pans for 5 minutes, then turn out onto a rack to cool completely. —*Lydia Shire*

MAKE AHEAD The bread can be kept, tightly wrapped and frozen, up to one month.

RICH TURKEY STOCK

MAKES ABOUT 7 CUPS

- 5 pounds turkey parts, such as wings, necks and drumsticks
- 9 cups water
- Reserved turkey neck and giblets (except the liver)
- 1 large onion, thickly sliced
- 1 large carrot, thickly sliced
- 1 large celery rib, thickly sliced
- 2 garlic cloves, sliced

1 teaspoon kosher salt

Freshly ground pepper

I. Preheat the oven to 400°. Put the turkey parts in a flameproof roasting pan and roast for about 1 hour, turning occasionally, until well browned. Transfer the turkey parts to a large pot.

2. Set the roasting pan over two burners. Add 1 cup of the water and boil over moderately high heat, scraping up the brown bits from the bottom of the pan. Add the liquid to the pot.

3. Add the turkey neck and giblets to the pot along with the onion, carrot, celery, garlic, salt, generous pinches of pepper and the remaining 8 cups of water. Bring to a boil over high heat. Reduce the heat to moderately low and simmer, partially covered, until the meat is falling off the bones and the gizzard is very tender, about 2 hours.

4. Strain the stock. Finely dice the gizzard and heart and reserve for the gravy. Skim the fat from the stock before using.

MAKE AHEAD The stock and giblets can be refrigerated separately for up to two days; any leftover stock can be frozen for up to one month.

Turkey and Mushroom Potpie

8 SERVINGS

4 cups turkey stock, chicken stock or canned low-sodium chicken broth

1 pound large Yukon Gold potatoes, peeled and cut into 1/3-inch dice

1 teaspoon dried thyme

Salt

3 tablespoons unsalted butter

2½ tablespoons vegetable oil

1 pound white mushrooms, quartered

Freshly ground pepper

1 pound fresh shiitake mushrooms, stemmed and thinly sliced

1 large onion, coarsely chopped

4 ounces lean prosciutto, finely chopped

1/3 cup all-purpose flour blended with 1/3 cup water

1 pound cooked turkey, cut or torn into 3/4-inch pieces

1/3 cup coarsely chopped parsley

1 large sheet of thawed frozen puff pastry (8½ to 14 ounces)

1 large egg, lightly beaten

I. Butter a 13-by-9-by-2-inch baking dish. In a saucepan, combine the turkey stock, potatoes, thyme and a large pinch of salt and bring to a boil over high heat. Reduce the heat to low, cover and simmer until the potatoes are tender, about 10 minutes.

2. Meanwhile, in a large skillet, melt 1 tablespoon of the butter in 1 tablespoon of the oil. Add the white mushrooms, season with salt and pepper and sauté over moderately high heat until the

mushrooms are golden, about 5 minutes. Transfer the mushrooms to a bowl. Repeat the process with one more tablespoon each of the butter and oil and the shiitakes. Add the shiitakes to the white mushrooms.

3. In the same skillet, melt the remaining 1 tablespoon of butter in the remaining ½ tablespoon of oil. Add the onion and the prosciutto and sauté over moderately high heat until the onion softens, about 5 minutes. Remove the skillet from the heat and add the mushroom mixture.

4. Strain the turkey stock into the skillet. Add the flour-and-water mixture and bring to a boil over moderate heat, stirring constantly. Add the turkey, potatoes and parsley to the skillet and season the mixture with salt and pepper. Spread the filling in the baking dish and let cool. ➤

Turkey and Mushroom Potpie

5. Preheat the oven to 400°. If necessary, roll out the puff pastry on a lightly floured surface to a 14-by-10-inch rectangle. Moisten the rim of the baking dish with water and cover the filling with the pastry dough, pressing the dough firmly against the rim of the baking dish; tuck the edges under. Make a few slits in the pastry and brush it with the beaten egg. Bake the potpie for 45 minutes to 1 hour, or until the top is golden. Let the potpie stand for 10 minutes before serving. *—Diana Sturgis*

WINE 1995 Bonterra Chardonnay

Turkey Chili Potpie with Corn-Bread Crust

8 SERVINGS

Always-appealing potpie becomes easy when covered with a corn-bread rather than a pastry crust.

- 1 large onion, cut into large pieces
- 5 garlic cloves, crushed
- 1 large red bell pepper, cut into large pieces
- 1 large green bell pepper, cut into large pieces
- ¼ cup plus 3 tablespoons vegetable oil
- ¼ cup pure hot chile powder
- One 35-ounce can whole peeled tomatoes, coarsely chopped, with their juices
- 3 teaspoons salt
- 1¼ pounds cooked turkey, cut or torn into ¾-inch pieces
- One 19-ounce can black beans, drained and rinsed
- ⅓ cup finely chopped cilantro
- 1 cup all-purpose flour
- 1 cup yellow cornmeal
- 1 tablespoon sugar
- 2 teaspoons baking powder
- 1 cup milk
- 2 large eggs

I. Preheat the oven to 400°. Butter a 13-by-9-by-2-inch baking dish. In a food processor, finely chop the onion and garlic; transfer to a bowl. Finely chop the bell peppers in the processor.

2. Heat the ¼ cup of oil in a large heavy skillet. Add the onion, garlic and chile powder and cook over high heat, stirring, until softened, about 5 minutes. Add the chopped bell peppers and cook, stirring, until slightly softened, about 5 minutes. Stir in the tomatoes with their juices and 2 teaspoons of the salt and cook for 10 minutes. Add the turkey, black beans and cilantro and spread in the prepared baking dish.

3. In a bowl, sift together the flour, cornmeal, sugar, baking powder and the remaining 1 teaspoon of salt. In another bowl, whisk the milk, eggs and the remaining 3 tablespoons of oil. Stir the egg mixture into the dry ingredients and spoon over the filling; the topping will spread as it bakes. Set the dish on a baking sheet. Bake for about 35 minutes, or until the crust is golden. Let stand 10 minutes before serving. *—Diana Sturgis*

WINE 1996 Morgan Sauvignon Blanc

Turkey and Oyster Potpie with Biscuit Topping

8 SERVINGS

- 3 tablespoons unsalted butter
- 2 medium leeks, white and tender green, thinly sliced
- 2 large celery ribs, finely chopped
- About 1½ cups turkey stock, chicken stock or canned low-sodium chicken broth
- 3 dozen shucked oysters, liquor reserved separately
- 2 cups plus 3 tablespoons all-purpose flour
- 1 pound cooked turkey, cut or torn into ¾-inch pieces
- ½ cup heavy cream
- ¼ cup coarsely chopped parsley
- Salt and freshly ground pepper
- 1 tablespoon baking powder
- 4 tablespoons cold unsalted butter, cut into bits
- ¼ cup freshly grated Parmesan
- ⅔ cup milk
- ½ cup heavy cream

I. Preheat the oven to 450°. Melt the butter in a large skillet. Add the leeks and the celery and cook over moderate heat, stirring, until the vegetables are softened, about 10 minutes. In a measuring cup, add enough turkey stock to the oyster liquor to make 2 cups.

2. Stir 3 tablespoons of the flour into the leek mixture and cook for 1 minute. Stir in the turkey-stock mixture and bring to a simmer. Add the turkey, cream and parsley and season with salt and pepper. Butter a 12-by-8-by-2-inch baking dish and spread the filling in it. Arrange the oysters on top.

3. In a large bowl, stir together the remaining 2 cups flour, the baking powder and ¼ teaspoon salt. Quickly rub in the butter with your fingertips. Stir in half of the Parmesan cheese. Mix the milk and cream and gently stir this liquid into the dry ingredients until just combined.

4. Drop rounded teaspoons of the biscuit topping onto the oysters and filling; the topping will spread as it bakes. Sprinkle with the remaining cheese, set the dish on a baking sheet and cook the potpie for about 30 minutes, or until the topping is golden and crusty. Let the potpie stand for 10 minutes before serving. *—Diana Sturgis*

WINE 1996 Lucien Albrecht Riesling

Hot and Tart Turkey

2 SERVINGS **L**

This recipe is Sichuan in concept, but without the excessive oiliness that often characterizes the food of China's western provinces. It's good served over rice.

- 1 cup chicken stock
- 3 tablespoons ketchup
- 2 teaspoons plus 1 tablespoon Shao-Hsing wine or dry sherry
- 2 teaspoons cornstarch
- 1½ teaspoons sugar

Hot and Tart Turkey

1½ teaspoons white vinegar

½ teaspoon salt

Freshly ground white pepper

6 ounces turkey cutlets, cut into
2-by-1-inch strips

1 teaspoon Sichuan Peppercorn Oil
(recipe follows)

1½ teaspoons minced garlic

1 teaspoon minced ginger

6 scallions, white parts only,
sliced diagonally ¼ inch
thick

2 to 3 Thai chiles, thinly sliced (with
seeds)

2 celery ribs, cut into 2-by-¼-inch
matchstick strips

1 medium cucumber—peeled,
seeded and cut into 2-by-¼-inch
matchstick strips

½ medium red bell pepper, cut
into 2-by-¼-inch matchstick
strips

1. Combine ¼ cup of the chicken stock, the ketchup, the 2 teaspoons wine, the cornstarch, sugar, vinegar, ¼ teaspoon salt and white pepper to taste in a medium bowl.

2. Add the remaining ¾ cup chicken stock to a wok and bring to a boil over high heat. Add the turkey and cook, stirring, until just opaque, about 2 minutes. Drain the turkey and set aside 1 tablespoon of the stock; reserve the rest of the stock for another use.

3. Wipe out the wok and set it over high heat for 40 seconds. Add the Sichuan Peppercorn Oil and when a wisp of white smoke appears, add the garlic, ginger and the remaining ¼ teaspoon salt and stir-fry for 10 seconds. Add the scallions and Thai chiles and stir-fry for 30 seconds. Add the celery, cucumber and red bell pepper and stir-fry until crisp-tender, about 1 minute. Add the reserved 1 tablespoon stock and the turkey and cook for 1 minute. Add the remaining 1 tablespoon wine and cook for 30 seconds.

4. Make a well in center of the wok; stir the sauce and add it to the well. Stir in the vegetables and turkey. Cook until thick and bubbling. Serve immediately.

SICHUAN PEPPERCORN OIL

MAKES 1 CUP

2 tablespoons Sichuan
peppercorns

1 cup peanut oil

Heat a wok over high heat for 30 seconds. Add the Sichuan peppercorns. Reduce the heat to low and stir the peppercorns until fragrant, about 2 minutes. Add the peanut oil and bring to a boil over moderate heat. Reduce the heat to moderately low. Cook until the peppercorns blacken, 4 to 5 minutes, and then strain the oil. —*Eileen Yin-Fei Lo*

MAKE AHEAD The peppercorn oil can be stored in a cool place for up to two months.

WINE Turkey is usually mild; this dish is anything but. Fiery and sweet, it needs a slightly sweet wine for balance. Look to Germany for an aromatic, not-quite-dry Riesling, such as the 1995 Carl Graff Urziger Schwarzlay QbA or the 1995 Heyl Schloss Mathildenhof Kabinett.

Pinot-Noir-Glazed Squabs with Roasted Vegetables

4 SERVINGS

Red wine in the marinade tenderizes and colors the squabs, so they emerge brown, crisp-skinned and juicy. I add honey to offset the wine's acidity. Try this marinade with any kind of poultry or game bird. If using squabs, have your butcher cut out the backbones and remove the breastbones; cut larger birds into serving pieces before marinating.

1 cup olive oil

2 tablespoons Dijon mustard

1 tablespoon honey

1 cup Pinot Noir

Four 1-pound squabs, butterflied
and breastbones removed

2 medium yellow squash, cut into
1-inch rounds

2 medium zucchini, cut into
1-inch rounds

1 pound white mushrooms,
stemmed

2 red bell peppers, cut into
1-inch pieces

1 red onion, halved and sliced
lengthwise

2 teaspoons finely chopped thyme

1 teaspoon finely chopped sage

Salt and freshly ground pepper

1 tablespoon vegetable oil

1. In a medium bowl, combine the olive oil, mustard and honey. In a small saucepan, boil the Pinot Noir until it is reduced to ¼ cup, about 7 minutes. Gradually whisk the hot wine into the marinade; let cool. Pour half of the marinade into a large, sturdy resealable plastic bag and add the squabs. Let marinate, refrigerated, for 2 hours or overnight.

2. Preheat the oven to 425° and position a rack in the upper third. In a large bowl, toss the vegetables and herbs with the remaining marinade and let stand for 15 minutes. Transfer to a large rimmed baking sheet, season with salt and pepper and roast for about 30 minutes, or until crisp-tender. Drain the vegetables in a colander for a few minutes, then return them to the baking sheet and roast for about 5 minutes more, or until tender. Transfer the vegetables to a large platter, cover loosely and keep warm.

3. Remove the squabs from the marinade and pat them dry with paper towels. Heat the vegetable oil in a large heavy skillet. Season the squabs with salt and pepper and add them to the skillet, skin-side down. Cook over moderately high heat until the skin of the squabs is dark brown, about 3 minutes. Transfer the squabs to a baking sheet, skin-side up, and roast them for 10

minutes for medium rare. Arrange the roasted squabs on the vegetables and serve immediately. *—Cory Schreiber*
WINE 1995 Eyrie Vineyards Yamhill County Pinot Noir. Game birds and Pinot Noir are a time-honored pairing. The 1995 Eyrie displays an amazing range of tastes, including strawberry, tea and dried cherries, yet is subtle enough to allow the flavor of the squabs to come through.

Spinach-Stuffed Quail with Apple Frisée Salad

4 SERVINGS

- ½ cup golden raisins
- ¼ cup apple cider
- ½ cup finely chopped walnuts, toasted
- 2 tablespoons olive oil
- ¼ cup minced shallots
- 1½ pounds fresh spinach—stemmed, blanched and chopped, or one 10-ounce package frozen chopped spinach, thawed and squeezed

Salt and freshly ground pepper

- ½ cup balsamic vinegar
- 4 tablespoons unsalted butter
- 8 partially boned quail
- 2 tablespoons vegetable oil

Apple Frisée Salad (recipe follows)

1. Preheat the oven to 400°. In a small saucepan, combine the raisins and cider and bring to a boil over moderately high heat. Cover and set aside to plump the raisins, about 10 minutes.

2. Toast the walnuts in a pie pan in the oven for about four minutes, or until lightly browned. Increase the oven temperature to 500°.

3. In a medium skillet, heat the olive oil. Add the shallots and cook over moderate heat, stirring often, until softened but not browned, about 3 minutes. Stir in the spinach, walnuts and raisins with any cider. Season with salt and pepper and let cool to room temperature.

4. In a small saucepan, boil the vinegar until reduced by half, about 10 minutes. Stir in 2 tablespoons of the butter and set aside.

5. Season the quail cavities with salt and pepper. Fill each quail with 2 tablespoons of the spinach stuffing. Using butcher's twine, tie the legs of each quail together, then tie the wings behind.

6. In a large skillet, melt the remaining 2 tablespoons of butter in the vegetable oil over high heat. Add the quail in batches and cook, turning often, until browned on all sides. Set the quail on a rack in a roasting pan and brush generously with the reduced balsamic-vinegar mixture; season with salt and pepper. Roast for 5 to 7 minutes, or until the skin is browned and the flesh is barely pink at the leg joint. Discard the twine from the quail and serve the quail with the frisée salad.

APPLE FRISÉE SALAD

4 SERVINGS

- ¼ cup balsamic vinegar
- 1 tablespoon honey
- 1 teaspoon Dijon mustard
- ½ teaspoon salt
- ¼ teaspoon freshly ground pepper
- 3 tablespoons olive oil
- 3 medium apples, preferably different colors, cored and thinly sliced
- 2 heads frisée lettuce (½ pound total)

In a large bowl, whisk together the vinegar, honey, mustard, salt and pepper. Gradually whisk in the oil. Add the sliced apples and frisée, toss well and serve. *—Sarah Stegner*
MAKE AHEAD The quail can be prepared through Step 3 up to one day in advance.
WINE 1990 Jean-Marc Boillot Volnay. Choose a Volnay from Burgundy for its finesse and elegance to balance the fragility of the quail.

Roast Quail with Hazelnuts and Port

6 SERVINGS

Good organization is essential to having the different elements—birds, sauce and pancakes—hot and ready to serve at the same time. You should start frying the pancakes as soon as the quail goes into the oven. Have the butcher truss the quail so they keep their shape during cooking.

- 6 tablespoons cold unsalted butter
- ½ cup thinly sliced shallots
- 2 cups ruby port
- 2 cups chicken stock or canned low-sodium broth
- 1 cup hazelnuts (about 5 ounces)
- 2 tablespoons clarified unsalted butter (see p. 22)
- 6 partially boned quail, trussed

Salt and freshly ground pepper
Sour-Cherry Pancakes (recipe follows)

1. In a medium stainless-steel saucepan, melt 1 tablespoon of the cold butter. Add the shallots and cook over moderately low heat, stirring, until softened but not browned, about 2 minutes. Add the port and boil over moderately high heat until reduced to ¾ cup, about 15 minutes. Add the stock and boil until reduced to 1⅓ cups, about 15 minutes. Strain the sauce into a small stainless-steel saucepan, pressing on the solids.

2. Preheat the oven to 350°. Spread the hazelnuts on a pie plate and toast in the oven until fragrant, about 10 minutes. Wrap the nuts in a kitchen towel and rub them against each other to remove the skins; let cool completely.

3. In a food processor, grind half of the hazelnuts to a paste; transfer the paste to a small bowl. Finely chop the remaining hazelnuts and stir them into the hazelnut paste with 1 tablespoon of the clarified butter. ➤

Roast Quail with Hazelnuts and Port

4. Preheat the oven to 475°. In a large heavy skillet, warm ½ tablespoon of the clarified butter. Add three of the quail, breast-side down, and season with salt and pepper. Cook the quail over high heat until browned, about 2 minutes. Transfer the quail, breast-side up, to a buttered baking sheet and season with salt and pepper. Wipe out the skillet and repeat with the remaining ½ tablespoon of clarified butter and three quail; let cool.

5. Pat the hazelnut mixture onto the quail and roast in the center of the oven for 4 to 5 minutes for medium rare. Let the quail rest for about 10 minutes before serving.

6. Meanwhile, rewarm the sauce over moderate heat. Cut the remaining 5 tablespoons of cold butter into ½-inch dice. Briskly whisk in the butter over low heat, one piece at a time, until smooth. Season with salt and pepper. Keep the sauce warm off the heat.

7. Set one pancake on each warmed plate, top with a quail and pour about 2 tablespoons of the sauce around each bird. Pass the remaining pancakes and sauce separately.

menu

Potato-Chip Tower with Scallops and Caviar (p. 36)

1992 RAVENEAU VALMUR CHABLIS

Roast Quail with Hazelnuts and Port (p. 207)

1988 LEROY SAVIGNY-LÈS-BEAUNE LES NARBANTONS

Apricot Soup (p. 380)
Pistachio Biscotti (p. 357)

NONVINTAGE VEUVE CLICQUOT DEMI-SEC CHAMPAGNE

SOUR-CHERRY PANCAKES

MAKES TWELVE 3-INCH PANCAKES

- ½ cup dried sour cherries (about 3 ounces)
- 1 cup red wine
- 3 large eggs
- 1 tablespoon olive oil
- ½ cup all-purpose flour
- 1 teaspoon kosher salt
- ½ teaspoon freshly ground pepper
- ½ teaspoon baking powder
- ¼ cup water
- 2 large egg whites
- 2 tablespoons plus 2 teaspoons clarified unsalted butter (see p. 22)

1. In a small stainless-steel saucepan, simmer the dried cherries in the wine over moderate heat until the cherries are plumped, about 15 minutes. Drain the cherries and reserve the wine for another use.

2. In a large bowl, whisk the whole eggs with the oil, flour, salt, pepper, baking powder and water. Transfer the mixture to a food processor or blender and blend until smooth. Return the batter to the bowl. In a medium bowl, beat the egg whites until they hold stiff peaks. Using a spatula, fold them into the pancake batter.

3. In a large heavy skillet, heat 2 teaspoons of the clarified butter. Gently stir the pancake batter. Then make three pancakes using about 3 tablespoons of batter for each. Sprinkle about 8 cherries on each of the pancakes and cook over moderately high heat until golden on the bottom, about 2 minutes. Turn the pancakes and cook them on the second side for 1 minute. Transfer the pancakes to a baking sheet and keep them warm. Repeat the process with the remaining butter and pancake batter. —*Joachim Splichal*

MAKE AHEAD The batter for the Sour-Cherry Pancakes can be made in advance and kept in the refrigerator for up to two hours.

WINE 1988 Leroy Savigny-lès-Beaune Les Narbantons. Game birds and a great red Burgundy—need I say more? This is a delicious fruit-driven Pinot Noir from the Côte de Beaune that is just starting to develop its full complexity. The bright red fruits add life to the aged port-wine sauce.

White-Wing-Dove-Style Grilled Quail

16 SERVINGS

- 16 partially boned quail, legs removed and reserved
- 3 jalapeño peppers, sliced crosswise ¼ inch thick
- 1 medium onion, halved lengthwise and sliced ¼ inch thick
- Salt and freshly ground pepper
- 16 thin slices of bacon
- 3 tablespoons unsulphured molasses
- 2 tablespoons olive oil
- 2 teaspoons sherry vinegar
- ⅓ cup cornmeal

1. Light a grill, preferably charcoal. Lay the quail breasts, skin-side down, on a work surface. Set a slice of jalapeño and a few slices of onion in the center of each of the quail breasts. Season the breasts with salt and pepper and fold them together to enclose the filling. Wrap a slice of bacon around each of the breasts and secure with a wooden toothpick.

2. In a small bowl, combine the molasses, oil and vinegar. Brush the stuffed quail and the legs with the glaze and sprinkle with the cornmeal. Season with salt and pepper.

3. Grill the quail breasts over a medium-hot fire, turning, until they are crisp and medium rare, about 9 minutes. Grill the quail legs, turning, until browned, about 4 minutes. Serve the quail hot off the grill. —*Robert Del Grande*

Grilled Duck Breasts with Apricot Mustard

20 SERVINGS

- 1 cup olive oil
- ¼ cup minced shallots
- 2 tablespoons chopped thyme

Freshly ground pepper

- 20 small skinless, boneless duck-breast halves

Salt

Apricot Mustard (recipe follows)

1. In a large bowl, combine the oil, shallots, thyme and a generous grinding of pepper. Add the duck breasts and marinate for 1 hour.

2. Light a charcoal grill. Season the duck breasts with salt and grill over a medium-hot fire for 3 to 4 minutes per side for medium rare. Slice the duck breasts crosswise at an angle and fan the slices on plates. Serve with the Apricot Mustard.

APRICOT MUSTARD

MAKES ABOUT 2½ CUPS

- 1 cup dried apricots (about ½ pound)
- ¾ cup dry white wine
- 1 small shallot, minced
- 2 large garlic cloves, minced
- ¼ cup tarragon vinegar
- ¼ teaspoon ground ginger
- ¼ teaspoon cayenne pepper
- ⅛ teaspoon ground allspice
- ⅛ teaspoon turmeric
- ⅛ teaspoon ground cardamom
- 1½ cups water
- 3 tablespoons Dijon mustard

Salt and freshly ground black pepper

1. In a medium stainless-steel saucepan, combine all of the ingredients except the water, mustard, salt and pepper. Add the water and simmer over moderately high heat until the apricots are soft, about 15 minutes. Remove from the heat and let cool.

2. Transfer the contents of the saucepan to a blender and puree until smooth. Strain the puree through a fine-meshed sieve into a bowl and stir in the Dijon mustard. Season with salt and black pepper. Thin the mixture with water if it seems too thick. Let cool, then transfer the mustard to a glass jar and refrigerate for up to one week. *–David Page*

Pinot-Noir-Braised Duck Legs

4 SERVINGS

These succulent duck legs with their crisp skin and flavorful sauce are a favorite on the Sunday menu at the Wildwood Restaurant & Bar in Portland, Oregon. The fruity qualities of the Pinot Noir wine underscore the dried fruit in the dish, and the acidity balances the heartiness of the duck.

- 4 large whole duck legs (about 4 pounds), trimmed

Salt and freshly ground pepper

- ½ cup Pinot Noir
- 5 cups chicken stock or canned low-sodium broth
- 2 heads of garlic, cloves separated and peeled
- 1 cup mixed dried fruit, such as tart cherries, apricots and prunes
- 8 thyme sprigs

1. Preheat the oven to 350°. Season the duck legs with salt and pepper. In a large heavy skillet, cook the duck legs over moderately high heat, skin-side down, until the skin is mahogany colored, about 15 minutes. Using a metal bulb baster or a large spoon, remove the fat from the pan as it is rendered. Turn the legs and cook them on the second side for about 3 minutes. Transfer the duck to a platter and pour off any remaining fat.

2. Add the wine to the skillet and boil until reduced by half, about 5 minutes. Add the stock, garlic, half of the dried fruit and the thyme and bring to a boil. Transfer the mixture to a 13-by-9-inch baking dish and set the duck legs, skin-side up, on top. Bake for 2 hours, or until the legs are very tender. Transfer the legs to a warm platter.

3. Pour the braising liquid into a 4-cup glass measure and let stand until the fat rises to the top, about 3 minutes. Skim off the fat and strain the liquid into a medium skillet, pressing hard on the solids. Bring to a boil over high heat. Add the remaining dried fruit and simmer the sauce for 5 minutes. Rewarm the duck in the sauce, skin-side up, to preserve its crispness. Serve the duck legs hot. *–Cory Schreiber*

WINE 1994 Thomas Willamette Valley Pinot Noir. The spice and dusty cherry components of the wine are a classic match for duck.

Duck-Leg Stew with Lentils and Green Olives

6 SERVINGS

- 2 tablespoons vegetable oil
- 6 Long Island duck legs

Salt and freshly ground pepper

- 1 medium onion, chopped
- 2 cups dry white wine
- 1 tablespoon chopped thyme
- 10½ cups water
- 1 tablespoon unsalted butter
- 2 medium carrots, diced
- 1 medium celery rib, diced
- 1 medium leek, white and light green, diced
- 3 cups green lentils (1½ pounds), washed
- 3 cups chopped fresh spinach
- 1 cup green olives
- 1½ tablespoons fresh lemon juice

1. Preheat the oven to 350°. Heat the oil in a large stainless-steel ovenproof skillet. Season the duck legs with salt and pepper and add them to the skillet, skin-side down. Cook the duck legs over moderately high heat until they are browned on one side, about 10 minutes. Turn and cook until browned, about 5 minutes longer. Transfer the duck legs

to a platter and pour off all but 2 table-spoons of the fat. Add the onion to the skillet and cook until just soft, about 3 minutes.

2. Return the duck to the skillet and add the wine, thyme and ½ cup of the water. Cover and bring to a boil, then cook in the oven for about 1½ hours, or until tender.

3. Meanwhile, melt the butter in a 4-quart saucepan over moderately high heat. Add the carrots, celery and leek and cook, stirring occasionally, until just soft, about 4 minutes. Stir in the lentils and the remaining 10 cups of water and bring to a boil. Reduce the heat to moderate, cover partially and cook until tender, about 30 minutes. Drain and season with salt.

4. Transfer the duck legs to a plate, cover them with aluminum foil and keep warm. Add the spinach, olives and le-mon juice to the skillet; cook for 6 min-utes to blend the flavors. Stir in the lentil mixture and season with salt and pepper. Spoon the stew into a large shallow bowl, arrange the duck legs on top and serve.   *–Gordon Hamersley*

MAKE AHEAD The duck stew can be refrigerated, covered, for up to two days. Remove the fat from the surface and reheat in a 350° oven before pro-ceeding with Step 3.

WINE With this earthy stew, try the red I call Châteauneuf meets Bordeaux: Domaine Cazes Côtes du Roussillon Vil-lages, a rich wine with soft tannins. Look for the 1993. Or opt for the more serious 1993 Selvapiana Chianti Rufina.

CHAPTER 10 pork veal

Grilled Pork Chops with Succotash (p. 221)

215   Pork Rib Roast with Pear Thyme Sauce

215   Pork Rib Roast Glazed with Honey Mustard

216   Sweet-Tea-Cured Roast Pork

217   Chile Citrus Pork with Sautéed Pears

218   Roast Pork with Balsamic Onion Marinade

218   Roasted Pork Loin with Sherry and Sautéed Red Onions

218   Roasted Pork Tenderloin with Lentils and Merlot Vinaigrette

219   Pork Tenderloin with Grapefruit and Curry

221   Grilled Pork Chops with Succotash

221   Caribbean-Spiced Grilled Pork Chops

222   Sherry-Glazed Pork Chops with Fried Sweet Onion Rings

222   Pork Chops with Creamed Corn and Chanterelles

223   Sweet-and-Sour Eggplant with Sautéed Pork

224   Sautéed Pork Scallops with Scallions and Capers

224   Easiest Barbecued Ribs

225   Spicy Ribs

225   Sausage and Broccoli Rabe with Polenta

227   Crumb-Crusted Ham with Orange Madeira Sauce

228   Roast Veal

228   Roasted Veal Shoulder Stuffed with Lemon, Capers and Parsley

228   Grilled Stuffed Veal Chops

230   Veal Shanks Braised in White Wine

230   Veal with Green Tea Leaves

232   Blanquette of Veal, Leeks and Peas

233   Veal Piccata with Orange, Capers and Tarragon

Pork Rib Roast with Pear Thyme Sauce

Pork Rib Roast with Pear Thyme Sauce

10 SERVINGS

This succulent roast pork is served with a sweet pear-cider glaze. Pear cider is available at specialty-food stores and many farmers' markets, or use apple cider. Although the ten-rib roast is best suited to serve ten people, it can stretch to serve unexpected guests; at carving time, cut down along both sides of each bone to produce slightly smaller rib portions and an extra slice of meat between each pair of ribs. Allow time for the prepared pork to refrigerate overnight before roasting.

One 10-rib pork loin roast (about 5½ pounds), trimmed of excess fat, ribs frenched (see box, p. 260)
3 garlic cloves, thinly sliced
2 tablespoons plus ½ teaspoon thyme leaves, plus 4 thyme sprigs
Kosher salt and freshly ground pepper
2 tablespoons olive oil
2 medium onions, peeled and cut into thick wedges with the root ends left intact
4 medium Bartlett pears—halved, cored and cut into thick wedges
1½ quarts pear cider or apple cider
½ small cinnamon stick
10 black peppercorns
1 whole clove
2 tablespoons minced shallots
30 tiny cherry tomatoes, for garnish

1. Make twenty small incisions all over the fatty side of the pork roast. Insert a slice of garlic in each slit. Season the meat all over with the 2 tablespoons thyme leaves, 1½ tablespoons of salt and 1 tablespoon of ground pepper. Cover the pork roast and refrigerate overnight.

2. Preheat the oven to 400°. Coat the bottom of a very large roasting pan with the oil. Set the pork roast in the pan, fat-side up, and surround it with the onion wedges. Roast the pork for 45 minutes. Add the pear wedges to the pan, turning them to coat with the drippings. Continue roasting the pork for 20 to 30 minutes longer, or until an instant-read thermometer inserted in the thickest part of the meat registers 150°. Set the pork roast on a large platter and surround it with the roasted pears and onions. Cover the pork roast, pears and onions with aluminum foil.

3. Meanwhile, in a large saucepan, combine the pear cider with the thyme sprigs, the cinnamon stick, the peppercorns and the clove. Boil the cider over high heat until it is reduced to 2½ cups, about 30 minutes.

4. Discard the fat from the roasting pan and set the pan over moderate heat. Add the shallots and cook, stirring, until wilted, about 3 minutes. Add the reduced pear cider and bring to a boil, scraping up any brown bits. Transfer the sauce to a small saucepan and simmer over moderate heat until reduced to 1 cup, about 8 minutes. Strain the sauce and add the remaining ½ teaspoon thyme leaves. Season with salt and pepper.

5. Carve the pork roast and arrange the chops on a platter. Arrange the roasted pears and onions around the pork and garnish with the cherry tomatoes. Serve the pork roast with the pear-cider sauce alongside. —George Mahaffey

WINE The 1995 Château Thivin Côte de Brouilly has enough acidity to cut through the sweetness of the pear sauce that accompanies this pork roast. As another alternative, the 1995 Eberle Côtes-de-Rôbles from California, a blend of Rhône varietals with ripe fruit flavors and graceful soft tannins, also marries well with the roast.

---

menu

HOMEMADE EGGNOG (P. 415)

———

Spinach and Crabmeat Soup with Country-Ham Croutons (p. 81)

1992 JOH. JOS. PRUM WEHLENER SONNENUHR AUSLESE RIESLING

———

Avocado Grapefruit Salad with Pomegranate Dressing (p. 51)

———

Hot-Smoked Salmon with Green-Apple Slaw (p. 43)

———

Pork Rib Roast with Pear Thyme Sauce (p. 215)

Creamy Butternut Squash, Potato and Tomato Gratin (p. 309)

Potato Bread with Dill and Caraway (p. 287)

1995 CHATEAU THIVIN COTE DE BROUILLY

———

Macadamia Shortbread with Fruit Compote and Banana Cream (p. 379)

Pork Rib Roast Glazed with Honey Mustard

4 SERVINGS

¼ cup honey
¼ cup Dijon mustard
1 teaspoon finely chopped rosemary
One 2½-pound pork rib roast, trimmed
Salt and freshly ground pepper
12 medium carrots

1. Preheat the oven to 425°. In a small bowl, stir together the honey, mustard and rosemary. Season the pork roast with salt and pepper and brush three-quarters of the honey mustard over the meat. Cover the roast and set aside for 20 minutes. ➤

Pork Rib Roast Glazed with Honey Mustard

2. Meanwhile, parboil the carrots in a large pot of salted water for 7 minutes. Drain the carrots, rinse them in cold water and pat them dry.

3. Set the pork roast on a rack in a large oiled roasting pan. Place the carrots in a single layer around the pork and roast for about 1 hour and 10 minutes, or until an instant-read thermometer inserted in the thickest part of the meat registers 150°. Every 10 to 15 minutes, carefully turn the carrots so that they cook evenly.

4. Transfer the pork roast to a carving board and cover it loosely with aluminum foil. Pour the remaining honey mustard over the carrots. Return the carrots to the oven and roast them, turning often, for about 10 minutes, or until very tender. Serve the pork roast on a warmed platter surrounded by the carrots.   *–Steven Chiappetti*
WINE 1990 Guigal Côte Rôtie. Côte Rôtie wins out over red Burgundy because of the sweet acidic glaze on the pork roast here. The spiciness that is found in Rhône wines nicely complements the dish.

Sweet-Tea-Cured Roast Pork

8 SERVINGS

This succulent pork rib roast combines two Southern classics—sweet tea and pork chops. Ask your butcher to remove the chine bone from the roast, make half-inch-deep incisions through the bone between the ribs and french the bones (see box, p. 260). You'll need to brine the pork for two days to guarantee juicy meat.

CURED PORK

16 orange pekoe tea bags
 2 quarts boiling water
 2 cups sugar
 1 cup kosher salt
 1 cup cider vinegar
 2 lemons, quartered
 2 quarts ice water
One 8-bone center rib roast of pork, trimmed of all visible fat (about 4½ pounds)

---

low-fat tricks

Denial isn't the style at the Inn at Blackberry Farm, outside Knoxville, Tennessee, but chef John Fleer still manages to minimize saturated fat in his food. Here are three of his tricks:

1. Use fruit juices or reduced wines rather than vinegar in salad dressings; because the reductions are not very acidic, they don't require much oil for balance.

2. Cure large cuts of meat and whole birds in a fat-free salt-sugar mixture to keep the meat tender and juicy. Chef Fleer likes to flavor his cure with tea, as in the Sweet-Tea-Cured Roast Pork, and to allow two days for the cure to really permeate the meat.

3. Serve meats with potent low-fat condiments such as Pickled-Pepper Relish (p. 58), Sweet-Onion Jam (p. 331) and Black-Eyed-Pea Salsa (p. 331) instead of buttery sauces.

SWEET-TEA RUB

 3 tablespoons minced lemon zest
 3 tablespoons plus 1 teaspoon finely chopped mint leaves
 1 tablespoon plus 1 teaspoon finely chopped thyme leaves
 5 lemon tea bags, opened

I. CURE THE PORK: Steep the tea bags in the boiling water until the tea is very strong, about 8 minutes. Remove the tea bags and stir in the sugar, salt and cider vinegar until the sugar and salt are dissolved. Pour the tea mixture into a large bowl, add the lemon quarters and the ice water and allow the brine to cool completely. Add the pork roast to the bowl; the roast should be entirely submerged in the brine. Cover the bowl with plastic wrap and refrigerate for 2 days.

---

menu

BLACKBERRY KIR ROYALE (P. 409)

Yellow-Tomato Gazpacho with Olivata Croutons (p. 71)

Roast Carrot Salad with Muscadine Vinaigrette (p. 58)

1995 MATANZAS CREEK SAUVIGNON BLANC

Sweet-Tea-Cured Roast Pork (p. 216)

Sweet-Onion Jam (p. 331)

Black-Eyed-Pea Salsa (p. 331)

Sesame-Dressed Haricots Verts in Roast Onions (p. 322)

1994 RIDGE GEYSERVILLE

Chocolate Buttermilk Cake with Blackberry Meringue (p. 341)

1996 LINDEN VINEYARDS LATE HARVEST VIDAL

2. MAKE THE SWEET-TEA RUB: Combine the lemon zest, mint, thyme, and lemon tea in a small bowl. Remove the pork roast from the brine and pat dry. Set the roast, meaty-side up, on a rack in a roasting pan and generously coat with the sweet-tea rub. Let the roast stand at room temperature until it is no longer cold, about 1 hour.

3. Preheat the oven to 375°. Roast the pork in the lower third of the oven for about 1 hour and 10 minutes or until an instant-read thermometer inserted in the center of the roast registers 135°. Let the pork rest for 15 minutes. Carve the roast by cutting between the bones. Arrange the chops on a large platter and serve. —*John Fleer*

WINE Young but ripe and juicy Zinfandel will marry nicely with these roasted pork chops. Try the 1994 Ridge Geyserville, a Zinfandel blend.

Chile Citrus Pork with Sautéed Pears

8 SERVINGS **L**

- 6 dried ancho chiles, stemmed and seeded
- 4 sun-dried-tomato halves (not oil-packed)
- 1 tablespoon canola oil
- 1 medium onion, chopped
- ½ cup fresh orange juice
- ¼ cup fresh lemon juice
- ¼ cup tomato paste
- 2 tablespoons finely grated orange zest
- 1 tablespoon coarsely chopped tarragon
- 1 teaspoon dried oregano

Kosher salt

- 2½ pounds trimmed boneless center-cut pork loin

Freshly ground pepper

- 3 large ripe Comice pears—peeled, cored and sliced lengthwise ⅓ inch thick
- 6 cups watercress, stemmed

1. In a bowl, soak the ancho chiles in hot water until they are softened, about 20 minutes. In another bowl, soak the sun-dried tomatoes in hot water until they are softened, about 15 minutes. Drain the chiles and the tomatoes; coarsely chop the chiles.

2. Heat the oil in a skillet. Add the onion, chiles and sun-dried tomatoes and cook over moderately low heat until softened, about 6 minutes. Then transfer the onion, chiles and tomatoes to a blender and add the orange juice, lemon juice, tomato paste, orange zest, tarragon, dried oregano and 2 tablespoons of kosher salt. Puree the chile paste until smooth.

3. Preheat the oven to 450°. Roast the pork in a roasting pan for about 15 minutes, or until it is starting to brown.

Spread 6 tablespoons of the chile paste on the pork. Lower the oven temperature to 375° and roast for 10 minutes. Spread another 2 tablespoons of the chile paste on the pork and roast for about 30 minutes more, or until an instant-read thermometer inserted in the meat reads 145°. Cover the pork with aluminum foil and let rest for 5 minutes. Season the roast pork with salt and pepper.

4. In a nonstick skillet, cook the pear slices over moderately high heat, without stirring, until they are tender and golden, about 4 minutes. Arrange the watercress and the pear slices on a serving platter. Slice the pork roast ¼ inch thick and arrange the slices of pork on top of the watercress and the pear slices. —*Charlie Palmer*

Chile Citrus Pork with Sautéed Pears

Roast Pork with Balsamic Onion Marmalade

4 SERVINGS Q

If you have good, strong veal stock in your freezer, skip Step 2 and add one cup of the veal stock in place of the reduced chicken broth in Step 4. Cook the marmalade, sauce base and pork roast simultaneously.

1 medium onion, thinly sliced
6 tablespoons balsamic vinegar
2 tablespoons sherry vinegar
2½ tablespoons sugar
Cracked black pepper
2 cups canned low-sodium chicken broth
4 tablespoons unsalted butter
1 tablespoon olive oil
1 pound pork tenderloin, preferably a thick portion, trimmed
Salt

ı. In a small stainless-steel saucepan, combine the onion, vinegars, sugar and ¼ teaspoon of cracked black pepper and bring to a boil over high heat. Reduce the heat to moderately low and

---

menu

Clams à la Marinière (p. 43)

———

Roast Pork with Balsamic
Onion Marinade (p. 218)

Endive and Roquefort
Salad (p. 54)

WINE Garlicky clams and hearty pork are a good excuse to try a Belgian beer, such as Palm Ale. The combination is also ideal for red wines—especially medium-bodied Bordeaux, with their mild tannins and balanced flavors. Consider a 1994 Saint-Estèphe, such as the Château Haut-Beauséjour or the Château de Pez.

---

cook, stirring occasionally, until the liquid is reduced to a thick syrup and the onion is soft, about 30 minutes. Refrigerate or leave at room temperature. Meanwhile, preheat the oven to 425°.

2. In a medium saucepan, cook the broth over high heat until reduced to 1 cup, 10 to 15 minutes.

3. In a large ovenproof skillet, melt 1 tablespoon of the butter in the oil over moderately high heat. When the foam subsides, season the pork lightly with pepper and cook in the skillet until browned on all sides, about 2 minutes per side. Transfer the pan to the oven; roast the meat for 8 to 9 minutes, or until an instant-read thermometer inserted in the thickest part reads 135°. Transfer the pork to a cutting board and let rest while you finish the sauce.

4. Meanwhile, discard the fat in the skillet. Return the pan to high heat. Add the reduced broth; boil over high heat, scraping up any brown bits, until reduced to ¼ cup, about 6 minutes. Off the heat, whisk in the remaining 3 tablespoons butter. Season with salt.

5. Slice the tenderloin across the grain and arrange on four plates. Spoon some marmalade next to the pork, drizzle with the pan sauce and serve. *–Jocelyn Bulow*

MAKE AHEAD The marmalade can be refrigerated in a jar for several days.

Roasted Pork Loin with Sherry and Sautéed Red Onions

8 SERVINGS

2 tablespoons unsalted butter
3 large red onions, thinly sliced
1 cup red pearl onions (about 5 ounces), blanched and peeled
Coarse salt and freshly ground pepper
One 3-pound boneless pork loin, tied, at room temperature
½ cup medium-dry sherry
2 tablespoons chopped flat-leaf parsley

ı. Melt the butter in a large heavy skillet. Add the sliced onions and cook over moderate heat until slightly softened, about 10 minutes. Reduce the heat to low, add the pearl onions and cook, stirring occasionally, until all of the onions are very soft, about 45 minutes. Season with salt and pepper.

2. Meanwhile, preheat the oven to 350°. Rub the pork loin all over with 1½ teaspoons of salt and ¾ teaspoon of pepper. Roast the pork for about 1 hour, or until the outside of the meat is browned and the internal temperature registers 150° on an instant-read thermometer. Transfer the roast to a warm platter and discard the strings. Cover loosely with aluminum foil; let stand for 15 minutes.

3. Skim any fat from the juices in the roasting pan, add the sherry and bring to a boil over moderately high heat, scraping up any brown bits from the bottom of the pan. Add the onions and parsley. Season with salt and pepper. Thinly slice the pork; serve with the onions and the sherry sauce. *–Rori Spinelli*

MAKE AHEAD The recipe can be prepared through Step 1 and refrigerated overnight.

Roasted Pork Tenderloin with Lentils and Merlot Vinaigrette

4 SERVINGS

Merlot gives this recipe earthy tones that make for a great autumn entrée. Adding bacon to the lentils would bring out the Merlot–a delicious match with smoked meats of any kind.

¾ cup olive oil
1 small fennel bulb, finely diced
1 small onion, finely diced
1 small carrot, finely diced
1 small celery rib, finely diced
1 cup Le Puy lentils (7½ ounces)
2½ cups water
1½ cups Merlot
2 tablespoons red-wine vinegar
Salt and freshly ground pepper

One 1-pound pork tenderloin, well
    trimmed and halved crosswise

½ teaspoon ground cumin

½ teaspoon ground fennel

1. In a heavy medium saucepan, heat
2 tablespoons of the oil. Add the fennel,
onion, carrot and celery and cook over
moderately high heat until the onion is
softened but not browned, about 5 minutes. Add the lentils to the saucepan
and stir to coat with the oil. Add the
water and bring to a simmer. Cover partially and cook over moderately low
heat, stirring occasionally, until the lentils are tender and the liquid is absorbed, about 40 minutes.

2. Meanwhile, preheat the oven to 450°.
In a medium saucepan, boil the Merlot
until it is reduced to 6 tablespoons, 10
to 12 minutes. Remove the saucepan
from the heat and whisk in the vinegar,
½ cup of the oil, 1¼ teaspoons of salt
and ½ teaspoon of pepper. Add this
vinaigrette to the lentils and cook over
low heat, stirring occasionally, for 5
minutes.

3. In an ovenproof skillet, heat the remaining 2 tablespoons oil. Season the
meat with salt and pepper and rub with
the ground cumin and fennel. Put the
pork in the hot skillet and sear until well
browned on all sides, about 6 minutes.
Place the skillet in the oven and cook
for 5 minutes. Let the pork stand, covered, for 5 minutes, then slice and serve
on top of the lentils.   *—Cory Schreiber*

MAKE AHEAD The lentils can be
cooked up to four hours ahead. Reheat
before serving.

WINE 1995 Eola Hills Wine Cellars Reserve Applegate Valley Merlot. This is
a smooth, soft and polished wine from
vineyards primarily in the Rogue Valley
in southern Oregon. Its ripe boysenber-
ry flavor, balanced by herbal and spice
components typical of Merlots from the
area, is a good foil for the lentils and
spices.

ABOVE: **Roasted Pork Loin with
Sherry and Sautéed Red Onions.**
RIGHT: **Roasted Pork Tenderloin with
Lentils and Merlot Vinaigrette.**

Pork Tenderloin with Grapefruit and Curry

4 SERVINGS **L**

4   dried chipotle chiles, stemmed
    and seeded

1   tablespoon garam masala or
    curry powder

1   cinnamon stick

½ cup ruby red grapefruit juice

1   tablespoon honey

1   tablespoon sugar

1   teaspoon cider vinegar

1   teaspoon kosher salt

1   tablespoon water

1   pound pork tenderloin, trimmed
    of visible fat

1   teaspoon vegetable oil

1. In a spice grinder or clean coffee mill,
grind the chipotles, garam masala and
cinnamon stick to a powder. In a large
stainless-steel baking dish, combine the
spice mixture with the grapefruit juice,
honey, sugar, vinegar, salt and water,

Grilled Pork Chops with Succotash

Sweet-and-Sour Eggplant with Sautéed Pork

6 SERVINGS

We've cooked this Chinese-flavored dish for years, often omitting the pork and serving the eggplant with stir-fried rice noodles as a vegetarian entrée. You can discard the chiles before serving if you're worried about biting into one.

    2 pounds small eggplants
    1 tablespoon coarse salt
About ½ cup olive oil
Four 6-ounce boneless pork loin
        chops, pounded ¼ inch thick and
        cut into ½-inch-wide strips
Table salt and freshly ground black
        pepper
    ¼ teaspoon cayenne pepper
    2 tablespoons sesame seeds
    2 medium onions, finely chopped
6 to 10 dried hot red chiles, such as
        árbol
    3 large garlic cloves, crushed
    2 tablespoons tomato paste
    ½ cup chicken stock or canned
        low-sodium broth
    ¼ cup red-wine vinegar
    3 tablespoons light brown sugar
    ½ cup cilantro leaves

1. Trim the eggplants and slice them crosswise ¼ inch thick. Put the slices in a colander, sprinkle with the coarse salt and let drain for 30 minutes. Squeeze the eggplant slices to remove the liquid, and then pat dry with paper towels.

2. Heat 1 tablespoon of the oil in a large nonstick skillet. Working in batches, arrange the eggplant slices in a single layer and cook over high heat until lightly browned, about 1 minute per side. Transfer to paper towels to drain. Cook the remaining eggplant, using 1 tablespoon of oil for each batch.

3. Heat another tablespoon of the oil in the skillet. Toss the pork with salt, pepper and the cayenne. Add half of the pork to the skillet; cook over high heat, stirring, until browned, about 2 minutes. Transfer

ABOVE: **Sherry-Glazed Pork Chops with Fried Sweet Onion Rings.** RIGHT: **Caribbean-Spiced Grilled Pork Chops.**

to a plate. Brown the remaining pork in 1 tablespoon of oil and add to the plate.

4. In a small skillet, toast the sesame seeds over moderate heat, stirring, until fragrant, about 3 minutes.

5. Heat 2 tablespoons of the oil in the large skillet. Add the onions. Cook over high heat, stirring occasionally, until golden, about 5 minutes. Add the chiles; cook until the skins begin to blister, 1 to 2 minutes. Lower the heat to moderate, add the garlic and cook for 1 minute. Add the tomato paste; cook, stirring, for 2 minutes. Stir in the stock, vinegar and brown sugar and cook for 2 minutes more.

6. Add the eggplant, pork and any juices to the skillet, toss well and cook until

heated through. Stir in the cilantro leaves and sesame seeds and serve. *–Susan Feniger and Mary Sue Milliken*

WINE 1995 Simi Rosé of Cabernet Sauvignon from California

223

Sautéed Pork Scallops with Scallions and Capers

Sautéed Pork Scallops with Scallions and Capers

4 SERVINGS

As I was browsing at the meat counter of my local market in Longboat Key, Florida, I saw pork loin that had been sliced almost as thin as scaloppine. My father used to cut it that way and cook the slices quickly in a pan in which he had softened some cut-up young spring onions with a few capers. Here in the States, I never see those sweet young onions that come to the market in Italy with their edible green tops on, but I do find scallions, a variety of onion that Italian farmers seem to ignore. The flavor of scallions is even richer than that of onions and not at all unsuited to this dish.

- 15 scallions
- 1 pound thinly sliced boneless top pork loin
- 2 tablespoons vegetable oil
- 2 tablespoons butter
- All-purpose flour, for dredging
- Salt and freshly ground pepper
- 1½ tablespoons capers (drained if packed in vinegar, rinsed and drained if packed in salt), chopped

1. Wash the scallions in two or three changes of cold water, and then slice them crosswise into ½-inch pieces.

2. Using a meat pounder, lightly pound the pork scallops to a ¼-inch thickness.

3. Put the oil and 1 tablespoon of the butter in a large skillet and turn the heat to high. When the oil is hot, lightly flour the pork scallops and add them to the pan. Brown them well on both sides, then transfer to a warm plate.

4. Reduce the heat to moderately low. Add the scallions to the skillet; season with salt and pepper. Cover and cook, stirring from time to time, until the scallions are very, very soft, about 20 minutes. Stir in the capers and the remaining 1 tablespoon butter.

5. Return the meat to the pan and season with salt and pepper. Cook over moderate heat just until the meat is warmed through, turning it over once or twice. Turn the contents of the skillet out onto a warm serving platter and bring to the table at once.   –*Marcella Hazan*

MAKE AHEAD You can prepare this dish through Step 4 several hours in advance. Reheat the scallions and capers thoroughly over moderate heat before putting in the meat.

Easiest Barbecued Ribs

4 SERVINGS

Most Southerners go to their favorite barbecue joint to eat 'cue, but these garlic-smothered, oven-roasted ribs are hard to beat. (Of course, you can cook them, covered, on a wood, charcoal or gas grill.) They take practically no time or effort, and I've never met a soul who didn't love them. Serve with coleslaw and iced tea.

- 6 whole heads of garlic
- 6 pounds whole slabs babyback pork ribs, at room temperature
- Salt and freshly ground black pepper
- Cayenne pepper

1. Preheat the oven to 350°. Place three heads of garlic on each of two large baking sheets and roast for 25 minutes. Season the ribs all over with salt, black pepper and cayenne. Place the ribs, meaty-side up, on the baking sheets with the garlic and roast for 1 hour and 15 minutes, turning them every 25 minutes. The ribs are done when they're nicely browned and the garlic is very soft. Remove the ribs and garlic to a cutting board.

2. Slice the root ends off the garlic heads and squeeze out the roasted garlic. Spread the roasted garlic in a thin

layer all over the ribs, and then season the ribs with salt. Cut the slabs of ribs apart, pile the ribs on a platter and serve. —*John Martin Taylor*

WINE A gutsy red is the way to go here–pick a California Zinfandel, such as the 1995 Ridge Sonoma Station or the 1994 Chateau Montelena.

Spicy Ribs

20 SERVINGS

If you happen to have two ovens with three racks each, by all means roast all of the ribs at once.

- 2 teaspoons sugar

Salt

- 12 whole slabs (sides) pork spareribs
- 3 cups fresh orange juice
- 2 cups unsulphured dark molasses
- 2 cups cider vinegar
- 1 cup tomato paste
- 24 garlic cloves, minced
- 2 tablespoons ground cumin
- 4 teaspoons cayenne pepper
- 4 teaspoons paprika
- 1 tablespoon ground coriander
- 2 teaspoons black pepper

I. Preheat the oven to 400°. Mix the sugar with 1 tablespoon of salt and sprinkle on both sides of the ribs. Put two slabs of ribs, meaty-side up, on each of six large broiler pans; fold the ends under if necessary. Cover the pans tightly with aluminum foil. Set one pan of ribs on each rack in your oven (refrigerate the rest) and roast for 10 minutes. Reduce the oven temperature to 325° and roast for 1½ hours longer.

2. In a large bowl, whisk all the remaining ingredients together with 4 teaspoons of salt. Uncover the ribs and turn them bony-side up. Brush 1 cup of the sauce over the ribs and bake, uncovered, for 30 minutes. Turn the ribs meaty-side up and brush with another 1½ cups of the sauce. Bake for about 1½ hours longer, or until very tender; rotate the pans and baste once with about ½ cup of the sauce halfway through.

3. Remove the ribs from the oven and lightly coat them with more of the sauce. Return the oven temperature to 400° and repeat with the remaining ribs and sauce.

4. Reheat the ribs if needed. Pour any remaining sauce into a bowl and serve on the side. —*Marcia Kiesel*

WINE The molasses glaze on these ribs suggests a beer, which won't get lost between bites.

Spicy Ribs

Sausage and Broccoli Rabe with Polenta

4 SERVINGS **Q**

Sausage and broccoli rabe are simmered in a flavorful tomato sauce and served over creamy polenta for a rustic Italian meal. If you like, pass freshly grated Parmesan cheese at the table.

- 1 pound broccoli rabe, tough stems removed
- ¼ cup olive oil
- 1⅓ pounds hot or mild Italian sausage
- 1 medium onion, chopped

2　garlic cloves, minced
¼　cup dry white wine
One 15-ounce can crushed tomatoes
　　in thick puree
1½　cups chicken stock or canned
　　low-sodium chicken broth
½　teaspoon dried thyme
2½　teaspoons salt
¼　cup chopped flat-leaf parsley
⅛　teaspoon freshly ground pepper
4½　cups water
1⅓　cups coarse or medium cornmeal

I. In a large pot of boiling salted water, cook the broccoli rabe until tender, about 2 minutes. Drain, then rinse in cold water and drain again thoroughly. Cut into 2-inch pieces and set aside.

2. Heat 1 tablespoon of the oil in a large heavy skillet. Add the sausage and cook over moderately high heat, turning occasionally, until browned and cooked through, about 10 minutes. Transfer the sausage to a plate and let cool slightly. Slice into ½-inch-thick rounds.

3. Pour off all but 2 tablespoons of the fat from the skillet. Add the onion and the garlic and cook over moderately low heat, stirring occasionally, until the onion is translucent, about 5 minutes. Stir in the wine and bring to a simmer. Stir in the sausage slices, the tomatoes, stock, thyme and 1¼ teaspoons of the salt. Bring to a simmer and cook for 20 minutes. Add the broccoli rabe, parsley and pepper to the skillet and return to a simmer.

Sausage and Broccoli Rabe with Polenta

4. Meanwhile, in a medium saucepan, combine the water and the remaining 1¼ teaspoons of salt and bring to a boil. Whisk in the cornmeal in a slow steady stream, then whisk in the remaining 3 tablespoons of oil. Reduce the heat and simmer, stirring frequently with a wooden spoon, until the polenta is thickened, about 20 minutes.

5. Spoon the polenta onto dinner plates and top with the sausage and broccoli rabe ragout.   —Susan Lantzius Rich

WINE This dish wants a red wine without a high level of tannins, which could combine with the broccoli rabe to create an unpleasant bitterness. One excellent choice: an Italian Barbera with minimal tannin, such as the 1995 Michele Chiarlo Barbera d'Asti.

Crumb-Crusted Ham with Orange Madeira Sauce

This recipe calls for a top-quality smoked ham. It shouldn't be too sweet or too salty, or one that's been sectioned and reshaped. Karl Ehmer makes a superior ham using an old German smoking recipe. It's available by mail from Citarella in New York City (212-874-0383).

12 SERVINGS

One 12- to 13-pound bone-in smoked ham (see above)

1½ cups medium-dry Madeira

2 cups coarse fresh bread crumbs

½ cup finely chopped flat-leaf parsley

3 large garlic cloves, minced

3 tablespoons unsalted butter, melted

2 tablespoons Dijon mustard

½ teaspoon kosher salt

2 large navel oranges

½ teaspoon finely grated orange zest

I. Preheat the oven to 325°. Set the ham in a large roasting pan, fat side up. Using a sharp knife, score the fat all over in a crosshatch pattern. Pour 1 cup of the Madeira over the ham and cover tightly with aluminum foil. Bake for about 3½ hours, or until heated through.

Crumb-Crusted Ham with Orange Madeira Sauce

2. In a medium bowl, toss the bread crumbs with the parsley. In a small bowl, combine the garlic, melted butter and mustard, then work into the bread crumbs with your fingers. Season with the salt.

3. Uncover the ham and baste with the pan juices, then transfer to a large platter. Pour the pan juices into a medium saucepan. Return the ham to the roasting pan and raise the oven temperature to 375°. Pat the bread-crumb mixture all over the top of the ham, pressing it firmly into the fat. Return the ham to the oven and bake for about 30 minutes longer, or until the bread-crumb coating is crisp and golden brown. Transfer the ham to a cutting board and let rest for 15 minutes.

4. Meanwhile, using a sharp knife, peel the oranges; remove all the bitter white pith. Working over a bowl to catch the juices, cut the oranges between the membranes to release the sections; you should have ½ cup of juice. Add the orange sections, orange juice and the remaining ½ cup of Madeira to the juices in the saucepan. Cover and simmer over low heat for 10 minutes. Remove from the heat, add the orange zest and keep warm.

5. Using a long, thin knife, carefully slice the ham, holding the crumbs in place with one hand while you cut. Arrange the ham slices on a platter. Sprinkle any fallen crumbs over the ham and serve with the orange sauce. —Marcia Kiesel

WINE 1989 Meerlust Merlot

Roast Veal

8 SERVINGS

One 3-pound boneless veal shoulder
    roast, tied
  2 tablespoons unsalted butter,
      1 tablespoon cut into 12 pieces
  3 large garlic cloves—1 minced and
      2 peeled
  1 tablespoon chopped sage
  1 teaspoon chopped rosemary
Salt and freshly ground pepper
  1 large carrot, coarsely chopped
  1 large celery rib, coarsely chopped
  1 large shallot, coarsely chopped
  2 tablespoons olive oil
 ⅔ cup dry white wine

1. Preheat the oven to 400°. Set the veal roast on a work surface, fat-side up. Make twelve 1-inch incisions over the top of the roast and insert a piece of butter in each hole. In a small bowl, combine the minced garlic with the sage, rosemary and ¼ teaspoon each of salt and pepper. Rub the garlic mixture over the top of the roast, then coat the meat with the remaining 1 tablespoon of butter.

2. Put the carrot, celery, shallot and the remaining two whole garlic cloves in an enameled cast-iron casserole that will hold the veal roast snugly. Add the roast, fat-side up, and drizzle the olive oil on top. Season the roast with salt and pepper.

3. Cover the casserole and roast the meat in the oven for 1½ hours, turning it every 30 minutes. The roast is done when an instant-read thermometer inserted in the thickest part registers 145° to 150°.

4. Transfer the roast to a carving board; let stand for 10 minutes. Set the casserole over high heat, add the wine and boil until the liquid has reduced to 1¼ cups, about 4 minutes. Strain through a coarse sieve, pressing the solids into the sauce. Skim off the fat and season with salt and pepper.

5. Carve the veal roast into eight slices. Pour any meat juices that have accumulated into the sauce and serve the roast at once.   *—Egi Maccioni*

WINE To go with the veal and its accompaniments, pick an elegant red with some depth of flavor. A Chianti Classico Riserva, such as the 1991 Antinori Badia a Passignano or the 1993 Castello Vicchiomaggio Riserva La Prima, would work well.

Roasted Veal Shoulder Stuffed with Lemon, Capers and Parsley

6 SERVINGS

Instead of starting at a higher temperature, this veal roasts at a steady 375°; the piquant stuffing adds so much interest to the roast that it doesn't need a deep golden crust.

  3 tablespoons olive oil
  1 large onion, finely chopped
  2 garlic cloves, minced
  1 cup dried bread crumbs
 ½ cup chopped flat-leaf parsley
 ¼ cup thinly sliced sun-dried
      tomatoes
  2 tablespoons drained capers,
      chopped
  1 tablespoon fresh lemon juice
Salt and freshly ground pepper
One 2½-pound veal shoulder, boned
    and trimmed

1. Preheat the oven to 375°. In a large skillet, heat 1 tablespoon of the oil. Add the onion and cook over moderately high heat, stirring often, until softened but not browned, about 5 minutes. Add the garlic and cook until fragrant, about 1 minute. Remove from the heat; let cool.

2. In a large bowl, combine the onion mixture with the bread crumbs, parsley, sun-dried tomatoes, capers, lemon juice and 1 tablespoon of the oil. Season with salt and pepper; stir to blend.

3. Lay the veal shoulder flat, boned-side up, on a large work surface and season

it generously with salt and pepper. Spread the filling over the top of the veal shoulder, leaving a 1-inch border on all sides. Roll up the meat and tie with butcher's twine; season with salt and pepper. Set the meat on a rack in a roasting pan and drizzle the remaining 1 tablespoon of olive oil over the top. Roast the veal for about 1 hour, or until an instant-read thermometer inserted in the thickest part of the meat registers 140° for slightly pink meat. Transfer the roasted veal to a carving board, cover it loosely with aluminum foil and let it stand for 10 to 15 minutes. Slice the stuffed veal shoulder and serve at once.   *—Sarah Stegner*

WINE 1991 Robert Mondavi Pinot Noir Reserve. This nicely balanced wine has plenty of heft and fruit to stand up to the solidity of the roast and the acidity of the lemon and capers.

Grilled Stuffed Veal Chops

4 SERVINGS

These chops are best grilled over a charcoal fire, but they can also be broiled or sautéed in butter and oil.

Salt
12 thin green beans, ends trimmed
  4 veal rib chops, cut 1-inch thick,
      protruding bones scraped clean
  2 firm, ripe plum tomatoes—
      peeled with a vegetable peeler,
      sliced ¼ inch thick and seeded
 ¼ pound fontina or mozzarella,
      sliced ¼ inch thick
  4 large basil leaves
Freshly ground black pepper
  1 tablespoon extra-virgin olive oil

1. Bring a small saucepan of water to a boil. Add 1 tablespoon of salt and the beans and cook until crisp-tender, about 3 minutes. Drain and pat thoroughly dry.

2. Lay each veal chop on a work surface in front of you. Using a thin sharp knife, slice the meat horizontally, stopping at

Roasted Veal Shoulder Stuffed with Lemon, Capers and Parsley

the bone. Working with one chop at a time, fold back one of the meat slices and pound the other one out as thinly as possible with a meat pounder, starting from the bone. Turn the chop over and repeat with the second slice of meat.

3. Open the veal chops in front of you and stuff each one with one-fourth of the tomato and cheese slices, 3 green beans and a basil leaf. The stuffing ingredients shouldn't protrude from the meat; trim them if necessary. Season with salt and pepper and fold over the flaps. Seal the edge of each chop with three toothpicks.

4. Light a charcoal grill. Brush the chops with the oil and grill for 2 minutes. Season with salt, turn the chops and season them on the second side. Grill the chops for 2 minutes longer or until just cooked through.   *–Marcella Hazan*

MAKE AHEAD The chops can be stuffed and sealed early in the day.

WINE Richness from the cheese enhances these sweet veal chops and points to a deep-flavored but not-too-powerful red. Consider a Rosso di Montalcino, such as the 1995 Altesino, or a Rosso di Montepulciano, such as the 1993 La Braccesca, both from Tuscany.

Grilled Stuffed Veal Chops

Veal Shanks Braised in White Wine

6 SERVINGS

- 6 tablespoons vegetable oil
- 6 large, meaty center-cut pieces of osso buco (about 5 pounds)

Salt and freshly ground pepper

- 4 medium carrots, cut into 2-inch pieces
- 1 large onion, chopped
- 1 tablespoon tomato paste
- 1 tablespoon minced garlic
- 3 cups dry white wine
- 1 teaspoon dried marjoram
- 2 cups water
- 1 teaspoon chopped fresh marjoram
- 2 cups packed chopped kale

Boiled Yukon Gold potatoes, for serving

1. Preheat the oven to 350°. Heat ¼ cup of the oil in a large skillet. Season the veal shanks with salt and pepper and brown them in the skillet over moderately high heat, about 8 minutes per side; transfer to a platter.

2. Reduce the heat to moderately low and add the remaining 2 tablespoons of oil. Add the carrots, onion, tomato paste and garlic and cook, stirring, until the onion is just soft, about 3 minutes. Return the veal and add the wine, dried marjoram and water. Cover and bring to a boil, then cook in the oven for about 2 hours, or until very tender.

3. Transfer the veal and vegetables to a large shallow bowl, cover and keep warm. Boil the liquid in the skillet over high heat until reduced to 2 cups, about 15 minutes. Add the fresh marjoram and kale; cook until the kale is tender, about 2 minutes. Pour the sauce over the veal. Serve with the potatoes.*–Gordon Hamersley*

WINE The simplicity of this dish gives you a lot of wine choices. Try an older Italian red, such as the 1989 Luigi Ferrando Carema with its mellow fruit. The 1989 or 1992 Eyrie Vineyards Pinot Noir Reserve, with more forward fruit, would not overpower the veal either.

Veal with Green Tea Leaves

2 SERVINGS **L**

Cooking with tea leaves is common in China, particularly in tea-growing regions such as Hangzhou, where fresh leaves are readily available. The tea contributes a subtle flavor and aroma to the dish.

- ⅓ cup brewed green tea
- 2 tablespoons oyster sauce
- 1½ teaspoons soy sauce
- 1½ teaspoons sugar
- ½ teaspoon white vinegar
- 1 tablespoon plus 2 teaspoons Shao-Hsing wine or dry sherry
- 2½ teaspoons tapioca starch
- 6 ounces lean veal loin
- 1½ teaspoons Shallot Oil (p. 336)

Pinch of salt

- 2 teaspoons green tea leaves
- ½ cup boiling water
- 2 tablespoons dried cloud ear mushrooms, soaked in hot water for 30 minutes
- ¾ cup chicken stock
- 6 thin asparagus spears, sliced ¼ inch thick on the diagonal
- 1 celery rib, cut into ¼-inch dice
- 2 small scallions, white parts only, thinly sliced
- 1 teaspoon minced fresh ginger
- 1 teaspoon minced garlic
- ¼ cup finely chopped red bell pepper
- ¼ cup thinly sliced water chestnuts

1. Combine the green tea, oyster sauce, soy sauce, sugar, vinegar, the 2 teaspoons wine and the tapioca starch in a small bowl and set aside.

2. Slice the veal across the grain ¼ inch thick, then cut the slices into 2-by-½-inch strips. In a small bowl, toss the veal with ¼ teaspoon of the Shallot Oil and the salt. Refrigerate for 1 hour.

3. Put the tea leaves in a bowl. Add the boiling water, cover and let steep for 10 minutes. Strain the tea, reserving only the leaves. Thoroughly rinse the soaked mushrooms in cold water; drain. ➤

Veal with Green Tea Leaves

4. Set a wok over high heat for 30 seconds. Add the stock and bring to a boil. Add the mushrooms, asparagus and celery and cook until the asparagus is bright green, about 1 minute. Drain the vegetables and reserve the stock for another use.

5. Wipe out the wok and set it over high heat for 40 seconds. Add the remaining 1¼ teaspoons of Shallot Oil and swirl to coat the wok. When a wisp of white smoke appears, add the scallions, ginger and garlic and stir-fry for 30 seconds. Stir in the veal, red bell pepper, water chestnuts, the remaining 1 tablespoon wine and the reserved tea leaves. Add the mushrooms, asparagus and celery and mix thoroughly.

6. Make a well in the center of the wok, pushing everything up the sides slightly. Stir the sauce and add it to the wok. Stir in the veal and vegetables and cook until thick and bubbling. Serve immediately. —Eileen Yin-Fei Lo

WINE This mild dish calls for a characterful, dry white with enough flavor to tie the meat, asparagus and other ingredients together. A California Pinot Blanc, such as the 1995 Murphy-Goode or the 1995 Lockwood, would work particularly well here.

Blanquette of Veal, Leeks and Peas

10 SERVINGS

Serve this rich, creamy stew with boiled peeled potatoes, buttered egg noodles or steamed rice.

- 4 pounds boneless veal shoulder or leg, cut into 2-inch chunks
- 2 large carrots, cut into 2-inch pieces
- 1 medium onion, chopped

Bouquet garni made with 2 cloves, 8 peppercorns, 2 bay leaves and 1 sprig of thyme

- 4 cups chicken stock or canned low-sodium broth
- 3 cups dry white wine
- 4 tablespoons unsalted butter
- 3 medium leeks, white and light green, thinly sliced
- 1 pound small white mushrooms, trimmed
- ½ cup water
- 1 tablespoon fresh lemon juice

Kosher salt

- 2 cups thawed frozen peas or halved snow peas
- 3 large egg yolks, at room temperature
- 1 cup heavy cream or crème fraîche, at room temperature
- 1½ tablespoons chopped tarragon

Freshly ground pepper

1. Preheat the oven to 350°. In a large enameled cast-iron casserole, cover the chunks of veal with cold water and bring the water to a boil over high heat, skimming as necessary. Drain the pieces of veal in a colander. Return the veal to the casserole and add the carrots, onion, bouquet garni, chicken stock and white wine. Cover and bring to a boil over high heat, then cook the veal stew in the oven for about 2½ hours, or until very tender.

2. Meanwhile, in a large stainless-steel skillet, melt the butter over moderately high heat. Add the leeks and the mushrooms and cook, stirring, for about 1 minute. Add the water, the lemon juice and 1 teaspoon of salt and reduce the heat to low. Cook until the leeks and the mushrooms are tender, about 10 minutes.

3. Transfer the veal stew to a colander set over a bowl. Discard the bouquet garni. Transfer the veal and the vegetables to a large shallow bowl, cover and keep warm. Pour the broth back into the casserole and boil over high heat until it is reduced to 2 cups, about 15 minutes. Add the peas to the casserole and cook until they are tender, about 2 minutes. Using a slotted spoon, remove

low-fat tips

1. **Use flavorful stock** in place of oil for stir-frying.
2. **Use lean cuts of meat** and trim all visible fat before cooking.
3. **Poach meat in stock** rather than in water to add flavor.
4. **Accompany all main courses** with plain rice and plenty of steamed or stir-fried vegetables.
5. **Use a well-seasoned wok** or cast-iron skillet. Season your wok by making an infused oil or cooking french fries (for the unconverted), then wiping the wok clean.
6. **If you do a lot of steaming**, invest in a stainless-steel wok.

the peas from the casserole and add them to the bowl with the veal and the vegetables.

4. In a small bowl, whisk the egg yolks and the cream. Whisk in ½ cup of the hot broth. Add the egg-yolk mixture to the casserole and whisk constantly over moderately low heat until the sauce thickens, about 8 minutes; do not let the sauce boil. Remove the sauce from the heat and continue whisking for a minute or two to stop the cooking. Stir in the tarragon and season the sauce with salt and pepper. Pour the sauce over the veal and vegetables in the bowl and serve. —Gordon Hamersley

MAKE AHEAD The veal stew can be refrigerated, covered, for up to two days. Remove the fat from the surface and reheat the stew in a 350° oven before proceeding.

WINE Such an elegant and yet simple dish as this blanquette of veal requires at least a semblance of luxury in the wine that accompanies it. You can splurge on a nutty 1994 Hanzell Chardonnay from California, or opt for the less pricey 1993 Lageder Chardonnay from Italy.

Veal Piccata with Orange, Capers and Tarragon

4 SERVINGS

This dish has been updated with sophisticated but decidedly non-Italian flavors. The classic Italian cooking technique—pounding the veal and sautéing it over high heat—remains the same. (A butcher can do the pounding for you.)

 1 pound veal, cut into scaloppine, pounded very thin

Salt and freshly ground pepper

All-purpose flour

 4 tablespoons unsalted butter

 2 tablespoons olive oil

 ½ cup fresh orange juice

 1 tablespoon finely julienned orange zest

 3 tablespoons capers

 1½ tablespoons sherry vinegar

 ¼ cup chopped tarragon

1. Season the veal with salt and pepper and coat lightly with flour. In a large stainless-steel skillet, melt 1 tablespoon of the butter in 1 tablespoon of the oil over high heat. Add half of the veal in a single layer and cook about 1 minute per side. Transfer the veal to a large serving platter and keep warm. Repeat the process with another tablespoon each of the butter and oil and the remaining veal.

2. Add the orange juice, orange zest, capers and vinegar to the skillet and bring to a boil over high heat. Cook, stirring, until slightly thickened. Add the remaining 2 tablespoons of butter and the tarragon and whisk until blended. Add up to 2 tablespoons of water if the sauce looks thick. Return the veal to the pan and turn each piece to coat with sauce. Transfer the veal to a large serving platter, pour the sauce on top and serve.   *–Erica De Mane*

WINE This elegant dish calls for an elegant wine. A Chardonnay is ideal. Consider the 1994 Antinori Cervaro della Sala or, from California, the 1995 Jekel.

CHAPTER 11 beef lamb game

Nine-Spice Rack of Lamb with Cucumber Relish (p. 251)

237   Spice-Crusted Rib-Eye Roast with Garlic Jus

237   Balsamic-Marinated Beef Tenderloin

238   Spicy Roast Beef with White-and-Black-Bean Ragout

239   Red-Cooked Beef with Cinnamon

240   Rio Rancho Steaks with Ancho Butter

241   Stuffed Rib-Eye Steaks with Chile Lime Relish

241   Grilled Beef Tenderloin with Merlot Sauce

242   Steak with Rosemary Oil

242   Seasoned Sliced Pan-Grilled Beef Steaks

243   Pan-Seared Strip Steaks with Red-Wine Onion Sauce

244   Pan-Seared Steaks with Vidalia Onions

245   Rosemary Flank Steak with Roasted Potatoes

245   Braised Short Ribs

245   Beef and Coconut Satays

246   Sesame Grilled Beef

246   Pepper Steak

248   Steamed Orange Beef

249   Green Chili

249   Parsley and Garlic Meatballs

249   Slow-Roasted Oxtail Stew with Pancetta

251   Nine-Spice Rack of Lamb with Cucumber Relish

251   Lamb with Onion Juice and Grilled Eggplant

252   Roasted Chiappetti Leg of Lamb with Pesto Stuffing

252   Roast Leg of Lamb with Orange and Herbs

253   Spiced Lamb Shanks with Almonds and Dates

254   Lamb Shanks on Polenta with a Parmesan Crust

255   Braised Lamb Shanks

256   Seared Lamb alla Romana

256   Georgian Lamb and Vegetable Stew

257   Lamb and Rosemary Potpies

259   Savory Vegetable and Lamb Stew

259   Balsamic-Glazed Rack of Venison

260   Roasted Venison with Beach-Plum Sauce

Spice-Crusted Rib-Eye Roast with Garlic Jus

Spice-Crusted Rib-Eye Roast with Garlic Jus

12 SERVINGS

This beautifully marbled cut of beef is perfect for showing off the best red wines. A crust of ground spices and roasted garlic whisked into the pan juices just before serving give this simple dish added depth of flavor.

1 teaspoon unsalted butter
1 large head of garlic, top third cut off
One 7-pound tied boneless rib-eye roast, at room temperature, bones reserved (total weight with bones about 8¾ pounds)
4½ cups water
Kosher salt
1 tablespoon whole black peppercorns
1 tablespoon coriander seeds
1 teaspoon cumin seeds
1 teaspoon anise seeds
Freshly ground pepper

1. Preheat the oven to 350°. Spread the butter over the cut-side of the garlic and wrap it loosely in aluminum foil, crimping the package to seal. Roast for about 45 minutes, or until very soft. Squeeze the soft garlic cloves from the skin and strain into a small bowl. Cover with plastic wrap.

2. Increase the oven temperature to 400°. Put the reserved rib bones in a roasting pan and roast for 30 minutes, or until browned. (Leave the oven on.) Transfer the rib bones to a medium saucepan. Cover the bones with 4 cups of the water and add ½ teaspoon of salt. Cover partially and simmer over low heat until the liquid is reduced to 1 cup, about 1½ hours. Strain the stock into a bowl.

3. Meanwhile, in a spice grinder or a mortar, grind the peppercorns, coriander, cumin and anise seeds to a coarse powder. Rub the spice mixture all over the roast and season it with salt. Set the meat on a rack in a roasting pan and roast in the center of the oven for 15 minutes. Reduce the temperature to 325° and roast for about 2 hours longer, or until an instant-read thermometer inserted in the center of the roast registers 120° for medium rare. Transfer the roast to a carving board. Cover loosely with aluminum foil; let rest for 10 to 15 minutes before slicing.

4. Pour the juices from the roasting pan into a glass measure and discard the fat. Set the roasting pan over two burners on moderately high heat. When the pan starts to sizzle, add the remaining ½ cup of water and simmer, scraping the bottom of the pan to loosen any browned bits. Stir in the reserved stock and simmer over low heat for a few minutes. Pour this jus into a small saucepan and add the reserved pan juices from the glass measure; keep the jus warm over very low heat.

5. Using a large, sharp knife, carve the roast into ½-inch-thick slices; add any meat juices to the jus. Whisk in 1 tablespoon of the roasted-garlic puree. Season the jus with salt and pepper and serve with the roast. —*Marcia Kiesel*

MAKE AHEAD The garlic puree can be refrigerated for up to three days.

WINE A supple red: Turley's 1994 Pahlmeyer Red Table Wine; Léoville Las Cases Bordeaux from France or Corison Cabernet Sauvignon from California

Balsamic-Marinated Beef Tenderloin

4 SERVINGS L

Grill sliced onions and zucchini along with the tenderloin to serve as a complement.

1 tablespoon kosher salt
1 pound center-cut beef tenderloin, trimmed of visible fat
¼ cup balsamic vinegar
¼ cup Barolo or other dry red wine
1 large shallot, coarsely chopped

menu

Smoked-Trout Spread (p. 14)
1995 J. FRITZ SAUVIGNON BLANC

Sweet Pea Soup with Chive Oil (p. 72)
1995 MARTINELLI GEWÜRZTRAMINER DRY SELECT

Crab Ravioli with Shallot Cream (p. 40)
1995 LANDMARK OVERLOOK CHARDONNAY

Spice-Crusted Rib-Eye Roast with Garlic Jus (p. 237)
1994 PAHLMEYER RED TABLE WINE

Pistachio Ricotta Napoleons with Oranges (p. 387)
1995 J. FRITZ LATE HARVEST ZINFANDEL

1 teaspoon coarsely chopped rosemary
1 teaspoon coarsely chopped sage
¼ teaspoon freshly ground pepper
1 teaspoon vegetable oil

1. Rub the salt all over the tenderloin for 1 to 2 minutes, then refrigerate the meat uncovered for 1 hour. In a blender, combine the vinegar, wine, shallot, rosemary, sage and pepper and puree.

2. Put the meat in a small stainless-steel baking dish. Pour the marinade over it, rubbing off the salt. Refrigerate for 1 hour, turning and basting every 15 minutes.

3. Light a grill. Using a damp paper towel, coat the grill with the oil. Remove the meat from the marinade and grill over a medium-hot fire, turning occasionally, until browned and medium rare, about 15 minutes. Transfer to a cutting board and let stand for 10 minutes. ➤

4. Strain the balsamic marinade into a small stainless-steel saucepan. Bring to a boil over moderately high heat and simmer for 30 seconds. Slice the beef tenderloin ⅓ inch thick and serve with the balsamic sauce.   *–Jim Cohen*

WINE 1994 De Loach Vineyards Estate Bottled Zinfandel from California

Spicy Roast Beef with White-and-Black-Bean Ragout

4 SERVINGS

A beef eye-of-round for four people cooks in about forty-five minutes, so it's a good cut to keep in mind for weekday dinners.

    2 teaspoons chili powder
    2 teaspoons ground cumin
    1 teaspoon ground coriander
    1 teaspoon dry mustard
    2 tablespoons vegetable oil
 1½ pounds beef eye-of-round
Salt and freshly ground pepper
    ¼ pound sliced bacon
    2 tablespoons unsalted butter

BELOW: **Balsamic-Marinated Beef Tenderloin.**
RIGHT: **Spicy Roast Beef with White-and-Black-Bean Ragout.**

    1 large onion, halved and thinly sliced
    1 garlic clove, minced
    1 small jalapeño pepper, minced
    1 cup cooked white beans, rinsed if canned
    1 cup cooked black beans, rinsed if canned
    1 tablespoon chopped cilantro leaves
Two 9-inch corn tortillas, cut into ½-inch-wide strips and fried (optional)

1. Preheat the oven to 450°. In a small bowl, combine the chili powder, cumin, coriander and mustard. Stir in the oil. Season the meat with salt and pepper; coat with the spice mixture, cover and let stand 30 minutes at room temperature.

2. Set the meat on a rack in a roasting pan and lay the bacon slices on top. Roast for 15 minutes. Reduce the oven temperature to 375° and roast for 25 to 30 minutes longer, or until an instant-read thermometer inserted in the thickest part of the meat registers 135° for medium rare. Discard the bacon, transfer the meat to a carving board and cover loosely with aluminum foil.

3. In a medium skillet, melt the butter. Add the onion and cook over moderately high heat, stirring often, until softened but not browned, about 5 minutes. Add the garlic and jalapeño and cook until the garlic is fragrant, about 1 minute. Stir in the white and black beans and the cilantro and cook until the beans are hot. Spoon onto plates.

4. Carve the meat into thin slices and arrange the slices on top of the beans.

Garnish the meat with the fried tortilla strips and serve. *—Steven Chiappetti*
WINE 1990 Château de Beaucastel Châteauneuf-du-Pape. The wine's spiciness and high alcohol level make it a good match for the fiery and earthy flavors of the beef and beans.

Red-Cooked Beef with Cinnamon

8 SERVINGS

Rice noodles are available at Asian markets, but you can substitute any long, broad noodle.

- 3 cups water
- 1 cup medium-dry sherry
- ¾ cup fresh orange juice
- ½ cup soy sauce
- ¼ cup honey
- 4 cinnamon sticks
- 1 tablespoon five-spice powder
- 1 tablespoon chopped garlic
- 1 tablespoon minced fresh ginger
- 1 teaspoon coriander seeds
- ½ teaspoon crushed red pepper
- ¼ cup vegetable oil

One 4-pound piece of boneless beef flanken or brisket

Salt and freshly ground pepper

- 1 medium onion, thinly sliced
- 1 pound wide or medium dried rice noodles
- 6 heads baby bok choy, halved lengthwise, or 1 pound Napa cabbage, cut into 1-inch pieces
- 1 medium red bell pepper—roasted, peeled, seeded and thinly sliced (optional)

Cilantro, for garnish

Mint sprigs, for garnish

1. Preheat the oven to 350°. In a medium stainless-steel bowl, combine the water, sherry, orange juice, soy sauce, honey, cinnamon, five-spice powder, garlic, ginger, coriander and crushed red pepper.
2. In a large enameled cast-iron casserole, heat the oil over moderately high heat. Season the beef with salt and

Red-Cooked Beef with Cinnamon

pepper. Add the beef to the casserole and cook until browned, about 5 minutes per side. Drain any fat.
3. Add the onion and the sherry mixture to the meat, cover and bring to a boil. Cook the meat in the oven for about 2½ hours, or until very tender; turn the meat halfway through cooking.
4. Meanwhile, in a large bowl, cover the noodles with cold water and let soften, 20 to 30 minutes. Drain and set aside.
5. Transfer the beef to a large platter, cover with aluminum foil and keep warm. Skim the fat from the broth and add the bok choy and red bell pepper, if using. Simmer over moderate heat until the bok choy is just tender, 3 to 5 minutes. Season with salt and pepper. Add the

noodles and simmer just to heat through.
6. To serve, cut the beef across the grain into ½-inch-thick slices. Transfer the noodles to six warm shallow bowls. Top the noodles with slices of beef, red bell pepper and bok choy. Ladle the broth over all and garnish with the cilantro and mint *—Gordon Hamersley*
MAKE AHEAD The recipe can be prepared through Step 3 and refrigerated for up to two days. Remove the fat from the surface of the broth and reheat in a 350° oven before proceeding.
WINE With this Chinese-inspired stew, try any of Turley Wine Cellars's 1994 single-vineyard Zinfandels, such as the Aida Vineyard, if you can find it. Or simply serve your favorite beer.

239

Rio Rancho Steaks with Ancho Butter, with New-Potato Salad with Grilled Red Onions (p. 64)

menu

CAFE ANNIE MARGARITAS (P. 412)

Refried Beans with Pickled Jalapeños (p. 327)

Tall Tim's Texas Toasts (p. 17)

White-Wing-Dove-Style Grilled Quail (p. 209)

Deep-in-the-Heart-of-Texas Chicken (p. 171)

Rio Rancho Steaks with Ancho Butter (p. 240)

New-Potato Salad with Grilled Red Onions (p. 64)

Spicy Coleslaw (p. 56)

Ginger Star Shortcakes with Summer Berries (p. 383)

Rio Rancho Steaks with Ancho Butter

16 SERVINGS

Any leftover smoky chile butter can be used to top grilled fish or roasted meat or stirred into polenta.

ANCHO BUTTER

- 2 ancho chiles, stemmed and seeded
- Boiling water
- 1 tablespoon olive oil
- ¼ medium onion, coarsely chopped
- 6 garlic cloves, coarsely chopped
- 2 sticks (½ pound) unsalted butter, softened
- 2 teaspoons fresh lime juice
- ½ teaspoon kosher salt
- ¼ teaspoon pure maple syrup

STEAKS

- ½ cup olive oil
- ¼ cup unsulphured molasses
- ¼ cup sherry vinegar
- 2 teaspoons pure chile powder, preferably ancho
- Six 1½-pound bone-in rib-eye steaks, about 3 inches thick
- Salt and freshly ground pepper

1. MAKE THE ANCHO BUTTER: In a heatproof bowl, soak the anchos in boiling water until softened, about 20 minutes. Drain the anchos and coarsely chop them.

2. Heat the oil in a small skillet. Add the onion and garlic and cook over low heat, stirring, until tender and lightly caramelized, about 4 minutes. Remove from the heat and let cool.

3. On a cutting board, chop the anchos and the onion together to make a coarse paste. Transfer to a bowl. Beat in the butter, lime juice, salt and maple syrup.

4. GRILL THE STEAKS: Light a grill, preferably charcoal. In a bowl, combine the oil, molasses, vinegar and chile powder. Brush the steaks on both sides with some of the mixture and season with salt and pepper. When the fire is hot, sear the steaks until well browned on the outside, about 3 minutes per side. Remove the steaks from the grill and spread the coals to cool them down. Return the steaks to the grill and brush with more of the molasses mixture. Grill slowly, turning and rotating, until rare to medium rare, about 8 minutes per side. Transfer to a large platter and let rest for 10 minutes. Thinly slice the steaks and serve with the ancho butter. *–Robert Del Grande*

MAKE AHEAD The ancho butter can be refrigerated for up to three days or frozen for up to one month. Let the butter soften before using.

Stuffed Rib-Eye Steaks with Chile Lime Relish

4 SERVINGS

We make our zesty relish with preserved malagueta peppers, a hallmark of Brazilian cooking. You can substitute any spicy pickled chiles, such as jalapeños or tabascos. Even without the relish, the roasted-serrano-stuffed steaks are a treat for any chile lover.

LIME RELISH

- 1 small onion, finely chopped
- 4 large garlic cloves, minced
- ¼ cup minced pickled chiles
- ¼ cup fresh lime juice
- 3 tablespoons coarsely chopped flat-leaf parsley
- 1 teaspoon coarse salt

STEAK

- 3 tablespoons olive oil
- 8 to 12 small serrano chiles, stemmed
- 16 medium garlic cloves, peeled

Four 10- to 14-ounce boneless rib-eye, sirloin or shell steaks, about 1½ inches thick

Salt and freshly ground pepper

I. MAKE THE LIME RELISH: Combine all of the ingredients in a mini-processor, blender or mortar and blend or grind to a paste.

2. PREPARE THE STEAK: Heat the oil in a small saucepan until shimmering. Add the serranos and sauté over moderate heat until the skins start to brown and blister, about 2 minutes. Transfer to paper towels. Add the garlic to the pan and cook over low heat until golden, 4 to 6 minutes. Transfer to paper towels and let cool.

3. Using a small knife, make six or seven 1-inch horizontal incisions along the edge of each steak. Stuff the incisions in each steak with 4 garlic cloves and 2 or 3 serranos.

4. Light a grill or preheat the broiler and position a rack as close to the heat source as possible. Season the steaks with salt and pepper. Grill or broil for 4 to 5 minutes per side for medium-rare. Serve at once with the lime relish. –*Susan Feniger and Mary Sue Milliken*

WINE 1994 Moulin de Lagrezette Cahors from France

Grilled Beef Tenderloin with Merlot Sauce

8 SERVINGS

The luxurious red-wine sauce relies on demiglace, reduced veal stock that's available at specialty-food stores and by mail order from D'Artagnan (800-327-8246) or More Than Gourmet (800-860-9385). If you can't find demiglace, substitute a rich veal, beef or chicken stock; don't use canned broth.

MERLOT SAUCE

- 10 medium shallots, thinly sliced
- 1 bottle (750 ml) Merlot
- 3 cups demiglace

BEEF AND VEGETABLES

- 16 fingerling or small new potatoes
- 1 pint pearl onions (about 32), preferably red, blanched and peeled
- 3½ tablespoons unsalted butter
- 1 teaspoon sugar

Salt

- 16 baby carrots
- 3 medium portobello mushrooms, stemmed

Olive oil, for brushing

Freshly ground pepper

Eight 5-ounce beef tenderloin fillets

HERB SALAD

- 1 cup chervil sprigs
- 1 cup flat-leaf parsley sprigs, tough stems removed
- ½ cup very coarsely chopped chives
- ½ cup tarragon leaves
- ¼ cup extra-virgin olive oil
- 2 tablespoons red-wine vinegar

Salt and freshly ground pepper

I. MAKE THE MERLOT SAUCE: Combine the shallots and wine in a heavy saucepan and boil over high heat

menu

Chive-Spiked Smoked Salmon on Chips (p. 14)

A FLIGHT OF CHARDONNAYS:
1994 ELKHORN PEAK WINERY
1995 KENT RASMUSSEN WINERY
1992 BARNETT VINEYARDS

Chilled Leek Terrine with Caviar (p. 29)

1995 ELKHORN PEAK WINERY
PINOT NOIR

Green Parsley Risotto with Sautéed Shrimp (p. 32)

1995 KENT RASMUSSEN WINERY
PINOT NOIR

Grilled Beef Tenderloin with Merlot Sauce (p. 241)

1994 AZALEA SPRINGS WINERY
MERLOT

Dried-Fruit Compote with Fresh Goat Cheese (p. 389)

1993 KENT RASMUSSEN WINERY
LATE HARVEST SAUVIGNON BLANC

Grilled Beef Tenderloin with Merlot Sauce

until reduced to 2 tablespoons, about 45 minutes. Add the demiglace and boil until reduced to 2 cups, 10 to 15 minutes. Strain the sauce and return it to the saucepan.

2. MAKE THE BEEF AND VEGETABLES: Preheat the oven to 425°. Spread the potatoes in a medium baking dish and bake for about 35 minutes, or until they are tender. Meanwhile, in a small skillet, cover the onions with water. Add 2 tablespoons of the butter, the sugar and a pinch of salt and bring the water to a boil over high heat. Cook until the water has evaporated, about 20 minutes. Stir constantly until the onions are glazed and lightly browned, about 3 minutes more.

3. In a saucepan, cover the carrots with cold water. Add salt and bring to a boil over high heat. Cook until the carrots are just tender, about 7 minutes. Drain, rinse under cold water and drain again. Melt the remaining 1½ tablespoons of butter in the saucepan, add the carrots and sauté until warmed through. Add the onions.

4. Meanwhile, light a charcoal grill or preheat the broiler. Brush the mushrooms with oil, season them with salt and pepper and grill or broil them for about 7 minutes per side, or until the mushrooms are tender and lightly charred. Let cool slightly, then slice the mushrooms. Season the beef with salt and pepper and grill or broil for about 5 minutes per side for rare meat.

5. TOSS THE HERB SALAD: In a bowl, combine the chervil, parsley, chives and tarragon. Add the oil and vinegar. Season the salad with salt and pepper and toss well.

6. Rewarm the potatoes in the oven and the onions and carrots on the stove. Reheat the sauce. Set a beef fillet on each plate. Top the beef fillets with the herb salad and spoon the sauce around. Arrange the mushrooms, the potatoes,

the onions and the carrots alongside the beef and serve. —*Pilar Sanchez*
WINE 1994 Azalea Springs Winery Merlot. You can't go wrong with portobellos and Merlot. God made that combo. Portobellos bring out the best in any red.

Steak with Rosemary Oil

4 SERVINGS **Q**

Once you've sautéed meat or poultry, it takes only a few more seconds to make a wonderful flavored oil. Just add a handful of fresh herbs or other seasonings to your sauté pan and cook them briefly (see "Instant Oils," right). Here I've spiffed up beefsteak with a fragrant rosemary oil. Serve with crusty bread and sautéed cherry tomatoes.

2½ tablespoons olive oil
1½ pounds well-trimmed boneless sirloin or rib-eye steak, cut ¾ inch thick
Salt and freshly ground pepper
Four 3-inch rosemary sprigs, bruised with the back of a heavy knife

I. In a large heavy skillet, heat 1 tablespoon of the oil. When it just begins to smoke, season both sides of the steak generously with salt and pepper and cook over moderately high heat for 3 minutes per side for medium rare. Transfer the steak to a warmed platter.
2. Add the remaining 1½ tablespoons of oil and the rosemary to the skillet and stir frequently until the rosemary begins to color, about 1½ minutes. Scrape the oil over the steak, garnish with the rosemary sprigs and serve. —*Judith Sutton*
WINE Red meat, red wine—what could be easier? To complement the flavor of the rosemary here, you'll want to stick with Cabernet Sauvignon, which has a hint of herbiness of its own. Among a number of possibilities to consider are the 1993 Chateau Montelena or the 1992 Burgess from California—or a Bordeaux, such as the 1992 Château Léoville Barton.

Seasoned Sliced Pan-Grilled Beef Steaks

6 SERVINGS

Italian beefsteak is rarely, if ever, quite as tender as the best American steaks, but what it lacks in mere tenderness it more than makes up for in taste. An Italian cook understands that grilling alone, however skillfully executed and however choice the cut of meat, is not sufficient to produce good flavor. Flavor is coaxed by a confident sprinkling of salt while the meat is cooking—not after it is served; by good olive oil; by pepper; and, on occasion, by the judicious use of garlic and herbs. In order to distribute the seasonings more thoroughly, Italians often cut a large grilled steak into several thick slices, thereby producing many more surfaces to coat. A steak served thus is called a *tagliata* from the Italian *tagliare*, to cut.

⅓ cup extra-virgin olive oil
12 medium garlic cloves, peeled

---

instant oils

To make these oils, add the flavoring plus a tablespoon or so of olive oil to the hot pan used to cook meat or poultry. Try these classic ideas, experiment with other herbs and spices or make up your own combinations.

Sage oil Cook leaves from a few small sprigs just until crisp and lightly browned. The fried sage leaves can be used as a garnish.

Garlic oil Cook three to four smashed peeled cloves over low heat until pale gold (the garlic will turn bitter if it darkens); discard the garlic.

Chile oil Cook four or more small dried chiles for thirty seconds; discard the chiles.

Scallion oil Split three scallions lengthwise and cook for one to two minutes, or until lightly browned; discard the scallions.

ABOVE: **Making rosemary oil.**
RIGHT: **Steak with Rosemary Oil,
with Sautéed Cherry Tomatoes
with Shallots (p. 320).**

1 or 2 sprigs of rosemary
  2 boneless rib or strip steaks,
     cut 2 inches thick
Salt and freshly ground pepper

1. Put the oil and garlic cloves in a large skillet and turn the heat to moderately high. Cook, stirring two or three times, until the garlic is pale gold, about 3 minutes. Remove from the heat and stir in the rosemary; set aside.

2. Heat a cast-iron skillet or stovetop grill over high heat. When the pan is very hot, add the steaks–they should sizzle instantly and quickly begin to smoke. Cook the steaks until they are very dark brown on one side, about 3 minutes. Turn the steaks, sprinkle with salt and brown the other side.

3. Transfer the pan-grilled steaks to a cutting board and slice them on an angle about ½ inch thick; the meat should be quite, quite rare.

4. Reheat the rosemary oil over moderately high heat. As the oil begins to heat up, put in the steak slices and any juices they may have released. Cook for 1 minute, turning the slices and seasoning with pepper. Transfer the meat to a warm platter and pour all the pan juices on top, holding back the rosemary and garlic. Serve piping hot. –*Marcella Hazan*

Pan-Seared Strip Steaks with Red-Wine Onion Sauce

4 SERVINGS **Q**

Freshly ground pepper
Four 8-ounce New York strip steaks
  1 tablespoon vegetable oil
  3 tablespoons unsalted butter
  ½ medium red onion, sliced
     ¼ inch thick
  ½ cup dry red wine, such as
     Côtes du Rhône
  1 cup plus 1 tablespoon beef stock
     or canned low-sodium broth
  1 teaspoon arrowroot
Salt
  1 tablespoon minced flat-leaf parsley

1. Preheat the oven to 200°. Pepper both sides of the steaks.

2. In a large heavy stainless-steel skillet, heat the oil over high heat. When it begins to smoke, add two of the steaks and sear them for 2 minutes on each side. Transfer to a heatproof plate. Keep warm in the oven and repeat with the remaining 2 steaks.

3. Discard the oil. Add the butter to the pan. Add the onion; cook over high heat, stirring, until browned, 2 to 3 minutes. Add the wine and the 1 cup stock. Boil over moderately high heat until the liquid is reduced to ½ cup, about 4 minutes.

4. Dissolve the arrowroot in the remaining 1 tablespoon of stock and stir into the sauce. Remove the pan from the heat, add the steak juices and season with salt and pepper. Spread the onion sauce on warmed plates, top with the steaks and serve at once, garnished with the parsley.   —*Bob Chambers*

WINE A full-throttle, deep and fruity Zinfandel is best: try the 1994 Seghesio or the 1994 Sebastiani Old Vine.

LEFT: **Pan-Seared Steaks with Vidalia Onions.** BELOW: **Pan-Seared Strip Steaks with Red-Wine Onion Sauce, with Mashed Yukon Golds (p. 310).**

Pan-Seared Steaks with Vidalia Onions

4 SERVINGS

Everyone thinks that we Southerners do most of our cooking on the grill, but the meat eaters I know prefer their steaks pan-seared. I don't usually cook sweet onions because they tend to be watery, but in this dish, they're perfect.

Four ½-pound boneless strip steaks (about 1-inch thick)
Freshly ground pepper
Coarse salt
  4 tablespoons unsalted butter
  1 very large Vidalia or other sweet onion, finely chopped
  ½ cup spicy young red wine, such as Côtes du Rhône

I. Set a large cast-iron skillet over high heat. Season the steaks generously on both sides with pepper. When the skillet is searing hot, season the steaks with salt, add them to the skillet and cook for 2 minutes. Shake the skillet; the steaks should be seared enough to loosen. Using tongs, turn the steaks and cook until they are browned on the second side but still quite rare, about 2 minutes. Shake the skillet again to loosen the steaks. Transfer the steaks to ovenproof plates and keep warm in a low oven.

2. Immediately add the butter and the chopped Vidalia onion to the skillet and cook over moderate heat, shaking often, until the onion is softened, about 5 minutes. Add the wine and bring to a boil over high heat, scraping up any brown bits from the bottom of the skillet. Using a slotted spoon, transfer the onion to the plates. Boil the wine sauce until it is reduced and tasty and then season it with salt and pepper. Pour the sauce over the steaks and serve immediately.   —*John Martin Taylor*

WINE Red meat with a red-wine sauce is big-red territory. Go for the 1993 Guigal Côtes du Rhône or the 1994 Rosemount Estate McLaren Vale Shiraz from Australia.

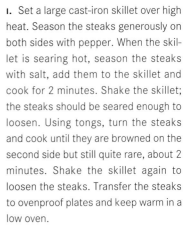

menu

Pan-Seared Strip Steaks with Red-Wine Onion Sauce (p. 243)

Steamed spinach

Mashed Yukon Golds with Buttermilk (p. 310)

1994 SEGHESIO ZINFANDEL

1994 SEBASTIANI OLD VINE ZINFANDEL

———

Banana-Split Tart (p. 369)

Rosemary Flank Steak with Roasted Potatoes

6 SERVINGS **L**

- 6 tablespoons canola oil
- 3 medium Spanish onions—1 thinly sliced, 2 cut into thin wedges attached at the root end
- 3 garlic cloves, thinly sliced
- 2 shallots, thinly sliced
- 1/3 cup minced rosemary
- 2 tablespoons red-wine vinegar
- 1 teaspoon ground cumin
- 1/2 teaspoon cayenne pepper
- 1¾ pounds trimmed flank steak
- 2 pounds small unpeeled new potatoes, quartered
- 2 tablespoons balsamic vinegar
- 1 tablespoon olive oil

Salt and freshly ground pepper

1. Heat the canola oil in a large stainless-steel skillet. Add the sliced onion, garlic and shallots and cook over moderately low heat, stirring, until softened, about 5 minutes. Add the rosemary and cook for 1 minute. Add the red-wine vinegar, cumin and cayenne pepper and let cool.

2. Scrape the marinade into a large, sturdy resealable plastic bag. Add the flank steak and spread the marinade over it. Seal the bag and refrigerate for 1 to 4 hours, turning the bag twice.

3. Preheat the oven to 400°. In a large bowl, gently toss the potatoes, onion wedges, balsamic vinegar and oil; season lightly with salt and black pepper. Spread the vegetables in a large non-stick roasting pan. Roast for about 40 minutes, stirring once, until tender and browned.

4. Light a grill or heat a large cast-iron grill pan. Scrape the marinade off the steak. Grill the steak over moderately high heat for about 15 minutes, turning once, until browned and medium-rare. Cover with aluminum foil; let rest for 5 minutes. Season with salt and pepper. Thinly slice across the grain. Serve with the potatoes and onions. *–Charlie Palmer*

Braised Short Ribs

6 TO 8 SERVINGS

- 1/4 cup vegetable oil
- 8 meaty beef short ribs (about 5 pounds)

Salt and freshly ground pepper

- 2 medium carrots, finely chopped
- 2 celery ribs, finely chopped
- 1 small onion, finely chopped
- 1/4 cup tomato paste
- 1 cup cider vinegar
- 2 cups chicken stock or canned low-sodium broth
- 1 cup drained and coarsely chopped canned Italian tomatoes
- 3 tablespoons dark brown sugar
- 2 tablespoons molasses

1. Preheat the oven to 375°. In a large enameled cast-iron casserole, heat the oil. Season the ribs with salt and pepper. Add the ribs in batches and brown them on all sides over moderately high heat. Remove the ribs to a plate and pour off all but 2 tablespoons of fat from the casserole. Add the carrots, celery and onion and cook, stirring often, until browned, about 10 minutes. Stir in the tomato paste and cook for 4 minutes longer. Pour in the vinegar and boil over high heat, scraping up any brown bits. Stir in the stock, tomatoes, brown sugar and molasses, add the ribs and bring to a boil.

2. Cover and braise the ribs in the oven for about 2 hours, turning them occasionally, until the meat is very tender. Remove the ribs to a large platter and cover with aluminum foil to keep warm. Skim off all the fat from the cooking liquid. Pour the contents of the casserole through a fine strainer, pressing hard on the vegetables. Bring the sauce to a boil and season with salt and pepper. Pour over the ribs and serve. *–Warren Katz*

WINE Gutsy flavors call for a red with palate-cleansing tannins. That's Cabernet Sauvignon. Go for a California bottling, such as the 1993 Conn Creek Limited Release or the 1993 Mount Veeder.

Beef and Coconut Satays

4 SERVINGS

Satays are Indonesia's national dish and culinary common denominator: these little kebabs are served in elegant hotel restaurants, from roadside pushcarts and just about everywhere in between. This beef and coconut version, a specialty of the island of Madura, near Java, owes its distinctive flavor and texture to shredded coconut. The meat mixture is traditionally flavored with *ketjap manis*, a sweet soy sauce available at Asian markets; I've used soy sauce and molasses in its place, but use *ketjap manis* if you can find it.

- 10 ounces lean ground beef
- 1/2 cup shredded sweetened coconut
- 1/2 tablespoon soy sauce
- 1/2 tablespoon unsulphured molasses
- 2 teaspoons finely grated fresh ginger
- 1 teaspoon fresh lime juice
- 3/4 teaspoon salt
- 1/2 teaspoon turmeric
- 1/2 teaspoon freshly ground pepper
- 2 tablespoons vegetable oil, plus more for grilling

1. In a bowl, combine the ground beef, coconut, soy sauce, molasses, ginger, lime juice, salt, turmeric, pepper and the 2 tablespoons of oil. Mix with your hands to combine the ingredients.

2. With lightly moistened hands, roll 1 tablespoon of the meat mixture around a bamboo skewer into a 6-inch-long strip about 1/3 inch thick. Repeat until all of the meat mixture is used up.

3. Light a grill. When the fire is hot, oil the grill. Arrange the skewers at the edge of the grill (so they don't burn) and cook the satays, turning often, until the meat is lightly charred and just cooked through, 3 to 4 minutes. Serve the satays at once. *–Steven Raichlen*

MAKE AHEAD The satays can be refrigerated overnight after Step 2.

BEER Geary's London-Style Porter, from Maine, stands up to the highly seasoned beef without being too heavy.

Sesame Grilled Beef

6 SERVINGS

Korean barbecue comes in two main varieties, one of which is *bul kogi*. This type of barbecue consists of thin shavings of beef steeped in a salty-sweet sesame marinade and cooked until crisp on a charcoal grill that resembles an inverted wok. The sugar and sesame oil caramelize during cooking, giving the meat a candied sweetness. The dish takes its name from the Korean words for *fire* and *meat*. *Bul kogi* is eaten like moo shu or fajitas, using a lettuce leaf instead of a pancake or tortilla. You roll the meat in a romaine lettuce leaf, dip it in sauce and eat it. The result is a fabulous contrast of sweet and salty, pungent and fruity, crisp and chewy.

global barbecuespeak

anticuchos Peruvian spicy kebabs, usually made with beef heart.
barbacoa Mexican pit-roasted, spice-marinated lamb or kid.
bistecca alla fiorentina Tuscan olive-oil-marinated grilled steak.
grillade French grilled steaks or chops.
kofta Middle Eastern ground kebabs.
laab Thai grilled meat salads.
lechón asado Puerto Rican marinated pit-roasted pig.
mechoui Moroccan spit-roasted lamb.
shawarma Middle Eastern spiced lamb or turkey roasted on a vertical spit.
souvlaki Greek lamb shish kebab.
spiedini Italian shish kebab.
teriyaki Japanese barbecue.
tikka Indian grilled or spit-roasted poultry.
yarng Thai barbecue.
yakitori Japanese grilled chicken.

MARINATED MEAT

- 2 pounds shell steak or sirloin, sliced across the grain ¼ inch thick
- ½ cup soy sauce
- ⅓ cup sugar
- 3 tablespoons sake or dry sherry
- 8 garlic cloves, minced
- 4 scallions, minced
- 2 tablespoons Asian sesame oil
- 2 tablespoons toasted sesame seeds
- ½ teaspoon freshly ground pepper

DIPPING SAUCE

- ½ cup soy sauce
- ½ cup sake
- ¼ cup sugar
- 1 Asian pear—peeled, cored and finely chopped
- 4 scallions, finely chopped
- ¼ medium onion, finely chopped
- 2 tablespoons sesame seeds, toasted

SERVING

- 1 head of romaine lettuce, separated into leaves

1. MARINATE THE MEAT: With a meat pounder, pound the meat between two sheets of plastic wrap until you have wide, thin strips. In a shallow bowl, combine the soy sauce, sugar and sake; stir to dissolve the sugar. Stir in the remaining ingredients. Add the meat and turn to coat with the marinade. Set aside to marinate for 1 hour, turning the meat from time to time.

2. MAKE THE DIPPING SAUCE: In a medium bowl, combine the soy sauce, sake and sugar; stir to dissolve the sugar. Add the Asian pear, scallions, onion and sesame seeds. Pour the sauce into six small bowls.

3. Light a grill. When the fire is hot, arrange the meat on the grill and cook for 1 to 2 minutes per side, or until nicely browned. Transfer the meat to a platter and arrange the romaine leaves alongside. To eat, wrap a piece of meat in a lettuce leaf, dip the bundle in the Asian pear sauce and pop it into your mouth. *–Steven Raichlen*

BEER The aggressive hops in American brown ales will contrast beautifully with the seasonings here, and the chocolatey malt will stand up to the beef. Consider Brooklyn Brown Ale from New York.

Pepper Steak

2 SERVINGS L

With lots of peppers and not much steak, this is excellent diet food. To make half a teaspoon of ginger juice, put a teaspoon of finely grated fresh ginger in a tea strainer and press to extract the juice.

MARINATED BEEF

- 1 teaspoon Shao-Hsing wine or dry sherry
- ½ teaspoon ginger juice (see above)
- 1 teaspoon cornstarch

Pinch of freshly ground white pepper

- ¼ pound trimmed London broil, thinly sliced against the grain

SAUCE

- ¼ cup chicken stock
- 1 tablespoon oyster sauce
- 2 teaspoons Shao-Hsing wine or dry sherry
- 2 teaspoons cornstarch
- ¾ teaspoon dark soy sauce
- ½ teaspoon sugar
- ¼ teaspoon Asian sesame oil

Pinch of freshly ground white pepper

- 2 teaspoons peanut oil
- 1 teaspoon minced fresh ginger
- 2 medium green bell peppers, thinly sliced lengthwise
- 2 tablespoons chicken stock
- 1½ tablespoons fermented black beans, rinsed
- 1 teaspoon minced garlic

Salt

1. MARINATE THE BEEF: In a medium bowl, combine the wine, ginger juice, cornstarch and pepper. Add the beef; toss well. Set aside to marinate for 20 minutes. ➤

Sesame Grilled Beef

2. MAKE THE SAUCE: Combine the stock, oyster sauce, wine, cornstarch, soy sauce, sugar, sesame oil and white pepper in a small bowl.

3. Set a wok or large skillet over high heat for 30 seconds. Add 1 teaspoon of the peanut oil and stir to coat the wok. When a wisp of white smoke appears, add the minced ginger and stir-fry for 10 seconds. Add the green bell peppers and stir-fry for 45 seconds. Add 1 tablespoon of the chicken stock and stir-fry until the peppers turn bright green, about 2 minutes. Transfer the peppers to a plate.

4. Return the wok to the burner and add the remaining 1 teaspoon peanut oil; stir to coat the wok. When a wisp of white smoke appears, add the black beans and the garlic and stir-fry until fragrant, about 45 seconds. Add the

beef and its marinade; spread the meat in an even layer and let cook undisturbed for 30 seconds. Turn the beef, add the remaining 1 tablespoon of stock and stir well.

5. Return the green bell peppers to the wok and stir-fry for 1 minute. Make a well in the center of the wok, pushing everything up the sides slightly. Stir the sauce and pour it in. Stir until the sauce boils and thickens, about 1 minute. Add a pinch of salt and serve the pepper steak hot.   *–Eileen Yin-Fei Lo*

WINE The right red for this savory beef? A medium-bodied Bordeaux, such as the 1993 Château Prieuré-Lichine or a lighter Australian Cabernet Sauvignon, such as the 1993 Chateau Tahbilk. Both have the depth of flavor and the acidity to stand up to the seasoning and the bell peppers.

Pepper Steak

Steamed Orange Beef

4 SERVINGS **L**

Many people know orange beef as a twice-fried, sugar-laden dish. This version, made with ground sirloin, has all the defined flavor of the familiar dish without any of the heaviness. The beef is best enjoyed wrapped up in a leaf of cold iceberg lettuce. If you're serving it as a main course, you may want to double the portions.

MEAT MIXTURE

- ½ **pound lean ground sirloin**
- ½ **cup thinly sliced scallions**
- ⅓ **cup finely diced water chestnuts**
- ¼ **cup chicken stock**
- 1½ **tablespoons minced orange zest**
- 1 **tablespoon Shao-Hsing wine or dry sherry**
- 1 **tablespoon oyster sauce**
- 1 **tablespoon dark soy sauce**
- 1 **tablespoon cornstarch**
- 2 **teaspoons finely grated fresh ginger**
- 1 **teaspoon Shallot Oil (p. 336)**
- 1 **teaspoon sugar**
- ½ **teaspoon white vinegar**

Salt and freshly ground white pepper

- ¼ **cup finely diced red bell pepper**
- 2 **tablespoons minced coriander (cilantro)**
- 8 **iceberg lettuce leaves**

I. MAKE THE MEAT MIXTURE: Combine all of the ingredients in a large bowl; stir in one direction until well mixed. Transfer to a shallow steamproof bowl.

2. Set the bowl in a steamer basket over boiling water and steam until the meat is cooked through, about 15 minutes. Remove the bowl from the steamer and sprinkle the beef with the red bell pepper and coriander. Serve with the lettuce leaves.   *–Eileen Yin-Fei Lo*

WINE A light, low-tannin red, such as the 1995 Antinori Santa Christina Sangiovese from Italy or the 1994 Montevina Terra d'Oro Barbera from California, would suit this delicate, subtle dish.

Green Chili

10 SERVINGS

If you can't find pure chile powder, use equal parts hot and sweet Hungarian paprika. Like all spices, paprika is best when it's fresh.

- 2 tablespoons vegetable oil
- 5 pounds beef chuck, cut into 1-inch cubes

Salt and freshly ground pepper
- 2 large onions, chopped
- 4 garlic cloves, chopped
- 6 tablespoons pure chile powder
- 2 teaspoons ground cumin

One 12-ounce bottle of beer
- 2 cups water
- 1 red bell pepper, chopped
- 1 yellow bell pepper, chopped

Two 4-ounce cans whole green chiles, drained and chopped

1. In a Dutch oven, heat ½ tablespoon of the oil. Add one-quarter of the beef cubes, season them with salt and pepper and cook over high heat, without stirring, until they are brown on the bottom, about 3 minutes. Transfer the cubes of beef to a bowl and repeat with the remaining oil and beef. Add the onions to the pot and cook over moderate heat, stirring, until softened but not browned, about 5 minutes. Add the garlic, chile powder and cumin to the pot and cook, stirring, until fragrant, about 4 minutes.

2. Return the browned beef with any accumulated juices to the pot and stir well. Add the beer and the water and bring to a boil. Simmer over low heat, stirring occasionally, until the beef is very tender, about 2 hours. Stir in the red and yellow bell peppers and cook until softened, about 12 minutes. Add the green chiles and simmer until the chili is heated through, about 5 minutes. Season the chili with salt and pepper and serve. —*John Hopkins*

MAKE AHEAD The chili can be refrigerated for up to two days.

Parsley and Garlic Meatballs

8 SERVINGS

Lightly flatten these herb-flecked meatballs before sautéing and then finish them in broth to keep them moist.

- 3 slices of white bread, crusts trimmed
- ⅓ cup milk
- 1½ pounds lean ground beef
- 3 tablespoons vegetable oil
- 1 medium onion, finely chopped
- 3 large garlic cloves, finely chopped
- ¼ cup minced flat-leaf parsley
- ½ teaspoon ground cumin

Salt and freshly ground pepper
- 2 cups chicken stock or canned low-sodium broth

1. In a small bowl, soak the bread in the milk for 5 minutes. Squeeze the bread and discard the milk. In a large bowl, combine the ground beef with the bread, 1 tablespoon of the oil, the onion, garlic, parsley, cumin, 1½ teaspoons of salt and ½ teaspoon of pepper and mix well. Shape the mixture into 2-inch meatballs, and then flatten the meatballs slightly.

2. Heat another tablespoon of the oil in a large nonstick skillet. Add half of the meatballs and cook over moderately high heat, turning once, until browned on both sides, about 5 minutes. Transfer the meatballs to a bowl and wipe out the skillet. Repeat with the remaining 1 tablespoon oil and the uncooked meatballs.

3. In a large saucepan, bring the chicken stock to a simmer. Season with salt and pepper and add the meatballs. Simmer over moderate heat, stirring occasionally, until the meatballs are heated through, about 10 minutes. Transfer the meatballs and broth to a bowl and serve. —*Michel Benasra*

MAKE AHEAD The cooked meatballs can be refrigerated in the broth overnight. Reheat gently.

Slow-Roasted Oxtail Stew with Pancetta

4 SERVINGS

Unsweetened chocolate and dried fruit add depth to this hearty stew, though their flavors are barely perceptible.

- 2 tablespoons olive oil
- 5 pounds trimmed oxtails, cut into 2-inch lengths

Salt and freshly ground pepper
- 2 cups red wine
- 2 cups beef stock or canned low-sodium broth
- 2 medium onions, coarsely chopped
- 2 large carrots, coarsely chopped
- 2 celery ribs, coarsely chopped
- ¼ cup finely grated unsweetened chocolate (about ½ ounce)
- 1 tablespoon tomato paste
- 2 bay leaves
- ½ cup pitted prunes (about 4 ounces)
- 1 cup warm water
- ½ pound pancetta, cut into ½-inch dice
- 1¼ pounds pearl onions, blanched and peeled

Cooked pappardelle or wide noodles

1. Preheat the oven to 325°. Heat the oil in a large flameproof casserole. Season the oxtails with salt and pepper and cook over moderately high heat, turning often, until browned all over, about 20 minutes. Transfer the oxtails to a platter.

2. Pour off any fat from the casserole and add the wine and stock. Bring to a boil over high heat, stirring to incorporate any brown bits from the bottom of the pan. Return the oxtails to the casserole and add the onions, carrots, celery, chocolate, tomato paste and bay leaves. Cover and return to a simmer, then transfer to the oven and bake for about 4 hours, turning the oxtails often, until the meat is meltingly tender; add about ½ cup of water after 3 hours if the liquid has evaporated. ➤

Nine-Spice Rack of Lamb with Cucumber Relish

3. Meanwhile, in a small bowl, soak the prunes in the water until plumped, about 20 minutes; drain.

4. Transfer the oxtails to a large platter and cover to keep warm. Strain the cooking liquid through a sieve and skim off the fat. Add water, if necessary, to make 2½ cups of liquid. Return the liquid to the casserole and add the plumped prunes.

5. In a large skillet, cook the pancetta over moderately high heat, stirring often, until browned, about 5 minutes. Pour off any fat, add the pearl onions and cook, stirring often, until golden, about 7 minutes. With a slotted spoon, transfer the pancetta and onions to the casserole and simmer until the onions are tender, about 5 minutes. Pour the sauce over the oxtails and serve with the pappardelle.   *–Marsha McBride*

MAKE AHEAD The stew can be refrigerated for up to two days.

WINE This meaty stew gains a fruity dimension from the prunes, so a fruity, sturdy red, such as a California Cabernet Sauvignon, is a solid choice. Try the 1994 Hanna or the 1994 Joseph Phelps.

Nine-Spice Rack of Lamb with Cucumber Relish

4 SERVINGS
You can use this spice rub on any cut of lamb (or on steak). The crusty chops are sensational set off against the cool relish. Cultivated mint can replace the wild, if necessary.

  2 large European cucumbers—peeled, halved lengthwise, seeded and cut into 1-inch pieces
  ½ cup wild mint leaves
Kosher salt
One 1-inch-long cinnamon stick
  1 teaspoon sesame seeds
  1 teaspoon fenugreek seeds
  1 teaspoon cumin seeds
  1 teaspoon blade mace

  ½ teaspoon cardamom seeds
  ½ teaspoon crushed red pepper
  1 whole clove
  ¼ teaspoon freshly grated nutmeg
Two 8-rib racks of lamb, frenched (see box, p. 260)
  2 tablespoons peanut oil
Freshly ground black pepper

1. In a food processor, combine the cucumbers, mint and ½ teaspoon of kosher salt. Pulse until minced but not pureed. Transfer the cucumber mixture to a coarse strainer set over a bowl. Let drain in the refrigerator for at least 1 hour and up to 3 hours.

2. Preheat the oven to 500°. In a small skillet, combine the cinnamon, sesame seeds, fenugreek seeds, cumin seeds, mace, cardamom seeds, crushed red pepper and clove. Toast the spices over moderately high heat until fragrant, about 2 minutes; shake the pan frequently. Transfer the spices to a plate to cool. Coarsely grind the spices in a spice grinder or mortar. Transfer the spices to a small bowl and stir in the nutmeg.

3. Using a sharp knife, score shallow X marks in the fat of the lamb racks. Rub the spice mixture over both sides of the racks. Heat two large ovenproof skillets over high heat for 2 minutes. Add 1 tablespoon of the oil to each skillet. When the oil is very hot, add a rack of lamb to each of the skillets, fat-side down. Cook the lamb racks until they are browned, about 2 minutes. Turn the lamb racks over and cook for 2 minutes on the bony side. Turn the lamb racks again, fat-side down, and transfer the skillets to the oven. Roast the racks for 15 minutes for medium rare. Remove from the oven and cover loosely with aluminum foil. Let the racks rest for 10 minutes.

4. Transfer the cucumber relish from the strainer to a bowl and season with salt and black pepper. Carve the lamb

racks into chops and serve them with the relish. *–Jean-Georges Vongerichten*

MAKE AHEAD The spice mixture can be stored in a tightly covered jar for up to two days.

WINE 1993 Paolo Scavino Barbera d'Alba Affinato in Carati. With huge red fruit, licorice and rose-petal nuances, acidity and a sweet oak background, this wine is a natural for the sweet-spicy nature of this dish.

Lamb with Onion Juice and Grilled Eggplant

4 SERVINGS
To be strictly authentic, this Turkish recipe would be made with lamb tenderloin, which costs a sultan's fortune. I've retooled the recipe for the more affordable and readily available rack of lamb. I love the smoky flavor you get from grilling racks directly over the flames, but this method does require constant attention: as the fat melts, flare-ups are inevitable and unwatched racks will burn. Although it's not traditional, I like to marinate the lamb in sturdy resealable plastic bags, which keep the onion aromas from permeating the refrigerator.

  1 large white onion, finely chopped
  1 cup whole milk
  1 cup extra-virgin olive oil
Freshly ground pepper
  2 racks of lamb, chine bones removed, rib bones frenched (see box, p. 260)
  1 cup whole-milk yogurt
  2 long, slender eggplants (1 pound)
  1 small green bell pepper
  1 garlic clove, minced
  2 tablespoons unsalted butter
  1 teaspoon fresh lemon juice
Salt

1. In a blender or food processor, puree the onion. Strain the puree through a double layer of cheesecloth or a fine-meshed strainer into a deep baking dish; you should have about ½ cup of juice. Stir in the milk, oil and 1 teaspoon of freshly ground pepper. Add the lamb racks and coat with the marinade. Cover and refrigerate for 24 hours, turning the racks from time to time.

2. Scoop the yogurt into a fine stainless-steel strainer set over a bowl and let drain overnight in the refrigerator.

3. Light a grill. When the fire is hot, grill the eggplants and green bell pepper, turning often, until they are charred on all sides and very soft, about 10 minutes for the bell pepper and 30 minutes for the eggplants. Transfer the charred vegetables to a plate and let cool. Scrape the charred skins off the eggplants and bell pepper. Core and seed the bell pepper.

4. In a food processor or blender, puree the eggplants and bell pepper with the garlic. Add the drained yogurt, butter and lemon juice; process until smooth. Transfer to a saucepan and simmer over moderate heat for 2 minutes. Season with salt and pepper and set aside.

5. Drain the lamb racks, reserving the marinade. Generously season the lamb racks with salt. Grill the lamb racks over a hot fire, starting bony-side down and turning with tongs as needed; baste the racks with the marinade during the first 15 minutes of cooking and rotate them, moving them away from the coals if the meat starts to burn. If the tips of the bones begin to char, wrap them in aluminum foil. Stand the lamb racks on their ends and sear until browned. Total cooking time will be about 30 minutes, depending on the size of the lamb racks; medium-rare meat will measure 125° to 130° on an instant-read thermometer. Remove the lamb racks from the grill and let them rest for 10 minutes before carving.

6. To serve, reheat the eggplant sauce. Spread it on plates or a platter. Carve the lamb racks into chops, cutting down between the ribs. Arrange the lamb chops on the eggplant sauce and serve at once. *–Steven Raichlen*

BEER Trappist ales are brewed with special yeasts that impart unique flavors, such as black currants and spices. Slightly sweet, reddish amber Chimay Rouge, from Belgium, has a firm and malty body that pairs well with all red meats and offsets the smoky flavors in this dish.

Roasted Chiappetti Leg of Lamb with Pesto Stuffing

4 SERVINGS

- 1 cup basil leaves
- ¼ cup pine nuts
- ¼ cup freshly grated Parmesan
- 4 garlic cloves
- 2 tablespoons hot water
- ¼ cup olive oil, plus more for brushing
- 1 cup dried bread crumbs

One 1½-pound butterflied and well-trimmed leg of lamb

Salt and freshly ground pepper

- 1 medium eggplant, halved lengthwise and sliced crosswise ½ inch thick
- 4 medium tomatoes, sliced ½ inch thick

I. Preheat the oven to 425°. In a blender, combine the basil, pine nuts, Parmesan, garlic and water with the ¼ cup oil. Blend, stopping and scraping the sides of the blender as necessary, until a thick paste forms. Transfer the pesto to a bowl and stir in the bread crumbs.

2. Lay the butterflied leg of lamb flat, boned-side up, on a large work surface and season it generously with salt and pepper. Spread the pesto over the lamb, leaving a 1-inch border on all sides. Roll up the lamb and tie it with butcher's twine; season with salt and pepper. Set the stuffed leg of lamb on a rack in a large roasting pan and brush it with more oil. Arrange the eggplant and tomato slices in a single overlapping layer around the lamb. Brush the vegetables with oil and season well with salt and pepper.

3. Roast the leg of lamb for 15 minutes. Reduce the oven temperature to 375° and roast the lamb for 30 minutes longer, or until an instant-read thermometer inserted in the thickest part of the meat registers 140° for slightly pink meat. Transfer the leg of lamb to a carving board and cover it loosely with aluminum foil; let it stand for about 10 minutes. Slice the stuffed leg of lamb and serve it with the roasted eggplant and tomato slices. *–Steven Chiappetti*

WINE 1989 Château Pichon Lalande Pauillac. Young and more affordable than an older vintage, this gutsy, Cabernet Sauvignon–dominant Bordeaux balances the assertive flavors of the pesto.

Roast Leg of Lamb with Orange and Herbs

8 SERVINGS

Meaty leg of lamb gets a sweet tang from the orange-juice-based pan sauce.

- 2 large garlic cloves, minced
- 2 teaspoons finely grated orange zest
- 1 tablespoon finely chopped flat-leaf parsley
- 1 teaspoon finely chopped rosemary
- 1 teaspoon finely chopped thyme

Pinch of ground cumin

- 3 tablespoons plus 1 teaspoon olive oil

Salt and freshly ground pepper

One 8½-pound leg of lamb, trimmed of excess fat

- ½ cup fresh orange juice
- ¾ cup dry white wine
- 4 medium onions, peeled and halved crosswise
- 8 small carrots, halved lengthwise
- 1½ cups water, plus more if needed

1. In a small bowl, combine the garlic, orange zest, parsley, rosemary, thyme, cumin and the 1 teaspoon oil. Add a pinch each of salt and pepper.

2. Using a small sharp knife, make about twenty-five evenly spaced 1-inch incisions in the meaty sections of the lamb. Stuff about ½ teaspoon of the orange-herb paste into each incision. Turn the lamb fat-side up and rub with 1 tablespoon of the oil and then 2 tablespoons of the orange juice.

3. Preheat the oven to 450°. In a large stainless-steel roasting pan, combine ¼ cup of the wine and the remaining 2 tablespoons of olive oil. Arrange the onions and the carrots cut-side down in the roasting pan, set the leg of lamb on top and season with salt and pepper. Roast the leg of lamb in the center of the oven for 20 minutes. Pour the remaining ½ cup of wine and ½ cup of the water into the roasting pan and reduce the oven temperature to 325°. Continue roasting the leg of lamb for 1 hour and 20 minutes, basting a few times and adding up to ½ cup more water if the roasting pan gets dry.

4. Pour 2 tablespoons of the orange juice over the leg of lamb and raise the oven temperature to 400°. Roast the leg of lamb for about 30 minutes longer, or until the meat is medium-rare and an instant-read thermometer inserted in the meaty part of the leg registers 130°. Transfer the leg of lamb to a carving board, cover it loosely with aluminum foil and let it rest for 10 minutes. Transfer the carrots and onions from the roasting pan to a plate and keep them warm in a low oven.

5. Set the roasting pan on two burners over moderately high heat. Add the remaining ¼ cup of orange juice and boil for 3 minutes, scraping up the brown bits. Add the remaining 1 cup of water to the roasting pan and boil until the sauce is reduced and flavorful,

about 5 minutes. Pour the pan sauce into a serving bowl and skim the fat from the surface. Add any juices from the lamb and season the sauce with salt and pepper. Carve the leg of lamb and serve with the roasted carrots and onions; pass the pan sauce separately at the table. —*Marcia Kiesel*

MAKE AHEAD The leg of lamb can be prepared through Step 2 and refrigerated for up to one day. Let the lamb return to room temperature before proceeding with the recipe.

---

menu

Skillet-Toasted Almonds (p. 13)

Green-Olive Tapenade (p. 13)

Garlic Shrimp (p. 23)

HIDALGO LA GITANA
MANZANILLA SHERRY

1995 DR. KONSTANTIN FRANK
DRY JOHANNISBERG RIESLING

Smoky Escarole and Carrot Soup (p. 81)

1995 GEORGES DUBOEUF
CHIROUBLES

LIVIO FELLUGA TOCAI FRIULANO

Roast Leg of Lamb with Orange and Herbs (p. 252)

Potato and Fennel Gratin (p. 310)

Swiss Chard and Shallots (p. 323)

1990 CHÂTEAU COUFRAN
BORDEAUX

SHAFER VINEYARDS STAGS LEAP
DISTRICT CABERNET SAUVIGNON

Sweet Goat-Cheese and Walnut Tartlets (p. 371)

COCKBURN'S 10 YEARS OLD
TAWNY PORTO

FONSECA BIN 27 PORTO

Spiced Lamb Shanks with Almonds and Dates

6 SERVINGS

3 dried ancho chiles, stemmed and seeded
2 cups boiling water
¼ cup blanched whole almonds
2 teaspoons whole allspice berries
2 teaspoons fennel seeds
1¼ teaspoons whole cloves
1¼ teaspoons cinnamon
1¼ teaspoons nutmeg
6 tablespoons vegetable oil
2 large onions—1 finely chopped, 1 coarsely chopped
12 pitted dates, chopped
4 teaspoons sherry vinegar
¼ cup olive oil
Salt and freshly ground pepper
6 lamb shanks (about 1 pound each), trimmed of fat
15 garlic cloves, peeled
4 medium carrots, cut into 2-inch pieces
2 tablespoons tomato paste
4 cups chicken stock or canned low-sodium broth
3 cups red wine

1. Preheat the oven to 350°. In a heatproof bowl, cover the chiles with the boiling water and set aside until softened, about 20 minutes. Drain and chop the chiles.

2. Meanwhile, put the almonds on a baking sheet and toast them in the oven, stirring once, for about 8 minutes, or until golden brown. Let cool, then coarsely chop the almonds.

3. In a small skillet, toast the allspice, fennel seeds and cloves over moderate heat, shaking the pan, until fragrant, about 1 minute; let cool. Grind to a powder in a spice grinder or a mortar. Empty into a bowl and mix in the cinnamon and nutmeg.

4. In a small skillet, heat 2 tablespoons of the vegetable oil over moderately high heat. Add the finely chopped onion

and 2 teaspoons of the spice mixture. Reduce the heat to low and cook, stirring, until the onion is tender, about 10 minutes. Scrape the spiced onion into a food processor and add the chiles, dates and vinegar. Process to a coarse paste. With the machine on, add the olive oil in a thin steady stream. Scrape the mixture into a bowl and stir in the almonds. Season with salt and pepper.

5. In a large enameled cast-iron casserole, heat the remaining ¼ cup vegetable oil. Season the lamb shanks with salt and pepper. Add them to the casserole and brown over moderately high heat, about 4 minutes on each side;

Lamb Shanks on Polenta with a Parmesan Crust

transfer to a platter. Add the coarsely chopped onion, the garlic, carrots, tomato paste, the remaining spice mixture and 3 tablespoons of the chile-almond paste to the casserole and cook, stirring, until fragrant, about 3 minutes. Stir in the stock and wine and add the shanks.

6. Cover the casserole and bring the liquid to a boil and then cook the shanks in the oven, turning once, for about 2½ hours, or until very tender.

7. Transfer the lamb shanks and the carrots to a large platter; cover them with aluminum foil and keep warm. Boil the stewing liquid over high heat until

reduced and flavorful, about 10 minutes. Spread 2 tablespoons of the chile-almond paste over each of the lamb shanks and place on a dinner plate along with some carrots. Spoon a generous amount of sauce over the lamb shanks and serve. –*Gordon Hamersley*

MAKE AHEAD The chile-almond paste can be refrigerated for up to three days. Bring to room temperature before proceeding with Step 5. The lamb stew can be refrigerated for up to two days. Remove the fat from the surface and reheat in a 350° oven before proceeding with Step 7.

WINE Try the rich, spicy flavors of the 1992 or 1993 Charvin Châteauneuf-du-Pape. Other options: the softer, older 1990 Marqués de Riscal, a leathery Rioja Reserva, or the 1988 or 1989 Vallformosa Penedés Gran Reserva. There is a strong affinity between the sherrylike raisin tones of Spanish wines and the dates and spices in this North African-accented stew.

Lamb Shanks on Polenta with a Parmesan Crust

6 SERVINGS

Stews are usually soupy affairs, with chunks of meat and vegetables in a flavorful broth. But here stewed lamb shanks are set on polenta, covered with garlicky Parmesan bread crumbs and browned in the oven. The broth is served separately.

¼ cup vegetable oil

6 lamb shanks (about 1 pound each), trimmed

Salt and freshly ground pepper

4 medium carrots, cut into 2-inch lengths

1 medium onion, coarsely chopped

12 garlic cloves—11 chopped, 1 minced

2 tablespoons tomato paste

1 tablespoon dried rosemary

3 cups dry white wine

3 cups chicken stock or canned low-sodium broth

8 cups warm water

2 cups coarse yellow cornmeal

3 tablespoons unsalted butter

½ cup freshly grated Parmesan (about 1½ ounces)

1½ cups fresh bread crumbs

1 shallot, thinly sliced

1 tablespoon chopped parsley

Rosemary sprigs, for garnish

1. Preheat the oven to 350°. In a large enameled cast-iron casserole, heat the oil over moderately high heat. Season the lamb shanks with salt and pepper. Add the lamb shanks in batches to the casserole and cook them until they are browned, about 5 minutes per side; transfer the shanks to a platter. Add the carrots, onion, chopped garlic, tomato paste and rosemary to the casserole and cook, stirring, until fragrant, about 3 minutes.

2. Return the lamb shanks to the casserole and add the wine and the chicken stock. Cover and bring the liquid to a boil, then cook the lamb stew in the oven, turning once, for about 2½ hours, or until very tender.

3. While the lamb shanks are cooking, make the polenta: In a large saucepan, bring 4 cups of the water to a boil. In a bowl, combine the cornmeal with the 4 remaining cups of warm water. Whisk 1 teaspoon of salt and the cornmeal mixture into the saucepan until the mixture begins to thicken. Reduce the heat to low and cook, whisking vigorously every 5 minutes or so, until the polenta is thick and creamy, about 1 hour. Remove the saucepan from the heat and stir in 2 tablespoons of the butter and ¼ cup of the Parmesan. Season the polenta with salt and pepper. Cover the polenta and keep it warm.

4. Melt the remaining 1 tablespoon butter. In a bowl, combine the butter, bread crumbs, shallot, parsley, minced garlic and the remaining ¼ cup of Parmesan. Season with salt and pepper.

5. Increase the oven temperature to 400°. Spoon the polenta onto a large ovenproof platter or other serving piece and set the lamb shanks on top. Ladle ¼ cup of the cooking broth over each of the shanks. Pat each lamb shank with ¼ cup of the Parmesan crumbs. Arrange the roasted vegetables around the lamb shanks. Bake the lamb shanks on the top shelf of the oven for about 15 minutes, or until the Parmesan crumbs are browned. Garnish with the rosemary and serve. Pass the remaining broth separately. *–Gordon Hamersley*

MAKE AHEAD The lamb can be prepared through Step 2 and refrigerated, covered, for up to two days. Remove the fat from the surface of the stew and reheat in a 350° oven before proceeding with the recipe.

WINE Try a red, such as the 1988 or 1992 Domaine de Trevallon Coteaux d'Aix en Provence. This delicious wine is the perfect match for both the cheese and the rich meat.

Braised Lamb Shanks

4 SERVINGS

1 tablespoon unsalted butter

2 tablespoons olive oil

Two 1-pound lamb shanks, each cut in half crosswise by a butcher

Salt

1 medium onion, finely chopped

One 16-ounce can peeled Italian tomatoes, chopped, with their liquid

6 cloves garlic, chopped

1 cup dry white wine

½ cup water

12 large parsley stems

12 juniper berries, crushed

7 large thyme sprigs

⅓ cup chopped flat-leaf parsley

stew meat

The usual recommended cut for stewing is not always the best. For instance, in every cookbook I've ever read, the meat of choice for beef stew is chuck or rump. Although both are certainly good and flavorful cuts, I find it hard to get a meltingly tender result with them. Here are the cuts I like best:

For beef, I like flanken (short ribs) or the large end of a brisket.

For lamb, I think that the shank has a great flavor. When I don't want the bone I prefer to use two- to three-inch cubes of shoulder.

For veal, I like the shoulder as well as the so-called osso buco cut (shanks sawed into two-inch slices).

For pork, I use the butt to get a chunky stew and I love to braise big country-style ribs. For a really big taste, stew smoked pork hocks– or try asking your butcher for pig tails, ears and snouts. We get squeals of horror from our daughter but are they ever delicious with spicy black beans. *–Gordon Hamersley*

1. Preheat the oven to 350°. In a large enameled cast-iron casserole, melt the butter in the oil over moderately high heat. Season the lamb shanks with salt, add them to the casserole and cook, turning, until the shanks are browned on all sides. Remove the shanks to a plate and pour off all but 1 tablespoon of fat. Add the onion and cook, stirring, until slightly golden, 3 to 5 minutes. Add the tomatoes and garlic and cook over high heat for 3 minutes. Add the lamb shanks, wine, water, parsley, juniper berries and thyme; bring to a boil.

2. Cover the casserole and transfer it to the oven. Cook for 30 minutes, turn the lamb shanks and cook for 1½ hours, or until the lamb is tender. Discard the

ABOVE: **Braised Lamb Shanks, with Pasta with Olive Oil, Garlic and Parsley (p. 89).** LEFT: **Seared Lamb alla Romana.**

Brown on all sides over high heat, about 5 minutes; remove to a plate. Repeat with the second half and then return the first batch to the skillet and add the artichokes. Pour the sauce over the lamb and artichokes, stir well and cook for 1 minute. Season with salt and black pepper, sprinkle with the parsley and serve immediately. *—Michael Romano*

MAKE AHEAD The sauce can be refrigerated for up to three days. Bring to room temperature before proceeding with Step 2.

WINE 1994 Bonny Doon Le Cigare Volant. Here's a Syrah blend, a spicy and yummy Rhône-style red that loves lamb in any guise.

herb stems and stir in the chopped parsley before serving. *—Joshua Eisen*

MAKE AHEAD The cooked shanks can be refrigerated for up to two days.

Seared Lamb alla Romana

4 SERVINGS **Q**

This speedy lamb dish offers lots of flavor in a matter of minutes.

- ¼ cup chopped sun-dried tomatoes in oil, drained
- 3 garlic cloves, sliced
- 4 anchovy fillets, drained
- 1 teaspoon finely chopped rosemary
- ¼ teaspoon crushed red pepper

Kosher salt and freshly ground black pepper

- ½ cup dry white wine
- 2 tablespoons olive oil
- 1½ pounds tender lamb leg meat, cut into 1-inch cubes
- 1 cup frozen artichoke hearts— thawed, drained and cut into 1-inch pieces (optional)
- 2 tablespoons chopped flat-leaf parsley (optional)

1. In a food processor, combine the sun-dried tomatoes, garlic, anchovies, rosemary, crushed red pepper, ½ teaspoon of salt and a large pinch of black pepper. Process to a coarse paste. Add the wine and process to blend. Scrape the sauce into a small bowl.

2. In a large stainless-steel skillet, heat the oil. Add half the lamb to the skillet and season with salt and black pepper.

Georgian Lamb and Vegetable Stew

4 SERVINGS

I discovered this spicy, herb-packed stew in the Republic of Georgia. The herbs are practically a vegetable here, so more is better, but keep the amounts of cilantro and basil roughly equal.

- 2 to 4 cups coarsely chopped cilantro
- 2 to 4 cups coarsely chopped basil
- 5 garlic cloves, smashed
- 1 jalapeño pepper, stemmed and seeded (optional)

2 pounds boneless lamb shoulder, trimmed and cut into 2-inch chunks

Salt and freshly ground pepper

4 small onions, each peeled and cut lengthwise into 8 wedges

1 small eggplant, cut into 1½-inch cubes

1 pound Red Bliss potatoes, peeled and cut into 1½-inch cubes

1 pound tomatoes, cored and coarsely chopped, or one 28-ounce can plum tomatoes, chopped, with their liquid

¼ cup extra-virgin olive oil

¾ cup water

I. Preheat the oven to 300°. In a food processor, combine the cilantro, basil, garlic and jalapeño and pulse until the mixture is finely chopped.

2. In a medium bowl, toss the lamb with half of the herb mixture, ¼ teaspoon of salt and a generous pinch of pepper. In another bowl, combine the onions, eggplant, potatoes and tomatoes with the remaining herb mixture, ¼ teaspoon of salt and a generous pinch of pepper.

3. Pour the oil into a 4-quart enameled cast-iron casserole. Layer half of the herbed lamb in the casserole, season lightly with salt and pepper and cover the lamb with half of the vegetables. Season with salt and pepper and repeat with the remaining lamb and vegetables, lightly seasoning each layer. Add the water, cover tightly and bake the stew in the oven for about 4 hours, or until the meat and the vegetables are very tender.   *–Darra Goldstein*

MAKE AHEAD The stew can be refrigerated, covered, for up to three days.

WINE The spicy richness of this lamb dish signals not just a red, but a hearty one to match the intensity of the stew. Think Rhône red from France, such as the 1995 Chapoutier Crozes-Hermitage Les Meysonniers or the 1995 Alain Graillot Crozes-Hermitage.

Lamb and Rosemary Potpies

6 SERVINGS

These tempting individual pies are filled with a savory lamb and vegetable stew and topped with simple shortcrust pastry. They are fine on their own or with a small green salad.

PASTRY

2 cups all-purpose flour

Salt

1 stick (4 ounces) cold unsalted butter, cut into ½-inch pieces

⅓ cup solid vegetable shortening, chilled

¼ cup ice water

LAMB STEW

¼ cup olive oil

4 pounds lamb stew meat, trimmed and cut into ¾-inch pieces

Salt and freshly ground pepper

2 large onions, cut into 1-inch pieces

2 large carrots, cut into 1-inch pieces

2 tablespoons minced garlic

2 tablespoons finely chopped thyme

2 tablespoons finely chopped rosemary

½ cup all-purpose flour

2 quarts chicken stock or canned low-sodium broth

2 bay leaves

¼ cup finely chopped flat-leaf parsley

I. MAKE THE PASTRY: In a food processor, pulse the flour with a generous pinch of salt. Add the butter and shortening and pulse until the mixture resembles coarse meal. Add the ice water and pulse just until the dough comes together. Pat into a 6-inch log, wrap in plastic and refrigerate for at least 1 hour or overnight.

2. MAKE THE LAMB STEW: Heat 1 tablespoon of the oil in a large enameled cast-iron casserole. Season the lamb lightly with salt and pepper and add about one-quarter of it to the casserole in a single layer. Cook the lamb over moderately high heat until browned all over, about 7 minutes. Transfer to a platter and brown the remaining lamb in three batches, using 1 tablespoon of oil for each batch.

3. Add the onions, carrots, garlic, thyme and rosemary to the casserole and cook over moderately low heat, stirring occasionally, until barely softened, about 5 minutes. Return the lamb to the casserole and cook over high heat for 1 minute. Sprinkle in the flour and stir to coat the lamb and vegetables. Cook until lightly browned, about 30 seconds. Add the stock, bay leaves and a pinch each of salt and pepper and bring the stew to a boil. Cover the casserole and cook over low heat until the meat is tender, about 1¼ hours.

4. Using a slotted spoon, transfer the lamb and vegetables to a platter and let

Lamb and Rosemary Potpies

FROM TOP: **Parsley and Garlic Meatballs** (p. 249), **Lemon Chicken with Golden Raisins** (p. 190), **Savory Vegetable and Lamb Stew**, and **Roasted Sweet Peppers in Tomato Sauce** (p. 320).

cool to room temperature. Set the casserole over high heat and boil until the sauce is thickened and reduced to 4 cups, about 20 minutes. Stir in the parsley, season with more salt and pepper and let cool. Discard the bay leaves and return the meat and the vegetables to the sauce.

5. Cut the pastry into six equal pieces. On a lightly floured surface, roll each piece out to a rough 7-inch round about ⅛ inch thick. Using a plate or bowl, cut out a 6-inch disk from each round. Cut four small vents in each disk.

6. Preheat the oven to 425°. Spoon the stew into six 10-ounce ovenproof bowls, pie dishes or deep gratin dishes; they should be about 5 inches wide and 2 inches deep. Arrange the crusts on top. Fold any overhanging dough underneath, leaving a ½-inch border, and crimp the edges. Set the bowls on a large rimmed baking sheet; bake for about 25 minutes, or until the crusts are golden. Let cool 10 minutes before serving. –*James Henahan*

WINE Homey lamb potpies call for a satisfying, flavorful red. Consider a Rioja from Spain, such as the 1988 Bodegas Montecillo Reserva, or a California Cabernet Sauvignon, such as the 1993 Chateau Montelena Calistoga Cuvée.

Savory Vegetable and Lamb Stew

8 SERVINGS

Beef stew meat can be substituted for the lamb in this comforting stew.

- 1 tablespoon plus 1 teaspoon olive oil
- 2 pounds boneless lean lamb stew meat, such as shoulder, cut into 2-inch chunks

Salt and freshly ground pepper

- 1 large onion, cut lengthwise into 8 wedges
- 1 cinnamon stick
- ½ teaspoon turmeric

Pinch crumbled saffron threads (optional)

- 1 quart chicken stock or canned low-sodium broth
- 1 quart water
- 5 medium carrots, quartered lengthwise and halved crosswise
- 3 large celery ribs, halved lengthwise and quartered crosswise
- 5 small zucchini, halved lengthwise and crosswise
- 10 small pattypan squash, trimmed

Two 15-ounce cans chickpeas, drained and rinsed

1. Heat the 1 tablespoon oil in a large heavy Dutch oven. Generously season the lamb with salt and pepper. Working in three batches, sauté the meat over moderately high heat until browned all over, about 5 minutes per batch. Transfer the meat to a platter.

2. Add the remaining 1 teaspoon of oil to the Dutch oven and cook the onion over moderate heat, turning once, until browned on all sides, about 4 minutes. Transfer the onion to the platter.

3. Return the meat to the pot. Add the cinnamon stick, turmeric, saffron, if using, and the stock and water and bring to a simmer over high heat. Reduce the heat to moderately low and simmer until the meat is tender, about 1 hour.

4. Add the carrots, celery and onion to the Dutch oven and return to a simmer. Cook until the carrots are almost tender, about 15 minutes. Add the zucchini, pattypan squash and chickpeas and cook until the zucchini and squash are just tender, about 10 minutes longer. Discard the cinnamon stick and season the stew with salt and pepper. Transfer to bowls and serve. –*Michel Benasra*

Balsamic-Glazed Rack of Venison

4 SERVINGS **L**

You can substitute other venison cuts, including tenderloin and leg steaks, for the elegant racks here. Red cabbage makes an excellent accompaniment.

- ¼ cup balsamic vinegar
- 2 tablespoons olive oil
- 1½ tablespoons ketchup
- 1 tablespoon Worcestershire sauce

Kosher salt and coarsely ground pepper

- 1 tablespoon canola oil

Two 1¼-pound venison racks, 4 chops each, frenched (see box, p. 260)

1. In a bowl, combine the vinegar, olive oil, ketchup, Worcestershire sauce, ¾ teaspoon of salt and ½ tablespoon of pepper.

2. Preheat the oven to 450°. In a stainless-steel ovenproof skillet, heat the canola oil until shimmering. Set the venison racks bone-side up in the skillet. Sear them over high heat, turning once, until browned, about 1½ minutes per side. Put the skillet in the oven and roast for about 20 minutes, brushing the racks three times with the glaze, until the meat is rare and an instant-read thermometer inserted in the meat reads 125°. Cover with aluminum foil and let rest for 10 minutes. Season with salt and pepper. ➤

five meaty tips

These principles apply to all cuts of meat, but are most important for cuts that have less fat to tenderize them.

1. **Get more flavor** from oil-based marinades by first sautéing onions, chiles or spices in the oil

2. **Don't let meat sit too long** in highly acidic marinades or it will get chewy.

3. **Salt meat lightly** or not at all before cooking, so juices won't be drawn out.

4. **Sear steaks over high heat.** Low-fat roasts should also be cooked at high temperatures.

5. **Keep the heat low when braising or stewing**; if the meat boils, it toughens.

Balsamic-Glazed Rack of Venison

3. Add the remaining balsamic glaze to the skillet and bring to a boil over high heat, stirring to scrape up the brown bits. Cut the venison into chops and serve with the sauce. *–Charlie Palmer*

Roasted Venison with Beach-Plum Sauce

20 SERVINGS

This recipe originally called for spit-roasting a bone-in leg of venison but has been adapted for the home oven, for either a whole leg or boneless roasts. If you have access to a large rotisserie, cook the venison over a medium fire for one-and-a-half to two hours, or until the internal temperature measures 125°. Whichever method you choose, save any pan juices and carving juices to add to the sauce.

- ¼ **cup plus 2 tablespoons vegetable oil**
- ½ **cup chopped thyme leaves**
- 10 **garlic cloves, minced**
- ¼ **cup cracked black peppercorns**
- 2 **tablespoons crushed and chopped juniper berries**
- 1 **whole leg of venison (15 to 17 pounds), hip bone and shank end removed and reserved, roast tied, or one 9-pound boneless Denver leg of venison (see box, opposite page), ½ pound reserved for the sauce, the rest tied into 4 even-size roasts**

Kosher salt
Beach-Plum Sauce (recipe follows)

1. In a small bowl, combine the ¼ cup oil with the thyme, garlic, peppercorns and juniper berries.

2. Set the bone-in roast on a rack in a large roasting pan; alternatively, set the boneless roasts on a rimmed baking sheet, leaving as much room between them as possible. Rub with the seasoning mixture, coating completely. Cover with plastic wrap; refrigerate overnight. Bring to room temperature before proceeding.

3. COOK THE BONE-IN ROAST: Preheat the oven to 350°. Rub the meat with the remaining 2 tablespoons of oil and season with salt. Roast the venison in the center of the oven for 1 hour. Turn the roast, baste with the pan juices and roast for 1 hour longer. Turn the roast once more and cook for about 20 minutes longer for medium-rare, or until an instant-read thermometer inserted in the thickest part of the meat registers 125°. Let rest 20 minutes before carving.

COOK THE BONELESS ROASTS: Preheat the oven to 500°. Rub the meat with the remaining 2 tablespoons of oil and season with salt. Roast in the upper third of the oven for 25 to 30 minutes for medium rare or until an instant-read thermometer inserted in the thickest part of each roast registers 125°. Let rest for 10 minutes before carving.

4. To serve, untie the roasts. Stand the bone-in roast on a large carving board with the shank end facing up. Carve slices from the side, slicing the meat straight down to the bone; slicing against the grain produces a more tender piece of meat. Carve the boneless roasts into ¼-inch-thick slices. Serve at once with the Beach-Plum Sauce.

BEACH-PLUM SAUCE

MAKES ABOUT 2 CUPS

If beach-plum jelly, made from the wild plums that grow all over coastal Massachusetts, is hard to find, substitute the traditional red-currant jelly.

- ½ pound venison scraps, plus any bones
- 2 medium carrots, chopped
- 2 celery ribs, chopped
- 1 medium onion, chopped
- ¼ cup vegetable oil
- 1 cup red-wine vinegar
- 3 cups rich veal stock (see "Venison," below)
- 1 cup red wine
- 6 parsley stems
- 4 thyme sprigs
- 4 juniper berries
- 2 bay leaves
- 2 tablespoons cracked peppercorns
- 2 tablespoons all-purpose flour
- 1 cup beach-plum jelly
- 2 tablespoons unsalted butter

Kosher salt

I. Preheat the oven to 400°. In a large roasting pan, combine the venison scraps and bones with the carrots, celery, onion and 2 tablespoons of the oil; toss well. Roast for 30 to 40 minutes, stirring occasionally, until well browned. Transfer to a large saucepan.

venison

The "Denver leg" in the recipe for Roasted Venison with Beach-Plum Sauce is widely available at better butchers. It comes separated into perfectly lean, trimmed pieces, which are then tied into manageable roasts. The venison (and the stock for the sauce) can be ordered from D'Artagnan (973-344-0565).

2. Set the roasting pan over two burners. Add the vinegar. Deglaze the pan over moderate heat, scraping to loosen the brown bits. Pour the vinegar into the saucepan. Add the stock, wine, parsley, thyme, juniper, bay leaves and 1 tablespoon peppercorns. Simmer over moderately low heat, skimming occasionally, until very flavorful, about 1 hour.

3. Meanwhile, in a small skillet, combine the remaining 2 tablespoons of oil with the flour. With a wooden spoon, stir the mixture over moderately low heat until light brown, about 5 minutes. Scrape the roux into a bowl.

4. Once the sauce has reduced, whisk 1 cup into the roux; whisk the roux mixture into the simmering sauce until thoroughly blended. Cook over very low heat for 45 minutes, whisking occasionally. Add the jelly and simmer for 15 minutes. Strain into a medium saucepan and add the remaining 1 tablespoon peppercorns.

5. Add any juices reserved from carving the venison and then whisk in the butter, 1 tablespoon at a time. Season the sauce with salt and serve it with the venison.   –Jasper White

Roasted Venison with Beach-Plum Sauce

CHAPTER 12 other main dishes

Bean Salad with Fresh Salmon and Dill (p. 279)

265   Stuffed Peppers with Couscous and Artichokes

265   Stuffed Zucchini Pesaro-Style

266   Grilled Eggplant Parmesan

266   Erica's Eggplant Parmesan

267   Vegetable Mixed Grill

267   New World Ciambotta

268   Summer Bean Stew

268   Vegetable and Sun-Dried-Tomato Tagine

269   Winter Vegetable Stew with a Cheddar Crust

271   Quick Onion Pullao

271   Summer Squash, Sweet Pepper and Polenta Casserole

272   Steamed Bean Curd with Scallions

272   Pan-Fried Bean Cakes

273   Black-Bean and Roasted-Vegetable Burritos

273   Poached Eggs Diavolo on Polenta

274   Huevos Rancheros

275   Caramelized-Onion and Asparagus Frittata

275   Cowboy Frittata

275   Savory Artichoke Bread Pudding

276   Ham and Cheese Strata

276   Warm Green Salad with Lobster and Oranges

276   Black-Bean and Rice Salad with Fresh Crab

277   Pan-Roasted Salmon with Orange Vinaigrette

279   Bean Salad with Fresh Salmon and Dill

279   Tortilla Salad

279   Fried-Chicken Salad

281   Quails with Beet and Goat-Cheese Salad

281   Chimichurri Mixed Grill

282   Spicy Thai Beef Salad

282   Mediterranean Pepper Salad with Sausages

283   Chilled Make-Ahead Summer Oatmeal

Stuffed Peppers with Couscous and Artichokes

Stuffed Peppers with Couscous and Artichokes

4 SERVINGS

Bell peppers welcome almost any savory stuffing, not just the usual mix of beef or sausage and rice. Couscous makes a great alternative.

- 1 lemon, halved
- 24 baby artichokes (2 pounds)
- 1 cup couscous
- Salt and freshly ground black pepper
- 2 tablespoons unsalted butter, cut into small pieces
- About 1 cup chicken stock or canned low-sodium broth
- 3 tablespoons olive oil, plus more for coating the peppers
- 2 shallots, thinly sliced
- ½ cup water
- ¼ pound thinly sliced prosciutto, chopped
- ½ cup Niçoise olives, halved and pitted
- ½ cup pine nuts, toasted
- ¾ cup freshly grated Parmigiano-Reggiano
- 8 medium yellow bell peppers

I. Preheat the oven to 400°. Squeeze the juice from the lemon into a large bowl of cold water. Cut off the stems of the artichokes. Trim the tops and pull off the tough outer leaves. Halve the artichokes lengthwise, then thinly slice crosswise. Drop the artichokes into the acidulated water.

2. Put the couscous in a heatproof bowl, season with salt and pepper and scatter the butter all over. In a small saucepan, bring the stock to a boil and stir it into the couscous; cover and set aside for about 8 minutes. Fluff with a fork; it should be soft. If not, add a little hot water.

3. Meanwhile, in a large stainless-steel skillet, heat the 3 tablespoons of oil. Drain the artichokes. Add them to the skillet with the shallots, season with salt and pepper and cook over moderate heat, stirring, until the artichokes are beginning to brown, about 8 minutes. Reduce the heat to moderately low, add the water and cook until tender, about 4 minutes. Add the artichokes and the shallots to the couscous and let cool slightly. Add the prosciutto, olives, pine nuts and half the cheese to the couscous. Season with salt and pepper and toss gently.

4. Cut off the tops of the peppers and scoop out the seeds and ribs. Lightly brush the peppers with oil and fill them with the couscous mixture. Sprinkle the remaining cheese on top of the couscous. Stand the peppers upright in a 13-by-9-inch baking dish. Pour about ½ inch of water into the dish and cover the peppers loosely with aluminum foil. Bake for 30 minutes, or until the peppers are barely tender. Set the reserved tops on the peppers and bake for another 30 minutes, or until the peppers are tender. Serve the stuffed peppers warm or at room temperature. *—Erica De Mane*

MAKE AHEAD The peppers can be refrigerated, covered, overnight. Return the peppers to room temperature before reheating, covered with aluminum foil, in a 325° oven.

WINE The best foil for the complicated flavors here is a simple, crisp white. Try a Sicilian one, such as the 1995 Regaleali Bianco, or a Chilean Sauvignon Blanc, such as the 1995 Los Vascos.

Stuffed Zucchini Pesaro-Style

4 SERVINGS

From my earliest days as a cook, I have enjoyed exploring the potential of a hollowed zucchini and have found it can contain a diverse number of good things: ground pork and such pork products as prosciutto and pancetta, ground lamb and rice, or rice with wholly vegetarian accompaniments such as onions, tomatoes and herbs. Here is a dish I had in the Marches seaside town of Pesaro. The zucchini contain veal—the meat with the most delicate taste—which stays unusually juicy within its moist vegetable cocoon.

- 8 medium zucchini
- ¼ cup extra-virgin olive oil
- 10 ounces ground veal
- 2 garlic cloves, peeled and lightly smashed
- ⅔ cup freshly grated Parmigiano-Reggiano
- Salt and freshly ground pepper
- 1 small onion, finely chopped
- ½ cup dry white wine
- 1 pound firm, ripe tomatoes— peeled, seeded and cut into several pieces, or 1 cup canned Italian plum tomatoes, cut up, with their juices

I. Soak the zucchini in cold water for 30 minutes. Scrub them under cold running water with a brush to remove any grit. Slice off both ends and, using an apple corer, hollow out the zucchini; the aim is to scoop out their centers, leaving tubes with thin walls that will hold the meat stuffing. Be careful not to pierce the skins. Chop the scooped-out zucchini flesh rather fine and set aside.

2. Put 1 tablespoon of the oil in a large skillet and turn the heat to moderately high. When the oil is hot enough to sizzle instantly on contact with meat, add the ground veal and cook it until lightly browned, turning it a few times, about 4 minutes. Use a slotted spoon to transfer it to a bowl. Do not clean out the skillet.

3. Put another tablespoon of the oil in the skillet. Add the garlic cloves and cook over moderately high heat, stirring frequently, until golden, about 2 minutes. Remove the garlic cloves with a slotted spoon and discard.

4. Add the chopped zucchini flesh to the skillet and brown it lightly over moderate heat, turning it from time to time, 5 to 6 minutes. Transfer the zucchini to the bowl of veal. Add the Parmigiano-Reggiano to the bowl and season with

salt and pepper. Mix the ingredients to combine them uniformly. Fill the zucchini with the stuffing, packing it snugly.

5. Put the remaining 2 tablespoons of oil in a heavy 12-inch skillet and turn the heat to moderately high. As soon as the oil is hot, put in as many zucchini as will fit loosely in a single layer. Brown the zucchini on all sides, turning them as necessary; if a little bit of the stuffing falls out, it's of no consequence. Use a slotted spoon to transfer the browned zucchini to a platter. Repeat with any remaining zucchini. Do not clean out the pan.

6. Add the onion to the pan and cook over moderately high heat, stirring, until lightly golden, about 3 minutes. Return all of the zucchini to the skillet and add the wine. While the wine bubbles away, use a wooden spoon to scrape any residue from the bottom of the pan. Sprinkle the zucchini lightly with salt. Add the tomatoes with their juices and turn over the contents of the pan once or twice. Cover, reduce the heat to low and cook for 30 to 40 minutes, gently turning the zucchini from time to time. When the zucchini are very tender and the sauce is richly flavored, remove from the heat. Let stand for about 5 minutes before serving. –Marcella Hazan
MAKE AHEAD The stuffed zucchini can be prepared several hours in advance and reheated.

Grilled Eggplant Parmesan

6 SERVINGS **L**

1 tablespoon olive oil
1 large onion, chopped
1 small carrot, halved
1 small celery rib, halved
1 rosemary sprig
One 35-ounce can Italian peeled tomatoes
Salt and freshly ground pepper
3 pounds Asian eggplants, ends trimmed, sliced lengthwise ⅓ inch thick

6 ounces part-skim mozzarella, shredded (about 1¾ cups)
¼ cup freshly grated Parmesan
2 tablespoons finely shredded basil leaves

I. Heat 2 teaspoons of the oil in a medium stainless-steel saucepan. Add the onion and cook over moderate heat, stirring, until wilted, about 3 minutes. Tie the carrot, celery and rosemary together with cotton string and add to the saucepan along with the tomatoes and their juices. Season with a pinch each of salt and pepper and simmer over low heat, stirring to break up the tomatoes, until the sauce is slightly reduced, about 25 minutes. Discard the vegetable bundle.

2. Pass the sauce through a food mill; alternatively, transfer the sauce to a food processor and process to a coarse puree. Season with salt and pepper.

3. Light a grill. Using a damp paper towel, coat the grill with the remaining 1 teaspoon of oil. Season the eggplant slices with salt and grill over a medium-low fire, turning once, until tender and golden brown, about 12 minutes.

4. Preheat the oven to 400°. Spread ½ cup of the tomato sauce in a stainless-steel 11-by-8-inch baking dish. Arrange one-third of the eggplant in the dish, cover with one-third of the mozzarella and sprinkle with 1 tablespoon of the Parmesan. Make another layer, using 1 cup of the sauce, one-third each of the eggplant and mozzarella and 1 tablespoon of Parmesan. Top with the remaining ½ cup of sauce, eggplant, mozzarella and 2 tablespoons Parmesan. Bake in the upper third of the oven for about 30 minutes, or until bubbling hot and lightly browned on top. Sprinkle with the shredded basil leaves and serve. –Jim Cohen
MAKE AHEAD The tomato sauce can be refrigerated for up to three days. Reheat gently before proceeding.
WINE 1993 Monsanto Chianti Classico Riserva from Tuscany, Italy

Erica's Eggplant Parmesan

4 SERVINGS

My mother always made eggplant parmigiana with thick slices of breaded and fried eggplant and a dark tomato sauce. The result was good but heavy. Here's a lighter version, made with baked eggplant and a briefly cooked tomato sauce.

2 medium eggplants, sliced crosswise ⅓ inch thick
Salt and freshly ground pepper
¼ cup olive oil, plus more for brushing
8 scallions, thinly sliced
¼ teaspoon dried savory
Two 35-ounce cans Italian peeled tomatoes, drained and finely chopped in a food processor
¼ pound Italian fontina, grated or chopped
1 cup heavy cream
1 large egg
¾ cup grated grana padano cheese

I. Preheat the oven to 425°. Brush three baking sheets with oil. Arrange the eggplant slices on the sheets in one layer, season with salt and pepper and drizzle with 1 tablespoon of the oil. Bake for about 20 minutes, or until the bottoms are lightly browned; turn and bake for 20 minutes, or until browned on the other side.

2. In a large stainless-steel skillet, heat the remaining 3 tablespoons of oil. Add the scallions and savory and cook over moderate heat, stirring, until softened, 2 to 3 minutes. Add the tomatoes, season with salt and pepper and cook over high heat until slightly thickened, about 8 minutes.

3. In a small saucepan, melt the fontina in the cream over moderate heat, whisking until smooth. Season with salt. Remove the pan from the heat, let cool slightly and whisk in the egg.

4. Spread ¾ cup of the tomato sauce over the bottom of a 13-by-9-inch baking dish. Arrange one-third of the eggplant slices in the dish, overlapping only slightly. Pour in one-third of the fontina cream and sprinkle with one-third of the grana padano. Continue layering the to- mato sauce, eggplant, fontina cream and grana padano two more times. Bake for about 30 minutes, or until bubbling and lightly browned on top. Let rest for 10 minutes before serving. *–Erica De Mane*

WINE Tomato sauce, cheese and scal- lions pair best with a Chianti Classico. Look for the 1991 Ruffino Tenuta Santedame or the 1994 Carpineto.

Vegetable Mixed Grill

4 SERVINGS

This mixed grill of vegetables has many virtues, not the least of which is that it's the best way I've found to cook okra.

- 1 pound okra
- 1 pound thick asparagus, ends trimmed
- ½ pound fresh shiitake or large button mushrooms, stems removed
- 6 slender Asian eggplants, halved lengthwise
- 2 tablespoons Asian sesame oil

Salt and freshly ground pepper

- ⅓ cup white miso
- 1 tablespoon sake
- 1 tablespoon mirin
- 1 tablespoon sugar
- 1 tablespoon mayonnaise
- 2 teaspoons toasted sesame seeds

I. Trim the stems off the okra; do not cut into the pods. Arrange the okra side by side and thread them in small groups on two parallel bamboo skewers. Treat the asparagus the same way. Thread the shiitake caps onto a skewer, three or four per skewer; the caps should lie flat. Using a sharp knife, make shallow crisscross cuts on both sides of each eggplant half. Transfer all of the veg- etables to a platter. Brush the vegeta- bles with the sesame oil; season with salt and pepper.

Vegetable Mixed Grill

2. In a small bowl, whisk the miso with the sake, mirin, sugar and mayonnaise.
3. Light a grill. When the fire is hot, grill the eggplants, cut-side down, for 3 to 4 minutes or until nicely browned. Turn the eggplants and brush with the miso sauce. Grill for 6 to 8 minutes longer, until the bottoms are nicely browned and the flesh is soft. Transfer the egg- plants to a platter and sprinkle with ½ teaspoon of the sesame seeds.
4. Grill the okra, asparagus and shiitakes, turning, for about 4 minutes or until nicely browned and cooked through. Transfer to the platter, sprinkle with the remaining 1½ teaspoons of sesame seeds and serve.   *–Steven Raichlen*
BEER Belgian wheat beer pairs won- derfully with vegetables because it's light and dry. Try Blanche de Bruges, which is flavored with coriander, orange peel and aromatic peppers.

New World Ciambotta

4 SERVINGS

The traditional southern Italian ciambot- ta contains eggplant, tomatoes, pota- toes and sometimes bell peppers. I've dropped the eggplant and added sweet corn, for an American accent.

- 6 tablespoons olive oil
- 1½ pounds red-skinned new potatoes, cut into ¾-inch dice
- 1 red bell pepper, cut into ¾-inch dice
- 6 scallions, thinly sliced
- 1 pound small zucchini, cut into ¾-inch dice
- 2 cups fresh corn kernels
- 3 garlic cloves, minced
- 1 pound ripe plum tomatoes, chopped
- 2 tablespoons minced basil
- ½ teaspoon dried thyme

Salt and freshly ground pepper

- ¾ cup plain dry bread crumbs

1. Preheat the oven to 400°. In a large stainless-steel skillet, heat 2 tablespoons of the oil. Add the potatoes and cook over moderate heat, stirring occasionally, until brown and just tender, about 10 minutes. Using a slotted spoon, transfer the potatoes to a 13-by-9-inch baking dish. Heat another tablespoon of the oil in the skillet. Add the red bell pepper and cook, stirring occasionally, until tender, 4 to 5 minutes. Add the scallions and cook, stirring, until tender, about 1 minute. Transfer to the baking dish.

2. Heat another 2 tablespoons of the oil in the skillet. Add the zucchini and cook, stirring, until just tender, 3 to 4 minutes; transfer to the baking dish. Add the corn and garlic to the skillet and cook until crisp-tender, about 2 minutes; transfer to the baking dish. Add the tomatoes, basil and thyme to the baking dish, season with salt and pepper and toss gently.

3. Heat the remaining 1 tablespoon of oil in the skillet. Add the bread crumbs and cook over moderate heat, stirring, until lightly toasted. Sprinkle the bread crumbs evenly over the vegetables and bake for 30 to 35 minutes, or until hot. Serve immediately.   –Erica De Mane

WINE Rustic and hearty, this vegetable medley needs an assertive white, such as a Vernaccia di San Gimignano. Look for the 1995 San Quirico or the 1995 Teruzzi & Puthod Terre di Tufi.

Summer Bean Stew

6 SERVINGS L

1   tablespoon plus 2 teaspoons extra-virgin olive oil
1   large onion, coarsely chopped
2   large garlic cloves, minced
One 35-ounce can Italian plum tomatoes—seeded and coarsely chopped, juices reserved
2   pounds Yukon Gold potatoes, peeled and cut into 1½-inch chunks

3   cups vegetable stock or water
2   bay leaves
1   teaspoon sweet paprika
½   teaspoon dried thyme
¼   teaspoon saffron threads, crumbled (optional)
Salt and freshly ground pepper
¾   pound young green beans, cut into 1½-inch lengths
1   large red bell pepper, cut into ¾-inch dice
1   medium zucchini, cut into 1½-inch chunks
1½   cups fresh or frozen baby lima beans
Hot sauce

1. Heat the 2 teaspoons oil in a stainless-steel saucepan. Add the onion and cook over moderate heat, stirring, until just beginning to brown, about 5 minutes. Add the garlic and stir until it is fragrant, about 1 minute. Add the tomatoes, potatoes, stock, bay leaves, paprika, thyme, saffron, if using, and a large pinch each of salt and pepper. Cover partially, bring to a boil and cook until the potatoes are just tender, 10 to 12 minutes.

2. Add the green beans and the red bell pepper to the saucepan. Cover partially and cook until the vegetables are crisp-tender, about 5 minutes. Add the zucchini and lima beans and cook until the vegetables are tender but not falling apart, about 5 minutes. Season with salt and pepper. Serve in bowls, drizzled with the remaining 1 tablespoon of oil and hot sauce.–David Hirsch, Linda Dickinson and Susan Harville

WINE The citrusy acidity of Sauvignon Blanc stands up to tomatoes and its herbaceous character makes it a natural partner to peppers, zucchini and green beans. Look for lively examples, such as the 1995 Quivira from California or the 1995 Domaine Vacheron Sancerre from France.

Vegetable and Sun-Dried-Tomato Tagine

4 SERVINGS

Sun-dried tomatoes add a robust sweetness to this spicy tagine, which enriches the other vegetables.

¼   cup olive oil
1   medium onion, finely chopped
2   garlic cloves, crushed
2   teaspoons ground cumin
½   teaspoon turmeric
Pinch of cayenne pepper
2   cups tomato juice
12   oil-packed sun-dried tomato halves
6   pitted prunes
Salt
1   large Idaho potato, peeled and sliced ¼ inch thick
2   medium carrots, sliced ¼ inch thick
1   small eggplant, sliced ¼ inch thick
1   medium zucchini, sliced ¼ inch thick
10   pitted oil-cured black olives, preferably Niçoise
1   cup cooked chickpeas, drained and rinsed if canned
Freshly ground black pepper
Harissa (recipe follows)

1. Preheat the oven to 350°. Heat the oil in a medium flameproof casserole. Add the onion and the garlic and cook over moderately high heat, stirring often, until the onion is translucent, 5 to 7 minutes. Add the cumin, turmeric and cayenne to the casserole and cook, stirring constantly, until fragrant, about 2 minutes.

2. Stir in the tomato juice, sun-dried tomatoes and prunes, season with salt and bring to a boil. Reduce the heat to moderately low and simmer until the sauce has thickened, about 20 minutes. Stir in the potato, carrots, eggplant, zucchini, olives and chickpeas.

Add just enough cold water to the casserole to cover the vegetables, mix well and bring to a simmer. Season with salt and black pepper.

3. Cover the casserole and transfer to the oven. Bake, stirring occasionally, for about 1 hour or until the vegetables are tender. Let cool slightly and serve with the Harissa.

HARISSA
MAKES ABOUT ¾ CUP
This potent North African condiment is especially good and spicy when made at home, but it's also available at Middle Eastern groceries.

1½   cups (loosely packed) hot dried red chiles (about 1 ounce)
⅓   cup olive oil
3   garlic cloves, minced
1   teaspoon caraway seeds, ground in a spice grinder or mortar
1   teaspoon ground coriander
½   teaspoon ground cumin
Salt

I. In a small saucepan, cover the dried red chiles with water. Boil the water over moderately high heat until the chiles are slightly softened, about 2 minutes. Cover and let the chiles soak for 1 hour.

2. Drain the chiles, reserving the soaking liquid, and transfer them to a food processor. Add the oil, garlic, caraway seeds, coriander and cumin and season with salt. Puree until smooth, adding enough of the reserved chile-soaking liquid to process the sauce. Transfer to a bowl.   –Gary Danko

MAKE AHEAD The Harissa can be refrigerated for up to one week.

WINE A tart California Sangiovese has just the right acidity to match the intense flavor of the tomato juice and the sun-dried tomatoes in this tagine. Look for the 1994 Shafer Firebreak or the 1994 Silverado.

Winter Vegetable Stew with a Cheddar Crust
In a pinch, use chicken stock or canned low-sodium broth in place of the Mushroom Broth.

6 SERVINGS
4   tablespoons unsalted butter
¼   cup olive oil
1   large red onion, cut crosswise into ⅓-inch-thick rounds
3   medium carrots, cut into 1-inch pieces
1   celery root (about 1 pound), peeled and cut into 1-inch pieces
1   butternut squash (about 1½ pounds), peeled and cut into 1½-inch pieces
1   acorn squash (about 1½ pounds), peeled and cut into 1½-inch pieces
3   parsnips, peeled and quartered lengthwise
5   medium portobello mushrooms (about 1 pound), stems reserved for broth, caps cut into 1-inch pieces
4   cups Mushroom Broth (recipe follows)
Salt and freshly ground pepper
¼   teaspoon dried marjoram
CHEDDAR BISCUIT CRUST
2   cups all-purpose flour
4   teaspoons baking powder
1½   teaspoons minced garlic
½   teaspoon salt
¼   teaspoon coarsely ground pepper
1   stick (4 ounces) cold unsalted butter, cut into small cubes
1   cup shredded sharp cheddar (4 ounces)
1   cup heavy cream

I. Preheat the oven to 400°. In a large stainless-steel skillet, melt 1 tablespoon of the butter in 1 tablespoon of the oil over moderately high heat. Add the onion and the carrots and cook, stirring occasionally, until the vegetables are browned all over, about 10

minutes. Transfer the vegetables to a large roasting pan.

2. Add another tablespoon each of butter and oil to the skillet. Add the celery root and butternut squash and cook, stirring occasionally, until browned all over, about 10 minutes; transfer to the roasting pan. Repeat the cooking process using another tablespoon each of butter and oil and the acorn squash and parsnips. Add the remaining tablespoon each of butter and oil. Add the portobellos and cook, stirring occasionally, until tender and browned all over, about 6 minutes; transfer to the roasting pan and stir to mix.

3. Add the Mushroom Broth to the skillet and bring to a simmer over high heat, scraping up any brown bits. Pour the broth over the vegetables. Season with salt and pepper and add the marjoram. Cover with aluminum foil and cook the vegetables in the oven for about 45 minutes, or until just tender when pierced. Increase the oven temperature to 450° and cook, uncovered, for 5 minutes longer.

4. Meanwhile, MAKE THE CHEDDAR BISCUIT CRUST: In a medium bowl, stir together the flour, baking powder, garlic, salt and pepper. Using a pastry cutter or two knives, cut in the butter until the mixture resembles coarse meal. Stir in the cheese. Add the cream and mix lightly with a wooden spoon until the dough just holds together. Cover and set aside.

5. Using a large spoon, dollop the biscuit dough on the vegetable stew; there will be some bald spots. Bake for about 20 minutes, or until the crust is cooked through and golden.

MUSHROOM BROTH
MAKES 4 CUPS
¼   cup vegetable oil
1½   pounds white mushrooms, finely chopped

Winter Vegetable Stew

Reserved portobello mushroom
    stems, brushed clean
½ Spanish onion, coarsely
    chopped
2 teaspoons chopped garlic
2 cups dry white wine
½ cup soy sauce
½ cup dried mushrooms,
    such as porcini or shiitake
    (½ ounce)
Pinch of salt
½ teaspoon herbes de Provence
    or dried thyme
6 cups water

1. In a large stainless-steel saucepan, heat the oil over moderately high heat. Add the white mushrooms, the portobello-mushroom stems, the onion and the garlic and cook, stirring, until the mushrooms release their liquid, about 5 minutes.

2. Add the white wine, soy sauce, dried mushrooms, salt, herbes de Provence and water to the saucepan and bring the liquid to a boil. Cover, reduce the heat to moderate and simmer until the liquid is reduced to about 4 cups, about 1 hour.

3. Pour the broth through a fine strainer into a heatproof bowl. Strain again, leaving any particles at the bottom of the bowl.   *–Gordon Hamersley*

MAKE AHEAD The Mushroom Broth can be made up to four days in advance and refrigerated.

WINE If you want to emphasize the richness of the vegetables and the biscuit crust on this Winter Vegetable Stew, choose a robust Gigondas, such as the soft, round, earthy-but-lighter-than-most 1993 Domaine du Pourra. For a more offbeat partnering, go for a Fontodi Chianti Classico Riserva from 1985, 1986 or 1988; these wines will be more mellow than the later vintages. The simpler choice would be a really good Côtes du Rhône: the 1994 Domaine de la Solitude.

Quick Onion Pullao

2 TO 4 SERVINGS

Here's a quick way of turning yesterday's plain rice into a fragrant, pale yellow vegetarian delight with turmeric-tinted onions and bright flecks of green chile. Serve with plain yogurt and a simple salad.

¼ cup raw cashews
3 tablespoons vegetable oil
¼ teaspoon asafetida (optional)
1 teaspoon mustard seeds
1 teaspoon turmeric
1 pound onions (3 to 4), thinly
    sliced into rings or half circles
4 jalapeño peppers, minced
2 tablespoons minced fresh
    ginger
5 fresh or dried curry leaves
1½ teaspoons salt
1 teaspoon sugar
4 cups cooked Govindobhog Rice
    (p. 307) or Basmati Rice (p. 307)
¼ cup fresh lime juice

1. In a small heavy skillet, toast the cashews over high heat, stirring constantly, until golden. Remove from the heat and stir for 15 seconds, then transfer to a plate.

2. In a large saucepan, heat the oil until it shimmers. Add the asafetida and stir briefly to dissolve, then stir in the mustard seeds. When they stop popping, stir in the turmeric. Add the onions, jalapeños, ginger and curry leaves and stir to coat with the oil.

3. Lower the heat to moderate and cook, stirring frequently, until the onions start to brown, about 8 minutes. Stir in the salt and sugar. Add the rice; gently turn and stir until well mixed and heated through. Drizzle in the lime juice and cook, stirring, for 30 seconds. Discard the curry leaves. Mound the pullao on a deep platter, top with the cashews and serve.   *–Jeffrey Alford and Naomi Duguid*

WINE 1995 Dry Creek Dry Chenin Blanc

Summer Squash, Sweet Pepper and Polenta Casserole

4 SERVINGS

This firm-textured casserole, full of garden-fresh vegetables, can be sliced like a pie and served at room temperature.

½ tablespoon unsalted butter
½ tablespoon olive oil
1 small onion, coarsely chopped
1 red bell pepper, cut into
    ½-inch dice
2 small red-skinned new
    potatoes, peeled and cut into
    ¼-inch dice
2 large garlic cloves, minced
1 medium yellow squash, cut into
    ¾-inch dice
1 medium zucchini, cut into
    ¾-inch dice
½ cup polenta
¼ cup all-purpose flour
¼ cup freshly grated Parmesan
1 tablespoon thyme leaves
1 teaspoon salt
1 teaspoon freshly ground pepper
1 cup milk
2 large eggs
6 tablespoons grated Gruyère
    (2 ounces)

1. Preheat the oven to 350°. Generously butter a 9-inch round baking dish. In a large heavy skillet, melt the butter in the oil over moderately high heat. Add the onion, red bell pepper and potatoes and cook, stirring, for 3 minutes. Stir in the garlic and cook until the vegetables are partially softened but not browned, about 2 minutes. Add the squash and zucchini to the skillet and cook, stirring, until they are almost tender, 4 to 5 minutes. Set the vegetables aside.

2. In a large bowl, toss together the polenta, flour, Parmesan, thyme, salt and pepper. In a separate bowl, whisk together the milk and eggs, then whisk them into the polenta mixture until combined. Stir the reserved vegetables into the loose batter and spread the

mixture in the prepared baking dish. Bake the casserole on the middle shelf of the oven for 25 to 30 minutes, or until firm. Sprinkle the Gruyère on top. Bake for about 7 minutes, or until golden around the edges. Serve the summer-squash casserole hot or at room temperature.   *–Georgeanne Brennan*

Steamed Bean Curd with Scallions

4 SERVINGS **L**

- ¾ cup vegetable broth
- 1 tablespoon oyster sauce
- 1 tablespoon cornstarch
- 1 teaspoon dark soy sauce
- ½ teaspoon sugar
- ¼ teaspoon salt
- 4 fresh bean-curd cakes (about 1 pound)
- 2 teaspoons peanut oil

Summer Squash, Sweet Pepper and Polenta Casserole

- 4 scallions, white parts quartered lengthwise, green parts cut into 1½-inch pieces

1. Combine the vegetable broth, oyster sauce, cornstarch, soy sauce, sugar and salt in a small bowl.

2. Place the bean-curd cakes on a heatproof dish in a steamer basket and steam for 10 minutes.

3. Meanwhile, heat a wok over high heat for about 30 seconds. Add the oil and stir to coat. When a wisp of white smoke appears, add the scallions and stir-fry until bright green, about 30 seconds. Transfer to a warmed plate.

4. Stir the sauce and add it to the wok. Cook over low heat, stirring, until the sauce thickens and becomes dark and glossy. Stir in the scallions. Pour the sauce over the steamed bean curd and serve.   *–Eileen Yin-Fei Lo*

WINE Oyster and soy sauces add saltiness to this otherwise mild dish, making it a good candidate for a medium-bodied, fruity white. Because the scallions add an herbal note, Sauvignon Blanc is a particularly good choice here. Look for California examples, such as the 1995 Fetzer Barrel Select or the 1995 Matanzas Creek.

Pan-Fried Bean Cakes

4 SERVINGS

There's nothing new about refrying beans, but typical of the current approach to regional foods, these cakes are lightened with beaten egg white and served with fresh tomatoes. You can use just about any canned, frozen or leftover beans for this dish. Serve with a green salad.

- 1 pound ripe tomatoes
- 2 cups cooked beans or black-eyed peas
- 2 tablespoons chopped mixed herbs, such as parsley, basil and oregano
- 1 large egg, separated
- 1 small onion, minced
- 1 garlic clove, minced
- 1 teaspoon chili powder

Salt and freshly ground pepper

- ¾ cup fine dry bread crumbs
- 3 tablespoons vegetable oil
- ½ teaspoon fresh lemon juice

1. Peel and finely chop the tomatoes and let them drain in a sieve set over a bowl. Meanwhile, in a medium bowl, mash the cooked beans with 1 tablespoon of the herbs, the egg yolk, onion, garlic and chili powder; leave a few of the beans whole for texture. Season with salt and pepper.

2. In a small bowl, beat the egg white until it holds soft peaks, then fold it into the mashed beans. Using moistened hands, form the mixture into eight patties, each about ½ inch thick. Coat the patties well with the bread crumbs.

3. In a large heavy skillet, heat 1½ tablespoons of the oil. Fry four of the patties over moderately high heat until golden brown, about 2 minutes per side. Transfer to a baking sheet and keep warm in a low oven. Wipe out the skillet and repeat with the remaining oil and bean patties.

4. In a small glass or stainless-steel bowl, toss the chopped tomatoes with the remaining herbs and the lemon juice. Season the tomatoes with salt and pepper. Serve the fried bean cakes topped with the tomatoes. –*John Martin Taylor*

WINE What's needed here is a straightforward refreshing dry white, such as a Mâcon from France. Look for the 1995 Georges Duboeuf Fête des Fleurs or the 1995 Les Charmes Mâcon-Lugny.

Black-Bean and Roasted-Vegetable Burritos

Black-Bean and Roasted-Vegetable Burritos

8 SERVINGS **L**

Hearty black beans, sweet roasted vegetables, smoky chipotles and cheddar cheese fill these vegetarian burritos. The vegetables can be grilled rather than roasted.

Vegetable-oil cooking spray
- 4 medium red, green and yellow bell peppers, cut into 3-by-¼-inch matchstick strips
- 1 large onion, sliced crosswise ¼ inch thick
- 1 medium zucchini, cut into 3-by-¼-inch matchstick strips
- 1 tablespoon fresh lemon juice
- 2 teaspoons extra-virgin olive oil
- 1 teaspoon dried oregano

Salt and freshly ground pepper
- 3 cups cooked black beans, drained and rinsed if canned
- 2 scallions, finely chopped
- 2 canned chipotle chiles–stemmed, seeded and minced
- 3 garlic cloves, minced
- 2 tablespoons finely chopped cilantro
- 1 to 2 tablespoons fresh lime juice

Eight 10-inch flour tortillas
- 1 cup grated low-fat cheddar (about 3 ounces)
- 3 ripe tomatoes, seeded and minced

I. Preheat the oven to 475°. Lightly coat a shallow roasting pan or rimmed baking sheet with vegetable-oil cooking spray. In a large bowl, combine the bell peppers, onion, zucchini, lemon juice, oil, oregano and a pinch each of salt and pepper. Transfer the vegetables to the pan and roast for 20 to 25 minutes, stirring, until crisp-tender.

2. In a stainless-steel saucepan, coarsely mash half of the black beans with the scallions, chipotle chiles, garlic and cilantro. Add the remaining black beans and season with the lime juice, salt and pepper. Cook the bean mixture over moderate heat, stirring, until warmed through, about 6 minutes.

3. Heat a large cast-iron skillet or griddle over moderate heat. Heat the tortillas, one at a time, until just softened, about 15 seconds per side. Transfer to plates and pile the beans and vegetables on top. Sprinkle with the cheese and roll up the tortillas. Top with the tomatoes and serve. –*David Hirsch, Linda Dickinson and Susan Harville*

WINE Peppers, onions, cheddar and garlicky beans–these direct flavors call for a gutsy red, such as a California Zinfandel. Look for the 1994 Marietta or the 1994 Bannister Dry Creek Valley.

Poached Eggs Diavolo on Polenta

4 SERVINGS **L**

Low-fat sauces and accompaniments can dress up pared-down egg dishes. Here, soft polenta and a wicked tomato sauce make a serving of a single poached egg much more satisfying.
- 2 teaspoons olive oil
- 1 shallot, minced

One 14-ounce can Italian peeled tomatoes, with their liquid
- 1 tablespoon tomato paste
- 2 teaspoons Tabasco sauce

273

½ teaspoon dried oregano

Salt and freshly ground pepper

1¼ cups instant polenta

2 teaspoons unsalted butter

4 large eggs

2 tablespoons finely chopped
flat-leaf parsley

1. Heat the oil in a medium nonstick skillet. Add the shallot to the skillet and cook over low heat until golden, 4 to 5 minutes. Add the tomatoes and their liquid to the skillet, breaking up the tomatoes with a spoon. Stir in the tomato paste, Tabasco and oregano. Bring the sauce to a boil over high heat, then lower the heat to moderate and simmer for 15 minutes, stirring occasionally. Season the sauce with salt and pepper and keep warm.

2. Fill a large skillet with water, add ½ teaspoon salt and bring to a simmer over moderate heat.

Huevos Rancheros

3. Meanwhile, bring 4½ cups of water to a boil in a medium heavy saucepan. Add 1¼ teaspoons salt and whisk in the polenta. Cook over moderate heat, stirring, until the polenta is cooked through and pulls away from the side, about 10 minutes. Stir in the butter. If the polenta is too stiff, stir in a little more water. Mound the polenta on four warm plates. Top the polenta with half of the tomato sauce.

4. Crack each egg into a separate small bowl or dish. Slide the eggs quickly into the simmering water in the skillet and cook until the whites are set and the yolks are soft, about 3 minutes.

5. Working quickly, use a slotted spoon to set one of the poached eggs on top of each serving of the polenta. Spoon the remaining tomato sauce over the poached eggs, sprinkle with the parsley and serve.   *—Elaine Corn*

Huevos Rancheros

4 SERVINGS **L**

In my hometown of El Paso, Texas, where it's easy to buy fresh tortillas, we wouldn't bother toasting them. However, if you can't find fresh ones, go ahead and heat the tortillas in the skillet as directed. I've held back some cheese and replaced some whole eggs with whites; the rest of the recipe is straight from El Paso.

1 teaspoon vegetable oil

1 medium onion, coarsely
chopped

2 large garlic cloves, minced

1 jalapeño pepper, seeded and
minced

1 tablespoon minced cilantro

1 teaspoon pure chile powder

One 10-ounce can enchilada
sauce

One 8-ounce can tomato sauce

1 teaspoon dried oregano,
preferably Mexican

4 corn tortillas

Vegetable-oil cooking spray

1 cup canned low-fat refried
beans

4 tablespoons water

1 cup loosely packed grated
Monterey jack (2 ounces)

4 large eggs, lightly beaten

4 large egg whites

egg tips

1. **Eggs shouldn't be stored in the refrigerator door.** They'll keep better in their carton on an inside shelf.

2. **Properly refrigerated eggs** should be used within five weeks of the sell-by date on the box.

3. **Hard-cooked eggs** should be used within one week.

4. **The Grade A designation** is based on the appearance of the egg shell and the quality of the white and the yolk. It has nothing to do with freshness.

¼ cup prepared salsa

Salt and freshly ground pepper

1 teaspoon unsalted butter

1. Preheat the broiler. Heat the oil in a large nonstick skillet. Add the onion, garlic and jalapeño pepper and cook over moderately high heat, stirring, until softened, about 4 minutes. Add the cilantro and the chile powder to the skillet and cook, stirring, for 30 seconds. Add the enchilada sauce, the tomato sauce and the oregano. Reduce the heat to moderate and simmer, stirring occasionally, until the sauce is thickened, about 5 minutes. Cover the sauce and keep it warm.

2. Heat a medium nonstick skillet over moderately high heat. Lightly coat the corn tortillas on both sides with some vegetable-oil cooking spray. Toast one corn tortilla at a time in the skillet, about 15 seconds per side. Dip one side of the toasted tortilla into the tomato sauce and set it, coated-side up, on a baking sheet. Repeat with the remaining corn tortillas.

3. In a medium saucepan, combine the refried beans with 2 tablespoons of the water and warm over moderately low heat. Spread ¼ cup of the beans on each of the tortillas and top each one with grated Monterey jack. Broil the tortillas for about 1 minute, or until the cheese is melted; keep warm.

4. In a bowl, beat the eggs, egg whites, salsa and the remaining 2 tablespoons of water; season with salt and pepper. Heat the butter in the medium skillet until it is foaming. Add the egg mixture and cook over moderately high heat, pushing the eggs into the center of the pan, until the eggs are set but still soft, about 2 minutes.

5. Transfer the tortillas to four plates. Top the tortillas with the scrambled eggs and a little sauce and serve immediately, with a bowl of the remaining sauce alongside.　　　*—Elaine Corn*

Caramelized-Onion and Asparagus Frittata

6 SERVINGS **L**

1 teaspoon vegetable oil

2 large onions, finely chopped

12 fresh asparagus spears, trimmed and peeled

4 large eggs

3 large egg whites

1 tablespoon water

Salt and freshly ground pepper

Coarsely chopped parsley

1. Heat the oil in a medium nonstick ovenproof skillet. Add the onions and cook over moderately high heat, stirring, until sizzling, about 2 minutes. Reduce the heat to moderately low and cook, stirring frequently, until the onions are well browned, about 30 minutes longer.

2. Meanwhile, in a skillet of boiling salted water, cook the asparagus until tender, 3 to 4 minutes; drain and set aside.

3. Preheat the broiler. In a bowl, whisk the whole eggs, egg whites and water until frothy, then season with salt and pepper. Pour the eggs over the hot onions in the skillet and let set for 1 minute. Cover and cook until the eggs are set around the edges but still soft in the center, 2 to 3 minutes.

4. Arrange the asparagus on top of the frittata, then slip the pan under the broiler and cook for 30 to 60 seconds, or until the omelet puffs up and lightly browns. Slide the frittata onto a serving plate and sprinkle with the chopped parsley. Cut the frittata into six wedges and serve.　　　*—Elaine Corn*

Cowboy Frittata

8 SERVINGS

4 slices of bacon, chopped

1 medium onion, chopped

12 large eggs

¾ teaspoon salt

½ teaspoon freshly ground pepper

½ cup salsa

1 cup shredded cheddar

1. Preheat the oven to 400°. In a large ovenproof skillet, cook the bacon over moderately low heat until slightly crisp, about 5 minutes. Add the onion and cook, stirring, until softened but not browned, about 4 minutes.

2. In a bowl, lightly beat the eggs with the salt and pepper. Add the eggs to the skillet and, using a spatula, gently pull the cooked eggs to the center while tilting the skillet to allow the uncooked portion to flow to the edges, about 3 minutes. When the eggs start to form a cohesive mass, place the skillet in the oven and bake for about 6 minutes, or until the eggs are set. Remove from the oven; top the eggs with the salsa and then the cheese. Return the skillet to the oven and bake for about 2 minutes, or until the cheese is melted. Cut the frittata into wedges and serve hot or warm.　　　*—John Hopkins*

Savory Artichoke Bread Pudding

8 SERVINGS **Q**

This rich, main-course bread pudding is flavored with nutty Gruyère cheese and tender artichoke hearts.

4 tablespoons unsalted butter

Two 9-ounce packages frozen artichoke hearts, thawed

2 large shallots, finely chopped

½ teaspoon dried thyme

Salt

¾ pound crusty bread, cut into 1-inch cubes

¾ cup grated Gruyère (about 2 ounces)

5 cups milk

5 large eggs

4 egg yolks

½ teaspoon freshly ground pepper

⅓ cup freshly grated Parmesan

1. Preheat the oven to 350°. Melt the butter in a large skillet. Add the artichoke hearts, shallots and thyme, season with salt and cook over moderately high heat, stirring occasionally, until the shallots have softened, about 5 minutes.

2. Meanwhile, spread the bread cubes in a 13-by-9-inch baking dish. Add the artichoke-heart mixture and the Gruyère and toss well. In a bowl, whisk the milk with the eggs, egg yolks, pepper and ½ teaspoon of salt. Pour the custard evenly over the bread and sprinkle with the Parmesan.

3. Set the baking dish in a large roasting pan. Add enough hot water to the pan to reach halfway up the sides of the baking dish. Bake for about 50 minutes, or until the custard is set and the top of the pudding is well browned. Let cool slightly before serving. *–Jan Newberry*

Ham and Cheese Strata

4 SERVINGS **Q**

For this rich, tasty main course, soak the bread in the egg mixture while you cut up the other ingredients.

 8 large eggs
1½ cups milk
 ½ teaspoon salt
 ½ teaspoon freshly ground pepper
 4 cups 1-inch cubes of Italian bread

Ham and Cheese Strata

 6 ounces Virginia ham, cut into ½-inch dice (1½ cups)
 6 ounces Gouda, cut into ¾-inch dice (1½ cups)
 ½ cup julienned sun-dried tomatoes, drained
 ¼ cup plus 1 tablespoon snipped chives
 1 cup coarsely grated cheddar (about 4 ounces)

1. Preheat the oven to 425°. In a large bowl, whisk together the eggs, milk, salt and pepper. Stir in the bread; let soak. Add the ham, Gouda, tomatoes and ¼ cup of chives to the egg mixture and stir.

2. Butter a shallow 2-quart baking dish; pour in the egg mixture. Sprinkle the cheddar on top. Bake for 25 minutes, or until puffed and golden. Let cool slightly, sprinkle with the remaining chives and serve. *–Diana Sturgis*

Warm Green Salad with Lobster and Oranges

4 SERVINGS

This fragrant salad is from *Lobster at Home* (Scribner).

 2 tablespoons fine sea salt
Two 1¼-pound live lobsters
 2 minneola tangelos or navel oranges
 ⅓ cup extra-virgin olive oil
Freshly ground pepper
 4 shallots, minced
 1 teaspoon finely grated lemon zest
 3 tablespoons sherry vinegar
 4 large basil leaves, finely shredded
 8 cups mixed hearty greens, such as frisée, radicchio, mizuna, spinach and Belgian endive

1. Fill a large stockpot with 2 inches of water, add the salt and bring to a boil over high heat. Put the lobsters in the boiling water, head first, and cook until they start to turn red, about 4 minutes. Transfer the lobsters to a bowl to cool.

2. Remove the meat from the lobster knuckles and claws; keep the claw

meat in one piece if possible. Twist the tails off the bodies. Split the tails lengthwise and remove the tail meat. Pull out and discard the black intestinal vein. Cut each tail half into three pieces. Transfer the meat to a bowl.

3. Cut the zest from one tangelo into a fine julienne. Peel both tangelos and, working over a bowl, cut in between the membranes to release the sections. Squeeze the membranes to extract the juice; measure out ¼ cup of juice and set aside.

4. Shortly before serving, in a large stainless-steel saucepan, warm the oil over moderate heat. Add the lobster meat, season with pepper and stir until just cooked through; return the lobster to the bowl. Add the shallots and citrus zests to the pan and cook for 1 minute. Add the tangelo juice, vinegar and basil and season with salt and pepper. Add the greens and toss just until warm, about 1 minute.

5. Arrange the greens on plates and garnish with the reserved lobster and tangelo sections. Spoon any remaining dressing on top of the salad and serve at once. *–Jasper White*

WINE 1993 Bouscaut Bordeaux Blanc or 1994 Talbot Bordeaux Blanc

Black-Bean and Rice Salad with Fresh Crab

4 SERVINGS

Throughout the South, a hot pilaf of beans, salt pork and rice is known as hoppin' John; here the combination is served cold with fresh crabmeat. Try any cooked beans in this dish. If you use beans from a can, make sure it contains nothing but beans, water and salt, and rinse the beans well. Serve the salad with tomato slices or in hollowed-out tomatoes.

 ⅔ cup long-grain white rice
1⅓ cups water
 ½ teaspoon salt

1½ cups cooked black beans or one 19-ounce can, drained and rinsed

½ pound lump crabmeat, picked over

6 scallions, white and tender green, thinly sliced

¼ cup extra-virgin olive oil

1 celery rib, finely chopped

2 tablespoons minced parsley

1½ tablespoons fresh lemon juice

Freshly ground pepper

Hot sauce

1. In a saucepan, combine the rice with the water and salt. Cover and bring to a boil, then cook over low heat until the rice is tender and the water is absorbed, about 17 minutes. Let cool.

2. In a bowl, combine the rice with all of the remaining ingredients except the hot sauce and stir gently, making sure not to mash the crabmeat or beans. Refrigerate for at least 1 hour so the flavors can blend. Serve the salad at room temperature. Pass the hot sauce separately. —*John Martin Taylor*

MAKE AHEAD The salad can be refrigerated for up to two days.

WINE Pour a fruity California sparkling white, such as the nonvintage Domaine Chandon Reserve Cuvée 490 or the 1991 Schramsberg Blanc de Blancs, to contrast with the up-front flavors here.

Pan-Roasted Salmon with Orange Vinaigrette

4 SERVINGS **Q**

Try substituting arugula for the fresh baby spinach, and for added depth and complexity, use blood oranges when they are available. You might also want to try cooking the salmon with its skin. Make sure to allow the skin to crisp up in the pan before serving, skin-side up.

½ cup fresh orange juice

½ cup balsamic vinegar

2 tablespoons extra-virgin olive oil

2 tablespoons minced white onion

1 anchovy fillet, drained and minced

Pan-Roasted Salmon with Orange Vinaigrette

1 tablespoon finely grated orange zest

2 teaspoons each coarsely chopped parsley, basil and mint

Kosher salt and freshly ground pepper

1 large bunch baby spinach (about 4 ounces), stemmed

1 medium fennel bulb—halved, cored and thinly sliced crosswise

1 small head of radicchio, torn into 2-inch pieces

2 tablespoons pure olive oil

Four 6-ounce skinless salmon fillets

1. Preheat the oven to 450°. In a stainless-steel bowl, combine the orange juice, vinegar, extra-virgin olive oil, onion, anchovy, orange zest and fresh herbs. Season with salt and pepper. Place the spinach, fennel and radicchio in a heatproof bowl.

2. In a large stainless-steel ovenproof skillet, heat the pure olive oil. Season the salmon fillets with salt and pepper and add them to the skillet, skinned-side down. Cook the fillets over high heat for 1 minute. Transfer the skillet to the oven and roast the salmon fillets until they are just cooked through, about 6 minutes. Remove the salmon to a plate.

3. Wipe out the skillet and add the vinaigrette. Bring to a simmer over high

Bean Salad with Fresh Salmon and Dill

heat, then pour the hot vinaigrette over the greens and toss to mix. Arrange the slightly wilted greens on four plates, set a piece of salmon on top of each and serve. —*Michael Romano*

MAKE AHEAD The vinaigrette can be refrigerated for up to two days. Bring to room temperature before proceeding with the recipe.

WINE 1996 Mulderbosch Sauvignon Blanc. This wine's ripe, intensely citrusy fruit is a fine match for the pan-roasted salmon.

Bean Salad with Fresh Salmon and Dill

4 SERVINGS

Cannellini beans dressed with good olive oil are a staple first course in Italian trattorias. Combine them with salmon and dill—two very un-Italian ingredients—and you get an elegant main course with clean, direct flavors.

1½ cups dried cannellini beans (10 ounces), soaked overnight and drained
2 quarts water
1 small onion, halved
1 carrot, halved
4 garlic cloves, lightly smashed
2 bay leaves
1 medium fennel bulb, finely diced, stalks, core and fronds reserved
Salt and freshly ground pepper
1 tablespoon chopped dill
½ cup good fruity olive oil
Two 8-ounce skinless salmon fillets

1. Place the beans in a large pot. Add the water, onion, carrot, garlic, bay leaves and the reserved fennel stalks and core. Bring to a boil, reduce the heat to very low, cover and simmer until the beans are tender, about 1 hour. Season the beans with salt and pepper during the last 10 minutes of cooking.

2. Drain the beans and discard all the cooked vegetables. Coarsely chop the fennel fronds. Transfer the beans to a large serving platter and, while still warm, add the dill, diced fennel bulb, fennel fronds and all but 1 tablespoon of the oil. Season with salt and pepper and toss gently to combine.

3. In a medium nonstick skillet, heat the remaining 1 tablespoon oil. Season the salmon on both sides with salt and pepper, add to the skillet and cook over moderate heat on one side until brown and crusty, about 3 minutes. Gently flip the salmon and cook on the other side until just cooked through, about 4 minutes. Transfer to a plate to cool slightly. Break into large flakes and toss gently with the beans. Serve warm or at room temperature. —*Erica De Mane*

MAKE AHEAD The cooked beans can be refrigerated, covered, for up to two days. Bring to room temperature before proceeding with Step 3.

WINE A round, full-bodied white, such as the 1995 Falesco Grechetto or the 1995 Mazzocco River Lane, a California Chardonnay, would set off the flavors of the salad and complement the richness of the salmon and the olive-oil dressing.

Tortilla Salad

4 SERVINGS ⦿

Use either corn or flour tortillas, depending on what you have on hand.

3 tablespoons fresh lime juice
½ small fresh red chile pepper, seeded and minced
¼ teaspoon salt
2 tablespoons vegetable oil, plus more for frying
Six 8-inch corn or flour tortillas, quartered
6 cups baby salad greens
1 ripe mango, peeled and cut into 1-inch chunks
1 cup cooked black beans, rinsed
½ small red onion, thinly sliced
1 pound cooked shrimp or smoked chicken breasts, cut into thin strips
¼ cup mild goat cheese, such as Montrachet

1. In a small glass or stainless-steel bowl, combine the lime juice, chile, salt and the 2 tablespoons of oil.

2. In a large skillet, heat ⅛ inch of oil over moderately high heat until almost smoking. Add as many tortilla quarters as will fit without overlapping and fry until crisp and golden, about 2 minutes per side. Transfer the chips to paper towels to drain and repeat with the remaining tortillas.

3. In a large bowl, toss the greens with 1½ tablespoons of the dressing. Mound the greens on a large platter. Add the mango, black beans, onion and 3 tablespoons of the dressing to the bowl and toss, then arrange over the greens. Distribute the shrimp on top, then crumble the cheese over the salad. Arrange the tortilla chips around the platter to use as scoops and serve. —*Victoria Wise*

WINE Shrimp, goat cheese and a lime-juice dressing narrow the wine choices to a tart, assertive white. That's Sauvignon Blanc territory. California offers a number of choices, such as the 1995 Caymus.

Fried-Chicken Salad

4 SERVINGS

Fried chicken has become such a popular fast food that few Americans cook it at home anymore. In this new salad, strips of chicken breast are sautéed in olive oil and served over greens that have been tossed in a sherry-vinegar dressing.

¼ cup plus 2 tablespoons extra-virgin olive oil
¼ cup all-purpose flour
Salt and freshly ground black pepper
¼ teaspoon cayenne pepper
4 skinless, boneless chicken-breast halves, cut crosswise into ¾-inch strips
1 shallot, minced
3 tablespoons sherry vinegar
½ pound mesclun

Fried-Chicken Salad

1. In a skillet, heat the oil. Meanwhile, in a shallow bowl, combine the flour with 1 teaspoon salt, ¼ teaspoon black pepper and the cayenne. Dredge the chicken pieces in the flour, shaking off any excess. Add the chicken pieces to the skillet and cook them over moderately high heat until crisp, about 2 minutes per side. Using a slotted spoon, transfer the fried chicken pieces to a plate. Season the fried chicken lightly with salt.

2. Add the shallot to the skillet and cook over moderately low heat, stirring, until softened but not browned. Add the vinegar to the skillet and bring to a boil, scraping up any brown bits. Let the dressing cool slightly.

3. In a large bowl, toss the mesclun with the warm shallot dressing and then season the salad with salt and black pepper. Arrange the dressed greens on four plates. Top each of the salads with some of the fried chicken pieces and serve.   —*John Martin Taylor*

WINE The sharp flavor accents here call for a round and fruity white for balance. Pick a California Chardonnay, such as the 1995 Bernardus or the 1995 Estancia Pinnacles.

Quails with Beet and Goat-Cheese Salad

4 SERVINGS

- 16 small beets (1 to 2 ounces each)
- 3 oranges
- ½ cup plus 2 teaspoons extra-virgin olive oil

Salt and freshly ground pepper

- 2 tablespoons red wine
- 1½ teaspoons red-wine vinegar
- ½ teaspoon fennel seeds
- 8 partially boned quails
- ¼ cup balsamic vinegar
- 2 ounces soft goat cheese, cut into ½-inch pieces
- 4 ounces mesclun (optional)

I. Preheat the oven to 350°. Put the beets in a 9-inch-square glass baking dish. Squeeze the juice from two of the oranges over the beets. Add ¼ cup of the oil and season with salt and pepper. Cover the baking dish tightly with aluminum foil and bake the beets for 50 minutes to 1 hour, or until they are tender when pierced. Peel and quarter the beets while they are still warm and return them to the baking dish. Add the wine, red-wine vinegar and the juice of the remaining orange to the baking dish. Season with salt and pepper and toss well. Let stand for 30 minutes at room temperature or overnight in the refrigerator.

2. Meanwhile, in a small skillet, toast the fennel seeds over moderately low heat until fragrant, about 1 minute. Let cool, then coarsely crush the fennel seeds; set aside.

3. In a bowl, combine the quails with the balsamic vinegar and ¼ cup of oil. Let stand for 10 minutes.

4. In a large heavy skillet, heat 1 teaspoon of the olive oil. Season four of the quails with salt and pepper and cook over moderately high heat, turning once, until the quails are browned on both sides and the breasts are medium rare, about 6 minutes; keep the quails

warm. Wipe out the skillet and repeat the process with the remaining olive oil and quails.

5. Spoon the beets onto a platter and sprinkle them with the fennel seeds and the goat cheese. Season the beet salad with pepper. Set the quails on top of the beet salad, garnish the platter with mesclun and serve. *–Cory Schreiber*

MAKE AHEAD The recipe can be prepared a day ahead through Step 2.

WINE 1995 WillaKenzie Estate Oregon Gamay Noir. This wine is reminiscent of a good cru-Beaujolais. The WillaKenzie has blackberry and plum flavors as well as some tart cherry at the finish. Both the dish and the wine share a rustic character.

Chimichurri Mixed Grill

12 SERVINGS

I like this mixed grill best made with spicy merguez and Italian cheese and parsley sausage.

- 1¼ cups white-wine vinegar
- 1 cup finely chopped parsley
- ½ cup olive oil
- 4 large garlic cloves, minced
- 1 jalapeño pepper, minced
- 2 tablespoons kosher salt
- 3 pounds hot sausage, coiled or links
- 3 pounds sweet sausage, coiled or links
- 2 dozen chicken wings, split into drumettes and wing pieces
- 4 dozen littleneck clams, scrubbed

Chimichurri Mixed Grill

I. To make the chimichurri sauce, combine the vinegar, parsley, oil, garlic, jalapeño and salt in a bowl. Let the chimichurri sauce stand at room temperature for 1 to 4 hours.

2. Light a grill. For coiled sausage, cross two long skewers through the sausage, making an X. For sausage links and the chicken wings, pierce each piece crosswise with two parallel wooden skewers, held about ½ inch apart, threading four or five rows on each pair of skewers. Grill everything over a moderately hot fire, turning once or twice, until crusty and cooked through. Transfer the sausages and chicken wings to a large platter and cover loosely with aluminum foil.

3. Stoke the fire with additional charcoal; for gas grills, increase the heat to high. Add 1 tablespoon of the sauce to each of two 10-inch metal cake pans and divide the clams between them. Set the pans on the grill, cover the grill and steam the clams until they open, about 8 minutes. Serve the mixed grill at once and pass the remaining sauce separately. —Marcia Kiesel

Spicy Thai Beef Salad

4 TO 6 SERVINGS

In this dish from northeast Thailand, the beef is lightly grilled or broiled, thinly sliced and cooked again briefly in a hot dressing. Serve with rice.

- 1 pound beef sirloin steak, cut about ¾ inch thick

---

piquillo peppers

The jarred piquillo peppers called for in the recipe for Mediterranean Pepper Salad with Sausages are available at specialty-food stores and by mail from Zingerman's (313-769-1625). Or substitute four roasted red bell peppers, peeled, seeded and cut into thin strips, then mixed with a large pinch of cayenne.

- 1 teaspoon freshly ground pepper
- ½ cup beef or chicken stock or canned low-sodium broth
- 3 tablespoons fresh lime juice
- 2 tablespoons Thai fish sauce (nam pla)
- 1 teaspoon sugar
- ⅓ cup thinly sliced shallots, separated into rings
- 4 scallions, halved lengthwise and cut into ½-inch pieces
- 2 bird or serrano chiles, minced
- ½ cup mint leaves

ACCOMPANIMENTS

- 1 small green cabbage—cored, cut into wedges and separated into leaves
- 8 to 10 Bibb lettuce leaves
- 5 to 6 Chinese long beans, trimmed and cut into 2-inch pieces
- 3 scallions, white and tender green, halved lengthwise
- 1 seedless European cucumber, peeled and sliced ¼ inch thick

I. Light a charcoal grill or preheat the broiler. Rub the sirloin steak with the freshly ground pepper. Sear the steak about 3 inches from the heat for about 1½ minutes on each side; the meat should be very rare. Slice the meat very thinly against the grain.

2. In a medium stainless-steel saucepan, combine the stock, lime juice, fish sauce and sugar and bring to a boil. Add the slices of steak to the saucepan and stir quickly to coat them with sauce. Immediately pour the steak and the dressing into a bowl. Add the shallots, the scallions, the chiles and the mint leaves and toss gently. Mound the beef salad on a plate. Serve the salad with a platter containing at least three of the accompaniments. —Jeffrey Alford and Naomi Duguid

WINE 1994 Hogue Cellars Merlot

Mediterranean Pepper Salad with Sausages

4 SERVINGS

The Spanish generally favor bell peppers over spicier chiles. However, we were recently introduced to piquillo peppers, native to the Navarre region of northern Spain. They're as sweet as red peppers but with a delicate and delightful punch, plus fire-roasting adds a smoky flavor. This salad also makes a piquant garnish for grilled swordfish or a tasty hors d'oeuvre mounded on toasts.

- 8 flat anchovy fillets
- One 7-ounce jar piquillo peppers— drained and cut crosswise into ¼-inch rings, 1 tablespoon of the liquid reserved (see box, left)
- ¼ small red onion, thinly sliced
- 1 small garlic clove, mashed
- ¼ cup loosely packed basil leaves, julienned
- 2½ tablespoons extra-virgin olive oil
- 1 tablespoon red-wine vinegar
- 1 tablespoon nonpareil capers
- Salt and freshly ground pepper
- 1½ pounds sweet Italian sausages

I. In a small bowl, soak the anchovies in cold water for 10 minutes. Drain the anchovies, pat them dry and cut them into thin lengthwise strips.

2. In a medium bowl, combine the piquillo peppers and their reserved liquid with the anchovies, onion, garlic, basil, oil, vinegar and capers. Season with salt and pepper and let stand at room temperature for 30 minutes or refrigerate for up to 2 days.

3. Light a grill or heat a grill pan or cast-iron skillet. Grill or cook the sausages over moderately high heat, turning, until they are browned and cooked through, 15 to 20 minutes. Set the sausages on plates and spoon the piquillo-pepper salad alongside. —Susan Feniger and Mary Sue Milliken

Chilled Make-Ahead Summer Oatmeal

4 SERVINGS **Q**

What's a recipe for cereal doing among these main dishes? Many years ago, when I was *chef de cuisine* at Chez Max in Zurich, Switzerland, the cooks there would make up big batches of rich and nutty muesli in the summer, and we'd very happily eat it chilled for dinner. For a sweeter, fruitier taste, use the fruit-flavored yogurt and fruit nectar called for below. You can fold one-quarter cup of well-chilled whipped cream into the oatmeal just before serving for a real Swiss-style treat.

16 ounces plain or fruit-flavored yogurt

2 cups instant or old-fashioned oatmeal, or unsweetened Swiss-style muesli

2 cups peach or apricot nectar, milk, rice milk or soy milk, or a combination

2 large peaches, processed to a coarse puree

1 cup blueberries

3 tablespoons whole almonds, coarsely chopped

1 tablespoon pumpkin seeds or sunflower seeds

Pinch of ground cinnamon

Pinch of ground cardamom

In a large serving bowl, combine all of the ingredients and mix thoroughly. Cover the oatmeal with plastic wrap and refrigerate overnight. Serve the oatmeal chilled.　　*—Michael Romano*

CHAPTER 13 bread pizza sandwiches

Grilled Eggplant and Cheese Pizzas (p. 291)

287   Honeymoon French Toast

287   Country Loaf

287   Potato Bread with Dill and Caraway

288   Broccoli Bread

288   Crispy Corn Bread

288   Jalapeño Corn Bread

289   Cheese Biscuits

289   Blue-Cornmeal Pancakes

289   Focaccia with Black Olives

290   Pizza with Parsley Pesto and Potatoes

291   Grilled Eggplant and Cheese Pizzas

293   Wild-Mushroom and Cheese Pizzas

294   Bull's-Eyes with Mushrooms and Fontina

294   Parmesan-Crusted Vegetarian Sandwiches

295   Shrimp-and-Avocado Pockets

295   Salmon Burgers with Green Tartare Sauce

297   Tuna Burgers with Sesame Slaw

297   Turkey Sandwiches with Cranberry Apricot Relish

298   The Reubenesque

298   Quesadillas

299   Smoky Cubano Sandwiches

300   Orwasher's Special

301   B.O.A.T. Sandwiches

Honeymoon French Toast

Honeymoon French Toast

2 LARGE SERVINGS

For a hearty French toast, soak whole-grain bread in a maple-syrup-infused batter. If you prefer, you can substitute a firm-textured white bread. Serve fresh mango alongside.

- 3 large eggs
- ½ cup milk
- ¼ cup granulated sugar
- ¼ cup pure maple syrup plus more, preferably warmed, for serving
- 1½ teaspoons pure vanilla extract
- ½ teaspoon cinnamon

Six ½-inch-thick slices whole-grain bread

4 to 5 tablespoons unsalted butter

- 2 teaspoons confectioners' sugar, for garnish

I. In a large shallow bowl, whisk together the eggs, milk, sugar, the ¼ cup of maple syrup, the vanilla and cinnamon until the sugar is dissolved.

2. Soak the bread slices in the egg mixture, one slice at a time, for about 1 minute, and then transfer to a tray or baking sheet; don't oversoak or the bread will fall apart.

3. Melt 2 tablespoons of the butter in each of two large heavy skillets. Add the bread to the skillets and cook over moderately low heat, turning once, until golden brown, about 5 minutes per side; if the pans are dry when you turn the toast, swirl in a little more butter. Transfer the French toast to plates and dust with the confectioners' sugar. Serve the French toast at once with the warm maple syrup.   —Jonathan Eismann

Country Loaf

MAKES ONE 2½-POUND LOAF

With slow risings, this bread develops a wonderful texture, crisp on the outside and chewy on the inside. If you have your own sourdough starter going, you can use it in place of the recipe given here.

About 4 cups bread flour

- ¾ cup whole-wheat flour
- ¾ teaspoon active dry yeast
- 2½ teaspoons salt

Sourdough Starter (recipe follows)

- 1 cup lukewarm water
- ½ cup beer or pale ale
- 2½ tablespoons olive oil
- 2 tablespoons milk
- 3 tablespoons cornmeal

I. In the bowl of a standing electric mixer fitted with a dough hook, combine 3 cups of the bread flour with the whole-wheat flour, yeast and salt.

2. In a pitcher, stir together the Sourdough Starter, water, beer, oil and milk. With the mixer set at low speed, gradually pour the liquid into the dry ingredients, and then increase the speed to medium and knead for 7 minutes. Stop the machine occasionally to scrape down the inside of the bowl with a spatula. The dough will be sticky.

3. Spread ½ cup of the bread flour on a work surface. Scrape the dough onto the surface and knead vigorously by hand for 5 minutes, using just enough additional flour to prevent the dough from sticking. Transfer the dough to a lightly oiled large bowl; turn to coat with oil. Cover with plastic wrap and leave in a warm place until the dough has doubled in bulk, 2½ to 3 hours.

4. Turn the dough out onto a freshly floured surface, knead it briefly and shape it into an oval. Sift 2 tablespoons of the bread flour over a large baking sheet, then sprinkle it with the cornmeal. Transfer the dough to the sheet and gently stretch it into a long flat loaf about 2 inches high. Dust the rough surface of the loaf lightly with more of the bread flour, cover with a linen dish towel and let rise at room temperature for 2 hours.

5. Meanwhile, preheat the oven to 450° and position a rack in the lower third of the oven. With a knuckle, indent the dough in six spots. Bake the bread for 30 to 35 minutes, or until the loaf is golden brown.

SOURDOUGH STARTER

MAKES ABOUT 1½ CUPS

- 1 cup bread flour
- 1 cup water
- ¼ teaspoon active dry yeast

In a 1-quart pitcher, stir together the flour, water and yeast. Cover the pitcher almost completely with plastic wrap and let stand at room temperature overnight. For a stronger sour flavor, let the starter stand in the refrigerator for up to 2 days.   —Darra Goldstein

MAKE AHEAD In Step 3 of the bread recipe, the dough can rise overnight in the refrigerator.

Potato Bread with Dill and Caraway

MAKES 2 LOAVES

- 4 large Idaho potatoes (about 2 pounds)
- 2 envelopes active dry yeast
- 2 cups lukewarm water

About 8 cups unbleached bread flour

- ½ cup nonfat dry milk powder
- 3 tablespoons sugar
- 3 tablespoons finely chopped dill
- 2 tablespoons salt
- ¼ cup caraway seeds
- 4 large eggs—3 eggs lightly beaten

I. Preheat the oven to 400°. Prick the potatoes all over and bake for about 45 minutes, or until tender. Let cool completely, then peel the potatoes and pass them through a ricer. Measure out 3½ cups of potatoes.

2. In a very large bowl, stir the yeast into the water and let stand for about 5 minutes, or until the yeast is foamy. In another bowl, combine 6½ cups of the flour, the powdered milk, sugar, dill, salt and half of the caraway seeds. Using your hands, work the potato pulp into

the flour mixture. Add the potato mixture and the beaten eggs to the dissolved yeast and mix vigorously until it comes together into a loose, lumpy dough. Scrape the dough out onto a lightly floured work surface and knead, adding up to 1½ cups more flour to make a smooth, satiny dough that is just slightly sticky. Put the dough in a large, lightly buttered bowl, cover it with plastic and set it aside in a warm place until it is doubled in volume, about 45 minutes.

3. Butter two large baking sheets. Punch down the dough and knead it briefly. Cut the dough into twenty-four even pieces and shape each piece into a round ball. On one baking sheet, arrange half of the dough balls in two rows, with the pieces lightly touching each other. Use the remaining dough balls to form the second loaf. In a small bowl, beat the remaining egg with 1 tablespoon of water. Brush the tops of the loaves all over with the egg wash and then sprinkle with the remaining caraway seeds. Cover the loaves with plastic wrap and let stand in a warm place until doubled in volume, about 40 minutes.

4. Preheat the oven to 375°. Bake the loaves for about 30 minutes, until they are richly golden. Cover the loaves with aluminum foil after 5 minutes of baking to prevent them from burning. Rotate the loaves halfway through baking. After 30 minutes, remove the foil and bake the bread for about 8 minutes, or until the loaves are evenly browned. Transfer the loaves to racks to cool. Serve the potato bread warm or at room temperature.   –*George Mahaffey*

MAKE AHEAD The potato bread can be baked a day ahead; wrap the loaves well and let stand at room temperature. If you want to serve the bread warm, wrap the loaves in aluminum foil and heat in a 350° oven.

Broccoli Bread

MAKES 2 LOAVES

For a heartier bread, roll pepperoni slices into the dough.

- ¾ pound broccoli, stems peeled
- 2 tablespoons olive oil
- 2 large garlic cloves, minced
- 4 oil-packed sun-dried-tomato halves, drained and chopped
- 2 tablespoons chopped black olives, such as Kalamata
- ¼ to ½ teaspoon crushed red pepper

Salt and freshly ground black pepper
- ½ pound frozen bread dough, thawed and cut in half
- ½ cup crumbled feta
- ¼ cup freshly grated Parmesan

1. Preheat the oven to 350°. Cook the broccoli in boiling salted water for 3 minutes. Drain and chop.

2. In a large skillet, heat the oil. Add the garlic and cook over moderate heat until fragrant, about 30 seconds. Add the sun-dried tomatoes, olives and crushed red pepper and cook for 1 minute. Add the broccoli and season with salt and black pepper.

3. On a lightly floured work surface, roll each piece of dough into a 12-by-9-inch rectangle. Spoon half of the broccoli mixture down one longer side of each rectangle, about 2 inches from the edge. Top each with half of the feta and Parmesan. Roll the dough up around the filling; fold in the sides.

4. Bake the bread for about 40 minutes, or until brown. Let cool slightly, and then slice and serve.   –*Marcia Kiesel*

Crispy Corn Bread

MAKES TWO 9-INCH ROUND LOAVES

Once the ingredients have all been measured out, making corn bread is a speedy process. The cast-iron skillet and the oil in it must be hot to make the bottom crust crisp.

- 3 tablespoons vegetable oil
- 1½ cups all-purpose flour
- ¼ cup plus 2 tablespoons sugar
- 2 tablespoons baking powder
- 2 teaspoons salt
- 2½ cups cornmeal, preferably stone-ground
- 2 cups milk
- 4 large eggs, lightly beaten
- 6 tablespoons unsalted butter, melted

1. Preheat the oven to 425°. Warm two 9-inch cast-iron skillets over moderate heat. Add 1½ tablespoons of the oil to each and heat.

2. Meanwhile, in a bowl, sift the flour with the sugar, baking powder and salt. Stir in the cornmeal. Add the milk and eggs and stir lightly. Add the melted butter and stir just until blended. Scrape the batter into the hot skillets; the oil should bubble. Bake for about 18 minutes, or until the center springs back when gently pressed. Transfer to a rack to cool. Serve warm.   –*Marcia Kiesel*

Jalapeño Corn Bread

MAKES ONE 12-BY-4½-INCH LOAF

This sweet and hot corn bread is delicious on its own or, of course, with butter. If you don't have a twelve-inch loaf pan, make the corn bread in two eight-by-five-inch pans instead.

- 1 tablespoon olive oil
- ¼ cup finely chopped seeded jalapeño peppers
- ¼ cup finely chopped red bell pepper
- ¼ cup fresh or thawed frozen corn kernels
- ¾ cup sugar
- ½ cup water
- ½ cup vegetable oil
- 1¾ cups all-purpose flour
- 1¼ cups medium-grind cornmeal
- 1 tablespoon baking powder
- 1½ teaspoons kosher salt
- 4 large eggs, lightly beaten

I. Preheat the oven to 400°. Butter a 12-by-4½-inch loaf pan. Heat the olive oil in a small skillet. Add the jalapeños, red bell pepper and corn kernels and cook over moderate heat, stirring, until wilted, about 4 minutes. Scrape onto a plate and let cool completely.

2. In a large bowl, dissolve the sugar in the water. Stir in the vegetable oil. In a medium bowl, sift together the flour, cornmeal, baking powder and salt. Using an electric mixer, beat the dry ingredients into the sugar mixture. Add the eggs and the pepper-and-corn mixture and beat until just blended.

3. Scrape the batter into the prepared pan and bake for about 45 minutes, or until the bread is golden brown and a cake tester inserted in the center comes out clean; if the top browns too quickly, cover with aluminum foil. Turn the corn bread out onto a rack to cool before slicing.   *–Tim Keating*

MAKE AHEAD The corn bread can be wrapped well and frozen for up to one week or kept at room temperature for up to two days.

Cheese Biscuits

MAKES ABOUT 16 BISCUITS
Rendered bacon fat adds a rich flavor and tenderness to biscuits. When frying bacon, pour off the fat and save it in the refrigerator. If you wish, you can use all bacon fat in these biscuits.

- 2 cups all-purpose flour
- 1 tablespoon baking powder
- ½ teaspoon salt
- ¼ teaspoon baking soda
- 4 tablespoons solid vegetable shortening
- 2 tablespoons rendered bacon fat
- ¾ cup milk
- ¾ cup grated Monterey jack

I. In a bowl, mix the flour with the baking powder, salt and baking soda. Using a pastry blender, cut in the shortening and the bacon fat until the mixture

resembles coarse meal. Add the milk and stir lightly to combine. Let the dough rest for 20 minutes at room temperature or in the refrigerator. Gently knead in the cheese.

2. Preheat the oven to 450°. On a lightly floured surface, gently roll out the dough ½ inch thick. Using a 2-inch round biscuit cutter, cut out sixteen biscuits; re-form any scraps into another biscuit. Place the biscuits on a lightly greased baking sheet. Bake for about 10 minutes, or until golden brown. Serve at once. *–John Hopkins*

Blue-Cornmeal Pancakes

MAKES 32 SMALL PANCAKES
Blue cornmeal, a specialty of the Southwest, gives these pancakes a blue-gray hue. Finely milled from dried blue corn, it is available in health-food shops; the yellow variety can be substituted.

- ¾ cup blue cornmeal
- 1½ cups all-purpose flour
- 2 tablespoons sugar
- 1 tablespoon plus 1 teaspoon baking powder
- ¾ teaspoon salt
- ⅔ cup milk
- 1 large egg, lightly beaten
- 3 tablespoons vegetable oil, plus more for frying

Soft unsalted butter, for serving
Pure maple syrup, for serving

I. In a skillet, stir the cornmeal over moderately high heat until lightly toasted, about 4 minutes. Transfer to a plate to cool. In a bowl, mix the cornmeal with the flour, sugar, baking powder and salt. Stir in the milk, egg and the 3 tablespoons of oil until blended.

2. In a skillet, heat a film of oil. Add 2 tablespoons of batter per pancake and cook over moderate heat until bubbles appear on the surface, about 3 minutes. Flip the pancakes and cook for about 2 minutes; reduce the heat if they brown too much. Repeat for each batch. Serve hot with butter and syrup. *–John Hopkins*

Blue-Cornmeal Pancakes

Focaccia with Black Olives

4 SERVINGS **L**
Focaccia is traditionally drizzled liberally with olive oil. Here, the dough is lightly brushed with extra-virgin olive oil before baking and again just before serving. The flavor hits your palate with the first bite, giving the impression that there's more oil than there really is.

- 1 tablespoon all-purpose flour, for rolling out the dough
- 1 pound store-bought pizza dough
- 1 tablespoon extra-virgin olive oil
- 1 tablespoon minced thyme or rosemary leaves
- 1 cup fleshy black olives, such as Kalamata or Gaeta

I. Preheat the oven to 450°. Place a pizza stone or a heavy sheet pan in the oven to heat for at least 30 minutes.

2. Sprinkle the flour on a work surface. Flatten the dough into a disk and roll it out into a rough 12-inch round. Transfer the dough to a cookie sheet lined with parchment paper. Prick the dough all over with a fork and brush with ½ tablespoon of the oil. Sprinkle with the thyme, cover the dough lightly with plastic wrap and set aside to rise until puffy, about 20 minutes.

3. Pit the olives: On a work surface, tap the olives with a heavy object, such as

Making Focaccia with Black Olives: brushing the dough with oil, RIGHT; pitting the olives, TOP RIGHT; and the finished focaccia, ABOVE.

a stone or a meat pounder, to split them open. Remove the pits. Chop the olives very coarsely and scatter them evenly over the focaccia dough; press the olive pieces in gently.

4. Slide the focaccia on the parchment paper onto the hot pizza stone or pan in the oven. Bake for 15 to 20 minutes, or until the edges are browned. Remove the focaccia from the oven and brush with the remaining ½ tablespoon of oil. Cut the focaccia into wedges and serve at once.   *–Sally Schneider*

Pizza with Parsley Pesto and Potatoes

4 SERVINGS

Parsley pesto makes a wonderful change from basil and lends a beautiful shade of green to the potatoes.

- 1 **pound Red Bliss potatoes, sliced ⅓ inch thick**

Salt

- 1 **cup packed flat-leaf parsley**
- 2 **tablespoons chopped walnuts**
- 1 **garlic clove, minced**
- ½ **cup extra-virgin olive oil**

Pizza Dough (recipe follows)

- ¾ **cup shredded Italian fontina**
- ¼ **cup freshly grated Parmigiano-Reggiano**

1. Set a pizza stone or oven tiles in the bottom third of the oven. Preheat the oven to 400°, allowing at least 45 minutes for the stone to heat. Meanwhile, arrange the potatoes in a single layer on a lightly oiled baking sheet, sprinkle with salt and bake in the upper third of the oven for about 30 minutes, or until tender. Let cool slightly.

2. In a food processor, combine the parsley, walnuts, garlic and ½ teaspoon of salt; pulse until finely chopped. With the machine on, add the oil in a thin stream and process until the pesto is smooth.

3. Raise the oven temperature to 500°. Roll or stretch one piece of the Pizza Dough into an 8-inch round. Place the dough on a floured pizza peel or inverted cookie sheet and arrange one-quarter of the potatoes on top, leaving a ½-inch border of dough. Drizzle the potatoes with one-quarter of the pesto and top with one-quarter of the fontina and

Parmigiano-Reggiano. With a quick motion, slide the pizza onto the hot stone and bake for about 8 minutes, or until the cheese is bubbling and the bottom of the crust is golden and crisp. Transfer the cooked pizza to a plate and serve hot. Repeat with the remaining dough, potatoes, pesto and cheeses.

PIZZA DOUGH

MAKES FOUR 8-INCH PIZZA CRUSTS

About 2 cups unbleached all-purpose flour

- 1 **envelope active dry yeast**
- 1 **cup lukewarm water**
- ½ **cup whole-wheat flour**
- 1 **teaspoon salt**

1. In a large bowl, combine ¼ cup of the all-purpose flour with the yeast and ¾ cup of the water. Set aside, uncovered, in a warm place until bubbly, about 30 minutes. Stir in the whole-wheat flour, the remaining all-purpose flour and the salt to form a soft dough. Add the remaining ¼ cup water.

2. Scrape the pizza dough onto a lightly floured work surface and knead until silky and elastic, about 5 minutes; add just enough all-purpose flour to keep the dough from sticking. Transfer the pizza dough to a lightly oiled bowl, cover and let the dough rise until doubled in bulk, about 1½ hours.

3. Punch down the pizza dough, cover and let it rise for 30 minutes. Turn the pizza dough out onto the work surface and divide it into four pieces. Let the pizza dough rest for 10 minutes before shaping.   *–Darra Goldstein*

MAKE AHEAD The pizza dough can rise overnight in the refrigerator at the end of Step 2.

WINE Olive oil, walnuts, and fontina and Parmigiano-Reggiano cheeses provide this pizza with rich flavors that will set off a full-flavored red. Go for a gutsy Zinfandel, such as the 1994 Tessera Old Vine or the 1994 Kenwood Jack London.

Grilled Eggplant and Cheese Pizzas

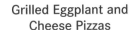

8 SERVINGS **L**

These low-fat pizzas, topped with pungent grilled eggplant and two kinds of cheese, were inspired by those served at Al Forno in Providence, Rhode Island. Serve the pizzas as they come off the grill and then continue making more.

- 2 packages active dry yeast (¼ ounce each)
- 3 cups lukewarm water (105° to 115°)
- 4 cups bread flour
- About 4 cups all-purpose flour
- Kosher salt
- 1 tablespoon plus 2 teaspoons olive oil
- 8 small garlic cloves, minced
- Eggplant Caviar (recipe follows)
- ½ cup freshly grated Parmesan or 1½ ounces shaved Parmesan
- 6 ounces feta or ricotta salata, sliced or crumbled
- 1 cup flat-leaf parsley leaves

I. In a large bowl, sprinkle the yeast over the warm water and let stand until foamy, about 5 minutes. Stir in the bread flour, then add 4 cups of all-purpose flour and 2½ teaspoons of kosher salt. Transfer the pizza dough to a lightly floured surface and knead briefly, adding more all-purpose flour as necessary to form a smooth, slightly sticky dough. Coat a large bowl with vegetable-oil cooking spray and add the pizza dough. Lightly spray plastic wrap and cover the dough with it. Let the pizza dough rise in a warm place until it is doubled in bulk, about 1½ hours. Punch the pizza dough down and divide it into eight balls. Flatten each ball of dough into a disk.

2. Arrange the disks of pizza dough on two lightly floured large baking sheets. Cover the disks with lightly sprayed plastic wrap and let stand at room temperature until the dough has doubled in bulk, about 1 hour. ➤

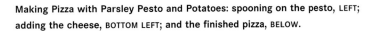

Making Pizza with Parsley Pesto and Potatoes: spooning on the pesto, LEFT; **adding the cheese,** BOTTOM LEFT; **and the finished pizza,** BELOW.

Grilled Eggplant and Cheese Pizzas

3. Light a grill. Pour ½ teaspoon of the oil onto an unrimmed baking sheet, add a pizza-dough disk and turn to coat it with the oil. Working on the baking sheet, stretch the disk of dough out to a 12-inch round.

4. Using a damp paper towel, coat the grill with 1 teaspoon of the oil. Carefully transfer the round of pizza dough to the grill and cook over a hot fire, rotating occasionally, until crusty and dark brown on the bottom, about 3 minutes. Turn the crust over and sprinkle 1 minced garlic clove on top. Spread about ⅓ cup of the Eggplant Caviar on the pizza crust and top it with 1 tablespoon of the Parmesan and then one-eighth of the feta. Cook the pizza, rotating occasionally, until it is crusty on the bottom, about 3 minutes. Garnish the pizza with a few parsley leaves, cut it into wedges and serve. Repeat the process with the remaining ingredients to make seven more pizzas.

EGGPLANT CAVIAR

MAKES ABOUT 3 CUPS

Grilled eggplant caviar is also wonderful on bruschetta and with grilled fish and poultry.

- 2 medium green bell peppers
- 2 teaspoons vegetable oil
- 2 large eggplants (about 3 pounds), sliced crosswise 1 inch thick
- 2 large onions, sliced crosswise 1 inch thick
- ¼ cup water
- 3 garlic cloves, coarsely chopped
- One 6-ounce can tomato paste
- 2 tablespoons red-wine vinegar
  Salt and freshly ground pepper

I. Light a grill. When the fire is hot, grill the green bell peppers, turning, until they are blackened and blistered all over, about 3 minutes per side. Working over a strainer set over a bowl, remove the charred skin, stems and seeds from the bell peppers, reserving the pepper juices. Then cut the bell peppers into thin strips.

2. Using a damp paper towel, coat the grill with 1 teaspoon of the oil. Grill the eggplant slices until tender and golden brown on both sides, about 10 minutes. Let cool slightly, discard the eggplant skin and chop the eggplant. Coat the grill with the remaining 1 teaspoon of oil and grill the onion slices, turning, until lightly charred and tender, about 15 minutes. Chop the onions.

3. Put the bell-pepper strips and the reserved pepper juices in a large non-stick skillet and bring to a simmer over moderate heat. Add the water and the garlic and simmer, stirring, for 3 minutes. Stir in the tomato paste and simmer for 5 minutes. Add the chopped eggplant and onion and cook, stirring, until heated through, about 3 minutes. Transfer the mixture to a food processor, add the vinegar and process to a coarse puree. Season with salt and pepper. —*Jim Cohen*

MAKE AHEAD The disks of pizza dough can be frozen, wrapped separately, for up to two months; thaw before proceeding with Step 2 of the pizza recipe. The Eggplant Caviar can be refrigerated for up to five days. Let return to room temperature before using.

WINE 1994 Banfi Cellars Argusto Dolcetto d'Acqui from Piedmont, Italy

Wild-Mushroom and Cheese Pizzas

10 SERVINGS

- 1½ teaspoons active dry yeast
- ½ teaspoon sugar
- 1 cup lukewarm water (105° to 115°)
- ¼ cup plus 1 tablespoon extra-virgin olive oil, plus more for brushing
- Fine sea salt
- About 2½ cups all-purpose flour
- 1½ pounds assorted wild mushrooms, such as oysters and chanterelles, thickly sliced
- 1 large shallot, minced
- Freshly ground pepper
- 4 ounces fontina, grated, or 5 ounces soft mild cheese, such as Stracchino or Taleggio

I. In a large bowl, dissolve the yeast and sugar in ¼ cup of the lukewarm water and set aside until foamy, about 10 minutes. Add the 1 tablespoon oil, 1 teaspoon of salt and the remaining ¾ cup of water. Stir in as much of the flour as possible. Turn the pizza dough out onto a lightly floured surface and knead it until silky, adding a little more flour if necessary; the dough should be soft but not sticky. Shape the pizza dough into a ball and transfer it to a lightly oiled bowl. Cover and let the dough rise in a warm place until it is doubled in bulk, about 1 hour.

2. Punch the dough down and shape it into ten balls. Set the balls of pizza dough on a lightly oiled baking sheet, cover them with lightly oiled plastic wrap and refrigerate for at least 1 hour or overnight.

3. Heat the remaining ¼ cup of oil in a large skillet. Add the mushrooms and shallot, season with salt and pepper and cook until the liquid evaporates and the mushrooms begin to brown, about 9 minutes.

4. Preheat the oven to 550° or as hot as it will go. Put a pizza stone in the oven or generously brush two large baking sheets with oil. Working with one ball of pizza dough at a time, punch it down, then stretch it or roll it out to a 6-inch circle. Sprinkle or spread some of the cheese on the pizza dough and top with some of the mushrooms.

5. Working in batches, bake the pizzas until the crusts are golden and the bottoms are crisp, about 7 minutes on a pizza stone or 11 minutes on a baking

ABOVE: **Parmesan-Crusted Vegetarian Sandwiches.**
TOP: **Wild-Mushroom and Cheese Pizza.**

sheet. Let the mushroom-and-cheese pizzas cool slightly on a rack before serving.   –*Reed Hearon*
MAKE AHEAD Step 3 can be done a day ahead. Refrigerate the mushrooms but let them return to room temperature before using.

Bull's-Eyes with Mushrooms and Fontina

4 SERVINGS
Eggs fried in hollowed-out bread slices, or bull's-eyes, are one of my favorite breakfasts; when you fill the bread with spicy mushrooms, cheese and salsa, you have more of a meal. Ideally, the eggs should be cooked so that the yolks are almost firm yet ever so slightly runny. If you like, you can cook the yolks less and serve the sandwiches with knives and forks.

- 5 tablespoons unsalted butter
- 2 shallots, thinly sliced
- ¾ pound mushrooms, stemmed and thinly sliced
- 1 tablespoon fresh lemon juice
- Salt and freshly ground pepper
- 1 teaspoon hot paprika
- 8 slices of whole wheat bread, with a 2-inch square cut out of each center
- 8 large eggs
- 2 ounces fontina or Monterey jack, cut into 8 slices
- 1 tablespoon plus 2 teaspoons prepared salsa

1. Melt 1 tablespoon of the butter in a large skillet. Add the shallots and cook over moderate heat, stirring, until wilted, about 3 minutes. Raise the heat to high and add the mushrooms and lemon juice. Cook, stirring occasionally, until the mushrooms release their liquid. Season the mushrooms with salt and pepper and cook until the liquid has evaporated and the mushrooms start to brown, about 4 minutes. Add the paprika and cook, stirring, until fragrant, about 2 minutes. Transfer the mushrooms to a bowl.

2. Wipe out the skillet and melt another tablespoon of the butter. Arrange two slices of hollowed-out bread in the skillet and break an egg into each hole. Cook over low heat until the bread is well-browned on the bottom and the yolks are partially set, about 3 minutes. Turn the bread over and cook the second sides until the yolks are barely set, about 3 minutes more. Turn the bread again, set a slice of cheese on each toast and season with salt and pepper.

3. Spread one heaping teaspoon of salsa on one of the toasts and cover with ⅓ cup of the mushrooms; invert the other toast on top, cheese-side down. Transfer the sandwich to a plate. Repeat with the remaining ingredients to make three more bull's-eyes. –*Marcia Kiesel*
WINE Eggs aren't easy to match–they tend to flatten wine flavors–but the wine-friendly mushrooms, shallots and cheese make a straightforward, round and fruity white the natural choice. Try a Pinot Blanc, such as the 1996 Pierre Sparr from Alsace or the 1995 Mirassou from northern California.

Parmesan-Crusted Vegetarian Sandwiches

4 SERVINGS
Cheese is a key ingredient in skillet sandwiches. In most cases, melted cheese inside the sandwich holds everything together. Here, though, the cheese is on the outside, making a crisp crust on the bread. Smooth avocados do the job of binding the sandwich.

- 6 tablespoons unsalted butter, softened
- ¼ cup freshly grated Parmesan
- Salt and freshly ground pepper
- 8 thick slices of firm white or oatmeal bread
- 1 tablespoon plus 2 teaspoons mayonnaise
- 1 tablespoon plus 1 teaspoon Dijon mustard
- 2 ripe avocados
- 2 tablespoons fresh lime juice
- 12 thin tomato slices
- 4 thin red-onion slices
- 2 cups alfalfa sprouts

1. In a small bowl, blend the butter with the Parmesan and season with salt and pepper. Spread one side of each bread slice with the Parmesan butter. In another small bowl, blend the mayonnaise with the mustard. Halve and pit the avocados and thinly slice them lengthwise.

Sprinkle the avocado slices with the lime juice.

2. Put two to three slices of bread, buttered-side down, in a large skillet set over moderate heat. Cook until the bottoms are crisp and deep brown, about 3 minutes. Remove from the pan and repeat with the remaining bread.

3. Put four of the cheese toasts on a work surface, browned-side down. Arrange an avocado half and three slices of tomato on each toast and season with salt and pepper. Top each with one slice of onion, 1 tablespoon of the mustard-mayonnaise and ½ cup of alfalfa sprouts. Top with the remaining cheese toasts, browned-side up. *–Marcia Kiesel*

WINE The vegetables would suggest a light white as a flavor foil, but the cheese gives the sandwich enough richness to pair with a round, fruity California Chardonnay, such as the 1996 Meridian Santa Barbara or the 1996 Alexander Valley Vineyards Wetzel Family Estate.

sandwich tips

To build a neat, easy-to-eat grilled sandwich, follow these suggestions:

Use firm bread that won't disintegrate when you pile on the ingredients.

Slice vegetables, meats and cheeses evenly and on the thin side so that they stack up well.

Press cheese sandwiches down in the skillet to keep them compact and to ensure that the cheese melts evenly. If the sandwich is not too tall, you can push it down with your hand; if it's bulky, weight it down with a small skillet or with a large onion or potato.

Use a serrated knife and a gentle sawing motion to cut the sandwich after it is made. Don't push down; let the knife do the work.

Shrimp-and-Avocado Pockets

6 SERVINGS

Here's a no-cook recipe for those times when you don't want to turn on the stove.

- 3 tablespoons fresh lemon juice
- 1 garlic clove, minced
- 1 teaspoon salt
- ¼ teaspoon freshly ground pepper
- ¼ cup olive oil
- 1½ pounds cooked shelled shrimp, cut into ½-inch pieces
- 2 ripe Hass avocados, cut into ½-inch pieces
- 1 small red bell pepper, finely chopped
- 1 small red onion, finely chopped
- ¼ cup coarsely chopped cilantro
- 1½ cups torn frisée
- 6 pitas

In a large bowl, whisk the lemon juice with the garlic, salt and pepper. Gradually whisk in the oil. Add all of the remaining salad ingredients and toss well. Stuff the pitas with the shrimp salad and serve. *–Diana Sturgis*

Salmon Burgers with Green Tartare Sauce

6 SERVINGS

For this recipe, you can use scraps of salmon fillet, since the fish is going to be chopped anyway. I like to serve these tender fish cakes on toasted Indian nan bread, but you can also use soft rolls or semolina buns.

- 1½ pounds skinless salmon fillet, finely chopped by hand
- 1 cup finely diced red and green bell peppers
- ¼ cup finely chopped scallions
- ¼ cup heavy cream
- 2 teaspoons Tabasco sauce
- 2 teaspoons kosher salt
- Freshly ground black pepper
- 1 large egg white
- 1½ tablespoons vegetable oil
- 1 tablespoon unsalted butter, cut into 6 pieces

- 6 grilled or toasted nan breads, cut in half
- Green Tartare Sauce (recipe follows)
- 6 thick slices cut from a large ripe tomato
- 1½ cups lightly packed tender salad greens

I. In a large bowl, combine the salmon with the red and green bell peppers, scallions, heavy cream, Tabasco, salt and pepper to taste. Mix lightly but thoroughly.

2. In a small bowl, beat the egg white until stiff. Using a spatula, gently fold the egg white into the salmon mixture. Form the mixture into six patties about ½ inch thick.

3. Preheat the oven to 300°. In a large skillet, heat 1 tablespoon of the oil until shimmering. Add three of the salmon burgers, sliding a piece of butter under each one. Cook the burgers over moderately high heat until they are well browned, about 3 minutes. Flip the burgers, reduce the heat to moderate and cook until well browned and just cooked through, about 3 minutes longer. Transfer the burgers to a cookie sheet and keep warm in the oven. Repeat with the remaining oil, burgers and butter.

4. Set the salmon burgers on six of the nan halves. Top each with a heaping tablespoon of Green Tartare Sauce, a slice of tomato and ¼ cup of the greens. Set the remaining nan halves on top and serve. Pass the extra tartare sauce at the table.

GREEN TARTARE SAUCE

MAKES ABOUT 1 CUP

Try to make this a day ahead to allow the piquant flavors to develop. Leftover sauce is delicious on tuna sandwiches or with fish or chicken.

- 1 large shallot, chopped
- 3 tablespoons chopped capers
- ¼ cup chopped cornichons or gherkins

Salmon Burgers with Green Tartare Sauce

¾ cup mayonnaise

3 tablespoons chopped chives

3 tablespoons chopped parsley

2 tablespoons chopped dill

1 teaspoon fresh lemon juice

½ teaspoon Dijon mustard

½ teaspoon freshly ground
pepper

¼ cup olive oil

In a food processor, combine the shallot, capers and cornichons and pulse until finely chopped. Add the mayonnaise, chives, parsley, dill, lemon juice, mustard and pepper and process to blend. With the machine on, add the oil to the tartare sauce in a slow steady stream. —*Rick Moonen*

MAKE AHEAD The uncooked salmon burgers can be refrigerated for up to six hours. The sauce can be refrigerated for up to three days. Bring to room temperature before using.

WINE A Chenin Blanc, such as the 1995 Hogue Cellars from Washington State or the 1995 Pine Ridge from California, would be a good choice.

Tuna Burgers with Sesame Slaw

4 SERVINGS **L**

Japanese nori, or seaweed, and wasabi powder are available at Asian markets and health-food stores.

1 pound fresh yellowfin or bluefin
tuna fillet, finely chopped

3 tablespoons minced chives

1 tablespoon extra-virgin olive oil

Kosher salt and freshly ground
pepper

2 tablespoons sesame seeds

1 medium head green cabbage
(1½ pounds)—halved, cored and
shredded

2 medium carrots, grated

2 tablespoons rice vinegar

½ teaspoon Asian sesame oil

4 non-fat hamburger buns or
kaiser rolls

¼ cup plus 1 tablespoon soy sauce

1 tablespoon honey mustard

½ tablespoon wasabi powder

One 8-inch-square sheet of nori, cut
into thin strips (optional)

1. In a large bowl, lightly mix the tuna with the chives and the olive oil and season with ½ teaspoon of salt and a large pinch of pepper. Shape the mixture into four burgers, then cover and refrigerate.

2. In a small skillet, toast the sesame seeds over moderate heat, shaking the pan, until golden, about 3 minutes. Transfer the seeds to a plate to cool. In a large bowl, toss the shredded cabbage with the carrots, toasted sesame seeds, vinegar and sesame oil. Season with salt and pepper, cover and refrigerate the slaw for up to 4 hours.

3. Light a grill. When the fire is very hot, grill the tuna burgers, turning once, until they are nicely charred and still very rare, about 1 minute per side. Grill the hamburger buns, cut-side down, until they are toasted.

4. In a large skillet, combine the soy sauce, mustard and wasabi and bring to a boil over moderately high heat. Add the tuna burgers and cook, turning once, until glazed with sauce but still rare, about 1 minute. Set the burgers on the buns. Fold the nori into the slaw and serve alongside. —*Jim Cohen*

MAKE AHEAD The uncooked tuna burgers can be refrigerated overnight.

WINE 1994 Delheim Pinotage from Stellenbosch, South Africa

Turkey Sandwiches with Cranberry Apricot Relish

2 SERVINGS

This recipe will leave you with some of the sweet, tangy cranberry relish left over. The relish keeps well and can be served with roast pork, chicken or turkey, whether served on their own or as sandwiches.

Tuna Burgers with Sesame Slaw

RELISH

6 ounces fresh or frozen cranberries

¼ cup canned apricot nectar

¼ cup sugar

1 tablespoon honey

1 tablespoon port

¼ teaspoon pure vanilla extract

2 tablespoons water

2 tablespoons dried currants

2 tablespoons thinly sliced dried
apricots

SANDWICHES

4 slices white bread, toasted

4 romaine lettuce leaves

6 ounces sliced roasted turkey

Salt and freshly ground pepper

8 scallions, green part only

1. MAKE THE RELISH: In a medium stainless-steel saucepan, combine the cranberries, apricot nectar and sugar and bring to a boil over moderately high heat. Reduce the heat to low, cover and cook, stirring occasionally, until slightly reduced, about 20 minutes.

2. In a small stainless-steel saucepan, combine the honey, port, vanilla and water. Bring the mixture to a boil over high heat. Remove from the heat and stir in the currants and apricots. Let steep for 15 minutes.

3. Drain the cranberries, reserving ¼ cup of the cooking liquid. Stir the dried fruit mixture into the cranberries and then add the reserved cooking liquid. Let cool.

4. MAKE THE SANDWICHES: Spread two slices of the bread with about 1½ tablespoons each of the relish. Top with some of the lettuce and the turkey; season with salt and pepper. Top with the scallions and the remaining lettuce and bread slices.   —*Jonathan Eismann*

MAKE AHEAD The relish can be refrigerated for up to one week. The sandwiches can be refrigerated for up to three hours.

WINE A very fruity, berrylike wine with direct flavors is best for these turkey sandwiches. Try a Beaujolais or a light Pinot Noir, served slightly cool to underscore their fruitiness. Look for the 1995 or 1996 Beaujolais-Villages from Georges Duboeuf or the 1994 Saintsbury Carneros Pinot Noir.

Turkey Sandwiches with Cranberry Apricot Relish

The Reubenesque
4 SERVINGS

Based on the ever-popular Reuben, this grilled sandwich is made with smoked turkey instead of corned beef and coarsely chopped coleslaw instead of sauerkraut.

    2 tablespoons ketchup
    2 tablespoons mayonnaise
 3½ cups thickly sliced green
       cabbage
   ½ small onion, thinly sliced
   ¼ cup coarsely chopped sweet
       gherkins
   ½ teaspoon kosher salt
   ¼ teaspoon freshly ground pepper
    4 tablespoons unsalted butter
    8 slices of rye bread
   ¾ pound Jarlsberg cheese, cut into
       16 thin slices
    1 pound smoked turkey breast,
       cut into 16 slices

1. In a medium bowl, mix the ketchup and the mayonnaise. Add the cabbage, onion, gherkins, salt and pepper and toss to coat.

2. Melt 1 tablespoon of the butter in a large skillet. Add two slices of the bread to the skillet and top each with two slices of cheese, then four slices of turkey, about ½ cup of the coleslaw, two more slices of cheese and another slice of bread. Cook the sandwiches over moderately low heat until the bottoms are toasted and the cheese on the bottom is melted, about 4 minutes. Turn the sandwiches over, press them down and add another tablespoon of butter to the skillet. Cook until the second sides are browned, about 4 minutes. Transfer to plates. Repeat with the remaining ingredients to make two more sandwiches.   —*Marcia Kiesel*

WINE These grilled sandwiches don't require a subtle match, just a fruity Beaujolais-Villages from France, such as the 1996 Louis Jadot or the 1996 Georges Duboeuf.

Quesadillas
4 SERVINGS **Q**

   ½ pound mild sausage meat
Eight 8-inch flour or corn tortillas
    2 cups coarsely grated Monterey
       jack, Muenster or mozzarella
       (about 5 ounces)
    2 large poblanos or other mildly
       hot chiles, seeded and cut into
       thin strips
   ¼ cup pumpkin seeds, toasted
Vegetable oil, for frying
    2 cups small cilantro sprigs
    1 tablespoon fresh lime juice
Salt
    1 cup fresh tomato salsa

1. In a medium skillet, cook the sausage over moderate heat, stirring to break it up, until no trace of pink remains, about 8 minutes. Remove from the skillet with a slotted spoon and let cool briefly.

2. Set four tortillas on a work surface and top them with the sausage meat, the grated cheese and the poblano strips. Sprinkle the toasted pumpkin seeds on top and cover with the remaining tortillas.

3. Heat ⅛ inch of oil in a large heavy skillet until shimmering. Add one of the quesadillas and fry over moderately high heat until it is puffed and golden on the bottom, about 30 seconds. Press the quesadilla down with a spatula, flip and fry the other side for 30 seconds. Drain on paper towels and repeat the process with the remaining ingredients.

4. In a medium bowl, toss the cilantro, lime juice and a pinch of salt. Quarter the quesadillas if desired. Garnish with the cilantro sprigs and the salsa. Serve immediately.   —*Victoria Wise*

MAKE AHEAD The quesadillas can be made through Step 2 and refrigerated for up to one day. Return to room temperature before proceeding.

WINE Hearty reds, especially California Zinfandels, are made for foods like this. Look for fruity examples, such as the 1994 Chateau Montelena.

tortilla tips

1. **To store** Tortillas are always best when they're fresh, but if necessary they can be wrapped in plastic (be sure the package is airtight) and refrigerated–for up to three days for corn tortillas and up to four for flour tortillas. Flour tortillas can be frozen, but frozen corn tortillas have a tendency to crack.

2. **To serve tortillas warm as a bread** Microwave unwrapped tortillas for fifteen to thirty seconds. Or wrap in a damp cloth or towel and warm in a 200° oven.

3. **To serve crisp** Grill tortillas over an open fire or in a grill pan; deep-fry or bake them; or hold them with tongs over a stovetop gas burner until they are slightly crunchy but still pliable.

4. **To use stale tortillas** Cut tortillas into wedges and bake or fry. Serve the wedges as chips for guacamole, salsa and other dips or serve with refried beans.

Smoky Cubano Sandwiches

4 SERVINGS

Garlicky roast pork, popular at Cuban restaurants, makes the best filling for this hearty sandwich; or use smoked pork loin from a good deli or succulent roast pork from a Chinese restaurant. Traditionally, a thin layer is sliced off the top and bottom of each roll, so that it toasts evenly.

- 1 medium onion, thinly sliced
- 1 medium jalapeño pepper, seeded and thinly sliced
- ¼ cup coarsely chopped cilantro
- 3 tablespoons olive oil
- 2 tablespoons fresh lemon juice
- ¼ teaspoon finely grated lemon zest

Salt and freshly ground pepper

- 4 kaiser or hard rolls, trimmed and halved

Quesadillas

Vegetable oil
- ½ red bell pepper, thinly sliced
- 10 ounces smoked mozzarella, cut into 16 thin slices
- 1 pound roast pork, cut into 16 slices

I. In a bowl, combine the onion, jalapeño, cilantro, olive oil, lemon juice and lemon zest and season with salt and pepper. Spread 2 tablespoons of the onion relish on each kaiser-roll half.

2. Set a large skillet over moderate heat and coat it with a thin layer of vegetable oil. Place two kaiser-roll halves in the skillet, relish-side up, and top each one with half of the red-pepper slices, two of the mozzarella slices, four of the pork slices and then two more mozzarella slices. Reduce the heat to low and cover each of the sandwiches with another kaiser-roll half, relish-side down. Weight down the sandwiches with a

medium skillet and cook until the bottoms of the sandwiches are toasted and the bottom layer of cheese has melted, about 4 minutes. Turn the sandwiches, add a little more oil to the skillet and brown the second sides, about 4 minutes. Transfer the sandwiches to plates and repeat the process with the remaining ingredients to make two more sandwiches.   –*Marcia Kiesel*

WINE The cranked-up flavors in these grilled sandwichs call for a simple fruity-but-dry rosé or blush wine to play background. Top choices are the 1996 De Loach White Zinfandel and the 1996 Sanford Pinot Noir Vin Gris, both from California.

Orwasher's Special

4 SERVINGS

The raisin pumpernickel bread complements the flavors of the curry and cheddar cheese perfectly. If you can't get it, use regular pumpernickel bread and throw a handful of raisins into the curry mixture.

- 1 teaspoon curry powder
- 1 Granny Smith apple—peeled, cored and cut into ¼-inch matchstick strips
- 2 teaspoons fresh lemon juice
- ½ medium onion, thinly sliced
- 2 tablespoons mayonnaise
- Salt and freshly ground pepper
- 4 tablespoons unsalted butter
- Eight ½-inch-thick slices of raisin pumpernickel bread
- ½ pound sharp cheddar, cut into 8 thin slices
- ¾ pound baked cured ham, cut into 16 slices
- 2 cups arugula, torn into bite-size pieces

1. In a small skillet, stir the curry powder over moderately high heat until fragrant, about 15 seconds; let cool. In a medium bowl, toss the apple with the lemon juice. Add the onion, mayonnaise, toasted curry powder and a pinch each of salt and pepper and toss again.

2. Melt 1 tablespoon of the butter in a large skillet. Set two slices of bread in

Smoky Cubano Sandwiches

the skillet and top each with a slice of cheddar, four slices of ham, 1/3 cup of the curried apple, another slice of cheddar and a slice of bread. Weight down the sandwiches with a medium, heavy skillet and cook over moderate heat until the bottoms are toasted and the cheese on the bottom has melted, about 5 minutes. Turn the sandwiches over, press them down and add one more tablespoon of butter to the skillet. Brown the second sides, about 5 minutes. Separate the sandwiches between the ham slices and add 1/2 cup of the arugula to each, then reassemble the sandwiches. Transfer to plates and repeat the process with the remaining ingredients to make two more sandwiches. —Marcia Kiesel

WINE What's needed here is a white with a spicy-fragrant attitude to match the ham, curry and arugula. Try an Alsace Tokay Pinot Gris, such as the 1995 Léon Beyer or the 1993 Hugel Cuvée Tradition.

B.O.A.T. Sandwiches

6 SERVINGS

Made with bacon, olive paste, arugula and tomatoes, these sandwiches are a twist on the ordinary B.L.T. If you'd rather not cook, use thin slices of pro-sciutto—uncooked—instead of the bacon.

12 bacon slices (12 ounces)

1/3 cup mayonnaise

1 tablespoon black olive paste

1 teaspoon red-wine vinegar

12 slices peasant bread, toasted

1 bunch of arugula (5 ounces), large stems discarded

3 tomatoes, thinly sliced

ı. In a large skillet or a microwave oven, cook half of the bacon until crisp, about 5 minutes; drain. Repeat with the remaining bacon.

2. Stir together the mayonnaise, olive paste and vinegar and spread the mixture on half the bread slices. Top with the bacon, arugula, tomatoes and the remaining bread slices. —Diana Sturgis

CHAPTER 14 rice potatoes

Squash-Blossom Rice (p. 308)

305   Brown-Bag Sushi

305   Japanese Rice

305   Sushi Rice

306   Wehani Rice

306   Thai Jasmine Rice

306   Thai Sticky Rice

307   Black Thai Sticky Rice

307   Basmati Rice

307   Govindobhog Rice

307   Chelo

308   Golden Rice Pilaf with Spices

308   Wild Rice with Grapes and Toasted Almonds

308   Squash-Blossom Rice

309   Herbed Rice Salad

309   Creamy Butternut Squash, Potato and Tomato Gratin

310   Potato and Fennel Gratin

310   Mashed Yukon Golds with Buttermilk

310   Roasted-Garlic Mashed Potatoes

312   Toasted-Barley Mashed Potatoes

312   Mashed Turnips and Potatoes

312   Oven-Roasted Potatoes with Orange Zest

313   Dutch-Oven Potatoes

313   Two-Potato Pancakes

313   Maple-Glazed Sweet Potatoes and Apples

Brown-Bag Sushi

Brown-Bag Sushi

MAKES 2 DOZEN PIECES

These look humble, but they're one of the most delicious, I-want-more foods we know. Called *inari-zushi* in Japanese, they are easy and fun to make. The main ingredient is Japanese-style fried tofu, called *abura-age*; do not use Chinese-style fried tofu.

Twelve 5-by-2-inch Japanese-style fried tofu rectangles (abura-age)

Boiling water

1½ cups reconstituted hon-dashi (instant Japanese fish stock), light vegetable stock or water

5 tablespoons mirin

5 tablespoons Japanese soy sauce

3 tablespoons sugar

¼ cup sesame seeds

Sushi Rice (right)

Japanese pickled ginger, for serving

1. Put the fried tofu rectangles in a large heatproof bowl and pour boiling water over them to cover; drain immediately. When cool enough to handle, squeeze out the water. Cut the rectangles in half crosswise, making twenty-four almost-square pieces, each with one side that opens to form a pocket.

2. In a large stainless-steel saucepan, combine the stock with the mirin, soy sauce and sugar and bring to a boil over high heat. Add the tofu squares and stir to moisten. Cover with a lid that will keep the tofu submerged and simmer gently over low heat for 15 minutes. Transfer the tofu to a plate and let cool. Before using, gently squeeze the tofu to release any liquid and pat dry with paper towels.

3. In a small skillet, toast the sesame seeds over moderate heat, stirring, until fragrant, about 3 minutes. Let the seeds cool on a plate.

4. Shape about 3 tablespoons of the rice into a flattened oval and slide into a tofu pocket to just fill it. Repeat with remaining rice and tofu. Cover with a damp cloth until ready to eat. Coat the sushi with the sesame seeds and serve with a generous pile of pickled ginger and a small bowl of the extra sesame seeds for dipping. –*Jeffrey Alford and Naomi Duguid*

Japanese Rice

MAKES ABOUT 5½ CUPS

Japanese rice is a short- to medium-grain white rice. When properly cooked, it tends to form clumps. Serve it plain with any savory dish or as part of a simple meal of miso soup and Japanese pickles or a salad. We love it topped with fried shallots and a well-seasoned fried egg. The American-grown brand we like best is Kokuho Rose.

2 cups Japanese rice

2⅓ cups water

1. Put the rice in a medium bowl and cover with cold water. Rub the rice and swirl it vigorously with your hand, then drain. Repeat three or four times, or until the water is clear. Drain the rice in a sieve; for optimal texture, leave it in the sieve for 30 minutes.

2. Transfer the rice to a heavy 3½-quart saucepan. Add the 2⅓ cups water (use a little less water if the package is labeled "new rice") and bring to a vigorous boil over high heat. Cover tightly and cook over moderately low heat for 5 minutes, then reduce the heat to very low and cook for 10 minutes longer; do not peek at the rice as it cooks. Remove from the heat; let stand for at least 10 minutes before serving. –*Jeffrey Alford and Naomi Duguid*

Sushi Rice

MAKES ABOUT 5½ CUPS

To turn Japanese Rice into sushi rice, simply cook the rice with a little less water and flavor it with vinegar, sugar and salt. You can wrap sushi rice in nori (seaweed) for a quick snack or use it to make Brown-Bag Sushi (left).

rice tips

1. **Look for clean, intact grains** when buying rice loose. One pound of raw rice equals about two cups.

2. **Store rice** in a cool, dry, dark place.

3. **Refrigerate cooked rice** in a well-sealed container. With the exception of parboiled (converted) types, most rices will harden if they are exposed to cold.

4. **Reheat cold rice** with a sprinkling of water in a microwave oven or in a covered pot over low heat. Varieties with distinct grains, such as black Thai sticky rice and Wehani, can also be reheated by rinsing in boiling water.

5. **Leftover rice** is great to have on hand for stirring into soups and broths and for making fried rice—it may be the world's best vehicle for turning leftovers into something fresh and new.

2 cups Japanese rice

⅓ cup rice vinegar

1½ tablespoons sugar

¾ teaspoon salt

1. Rinse and cook the rice following the method for Japanese Rice (left), using only 2 cups of water in Step 2.

2. Meanwhile, in a small stainless-steel saucepan, combine the vinegar, sugar and salt. Bring to a boil over moderate heat, stirring to dissolve the sugar. Let the mixture cool.

3. Turn the cooked rice out into a large shallow wooden bowl or onto a work surface and spread it out in an even layer. Fan the rice to cool it and dissipate the steam. As you fan, pour half of the vinegar mixture over the rice; use a spatula to gently toss and evenly season the rice. Add the remaining vinegar mixture; continue to toss and turn the rice gently while fanning until the steam is

Govindobhog Rice

Basmati Rice

Black Thai Sticky Rice

Japanese Rice

Thai Jasmine Rice

Wehani Rice

Thai Sticky Rice

gone. Cover the cooled rice with a well-moistened cotton cloth (not plastic wrap) and set aside until ready to use. *–Jeffrey Alford and Naomi Duguid*

MAKE AHEAD The rice can stand at room temperature, covered, for up to eight hours. The vinegar and salt preserve the rice and prevent fermentation. Do not refrigerate.

Wehani Rice

MAKES ABOUT 3 CUPS

Wehani is a designer rice that was developed in northern California by Harlan Lundberg. It is a beautiful brownish red, with long grains; when cooked, it resembles a red-tinted brown rice. Because it is unpolished, Wehani needs longer cooking than polished varieties and remains somewhat chewy. Its hearty texture and fresh grain taste make it an ideal partner for robust dishes like stews and roasted or grilled meats.

  1 **cup Wehani rice**

2¼ **cups water**

 ½ **teaspoon salt**

Rinse the rice. In a medium saucepan, combine the rice with the water and salt. Bring to a rolling boil and stir gently. Cover, reduce the heat to very low and cook for 40 minutes. Remove the rice from the heat; let stand 45 minutes to allow the starches to firm up before serving. *–Jeffrey Alford and Naomi Duguid*

Thai Jasmine Rice

MAKES ABOUT 5½ CUPS

Jasmine rice is the grain of choice in central and southern Thailand. Once cooked, this aromatic long-grain white rice is very slightly sticky. It's versatile enough to eat every day, and any leftovers make excellent fried rice. Look for brands grown in Thailand, such as Peacock or Milagrosa. Or use an American rice labeled "fragrant."

  2 **cups Thai jasmine rice**

2½ **cups cold water**

1. Put the rice in a medium bowl and cover with cold water. Rub the rice and swirl it several times with your hand, then drain. Repeat two more times, or until the water is clear. Drain.

2. Transfer the rice to a heavy 3½-quart saucepan. Add the 2½ cups water to the saucepan and bring to a boil over high heat; boil for 15 seconds. Cover the pan tightly and reduce the heat to very low. Cook the rice without peeking for 20 minutes. Remove the rice from the heat and let stand, still covered, for 10 minutes. Stir the rice gently, then replace the lid until serving time. *–Jeffrey Alford and Naomi Duguid*

Thai Sticky Rice

MAKES ABOUT 4½ CUPS

In the north and northeast of Thailand, Laos and parts of Vietnam and southern China, long-grain sticky rice is the staple grain. When cooked, the opaque white, distinct grains are tender, slightly sweet and chewy but not gluey. Sticky rice is sometimes labeled "sweet rice" or "glutinous rice." To eat sticky rice the way the Thais do, pick up a clump, squeeze it gently into a ball and then dip it in sauce or use it as a scoop to pick up other foods.

  2 **cups Thai sticky rice**

1. Put the rice in a large bowl and cover with 3 inches of cold water. Let soak for at least 8 and up to 24 hours.

2. Drain the rice and put it in a cheesecloth-lined steamer basket, Chinese steamer or large sieve. Set the steamer in a large saucepan over boiling water. Cover tightly and steam the rice for 25 minutes; the rice must be over, not in, the water. Be sure that the saucepan doesn't run dry; add additional water if necessary.

3. Put the rice in a basket or bowl. Cover with a cloth to keep the rice warm and prevent it from drying out. *–Jeffrey Alford and Naomi Duguid*

Black Thai Sticky Rice

MAKES ABOUT 4½ CUPS

This is a beautiful unpolished long-grain rice that is quite chewy when cooked. The black bran keeps the grains separate and gives the rice a lightly sweet, mild grain flavor. In Thailand, black rice is generally soaked and cooked together with white Thai sticky rice (the colors blend, producing a wonderful dark purple) and then used to make desserts, but inventive American chefs are now using black rice in savory dishes.

2 cups black Thai sticky rice

1. Put the rice in a large bowl and cover with 3 inches of cold water. Let soak for at least 8 and up to 24 hours.
2. Drain the rice and put it in a cheese-cloth-lined steamer basket, Chinese steamer or large sieve. Set the steamer in a large saucepan over boiling water. Cover tightly and steam the rice for 35 minutes; the rice must be over, not in, the water. Be sure that the pan doesn't run dry; add water if necessary.
3. Put the rice in a basket or bowl; cover with a cloth to keep it warm and prevent it from drying out. *–Jeffrey Alford and Naomi Duguid*

Basmati Rice

MAKES ABOUT 5½ CUPS

Basmati rice grows in the Himalayan foothills of northern India and Pakistan. It's a very long-grained white rice that expands greatly, especially lengthwise, as it cooks. The dry, distinct and fluffy grains make it ideal for Persian and Moghul (North Indian) dishes, but it's also an excellent everyday rice. If you prefer, skip the preliminary soaking and follow the directions and proportions for cooking Thai jasmine rice.

2 cups basmati rice
4 cups water
1 teaspoon salt

1. Put the rice in a medium bowl and cover with cold water. Rub the rice and

swirl it vigorously with your hand, then drain. Repeat three or four times, or until the water is clear.
2. Transfer the rice to a heavy 3½-quart saucepan. Add the 4 cups water and the salt and stir gently to mix. Let soak for at least 30 minutes and up to 2 hours.
3. Bring the rice, in its soaking liquid, to a boil over high heat. Lower the heat to maintain a bare simmer. Half cover the pan and simmer for 15 minutes; the water will evaporate and steam holes will appear on the surface of the rice.
4. Cover the pan with the lid wrapped in a cotton towel, reduce the heat to very low and let the rice steam for 35 minutes. Remove from the heat and let stand, without lifting the lid, for at least 10 minutes. The rice will be fluffy and there will be a tasty, crusty layer on the bottom of the pan. *–Jeffrey Alford and Naomi Duguid*

Govindobhog Rice

MAKES ABOUT 6½ CUPS

In Calcutta we were introduced to this princely rice, which has a delicate, somewhat sweet flavor. Govindobhog is a long-grain white rice on a miniature scale, like a baby basmati. If you come across it, buy plenty, then enjoy it as an everyday plain rice or as an alternative to basmati in Chelo (right), a delicious Persian pilaf.

2 cups govindobhog rice
10 cups water
1 tablespoon salt

1. Put the rice in a medium bowl and cover with cold water. Rub the rice and swirl it with your hand, then drain. Repeat three or four times or until the water is clear. Drain well.
2. Bring the 10 cups water to a vigorous boil in a large saucepan. Add the salt and sprinkle in the rice. Return the water to a rolling boil, stirring occasionally. Boil until the rice is just barely cooked through but still firm, 6 to 8 minutes.

Chelo, with Chicken Kebabs (p. 192)

3. Drain the rice in a sieve and immediately return it to the pot. Cover with a cotton cloth and a tight-fitting lid and let stand off the heat for 15 minutes to steam and firm up. Gently stir the rice to break up any clumps and serve. *–Jeffrey Alford and Naomi Duguid*

Chelo

6 SERVINGS

The goal in cooking this dish is to end up with separate fluffy grains of rice that are not at all moist. The tastiest part of this Persian-style pilaf is the *tahdig*, or crust, that forms on the bottom of the pan. Serve with Chicken Kebabs (p. 192), sliced cucumbers and radishes, fresh herb sprigs and plain yogurt.

2½ cups basmati rice
4 tablespoons salt
4 quarts water
¼ cup vegetable oil or melted butter
2 tablespoons plain yogurt
1 large egg
Generous pinch of saffron threads,
    dissolved in ¼ cup boiling water

1. Wash the rice thoroughly. Transfer it to a large bowl and add 3 tablespoons of the salt and enough water to cover

by 2 inches. Let the rice soak for 2 to 3 hours. Drain well.

2. In a large heavy saucepan, bring the 4 quarts of water to a vigorous boil. Add the remaining 1 tablespoon salt and gradually sprinkle in the rice. Stir gently and bring back to a boil. Boil the grains just until tender outside but still slightly resistant at the core, about 4 minutes. Drain the rice in a sieve. Rinse under tepid water to cool.

3. Return the saucepan to high heat and add the oil. In a bowl, whisk the yogurt and egg together, then stir in ⅔ cup of the rice. Carefully spread the mixture evenly over the bottom of the pan in the sizzling oil. Gradually sprinkle the rest of the rice into the pan in a mound. Poke four deep holes in the rice.

4. Cover the saucepan with a lid wrapped in a cotton towel and cook over moderately high heat until steam builds up, about 1 minute. Reduce the heat to moderately low and cook for 30 minutes; the rice is done when the grains are tender and fluffy. Set the saucepan in 1 inch of cold water for 1 minute to cool down the rice.

Wild Rice with Grapes and Toasted Almonds

5. Scoop ½ cup of the cooked rice into a bowl and toss with the dissolved saffron. Mound the rest of the rice on a platter. Top with the saffron rice. Scrape the crust from the bottom of the pan, arrange it on the rice and serve. *–Jeffrey Alford and Naomi Duguid*

Golden Rice Pilaf with Spices
4 SERVINGS **L**

    1   teaspoon vegetable oil
    ½   medium onion, finely chopped
    1½ cups long-grain white rice
    1   teaspoon turmeric
    1   bay leaf
Small pinch of saffron (optional)
    3   cups water
Salt

Heat the oil in a medium saucepan. Add the onion and sauté over moderate heat until translucent, about 2 minutes. Add the rice, turmeric, bay leaf and saffron, if using, and stir until the rice is coated. Add the water, season with salt and bring to a boil. Stir the rice, cover and simmer over low heat until the rice is tender, about 17 minutes. Discard the bay leaf and serve.   *–Marvin Woods*

Wild Rice with Grapes and Toasted Almonds
6 SERVINGS **L**

This versatile nutty, fruity wild rice makes a pretty side dish, or use it to stuff grape leaves for hors d'oeuvres.

    3   cups Vegetable Stock (p. 312) or
        water
    1   cup wild rice (about 6 ounces),
        rinsed and drained
    1   teaspoon minced garlic
    1   tablespoon minced oregano
    2   teaspoons minced thyme
    1   bay leaf
    ¼   cup sliced blanched almonds
    ½   cup seedless red grapes, halved
    2   medium scallions, thinly sliced
    1   tablespoon crumbled feta (optional)
Salt and freshly ground pepper

I. In a medium saucepan, bring the stock to a boil. Add the wild rice, garlic, oregano, thyme and bay leaf and return to a boil over moderate heat. Reduce the heat to low, cover and cook until the rice is tender, about 40 minutes. Drain any excess liquid, return the rice to the pan and discard the bay leaf. Cover and let stand for 10 minutes.

2. Meanwhile, in a small heavy skillet, toast the almonds over moderate heat, stirring constantly, until golden, 6 to 8 minutes. Transfer to a plate to cool.

3. Transfer the rice to a bowl and stir in the grapes, the scallions and the feta, if using. Season with salt and pepper. Stir in the almonds and serve.   *–Cary Neff*

Squash-Blossom Rice
4 SERVINGS

This rice pilaf with squash blossoms has bright yellow flecks and a delicate, unusual flavor. If you don't have a kitchen garden or access to a farmers' market, use a half cup finely chopped baby summer squash and add a pinch of saffron.

    1   tablespoon unsalted butter
    1   tablespoon olive oil
    2   large shallots, minced
    1   cup long-grain rice
    8   squash blossoms, trimmed and
        thinly sliced (about 2 ounces)
    1   cup chicken stock or canned
        low-sodium broth
    1   cup water
Salt and freshly ground pepper

In a heavy saucepan, melt the butter in the oil over moderate heat. Add the shallots and cook, stirring, until softened but not browned, about 1 minute. Stir in the rice and cook until it begins to turn opaque, about 2 minutes. Add the squash blossoms, stock and water. Season with salt and pepper and bring to a boil. Cover and simmer over low heat until the liquid is absorbed and the rice is tender, about 20 minutes. Serve the rice hot.   *–Georgeanne Brennan*

Herbed Rice Salad

6 SERVINGS

1½ cups long-grain rice

3 cups water

Salt

2 tablespoons fresh lemon juice

1½ tablespoons minced shallots

2 teaspoons Dijon mustard

¼ cup extra-virgin olive oil

Freshly ground pepper

1 medium seedless cucumber, peeled and cut into ¼-inch dice

1 cup frozen petite peas, thawed

3 tablespoons chopped flat-leaf parsley

1½ tablespoons chopped dill

1. In a medium saucepan, combine the rice with the water and 1 teaspoon of salt and bring to a boil over high heat. Cover the saucepan, reduce the heat to low and cook for 18 minutes. Remove from the heat and let stand, covered, for 5 minutes. Fluff the rice and transfer to a large rimmed baking sheet to cool completely.

2. In a small glass or stainless-steel bowl, combine the lemon juice, shallots and mustard. Whisk in the oil in a thin, steady stream. Season with salt and pepper.

3. In a bowl, toss the rice with the cucumber, peas, parsley and dill. Just before serving, stir in the dressing; season with salt and pepper. *–Katrin Theodoli*
MAKE AHEAD The rice and dressing can stand separately at room temperature for up to three hours.

Creamy Butternut Squash, Potato and Tomato Gratin

12 SERVINGS

2 medium butternut squash (about 3 pounds) – peeled, halved, seeded and sliced crosswise 1/16 inch thick

Salt and freshly ground pepper

4 medium Idaho potatoes (about 1½ pounds), peeled and sliced 1/16 inch thick

Squash-Blossom Rice

5 medium tomatoes, peeled and thinly sliced

3½ cups heavy cream

1 tablespoon finely chopped garlic

1 teaspoon chopped thyme

½ teaspoon freshly grated nutmeg

1½ cups fresh bread crumbs

¼ cup freshly grated Parmesan

2 tablespoons finely chopped parsley

1 tablespoon finely chopped chives

1. Preheat the oven to 350°. Butter a 10-by-12-by-2-inch baking dish. Arrange half of the squash slices in a layer in the baking dish, overlapping them slightly. Season with salt and pepper. Cover with half of the potato slices, overlapping them slightly, and season with salt and pepper. Top with half of the tomato slices and season with salt and pepper. Repeat the layering with the remaining vegetables.

2. In a medium saucepan, combine the cream, garlic, thyme and nutmeg and bring the mixture slowly to a boil. Pour the cream mixture over the vegetables. Cover the gratin with aluminum foil and bake for about 45 minutes, or until the vegetables are tender when pierced with a knife.

3. Meanwhile, in a small bowl, combine the bread crumbs, Parmesan, parsley and chives. Sprinkle the bread-crumb mixture evenly over the gratin. Increase the oven temperature to 400° and continue baking the gratin, uncovered, for 20 to 25 minutes, or until the crust is

golden brown. Let rest for 10 minutes before serving.   *–George Mahaffey*

MAKE AHEAD The baked gratin can be refrigerated overnight. Reheat, covered, in a 300° oven for forty-five minutes. Uncover and cook until the top of the gratin is crisp.

Potato and Fennel Gratin

10 SERVINGS

If you're wondering whether you need another potato gratin recipe in your repertoire, this creamy, caramelized anise-flavored version will leave no doubt in your mind.

  2 tablespoons unsalted butter
  3 tablespoons extra-virgin olive oil
  3 large fennel bulbs–halved lengthwise, cored and thinly sliced
Salt and freshly ground pepper
  1 cup dry homemade bread crumbs
  4 pounds Yukon Gold potatoes, peeled and sliced ⅟₁₆ inch thick
1½ cups heavy cream
1½ cups chicken stock or canned low-sodium broth

I. In a large deep skillet, melt the butter in 1 tablespoon of the olive oil. Add the fennel, cover and cook over moderate heat until the fennel is wilted, about 6 minutes. Uncover and cook, stirring occasionally, until very soft and just caramelized, about 12 minutes. Season with salt and pepper; let cool slightly.

2. In a small bowl, combine the bread crumbs with the remaining 2 tablespoons oil. Season lightly with salt and pepper; set aside.

3. Preheat the oven to 350° and butter a 13-by-9-inch baking dish. Spread one-third of the potatoes in an even layer in the dish. Season lightly with salt and pepper and top with one-third of the fennel. Repeat the layering with the remaining potatoes and fennel, seasoning the layers and ending with the fennel.

4. In a large measuring cup, combine the cream and stock and pour over the vegetables, rearranging the fennel if it's dislodged by the liquid. Cover the dish tightly with aluminum foil and bake for about 1 hour, or until the potatoes are just tender; set a baking sheet underneath the dish to catch any drips. Remove the foil, sprinkle the top with the bread crumbs and bake for about 30 minutes longer, or until the top of the gratin is golden brown and the potatoes are very tender. Let the gratin rest for 10 minutes before cutting. *–Grace Parisi*

MAKE AHEAD The gratin can be refrigerated overnight. Reheat, covered, in a 350° oven before serving. Uncover and cook until the top of the gratin is crisp.

Mashed Yukon Golds with Buttermilk

6 SERVINGS **Q**

2¼ pounds medium Yukon Gold potatoes, peeled and quartered
  1 tablespoon kosher salt
¾ cup buttermilk
  4 tablespoons unsalted butter
¼ cup chopped chives
Freshly ground pepper

In a large saucepan, cover the potatoes with cold water and add the salt. Boil over high heat until tender, 15 to 18 minutes. Drain, reserving ⅓ cup of the cooking liquid. Pass the potatoes through a ricer or food mill set over the pan. Stir in the buttermilk, butter and chives. Season with pepper. Add the reserved water to desired consistency and rewarm over moderately low heat before serving.   *–Bob Chambers*

Roasted-Garlic Mashed Potatoes

4 SERVINGS **L**

These old-fashioned lumpy mashed potatoes have a light tang from the buttermilk. I usually use about three tablespoons of Roasted-Garlic Puree to flavor the potatoes, but you can add more or less to suit your taste.

1¼ pounds Yukon Gold potatoes
Salt
¾ cup warm buttermilk
Roasted-Garlic Puree (recipe follows)
  1 tablespoon unsalted butter
Freshly ground pepper

I. Put the potatoes in a medium saucepan, add 1 teaspoon of salt and cover with cool water. Bring to a boil over high heat. Reduce the heat and simmer until the potatoes are very tender, about 45 minutes. Drain the potatoes, reserving ¼ cup of the cooking liquid.

2. Coarsely mash the potatoes. Beat in the warm buttermilk with a wooden spoon, adding a little of the reserved potato-cooking liquid if needed. Blend in the Roasted-Garlic Puree. Stir in the butter and season with salt and pepper. Serve hot.

ROASTED-GARLIC PUREE

MAKES ABOUT ¼ CUP

  2 heads of garlic, papery outer skin peeled off
  1 thyme sprig
½ teaspoon olive oil
  2 tablespoons water

Preheat the oven to 400°. Put the garlic in the center of a 9-inch-square piece of aluminum foil. Add the thyme and drizzle

Roasted-Garlic Mashed Potatoes

Potato and Fennel Gratin, with Roast Leg of Lamb with Orange and Herbs (p. 252) and Swiss Chard and Shallots (p. 323)

with the oil and water. Bring the foil corners together and crimp to form an airtight seal. Bake for 30 minutes, or until the garlic feels tender; let cool. Squeeze the pulp into a small bowl and mash to a puree with a fork. *—Sally Schneider*

Toasted-Barley Mashed Potatoes

4 SERVINGS **L**

These simple, hearty mashed potatoes owe their rich creaminess to buttermilk and their appealing texture to toasted pearl barley.

½ cup pearl barley

3 cups Vegetable Stock (recipe follows) or chicken stock, or 2 cups canned chicken broth mixed with 1 cup of water

4 thyme sprigs

1 pound red-skinned or Yukon Gold potatoes, peeled and quartered

½ cup low-fat (1.5%) buttermilk, warmed

Salt and freshly ground pepper

1. In a medium saucepan, cook the barley over moderately high heat, stirring frequently, until toasted, 8 to 10 minutes. Add the Vegetable Stock and thyme and bring to a simmer. Reduce the heat to low and cook, stirring often, until tender, about 35 minutes. Drain the barley. Discard the thyme sprigs.

Toasted-Barley Mashed Potatoes

2. Meanwhile, in another medium saucepan, cover the potatoes with water. Bring to a boil over moderate heat and cook until the potatoes are tender, about 20 minutes. Drain, return to the pan and keep warm.

3. Pass the potatoes through a ricer or food mill or mash with a potato masher. Stir in the barley and warm buttermilk, season with salt and pepper and serve.

VEGETABLE STOCK

MAKES ABOUT 9 CUPS

1 onion, coarsely chopped

2 carrots, coarsely chopped

3 celery ribs, coarsely chopped

1 leek, coarsely chopped

6 fresh oregano sprigs or 1 teaspoon dried

6 fresh thyme sprigs or 1 teaspoon dried

1 bay leaf

½ tablespoon whole peppercorns

12 cups water

Combine the onion, carrots, celery, leek, oregano, thyme, bay leaf, peppercorns and water in a pot. Bring to a boil over moderately high heat and then simmer over moderately low heat for 1 hour. Strain the stock. *—Cary Neff*

MAKE AHEAD The stock can be refrigerated for up to one week or frozen for up to one month.

Mashed Turnips and Potatoes

20 SERVINGS

5 pounds turnips, peeled and cut into 2-inch chunks

2½ pounds all-purpose potatoes, peeled and cut into 2-inch chunks

2 cups milk

1 cup heavy cream

2 sticks (½ pound) unsalted butter, at room temperature

Salt and freshly ground pepper

1. In a large pot, cover the turnips and the potatoes with cold water and boil

over high heat until the potatoes are tender and the turnips are almost tender, about 20 minutes. Drain well. Return to the pot and shake over high heat to dry them out.

2. In a medium saucepan, warm the milk and the cream over low heat; set aside. In a large bowl, mash the potatoes and the turnips well but leave some lumps. Mix in the warmed milk and cream and the butter. Season the potatoes and turnips with salt and pepper and serve hot. *—Chris Schlesinger*

Oven-Roasted Potatoes with Orange Zest

12 SERVINGS

3 pounds small red-skinned potatoes

Salt

3 tablespoons olive oil

Freshly ground pepper

Zest from 2 medium oranges, cut into fine julienne strips

1. Preheat the oven to 375°. In a large saucepan, cover the potatoes with cold water, add salt and bring to a boil over moderately high heat. Reduce the heat to moderately low and simmer until the potatoes are just tender, about 20 minutes. Drain and pat dry with paper towels.

2. Spread the potatoes in a large flame-proof roasting pan, add the oil and stir well to coat. Season with salt and pepper. Roast in the oven for about 20 minutes, stirring often, until lightly browned and very tender.

3. Meanwhile, bring a small saucepan of water to a boil. Add the orange zest and boil for 2 minutes. Drain and rinse with cold water. Drain on paper towels.

4. Just before serving, set the roasting pan over moderate heat. Add the orange zest to the potatoes and cook, stirring often, until the zest is slightly softened, about 5 minutes. Season with salt and pepper and serve. *—The Mondavi family*

MAKE AHEAD The boiled potatoes can be refrigerated for up to two days.

Dutch-Oven Potatoes

8 SERVINGS

- 6 slices of bacon, cut into 2-inch pieces
- 4 russet potatoes, scrubbed and sliced crosswise ¼ inch thick
- 1 medium onion, chopped
- 1 green bell pepper, chopped

Salt and freshly ground pepper

Preheat the oven to 425°. In a Dutch oven or large ovenproof skillet, cook the bacon over moderately low heat until it is slightly crisp, about 5 minutes. Add the potatoes and stir to coat them with the bacon fat. Press the potatoes snugly into the pot and bake them for 10 minutes. Stir the potatoes, press them into the pot again and bake them for 20 minutes. Add the onion and the green bell pepper to the pot, season with salt and pepper and stir well. Press the vegetables firmly and bake for 20 minutes more, or until the potatoes are crusty. Serve at once. —*John Hopkins*

Two-Potato Pancakes

6 SERVINGS

These crisp white and orange pancakes are great with roast meat or poultry and almost any fish.

- 1 large russet potato, peeled and coarsely shredded
- 1 large sweet potato, peeled and coarsely shredded
- ¼ cup coarsely chopped scallions
- ½ teaspoon finely chopped thyme
- ¾ teaspoon salt
- ½ teaspoon freshly ground pepper
- 2 tablespoons vegetable oil

1. In a large bowl, toss the russet potato and the sweet potato with the scallions, thyme, salt and pepper.

2. In a heavy 9- to 10-inch nonstick skillet, heat 1 tablespoon of the oil. Spread half of the potato mixture evenly in the skillet and cook over moderately high heat until firm and browned on the bottom, about 5 minutes longer. Transfer the potato pancake to a large baking sheet; keep warm in a low oven. Repeat with the remaining oil and potato mixture. Cut each potato pancake into six wedges and serve hot. —*James Henahan*

Maple-Glazed Sweet Potatoes and Apples

20 SERVINGS

This dish is sure to win over even the youngest and pickiest eaters.

- 1 stick (4 ounces) plus 4 tablespoons unsalted butter
- 6 sweet potatoes (4½ pounds), peeled and sliced ¼ inch thick
- 6 large Granny Smith apples (3 pounds)—peeled, halved, cored and sliced ¼ inch thick
- 2 cups pure maple syrup
- 1½ cups apple cider
- 1 teaspoon salt

1. Preheat the oven to 350°. Grease two very large shallow baking dishes using 2 tablespoons of the butter for each. Alternating sweet-potato and apple slices, arrange the slices in the baking dishes in a single layer of concentric circles.

2. In a medium saucepan, combine the maple syrup, cider, the stick of butter and the salt. Simmer over moderate heat for 5 minutes. Pour half of the mixture over the slices in each of the baking dishes. Cover securely with aluminum foil.

3. Bake in the center of the oven for 40 minutes, or until the apples release their liquid. Remove the dishes from the oven, uncover and baste the apples and sweet potatoes with the pan juices. Increase the oven temperature to 450°. Place the dishes in the upper third of the oven. Continue baking for about 35 minutes longer, basting a few more times, until the potatoes are tender and nicely glazed. Serve hot. —*Jasper White*

MAKE AHEAD The recipe can be prepared up to one day in advance and refrigerated. Reheat, covered, in a 400° oven for twenty-five minutes.

CHAPTER 15 vegetables

Roasted Root Vegetables (p. 325)

317   Nicola's Stuffed Artichokes

317   Artichokes Simmered with Lemon and Honey

317   Sautéed Baby Artichokes with Lemon and Garlic

318   Braised Spring Vegetables

318   Sugar Snap Peas with Mint Oil

318 Skillet Ramp Gratin

319 Asparagus with Toasted Almonds and Garlic

319 Fried Zucchini Blossoms

319 Zucchini with Spicy Harissa

319 Peperonata

320 Roasted Sweet Peppers in Tomato Sauce

320 Braised Red Radishes

320 Sautéed Cherry Tomatoes with Shallots

320 Stuffed Tomatoes with Vegetables and Pine Nuts

321 Steamed Eggplant with Garlic Sauce

321 Roasted Tomato and Eggplant Tian

322 Sesame-Dressed Haricots Verts in Roast Onions

322 Sautéed Mushrooms with Walnuts and Herbs

322 Shiitake-Mushroom Sauté with Watercress

323 Sautéed Fall Greens with Caraway

323 Swiss Chard and Shallots

323 Jamaican Bok Choy

323 Carrots with Coriander and Caraway

324 Winter-Squash and Carrot Puree

324 Smoked Acorn Squash

324 Curried Cauliflower and Potatoes

324 Brussels Sprouts with Walnuts, Balsamic Vinegar and Mint

324 Stir-Fried Cabbage with Cashews

325 Roasted Root Vegetables

325 Summer Stew with Navy Beans and Okra

326 Cannellini Beans with Sage

326 Cuban Black Beans

327 Barbecued Baked Beans

327 Refried Beans with Pickled Jalapeños

Nicola's Stuffed Artichokes

Nicola's Stuffed Artichokes

12 SERVINGS

Braised artichokes are filled with savory garlic-and-dill-flavored rice. Don't use large artichokes; they're unwieldly to clean and cook.

- 12 medium artichokes
- Juice of 2 lemons
- 1 cup long-grain rice
- 9 medium scallions, thinly sliced
- 8 garlic cloves, minced
- ½ cup plus ⅓ cup minced dill
- ½ cup olive oil
- 2 teaspoons salt
- ¼ teaspoon freshly ground pepper
- 3 cups water
- 4 cups hot water

1. Using a serrated knife, trim the stems and 1½ inches from the top of one artichoke. Remove the small outer leaves and a layer of the larger ones. Using a melon baller or spoon, scoop out the center cone of leaves and the furry choke and drop the artichoke into a large bowl of water mixed with the lemon juice. Repeat with the remaining artichokes.

2. In a medium bowl, combine the rice, half of the scallions and garlic, the ½ cup of dill, 3 tablespoons of the oil, 1½ teaspoons of the salt and the pepper. Drain the artichokes well and loosely stuff the centers with the filling; the rice will expand during cooking.

3. In one very large or two large stainless-steel saucepans, combine the remaining scallions, garlic, ⅓ cup of dill and 5 tablespoons of oil with the remaining ½ teaspoon of salt. Arrange the stuffed artichokes on top. Gently pour the 3 cups water over and around the artichokes and bring to a boil over high heat. Cover, reduce the heat to moderately low and cook, spooning the juices over the rice occasionally, until the rice is tender and a leaf can easily be pulled from an artichoke, about 50 minutes. Add 2 cups of the hot water twice during cooking.

Transfer the artichokes to a platter and spoon the sauce around them. Serve the artichokes warm or at room temperature.   —*Nicola Kotsoni*

Artichokes Simmered with Lemon and Honey

12 SERVINGS

Tangy yet sweet, these flavorful artichokes are based on a traditional Greek-Jewish recipe.

- 18 baby or 6 large artichokes
- 1 lemon, halved
- 1 cup water
- ¾ cup fresh lemon juice
- ¼ cup honey
- ¼ cup olive oil
- Salt and freshly ground pepper

1. If using baby artichokes, pull off the tough outer leaves and trim the tops of the remaining leaves. If using large artichokes, pull off the dark green outer leaves until you reach the pale green leaves at the base; cut across the leaves about 1 inch from the base. Cut both baby and large artichokes in half lengthwise; scoop out the chokes. Using a vegetable peeler or paring knife, peel the stems and trim away any dark green. Rub the artichokes all over with the lemon halves.

2. In a medium stainless-steel saucepan, combine the water with the lemon juice, honey, oil and ½ teaspoon of salt. Snugly fit the artichokes in the pan. Cover and bring to a boil over high heat, then reduce the heat to low and cook until the artichokes are tender when pierced with a knife, about 15 minutes for large and 10 minutes for small. Transfer the artichokes to a plate.

3. Boil the liquid in the pan over high heat until reduced to ½ cup, about 10 minutes. Season with salt and pepper. Cut the artichokes into wedges and pour the reduced liquid on top. Serve at room temperature.   —*Peter Hoffman*

MAKE AHEAD The cooked artichokes can be refrigerated overnight.

Sautéed Baby Artichokes with Lemon and Garlic

Sautéed Baby Artichokes with Lemon and Garlic

4 SERVINGS

Baby artichokes, though little, are in fact mature vegetables. Accented with garlic and lemon, they make a lovely side dish.

- ¼ cup fresh lemon juice
- 1½ pounds smallest baby artichokes (about 14)
- 2 teaspoons unsalted butter
- 1½ tablespoons extra-virgin olive oil
- 1 large garlic clove, thinly sliced
- Salt and freshly ground pepper

1. Bring a medium saucepan of water to a boil. Add 3 tablespoons of the lemon juice to a large bowl of water. Working with one artichoke at a time, pull off the dark outer leaves and trim ½ inch off the top. Halve each artichoke lengthwise, then drop into the lemon water.

2. Drain the artichokes. Blanch in the boiling water until tender when pierced with a knife, about 3 minutes. Drain well.

3. Meanwhile, melt 1 teaspoon of the butter in the oil in a large stainless-steel skillet. Add the garlic; cook over high heat for 10 seconds. Add the artichokes. Season with salt and pepper. Cook, turning once, until golden brown, about 5 minutes. Stir in the remaining 1 tablespoon of lemon juice and 1 teaspoon of butter and serve.   —*Grace Parisi*

ABOVE: **Peperonata.** LEFT: **Skillet Ramp Gratin.**

Braised Spring Vegetables

8 SERVINGS

- 3 tablespoons fresh lemon juice
- 8 baby artichokes (about 1 pound)
- ¼ cup plus 1 tablespoon extra-virgin olive oil
- 1 large red onion, thinly sliced

Salt and freshly ground pepper

- 4 cups fresh young peas (about 4 pounds in the pod) or thawed frozen peas
- 2 cups fresh peeled fava beans (about 2 pounds in the pod)
- 2 cups water
- 3 tablespoons finely chopped mint

- 2 tablespoons coarsely chopped flat-leaf parsley

1. Stir 1 tablespoon of the lemon juice into a large bowl of water. Working with one artichoke at a time, pull off the dark outer leaves and trim ½ inch off the top; peel the stem. Quarter the artichoke lengthwise and then, after scraping out the choke with a spoon, drop it into the lemon water.

2. Heat 2 tablespoons of the oil in a large heavy saucepan. Add the onion and cook over moderately low heat, stirring, until translucent, about 8 minutes. Drain the artichokes well, add them to the saucepan and season with salt and pepper. Reduce the heat to low and cook, stirring, until just tender, about 12 minutes. Add the peas, beans and water. Cover partially and cook over low heat until the vegetables are tender, about 6 minutes.

3. Add the mint and parsley; season with salt and pepper. Stir in the remaining 3 tablespoons oil and 2 tablespoons lemon juice. Serve warm or at room temperature. *–Ruth Rogers and Rose Gray*

MAKE AHEAD The braised vegetables can be refrigerated overnight. Reheat gently and proceed with Step 3.

Sugar Snap Peas with Mint Oil

4 SERVINGS

Use the leftover fragrant mint oil as a marinade for chicken, lamb chops or firm white-fleshed fish, or mix it with lemon juice for a refreshing salad dressing.

- ⅓ cup mint leaves
- ⅓ cup canola oil

Salt and freshly ground pepper

- ½ pound sugar snap peas, strings removed

Lemon wedges, for serving

1. In a medium saucepan of boiling water, blanch the mint just until limp and bright green, about 30 seconds. Using a slotted spoon, transfer the mint to a blender; pulse until finely chopped. With the machine on, add the oil in a thin stream and blend until pureed. Transfer to a bowl. Season with salt and pepper.

2. Add salt to the boiling water. Blanch the peas until bright green and just tender, about 3 minutes. Drain well, transfer to a bowl and toss with about 1 tablespoon of the mint oil. Serve with lemon wedges. *–Grace Parisi*

Skillet Ramp Gratin

4 SERVINGS

Ramps, or wild leeks, have broad dark-green leaves and pink-hued bulbs. This rustic gratin can also be made with young, tender leeks or scallions, both of which require a little more cooking.

- 2 tablespoons unsalted butter
- ½ cup fresh bread crumbs
- ½ cup grated Gruyère (about 2 ounces)
- ¾ pound thin ramps, trimmed

Salt and freshly ground white pepper

- ⅔ cup heavy cream

1. Melt 1 tablespoon of the butter in a large ovenproof skillet. Add the bread crumbs and toast over high heat, stirring occasionally, until lightly golden, about 2 minutes. Transfer to a plate to cool, then toss with the Gruyère.

2. Heat the broiler. Melt the remaining 1 tablespoon of butter in the skillet until just brown. Add the ramps, all facing in one direction, and cook over high heat until limp and lightly golden, 3 to 4 minutes. Season with salt and pepper, add the cream and cook until bubbling, about 1 minute. Remove from the heat; sprinkle with the bread-crumb mixture.

3. Set the skillet under the broiler. Broil about 30 seconds, or until lightly browned and bubbling, and serve. –*Grace Parisi*

Asparagus with Toasted Almonds and Garlic

4 SERVINGS

¾ pound pencil-thin asparagus

2 tablespoons olive oil

Scant ¼ cup slivered almonds

2 garlic cloves, thinly sliced

Salt and freshly ground pepper

1 tablespoon sherry vinegar

1 teaspoon unsalted butter

1. Bring 1 inch of water to a boil in a large stainless-steel skillet. Add the asparagus. Cook just until tender and bright green, about 3 minutes. Drain; pat dry.

2. Wipe out the skillet and set over high heat. Add the oil and heat. Add the almonds; cook, stirring, 30 seconds. Add the asparagus and garlic. Season with salt and pepper. Cook, stirring often, until the garlic and almonds are golden and the asparagus is just beginning to brown, about 4 minutes. Stir in the vinegar and butter; season with salt and pepper. Put on a platter and serve. –*Grace Parisi*

Fried Zucchini Blossoms

8 SERVINGS

2 large eggs

2 tablespoons olive oil

1½ cups all-purpose flour, plus more for dusting

Salt

One 12-ounce bottle of beer

1 quart vegetable oil, for deep-frying

40 zucchini blossoms

1. In a large bowl, beat the eggs and olive oil with a fork. Sift the 1½ cups of flour and 1 teaspoon of salt over the eggs and stir. Add the beer and blend but do not overbeat; a few lumps are fine.

2. In a large saucepan, heat the oil to 375°. Meanwhile, remove the pistils from the zucchini blossoms, snapping them off at the base.

3. In a bowl, toss the blossoms with flour to coat thoroughly. Working with one blossom at a time, shake off the excess flour and dip the blossom in the batter, allowing excess batter to drip off. Drop the blossoms into the hot oil–five or six at a time–and fry, turning once, until golden brown, about 1 minute per side. Briefly drain the blossoms on a rack set over a baking sheet. Sprinkle lightly with salt and serve at once. –*Egi Maccioni*

Zucchini with Spicy Harissa

12 SERVINGS

12 medium zucchini

2 tablespoons pure olive oil

3 to 4 tablespoons fresh lemon juice

Kosher salt and freshly ground pepper

Spicy Harissa (recipe follows), for serving

Preheat the oven to 350°. Set the zucchini on a rimmed baking sheet and rub them with the oil. Bake for 30 to 40 minutes, or until tender when pierced. When cool enough to handle, cut off and discard the stem ends and coarsely chop the zucchini. Season to taste with the lemon juice and salt and pepper. Serve warm, with the harissa.

MAKE AHEAD The zucchini can be cooked, chopped and refrigerated, covered, for up to a day. Reheat and season.

SPICY HARISSA

MAKES ¾ CUP

Harissa is North Africa's famous fiery condiment. I use sweet, rich ancho chiles to make the paste less incendiary.

1 teaspoon cumin seeds

1 teaspoon coriander seeds

4 ancho chiles

1 cup loosely packed parsley leaves

1 cup loosely packed cilantro leaves

4 garlic cloves

¼ to ⅓ cup extra-virgin olive oil

1. In a small skillet, toast the cumin and coriander seeds over moderate heat, stirring, until lightly browned and fragrant, about 2 minutes.

2. Put the anchos in a small saucepan, cover with water and bring to a boil. Remove from the heat and let cool. Remove the stems and scrape the seeds from the chiles. In a food processor, combine the anchos, parsley, cilantro, garlic and the toasted cumin and coriander seeds and process until smooth. Add enough of the oil to the mixture to make a very thin paste. –*Peter Hoffman*

MAKE AHEAD The harissa can be refrigerated, covered, up to five days.

Peperonata

8 SERVINGS

This vegetable stew is best made a day ahead so the flavors can blend.

3 bell peppers–1 green, 1 red and 1 yellow–sliced ½ inch thick

2 large tomatoes, coarsely chopped

2 medium carrots, thinly sliced

1 large white onion, thinly sliced

1 medium zucchini, sliced crosswise ¼ inch thick

1 large garlic clove, sliced

⅓ cup olive oil

¼ cup chopped basil

1 tablespoon chopped parsley

Salt and freshly ground pepper

½ cup water

Combine all of the ingredients in a large enameled cast-iron casserole. Cover and simmer over low heat, stirring occasionally, until the carrots are tender, about 45 minutes. Season with salt and pepper. –*Egi Maccioni*

MAKE AHEAD The peperonata can be refrigerated for up to three days. Reheat gently before serving.

Braised Red Radishes

Roasted Sweet Peppers in Tomato Sauce

MAKES 3 CUPS

- 4 large red bell peppers
- 4 large green bell peppers
- 1 tablespoon olive oil
- 6 garlic cloves, thinly sliced

One 14-ounce can peeled Italian tomatoes, drained and chopped

- ½ teaspoon salt

Dash of harissa or Tabasco sauce

1. Preheat the oven to 425°. Arrange the red and green bell peppers on a baking sheet and roast for about 35 minutes, turning occasionally, until the skins are blistered all over. Transfer the bell peppers to a bowl, cover with plastic wrap and let steam for 15 minutes.

2. Peel the green bell peppers and discard the cores, seeds and ribs. Cut the green peppers into thick strips and put them in a medium bowl. Working over a strainer set over the bowl to catch the juices, peel the red bell peppers and discard the cores, seeds and ribs. Cut the red peppers into thick strips and add them to the bowl.

3. Heat the oil in a medium saucepan. Add the garlic and cook over moderately low heat, stirring, until translucent, about 4 minutes. Add the tomatoes and salt and simmer until slightly thickened, about 10 minutes. Add the green and red bell-pepper strips and the red-pepper juices; simmer gently over low heat until thickened, about 30 minutes. Stir in the harissa; serve warm. —*Michel Benasra*

MAKE AHEAD This recipe can be made ahead and refrigerated overnight. Reheat over low heat.

Braised Red Radishes

4 SERVINGS

Braising softens the bright red of radishes to a pretty pink and gives them a sweet turniplike flavor. It's an unexpected treatment for an underused vegetable.

- 30 red radishes with greens (about 2 pounds), greens trimmed to ¼ inch

Kosher salt

- ¾ teaspoon sugar
- ¼ cup extra-virgin olive oil
- 1½ cups water

1. Put the radishes in a medium saucepan and add 1 teaspoon of salt, the sugar, oil and water. Bring to a boil over high heat, then lower the heat to moderate, cover and simmer until the radishes are tender, about 15 minutes.

2. Using a slotted spoon, transfer the radishes to a serving bowl. Boil the cooking liquid over high heat until reduced to ¼ cup, about 15 minutes. Season the liquid with salt and pour it over the radishes. —*Seen Lippert*

Sautéed Cherry Tomatoes with Shallots

4 SERVINGS **Q**

- 1 tablespoon unsalted butter
- 2 large shallots, minced
- 2 pints cherry tomatoes, preferably small to medium

Salt and freshly ground black pepper

In a large heavy stainless-steel skillet, melt the butter over moderately high heat. Add the shallots and cherry tomatoes and season with salt and pepper. Cook, stirring occasionally, until the tomatoes start to soften (a few of the skins will split) and the shallots are golden, about 3 to 4 minutes. Serve immediately. —*Judith Sutton*

Stuffed Tomatoes with Vegetables and Pine Nuts

12 SERVINGS

- 12 ripe medium tomatoes
- 5 medium scallions, thinly sliced
- 1 medium white onion, minced
- 1 medium carrot, coarsely grated
- 1 tablespoon minced flat-leaf parsley
- 2¼ teaspoons minced dill
- ¾ teaspoon dried mint
- 2¼ teaspoons salt
- ¼ teaspoon freshly ground pepper
- ½ cup plus 1 tablespoon olive oil
- ½ cup long-grain rice
- ½ cup pine nuts (about 3 ounces), preferably toasted
- ¾ cup plain bread crumbs
- ¼ cup vegetable stock, chicken stock or water

1. Slice ½ inch off the top of each tomato and set aside. Working over a strainer set over a bowl, gently squeeze the juice and seeds from the tomatoes. Using a spoon, lightly scrape the pulp from the tomatoes onto a cutting board. Finely chop the pulp and reserve it. Arrange the hollowed tomatoes in a 13-by-9-inch glass or stainless-steel baking dish.

2. In a medium stainless-steel saucepan, combine the scallions, onion, carrot, parsley, dill, mint, salt, pepper and 3 tablespoons of the oil. Stir in 1 cup of the strained tomato juice and ½ cup of the pulp. Add the rice and pine nuts. Bring to a simmer over moderate heat, stirring often. Cover; reduce the heat to moderately low. Cook until the rice is barely tender, about 20 minutes. Let cool slightly.

3. Meanwhile, preheat the oven to 400°. Toss the bread crumbs with 2 tablespoons of the oil. Stuff the tomatoes with the rice filling and top with any remaining tomato pulp. Drizzle ¼ cup of the tomato juice, the remaining ¼ cup of oil and the stock over and around the stuffed tomatoes and mound the bread crumbs on top. Arrange the tomato tops alongside the tomatoes and bake for 25 to 30 minutes, or until the tomatoes are tender but not collapsed and the crumbs are browned. Cover each tomato with a top and serve warm or at room temperature. *–Charles Bowman*

Steamed Eggplant with Garlic Sauce

4 SERVINGS **L**

This is a dish with Sichuan and Hunan roots. Customarily, the eggplant is deep-fried, then stir-fried. I've reduced the fat content by steaming the eggplant instead. The texture is a bit different, but the flavors are still defined and intense.

SAUCE

- 1 tablespoon dark soy sauce
- 2 teaspoons oyster sauce
- 2 teaspoons sugar
- 1 teaspoon cornstarch dissolved in 1 tablespoon water
- 1 teaspoon distilled white vinegar
- ½ teaspoon Shao-Hsing wine or dry sherry
- ½ teaspoon crushed red pepper
- ¼ teaspoon salt

- 1 pound medium eggplants, peeled
- 1½ teaspoons peanut oil
- 2 teaspoons minced garlic
- 1½ tablespoons vegetable stock or water

I. MAKE THE SAUCE: Combine all of the ingredients in a small bowl.

2. Slice the eggplants lengthwise ½ inch thick and then cut the slices lengthwise into ½-inch strips. Put the eggplant on a heatproof plate and steam over boiling water until tender, 20 to 25 minutes. Carefully remove the plate and set aside.

3. Set a wok over high heat for 30 seconds. Add the oil and stir to coat. When a wisp of white smoke appears, add the garlic and stir-fry until golden, about 10 seconds. Stir in the eggplant. Add the stock and cook until the eggplant begins to fall apart, about 3 minutes.

4. Make a well in the center of the wok, pushing the eggplant up the side slightly. Stir the sauce and add it to the wok. Stir the eggplant into the sauce and cook until bubbling and thick, about 2 minutes. Transfer the eggplant to a warmed bowl and serve. *–Eileen Yin-Fei Lo*

WINE Look to Italy for a straightforward, crisply tart dry white that won't compete with the garlicky eggplant. Try the 1995 Alois Lageder Pinot Grigio and the 1994 or 1995 Pieropan Soave.

Roasted Tomato and Eggplant Tian

4 SERVINGS

If you like, serve this tian, or gratin, as a light main course with a green salad.

- 2 tablespoons olive oil
- 1½ pounds ripe tomatoes, sliced ¼ inch thick
- 1 pound eggplant, preferably Asian, sliced crosswise ¼ inch thick

Salt and freshly ground pepper

- ¾ teaspoon chopped sage
- ¾ teaspoon chopped marjoram
- ½ cup grated Monterey jack
- 1 tablespoon freshly grated Parmesan

I. Preheat the oven to 400°. Spread the oil on two baking sheets. Arrange the tomato slices in a single layer on one sheet and the eggplant slices on the other. Season the vegetables with salt and pepper and sprinkle with the herbs. Bake the vegetables for 30 minutes, then turn the slices and bake for 10 minutes longer, or until the eggplant is golden on both sides and the tomatoes

picking tips

One of the luxuries of growing your own vegetables is being able to pick them at the proper size and maturity for the dish you want to prepare.

Eggplant It's no use trying to make a delicate mousse with a large, intensely flavored eggplant. Opt for a moussaka or eggplant Parmesan to take advantage of a mature specimen.

Tomatoes Early in the season, tomatoes are best raw, in salads. Later, when the flavor is concentrated, I make roasted-tomato sauces and rich soups.

Squash Pick small squash for quick sautéing and medium-size ones for slower cooking in a casserole. I feed oversize squash, with spongy interiors and big seeds, to my neighbors' sheep.

Turnips Tiny turnips cook through in a minute or two; I serve them sliced, as a side dish. Large turnips should be cooked in stews or baked slowly.

Fennel Baby fennel is perfect shaved raw into salads; bigger bulbs are better braised. *–Georgeanne Brennan*

are jamlike. Remove from the oven and reduce the heat to 350°.

2. Using a spatula, transfer one third of the tomatoes in an even layer to a 9-inch square baking dish. Cover with half of the eggplant and one third of the Monterey jack. Repeat. Top with the remaining tomatoes and add any tomato juices from the baking sheet. Sprinkle with the remaining Monterey jack and the Parmesan. Bake for 20 minutes, or until lightly golden. Cover with aluminum foil and set aside for about 15 minutes before serving. *–Georgeanne Brennan*

WINE The cheeses point to a medium-bodied red as the best accompaniment. Consider a Rioja from Spain, such as the 1994 Paternina Banda Azul Crianza or the 1993 Conde de Valdemar Crianza.

Sesame-Dressed Haricots Verts in Roast Onions

8 SERVINGS

8 medium Vidalia or other
   sweet onions
Salt and freshly ground pepper
1 cup chicken stock or canned
   low-sodium broth, skimmed of fat
1½ teaspoons white sesame seeds
2 tablespoons Champagne vinegar
¼ cup extra-virgin olive oil
1½ teaspoons Asian sesame oil
½ teaspoon black sesame seeds
Salt
1½ pounds haricots verts or
   thin green beans
6 scallions, white and tender green,
   thinly sliced diagonally
½ small red onion, finely diced

1. Preheat the oven to 400°. Peel the onions, leaving the root ends intact. Cut off the onion tops and scoop out the centers with a spoon or melon baller, leaving the outer two layers intact. Arrange the hollowed-out onions in a large baking dish and season them well inside and out with salt and pepper. Pour the stock into the baking dish, cover with aluminum foil and bake for about 35 minutes, or until the onions are tender. Using a slotted spoon, transfer the onions to a large platter and let cool.

2. Meanwhile, in a small dry skillet, toast the white sesame seeds over moderately high heat, stirring, until lightly browned, about 2 minutes; let cool. In a small bowl, whisk together the vinegar, olive oil, sesame oil, white and black sesame seeds and a pinch of salt.

3. In a large saucepan of lightly salted boiling water, cook the beans until just tender, about 6 minutes. Drain, cool under running water and drain again; pat dry with paper towels. Cut the beans into 1-inch lengths and transfer them to a large bowl. Add the scallions, the red onion and the sesame dressing, season with salt and toss. Fill the onions with the bean salad and serve. *–John Fleer*

MAKE AHEAD The roasted onions, dressing and cooked beans can be refrigerated separately overnight. Let return to room temperature before serving.

Sautéed Mushrooms with Walnuts and Herbs

12 SERVINGS

The leftovers of the Georgian herb-and-nut paste used in this mushroom sauté will work well with chicken. Try it also with pasta and Parmesan cheese, or use it as a spread for crostini.

1 cup walnut pieces (4 ounces)
½ cup plus 1 tablespoon chopped
   parsley
½ cup plus 1 tablespoon chopped
   cilantro
2 garlic cloves, quartered
Salt and freshly ground pepper
5 tablespoons olive oil
1 tablespoon unsalted butter
2 pounds cremini mushrooms,
   trimmed and quartered
¼ cup kosher chicken stock or
   canned low-sodium broth

1. Preheat the oven to 400°. Put the walnuts on a rimmed baking sheet and toast in the oven for about 4 minutes, or until lightly browned. Transfer the nuts to a plate to cool completely. In a small food processor or mini-chopper, combine the nuts with ½ cup each of the parsley and cilantro, the garlic and a large pinch each of salt and pepper. Process to a paste. Add 3 tablespoons of the oil and process briefly to blend. Scrape the mixture into a small bowl and cover with plastic wrap.

2. In a large skillet, melt ½ tablespoon of the butter in 1 tablespoon of the oil over high heat. Add half of the mushrooms, season with salt and pepper and cook, stirring, until browned, about 3 minutes. Reduce the heat to low and cook the mushrooms until the liquid evaporates and they brown again, about 8 minutes. Transfer the mushrooms to a large plate and repeat with the remaining oil, butter and mushrooms.

3. Return all of the mushrooms to the skillet and add ½ cup of the nut paste. Stir in the chicken stock, 1 tablespoon at a time, to make a sauce. Season with salt and pepper and transfer the mushrooms to a large shallow dish. Serve the sautéed mushrooms warm or at room temperature, sprinkled with the remaining 1 tablespoon each of parsley and cilantro. *–Peter Hoffman*

MAKE AHEAD The nut paste can be refrigerated for up to three days.

Shiitake-Mushroom Sauté with Watercress

4 SERVINGS **L**

2 teaspoons olive oil
1 small red bell pepper, cut into
   ½-inch dice
2 garlic cloves, minced
1 pound fresh shiitake mushrooms,
   stems discarded and caps thinly
   sliced
¼ cup chicken stock or canned
   low-sodium broth, defatted
2 tablespoons fresh lemon
   juice
Salt and freshly ground pepper
1 bunch watercress, tough stems
   removed
1 tablespoon finely chopped mint

1. Heat the oil in a large stainless-steel skillet. Add the red bell pepper and the garlic and cook over moderate heat, stirring constantly, for 2 minutes. Add the mushrooms and stock. Cook, stirring occasionally, until tender, about 5 minutes. Stir in the lemon juice, season with salt and pepper and let cool slightly.

2. Arrange the watercress on a large plate and spoon the mushrooms on top. Sprinkle the mushrooms with the mint and serve. *–Amanda Cushman*

Sautéed Fall Greens with Caraway

8 SERVINGS

- 1 teaspoon caraway seeds
- 2 tablespoons olive oil
- ½ pound beet greens, trimmed and cut into 2-inch strips
- 1 medium head of red oak leaf lettuce, cut into 2-inch strips
- ½ pound spinach, tough stems discarded
- ½ tablespoon fresh lemon juice
- ½ teaspoon finely grated lemon zest

Salt and freshly ground pepper

1. In a large heavy saucepan, toast the caraway seeds over moderate heat until fragrant, about 3 minutes. Transfer the seeds to a plate to cool. Coarsely crush them with the side of a large knife.

2. Heat the oil in the saucepan. Add the greens, in batches if necessary. Sauté over moderate heat until wilted, about 3 minutes. Stir in the lemon juice, lemon zest and caraway. Season with salt and pepper and serve. –*Rori Spinelli*

Swiss Chard and Shallots

8 SERVINGS

Red chard makes this earthy dish more festive, though you can use green chard instead. Cooking the chard stems and leaves separately ensures that the leaves won't overcook.

- 3 pounds red Swiss chard, rinsed, leaves and stems separated
- 2 tablespoons unsalted butter
- 2 tablespoons extra-virgin olive oil
- 8 large shallots, finely chopped

Salt and freshly ground pepper

1. Coarsely chop the chard leaves. Peel any strings from the thick stems as you would celery, then cut the stems into 1-inch pieces.

2. Bring a large pot of salted water to a boil. Meanwhile, in a heavy medium skillet, melt the butter in the oil. Add the shallots and cook over moderate heat, stirring occasionally, until softened,

about 5 minutes. Season with ½ teaspoon each of salt and pepper.

3. Add the chard stems to the boiling water and cook until tender, about 5 minutes. Using a slotted spoon, transfer to a bowl. Add the leaves to the pot and cook until tender, about 2 minutes. Drain well in a colander and transfer to another bowl.

4. Rewarm the shallots. Stir half into the chard stems and half into the chard leaves and season both with salt and pepper. Make a ring of the stems on a large platter and pile the leaves in the center. –*Diana Sturgis*

MAKE AHEAD The chard can be refrigerated after Step 1 for up to one day; keep the stems and leaves separate.

Jamaican Bok Choy

8 SERVINGS

- 1 tablespoon olive oil
- 16 heads of baby bok choy, trimmed, or 4 pounds large bok choy, leaves and upper stems only, cut into 2-inch pieces
- 2 garlic cloves, minced
- 1 to 2 teaspoons seeded minced Scotch bonnet chile
- 1 tablespoon unsalted butter

Salt and freshly ground pepper

Heat the oil in a large enameled casserole or a large wok. Add the bok choy and stir-fry over moderately high heat until starting to wilt, about 3 minutes. Add the garlic and chile and cook, stirring, until the garlic is fragrant, about 1 minute. Stir in the butter. Season the bok choy with salt and pepper and serve at once. –*Herb Wilson*

Carrots with Coriander and Caraway

12 SERVINGS

This aromatic carrot dish is typical of Tunisian-Jewish cooking.

- 1½ teaspoons coriander seeds
- 1 teaspoon caraway seeds

Carrots with Coriander and Caraway, TOP; Sautéed Mushrooms with Walnuts and Herbs, LEFT; and Artichokes Simmered with Lemon and Honey (p. 317), BOTTOM.

- 2 tablespoons olive oil
- 2 pounds medium carrots, thinly sliced crosswise on the diagonal
- ½ cup white-wine vinegar

1. Warm a large stainless-steel skillet over moderate heat. Add the coriander and caraway seeds and cook, shaking the pan, until fragrant, about 1 minute. Empty the coriander and caraway seeds onto a plate to cool. Using a spice grinder or a mortar and pestle, grind the seeds to a powder.

2. In the same skillet, warm the oil over high heat. Add the carrots and cook, stirring occasionally, until lightly browned, about 10 minutes. Add the ground coriander and caraway and cook, stirring, until fragrant, about 1 minute. Reduce the heat to low, add the vinegar and cook, stirring occasionally, until the carrots are tender, about 3 minutes. Transfer to a large shallow dish. Serve warm or at room temperature. –*Peter Hoffman*

MAKE AHEAD The carrots can be refrigerated, covered, overnight.

Winter-Squash and Carrot Puree

6 SERVINGS

Serve with golden roast turkey, goose or chicken, roast pork loin or baked ham for a classic pairing.

- 1 kabocha or buttercup squash (about 2¾ pounds), halved crosswise and seeded
- 4 carrots, thinly sliced
- 1 large garlic clove, thinly sliced
- ¼ teaspoon dried thyme
- 2 cups water
- Salt and freshly ground pepper
- 1 tablespoon unsalted butter, cut into small pieces

1. Preheat the oven to 350°. Set the squash, cut-side down, on a lightly oiled baking sheet. Bake for about 45 minutes, or until soft.

2. In a saucepan, combine the carrots, garlic, thyme and water. Cover and bring to a boil and then simmer over low heat until the carrots are very tender, about 20 minutes. Transfer the contents of the pan to a food processor; puree. Scoop the squash out of its skin and puree it with the carrots. Season with salt and pepper.

3. Spread the puree in a buttered shallow baking dish; dot with the butter. Bake for 20 minutes, or until hot, and serve. —*Diana Sturgis*

Smoked Acorn Squash

4 SERVINGS

The hollows of the halved squash hold a mixture of mustard and maple syrup that becomes a delicious sauce.

- Two 2-pound acorn squash, halved crosswise and seeded
- ¼ cup fresh orange juice
- 2 tablespoons pure maple syrup
- 2 teaspoons Dijon mustard
- 2 teaspoons unsalted butter
- Salt and freshly ground pepper
- Light Tea-Smoking Mixture (p. 25)

1. In a steamer basket set over 1 inch of boiling water, steam the squash halves, covered, over moderate heat until tender when pierced, about 20 minutes.

2. In a small bowl, combine the orange juice, maple syrup and mustard. Pour one-quarter of this mixture into the hollow of each squash half. Add ½ teaspoon of the butter to each and season with salt and pepper.

3. Smoke the squash, hollow-side up, with the tea-smoking mixture, according to the Basic Wok-Smoking Method (p. 25), for 15 minutes. Serve the smoked squash warm. —*Marcia Kiesel*

Curried Cauliflower and Potatoes

6 TO 8 SERVINGS

- ¾ pound all-purpose potatoes, peeled and cut into ½-inch dice
- One 3-pound head of cauliflower, cut into 1½-inch florets
- 3 tablespoons unsalted butter
- 2 tablespoons vegetable oil
- 1 small onion, finely chopped
- 2 large garlic cloves, minced
- 2 tablespoons curry powder
- 2 teaspoons fresh lemon juice
- ½ teaspoon salt
- 1 cup water

1. Boil the potatoes in salted water until just tender, about 5 minutes. Remove the potatoes with a slotted spoon. Add the cauliflower and cook until crisp-tender, about 5 minutes; drain.

2. In a large stainless-steel skillet, melt the butter in the oil over moderate heat. Add the onion and garlic and cook until soft, about 2 minutes. Add the curry powder and cook, stirring, for 2 minutes. Add the potatoes and cauliflower and cook, stirring occasionally, for 2 minutes longer.

3. Add the lemon juice, the salt and the water. Cook, scraping up the bottom, until the liquid is absorbed, about 5 minutes; serve. —*Diana Sturgis*

Brussels Sprouts with Walnuts, Balsamic Vinegar and Mint

20 SERVINGS

- 1½ cups walnuts
- 8 pints (8 pounds) Brussels sprouts, trimmed and scored on the bottom
- Ice water
- 4 tablespoons unsalted butter
- ½ cup balsamic vinegar
- Salt and freshly ground pepper
- ½ cup chopped mint

1. Preheat the oven to 400°. Spread the walnuts on a baking sheet and toast for about 6 minutes, until fragrant and lightly browned.

2. In a large pot of boiling salted water, cook the Brussels sprouts until bright green and almost tender, about 6 minutes; drain. Immediately plunge the Brussels sprouts into ice water to stop the cooking. Pat dry with paper towels.

3. In each of two large skillets, cook half of the butter over high heat until it begins to brown. Add the Brussels sprouts in an even layer and cook without stirring until they brown on the bottom, about 8 minutes. Add the vinegar and cook, stirring, until the vinegar reduces and glazes the Brussels sprouts, about 3 minutes. Season with salt and pepper, stir in the walnuts and mint and serve at once. —*Gordon Hamersley*

MAKE AHEAD The Brussels sprouts can be prepared through Step 2 and refrigerated for two days. Store the walnuts separately in an airtight container.

Stir-Fried Cabbage with Cashews

4 TO 6 SERVINGS

Serve with barbecued spareribs—a natural for this Chinese-inspired dish. The black-bean chile sauce is available at Asian specialty stores and some supermarkets.

- 2½ tablespoons tomato paste
- 2½ tablespoons soy sauce

2½ teaspoons balsamic vinegar

½ teaspoon Chinese black-bean
    chile sauce

¼ cup water

1½ tablespoons vegetable oil

1 garlic clove, minced

2 pounds Savoy cabbage, cut into
   2-inch pieces

½ cup roasted whole cashews

I. In a bowl, mix the tomato paste, soy sauce, vinegar, black-bean chile sauce and water.

2. Heat the oil in a wok. Add the garlic and stir-fry over moderately high heat for about 30 seconds. Add the cabbage and stir-fry until just wilted, about 5 minutes. Add the sauce mixture and stir-fry for 1 minute. Serve topped with the cashews.   *–Marcia Kiesel*

Roasted Root Vegetables

4 TO 6 SERVINGS

Let your own affinities inspire the choice of vegetables in this utterly satisfying recipe; you'll want about seven pounds total.

3 large carrots, peeled and
   cut into 2-inch chunks

3 large beets, peeled and cut
   into 1½-inch chunks

2 russet potatoes (8 ounces each),
   peeled and quartered

2 parsnips (5 to 6 ounces each),
   peeled and cut into 2-inch chunks

2 onions, peeled and quartered
   lengthwise

1 small rutabaga (1½ pounds),
   peeled and cut into 1-inch chunks

1 sweet potato (8 to 10 ounces),
   peeled and cut into 8 pieces

8 garlic cloves

¼ cup plus 2 tablespoons
   extra-virgin olive oil

¼ cup balsamic vinegar

Salt and freshly ground pepper

I. Preheat the oven to 425°. Position racks in the upper and lower thirds of the oven.

2. In a large glass or stainless-steel bowl, toss the vegetables with the oil, vinegar and a generous pinch each of salt and pepper. Transfer to two large baking sheets. Roast the vegetables, stirring once or twice, for about 45 minutes, or until all are tender and browned. Switch the baking sheets halfway through. Using a slotted spoon, transfer the vegetables to a large platter, leaving the oil behind, and serve.   *–Darra Goldstein*

WINE Root vegetables have a sweet, earthy character that's echoed by Pinot Noir. Look for West Coast examples with not-too-subtle flavors, such as the 1994 King Estate from Oregon or the 1994 Gundlach-Bundschu from California.

Roasted Root Vegetables

Summer Stew with Navy Beans and Okra

4 SERVINGS **L**

1 cup dried navy beans (about
   7 ounces), picked over and rinsed

2 bay leaves

2 garlic cloves, peeled, plus
   ½ teaspoon minced garlic

1½ quarts water

Salt

1 teaspoon vegetable oil

1 thin slice of bacon (about
   1½ ounces), finely chopped

½ medium onion, finely chopped

2 cups vegetable stock or
   water

2 teaspoons minced thyme

Summer Stew with Navy Beans and Okra, with Sesame-Coated Striped Bass (p. 134) and Golden Rice Pilaf with Spices (p. 308)

Cuban Black Beans

15 SERVINGS

There are two secrets to true Cuban black beans: preparing them without meat and allowing the cooked beans to "sleep" overnight to develop flavor. The finished beans can be seasoned to taste with sugar and vinegar.

- 1 pound dried black beans, rinsed and picked over
- 2 green bell peppers, 1 quartered lengthwise, 1 minced
- 2 bay leaves
- 8 cups water
- ½ cup plus 2 tablespoons olive oil
- 1 red bell pepper, minced
- 1 yellow bell pepper, minced
- 1 large white onion, minced
- 1 tablespoon ground cumin
- 1 tablespoon dried oregano
- ½ cup minced garlic
- ¼ cup tomato paste

Salt

1. Put the black beans, quartered green bell pepper and bay leaves in a large saucepan and add the water. Bring to a boil over moderately high heat. Reduce the heat to low, partially cover the saucepan and cook, stirring occasionally, until the beans are tender, about 2½ hours. Remove and discard the green-bell-pepper quarters and the bay leaves.

2. Meanwhile, heat the 2 tablespoons oil in a large skillet. Add the minced bell peppers and onion and cook over moderate heat until softened. Stir in the cumin and oregano. In a small saucepan, cook the garlic in the remaining ½ cup of oil over moderately low heat until golden brown.

3. When the beans are tender, add the sautéed pepper mixture, the garlic in its oil and the tomato paste. Season with salt and simmer gently for 5 minutes to blend the flavors. Cover and refrigerate overnight or for up to 3 days. Reheat gently before serving.   —Alex Garcia

1½ cups fresh or thawed frozen corn kernels

1 cup thickly sliced fresh or thawed frozen okra (about 5 ounces)

3 medium tomatoes, seeded and coarsely chopped

Freshly ground pepper

1. Put the beans in a bowl, cover with water and let soak overnight. Drain the beans, put in a medium saucepan and add the bay leaves, garlic cloves and water. Bring to a boil, reduce the heat to moderately low and cook, partially covered, until tender but not mushy, about 1 hour. Season with salt about 10 minutes before the beans are done. Drain and discard the bay leaves and garlic.

2. Heat the oil in a medium saucepan. Add the bacon and cook over moderate heat until just crisp; pour off any excess fat. Add the onion and minced garlic and cook, stirring, until softened, about 2 minutes. Add the beans, stock and thyme. Simmer over moderately low heat until the liquid is reduced by two-thirds, about 15 minutes. After 10 minutes, add the corn and okra and cook until tender. Stir in the tomatoes and cook until slightly softened, about 1 minute. Season the mixture with salt and pepper and serve.   —Marvin Woods

Cannellini Beans with Sage

8 SERVINGS

1½ cups dried cannellini beans, soaked overnight in cold water

12 cups cold water

12 large sage leaves

4 garlic cloves

½ cup olive oil

Salt and freshly ground pepper

Drain and rinse the beans. In a large saucepan, cover the beans with the cold water. Add the sage, garlic and 3 tablespoons of the oil and bring to a gentle boil over moderate heat. Reduce the heat to low and simmer, stirring often, until the beans are tender, about 1½ hours. Season with salt and pepper. Transfer the beans to a bowl, drizzle the remaining 5 tablespoons of oil on top and serve.   —Egi Maccioni

Barbecued Baked Beans

20 SERVINGS

3½ cups dried beans, such as cranberry, Great Northern or pinto (about 1½ pounds), rinsed and picked over

9 ounces thickly sliced bacon, cut into ½-inch dice

3 large green bell peppers, cut into ⅓-inch dice

2 medium yellow onions, cut into ⅓-inch dice

4 medium celery ribs, cut into ⅓-inch dice

1 jalapeño pepper, finely chopped (with seeds)

1 tablespoon finely chopped garlic

4 cups veal stock or canned low-sodium chicken broth

4 cups best-quality barbecue sauce

One 12-ounce can tomato paste

¼ cup molasses

Salt

1. Soak the beans overnight in a large bowl of cold water. Drain and rinse.

2. Put the beans in a large pot, add cold water to cover generously and bring to a boil. Reduce the heat to moderate and simmer until tender, about 1 hour.

3. Meanwhile, in a large enameled cast-iron casserole, cook the bacon over moderately high heat, stirring occasionally, until crisp. Remove and set aside.

4. Add the green bell peppers, onions, celery and jalapeño to the casserole and sauté over moderately high heat for 3 minutes. Add the garlic and sauté for 2 minutes longer. Stir in the reserved bacon and the stock, barbecue sauce, tomato paste and molasses. Bring to a simmer, stirring occasionally.

5. Preheat the oven to 400°. Drain the beans and add to the casserole. Bake for 1 hour, stirring gently every 15 minutes. Season with salt and serve. *–David Page*

MAKE AHEAD The beans can be refrigerated for up to three days. Bring to room temperature and reheat thoroughly in a low oven before serving.

Refried Beans with Pickled Jalapeños

15 SERVINGS

1 pound dried pinto beans, rinsed and picked over

2 ancho chiles—stemmed, seeded and coarsely chopped

2 quarts water, more if needed

¼ cup olive oil

2 slices of bacon, minced

1 medium onion, finely chopped

4 garlic cloves, minced

Kosher salt

½ pound extra-sharp cheddar, grated (2⅔ cups)

½ cup drained sliced pickled jalapeño peppers

Tortilla chips or warm flour tortillas

1. In a large saucepan, combine the beans, anchos and water and bring to a boil over moderate heat. Lower the heat, cover partially and simmer until the beans are very tender, about 2 hours. Add a little water if necessary to keep the beans just covered as they cook; let cool. Working in batches, puree the beans and their liquid in a food processor.

2. Heat the oil in a large heavy skillet. Add the bacon; cook over moderately high heat without browning until the fat is rendered, about 5 minutes. Add the onion and garlic and sauté until deep golden brown, about 10 minutes. Lower the heat to moderate, add the pureed beans and stir until thick and creamy, about 5 minutes; if the beans become dry, stir in a little water. Season with salt.

3. Spread half the beans in a large oven-proof skillet or baking dish; sprinkle with half the cheese. Cover with the remaining beans and cheese and the jalapeños.

4. Preheat the oven to 350°. Bake the beans for about 20 minutes, or until they are heated through and the cheese is melted. *–Robert Del Grande*

MAKE AHEAD Refrigerate the beans overnight in the skillet. Return to room temperature and proceed with Step 4.

CHAPTER 16 condiments dips sauces syrups

Creamy Low-Fat Arugula Pesto (p. 335), TOP; **Fresh Tomato Sauce with Pecorino (p. 334),** RIGHT; **Olive Caper Tapenade with Fresh Mint (p. 332),** BOTTOM; **and Sun-Dried-Tomato Aioli (p. 336),** LEFT.

331 Cranberry Apple Butter

331 Haroset

331 Black-Eyed-Pea Salsa

331 Pickled Jalapeños

331 Sweet-Onion Jam

332 Sofrito

332 Cool Cucumber Yogurt Dip

332 Goat Cheese with Piquillo-Pepper Puree

332 Olive Caper Tapenade with Fresh Mint

333 Mango Mignonette Sauce

333 White-Wine Herb Sauce

333 Red-Wine Mushroom Sauce

334 Fresh Tomato Sauce with Pecorino

334 Creamy Garlic Tomato Sauce

334 Dried-Chile Cream Sauce

334 Thai Lime Sauce

335 Chipotle Peanut Sauce

335 Creamy Low-Fat Arugula Pesto

336 Sun-Dried-Tomato Aioli

336 Crisp Shallots and Shallot Oil

336 Whiskey and White-Peppercorn Syrup

336 Honey, Rosemary and Lavender Syrup

336 Basil and Cinnamon Syrup

337 Alain Senderens' Syrup for Tropical Fruits

337 Vanilla-Bean Syrup

Cranberry Apple Butter

Cranberry Apple Butter

MAKES ABOUT 2 PINTS

- 6 pounds McIntosh apples, quartered and cored
- ½ cup water
- 2 cups cranberries
- 1 cup sugar
- 2 tablespoons honey

In a large enameled cast-iron casserole, combine the apples and water. Cover and cook over moderate heat, stirring often, until soft, about 20 minutes. Uncover and cook over low heat, stirring occasionally, until a thickened puree forms, about 45 minutes. Meanwhile, in a medium saucepan, cook the cranberries with the sugar over low heat, stirring occasionally, until a thick puree forms, about 15 minutes. Pass the hot cranberry puree through a coarse strainer. Then pass the apple puree through a coarse strainer and return it to the casserole. Cook over moderately low heat, stirring occasionally, until very thick, about 15 minutes. Add the honey and the cranberry puree and stir until blended. Transfer the mixture to a heatproof bowl and let cool completely. Pack into clean jars and refrigerate for up to 1 month. *—Marcia Kiesel*

Haroset

MAKES ABOUT 3 CUPS

In this Greek Passover recipe for haroset, dried fruits replace the fresh apples familiar to most American Jews. A sweet condiment, it is served with matzo as part of the ritual.

- 1 cup dried currants (4 ounces)

About 1 cup red wine

- 1 cup blanched almonds (4 to 5 ounces)
- ½ cup walnut pieces (2 ounces)
- ½ cup pine nuts (3 ounces)
- 1 cup pitted dates (6 ounces), coarsely chopped
- 1 teaspoon cinnamon
- ½ teaspoon ground cloves

1. In a medium glass or ceramic bowl, cover the currants with ¾ cup of the wine and let them soak until plumped, at least 5 hours or overnight.

2. Preheat the oven to 350°. Spread the almonds and walnuts on a baking sheet and bake for 4 minutes; stir in the pine nuts and bake for about 3 minutes longer, or until all the nuts are lightly toasted. Let the nuts cool, then chop them. Add the nuts, dates, cinnamon and cloves to the currants and wine and mix well. Stir in the remaining wine if the mixture is very stiff. *—Peter Hoffman*

MAKE AHEAD The haroset can be made up to one day ahead. Cover but do not refrigerate.

Black-Eyed-Pea Salsa

MAKES ABOUT 3½ CUPS

Serve this Southern-style salsa with Sweet-Tea-Cured Roast Pork (p. 216) or on its own as a salad.

- 2 cups shelled fresh or frozen black-eyed peas
- 1 cup thinly sliced scallions, white and tender green
- ½ cup finely diced red bell pepper
- ½ cup finely diced yellow bell pepper
- 2 teaspoons finely chopped flat-leaf parsley
- 1 teaspoon finely chopped jalapeño pepper
- 1 teaspoon minced garlic
- ¼ cup cider vinegar
- 2 tablespoons extra-virgin olive oil

Salt and freshly ground pepper

1. Bring a medium saucepan of lightly salted water to a boil. Add the black-eyed peas and cook until tender, about 20 minutes. Drain and let cool completely.

2. In a large glass or stainless-steel bowl, toss the black-eyed peas with the scallions, red and yellow bell peppers, parsley, jalapeño and garlic. In a small glass or stainless-steel bowl, whisk together the vinegar, oil and salt and pepper to taste. Toss with the salad. Let

stand at room temperature for 2 hours. Season the salsa with salt and pepper before serving. *—John Fleer*

MAKE AHEAD The salsa can be refrigerated overnight. Let return to room temperature before serving.

Pickled Jalapeños

MAKES 1 QUART

One Christmas season, I came upon a silver martini shaker and handblown glasses at a New Orleans antiques store. I bought them, added a jar of my pickled jalapeños and created the perfect Acadian-martini ensemble for a friend who loves the fiery cocktail.

- 1½ pounds jalapeño peppers, stems removed
- 1 quart distilled white vinegar
- 12 garlic cloves
- 6 bay leaves
- 2 tablespoons kosher salt
- 1 tablespoon black peppercorns

Bring all of the ingredients to a boil in a saucepan. Simmer over low heat until the jalapeños are very soft, about 15 minutes. Remove from the heat and let steep for 30 minutes. Discard the bay leaves and pour the jalapeños and their liquid into a 1-quart canning jar. Let cool to room temperature. Refrigerate for up to 1 month. *—Emeril Lagasse*

Sweet-Onion Jam

MAKES 1 CUP

Grenadine helps sweeten this onion jam and adds vibrant red color. The jam is great with most meats, especially grilled or roasted pork.

- 1 tablespoon unsalted butter
- 2 medium Vidalia or other sweet onions, cut into ¾-inch dice (about 2½ cups)
- ½ cup sugar
- ⅓ cup red wine
- ⅓ cup red-wine vinegar
- ⅓ cup grenadine

Salt

Melt the butter in a medium skillet. Add the onions and cook over moderate heat, stirring, until soft and just translucent, about 8 minutes. Add the sugar, wine, vinegar, grenadine and a pinch of salt to the skillet. Cook over low heat, stirring, until the liquid thickens and coats the back of a spoon, about 35 minutes. Transfer the onion jam to a bowl and let cool.   –John Fleer

MAKE AHEAD The onion jam can be refrigerated for up to five days. Let return to room temperature before serving.

Sofrito

MAKES 4 CUPS

Packages of this colorful Spanish seasoning make great gifts, along with a bag of Valencia rice.

- 4 cups small cilantro sprigs
- 1 cup flat-leaf parsley sprigs
- 10 garlic cloves, chopped
- 2 onions, chopped
- 2 jalapeño peppers, seeded and chopped
- 1 red bell pepper, chopped

Olive Caper Tapenade with Fresh Mint, LEFT; Sun-Dried-Tomato Aioli (p. 336), RIGHT; and Creamy Low-Fat Arugula Pesto (p. 335), BOTTOM.

Coarsely chop the cilantro and parsley together. In a food processor, combine the garlic, onions, jalapeños and bell pepper; process to a coarse paste. Add the cilantro and parsley and pulse until just combined. Pack into jars and refrigerate for up to a month. –Marcia Kiesel

Cool Cucumber Yogurt Dip

MAKES ABOUT 3 CUPS

This condiment is a refreshing appetizer on its own and a soothing accompaniment to spicy dishes. It needs the richness of whole-milk yogurt, available at health-food stores and most supermarkets.

- 2 English cucumbers, peeled and cut into ¼-inch dice
- Salt
- 1¾ cups whole-milk yogurt
- ⅔ cup sour cream
- ¾ teaspoon sugar
- 3 tablespoons red-wine vinegar
- 1 large garlic clove, mashed to a paste
- 3 tablespoons extra-virgin olive oil
- Freshly ground white pepper
- 3 tablespoons minced dill

1. In a colander set over a bowl, toss the cucumbers with ½ teaspoon of salt. Set a plate directly on the cucumbers and weigh it down with a heavy can. Let the cucumbers drain for at least 4 hours at room temperature or overnight in the refrigerator.

2. Meanwhile, put the yogurt in a strainer lined with a coffee filter. Set the strainer over a large bowl and let the yogurt drain in the refrigerator until very thick, at least 4 hours or overnight.

3. In a medium glass or stainless-steel bowl, combine the cucumbers, yogurt and sour cream. In a small glass or stainless-steel bowl, stir the sugar into the vinegar until dissolved. Add to the cucumbers along with the garlic and oil. Season with salt and pepper and refrigerate until chilled, about 2 hours. Stir in the dill and serve.   –Charles Bowman

Goat Cheese with Piquillo-Pepper Puree

MAKES ABOUT 1 CUP **Q**

Jarred piquillo peppers, from the Navarre region of Spain, are now available at specialty-food stores in the United States. Piquillos are richer in flavor than roasted red bell peppers and have a bit of heat. The best substitute is jarred roasted red peppers plus one-quarter teaspoon hot paprika. Serve the dip with crudités or crackers, use it as a filling for omelets or thin with a little water and toss with pasta or grilled vegetables.

- ⅓ cup drained piquillo peppers
- ¼ cup grated Asiago or good-quality provolone (about 1 ounce)
- 5½ ounces fresh goat cheese, softened

In a food processor, pulse the piquillo peppers and Asiago cheese until finely chopped. Add the goat cheese and process until smooth.   –Grace Parisi

MAKE AHEAD The puree can be refrigerated for up to one week. Let return to room temperature before serving.

Olive Caper Tapenade with Fresh Mint

MAKES ABOUT ⅔ CUP **Q**

You can make this slightly spicy tapenade with both oil-cured and brine-cured olives; just be sure to use large ones, which are easier to pit. Serve with grilled steak, chicken, scallops or firm-fleshed white fish or on burgers.

- ½ cup flat-leaf parsley leaves
- ¼ cup mint leaves
- ¼ cup extra-virgin olive oil
- 2 tablespoons capers, drained
- ⅛ teaspoon crushed red pepper
- 1 cup assorted olives (about 5 ounces), pitted

In a food processor, pulse the parsley, mint, oil, capers and pepper until finely chopped. Add the olives; pulse until finely chopped but not pureed. –Grace Parisi

MAKE AHEAD Refrigerate for up to three days; serve at room temperature.

Mango Mignonette Sauce

MAKES ABOUT 1¼ CUPS

Mango gives a tropical twist to this classic sauce for ice-cold oysters and clams.

- ¾ cup red-wine vinegar
- ½ cup minced mango
- ¼ cup minced shallots
- 1½ teaspoons freshly ground pepper

Combine all the ingredients in a medium bowl and serve over freshly shucked oysters and clams. *–Chris Schlesinger*

White-Wine Herb Sauce

MAKES ABOUT 1 CUP **Q**

Serve this sauce with chicken breasts or white-fleshed fish.

- 1 large shallot, minced
- 2 cups dry white wine
- 1 stick (4 ounces) cold unsalted butter, cut into 8 pieces
- ¼ cup finely chopped herbs, such as parsley, chives and tarragon

Salt and freshly ground pepper

In a medium stainless-steel saucepan, combine the shallot and wine and boil over high heat until reduced to ½ cup, about 20 minutes. (To make the sauce with pan juices, discard the fat from the sauté skillet, add the reduced wine and boil for 30 seconds, scraping the bottom of the pan with a wooden spoon to dissolve the brown bits.) Off the heat, whisk in the butter 1 tablespoon at a time to make a thick sauce. Return the pan to the heat briefly to warm the sauce if necessary; do not boil. Add the herbs, season with salt and pepper and serve. *–James Peterson*

Red-Wine Mushroom Sauce

MAKES ABOUT 2 CUPS **Q**

Demiglace is available at specialty-food stores or by mail-order from More Than Gourmet (800-860-9392) or D'Artagnan (800-327-8246). You can make the sauce without butter or demiglace, but it will be quite thin. Serve with red meat, chicken or full-flavored fish

Red-Wine Mushroom Sauce

- ¾ pound white or cremini mushrooms, thickly sliced, or wild mushrooms, halved or quartered, depending on size
- 2 tablespoons olive oil
- 2 cups full-bodied red wine, such as Merlot, Zinfandel or Rioja
- 1 medium shallot, minced
- 2 tablespoons store-bought demiglace
- 6 tablespoons cold unsalted butter, cut into small pieces

Salt and freshly ground pepper

1. In a large skillet, sauté the mushrooms in the oil over high heat for about 10 minutes, until softened and fragrant.

2. In a medium stainless-steel saucepan, combine the red wine, the sautéed mushrooms, the shallot and the demiglace. Boil the mushroom mixture over high heat, stirring occasionally, until reduced to 2 cups, about 20 minutes. (To make the mushroom sauce with pan juices, discard the fat from the sauté skillet, add the reduced wine mixture and boil for 30 seconds, scraping the bottom of the pan with a wooden spoon to dissolve the browned bits.) Off the heat, whisk the butter into the mushroom mixture to make a thickened sauce. Season the sauce with salt and pepper. *–James Peterson*

Fresh Tomato Sauce with Pecorino

MAKES ABOUT 2½ CUPS Q

Serve with pasta, shrimp, chicken or vegetables.

1¼ pounds ripe medium tomatoes, cored and halved crosswise
⅔ cup freshly grated Pecorino Romano (about 2½ ounces)
2 scallions, cut into 2-inch pieces
1 jalapeño pepper, seeded and coarsely chopped
1 tablespoon tomato paste
1½ teaspoons whole marjoram leaves
¼ cup extra-virgin olive oil
Salt and freshly ground pepper

1. Working over a strainer set over a bowl, remove the tomato seeds. Using a wooden spoon, press down on the seeds to extract as much juice as possible. Discard the seeds and reserve ¼ cup of the juice. Cut the tomatoes into chunks.

2. In a food processor, combine one-quarter of the tomatoes with the tomato juice, cheese, scallions, jalapeño, tomato paste and marjoram. Add the remaining tomatoes and pulse until coarsely chopped; the sauce should be chunky. Transfer the sauce to a bowl, stir in the oil and season with salt and pepper.   —Grace Parisi

Creamy Garlic Tomato Sauce

MAKES ABOUT 1 CUP Q

You can substitute six tablespoons of prepared mayonnaise for the home-made garlic mayonnaise made in Step 1 below. Just add the crushed garlic to it. Serve with fish or chicken.

1 small garlic clove, minced
¼ teaspoon kosher salt
1 egg yolk, at room temperature
⅓ cup extra-virgin olive oil
Large pinch of saffron threads
1 tablespoon water
2 medium tomatoes, coarsely chopped, or 1 cup drained canned tomatoes, coarsely chopped
½ cup fish or chicken stock or canned low-sodium broth
Salt and freshly ground pepper

1. Crush the garlic to a smooth paste. In a small bowl, combine the garlic, salt and egg yolk. Slowly whisk in the oil in a thin stream to make a thick, smooth mayonnaise. Set aside.

2. In a bowl, crumble the saffron threads into the water. Steep for at least 10 minutes.

3. In a medium stainless-steel saucepan, combine the tomatoes and stock. Cover and simmer gently over moderate heat for 10 minutes to blend the flavors and reduce. Puree the tomato mixture by pushing it through a coarse strainer set over a bowl. Stir in the saffron and its liquid.

4. Return the tomato sauce to the saucepan and bring to a simmer over moderate heat. (To make the sauce with pan juices, discard the fat from the sauté skillet, add the tomato sauce and bring to a simmer over moderate heat, whisking to dissolve the brown bits.) Off the heat, slowly whisk in the mayonnaise. Season with salt and pepper. Rewarm gently, if necessary, whisking constantly. Do not let the sauce boil or it will curdle.   —James Peterson

Dried-Chile Cream Sauce

MAKES ABOUT 1 CUP Q

Serve this sauce with chicken, red meat or full-flavored fish.

2 large dried chiles, such as anchos, guajillos, mulatos or pasillas—halved, stemmed and seeded
1 cup hot water
1 cup heavy cream
Salt
Cayenne pepper
Lime wedges, for serving

1. Soak the chiles in the hot water until softened, about 20 minutes. Drain and finely chop to a paste-like consistency.

2. In a small saucepan, combine the chiles with the cream and bring to a slow simmer over moderate heat, whisking. Remove from the heat and let steep for 5 minutes.

3. Simmer the sauce over low heat, whisking constantly, until it is the consistency of light cream, about 3 minutes. Season the cream sauce with salt and cayenne and serve it with lime wedges.   —James Peterson

Thai Lime Sauce

MAKES ABOUT ⅔ CUP Q

Serve this tangy sauce with pork loin chops, shrimp or chicken breasts. You'll need only about one-and-a-half tablespoons for each serving.

1 garlic clove, minced
1 small shallot, minced
1 jalapeño pepper, seeded and minced
1 teaspoon finely grated lime zest
1 teaspoon finely grated lemon zest
½ cup water

Fresh Tomato Sauce with Pecorino

2 tablespoons fresh lemon juice

1 tablespoon Thai fish sauce (nam pla)

1 tablespoon smooth peanut butter

¼ cup coconut milk

1 tablespoon finely chopped cilantro

In a small stainless-steel saucepan, combine the garlic, shallot, jalapeño and citrus zests. (To make the sauce with pan juices, discard the fat from the sauté skillet and make the sauce in the pan.) Cook over moderate heat for about 1 minute, whisking quickly to release the flavors; don't stand over the pan or the chile fumes may make you cough. Stir in the water and reduce the heat to moderately low. Add the lemon juice and fish sauce and simmer gently for 1 minute. Whisk in the peanut butter and coconut milk; simmer until thickened and flavorful, about 2 minutes. Add the cilantro. Taste and add more fish sauce if needed. *–James Peterson*

Chipotle Peanut Sauce

MAKES ABOUT 1 CUP **Q**

This sweet, nutty sauce gets subtle heat from chipotles. Serve with grilled beef, pork, chicken wings or shrimp or as a dip for blanched vegetables.

½ cup chunky peanut butter

½ cup unsweetened coconut milk

1 chipotle chile in adobo

1 quarter-size slice of fresh ginger, peeled and finely chopped

1 teaspoon soy sauce

1 teaspoon fresh lime juice

¼ teaspoon Asian sesame oil

¼ cup water

In a food processor, combine the peanut butter, coconut milk, chipotle and ginger; pulse until smooth. Transfer to a small saucepan and bring to a simmer over low heat. Cook, stirring, for 1 minute. Transfer to a bowl. Whisk in the remaining ingredients until smooth; refrigerate until chilled. *–Grace Parisi*

MAKE AHEAD The sauce can be refrigerated for up to one week.

Creamy Low-Fat Arugula Pesto, TOP; **Fresh Tomato Sauce with Pecorino,** RIGHT; **Olive Caper Tapenade with Fresh Mint (p. 332),** BOTTOM; **and Sun-Dried-Tomato Aioli (p. 336),** LEFT.

Creamy Low-Fat Arugula Pesto

MAKES 1¼ CUPS **Q**

Arugula gives this lean pesto its fresh tart flavor and peppery kick; farmer cheese and low-fat cream cheese lend creaminess. Serve the pesto as a dip with fresh vegetables, as a spread on grilled vegetable sandwiches or, thinned with a little pasta-cooking liquid, as a sauce for pasta.

3 large unpeeled garlic cloves

⅓ cup plus 1 tablespoon farmer cheese (3 ounces)

⅓ cup plus 1 tablespoon reduced-fat cream cheese (3 ounces)

2 scallions, cut into 2-inch pieces

1 large bunch of arugula (about 6 ounces)

Salt and freshly ground white pepper

1. In a small dry skillet, cook the garlic cloves over moderate heat, turning occasionally, until they are softened and blackened in spots, about 15 minutes. Let cool slightly. Peel and lightly crush the garlic.

2. Meanwhile, in a food processor, combine the cheeses and scallions and process until smooth. Add the garlic to the food processor and puree. Add the arugula to the food processor and pulse until it is finely chopped but not pureed. Season the arugula pesto with salt and pepper. *–Grace Parisi*

healthy pantry essentials

Balsamic Vinegar This sweet, mellow vinegar is wonderful in salad dressings, and it perks up stews, soups and sauces.

Canned Plum Tomatoes No pantry is complete without good-quality canned tomatoes to turn into sauces for pasta, polenta, fish and poultry and to add to braises, chilis and stews.

Dried Herbs and Spices Essentials include rosemary, thyme, coriander, cumin, cinnamon, allspice, ancho chile powder, crushed red pepper, bay leaves, curry and five-spice powder. For maximum flavor, replace them every few months. Also essential: sea salt, kosher salt and a peppermill.

Dry Goods Pasta, stone-ground cornmeal (for polenta), arborio rice and quick-cooking beans and legumes, such as rice beans, flageolets and red and green lentils, keep almost indefinitely and can be cooked in minutes.

Extra-Virgin Olive Oil Perhaps the most essential item in a healthy kitchen, olive oil is an excellent cooking medium, rich in monounsaturated fats. It adds marvelous flavor that's compatible with a very wide variety of foods.

No- or Low-Sodium Chicken Broth In lieu of homemade stock, canned broths are fine if boosted with other flavors. Defat canned broth and simmer it with leftover chicken parts or infuse it with assertive ingredients—Parmesan cheese rinds, fresh herbs and spices—or aromatics, such as garlic, ginger and leeks.

Vanilla Beans and Pure Vanilla Extract Vanilla brings out the natural sweetness and flavors of fruit, chocolate and nut desserts, making it possible to use less sugar.

Sun-Dried-Tomato Aioli

MAKES ABOUT ⅔ CUP **Q**

This rich sauce is dependent on best-quality dried tomatoes; we recommend the California Sun Dry brand. Serve the aioli with grilled beef, lamb or chicken or on grilled vegetable or crab-cake sandwiches.

- ¼ cup drained oil-packed sun-dried tomatoes
- 1 small garlic clove, smashed

Pinch of cayenne pepper

- ½ cup mayonnaise

In a food processor, pulse the sun-dried tomatoes with the garlic and cayenne until finely chopped, then puree until smooth. Add the mayonnaise and pulse just until blended. —*Grace Parisi*

MAKE AHEAD The aioli can be refrigerated for up to one week. Let return to room temperature before serving.

Crisp Shallots and Shallot Oil

MAKES ABOUT ⅔ CUP CRISP SHALLOTS AND 7 OUNCES SHALLOT OIL

- 1 cup peanut oil
- 1 pound large shallots, peeled and thinly sliced

Heat a wok over high heat for 40 seconds. Add the oil and shallots and cook, stirring occasionally, until softened, about 5 minutes. Reduce the heat to moderate and cook, stirring frequently, until the shallots are golden and crisp, about 10 minutes. Strain the oil. Drain the shallots on paper towels. —*Eileen Yin-Fei Lo*

MAKE AHEAD The oil can be refrigerated separately for up to two months.

Whiskey and White-Peppercorn Syrup

MAKES 1 CUP **L**

Serve this peppery syrup with oranges, bananas or cherries.

- 1½ cups water
- 3 tablespoons sugar
- ½ vanilla bean, split lengthwise

- 16 whole white peppercorns
- 1 tablespoon Irish whiskey, cognac or bourbon
- ¼ cup finely slivered lemon zest

In a small saucepan, combine the water and sugar. Scrape the seeds from the vanilla bean; add the seeds and bean to the pan along with the peppercorns. Simmer over moderate heat until reduced to 1 cup, about 10 minutes. Add the whiskey and lemon zest and simmer for 2 minutes. Cool to room temperature, then strain. —*Sally Schneider*

Honey, Rosemary and Lavender Syrup

MAKES 1 CUP **L**

I came up with this fragrant herb and flower syrup while living in a little house in the south of France that was surrounded by huge rosemary and lavender hedges. I used local lime-blossom honey to sweeten the syrup, but any fine golden honey will do nicely. Lavender flowers can be found at herb and spice shops and stores that sell flowers for sachets. Serve with peaches, nectarines, apricots, cherries, berries and figs.

- 1½ cups water
- 3 tablespoons mild golden honey
- ½ teaspoon lavender blossoms
- 1 sprig of rosemary

Combine all of the ingredients in a medium saucepan. Simmer over low heat until reduced to 1 cup, about 10 minutes. Cool to room temperature, then strain. —*Sally Schneider*

Basil and Cinnamon Syrup

MAKES 1 CUP **L**

Serve with peaches, nectarines and all kinds of berries.

- 1½ cups water
- 3 tablespoons sugar
- ½ cup finely shredded basil

One 2-inch piece of cinnamon stick

- 1 tablespoon fresh lemon juice

In a small saucepan, combine the water and sugar. Add the basil and cinnamon and simmer over low heat until reduced to 1 cup, about 10 minutes. Cool to room temperature, then strain. Stir in the lemon juice.   —*Sally Schneider*

Alain Senderens' Syrup for Tropical Fruits

MAKES 1 CUP **L**

This highly perfumed syrup, which I first tasted at L'Archestrate restaurant in Paris, is like an essence of exotic flowers. Serve with mango, pineapple, papaya and passion fruit.

1½ **cups water**
3 **tablespoons sugar**
4 **strips of lemon zest**
3 **strips of lime zest**
3 **coriander seeds**
2 **thin slices of fresh ginger**
1 **whole clove**
1 **sprig of mint**
½ **vanilla bean, split lengthwise**
1 **tablespoon fresh lime juice**

In a small saucepan, combine the water and sugar. Add the zests, spices and mint. Scrape the seeds from the vanilla bean; add the seeds and bean to the pan. Simmer over moderate heat for 8 minutes. Cool to room temperature; strain. Stir in the lime juice.   —*Sally Schneider*

Vanilla-Bean Syrup

MAKES 1 CUP **L**

Serve with almost any fruit, from melons and bananas to lychees.

1½ **cups water**
3 **tablespoons sugar**
1 **moist Mexican or bourbon vanilla bean, split lengthwise**

In a small saucepan, combine the water and sugar. Scrape the seeds from the vanilla bean; add the seeds and bean to the pan. Simmer over moderate heat until reduced to 1 cup, about 10 minutes. Cool to room temperature, then strain.   —*Sally Schneider*

aromatic syrups

Syrups such as the ones on these pages, flavored with delicate and unusual combinations of spices, citrus zests, herbs and spirits, can turn fresh fruit into charming desserts. I also use these syrups to moisten plain cakes and for poaching fresh and dried fruits. Flavored syrups are often as much as 50 percent sugar. I've found, however, that a much lighter reduced syrup, made with three tablespoons of sugar per cup of water, is sweet enough to carry the aromatics and enhance the fruit flavors without being cloying and adding calories. I often add a vanilla bean because it amplifies other flavorings as well as the natural sweetness of fresh fruit. All of these syrups can be refrigerated for up to one week, so keep them on hand to create impromptu desserts using any seasonal fruits available. —*Sally Schneider*

CHAPTER 17 cakes cookies

Chocolate Buttermilk Cake with Blackberry Meringue (p. 341)

341   Mandarin Chocolate Cake

341   Chocolate Buttermilk Cake with Blackberry Meringue

343   Bittersweet Chocolate Bombes

344   Fifteen-Minute Magic

344   Almond Cake with Citrus Syrup

346   Almond and Carrot Cake

347   Sableuse and Wild-Berry Compote

347   Stephanie's Poppy Cake

349   Mini Poppy-Seed Pound Cakes

349   Torta di Riso

349   Pumpkin Caramel Pudding Cakes

350   Pumpkin-Seed Cupcakes

351   Chocolate Pumpkin Brownies

352   Chocolate Ginger Crackles

353   Gingerbread Cookies

354   Frangipane Raspberry Squares

355   Mexican Wedding Cookies

355   Lemon Cornmeal Madeleines

356   Hazelnut Praline Balls

356   Clove and Lemon Butter Wafers

356   Rosemary Tuiles

356   Macadamia and Dried-Cherry Biscotti

357   Pistachio Biscotti

Mandarin Chocolate Cake

Mandarin Chocolate Cake

MAKES ONE 8-INCH CAKE

This moist layer cake is decorated with Modeling Chocolate, which resembles a pliable Tootsie Roll.

- 2 cups all-purpose flour, more for dusting
- 1 teaspoon baking soda

Pinch of salt

- 2 sticks (½ pound) unsalted butter, softened
- 5 ounces unsweetened baking chocolate, coarsely chopped
- 1¾ cups hot, strong-brewed coffee
- ¼ cup orange liqueur
- 2 cups sugar
- 2 large eggs
- 1 teaspoon pure vanilla extract

Chocolate Ganache Filling and Glaze (recipe follows)

Modeling Chocolate, for decorating (recipe follows)

1. Preheat the oven to 275°. Grease two 8-inch round cake pans with shortening. Line the bottoms with waxed paper and grease the paper. Dust the pans with flour, tapping out the excess.
2. In a bowl, whisk together the flour, baking soda and salt. In a large bowl, combine the butter, chocolate, hot coffee and liqueur; stir occasionally until the chocolate and butter melt. Stir in the sugar until dissolved and the mixture is completely cool. Add the flour mixture in two batches, whisking between additions. Whisk in the eggs and vanilla. Divide the batter evenly between the pans and bake in the middle of the oven for 1¼ hours, or until a toothpick inserted in the center of the cakes comes out clean. Let the cakes cool completely on a rack. Refrigerate for at least 6 hours or overnight.
3. To unmold the cakes, set one pan at a time over a burner on low heat for 10 seconds. Run a blunt knife around the cakes to loosen; invert onto a rack. Remove the paper. Split each cake in half horizontally to make four layers.

4. Place one cake layer on a stiff cardboard round on a wire rack and spread it with ½ cup of the ganache filling. Repeat with the remaining cake layers and ganache, ending with a plain cake layer. Pour the ganache glaze over the cake, spreading it around the top and sides with a metal spatula. Let the glaze drip for 2 to 3 minutes. Using two spatulas, transfer the cake to a plate. Decorate with the Modeling Chocolate and refrigerate briefly to set the glaze.

CHOCOLATE GANACHE FILLING AND GLAZE

MAKES ENOUGH FOR ONE 8-INCH CAKE

Ganache is a luxurious, silky-smooth mixture of chocolate and cream.

- 24 ounces bittersweet or semisweet chocolate, finely chopped
- 2 cups heavy cream

1. Put the chopped chocolate in a large heatproof bowl. In a medium saucepan, bring the cream just to a boil over low heat. Pour the cream over the chocolate, cover and let stand for 5 minutes. Whisk the ganache gently until silky and smooth.
2. To make the filling, transfer 1½ cups of the ganache to a medium bowl. Set the bowl over ice and whisk the ganache gently until thick and spreadable.

MODELING CHOCOLATE

MAKES ABOUT 1 CUP

- 8 ounces semisweet chocolate chips
- ¼ cup plus 1 tablespoon light corn syrup

1. Melt the chocolate in a metal bowl set over a pan of hot but not boiling water. Stir the chocolate with a wooden spoon until smooth, then stir in the corn syrup; the chocolate will stiffen almost immediately. Stir until completely combined. Transfer the chocolate to a sturdy plastic bag and refrigerate until firm.

2. Work the chocolate with your hands until pliable. Hand-shape into flowers, braids or ropes. Or pat it into a disk and roll it out to the desired thickness by hand or in a manual pasta machine and use it to make ribbons or for cutting out shapes. *–Colette Peters*

MAKE AHEAD Refrigerate the Modeling Chocolate for up to one month.

WINE A small glass of Grand Marnier– or a cup of espresso

Chocolate Buttermilk Cake with Blackberry Meringue

MAKES ONE 9-INCH CAKE

Filled with sweet, billowing blackberry meringue, this rich-tasting chocolate cake is a stunning dessert. If you prefer, you can make a plain meringue without the preserves or berries and garnish the cake with whatever fruit you like.

CHOCOLATE CAKE

Vegetable-oil cooking spray

- 3 cups all-purpose flour
- 2 cups granulated sugar
- ¾ cup unsweetened Dutch-process cocoa powder
- 2 teaspoons baking soda
- 1 teaspoon salt
- 2½ cups fresh or thawed frozen blackberries
- 1 cup low-fat (1.5%) buttermilk
- ⅔ cup vegetable oil
- 2 tablespoons distilled white vinegar
- 2 teaspoons pure vanilla extract

BLACKBERRY FILLING

- ¾ cup egg whites (about 6)
- 1½ cups granulated sugar
- ½ teaspoon cream of tartar
- 1½ cups seedless blackberry preserves, at room temperature
- 1 pint fresh or thawed blackberries, plus additional berries for garnish
- 2 tablespoons confectioners' sugar

1. MAKE THE CHOCOLATE CAKE: Preheat the oven to 350°. Coat two 9-by-2-inch round cake pans with vegetable-oil cooking spray and line the bottoms

Chocolate Buttermilk Cake with Blackberry Meringue

with parchment paper. Lightly spray the paper. In a large bowl, sift together the flour, granulated sugar, cocoa, baking soda and salt.

2. Pass the blackberries through a fine strainer set over a bowl; you should have 1 cup of puree. Whisk in the buttermilk, oil, vinegar and vanilla. Pour the blackberry mixture into the dry ingredients. Divide the batter evenly between the prepared pans and bake for about 40 minutes, or until the cakes pull away from the sides and the tops spring back when pressed. Let cool on a rack for 10 minutes; unmold and cool completely.

3. MAKE THE BLACKBERRY FILLING: In a large heatproof bowl set over a saucepan of simmering water, whisk the egg whites with the granulated sugar and cream of tartar until the sugar dissolves and the whites are hot to the touch, about 5 minutes. Transfer to a standing mixer and beat at high speed until the meringue cools to room temperature and is very thick, about 15 minutes. Stir the preserves until smooth; gently fold 1 cup into the meringue.

4. Using a serrated knife, split the cakes in half horizontally. Thinly spread the remaining 1/2 cup of preserves on three of the cut cake layers. Set one of the layers on a large plate, preserves-side up. Spread one-third of the meringue on top and press one-third of the blackberries into the meringue. Repeat with the two remaining preserves-spread cake layers and the remaining meringue and blackberries. Top with the final cake layer and let stand at room temperature for 1 to 3 hours. Just before serving, sift the confectioners' sugar over the top of the cake and garnish with the additional blackberries. *–John Fleer*

MAKE AHEAD Bake the cake a day in advance and keep at room temperature.

WINE Velvety chocolate cake begs for a sweet, spritzy wine, such as the 1996 Linden Vineyards Late Harvest Vidal.

Bittersweet Chocolate Bombes

MAKES 2 INDIVIDUAL BOMBES

If you like decadent chocolate cake with a runny center, cut the cooking time to about fifteen minutes.

>   3   ounces bittersweet chocolate, coarsely chopped
>   4   tablespoons unsalted butter
>   1   large egg
>   1   large egg yolk
>   1/3 cup granulated sugar
>   1/3 cup all-purpose flour
>   1   teaspoon confectioners' sugar

Fresh raspberries, for garnish (optional)

Mint leaves, for garnish (optional)

1. Preheat the oven to 350°. Butter two 1-cup ramekins and set on a small baking sheet. In a small saucepan, melt the chocolate and butter over low heat, stirring occasionally. Let cool completely.

2. In a medium bowl, combine the egg, egg yolk and granulated sugar. Set over a pan of simmering water; beat at high speed until thick and warm, about 4 minutes. Off the heat, beat until thick enough to form a slowly dissolving ribbon when a beater is lifted, about 2 minutes.

3. Fold the chocolate mixture into the egg mixture. Sift in the flour, gently folding it in. Divide the batter between the ramekins; bake for about 20 minutes, or until well risen and set around the sides but still soft in the center. Let cool for 2 minutes. Unmold each bombe onto a plate. Sift the confectioners' sugar on top, garnish with raspberries and mint leaves and serve. *–Jonathan Eismann*

Bittersweet Chocolate Bombes

Fifteen-Minute Magic

satiny smooth, scraping down the side as necessary, about 3 minutes. Add the amaretti mixture and the melted chocolate and pulse until blended.

4. Scrape the batter into the prepared pan. Bake in the middle of the oven for 25 to 30 minutes, or until the cake domes somewhat and the top is dry and slightly cracked. Let cool on a rack for 10 minutes. Run a blunt knife between the cake and pan and unmold; peel off the waxed paper and let cool right-side up on the rack.

5. Dust the top of the cake with the confectioners' sugar and cocoa. Serve at room temperature. *–Dorie Greenspan*

MAKE AHEAD The cake can be made through Step 4, wrapped airtight and kept at room temperature for three days or frozen for up to one month.

WINE A Tawny Porto, such as the Sandeman 20 Year Old, or an Italian Vin Santo, such as the 1989 Badia a Coltibuono

Almond Cake with Citrus Syrup

MAKES ONE 9-INCH CAKE

Warm lemony syrup is poured over this Spanish cake, making it moist and fragrant. The recipe is an adaptation of an almond and orange Passover cake from *The Book of Jewish Food* (Knopf) by Claudia Roden.

CITRUS SYRUP

- ⅓ cup sugar
- ¼ cup fresh lemon juice
- Finely grated zest of 1 large lemon
- ½ cup water

CAKE

- 1 tablespoon oil, for the pan
- 2 tablespoons matzo meal
- 1 cup granulated sugar
- 1 cup ground almonds (4 ounces)
- ½ cup finely chopped almonds (2¾ ounces)
- Finely grated zest of 1 large lemon
- 8 large eggs, separated
- Confectioners' sugar (optional)

Fifteen-Minute Magic

MAKES ONE 8-INCH CAKE

In this rich cake, a flavorful blend of amaretti and blanched almonds replaces the usual flour. Made in a food processor, the batter takes no more than fifteen minutes to put together. Serve the cake with whipped cream or vanilla ice cream.

- 3 ounces bittersweet chocolate, chopped
- 1 ounce unsweetened chocolate, chopped
- 6 large double amaretti
- ¾ cup blanched slivered almonds
- 1 stick (4 ounces) unsalted butter
- ½ cup granulated sugar
- 3 large eggs, at room temperature
- 1 teaspoon each confectioners' sugar and unsweetened cocoa powder, for dusting

I. Preheat the oven to 350°. Butter an 8-inch round cake pan; line the bottom with waxed paper and butter the paper. Dust the pan with flour, tapping out the excess. Melt the chocolates together in a bowl, either over a pot of simmering water or in a microwave oven.

2. In a food processor, pulse the amaretti with the almonds until evenly ground. Transfer to a sheet of waxed paper.

3. Add the butter, granulated sugar and eggs to the processor and cream until

Almond Cake with Citrus Syrup

I. MAKE THE CITRUS SYRUP: In a small stainless-steel saucepan, combine the sugar, lemon juice and zest with the water. Bring to a boil over moderate heat, stirring to dissolve the sugar. Simmer over moderately low heat for 2 minutes. Remove from the heat; let steep.

2. MAKE THE CAKE: Preheat the oven to 325°. Oil the bottom and side of a 9-by-3-inch springform pan and line the bottom with parchment paper; oil the paper. Evenly coat the bottom and sides with the matzo meal, tapping out any excess. Refrigerate the pan.

3. In a large bowl, using a wooden spoon, mix together the granulated sugar, almonds, lemon zest and egg yolks.

4. In a large bowl, preferably copper, whisk the egg whites until they form stiff peaks. Stir one quarter of the whites into the almond mixture to lighten it. Using a large rubber spatula, gently fold in the remaining whites in three additions.

5. Pour the mixture in the prepared pan. Bake on the lowest shelf of the oven for about 1 hour, or until golden and a toothpick inserted in the center comes out dry. Let cool 10 minutes. Run a knife around the cake edge, remove the pan side and invert onto a wire rack. Peel off the parchment and let cool to room temperature.

6. Reheat and strain the syrup. Transfer the cake to a plate and prick all over with a fork. Pour the syrup evenly over the cake and set aside at room temperature for at least 3 hours or overnight. Sift confectioners' sugar over the cake, if desired, and serve. *–Peter Hoffman*

Almond and Carrot Cake

Almond and Carrot Cake

MAKES ONE 10-INCH CAKE

The minute amount of oil in almonds supplies some of the shortening for this cake. Buy very fresh shelled almonds with their skins on. The skins are important because they deepen the flavor as well as the color of the cake. Flour and a little additional shortening come from ladyfingers, *savoiardi* as they are called in Italy. You can find them in supermarkets and in Italian food shops. The domestic supermarket variety is moister than those imported from Italy. If you are using moist ladyfingers, crisp them in a 325° oven for twenty minutes before grinding them. To section the oranges, peel them with a sharp knife, removing all of the bitter white pith. Cut in between the membranes to release the sections.

- 1 tablespoon butter
- 1¾ cups whole almonds with skins (9 ounces)
- 1 cup plus 2 tablespoons sugar
- 4 ounces ladyfingers
- 9 ounces carrots, peeled and cut into 1-inch pieces
- 1 tablespoon amaretto liqueur
- 2½ teaspoons baking powder
- 4 large eggs, separated
- ¼ teaspoon salt
- Fresh orange sections
- Sweetened whipped cream, for serving

I. Preheat the oven to 350°. Grease the bottom of a 10-inch springform pan with the butter.

2. Combine the almonds and sugar in a food processor and process until the nuts are finely ground. Transfer to a large bowl.

3. Coarsely crumble the ladyfingers into the processor and grind until very fine; add to the bowl. Process the carrots until very fine and add them to the bowl. Mix in the amaretto and baking powder, then blend in the egg yolks.

4. In another bowl, beat the egg whites with the salt until stiff peaks form. Mix 2 tablespoons of the beaten whites into the almond and carrot mixture to lighten it, then fold in the remaining whites.

5. Pour the batter into the prepared pan and bake on the top shelf of the oven for 50 to 60 minutes, or until a toothpick inserted in the center of the cake comes out clean. Transfer to a rack and let cool to lukewarm. Remove the cake from the pan. Garnish the top with orange sections. Serve the cake with whipped cream. —*Marcella Hazan*

MAKE AHEAD The ungarnished cake can be wrapped in aluminum foil and kept at room temperature up to five days.

WINE This dense, sweet and nutty cake is perfect for showcasing a honey-rich late-harvest dessert wine, such as the 1994 Dolce from California, or a classic Sauternes from Bordeaux, such as the 1990 Château Rieussec.

Sableuse and Wild-Berry Compote

MAKES ONE 8-INCH CAKE

You may never make pound cake again after tasting this wonderful buttery yellow cake. It's unusual not only in the proportions of ingredients but also in the mixing method and the inclusion of cornstarch. Take special care folding in the last addition of butter.

- 9 large egg yolks, at room temperature
- 1 large whole egg, at room temperature
- ⅔ cup sugar
- ⅔ cup all-purpose flour
- ⅔ cup cornstarch
- 1 stick plus 6 tablespoons (7 ounces) unsalted butter, melted and cooled

Wild-Berry Compote (recipe follows)

1. Preheat the oven to 350°. Butter an 8-inch square cake pan and line the bottom with parchment or waxed paper. Butter the paper.

2. In a standing electric mixer fitted with a whisk, beat the egg yolks with the whole egg and sugar at medium speed until pale yellow, light and fluffy, about 15 minutes.

3. Sift together the flour and the cornstarch. Gradually beat the flour mixture into the egg mixture on low speed, by the handful, adding more only when the previous handful has been absorbed. Increase the speed to medium and pour in the melted butter in three batches. Before the last addition of butter is completely incorporated into the batter, turn off the machine and fold with a large rubber spatula using gentle, circular motions until just combined.

4. Scrape the batter into the prepared pan. Using two sheets of aluminum foil, wrap the pan completely top and bottom. Fold the foil loosely at the top to allow room for expansion. Bake in the center of the oven for 40 minutes, or until the cake has risen and springs back when lightly pressed. Immediately unmold the cake onto a plate, peel off the parchment paper and turn the cake right-side up. Cool to room temperature. Serve with the compote.

WILD-BERRY COMPOTE

MAKES ABOUT 3 CUPS

The compote, like the cake, is best eaten the day it is made. Get hold of some wild berries if you can, but this is a good recipe for any berry.

- 1 cup sugar
- 6 tablespoons unsalted butter
- 1 cup water
- 4 cups mixed wild berries, such as huckleberries, currants, raspberries and blueberries

In a medium stainless-steel saucepan, combine the sugar, butter and water. Boil over moderately high heat until reduced to a thick, clear syrup, about 15 minutes. Gently stir in the berries and cook until they start to break up,

about 2 minutes. Pour the berry compote into a bowl; let cool to room temperature. —*Jean-Georges Vongerichten*

WINE 1996 Paolo Saracco Moscato d'Asti. This bright, slightly sparkling wine is low in alcohol and big on apricot and peach flavors.

Stephanie's Poppy Cake

MAKES ONE 8-INCH CAKE

This cake begins with two eight-inch round layers that are split in half horizontally and given a light soaking with a rum-flavored syrup; it's a nice French touch that keeps the cake moist and adds a subtle extra flavor. You will need a handheld or standing electric mixer.

CAKE

- 6 eggs, separated, at room temperature
- 1 cup plus 3 tablespoons granulated sugar
- 3 tablespoons poppy seeds
- 1 tablespoon pure vanilla extract
- 1 cup plus 2 tablespoons plain unbleached cake flour
- 6 tablespoons unsalted butter, melted and cooled

RUM SYRUP

- 2 tablespoons granulated sugar
- 6 tablespoons hot water
- 1½ tablespoons rum, or 2½ teaspoons pure vanilla extract

LEMON CURD

- 6 tablespoons unsalted butter
- 1⅔ cups granulated sugar
- 2 whole eggs
- 2 egg yolks

Grated zest of 1 lemon

- ¼ cup strained fresh lemon juice
- 1 tablespoon light or dark rum (optional)

LEMON BUTTER ICING

- 1½ sticks (6 ounces) unsalted butter, at room temperature
- 3 cups sifted confectioners' sugar
- ⅓ cup of the lemon curd

Poppy seeds, for sprinkling

I. MAKE THE CAKE: Preheat the oven to 350°. Butter two 8-inch round cake pans and line the bottoms with rounds of parchment or waxed paper. Butter the paper and flour the pans, tapping out the excess.

2. In a large bowl, beat the egg yolks. Gradually add the 1 cup of granulated sugar and beat until the mixture is as thick as mayonnaise. Beat in the poppy seeds and vanilla.

3. In another large bowl, using clean beaters, beat the egg whites at high speed for 6 seconds. Reduce the speed to moderately low and continue beating, gradually working your way back up to high speed. When soft peaks form, sprinkle in the remaining 3 tablespoons of granulated sugar and beat to stiff shining peaks.

4. Scoop one quarter of the whites into the yolk mixture and rapidly but delicately fold them in. Sift one third of the flour over the batter and fold it in along with one-third of the egg whites. Continue to fold in one third of the flour and one third of the egg whites at a time until everything has been incorporated; fold in the melted butter with the last of the egg whites.

5. Immediately turn the batter into the prepared pans. Bang the pans once lightly on your work surface to force any air bubbles out of the batter. Bake in the lower third of the oven for 20 to 25 minutes; the cakes are done when they just begin to shrink from the pans. Let the cakes cool on a rack for 30 minutes. Invert the cakes, peel off the paper and let cool completely.

6. MAKE THE RUM SYRUP: In a small saucepan, combine all of the ingredients and stir over low heat until the granulated sugar is completely dissolved.

7. MAKE THE LEMON CURD: In a medium stainless-steel saucepan, whisk all of the ingredients over very low heat until the bubbles begin to subside and a tiny wisp of steam appears; do not boil. Stir the curd over ice until cooled and lightly thickened.

8. MAKE THE LEMON BUTTER ICING: In a medium bowl, beat the butter until softened, then beat in the confectioners' sugar until light and fluffy. Beat in 1/3 cup of the cooled lemon curd until smooth.

Making Stephanie's Poppy Cake: slicing one of the layers in half horizontally, TOP RIGHT; spooning on the lemon curd, MIDDLE; frosting the cake, BOTTOM; and the finished cake, decorated with piped icing and poppy seeds, BELOW.

9. Cut a ¼-inch wedge out of the side of each cake; this will enable you to line up the layers when assembling the cake. Using a long serrated knife, slice each cake in half horizontally and set on a work surface, cut-side up.

10. Gently brush each cake layer with 2 tablespoons of the rum syrup. Center a bottom layer of cake on a platter and spread one third of the remaining lemon curd over it. Cover with the top layer, cut-sides together, taking care to line up the wedges. Spread the top with lemon curd. Repeat with the remaining cake and curd, ending with a cake layer.

11. Spread a very thin layer of the icing over the top and side of the cake to keep wandering crumbs in place. Then spread a ¼-inch layer of icing over the top and side. Decorate as you wish, but I suggest using a pastry bag fitted with a star tip. In any case, sprinkling the cake with poppy seeds can disguise certain ineptitudes.   –*Julia Child*

MAKE AHEAD Refrigerate the cake, uncovered, to firm up the icing. Then wrap in plastic and refrigerate for up to three days or freeze for up to one month. Either way, allow the cake to come to room temperature before serving.

Mini Poppy-Seed Pound Cakes

MAKES 5 DOZEN CAKES

CAKES

½   cup heavy cream
¾   cup light brown sugar
2   large eggs
1   teaspoon pure vanilla extract
1   cup all-purpose flour
⅓   cup poppy seeds (1½ ounces)
1   teaspoon baking powder
½   teaspoon salt

FROSTING

2   ounces cream cheese, softened
1   tablespoon heavy cream
½   teaspoon pure vanilla extract
½   cup confectioners' sugar

1. **MAKE THE CAKES:** Preheat the oven to 350°. Butter and flour mini-muffin pans. Whip the cream until it holds a peak. Using an electric mixer, beat the brown sugar and eggs until blended. Beat in the vanilla. Add the flour, poppy seeds, baking powder and salt and mix until just incorporated. Fold in the whipped cream.

2. Spoon the batter into the muffin pans, filling them three-quarters full. Bake for 8 to 10 minutes, or until the cakes spring back when gently pressed. Let cool in the pan for 1 to 2 minutes, then turn them out onto a wire rack to cool completely.

3. **MAKE THE FROSTING:** In a bowl, combine the first three ingredients. Blend with a fork until smooth. Add the confectioners' sugar; mix well. Frost the cakes with a small knife. –*Larry Hayden*

MAKE AHEAD Store the cakes in an airtight container for up to two days.

WINE Tokaji from Hungary has a distinct tart butterscotch note that echoes the tangy cream-cheese frosting. Try the 1991 Royal Tokaji Wine Company Aszú 5 Puttonyos or the 1992 Disznókó Tokaji Aszú 5 Puttonyos.

Torta di Riso

MAKES ONE 12-BY-8-INCH CAKE

2¼   cups milk
1⅔   cups water
Strips of zest from ½ orange
Strips of zest from ½ lemon
⅔   cup arborio rice
Unsalted butter and plain dry bread crumbs, for the baking dish
1⅓   cups ricotta cheese (about 10½ ounces)
3   large whole eggs, lightly beaten
3   large egg yolks, lightly beaten
½   cup granulated sugar
⅓   cup heavy cream
¼   cup all-purpose flour
3   tablespoons Sambuca
2¼   teaspoons baking soda
1½   teaspoons pure vanilla extract
Confectioners' sugar, for dusting

1. In a medium heavy saucepan, combine the milk with the water and the zest. Bring to a boil over moderate heat. Stir in the rice. Simmer over low heat, stirring occasionally, until tender, about 30 minutes. Let cool and remove the zests.

2. Meanwhile, preheat the oven to 375°. Generously butter a 12-by-8-inch glass baking dish and coat with bread crumbs.

3. In a medium bowl, gently whisk together all the remaining ingredients except the confectioners' sugar. Stir in the rice mixture and transfer to the prepared baking dish; spread it evenly. Bake the cake for 45 minutes, or until it is golden brown and set. Let cool 1 hour. Dust the cake lightly with confectioners' sugar and serve warm, at room temperature or chilled, cut into squares. –*Egi Maccione*

Pumpkin Caramel Pudding Cakes

MAKES 20 CAKES

If you like, serve these cakes with candied ginger ice cream. To make your own easily, fold finely chopped candied ginger into slightly softened top-quality vanilla ice cream. Or accompany with whipped cream and garnish with candied ginger.

CARAMEL

1⅔   cups sugar
¾   cup light corn syrup
2   tablespoons water
1   cup heavy cream
1   stick (4 ounces) unsalted butter, cut into pieces

PUDDING CAKES

Three 15-ounce cans unsweetened pumpkin puree
6   large eggs, separated
6   tablespoons unsalted butter, melted
2   teaspoons finely grated orange zest
1½   cups cake flour
2   tablespoons baking powder
¾   teaspoon cinnamon
¾   teaspoon freshly grated nutmeg
¾   teaspoon salt
¼   cup plus 2 tablespoons sugar

I. MAKE THE CARAMEL: In a small saucepan, combine the sugar, corn syrup and water. Simmer over moderate heat, stirring once or twice, until a deep amber caramel forms, about 15 minutes. Add the cream and butter and stir over moderate heat until the caramel is smooth, about 3 minutes. Pour the caramel into a heatproof bowl and set aside to cool.

2. MAKE THE PUDDING CAKES: Preheat the oven to 375°. Arrange two racks in the center part of the oven. Butter and sugar twenty 1/2-cup ramekins and place on two large baking sheets.

3. In a food processor, combine the caramel with the pumpkin puree, egg yolks, melted butter and orange zest. Process until smooth; transfer to a large bowl.

4. In another large bowl, sift the cake flour with the baking powder, cinnamon, nutmeg and salt. Whisk to combine. Fold the flour into the pumpkin-caramel mixture until blended.

5. In a large stainless steel bowl, beat the egg whites until soft peaks form.

Add the sugar and beat until firm peaks form. Gently fold the egg whites into the pumpkin batter until only a few streaks of white remain. Spoon a rounded 1/2 cup of the batter into each prepared ramekin. Bake for about 30 minutes, until the cakes are risen and set. Carefully unmold the hot cakes onto dessert plates and serve at once.   —*Lydia Shire*

MAKE AHEAD The pumpkin caramel cakes can be baked and refrigerated for up to one day in their ramekins. Reheat the cakes in a 400° oven for about ten minutes, or until warmed through; then unmold and serve immediately.

Pumpkin-Seed Cupcakes

MAKES 12 CUPCAKES

Serve these moist cupcakes slathered with cream-cheese frosting and covered in a riot of crunchy toasted pumpkin and sunflower seeds. The same batter can be baked in an eight-inch round cake pan as an impressive dessert, or in a ten-by-four-inch loaf pan as a lovely gift. If you prefer an unfrosted cake, generously sprinkle the batter with the raw seeds before baking; the seeds will toast into a delicious topping.

CUPCAKES

- 1 cup raw pumpkin seeds (about 5 ounces)
- 1 cup raw sunflower seeds (about 5 ounces)
- 1 2/3 cups all-purpose flour
- 1 1/2 teaspoons ginger
- 1 teaspoon cinnamon
- 3/4 teaspoon salt
- 1/2 teaspoon baking soda
- 1/2 teaspoon baking powder
- 1/2 teaspoon nutmeg
- 1/4 teaspoon ground cloves
- 1 1/2 cups granulated sugar
- 1/2 cup vegetable oil
- 2 large eggs, lightly beaten
- 1 scant cup canned pumpkin puree
- 1/3 cup warm water

FROSTING

- 6 ounces cream cheese, softened
- 6 tablespoons unsalted butter, softened
- 3/4 cup confectioners' sugar
- 1 teaspoon pure vanilla extract

I. MAKE THE CUPCAKES: Preheat the oven to 350°. Toast the pumpkin and sunflower seeds on a large rimmed baking sheet for about 12 minutes, stirring once or twice, until light golden. Let cool, then transfer to a small bowl.

2. Lightly oil a 12-cup muffin tin. In a medium bowl, sift together the flour, ginger, cinnamon, salt, baking soda, baking powder, nutmeg and cloves; stir with a whisk to combine. In another medium bowl, using an electric mixer, beat the granulated sugar with the vegetable oil. Add the eggs and beat at high speed until the mixture lightens in color. Reduce the speed to low and beat in the pumpkin puree and water.

3. Whisk the pumpkin mixture into the dry ingredients, scraping the bottom of the bowl to incorporate the flour. Spoon the batter into the prepared muffin cups

Pumpkin Caramel Pudding Cakes

Pumpkin-Seed Cupcakes

and bake for about 25 minutes, or until a toothpick inserted in the center comes out clean. Let cool in the pan for 10 minutes and then transfer the cupcakes to a rack to cool completely.

4. MAKE THE FROSTING: Meanwhile, beat the cream cheese with the butter until smooth. Beat in the confectioners' sugar and vanilla. Spread the frosting on the cupcakes with a small metal spatula or a knife. Roll the cupcakes in the toasted seeds to coat the top and then serve.   *–Peggy Cullen*

Chocolate Pumpkin Brownies

MAKES 24 BROWNIES

These marbled brownies combine the flavors of rich chocolate and spicy pumpkin. They have the perfect texture, falling somewhere between cakey and fudgy. Walnuts are optional; I like them, but some chocoholics say they interfere with the brownie.

PUMPKIN BATTER

1   tablespoon unsalted butter, softened

3   ounces cream cheese, softened

½   cup sugar

1   large egg

⅓   cup canned pumpkin puree

1 teaspoon pure vanilla extract

½ teaspoon cinnamon

½ teaspoon ginger

1 tablespoon all-purpose flour

CHOCOLATE BATTER

5½ ounces best-quality semisweet chocolate, finely chopped

1¼ sticks (5 ounces) unsalted butter, cut into 1-inch pieces

4 large eggs, at room temperature

1½ cups sugar

1 teaspoon pure vanilla extract

¼ teaspoon salt

1⅓ cups all-purpose flour

1 heaping cup large walnut pieces (about 4 ounces), optional

BELOW: Chocolate Pumpkin Brownies. BELOW RIGHT: Chocolate Ginger Crackles.

1. MAKE THE PUMPKIN BATTER: Preheat the oven to 350°. Lightly butter a 13-by-9-inch baking dish. In a small bowl, using an electric mixer, beat the butter with the cream cheese until smooth. Beat in the sugar, scraping the bowl occasionally. Beat in the egg and then add the pumpkin puree, vanilla, cinnamon and ginger. Stir in the flour.

2. MAKE THE CHOCOLATE BATTER: Combine the semisweet chocolate and butter in a medium heatproof bowl. Set the bowl over a saucepan with 1 inch of simmering water and stir occasionally until melted. In a large heatproof bowl, combine the eggs with the sugar, vanilla and salt; set the bowl over the saucepan of simmering water and, using an electric mixer, beat at low speed until blended. Increase the speed to medium and beat until the mixture is warm to the touch. Remove from the heat and continue to beat until the mixture is thick and fluffy, about 5 minutes. Using a large rubber spatula, fold in the melted chocolate. Sift the flour over the warm batter and fold it in just until combined. Fold in the walnut pieces, if using.

3. Spread the chocolate batter evenly in the prepared pan. Using a tablespoon, drop dollops of the pumpkin batter all over the top. Using the back of a butter knife, swirl the pumpkin into the chocolate; don't overdo it or the swirl pattern will be lost. Bake for about 50 minutes, or until a toothpick inserted in the center comes out clean. Let cool completely before cutting. *—Peggy Cullen*

Chocolate Ginger Crackles

MAKES ABOUT 2½ DOZEN

These moist cookies are known as crackles because as they bake the tops crack to form beautiful brown and white patterns.

1 cup granulated sugar

6 tablespoons unsalted butter, melted and slightly cooled

2 large eggs

¼ cup plus 2 tablespoons unsweetened cocoa powder

1 teaspoon pure vanilla extract

1 cup all-purpose flour

1 teaspoon baking powder

Pinch of salt

½ cup chocolate chips

⅓ cup minced candied ginger

½ cup confectioners' sugar

1. In a bowl, using an electric mixer, beat the granulated sugar with the butter. Mix in the eggs and then add the cocoa and vanilla; beat at medium speed until smooth and creamy. Scrape down the bowl and add the flour, baking powder and salt. Mix the dough for 2 minutes. Stir in the chocolate chips and ginger. Cover with plastic wrap and refrigerate at least 2 hours or overnight.

2. Preheat the oven to 350°. Line two baking sheets with parchment paper or aluminum foil. Form the dough into 1-inch balls and coat them generously with the confectioners' sugar. Arrange the balls 1 inch apart on the prepared baking sheets. Bake for about 12 minutes, or until the tops look cracked. Transfer to wire racks to cool.   *–Larry Hayden*

MAKE AHEAD Store in an airtight container for up to three days.

WINE Ruby Porto is one of the few sweet wines that work well with chocolate desserts–it contrasts with chocolate like a drizzle of raspberry sauce. Look for the Fonseca Bin 27 or the Sandeman Founders Reserve.

Gingerbread Cookies

6 DOZEN 3-INCH COOKIES

This old-fashioned cookie has a snappy molasses flavor. The dough is a little softer than sugar-cookie dough, so handle it gently when forming it into logs for chilling. When rolling it out, use plenty of flour on the work surface, but be sure to brush off any excess before transferring the cookies to the baking sheet. The cookies do not spread as they bake. Because the dough is chestnut brown, it can be difficult to see when the cookies are done. Here's the secret: When fully baked, the

edges will be very slightly darker and a finger pressed lightly in the center will not leave an impression. The cookies will be very crisp once they've cooled completely. For softer cookies, bake on black cookie sheets for about eight minutes.

4½ cups all-purpose flour

1 tablespoon plus 2 teaspoons ground ginger

1 tablespoon unsweetened cocoa powder

2 teaspoons cinnamon

1 teaspoon ground cloves

1 teaspoon baking soda

1 teaspoon salt

¼ teaspoon freshly grated nutmeg

1½ sticks (6 ounces) unsalted butter, softened

¾ cup firmly packed light brown sugar

1 large egg at room temperature, lightly beaten

1 cup unsulphured molasses

1. In a medium bowl, sift the flour with the ginger, cocoa, cinnamon, cloves, baking soda, salt and nutmeg; whisk to blend.

2. In a standing mixer fitted with the paddle or in a large bowl using a handheld mixer, cream the butter and brown sugar

Making Gingerbread Cookies: cutting the dough into shapes, ABOVE; the finished cookies, decorated with Royal Icing (p. 354), TOP.

until light and fluffy. Scrape down the bowl with a rubber spatula and beat for a few seconds more. Beat in the egg, then gradually beat in the molasses. Scrape down the bowl again and beat for a few more seconds. Beat in half the dry ingredients on low speed just until incorporated, then beat in the remainder. ➤

3. Scrape the dough onto a lightly floured work surface and form it into a log; divide the log into three even pieces. Flatten each piece to a ½-inch thickness and wrap well in plastic. Refrigerate until chilled, at least 3 hours.

4. Preheat the oven to 350°. On a well-floured surface, working with one piece at a time, roll out the dough ⅛ inch to ³⁄₁₆ inch thick. Brush off the excess flour. Cut the dough into shapes and transfer to ungreased cookie sheets. Bake the cookies in the center of the oven for about 10 minutes, or until they just begin to color. Let cool completely on a rack.

Frangipane Raspberry Squares

ROYAL ICING
MAKES ABOUT 2¼ CUPS

This icing is actually a thick meringue, made from egg whites and confectioner's sugar, that dries to an opaque enamel-like finish. Its brilliant white color makes it an excellent base for tinting; the pigments come through clear and true.

- 4 cups confectioners' sugar (about 1 pound), sifted, plus more if needed
- 3 egg whites

I. Combine 4 cups of the confectioners' sugar and the egg whites in a grease-free bowl. Using clean beaters, beat the whites on low speed. After 30 seconds, scrape down the bowl with a rubber spatula and gradually increase the speed to medium high. Beat until the icing is glossy and stiff peaks form when the beaters are lifted, 5 to 7 minutes.

2. If the icing is to be applied with a paint brush, stir in water, a few drops at a time, until the desired consistency is reached. If the icing is to be piped through a pastry bag fitted with a decorating tip, stiffen the icing by stirring in more confectioners' sugar. –*Peggy Cullen*

MAKE AHEAD The cookie dough can be refrigerated for up to five days or frozen for up to two months. The icing can be refrigerated, colored or not, in an airtight container for up to four days. Beat lightly with a fork before using.

Frangipane Raspberry Squares
MAKES ABOUT 4 DOZEN

The rich flavor of almonds and the sweet juiciness of raspberries make a delicious mouthful, but you can substitute blackberries or pineapple chunks.

PASTRY

- 6 tablespoons unsalted butter, cut into ½-inch pieces
- 2 tablespoons granulated sugar
- 1 large egg yolk
- 1 cup all-purpose flour

Pinch of salt

FILLING

- ¾ cup granulated sugar
- 1 stick (4 ounces) unsalted butter
- 3 large eggs
- ¼ cup all-purpose flour
- 1 teaspoon almond extract
- 1 cup blanched almonds, finely ground (5 ounces)
- 1½ cups fresh raspberries
- 2 tablespoons confectioners' sugar

I. MAKE THE PASTRY: Preheat the oven to 375°. Using an electric mixer, cream the butter and sugar. Add the egg yolk and mix well. Add the flour and salt. Mix on low speed until a dough forms; if it's dry, add 1 tablespoon water.

2. Press the dough evenly into a 9-inch square cake pan. Prick the dough with a fork and bake for 12 to 15 minutes, or until firm but not browned. Remove from the oven and set aside. Reduce the oven temperature to 350°.

3. MAKE THE FILLING: Using an electric mixer, cream together the sugar and the butter. Beat in the eggs. Add the flour and almond extract and beat just until blended. Stir in the almonds.

4. Distribute the berries over the pastry. Spread the filling evenly over the berries. Bake 40 to 50 minutes, or until the top is lightly browned and feels slightly firm to the touch. Cool in the pan for at least 30 minutes. Cut into 1¼-inch squares. Transfer to a rack and dust with the confectioners' sugar.   *–Larry Hayden*

Mexican Wedding Cookies

MAKES 16 COOKIES

    4 tablespoons unsalted butter, at
       room temperature
    2 tablespoons finely chopped pecans
    ¼ teaspoon pure vanilla extract
    ¾ cup confectioners' sugar
    ½ cup all-purpose flour
Pinch of salt

1. In a medium bowl, beat the butter, pecans and vanilla until creamy, about 1 minute. Beat in ⅓ cup of the confectioners' sugar. Sift in the flour and salt and mix well. Shape the dough into an 8-inch log, wrap in plastic and refrigerate until chilled, at least 1 hour or overnight.

2. Preheat the oven to 350° and line a large cookie sheet with parchment paper. Using a sharp knife, quarter the dough lengthwise, then cut the quarters crosswise into four equal slices. Roll each piece of dough into a ¾-inch ball and arrange about 1 inch apart on the cookie sheet. Bake for about 15 minutes, or until lightly golden. Let cool slightly.

3. In a large bowl, gently toss the cookies in the remaining confectioners' sugar. Let cool completely. *–Jonathan Eismann*

Lemon Cornmeal Madeleines

Lemon Cornmeal Madeleines

MAKES ABOUT 3 DOZEN

If you don't have a madeleine pan, bake these cakes in a mini-muffin pan.

    4 tablespoons unsalted butter, melted
    ½ cup all-purpose flour
    ½ cup cornmeal
    ½ cup sugar
Grated zest of 2 lemons
    1 teaspoon cream of tartar
    ½ teaspoon baking soda
Pinch of salt
    1 large egg
    ¼ cup plus 2 tablespoons heavy
       cream
    ½ teaspoon vanilla extract

1. Preheat the oven to 350°. Generously brush madeleine molds with some butter.

2. In a medium bowl, combine the flour, cornmeal, sugar, lemon zest, cream of tartar, baking soda and salt. In another bowl, slightly beat the egg. Whisk in the cream and vanilla, then add 2 tablespoons of the butter. Add the cream mixture to the dry ingredients and mix just until blended. Spoon the batter into the prepared molds, filling them halfway.

3. Bake for 10 to 12 minutes, or until the cakes spring back when pressed lightly. Cool briefly. Loosen the cakes with the point of a table knife and cool them on a rack.   *–Larry Hayden*

Hazelnut Praline Balls

MAKES ABOUT 3 DOZEN

These sandy cookies have ground hazelnut praline inside and out. You'll need a standing electric mixer to make them.

- 1 stick plus 2 tablespoons (5 ounces) unsalted butter, cut into ½-inch pieces and chilled
- ¼ cup packed dark brown sugar
- 1½ cups all-purpose flour
- ½ cup Hazelnut Praline (recipe follows), plus more for coating
- 1 teaspoon pure vanilla extract
- ½ teaspoon salt
- ½ teaspoon freshly grated nutmeg

1. Preheat the oven to 350°. Line one or two baking sheets with parchment paper.

2. In a standing electric mixer fitted with the paddle attachment, cream the butter with the brown sugar at medium-low speed. Add the flour, the ½ cup of praline, the vanilla, salt and nutmeg and beat until the mixture forms large crumbs. Roll the dough into 1-inch balls.

3. Arrange the balls 1 inch apart on the baking sheets and bake for about 20 minutes, or until the cookies are lightly browned and firm. While they are still warm, roll the tops of the cookies in praline; stir the praline occasionally to keep it from compacting. Cool on a rack.

HAZELNUT PRALINE

MAKES ABOUT 2 CUPS

This makes more than you'll need for the cookies; put the rest on ice cream.

- 1 cup granulated sugar
- 2 tablespoons water
- ¾ cup skinned hazelnuts (4 ounces)

Lightly oil a large baking sheet. In a small heavy saucepan, combine the sugar and water. Cook over high heat, stirring, until the sugar dissolves. When the mixture starts to boil, stop stirring and cook undisturbed until a light amber caramel forms. Add the nuts; stir to coat. Pour onto the baking sheet. Let cool until hard, at least 10 minutes. Break in small pieces and pulse in a food processor until ground to a fine powder. –Larry Hayden

WINE Praline's candylike scent and sugary flavor are much like an Asti Spumante's. Look for one of the sweeter examples, such as Gancia or Cinzano.

Clove and Lemon Butter Wafers

MAKES ABOUT 9 DOZEN **L**

- 5 tablespoons unsalted butter, softened
- ⅔ cup sugar
- 2½ teaspoons grated lemon zest
- ¾ cup unbleached all-purpose flour
- 1 large egg, at room temperature
- 3 tablespoons fresh lemon juice
- ¼ teaspoon pure vanilla extract
- ¼ teaspoon salt
- ¼ teaspoon ground cloves (scant)

1. Preheat the oven to 350°. Beat the butter with the sugar and lemon zest until light and fluffy. Beat in the flour, egg, lemon juice, vanilla, salt and cloves.

2. Lightly butter a cookie sheet. Drop scant teaspoons of the batter onto the sheet, 2 inches apart. Spread the batter with the back of a spoon to make 2-inch rounds. Bake in the middle of the oven for 12 minutes or until the edges start to brown. Cool on the sheet 1 minute to firm up. Use a metal spatula to transfer to a rack to cool. –Sally Schneider

Rosemary Tuiles

MAKES 3 DOZEN

To make cup-shaped tuiles for holding fruit or sorbet, spread the batter into three-inch rounds, bake and then cool over upside-down shot glasses.

- ¾ cup confectioners' sugar
- 3 large egg whites
- 7 tablespoons all-purpose flour
- 4 tablespoons unsalted butter, melted
- 2 teaspoons finely chopped rosemary

1. Preheat the oven to 400°. Butter 2 large heavy rimless baking sheets. In a medium bowl, mix the sugar and egg whites with a wooden spoon until blended. Stir in the flour and melted butter. Drop teaspoonfuls of batter on each baking sheet, spacing them 3 inches apart. Spread into thin 2-inch rounds using the back of a spoon. Sprinkle each cookie with a tiny pinch of rosemary.

2. Bake one sheet at a time for 4 to 6 minutes, or until the tuiles are golden around the edges. Using a metal spatula, quickly transfer to a rack to cool. If any harden on the baking sheet, return the sheet to the oven for about 1 minute to soften them. Wipe off the baking sheet; butter again between batches. –Apicius

WINE These herby cookies need a wine that's as aromatic as it is sweet. Try a lighter dessert wine, such as the 1995 La Famiglia de Robert Mondavi Malvasia Bianca from California or the 1995 Dr. Weins-Prüm Wehlener Sonnenuhr Riesling Auslese from Germany.

Macadamia and Dried-Cherry Biscotti

MAKES 2½ DOZEN

- 1 cup dried tart cherries (4 ounces)
- ½ cup kirsch or water
- 1 cup unsalted macadamia nuts (4 ounces)
- ¼ cup plus 2 teaspoons granulated sugar
- ¼ cup light brown sugar
- 6 tablespoons unsalted butter, softened
- 3 large egg whites
- 1 teaspoon pure vanilla extract
- 1½ cups all-purpose flour

1. In a small bowl, soak the dried cherries in the kirsch for 1 hour; drain.

2. Meanwhile, preheat the oven to 400°. Spread the nuts on a baking sheet and toast for about 5 minutes, stirring once, until golden brown. Let cool completely, then pulse the nuts in a food processor until coarsely chopped. Reduce the oven temperature to 325°. Line a baking sheet with parchment paper.

3. In a medium bowl, combine the ¼ cup of granulated sugar with the brown sugar. Add the butter and beat with an electric mixer until smooth. Beat in two of the egg whites and the vanilla until the mixture is creamy. Beat in the flour, then stir in the nuts and the drained cherries until evenly distributed; the dough will be soft and slightly sticky.

4. Working on a sheet of waxed paper, shape the dough into a 14-inch log. Roll the log onto the lined baking sheet. Beat the remaining egg white and brush it on the log. Sprinkle with the remaining 2 teaspoons of granulated sugar. Set the baking sheet on a second baking sheet and bake in the middle of the oven for about 1 hour, or until the log is golden and firm to the touch. Let cool on the baking sheet, about 3 hours or overnight.

5. Using a sharp serrated knife, carefully cut the log on a diagonal into ¼- to ⅓-inch-thick slices. Using a spatula, lay the slices on two baking sheets. Bake for 10 minutes, or until lightly colored. Gently turn and bake for 10 minutes more. Cool on the baking sheets. –*Larry Hayden*

WINE A Vin Santo from Tuscany, such as the 1991 Antinori or the 1988 Castello di Ama

Pistachio Biscotti

MAKES ABOUT 2 DOZEN

- 1 stick (4 ounces) unsalted butter, softened
- 1 cup (packed) light brown sugar
- 6 tablespoons granulated sugar
- 1 teaspoon vanilla extract
- ¾ teaspoon finely grated orange zest
- 1 large egg
- 1½ cups all-purpose flour
- ⅔ cup ground almonds (about 4 ounces)
- 1 teaspoon baking powder
- ½ teaspoon cinnamon
- ¼ teaspoon salt
- 1 cup shelled unsalted pistachios (about 5 ounces)

Macadamia and Dried-Cherry Biscotti

1. In a large bowl, using a wooden spoon, beat the butter with the sugars, vanilla and zest until creamy. Beat in the egg. Mix in the flour, almonds, baking powder, cinnamon and salt. Stir in the pistachios.

2. Form the dough into two 12-inch logs and wrap in waxed paper. Place on a small baking sheet and refrigerate until chilled, about 2 hours.

3. Preheat the oven to 325°. Line a large heavy baking sheet with parchment paper. Unwrap the logs and set them on the prepared baking sheet at least 3 inches apart. Bake for about 35 minutes, or until golden and dry to the touch. Let cool for about 30 minutes, then cut the logs on the diagonal into ¾-inch-thick slices. Line the baking sheet with fresh parchment and arrange the biscotti on the paper without touching each other. Bake for about 25 minutes, or until golden. Cool on a rack. –*Joachim Splichal*

MAKE AHEAD The logs can be refrigerated overnight or wrapped in aluminum foil and frozen for up to one month. Thaw before baking.

CHAPTER 18 tarts pies

Almond and Strawberry Tart (p. 362)

361   Strawberry Tart

361   Midsummer Fruit Tart

362   Almond and Strawberry Tart

364   Pear and Almond Tart

364   Pear and Hazelnut Tart

365   Caramel Apple Tart

366   Pumpkin and Apple Tart with Ginger

369   Citrus Custard Tarts with Caramelized Figs

369   Banana-Split Tart

370   Banana Tarts with Bittersweet Chocolate Sauce

371   Sweet Goat-Cheese and Walnut Tartlets

371   Pumpkin Cheesecake

372   Double-Decker Pumpkin Chiffon Pie

Strawberry Tart

Strawberry Tart

MAKES ONE 10-INCH TART

The pastry for this tart is painted with melted bittersweet chocolate. Serve the tart on its own or with whipped cream.

1½ cups all-purpose flour
¼ cup sugar
Pinch of salt
1½ sticks (6 ounces) cold unsalted butter, cut into ½-inch dice
1 large egg
1½ ounces bittersweet chocolate, melted
¼ cup seedless strawberry jam, melted
1½ pints fresh strawberries, hulled and halved lengthwise

I. In a food processor, pulse the flour, sugar and salt. Add the butter; pulse until the mixture resembles coarse meal. Add the egg; pulse until incorporated.

2. Preheat the oven to 375°. Butter a 10-inch tart pan with a removable bottom. Transfer the dough to a lightly floured surface and pat it into a disk. Roll between two sheets of waxed paper into a 12-inch round. Transfer to a baking sheet and refrigerate until firm, about 15 minutes. Peel off the top sheet of waxed paper, invert the dough into the pan and peel off the other sheet of waxed paper. Fit the dough into the pan; chill again for 10 minutes. Prick all over with a fork. Bake in the middle of the oven for about 20 minutes, or until evenly golden. Let cool on a rack.

3. Transfer the shell to a platter. Brush the bottom with the chocolate. Refrigerate until set, about 10 minutes. Brush half of the jam over the chocolate. Arrange the strawberries in the shell, cut-side down, overlapping slightly. Brush with the remaining jam. –*Katrin Theodoli*

WINE Champagne is often served with desserts based on strawberries because the Pinot Noir in the blend echoes the flavor of the berries. Pick a demi-sec, such as the Veuve Clicquot (look for the white label) or the Moët & Chandon.

Midsummer Fruit Tart

MAKES ONE 9-INCH TART

The tart base here consists of a cleverly constructed free-form crust that is baked with a thin layer of cheesecake filling. The crust is made from a rich cookie-like dough. In the 1960s, when quiche ruled supreme in kitchens across America, every ambitious cook had a quiche ring. You simply buttered the ring, set it on a buttered baking sheet and lined it with dough. Then quiche disappeared and so did the ring; if you happen to have one tucked in the back of a drawer, you could certainly use it here. If not, try my associate Stephanie's free-form solution. It seems a little fussy, I know, but it works admirably.

PASTRY

1½ cups unbleached all-purpose flour, plus more for dusting
½ cup cake flour, sifted
1 stick (4 ounces) cold unsalted butter, quartered lengthwise and crosswise
¼ teaspoon salt
1 tablespoon sugar
5 tablespoons cold vegetable shortening
1 large egg
1½ teaspoons pure vanilla extract

CHEESECAKE FILLING

4 ounces whipped cream cheese, at room temperature
2 tablespoons unsalted butter, softened
1 teaspoon cornstarch, sifted
2 tablespoons sugar
¼ cup sour cream, at room temperature
1 large egg
1½ teaspoons pure vanilla extract

FRUIT TOPPING AND APRICOT GLAZE:

1 cup apricot jam
3 tablespoons sugar
3 tablespoons white rum, cognac or orange liqueur (optional)

1 pint fresh strawberries, hulled and thickly sliced lengthwise
3 kiwis, peeled and sliced
½ cup fresh raspberries
½ cup fresh blackberries

I. MAKE THE PASTRY DOUGH: Measure the flours, butter and salt into the container of a food processor and turn on the machine for about 30 seconds to blend thoroughly. Add the sugar, shortening, egg and vanilla and process just until the dough masses together. On a lightly floured work surface, press the dough into a disk 1 inch thick, sprinkling on a little flour if the dough is sticky. Wrap in plastic; refrigerate for at least 1 hour, or until firm.

2. Set the dough on a lightly floured work surface and start beating it with your rolling pin, frequently rotating the dough as you gradually form a circular shape. When soft enough to roll, transfer the dough to a lightly floured 18-inch square of heavy-duty aluminum foil. Working rapidly so the dough remains cold, start rolling it out into a roughly circular shape $3/16$ inch thick; patch the dough in places as necessary. With a knife, trim the dough into a 12-inch round–you'll have a handful of leftover scraps to freeze for your next tart. Slide the dough on its foil onto a cookie sheet and freeze for 5 minutes.

3. Roll the edge of the dough up over itself to make a ¾-inch border. Then roll the border over onto itself, making an upstanding edge. With lightly floured fingers, pinch the thick, raised edge of the dough to form a rim ¾ inch tall and $3/16$ inch thick. Make the height even all around, since the filling will leak out at any low spots. Decorate the outside of the tart shell's rim by supporting the inside with your fingers as you press the outside with the tines of a table fork held vertically. Trim off any extra foil, cover the tart shell and freeze for at least 30 minutes. ➤

Midsummer Fruit Tart

Almond and Strawberry Tart

MAKES ONE 9½-INCH TART

Juicy ripe strawberries make a refreshing topping for a rich, buttery tart. If you hate to roll pastry, try this technique: Chill the dough and coarsely grate it into the tart pan, then pat it into the base and sides.

PASTRY

- 1⅔ cups all-purpose flour
- 1¼ sticks (5 ounces) cold unsalted butter, cut into ½-inch dice
- Pinch of salt
- ⅔ cup confectioners' sugar
- 2 large egg yolks

FILLING

- ½ pound whole blanched almonds
- ¾ cup superfine sugar
- 1½ sticks (6 ounces) unsalted butter, softened
- 2 large eggs, at room temperature
- 2 pints fresh strawberries, bottoms trimmed flat and berries quartered lengthwise
- 1½ tablespoons confectioners' sugar
- Crème fraîche, for serving

I. MAKE THE PASTRY: Preheat the oven to 350°. In a food processor, pulse the flour, butter and salt until the mixture resembles coarse bread crumbs. Pulse in the confectioners' sugar and then the egg yolks until incorporated and the pastry pulls away from the side of the bowl. Pat the pastry into a smooth round disk.

2. On a lightly floured surface, roll out the pastry to a 12-inch round. Transfer the round to a 9½-inch fluted tart pan with a removable bottom, fitting it into the side; trim the overhang. Line the pastry with aluminum foil and fill it with pie weights, dried beans or rice. Bake the tart shell for about 20 minutes, or until the edges are lightly colored. Remove the foil and the weights. Bake the tart shell for about 10 more minutes, or

4. MAKE THE CHEESECAKE FILLING: Preheat the oven to 350°. Using a handheld mixer, beat the cream cheese until it is smooth and fluffy, then cream in the butter. Slowly beat in the cornstarch, then the sugar, sour cream, egg and vanilla.

5. Prepare a folded strip of aluminum foil 1 inch wide and long enough to surround the tart shell with an inch extra. Butter the foil and pin the buttered side closely around the tart. Pour in the filling. Bake on the lower shelf of the oven for about 20 minutes, or until the shell is lightly browned and crisp. The filling will puff up to the top of the tart shell. Remove the tart to a rack; the filling will sink down. Let cool thoroughly to set the crust.

6. FINISH THE TART: Slide the tart onto a serving platter and remove the foil. Push the jam through a sieve into a 6-cup saucepan, stir in the sugar and rum and simmer over moderate heat for 2 minutes. Brush a thin layer of the glaze inside the tart. Arrange the strawberries in a circle around the inside edge. Overlap the kiwis inside and mound the berries in the center. Brush the warm glaze over the fruit and serve.   –*Julia Child*

WINE Nothing adds a grace note to a meal like a glass of chilled sweet wine with dessert. Here, the flavors of the berries and glaze harmonize well with sweet Rieslings, such as the 1995 Columbia Crest Reserve Ice Wine from Washington State or the 1994 Beringer Special Select Late Harvest from California.

until the pastry is dry and firm to the touch. Let the tart shell cool on a rack.

3. MAKE THE FILLING: In a food processor, pulse the almonds and ¼ cup of the superfine sugar until the nuts are finely ground. In a medium bowl, beat the butter with the remaining ½ cup of superfine sugar until the mixture is light and creamy. Add the butter mixture to the almonds and process until combined. Add the eggs to the almond mixture one at a time, processing until the mixture is smooth before putting in the next egg.

4. Spread the almond mixture in the tart shell. Bake the tart in the lower third of the oven for about 45 minutes, or until the top is golden. Let cool completely on a rack.

5. Remove the cooled tart from the pan. Transfer the tart to a large platter. Arrange the quartered strawberries upright on the tart and then sift the confectioners' sugar over the strawberries.

Serve the strawberry tart with crème fraîche. *–Ruth Rogers and Rose Gray*

MAKE AHEAD The tart can be made through Step 4 and left to stand at room temperature for up to six hours.

WINE Nonvintage Le Filigare Vin Santo. This Vin Santo has all the perfume and aroma of a classic Vin Santo without being too intense, making it a perfect spring wine. Other drier Vin Santos include the 1990 Selvapiana and the 1991 Isole e Olena.

Almond and Strawberry Tart

Pear and Almond Tart

MAKES ONE 11-INCH TART

Pears and almonds make an elegant combination in this adaptation of a tart from Lydie Marshall's *Chez Nous* (HarperCollins).

½ cup whole unskinned almonds

¼ cup sugar

Tart Shell (recipe follows)

2 pounds medium Bartlett pears—peeled, halved, cored, and each half cut into 4 wedges

½ cup orange marmalade, melted

1 cup sour cream

1. Preheat the oven to 450°. In a food processor, coarsely chop the almonds with 3 tablespoons of the sugar. Sprinkle half of the nut mixture in the Tart Shell.

2. Arrange the pear slices in overlapping concentric circles in the shell and brush them with the marmalade, reserving a scant tablespoon. Sprinkle the remaining nut mixture over the pears.

3. Reduce the oven temperature to 400°. Bake the tart in the bottom third of the oven for about 1 hour, or until the pears are tender and the pastry is golden. Transfer to a rack. Brush the pastry rim with the reserved marmalade. Let cool. Stir the remaining 1 tablespoon sugar into the sour cream and serve with the tart.

TART SHELL

MAKES ONE 11-INCH TART SHELL

1 stick (4 ounces) unsalted butter, cut into ½-inch bits

1 cup all-purpose flour

Pinch of salt

2 to 3 tablespoons ice water

1. Freeze the butter for 5 minutes. In a food processor, combine the flour, salt and butter and process for 10 seconds. Add 2 tablespoons of ice water and process for 10 more seconds; if necessary, add a little more water.

2. Mound the pastry on a work surface. Using the heel of your hand, push down and away on the bits of pastry to fully blend the flour and butter. Pat into a 6-inch disk, wrap in plastic and refrigerate for at least 15 minutes or overnight.

3. Preheat the oven to 400°. On a lightly floured surface, roll the pastry out to a 13-inch circle. Transfer the pastry to an 11-inch tart pan with a removable bottom, fitting the pastry evenly into the pan and trimming any overhang. Line the pastry shell with aluminum foil and fill with pie weights, dried beans or rice. Bake for 20 minutes, then remove the foil and weights and bake for 5 to 10 minutes longer, or until the pastry is lightly browned.   *–Mireille Giuliano*

Pear and Hazelnut Tart

To toast the hazelnuts, spread them in a pie plate and put them in a 400° oven for about eight minutes, or until fragrant and browned. Let cool. Rub the nuts together in a kitchen towel to remove the skins.

MAKES ONE 11½-INCH TART

PASTRY

2 cups all-purpose flour

½ cup hazelnuts, toasted (see above) and chopped

1 tablespoon cinnamon

½ teaspoon cloves

½ teaspoon allspice

2 sticks (½ pound) unsalted butter, diced and chilled

2 hard-cooked egg yolks, pressed through a strainer

1½ tablespoons finely grated lemon zest

¼ cup ice water

Pear and Almond Tart

FILLING

¾ cup granulated sugar

½ cup hazelnuts, toasted (see above) and chopped

2 tablespoons finely grated fresh ginger

5 Bosc pears—peeled, cored and cut into 1-inch dice

3 tablespoons all-purpose flour

THYME CREAM

1 cup heavy cream

½ cup confectioners' sugar

1½ teaspoons chopped thyme

I. MAKE THE PASTRY: In a food processor, combine the flour, hazelnuts, cinnamon, cloves and allspice and process until the nuts are finely ground. Add the butter, egg yolks and lemon zest and pulse until the mixture resembles coarse meal. Add the ice water and pulse just until the dough comes together. Scrape the dough onto a lightly floured work surface and knead briefly. Pat the dough into a disk, wrap in plastic and refrigerate until firm, about 1 hour.

2. Preheat the oven to 350°. Cut off a third of the dough and keep it refrigerated. On a lightly floured surface, roll out the remaining dough to a 13-inch round. Fold the dough in half and transfer it to an 11½-inch tart pan with a removable bottom. Unfold the dough and press it into the pan and up the side as evenly as possible. Refrigerate the shell.

3. On a lightly floured surface, roll out the remaining piece of dough to a 13-by-8-inch rectangle. Place the rectangle on a baking sheet and freeze until very firm. Using a pizza cutter or a sharp knife, cut the rectangle lengthwise into ten strips, cutting directly on the pan. Refreeze the strips until needed.

4. MAKE THE FILLING: In a food processor, combine ¼ cup of the granulated sugar with the hazelnuts and ginger and process to a coarse powder. In a large bowl, toss the pears with the remaining ½ cup of granulated sugar

Caramel Apple Tart

and the flour. Remove the tart shell from the refrigerator. Spread the hazelnut-and-ginger mixture over the bottom of the shell and top with the pears. Arrange the frozen dough strips over the filling in a lattice pattern.

5. Bake the tart in the center of the oven for about 1½ hours, or until the pastry is brown and the filling is bubbling. Let cool on a rack for at least 10 minutes.

6. MAKE THE THYME CREAM: Meanwhile, in a large bowl, whip the cream until soft peaks form. Add the confectioners' sugar and thyme. Beat until firm; don't overbeat. Serve the tart warm, with the whipped cream. –*Gordon Hamersley*

MAKE AHEAD The tart shell and lattice top can be frozen for up to a week.

Caramel Apple Tart

MAKES ONE 11-INCH TART

Caramel-coated apple slices bound with custard fill this deluxe deep-dish tart.

PASTRY

2¾ cups all-purpose flour

¾ teaspoon salt

2 sticks (½ pound) cold unsalted butter, cut into bits

⅓ cup ice water

2 tablespoons apple jelly, melted

FILLING

10 medium Golden Delicious apples

1¼ cups plus 3 tablespoons water

⅔ cup sugar

2 tablespoons unsalted butter

½ cup heavy cream

2 large eggs

1. MAKE THE PASTRY: In a food processor, pulse the flour and salt. Add the butter and pulse until it resembles coarse meal. Sprinkle in the water and pulse just until combined. Turn the dough out onto a lightly floured surface and shape into an 8-inch disk. Wrap in plastic; refrigerate until chilled, about 1 hour.

2. Preheat the oven to 400°. On a lightly floured surface, roll the dough to a 16-inch round about ⅜ inch thick. Transfer to an 11-inch fluted tart pan about 2 inches deep and trim any overhanging dough. Line the shell with aluminum foil; fill with pie weights, dried beans or rice. Bake about 30 minutes, or until lightly colored around the edge. Remove the foil and weights. Bake about 15 minutes longer, or until the base is dry and golden. Let cool. Brush the inside with the jelly.

3. MAKE THE FILLING: Peel, core and coarsely chop two of the apples and put them in a medium heavy saucepan. Add the 3 tablespoons of water, cover and cook over moderate heat until soft, about 10 minutes. Using a fork, mash the cooked apples to a puree.

4. Peel and core five of the apples and cut them into 1-inch chunks. In a large heavy saucepan, combine the sugar and ¼ cup of the water. Stir to dissolve the sugar, then bring to a boil and cook over moderately high heat until golden brown, about 8 minutes. Remove from the heat and carefully stir in the remaining 1 cup of water and the butter. Add the apple chunks, cover and cook over high heat until tender, 8 to 10 minutes. Strain the apples; return the syrup to the saucepan.

5. Peel, halve and core the remaining 3 apples. Cut each half lengthwise into eight slices. Add the slices to the syrup in the saucepan, cover and cook over high heat until tender, 3 to 5 minutes. Strain the apples and reserve the syrup separately; you should have about ¾ cup. In a small bowl, whisk the cream with ¼ cup of the reserved syrup. Whisk in the eggs.

6. Preheat the oven to 350°. Spoon the pureed apples into the tart shell. Spread the cooked apple chunks evenly on the puree. Arrange the apple slices in concentric circles on the puree and pour the custard over the top. Set the tart on a large baking sheet and bake for about 1 hour, or until the custard is set in the middle and the top is golden.

7. In a small saucepan, boil the remaining syrup over moderate heat until it is reduced to about ¼ cup. Drizzle the reduced syrup over the apple tart and serve warm.   —*The Frescobaldi family*

MAKE AHEAD The baked shell can stand overnight at room temperature.

WINE 1991 Frescobaldi Pomino Vin Santo or 1995 La Famiglia di Robert Mondavi Moscato Bianco. Vin Santo, Tuscany's "holy wine," is a late-harvest wine that is traditionally served with dessert. The long aging imparts honey-like, nutty qualities that pair brilliantly with the tart's apple and caramel flavors. With its aromas of orange blossoms, gardenias and ripe peaches, the effervescent Moscato Bianco captures the true character of the Muscat grape and is an excellent accompaniment to fruit-based desserts like the apple tart.

Pumpkin and Apple Tart with Ginger

MAKES ONE 11-INCH TART

This luscious dessert pairs two Thanksgiving favorites—pumpkin and apple—in a sophisticated tart spiked with fresh and ground ginger, allspice and black pepper. Serve it with whipped cream or vanilla ice cream.

PASTRY

- 1½ cups all-purpose flour
- 2 tablespoons sugar
- 1 teaspoon salt
- ½ teaspoon finely grated lemon zest
- 1 stick (4 ounces) plus 1 tablespoon unsalted butter, diced and chilled
- 4 to 5 tablespoons ice water

FILLING

- 3 large eggs
- 1 cup dark brown sugar
- 2 cups unsweetened pumpkin puree
- 1 cup heavy cream
- 2 tablespoons finely grated fresh ginger
- 2 tablespoons fresh lemon juice
- 2 teaspoons cinnamon
- 1 teaspoon salt
- 1 teaspoon pure vanilla extract
- ½ teaspoon ground ginger
- ½ teaspoon freshly ground pepper
- ¼ teaspoon ground allspice
- 2 Granny Smith apples— peeled, halved, cored and sliced ⅛ inch thick
- ¼ cup granulated sugar
- 2 tablespoons unsalted butter, melted
- 4 amaretti cookies, coarsely crumbled (about ⅓ cup)

1. MAKE THE PASTRY: In a food processor, combine the flour, sugar, salt and lemon zest; pulse to mix. Add the butter and pulse until it is in pea-size pieces. Transfer the dough to a lightly floured surface and drizzle on 4 tablespoons of the ice water; add more if the dough seems dry. Knead briefly to blend. Pat the dough into a disk, wrap in plastic and refrigerate until chilled, at least 1 hour.

2. Preheat the oven to 425°. On a lightly floured surface, roll the dough into a 15-inch round. Fit the dough into an 11-inch tart pan with a removable bottom; without stretching the dough, press it into the side. Trim the overhang to ½ inch and fold it in to reinforce the side.

3. Line the shell with aluminum foil and fill with pie weights, dried beans or rice. Set the pan on a baking sheet and bake for about 25 minutes, or until the side of the pastry is lightly colored. Remove the foil and weights and bake for about 5 minutes, or until the base of the shell is golden. Transfer to a rack to cool. Reduce the oven temperature to 400°. ➤

FROM TOP: Pear and Hazelnut Tart (p. 364), Pumpkin and Apple Tart with Ginger, and Pumpkin Caramel Pudding Cake (p. 349)

Citrus Custard Tarts with Caramalized Figs

4. MAKE THE FILLING: In a large bowl, using an electric mixer, beat the eggs with the brown sugar until light, about 2 minutes. Add the pumpkin puree, cream, fresh ginger, 1½ tablespoons of the lemon juice, 1½ teaspoons of the cinnamon, the salt, vanilla, ground ginger, pepper and allspice. Beat until thoroughly blended.

5. In a bowl, toss the apples with the granulated sugar, the butter and the remaining ½ tablespoon lemon juice and ½ teaspoon cinnamon.

6. Pour the filling into the cooled tart shell. Starting at the outside, overlap the apple slices in concentric circles over the filling. Bake for about 1 hour, or until the apples are tender and golden and the custard is set in the center. Let cool completely, then sprinkle with the amaretti crumbs.   *–Jody Adams*

Citrus Custard Tarts with Caramelized Figs

MAKES EIGHT 4½-INCH TARTS
Buttery citrus custard, made with lemon, grapefruit and orange juices and zests, fills elegant individual tart shells. The tarts should be refrigerated overnight before serving to firm up the custard.

PASTRY

2½ cups all-purpose flour
2 teaspoons sugar
¾ teaspoon salt
2 sticks (½ pound) cold unsalted butter, cut into ½-inch pieces
1 teaspoon finely grated lemon zest
¼ cup plus 3 tablespoons cold skim milk

FILLING

½ cup fresh lemon juice
¼ cup fresh grapefruit juice
¼ cup fresh orange juice
3 large eggs
1 cup sugar
4 tablespoons unsalted butter, cut into pieces
½ tablespoon finely grated lemon zest

½ tablespoon finely grated grapefruit zest
½ tablespoon finely grated orange zest
12 ripe fresh figs, preferably green and purple, cut into thin wedges
½ cup water

I. MAKE THE PASTRY: In a food processor, pulse together the flour, sugar and salt. Add the butter and lemon zest and pulse until the mixture resembles coarse meal. Add the milk and pulse just until combined. Transfer the dough to a lightly floured work surface and gently knead until smooth. Divide the dough in half and pat each half into a smooth disk. Wrap in plastic and refrigerate until chilled, about 1 hour.

2. Arrange eight 4½-inch fluted tart pans with removable bottoms on a baking sheet. Divide one disk of dough into four equal pieces and roll each piece out to a 6½-inch round. Fit each round into a tart pan, pressing it into the side, and trim the overhang. Repeat with the remaining dough and tart pans. Refrigerate the tart shells for 30 minutes.

3. Preheat the oven to 375°. Line each shell with aluminum foil and fill with pie weights, dried beans or rice. Bake about 25 minutes, or until the edges are lightly golden. Remove the foil and weights and bake about 7 minutes longer, or until the pastry bottoms are golden. Let cool.

4. MAKE THE FILLING: In a double boiler or heatproof bowl set over a saucepan of simmering water, whisk the citrus juices together with the eggs and ½ cup of the sugar until blended. Cook, stirring constantly with a wooden spoon, until the custard is smooth and thick, 10 to 12 minutes; do not let it boil. Remove from the heat. Stir in the butter.

5. Strain the custard into a bowl and stir in the citrus zests. Divide the custard among the tart shells and let cool completely. Cover with a sheet of waxed paper and refrigerate overnight.

6. Remove the tarts from the pans; arrange the figs on top. In a small saucepan, cook the remaining ½ cup of sugar with the water over moderate heat, stirring occasionally, until the sugar is dissolved and the syrup slightly thickened, about 5 minutes; let cool. Brush the syrup over the figs.   *–Rori Spinelli*

WINE Serve a luscious dessert wine with a ripe but tart flavor of its own, such as the 1994 Far Niente Dolce from California or the 1990 Château Guiraud Sauternes from France.

Banana-Split Tart

MAKES ONE 8-INCH TART **Q**

1¼ cups vanilla-cookie crumbs
1 teaspoon cinnamon
6 tablespoons unsalted butter, 5 of them melted
½ cup sugar
½ cup water
1 cup semisweet chocolate chips
1 teaspoon pure vanilla extract
½ cup sweetened coconut flakes
¼ cup sliced almonds
1 pint vanilla ice cream
1½ large ripe bananas, thinly sliced

I. Preheat the oven to 350°. In a bowl, combine the cookie crumbs and cinnamon. Stir in the melted butter. Press into an 8-inch pie plate and bake for about 6 minutes, until golden. Let cool.

2. In a small saucepan, combine the sugar with the water and boil for 1 minute. Off the heat, stir in the chocolate and the remaining 1 tablespoon of butter until melted. Stir in the vanilla and cool.

3. On a baking sheet, toast the coconut and almonds for about 5 minutes, or until golden. Scoop the ice cream into the pie shell and drizzle on some of the chocolate sauce. Pool some of the sauce around the ice cream and top with the sliced bananas. Sprinkle with the coconut and almonds and drizzle a bit of the chocolate sauce over all. Chill in the freezer. ➤

4. Serve the tart with the remaining sauce on the side. If the crust sticks, set the pie plate on a towel moistened with very hot water and let sit for 30 seconds . —*Bob Chambers*

Banana Tarts with Bittersweet Chocolate Sauce

MAKES TEN 5-INCH TARTS

- ⅔ recipe Pâte Brisée (recipe follows)
- 10 ounces bittersweet chocolate, finely chopped
- ½ cup milk
- ¼ cup plus 2 tablespoons heavy cream
- ½ cup plus 2 tablespoons dark rum

Sweet Goat-Cheese and Walnut Tartlets

- 2 tablespoons granulated sugar
- 3½ pounds ripe bananas, sliced diagonally ⅓ inch thick
- 1 cup light brown sugar
- 6 tablespoons unsalted butter, softened
- 1 pint vanilla ice cream

I. Preheat the oven to 400°. On a lightly floured surface, roll out the Pâte Brisée ⅛ inch thick. Using a small saucer, cut out ten 5-inch rounds and arrange them on two baking sheets. Chill until firm, about 10 minutes. Prick the dough rounds all over with a fork and cover with aluminum foil. Set another baking

sheet on top and bake for 20 minutes. Remove the top baking sheets and the foil and bake for about 5 minutes longer, or until golden and crisp. Using a spatula, transfer the rounds to a rack to cool.

2. In a medium saucepan, melt the chocolate over low heat, stirring occasionally; remove from the heat. Meanwhile, in a small stainless-steel saucepan, combine the milk, cream, the 2 tablespoons rum and the granulated sugar and bring to a boil over moderately high heat. Whisk the hot milk mixture into the melted chocolate until smooth.

3. Preheat the broiler. Lightly butter two nonstick baking sheets and arrange the banana slices on them in a single layer, overlapping only if necessary. In a small stainless-steel saucepan, combine the brown sugar and butter and cook over moderately high heat, stirring occasionally, until bubbling, about 2 minutes. Add the remaining ½ cup of rum and carefully ignite it. Cook until the flame subsides, then remove from the heat. Brush the banana with two-thirds of the caramel and broil for about 2 minutes, shifting the pan once or twice, until browned and sizzling. Arrange the banana slices on the pastry rounds in a flower pattern.

4. Spoon the remaining caramel over the bananas and transfer the tartlets to dessert plates. Top with a scoop of ice cream; drizzle with the chocolate sauce.

PÂTE BRISÉE

MAKES ENOUGH DOUGH FOR
TEN 5-INCH TARTS, PLUS TWENTY-
FIVE 2-INCH PASTRY ROUNDS
FOR SWEET-ONION AND TOASTED-
WALNUT ROUNDS (P. 18)

- 3¾ cups all-purpose flour
- 1½ teaspoons salt
- 12 ounces (3 sticks) unsalted butter, cut into ½-inch pieces
- ¾ cup ice water

In a large bowl, combine the flour and salt. Using a pastry blender, cut in the butter until the mixture resembles small peas. If the dough becomes too warm, briefly refrigerate it. Add the ice water and stir until the dough comes together. Turn the dough out onto a work surface and pat it into a ball. Divide the dough into thirds and pat each third into a 6-inch disk. Cover each disk with plastic wrap and refrigerate for at least 1 hour or overnight.   *–Maria Helm*

WINE The delicate honey and apricot flavors of the 1993 Domaine de Coyeux Muscat de Beaumes de Venise complement the brown sugar and caramelized banana flavors of the tart.

Sweet Goat-Cheese and Walnut Tartlets

MAKES EIGHT 4½-INCH TARTLETS

PASTRY

 1 cup walnuts (about 4 ounces)
1½ cups all-purpose flour
 3 tablespoons sugar
Salt
 1 stick (4 ounces) chilled unsalted butter, cut into ½-inch pieces
 1 large egg yolk
 2 tablespoons ice water

CANDIED WALNUTS

 ¾ cup walnuts (about 3 ounces)
 2 tablespoons sugar
 1 teaspoon unsalted butter

FILLING

 ½ pound cream cheese
 6 ounces mild, soft goat cheese, such as Montrachet
 ¼ cup sugar
 2 large eggs, lightly beaten
 2 teaspoons pure vanilla extract
 ¼ cup apricot or raspberry preserves, melted and strained

I. MAKE THE PASTRY: In a food processor, combine the walnuts, flour, sugar and a pinch of salt and pulse until finely ground. Add the butter and pulse until the mixture resembles coarse meal. In a small bowl, combine the egg yolk with the ice water, then add the

mixture to the processor and continue pulsing just until the dough forms a ball. Transfer the dough to a work surface and shape into a 12-inch log. Wrap in plastic and refrigerate for 30 minutes.

2. Preheat the oven to 375°. Cut the dough into eight equal pieces and flatten each piece slightly into a round. Using your fingers, press the dough into eight 4½-inch tartlet pans with removable bottoms; the pans should be about ¾ inch deep. Prick the bottoms a few times with a fork and bake the crusts directly on the oven rack for 15 to 18 minutes, or until golden and cooked through.

3. MAKE THE CANDIED WALNUTS: In a medium nonstick skillet, cook the nuts over moderately high heat, shaking the pan constantly, until toasted and fragrant, about 3 minutes. Add the sugar, lower the heat to moderate and cook, stirring constantly, until the sugar is melted and beginning to caramelize, about 2 minutes. Stir in the butter. Immediately transfer the walnuts to waxed paper or parchment paper. Let cool completely; break the clusters into smaller pieces.

4. MAKE THE FILLING: In a medium bowl, beat the cream cheese, goat cheese and sugar until smooth. Beat in the eggs and vanilla.

5. Preheat the oven to 350°. Brush the tartlet bottoms with half the preserves. Fill each tartlet with ¼ cup of the custard; smooth the tops. Set on a large baking sheet and bake in the lower third of the oven for about 15 minutes, or until the custard is just set. Transfer to a rack and let cool for 30 minutes. Brush with the remaining melted preserves and sprinkle with the candied walnuts. Serve warm or at room temperature.   *–Grace Parisi*

MAKE AHEAD Make the tartlets through Step 4 a day in advance. Let the shells stand at room temperature. Store the nuts in an airtight container. Refrigerate the custard; return to room temperature before baking.

Pumpkin Cheesecake

MAKES ONE 9½-INCH
CHEESECAKE

Here's a spin on the classic pumpkin pie: a luxurious pumpkin-flavored cheesecake. Don't be afraid to use unseasoned, unsweetened canned pumpkin here; the smooth texture and distinct but mellow flavor work just as well as fresh pumpkin puree.

 2 cups gingersnap crumbs (from about ½ pound cookies)
 ⅓ cup melted unsalted butter
Three 8-ounce packages cream cheese, softened
 1 cup granulated sugar
 ½ cup light brown sugar
 3 large eggs, lightly beaten
One 15-ounce can pumpkin puree
 ¼ cup heavy cream
 1 tablespoon pure vanilla extract
 1 teaspoon cinnamon
 1 teaspoon ginger
 ½ teaspoon freshly grated nutmeg
 2 cups sour cream, at room temperature

I. Preheat the oven to 350°. Butter a 9½- or 10-inch springform pan and coat lightly with flour. In a medium bowl, toss the gingersnap crumbs with the melted butter until evenly moistened. Press the crumbs into the bottom and 1 inch up the side of the prepared pan. Bake for about 12 minutes, or until the crust begins to color. Let the crust cool. Reduce the oven temperature to 325°.

2. In a large bowl, using an electric mixer, beat the cream cheese until smooth. Beat in ¾ cup of the granulated sugar and the brown sugar, then beat in the eggs in three additions until the mixture is thoroughly combined, scraping down the side of the bowl occasionally.

3. In a medium bowl, combine the pumpkin puree and heavy cream with 1 teaspoon of the vanilla and the cinnamon, ginger and nutmeg. Add the pumpkin

Pumpkin Cheesecake

mixture to the cream-cheese mixture. Beat until combined, scraping the bowl a few times.

4. Wrap aluminum foil loosely around the bottom and up the side of the springform pan. Pour the cheesecake batter into the prepared pan and set it in a large baking dish or roasting pan. Place in the middle of the oven and pour 1 inch of hot water into the baking dish. Bake the cheesecake for about 70 minutes, or until the edges are firm and the center of the cheesecake is still slightly shaky.

5. In a small bowl, combine the sour cream with the remaining ¼ cup granulated sugar and 2 teaspoons vanilla. Remove the pumpkin cheesecake from the water bath and pour on the sour-

cream mixture. Gently tap the pan to spread the sour-cream topping, and continue baking the cheesecake for 10 minutes more.

6. Transfer the cheesecake to a rack and let cool for 1 hour. Remove the foil and the side of the pan and refrigerate the cheesecake for at least 4 hours or overnight. If you like, remove the cheesecake from the bottom of the pan by sliding a metal spatula under the crust to loosen it completely, then use two large metal spatulas to transfer the cheesecake to a serving plate. Alternatively, you can serve the cheesecake on the pan bottom.   *—Peggy Cullen*

MAKE AHEAD The pumpkin cheesecake can be refrigerated for up to two days before serving.

Double-Decker Pumpkin Chiffon Pie

MAKES ONE 9-INCH PIE

This delectable two-tone dessert features the standard pumpkin-pie filling topped with a layer of fluffy pumpkin-flavored chiffon. Sweetened whipped cream completes the holiday picture.

PUMPKIN PIE

- 1 cup canned pumpkin puree
- ¼ cup granulated sugar
- ¼ cup light brown sugar
- ½ teaspoon cinnamon
- ½ teaspoon ginger
- ¼ teaspoon freshly grated nutmeg
- ¼ teaspoon ground allspice
- ¼ teaspoon unsweetened cocoa powder
- ¼ teaspoon salt
- 2 large eggs, lightly beaten
- ⅔ cup heavy cream
- 1 tablespoon molasses
- 1 teaspoon pure vanilla extract

Prebaked Pie Pastry (recipe follows)

PUMPKIN CHIFFON

- 1½ teaspoons unflavored powdered gelatin
- 2 tablespoons cold water
- 1 cup canned pumpkin puree
- ¼ cup light brown sugar
- ¼ teaspoon cinnamon
- ¼ teaspoon ginger
- ¼ teaspoon freshly grated nutmeg
- ⅛ teaspoon salt
- 2 large eggs, separated
- 2 teaspoons pure vanilla extract
- ½ cup heavy cream
- ⅓ cup plus 1½ tablespoons granulated sugar

I. MAKE THE PUMPKIN PIE: Preheat the oven to 350°. In a medium bowl, whisk the pumpkin puree with the granulated sugar, brown sugar, cinnamon, ginger, nutmeg, allspice, cocoa powder and salt. Whisk in the eggs, cream, molasses and vanilla. Pour the custard into the Prebaked Pie Pastry, spreading it evenly. Bake for 35 to 40 minutes, or until the surface is puffed, the edges are firm and the center is slightly shaky. Transfer to a rack and let cool completely.

2. MAKE THE PUMPKIN CHIFFON: In a small cup, sprinkle the gelatin over the cold water. In a medium saucepan, combine the pumpkin puree, brown sugar, cinnamon, ginger, nutmeg and salt. Put the egg whites in a clean medium bowl and cover with plastic wrap. Stir the egg yolks into the pumpkin mixture and bring just to a boil over moderately high heat, stirring gently. Whisk in the dissolved gelatin and the vanilla. Transfer to a bowl and let cool to room temperature.

3. In a medium bowl, beat the heavy cream with the 1½ tablespoons of granulated sugar until soft peaks form.

4. Whisk the remaining ⅓ cup of granulated sugar into the egg whites. Set the bowl over a saucepan with 1 inch of simmering water; using an electric mixer, beat the whites at low speed until warm to the touch. Remove from the heat and continue beating at high speed until the whites are glossy and hold semifirm peaks.

5. Fold the meringue into the pumpkin mixture just until incorporated. Fold in the whipped cream. Spoon the chiffon over the pumpkin pie and refrigerate until set, at least 1 hour and up to 6 hours.

PREBAKED PIE PASTRY

MAKES ONE 9-INCH PIE SHELL

- 1 cup plus 2 tablespoons all-purpose flour
- ¾ teaspoon sugar
- ¾ teaspoon salt
- 3½ tablespoons cold vegetable shortening, cut into small pieces
- 3 tablespoons cold unsalted butter, cut into ½-inch pieces
- 3 tablespoons ice water

1. In a food processor, blend the flour with the sugar and salt. Add the shortening and butter and pulse until the mixture resembles coarse meal. Drizzle in the ice water and pulse until the dough forms small clumps. Turn the dough onto a lightly floured work surface and press it out with the heel of your hand. Gather the dough together and flatten it into a 4-inch disk. Wrap in plastic wrap and refrigerate for at least 1 hour.

2. On a lightly floured surface, roll out the dough to a 12-inch round. Transfer to a 9-inch glass pie plate. Trim any overhanging dough and flute the edges. Prick the bottom of the shell all over with a fork and freeze until firm, about 20 minutes.

3. Preheat the oven to 450°. Line the frozen pie shell with aluminum foil and fill with pie weights, dry beans or rice. Bake for 20 to 25 minutes, or until the edges are slightly golden. Remove the foil and weights; bake for 5 to 8 minutes more, or until the center loses its raw look. The shell should be a little light; it will be baked again. Let cool on a rack before adding the filling. *–Peggy Cullen*

MAKE AHEAD The dough can be prepared through Step 1 and refrigerated overnight, or prepared through Step 2 and frozen for up to 1 month. The pie can be prepared through Step 1 and refrigerated overnight.

WINE The penetrating taste of pumpkin makes a precise flavor match tricky. Instead, look for a wine of equal sweetness, such as the 1996 Quady Essenzia from California or the nonvintage Prosper Maufoux Muscat Beaumes de Venise from France.

Double-Decker Pumpkin Chiffon Pie

CHAPTER 19 fruit desserts

Three-Citrus Custard with Fresh Figs (p. 389)

377   Blueberry and Banana Brown Betty

377   Strawberry and Rhubarb Pandowdy

378   Rhubarb Mango Crumble

378   Plum and Ginger Crisp

378   Polenta Cherry Cobbler

379   Macadamia Shortbread with Fruit Compote and Banana Cream

380   Apricot Soup

380   Tropical Fruit Soup

380   Summer Peach Clafoutis

381   Sweet Peaches with Creamy Zabaglione

381   Warm Polenta Pancakes with Peaches and Mascarpone

382   Peach and Raspberry Crumble

382   White Peaches with Crushed Raspberries

382   Raspberry Fool

382   Peach and Blueberry Crisp

383   Nectarine and Blackberry Cobbler

383   Meringue Bowl with Sorbet and Fruit

383   Ginger Star Shortcakes with Summer Berries

385   Baked Apples

385   Apple Pecan Crisp

387   Granny-Smith-Apple Sorbet with Muscat and Grappa

387   Panforte with Pears and Vanilla Cream

387   Pistachio Ricotta Napoleons with Oranges

389   Oranges in Champagne Syrup

389   Three-Citrus Custard with Fresh Figs

389   Figs Poached in Orange Muscat

389   Dried-Fruit Compote with Fresh Goat Cheese

Blueberry and Banana Brown Betty

Blueberry and Banana Brown Betty

6 SERVINGS

Making your own bread crumbs for this dessert is easy. Cut the bread in slices and then trim off the crusts. Tear the slices into pieces, drop them into a food processor and pulse into fine crumbs.

- 5 large egg yolks
- ½ cup granulated sugar
- Pinch of salt
- 1 pint half-and-half
- 1 vanilla bean, split
- One 3-inch cinnamon stick
- 2 cups fresh brioche crumbs
- ½ cup packed dark brown sugar
- 4 tablespoons unsalted butter, melted
- 1 teaspoon ground cinnamon
- 4 ripe bananas, sliced ¼ inch thick
- 1 pint blueberries

1. Preheat the oven to 325°. In a bowl, whisk the egg yolks with the granulated sugar and salt. In a heavy saucepan, combine the half-and-half, vanilla bean and cinnamon stick and cook over moderately high heat until bubbles appear around the edges. Gradually whisk the hot liquid into the yolks. Return the mixture to the saucepan and cook over low heat, stirring constantly with a wooden spoon, until the custard is thick enough to coat the back of the spoon, about 5 minutes; do not boil.

2. Spread the brioche crumbs in a baking pan and bake for about 5 minutes, or until lightly toasted. In a medium bowl, toss the crumbs with the brown sugar, butter and cinnamon.

3. In a shallow 2-quart baking dish or six individual ramekins, combine the bananas and blueberries. Strain the custard over the fruit. Sprinkle the crumb topping over all. Set the baking dish or ramekins in a roasting pan and pour 1 inch of hot water into the pan. Bake the dessert for about 20 minutes, or until it is heated through and the topping is golden. —*Bradley Ogden*

Strawberry and Rhubarb Pandowdy

6 SERVINGS

With strips of pastry covering the fruit, this is a personal interpretation of a pandowdy.

- ¾ cup all-purpose flour
- 4 tablespoons unsalted butter
- 4 tablespoons cream cheese
- 1 teaspoon pure vanilla extract
- 1½ pounds rhubarb, peeled if stringy and cut into ½-inch dice
- 1 pint strawberries, quartered
- 1 cup granulated sugar
- 1 tablespoon fresh lemon juice
- 2 teaspoons grated lemon zest
- 1 teaspoon grated fresh ginger
- 1 tablespoon crystallized sugar or coarsely crushed sugar cubes

1. Put the flour in a bowl and add the butter, cream cheese and vanilla. Cut or rub in the butter and cream cheese just until a dough is formed. Pat the dough into a square, wrap and refrigerate for 30 minutes.

2. Preheat the oven to 400°. In a shallow 2-quart baking dish, toss the rhubarb with the quartered strawberries, granulated sugar, lemon juice, lemon zest and ginger.

3. On a lightly floured surface, roll the dough into a rectangle about ⅛ inch thick. Cut the dough crosswise into 2-inch-wide strips. Lay the strips of dough over the rhubarb and strawberries, anchoring the strips to the side of the dish; trim if necessary. Sprinkle the strips with the crystallized sugar. Set the dish on a baking sheet and bake the pandowdy for about 45 minutes, or until the topping is golden and the fruit is bubbling. —*Bradley Ogden*

Strawberry and Rhubarb Pandowdy

Rhubarb Mango Crumble

4 TO 6 SERVINGS

- 1 pound rhubarb stalks, cut into ¾-inch pieces
- 1 large ripe mango, cut into ¾-inch cubes
- ½ cup plus ½ tablespoon sugar
- ⅔ cup all-purpose flour
- 3 tablespoons yellow cornmeal
- ½ teaspoon ground ginger
- ⅛ teaspoon freshly ground white pepper

Pinch of salt

- 5 tablespoons unsalted butter, cut into ½-inch pieces

Plum and Ginger Crisp

1. Preheat the oven to 425°. Generously butter a large baking dish. Add the rhubarb and mango, then 6½ tablespoons of the sugar. Toss gently to combine.

2. In a food processor, combine the remaining 2 tablespoons of sugar with the flour, cornmeal, ginger, pepper and salt; pulse a few times to mix. Add the butter; process just until the mixture begins to clump. Transfer to a bowl. Pinch to form large and small crumbs; sprinkle evenly over the fruit. Bake 25 to 30 minutes, or until bubbly and golden on top. If desired, set the dish under the broiler for a few seconds to brown the top. –*Grace Parisi*

Plum and Ginger Crisp

6 SERVINGS

- 2¾ pounds plums, quartered and pitted
- 1 cup granulated sugar
- 2 tablespoons fresh lemon juice
- 1 teaspoon grated fresh ginger
- ¼ teaspoon ground cardamom
- 1 cup all-purpose flour
- ¾ cup packed dark brown sugar
- ½ cup sliced almonds (2½ ounces)
- ½ teaspoon salt
- 1 stick (4 ounces) unsalted butter, cut into ½-inch dice

1. Preheat the oven to 375°. In a shallow 2-quart baking dish, toss together the plums, granulated sugar, lemon juice, ginger and cardamom.

2. In a bowl, mix the flour with the brown sugar, almonds and salt. Cut or rub in the butter until the mixture resembles coarse meal. Sprinkle the topping over the plums and set the dish on a baking sheet. Bake for about 45 minutes, or until the topping is lightly browned and the fruit is bubbling.   –*Bradley Ogden*

Polenta Cherry Cobbler

6 SERVINGS

- ¾ cup buttermilk
- 3 tablespoons polenta or cornmeal
- 1 teaspoon pure vanilla extract
- 1 cup all-purpose flour
- 1 cup plus 6 tablespoons granulated sugar
- 2½ teaspoons baking powder
- ⅛ teaspoon salt
- 3 tablespoons unsalted butter, cut into ½-inch dice
- 6 cups pitted sour cherries
- 1 teaspoon grated orange zest
- ¼ teaspoon ground star anise (optional)
- 1½ tablespoons crystallized sugar or crushed sugar cubes

1. In a medium bowl, whisk the buttermilk with the polenta and vanilla and set aside for 30 minutes.

2. Preheat the oven to 400°. In a large bowl, combine the flour, the 6 tablespoons of granulated sugar, the baking powder and the salt. Cut or rub in the butter until the mixture resembles coarse meal. Slowly stir in the buttermilk mixture to form a loose wet dough; don't overmix.

3. In a shallow 1½- to 2-quart baking dish, toss the cherries with the zest, star anise and the remaining 1 cup of granulated sugar. Drop spoonfuls of the topping over the cherries; sprinkle with the crystallized sugar. Set the dish on a baking sheet. Bake about 45 minutes, or until the topping is golden. *–Bradley Ogden*

Macadamia Shortbread with Fruit Compote and Banana Cream

10 SERVINGS

Though delicious together, all three parts of this dessert can stand alone. Or you might want to serve the banana cream with the fresh fruit, the shortbread and compote with plain whipped cream or the compote with ice cream.

SHORTBREAD

- 2   cups sifted all-purpose flour
- ½   cup rice flour
- ½   cup sugar
- ½   pound (2 sticks) cold unsalted butter, cut into pieces
- ½   cup unsalted macadamia nuts, preferably roasted, finely chopped
- ½   teaspoon pure vanilla extract
- ¼   teaspoon pure almond extract
- 3½ tablespoons cold milk

FRUIT COMPOTE

- 1   cup water
- 1   cup sugar
- ¼   cup dry sherry
- 1   whole clove
- ½   cinnamon stick
- 3   medium plums, cut into small wedges
- 1   large ripe mango, cut into ½-inch dice

Macadamia Shortbread with Fruit Compote

- 2   cups fresh raspberries
- 1   cup fresh blueberries
- 1   cup fresh blackberries

BANANA CREAM

- 1   large banana, cut into ½-inch dice
- 3   tablespoons sugar
- 1½ cups heavy cream
- 1   tablespoon molasses
- 1   tablespoon honey
- ¼   teaspoon cinnamon

I. MAKE THE SHORTBREAD: In a large bowl, combine the all-purpose flour, rice flour and sugar. Using a pastry cutter or two knives, cut the butter into the dry ingredients until the mixture resembles coarse meal. Add the macadamia nuts, vanilla and almond extracts and milk and stir just until a dough begins to form; do not overwork the dough. Form two thirds of the dough into a 9-inch disk and shape the remaining piece into a 7-inch log. Wrap each piece in plastic and refrigerate for 1 hour or up to 2 days.

2. Preheat the oven to 400°. Set the disk of dough on a lightly floured baking sheet and let stand at room tempera-ture for 15 minutes to soften slightly. Form the log of dough into ¾-inch balls and gently press the dough balls around the edge of the top of the shortbread. Bake for about 40 minutes, or until golden brown.

3. MAKE THE FRUIT COMPOTE: In a large saucepan, combine the water, sugar, sherry, clove and cinnamon stick. Bring to a boil over moderately high heat, stirring occasionally, until the sugar dissolves completely. Remove the clove and cinnamon stick and add the plums and mango. Simmer over moderate heat until the fruit is barely tender, about 5 minutes. Add the raspberries, blueberries and blackberries and simmer for 3 minutes longer. Transfer the compote to a bowl to cool slightly.

4. MAKE THE BANANA CREAM: Heat a nonstick skillet. Add the banana and sugar and stir over moderate heat until the sugar melts and caramelizes, about 3 minutes. Let cool completely. Transfer the caramelized banana to a blender. Add the cream, molasses, honey and cinnamon and blend until smooth. Transfer to a bowl. ➤

5. To serve, cut the shortbread into ten wedges with a serrated knife. Spoon the compote into ten shallow bowls; top with a wedge of shortbread and a dollop of banana cream. *—George Mahaffey*

MAKE AHEAD The baked shortbread can be stored in an airtight container for up to three days; reheat in a 325° oven just before serving. The fruit compote can stand at room temperature for up to six hours.

BELOW: **Summer Peach Clafoutis.**
BOTTOM: **Tropical Fruit Soup.**

Apricot Soup

6 SERVINGS

Serve this refreshing summer dessert soup with Pistachio Biscotti (p. 357)

- ¾ **cup plus 2 tablespoons sugar**
- 3 **cups water**
- 10 **large fresh apricots, pitted and quartered**
- 1 **cup dry Champagne, chilled**

1. In a medium stainless-steel saucepan, combine the sugar with 1 cup of the water and stir over moderately low heat until the syrup is clear, about 4 minutes. Pour into a heatproof bowl.

2. In the same saucepan, cover the apricots with the remaining 2 cups of water and bring to a boil. Cover and simmer over moderate heat, stirring occasionally, until pulpy, about 25 minutes. Stir in the syrup.

3. Strain the apricot soup through a fine sieve into a nonmetallic bowl and refrigerate until chilled or for up to 1 day. Stir in the Champagne just before serving the soup. *—Joachim Splichal*

WINE The key here is to drink a Champagne that's sweeter than the dessert. Nonvintage Veuve Clicquot demi-sec offers fruit components matched by just the right acidity.

Tropical Fruit Soup

8 SERVINGS

Any good-quality fruit sorbet, especially one with a tropical flavor, can be used to garnish the soup.

- 1 **ripe mango, peeled and cut into large chunks**
- 1 **large ripe peach, peeled and cut into large chunks**
- 1 **small ripe banana, halved**
- 1 **cup cubed fresh pineapple**
- 1 **cup unsweetened coconut milk**
- 1 **cup fresh orange juice**
- 2½ **tablespoons fresh lime juice**
- 1 **teaspoon sugar**
- 1 **pint fruit sorbet**

Mint sprigs, for garnish

In a blender, combine the mango, peach, banana, pineapple, coconut milk, orange juice, lime juice and sugar and blend until smooth. Pass the puree through a fine strainer. Refrigerate until well chilled, for at least 1 hour or up to 1 day. Pour the soup into eight small bowls and garnish each serving with a scoop of sorbet and a mint sprig. *—Herb Wilson*

Summer Peach Clafoutis

6 SERVINGS

To peel peaches easily, blanch them first in boiling water for one minute.

- 4 **large eggs**
- ½ **cup heavy cream**
- ½ **cup milk**
- 3 **tablespoons all-purpose flour**
- ¾ **cup sugar**
- 4 **tablespoons unsalted butter**
- 6 **medium ripe peaches—peeled, pitted and quartered**

1. Preheat the oven to 350°. In a blender, combine the eggs with the cream, milk and flour. Add ½ cup of the sugar; blend until smooth.

2. In a large heavy skillet, melt the butter over moderate heat. Add the peaches, sprinkle with the remaining ¼ cup of sugar and cook, stirring occasionally, until tender, about 4 minutes.

3. Butter a 10-inch round glass pie plate and pour in one-quarter of the batter. Spoon the peaches with their liquid into the dish and pour the remaining batter on top. Set the pie plate on a baking sheet and bake for about 1 hour, or until golden and just set. Transfer to a rack and let cool to room temperature before serving. *—Joachim Splichal*

MAKE AHEAD The clafoutis can be refrigerated overnight. Gently reheat in a 300° oven before serving.

WINE 1994 Arrowood Preston Ranch Late Harvest White Riesling. Rich in honeysuckle and apricot aromas, this wine is a natural with a custardy peach dessert.

Sweet Peaches with Creamy Zabaglione

8 SERVINGS

- 8 medium ripe peaches
- ¼ cup Cointreau or other orange liqueur
- ¼ cup plus 3 tablespoons granulated sugar
- 3 large egg yolks
- ⅓ cup marsala
- 1 cup heavy cream
- 1 tablespoon confectioners' sugar
- 8 amaretti-cookie halves, crumbled

1. Bring a large saucepan of water to a boil. Blanch 2 peaches at a time for 30 seconds. Using a slotted spoon, transfer the peaches to a bowl of cold water, then peel off the skin. Halve and pit the peaches and slice them ⅓ inch thick.

2. In a bowl, toss the sliced peaches with the Cointreau and the ¼ cup of granulated sugar. Refrigerate for 2 to 5 hours.

3. In a heatproof bowl, whisk the egg yolks with the remaining 3 tablespoons of granulated sugar until pale, about 2 minutes. Add the marsala and set over a saucepan of simmering water. Whisk constantly over low heat until very pale and thickened to the consistency of soft whipped cream, about 8 minutes. Set the bowl in a larger bowl of ice water to cool.

4. In another bowl, whip the cream and confectioners' sugar to soft peaks. Fold in the cooled zabaglione.

5. Arrange the peaches with any accumulated juices in eight dessert glasses or shallow soup plates. Spoon a generous dollop of the zabaglione cream on top and sprinkle with the amaretti.

MAKE AHEAD The zabaglione can be prepared through Step 4 and refrigerated overnight.

Warm Polenta Pancakes with Peaches and Mascarpone

4 SERVINGS

The flavors and textures of the juicy fruit, the rich, creamy cheese and the

soft pancakes come together to make a special dessert. The mascarpone melts onto the warm polenta, giving it a light, slightly tart flavor and balancing the sweetness. Other fruit—pears, apricots, plums, apples—or even jam can be used.

- 2 cups water
- ½ tablespoon unsalted butter
- ½ teaspoon salt
- 6 tablespoons polenta or cornmeal
- ½ cup mascarpone cheese
- 2 or 3 ripe peaches, peeled and thinly sliced
- 4 mint sprigs, for garnish (optional)

Sugar, for sprinkling

1. In a medium saucepan, bring the water to a boil over moderately high heat. Add the butter and salt and then slowly whisk in the polenta. Reduce the

TOP: **Warm Polenta Pancakes with Peaches and Mascarpone.** RIGHT: **Sweet Peaches with Creamy Zabaglione.**

heat to low and cook, whisking, until the polenta has somewhat thickened, about 20 minutes. Remove from the heat; let cool for 2 minutes. Whisk in ¼ cup of the mascarpone.

2. Spoon 2 tablespoons of the polenta onto an aluminum-foil-lined baking sheet and, using the back of a spoon, spread it into a 3-inch round pancake about ¼ inch thick. Repeat with the remaining polenta, forming twelve pancakes. Let stand at room temperature for 10 minutes.

3. Preheat the broiler. Broil the pancakes about 6 inches from the heat for 3 minutes, or until they are slightly dry on top. Overlap three pancakes on each of four warmed plates and top with 1 tablespoon of mascarpone, the peaches and a sprig of mint. Serve the dessert immediately and pass the sugar separately.   *–Georgeanne Brennan*

MAKE AHEAD Before they're broiled, the pancakes can be refrigerated, covered, for up to one day.

WINE A chilled glass of light and fruity, slightly sweet Moscato would add a delicious grace note to this dish. Look for the 1996 Santo Stefano Moscato d'Asti from Italy or the 1995 La Famiglia di Robert Mondavi Moscato Bianco from California.

the upper crust

When is a crisp not a crumble? It's all a matter of what's on top. Although there's some flexibility–your grandmother's cobbler may not be like Bradley Ogden's–here are widely accepted definitions for these homey baked fruit desserts:

1. **Betty** Topped with buttered crumbs (bread, cookie or graham cracker), sometimes mixed with sugar and spices.

2. **Cobbler** Topped with a thick biscuit, pastry or bread crust.

3. **Crisp (or crumble in England)** Topped with a mixture of flour, butter, sugar and sometimes nuts, rolled oats or spices.

4. **Pandowdy** Topped with a pastry crust that is sometimes partially baked before being scored, pressed into the fruit and returned to the oven until crisp.

Peach and Raspberry Crumble

6 SERVINGS

TOPPING

- ¾ cup all-purpose flour
- ¾ cup old-fashioned rolled oats
- ¼ cup packed dark brown sugar
- ¼ cup granulated sugar
- ½ teaspoon salt
- ¼ teaspoon cinnamon
- ⅛ teaspoon nutmeg
- ⅛ teaspoon allspice

Pinch of ground cloves

- 6 tablespoons unsalted butter, cut into ½-inch dice

FILLING

- 5 ripe peaches—peeled, quartered and pitted
- 1 pint fresh raspberries
- ¾ cup granulated sugar
- 1 tablespoon fresh lemon juice
- ½ teaspoon cinnamon

Seeds scraped from 1 split vanilla bean

I. Preheat the oven to 375°.

2. MAKE THE TOPPING: In a large bowl, toss all the dry ingredients. Cut or rub in the butter until the bits of butter are the size of split peas.

3. MAKE THE FILLING: In a shallow 2-quart baking dish, combine the fruit, granulated sugar, lemon juice, cinnamon and vanilla seeds. Sprinkle with the topping. Set on a baking sheet; bake about 45 minutes, or until the topping is golden and the fruit bubbling.   *–Bradley Ogden*

White Peaches with Crushed Raspberries

4 SERVINGS **L**

- 1½ cups fresh raspberries
- 4 teaspoons sugar
- 1 teaspoon fresh lemon juice
- 4 ripe white peaches, peeled and cut into ½-inch slices

In a medium bowl, using a fork, coarsely crush the berries with the sugar and juice. Let stand at least 5 minutes, fold in the peaches and serve. *–Sally Schneider*

Raspberry Fool

4 SERVINGS **Q**

This version of the traditionally smooth puree features crushed berries swirled with the whipped cream for more intense flavor and variety in texture.

- ½ pint fresh raspberries (6 ounces)
- 3 to 4 tablespoons sugar, preferably superfine
- 1 cup heavy cream, chilled

In a bowl, using a fork, crush the raspberries with 2 to 3 tablespoons of the sugar. Whip the cream with the remaining 1 tablespoon sugar until stiff peaks form. Gently fold in the crushed berries; leave some streaks. Cover and refrigerate until serving time.   *–Judith Sutton*

Peach and Blueberry Crisp

20 SERVINGS

- 2 cups all-purpose flour
- 2 cups light brown sugar
- 1 tablespoon cinnamon
- 1 teaspoon freshly grated nutmeg
- ½ teaspoon salt
- 2 sticks (8 ounces) cold unsalted butter, cut into ½-inch dice
- 6 pounds ripe peaches, peeled and cut into eighths
- 4 pints fresh blueberries
- 1 cup slivered blanched almonds (about 4½ ounces)

Vanilla ice cream, for serving

I. Preheat the oven to 375°. In a medium bowl, toss the flour with the sugar, cinnamon, nutmeg and salt. Using a pastry blender or two knives, cut in the butter until the mixture resembles small peas.

2. Butter two 13-by-9-inch glass or ceramic baking dishes. In a large bowl, toss the peaches with the blueberries and spread the fruit in the prepared baking dishes. Scatter the topping evenly over the fruit and sprinkle the almonds on top. Bake for about 45 minutes, or until the fruit is bubbling and the topping is crisp. Serve warm or at room temperature with vanilla ice cream.   *–David Page*

Nectarine and Blackberry Cobbler

4 SERVINGS

- 2 large nectarines, thinly sliced
- 1 pint fresh blackberries
- 1 teaspoon fresh lemon juice
- ½ cup sugar
- 1 cup plus 2 tablespoons all-purpose flour
- 1½ teaspoons baking powder
- ½ teaspoon salt
- 4 tablespoons cold unsalted butter, cut into tablespoons
- ¼ cup milk

Vanilla ice cream, for serving (optional)

1. Preheat the oven to 450°. Combine the nectarines, blackberries and lemon juice in a bowl. Mix the sugar and the 2 tablespoons flour; toss with the fruit.

2. In a medium bowl, mix the remaining 1 cup flour with the baking powder and salt. Cut in the butter until the pieces are the size of small peas. Stir in the milk. Gather the dough into a ball and transfer to a lightly floured surface. Roll the dough into an 8-inch square about ¼ inch thick.

3. Pour the fruit and its juices into an 8-inch square glass baking dish. Lay the dough on top of the fruit. Place a sheet of aluminum foil in the bottom of the oven to catch any drips. Bake the cobbler for 20 minutes, then reduce the heat to 300° and bake for about 5 minutes longer, or until the crust is golden and the fruit is bubbling around the sides. Serve warm with a scoop of ice cream, if desired. –Georgeanne Brennan

WINE Sweet nectarines, tart blackberries and a crumbly crust call for a full-fledged sweet dessert wine. A Late Harvest Riesling is the perfect choice, its scent echoing the fruit of the cobbler. Consider a Washington State example, such as the 1995 Chateau Ste. Michelle Late Harvest White Riesling or the 1995 Columbia Crest Ice Wine White Riesling.

Meringue Bowl with Sorbet and Fruit

10 TO 12 SERVINGS

The large, free-form meringue bowl will be lightly cracked around the edge and slightly soft in the center. This recipe is adapted from *Our Meals* (Riverhead Books).

- 6 large egg whites
- 1½ cups sugar
- ¼ teaspoon cream of tartar
- 2 pints sorbet
- 4 cups berries

1. Preheat the oven to 300°. Line a baking sheet with parchment paper. Using a plate as your guide, draw an 11-inch circle on the paper. Turn the paper over.

2. In a large heatproof bowl, combine the egg whites, sugar and cream of tartar. Set the bowl over 1 inch of simmering water and stir constantly until the whites are very warm and the sugar is completely dissolved, about 5 minutes.

3. Remove from the heat. Using an electric mixer, beat the egg whites until they form stiff, glossy peaks. Transfer the meringue to the outlined circle and use a rubber spatula to shape it into a wide-rimmed bowl with a 1-inch-thick base. Bake for 15 minutes. Reduce the oven temperature to 250° and bake for 1½ hours longer, or until the meringue is light brown and crisp. Let cool completely.

4. Carefully lift the bowl off the paper and transfer to a platter. Fill with scoops of the sorbet and the berries and serve at once. –Heather Watts and Jock Soto

Ginger Star Shortcakes with Summer Berries

16 SERVINGS

For a show-stopping dessert, fill gingerbread shortcakes with rich mascarpone cream and sweet ripe berries.

BERRIES

- 1½ pints fresh strawberries, hulled and sliced
- 1½ pints fresh blueberries

Meringue Bowl with Sorbet and Fruit

- 1½ pints fresh blackberries
- 1½ pints fresh raspberries
- 1 cup sugar

MASCARPONE CREAM

- ¾ pound mascarpone cheese (1½ cups) or cream cheese, at room temperature
- ¼ cup plus 2 tablespoons finely chopped candied ginger (about 1½ ounces)
- 3 tablespoons sugar
- 1½ teaspoons pure vanilla extract
- 3 cups chilled heavy cream

SHORTCAKES

- 4½ cups all-purpose flour
- 1 cup plus 1½ tablespoons sugar
- 1 tablespoon plus 1 teaspoon ground ginger
- 1 tablespoon baking powder
- 2 teaspoons ground cinnamon
- 1½ teaspoons baking soda
- 1 teaspoon ground allspice
- ½ teaspoon salt
- ½ teaspoon freshly ground white pepper
- ¾ cup chilled Molasses Butter (recipe follows), cut into 1-inch pieces
- 1⅓ cups buttermilk
- 2 large egg yolks

About ¾ cup Molasses Butter (recipe follows), softened, for serving

Ginger Star Shortcakes with Summer Berries

I. PREPARE THE BERRIES: In a large bowl, toss the berries with the sugar and let macerate at room temperature for at least 1 or up to 4 hours; stir gently from time to time.

2. PREPARE THE MASCARPONE CREAM: In a medium bowl, beat the mascarpone with the ginger, sugar and vanilla until well blended. Slowly beat in the heavy cream just until the mixture forms soft peaks. Refrigerate for up to 3 hours; whip briefly before serving.

3. PREPARE THE SHORTCAKES: Preheat the oven to 425° and lightly butter two baking sheets. In a large bowl, sift the flour with the 1 cup sugar, the ginger, baking powder, cinnamon, baking soda, allspice, salt and pepper; whisk to combine. Using a pastry cutter or two knives, cut in the Molasses Butter until the mixture resembles small peas.

4. In a large measuring cup, whisk the buttermilk and egg yolks. Stir 1 cup into the dry ingredients. Using your hands, squeeze the dough until smooth; if necessary, stir in a little more liquid, but don't let the dough become sticky. Reserve the remaining liquid for glazing.

5. Turn the dough onto a lightly floured surface and roll out to a ½-inch thickness. Using a lightly floured 3-inch star-shaped or round biscuit cutter, cut out as many shortcakes as you can. Pat the scraps together and continue cutting to make a total of sixteen shortcakes. Arrange the shortcakes on the prepared baking sheets so they don't touch, then brush the tops lightly with the remaining buttermilk mixture and sprinkle with the remaining 1½ tablespoons of sugar.

6. Bake the shortcakes, a tray at a time, for about 15 minutes, or until the bottoms are lightly browned. Cool on a wire rack for 5 minutes. Split with a serrated knife; set each base on a plate and spread with a thin layer of Molasses Butter. Mound berries on each. Add a dollop of mascarpone cream; cover with the top.

MOLASSES BUTTER
MAKES ABOUT 1½ CUPS

- 2 sticks (½ pound) unsalted butter, softened
- ¼ cup dark brown sugar
- ⅓ cup unsulphured molasses

In a medium bowl, beat the butter with the brown sugar until light and creamy. Beat in the molasses. —*Joe Abuso*

MAKE AHEAD The Molasses Butter can be refrigerated overnight.

Baked Apples
4 SERVINGS

To ensure that the apples don't split open as they bake, make a shallow horizontal cut around the middle of each one.

- 4 baking apples, such as Rome Beauty or Cortland, cored
- ¼ cup sugar
- 2 tablespoons finely chopped walnuts
- 2 tablespoons chopped raisins

Pinch of freshly ground cardamom
Pinch of freshly ground nutmeg
Pinch of cinnamon

- 2 teaspoons unsalted butter

Heavy cream, for serving (optional)

I. Preheat the oven to 400°. Set the apples in a small baking dish so they don't touch one another.

2. In a small bowl, mix together the sugar, walnuts, raisins, cardamom, nutmeg and cinnamon. Spoon into the apples and top each with ½ teaspoon of butter. Loosely cover with aluminum foil and bake for about 45 minutes, or until the apples are just tender when pierced. Serve warm or room-temperature, with heavy cream if desired. —*Darra Goldstein*

Apple Pecan Crisp
6 SERVINGS

This delicious winter fruit and nut dessert can be made just as easily in one medium baking dish.

- 1 cup pecans (about 4 ounces)
- ¼ cup plus 2 tablespoons all-purpose flour
- ¼ cup plus 2 tablespoons light brown sugar
- ½ cup plus 2 tablespoons granulated sugar
- 6 tablespoons cold unsalted butter, cut into ½-inch dice
- ½ cup old-fashioned rolled oats
- 2½ pounds Cortland or other tart cooking apples—peeled, quartered, cored and sliced crosswise ¼ inch thick
- ½ cup dried cranberries (about 2½ ounces)
- 1 pint vanilla ice cream

I. Preheat the oven to 350°. Spread the pecans on a baking sheet and bake for 6 to 8 minutes, or until lightly toasted. Let the pecans cool and then coarsely chop them. Leave the oven on.

2. In a food processor, pulse the flour with the brown sugar and ¼ cup of the granulated sugar until combined. Add the butter and pulse until the mixture resembles coarse meal. Transfer the crumbs to a bowl and stir in the toasted pecans and the oats.

3. Generously butter six individual baking dishes; they should be about 6 inches wide and 1 inch deep. In a medium bowl, toss the apples with the cranberries and the remaining 6 tablespoons granulated sugar. Divide the apple mixture among the prepared baking dishes and cover with the crumb topping. Set the dishes on a large baking sheet and bake in the bottom third of the oven for 45 to 50 minutes, or until the apples are tender when pierced and the topping is toasted. Serve warm with the ice cream. —*James Henahan*

WINE To end the meal with a celebratory flourish, serve sparkling wine—but avoid brut bottlings, which will taste thin and tinny next to the crisp. Instead, look for extra dry or demi-sec Champagnes from Moët & Chandon or Mumm, or Crémants from California producers, such as Schramsberg or Scharffenberger.

Granny-Smith-Apple Sorbet with Muscat and Grappa

Granny-Smith-Apple Sorbet with Muscat and Grappa

MAKES ABOUT 1 QUART

- 1 cup sugar
- 1 tablespoon honey
- 1 cup water
- 3 Granny Smith apples
- 1 cup muscat

Juice of 1 medium lemon

- 2 tablespoons grappa

1. In a small saucepan, combine the sugar, honey and water; bring to a boil over low heat. Cook until reduced by half, about 10 minutes. Let cool.

2. Meanwhile, peel and core the apples; cut into walnut-size pieces. In a food processor, combine the apples, syrup, muscat, lemon juice and grappa. Puree until creamy. Transfer to an ice-cream maker. Freeze until firm. —*Marcella Hazan*

Panforte with Pears and Vanilla Cream

4 SERVINGS

Fresh lemon juice

- 2 large ripe Bartlett pears—peeled, halved lengthwise, cored and thinly sliced crosswise, keeping the shape of each half intact
- 1½ cups coarsely chopped panforte (about 7½ ounces)
- 1 cup heavy cream
- 1 teaspoon pure vanilla extract

Preheat the oven to 425°. Sprinkle a few drops of lemon juice over the pears to prevent discoloring. Divide 1 cup of the panforte among four shallow heatproof dishes. In a small saucepan, bring the cream barely to a simmer; stir in the vanilla. Pour half of the cream over the panforte. Top each serving with a sliced pear half and the remaining cream. Sprinkle the remaining ½ cup of panforte on top. Set the dishes on a baking sheet and bake for about 10 minutes, until the cream is bubbling and the tops are brown. Serve warm or at room temperature. —*Diana Sturgis*

Pistachio Ricotta Napoleons with Oranges

8 SERVINGS

SPICED ORANGES

- 6 navel oranges
- ½ to ⅔ cup fresh orange juice
- ¾ cup granulated sugar
- 3 tablespoons fresh lemon juice

One 3-inch cinnamon stick

Scant ½ teaspoon whole cloves

Scant ½ teaspoon whole allspice berries

NAPOLEONS

- ⅓ cup shelled unsalted pistachios
- 3 tablespoons granulated sugar
- 1 teaspoon minced orange zest
- 6 unbroken sheets of phyllo dough
- 6 tablespoons unsalted butter, melted
- 1½ cups ricotta (¾ pound)

Confectioners' sugar, for dusting (optional)

1. MAKE THE SPICED ORANGES: Using a sharp knife, peel the oranges, removing all of the bitter white pith. Working over a bowl, cut in between the membranes to release the orange sections. Squeeze the juice from the membranes into a glass measure; add enough fresh orange juice to make 1 cup.

2. In a large stainless-steel skillet, combine the orange juice with the granulated sugar, lemon juice, cinnamon, cloves and allspice. Cook over low heat, stirring, until the sugar dissolves, then simmer for 10 minutes. Add the orange sections in an even layer and remove from the heat. Let stand for 30 minutes or, for a spicier flavor, up to 1 hour. Using a slotted spoon, carefully transfer the orange sections to a plate. Cover and refrigerate.

3. Bring the juices in the skillet to a boil over high heat. Cook until slightly syrupy and reduced to ¾ cup, about 5 minutes. Strain into a glass measure and let cool.

4. MAKE THE NAPOLEONS: Preheat the oven to 400°. Line a large baking sheet with parchment paper; lightly butter the paper. Combine the pistachios,

Pistachio Ricotta Napoleons with Oranges

2 tablespoons of the granulated sugar and the orange zest in a blender or food processor; pulse until coarsely ground. Reserve 2 tablespoons of the pistachio mixture for garnish.

5. Keeping the rest of the phyllo covered with a damp towel, brush one sheet liberally with some of the melted butter. Sprinkle 1 tablespoon of the pistachio mixture evenly over the entire surface. Continue layering the phyllo, melted butter and ground pistachios. Press the layers together gently. Trim ½-inch from all four sides to make a neat rectangle.

6. Cut the phyllo lengthwise into four strips, then cut the strips crosswise to form sixteen small rectangles. Using a metal spatula, carefully transfer the rectangles to the prepared baking sheet. Bake the phyllo for about 12 minutes, or until golden and crisp; turn the pan for even browning if necessary. Let cool completely on the baking sheet.

7. Press the ricotta through a fine sieve and stir in the remaining 1 tablespoon of granulated sugar.

8. Assemble the napoleons just before serving: Place a phyllo rectangle on each plate; top each with 3 tablespoons ricotta. Spoon some of the orange syrup over. Top with another phyllo rectangle,

Three-Citrus Custard with Fresh Figs

offset slightly. Spoon the orange sections onto the plates, drizzle more syrup all around and sprinkle with the reserved 2 tablespoons of pistachio mixture. Lightly dust the tops with confectioners' sugar if desired. —*Grace Parisi*

Oranges in Champagne Syrup

10 SERVINGS

- 10 medium navel oranges
- 3 tablespoons sugar
- 1 tablespoon plus 1 teaspoon honey
- 2 cups water
- 1¼ cups Champagne or sparkling wine (about half of a 750 ml bottle)

Mint leaves, for garnish

ı. Using a small sharp knife, peel the oranges, removing all of the bitter white pith. Working over a large glass dish to catch the juice, cut between the membranes to release the orange sections and drop them into the dish.

2. In a medium saucepan, combine the sugar, honey and 2 cups of water and bring to a boil over high heat, stirring until the sugar is dissolved. Pour the hot syrup over the oranges and let cool. Refrigerate until chilled, about 3 hours.

3. Spoon the oranges and syrup into ten bowls. Pour 2 tablespoons of the Champagne into each bowl, garnish with mint leaves and serve. —*Michel Benasra*

Three-Citrus Custard with Fresh Figs

8 SERVINGS

- 1 cup fresh lemon juice
- ½ cup fresh grapefruit juice
- ½ cup fresh orange juice
- 6 large eggs
- 1 cup sugar
- 1 stick (4 ounces) unsalted butter, cut into small bits
- 1 tablespoon finely grated lemon zest
- 1 tablespoon finely grated grapefruit zest
- 1 tablespoon finely grated orange zest

- 8 ripe fresh figs, preferably green and purple, cut into thick wedges

Butter cookies, for serving

ı. In a double boiler or a large heatproof bowl set over a saucepan with 1 inch of simmering water, whisk the citrus juices with the eggs and sugar until combined. Cook, stirring constantly with a wooden spoon, until smooth and thick, 10 to 12 minutes; don't let the custard boil. Remove from the heat and stir in the butter.

2. Strain the custard into a bowl and stir in the grated citrus zests. Stir for 1 minute to cool slightly, then cover with waxed paper or plastic wrap and refrigerate overnight.

3. Spoon the custard into shallow bowls or stemmed glasses; garnish with the figs. Serve with butter cookies. —*Rori Spinelli*

Figs Poached in Orange Muscat

8 SERVINGS **Q**

- 3 cups sweet orange muscat wine, such as Quady Winery's Essensia
- 1 vanilla bean, split lengthwise
- 2 teaspoons finely grated orange zest

5 to 6 star anise pods

- 1 pound moist and plump dried black Mission figs

Mascarpone cheese (optional)

In a medium saucepan, combine the muscat, vanilla bean, orange zest and star anise. Bring to a boil over moderately high heat. Add the figs and reduce the heat to moderately low. Cover and simmer, stirring often, until the figs are tender, about 40 minutes. Remove from the heat and serve warm with a dollop of mascarpone. —*Jan Newberry*

Dried-Fruit Compote with Fresh Goat Cheese

8 SERVINGS

- 1½ cups pitted prunes (¾ pound)
- 1½ cups dried figs (¾ pound)
- 1½ cups dried apricots (½ pound)
- 1 bottle (750 ml) Sauvignon Blanc

- ½ cup sugar
- ¾ cup dried cherries (3 ounces)
- 2 teaspoons finely chopped sage, plus whole leaves for garnish
- ½ pound fresh goat cheese, cut into 8 slices

ı. In a large saucepan, combine the prunes, figs, apricots, wine and sugar and bring to a boil over high heat. Reduce the heat to moderately high and cook, stirring often, until the liquid has reduced to a thick syrup and the fruits are very tender, about 25 minutes. Stir in the cherries during the last 5 minutes of cooking; let cool.

2. Stir the chopped sage into the compote and spoon the compote into eight bowls. Set a slice of goat cheese on each serving and garnish with sage leaves. —*Pilar Sanchez*

CHAPTER 20 other desserts

Assorted caramels (p. 401)

393   The Ultimate Chocolate Pudding

393   Bittersweet Chocolate Bread Pudding

394   White-Chocolate Bread Pudding

395   Maple Bread Pudding

395   Bread-and-Butter Pudding with Lemon Curd

395   Sweet Sticky Rice Treat

396   Espresso Gelati Sundaes

396   Bittersweet Chocolate Cream Sandwiches

397   St. Gallen Kloster Torte

399   Cognac Almond Truffles

399   Triple-Chocolate Candy-Cane Kisses

399   Chocolate Soufflé Symphony

401   Chocolate Honey Caramels

401   Creamy Caramels

401   Butterscotch Caramels

403   Lemon Orange Caramels

403   Caramel Meringues

404   Harvest Crunch

404   Crystal-Coated Walnuts

404   Peanut Brittle

405   Lark Creek Lollies

The Ultimate Chocolate Pudding

The Ultimate Chocolate Pudding

6 SERVINGS

Dress up this chocolate pudding for grown-ups with some sweetened vanilla-flavored whipped cream and either chocolate shavings or a dusting of cocoa powder.

- ¾ cup sugar
- 6 tablespoons unsweetened Dutch process cocoa powder
- 3 tablespoons cornstarch
- ¼ teaspoon salt
- 2 cups milk
- 6 ounces top-quality semisweet chocolate, finely chopped
- 1½ cups heavy cream
- 1 teaspoon pure vanilla extract

I. Working over a large bowl, sift ½ cup of the sugar with the cocoa, cornstarch and salt. Whisk in ½ cup of the milk to make a smooth paste; scrape the bottom of the bowl with a rubber spatula to be sure everything is well mixed.

2. Put the chocolate in a heatproof bowl. In a medium saucepan, combine the heavy cream with the remaining 1½ cups of milk and ¼ cup of sugar and bring just to a simmer over moderately high heat, stirring. Reduce the heat to moderately low and stir in the cocoa paste. Whisking constantly, boil the mixture for 1 minute. Strain the mixture over the chocolate in the bowl. Add the vanilla and stir until the pudding is smooth.

3. Pour the pudding into six glasses or 1-cup ramekins and let cool to room temperature. Cover the puddings and refrigerate them until set, at least 4 hours.   *–Peggy Cullen*

MAKE AHEAD The puddings can be refrigerated for up to two days.

WINE A cream sherry, such as Harveys or the Emilio Lustau Rare Cream Reserva Superior, will work well with these puddings–as will a cup of dark-roasted coffee

Bittersweet Chocolate Bread Pudding

6 SERVINGS

In this unusual bread pudding, cubes of brioche are frozen, then barely moistened with a bitter chocolate custard and used to line individual ramekins. The trufflelike mixture in the center melts into a sauce as it cooks. Ground star anise can be found in specialty-food shops, but if you can't find it, omit it altogether.

Bittersweet Chocolate Bread Pudding

- 4 ounces bittersweet chocolate, finely chopped
- ¼ cup boiling water
- 1 tablespoon unsalted butter, melted
- 6 tablespoons sugar, plus more for the ramekins
- 2 extra-large eggs
- 3 tablespoons unsweetened cocoa powder, preferably Dutch process
- 3 tablespoons all-purpose flour

393

Sweet Sticky Rice Treat

⅛ teaspoon finely ground star
anise (optional)

½ cup half-and-half

1½ tablespoons dark rum

One ¾-pound brioche or challah,
crusts removed, bread cut into
½-inch cubes and frozen

Vanilla or coffee ice cream, for
serving

1. In a medium heatproof bowl, combine the chocolate and boiling water and stir until completely melted and smooth. Refrigerate the filling until firm, for at least 1 hour and as long as overnight.

2. Preheat the oven to 350°. Brush six 4-ounce ramekins with the melted butter. Line the bottoms with rounds of waxed paper, butter the paper and sprinkle with sugar.

3. In a large bowl, beat the eggs and the 6 tablespoons of sugar with an electric mixer until pale and thick. Sift the cocoa powder, flour and star anise into a bowl. Whisk in the half-and-half and rum just until smooth. Lightly whisk in the beaten egg mixture.

4. Moisten 1 cup of frozen brioche cubes at a time in the chocolate custard until slightly saturated, about 30 seconds. Using a slotted spoon, drain the brioche cubes and use them to fill the ramekins halfway. Place 1½ tablespoons of the chocolate filling in the center of each ramekin. Moisten the remaining frozen brioche cubes in batches and fill the ramekins, mounding them slightly in the center. Discard any remaining chocolate custard.

5. Set the ramekins in a roasting pan and pour enough hot water into the pan to reach 1 inch up the sides. Cover the pan with aluminum foil and bake for about 25 minutes, or until the puddings are puffed and set. Remove the ramekins from the water bath and let cool for 10 minutes before unmolding.

6. Invert the bread puddings onto small dessert plates. Remove the waxed paper and serve warm with the sweetened whipped cream.   *–Heidi Steele*

White-Chocolate Bread Pudding

12 TO 16 SERVINGS

Incredibly rich and impossibly indulgent, this bread pudding delivers a double dose of chocolate–a triple dose if you garnish it with bittersweet chocolate shavings.

BREAD PUDDING

One 24-inch baguette, ends trimmed,
bread cut into 1-inch slices

4½ cups heavy cream

1½ cups milk

¾ cup sugar

15 ounces white chocolate, broken
into small pieces

3 large eggs

12 large egg yolks

WHITE-CHOCOLATE SAUCE

½ cup heavy cream

8 ounces white chocolate, broken
into small pieces

Bittersweet or semisweet chocolate
shavings, for garnish
(optional)

1. MAKE THE BREAD PUDDING: Preheat the oven to 275°. Stand the bread slices on a baking sheet and bake for 15 minutes, or until dry but not browned. Transfer the bread to a 13-by-9-by-2-inch baking dish in an even layer. Increase the oven temperature to 350°.

2. In a large saucepan, heat the cream with the milk and sugar until hot but not steaming. Remove from the heat, add the white chocolate and stir until melted.

3. In a large bowl, beat the eggs with the egg yolks. In a slow, thin stream, whisk the hot cream into the eggs until smooth. Pour the custard over the bread and let stand until soggy, about 20 minutes. Press the bread into the custard occasionally.

4. Cover the pudding with aluminum foil and bake for 1 hour. Remove the foil; bake for 20 minutes longer, or until golden and puffed. Let cool for at least 20 minutes.

5. MAKE THE WHITE-CHOCOLATE SAUCE: Bring the cream to a boil in a small saucepan. Remove from the heat, add the white chocolate and stir until completely smooth.

6. Cut the bread pudding into squares and decorate with the chocolate shavings. Serve warm, with the white-chocolate sauce. Garnish with the chocolate shavings, if using. —*Palace Café*

Maple Bread Pudding

10 SERVINGS

This silky dessert tastes like a cross between crème brûlée and French toast.

One ½-pound loaf firm sliced white sandwich bread, crusts removed

12 large egg yolks

1 cup plus 2 tablespoons pure maple syrup, plus more for serving

½ teaspoon vanilla extract

4 cups heavy cream

1. Preheat the oven to 350°. Lightly butter an 11-by-8-by-2-inch baking dish. Cut the bread into ½-inch cubes, spread on a large baking sheet and toast in the oven for 10 to 12 minutes, or until light golden. Spread evenly in the baking dish. Reduce the oven temperature to 325°.

2. In a large bowl, whisk together the egg yolks, maple syrup and vanilla. In a medium saucepan, warm the cream until just hot to the touch. Gradually whisk the cream into the egg mixture

and strain over the bread cubes. Press a piece of plastic wrap directly onto the bread so that all of it is completely submerged in the custard. Let stand at room temperature until the bread is completely soaked, about 30 minutes.

3. Remove the plastic wrap; cover the baking dish with aluminum foil. Set it in a larger roasting pan and pour hot water into the pan to reach halfway up the side of the dish. Bake for about 1 hour and 15 minutes, or until the custard is just set. Let cool for 20 minutes, drizzle with warm maple syrup and serve. —*Larry Hayden*

MAKE AHEAD The pudding can be refrigerated for up to three days. Reheat in a 350° oven.

Bread-and-Butter Pudding with Lemon Curd

10 SERVINGS

Only the bread crusts go into this bread pudding. The curd and berries are perfect foils to the pudding's mellow flavor.

LEMON CURD

1 stick (4 ounces) unsalted butter, softened

⅔ cup sugar

6 tablespoons fresh lemon juice

2 large eggs, lightly beaten

BREAD PUDDING

¾ cup golden raisins (optional)

2 tablespoons brandy

One 1-pound loaf country bread

4 tablespoons unsalted butter, melted

3 large eggs

3 large egg yolks

2 cups milk

1 cup heavy cream

1 cup sugar

Fresh berries, for garnish

1. MAKE THE LEMON CURD: Set a small bowl in a medium bowl of ice water. Combine the butter, sugar, lemon juice and eggs in a medium stainless-steel saucepan. Cook over moderate heat, stirring constantly, until thick and just starting to bubble, about 6 minutes.

Immediately strain the curd into the small bowl and stir over the ice water until just cooled. Remove the bowl from the ice water, press plastic wrap directly on the curd and refrigerate until cold.

2. MAKE THE BREAD PUDDING: In a small bowl, combine the raisins and brandy and let stand for 20 minutes. If not using raisins, add the brandy to the custard in Step 4.

3. Preheat the oven to 350°. Cut the crust from the bread in thick pieces and cut the crusts into ⅓-inch cubes; you should have about 5 cups. In a large bowl, toss the bread-crust cubes with the melted butter.

4. Strain the raisins, reserving the brandy. In a medium bowl, whisk the whole eggs and egg yolks to mix. Whisk in the milk, cream, sugar and reserved brandy. Strain the custard over the bread-crust cubes; stir in the raisins.

5. Transfer the bread mixture to an 11-by-8-by-2-inch baking dish and place in a larger ovenproof pan. Pour enough hot water into the pan to reach halfway up the side of the baking dish. Bake for about 45 minutes, or until golden and puffed and a toothpick inserted in the center comes out clean. Cool for at least 10 minutes; cut into squares. Serve warm, garnished with the berries. Pass the curd separately. —*Brian J. Karam*

MAKE AHEAD The curd can be refrigerated for up to three days. Bring to room temperature before serving.

Sweet Sticky Rice Treat

4 TO 6 SERVINGS

This ubiquitous Thai street snack is sweetened and enriched with coconut milk and palm sugar. Shake the can of coconut milk before pouring—the cream and milk tend to separate.

1 cup black Thai sticky rice

1 cup Thai sticky rice

1½ cups canned unsweetened coconut milk

Espresso Gelati Sundaes

¼ cup palm sugar or light brown sugar

½ teaspoon salt

Sliced fresh mango and starfruit, for garnish

1. In a large bowl, soak the black Thai sticky rice and the Thai sticky rice in plenty of water to cover for 6 to 24 hours. Drain.

2. Put the soaked sticky rice in a cheesecloth-lined steamer basket or a large sieve. Set the steamer in a saucepan of water, cover and bring to a vigorous boil; the water must not touch the rice. Steam the rice for 30 minutes, stirring gently halfway through. When done, the rice will be shiny, tender and a little chewy.

3. Meanwhile, in a small saucepan, warm the coconut milk over low heat. Stir in the palm sugar and the salt until dissolved. Keep the mixture warm over very low heat.

4. Transfer the cooked sticky rice to a bowl and gently fold in the warm coconut-milk mixture. Cover the sticky rice loosely with plastic wrap and allow it to stand at room temperature for at least 30 minutes and up to 4 hours. Serve the sticky rice in small bowls, topped with the sliced mango and starfruit. *–Jeffrey Alford and Naomi Duguid*

Espresso Gelati Sundaes

MAKES 10, PLUS LEFTOVER GELATI

These luxurious gelati are delightful topped with a drizzle of espresso, but they are also wonderful on their own. They're best when eaten on the day they're made.

CREAM GELATO

3 cups heavy cream

1 cup milk

½ cup half-and-half

Finely grated zest of 1 lemon

1 cup sugar

3 egg yolks

¼ cup light corn syrup

½ teaspoon pure vanilla extract

CHOCOLATE GELATO

1½ cups sugar

1½ cups unsweetened cocoa

1 cup light corn syrup

5 cups water

3 cups heavy cream

About 1 cup strongly brewed espresso, at room temperature

1. MAKE THE CREAM GELATO: In a heavy medium saucepan, combine the cream, milk, half-and-half, lemon zest and ¼ cup of the sugar. Bring to a simmer over moderate heat, stirring occasionally.

2. Meanwhile, in a bowl, whisk the egg yolks with the remaining ¾ cup of sugar. Whisk in the hot cream mixture and return the custard to the saucepan. Cook for 6 minutes, stirring constantly; do not let it boil. Strain the custard into a bowl and stir in the corn syrup and vanilla. Refrigerate the custard until chilled. Working in two batches, freeze the custard in an ice-cream maker according to the manufacturer's instructions. Transfer to a chilled bowl and store in the freezer.

3. MAKE THE CHOCOLATE GELATO: In a large heavy saucepan, combine the sugar, cocoa, ½ cup of the corn syrup and the water. Bring to a boil over moderately high heat and cook, stirring often, until the syrup is very thick and reduced to 3¼ cups, about 40 minutes.

4. Scrape the syrup into a bowl and stir in the remaining ½ cup of corn syrup and the cream. Refrigerate until chilled. Working in two batches, freeze the mixture in an ice-cream maker according to the manufacturer's instructions. Transfer to a chilled bowl and store in the freezer.

5. Place one to two scoops of the chocolate gelato into parfait glasses and add a scoop or two of the cream gelato. Drizzle the gelati with 1 to 2 tablespoons of the room-temperature espresso and serve. *–Reed Hearon*

MAKE AHEAD The chocolate and cream gelati can be frozen separately for up to two days.

Bittersweet Chocolate Cream Sandwiches

MAKES 4

¼ cup heavy cream

1 ounce bittersweet chocolate

½ cup mascarpone cheese

1 tablespoon sugar

1 teaspoon coffee liqueur

8 large imported waffle cookies (gaufrettes)

Fresh strawberries or raspberries

1. In a small saucepan, scald the cream over moderate heat. Add the chocolate and remove from the heat. Let stand until melted, about 3 minutes, and then stir until smooth.

2. In a bowl, whisk the mascarpone until fluffy. Whisk in the sugar, liqueur and chocolate cream. Refrigerate for 15 minutes, until firm. Spread four of the waffle cookies with the chilled chocolate cream, top with the remaining four cookies and refrigerate. Serve the chocolate cream sandwiches with the fresh berries. *–Amy Farges*

what is chocolate?

It's the food of the gods–at least that's the translation of the ancient Greek word for the genus of cacao, *Theobroma*, from which chocolate is derived. It comes in varieties ranging from so-bitter-one-taste-makes-you-shiver to so-sweet-it's-cloying, and in colors that range from mahogany to ivory.

Unsweetened (baking) chocolate is the most basic, just chocolate liquor and cocoa butter.

Bittersweet and semisweet chocolate are made by varying the amount of cocoa butter, sugar, vanilla (or vanillin) and lechithin. While one manufacturer's bittersweet may be another's semisweet, both contain at least 35 percent chocolate liquor by weight; that's the law in the United States.

Sweet chocolate, a designation that is often used by domestic chocolate producers, indicates at least 15 percent chocolate liquor and usually some sweeteners in addition to sugar.

Milk chocolate does indeed contain milk–although usually the powdered kind–and at least 10 percent chocolate liquor.

White chocolate is, quite literally, a chocolate of a different color–and composition. It's iffy right down to its name; yes, it's white, but it's really not chocolate. In most cases, what's called "white chocolate" is really a compound based on vegetable fat rather than the cocoa butter that makes real chocolate so luxurious. If white chocolate doesn't contain cocoa butter (many European brands do), it should be labeled white confectionery coating or summer coating–and used only for decorations.

St. Gallen Kloster Torte

MAKES ONE 10-INCH TORTE

This Swiss version of a traditional Viennese linzer torte uses cocoa powder in the dough.

- 2¼ cups all-purpose flour
- 1 cup finely ground almonds
- ½ cup granulated sugar
- ¼ cup unsweetened cocoa powder
- 2 teaspoons baking powder
- 1½ sticks (6 ounces) cold unsalted butter, cut into ½-inch dice
- ¼ cup milk

St. Gallen Kloster Torte

- 1 cup seedless raspberry jam

Confectioners' sugar, for dusting

1. Preheat the oven to 350°. Butter a 10-inch fluted tart pan with a removable bottom.

2. In a large bowl, toss together the flour, almonds, granulated sugar, cocoa and baking powder. Mix in the butter with your fingertips until the mixture resembles coarse crumbs. Stir in the milk. Gather up the dough and pat it into a smooth ball. Cut off one third of the dough and set it aside. ➤

Cognac Almond Truffles

3. On a lightly floured sheet of waxed paper, and using a floured rolling pin, evenly roll the larger piece of the dough into a 12-inch round. Invert the dough into the prepared springform tart pan and peel off the waxed paper. Fit the dough into the tart pan without stretching it and trim the edges of the dough flush with the tart-pan rim. Spread the raspberry jam over the dough in an even layer.

4. On a sheet of waxed paper, roll the remaining dough into a 10-inch square and cut the square into ten strips. Lay the strips lattice-fashion over the raspberry jam, anchoring the ends of the strips to the dough rim. Bake the torte in the middle of the oven for 45 minutes, or until the dough is firm. Let cool. Dust the torte with confectioners' sugar and serve. *–Nick Malgieri*

WINE Try a Ruby Porto, such as Fonseca Bin 27 or Warre's Warrior, with this chocolatey raspberry-filled torte.

Cognac Almond Truffles

MAKES ABOUT 3 DOZEN

After enjoying these chocolate truffles at our house, our guests are always delighted to receive a small box of them to take home.

- ½ **pound chopped bittersweet chocolate**
- 4 **tablespoons unsalted butter**
- 2 **large egg yolks**
- 1 **tablespoon cognac**
- ¾ **cup toasted sliced almonds**

1. Melt the chopped bittersweet chocolate in the top of a double boiler set over moderate heat. Stir in the butter until melted. Off the heat, whisk in the egg yolks until glossy. Add the cognac; refrigerate until solid.

2. Using a teaspoon, scoop small balls of the truffle mixture onto a baking sheet lined with waxed paper. Roll the truffles between your hands, then roll the truffles in the almonds. Refrigerate the almond-coated truffles for up to four days.   *–Jacques Pépin*

Triple-Chocolate Candy-Cane Kisses

MAKES ABOUT 3 DOZEN

This is a great way to use up all those candy canes that accumulate during the holidays.

- Four 3-ounce chocolate bars—
  2 semisweet chocolate, 1 milk chocolate and 1 white chocolate
- ½ **cup crushed candy canes**

Melt the three kinds of chocolate in three separate bowls. Stir half of the crushed candy canes into the dark chocolate. Reserve a bit of the crushed candy for sprinkling and stir the remainder into the milk chocolate and white chocolate. Drop teaspoons of the dark chocolate onto a parchment-paper-lined tray. Top with one dollop each of the milk chocolate and the white chocolate. Sprinkle with the remaining crushed candy. Let harden.   *–Diana Sturgis*

Chocolate Soufflé Symphony

6 SERVINGS

This recipe offers an amazing range of textures and temperatures—warm chocolate soufflés topped with fudgy ice-cold sorbet and thin, crisp chocolate cookie strands. Either the soufflés or the sorbet would be delicious served solo.

- 4 **large eggs, separated**
- 3½ **tablespoons sugar**
- 1½ **teaspoons all-purpose flour**
- 1 **stick plus 2 tablespoons (5 ounces) unsalted butter**

Chocolate Soufflé Symphony

- 6 **ounces extra-bittersweet chocolate, finely chopped**
- ½ **teaspoon fresh lemon juice**

Chocolate Sorbet (recipe follows)
Chocolate Spaghetti (recipe follows)

1. Preheat the oven to 375°. In a large bowl, whisk the egg yolks briefly. Gradually add 3 tablespoons of the sugar and the flour, whisking until the mixture is light and fluffy.

2. In a small saucepan, melt the butter over low heat. Remove from the heat. Add the chocolate; stir until completely

caramel variations

Nutty Caramels Prepare Creamy Caramels (opposite page). When stirring in the butter and vanilla in Step 4, add one-and-a-half cups toasted, coarsely chopped walnuts or unskinned almonds.

Coffee Caramels Prepare Creamy Caramels. Dissolve one tablespoon plus one teaspoon of instant espresso powder in one tablespoon of warm water. When stirring in the butter and vanilla in Step 4, add the espresso.

Spiced Caramels Prepare Creamy Caramels but reduce the vanilla to one-half teaspoon. In a small bowl, mix one-half teaspoon each of ground cinnamon, ground ginger and ground allspice, one-quarter teaspoon freshly grated nutmeg and one-sixteenth teaspoon ground cardamom. Add when stirring in the butter and vanilla in Step 4.

Nutty Butterscotch Caramels
Prepare Butterscotch Caramels (opposite page). When stirring in the vanilla in Step 3, add one-and-a-half cups toasted, coarsely chopped walnuts or unskinned almonds.

Nutty Chocolate Caramels Prepare Chocolate Honey Caramels (opposite page). When stirring in the butter and vanilla in Step 4, add one-and-a-half cups of toasted and coarsely chopped walnuts or unskinned almonds.

Mocha Caramels Prepare Chocolate Honey Caramels. Dissolve one-and-a-half tablespoons of instant espresso powder in one tablespoon of warm water. Omit the vanilla in Step 4 and stir in the espresso along with the butter.

Spiced Chocolate Caramels Prepare Chocolate Honey Caramels. In a small bowl, mix one-half teaspoon each of ground cinnamon, ground ginger and ground allspice, one-quarter teaspoon freshly grated nutmeg and a pinch of ground cardamom. Add when stirring in the butter and vanilla in Step 4.

melted. Let cool to room temperature. Stir the chocolate into the egg mixture.

3. Butter six ½-cup ramekins and coat them with sugar. In a large bowl, beat the egg whites with the lemon juice until soft peaks form. Add the remaining ½ tablespoon sugar and beat until firm and glossy. Using a rubber spatula, fold one-third of the egg whites into the chocolate mixture to lighten it. Fold in the remaining whites until just blended, with a few streaks of white remaining.

4. Carefully spoon the mixture into the ramekins, filling them three-quarters full. Set the ramekins in a baking dish and add enough hot water to the dish to reach halfway up the sides of the ramekins. Bake for about 10 minutes, or until the soufflés have risen nicely and are just slightly wobbly in the center.

5. Using oven mitts or large tongs, carefully remove the soufflés from the water bath and unmold each one onto a dessert plate. Top with a small scoop of the sorbet and garnish with a band of the spaghetti. Serve at once.

CHOCOLATE SORBET

MAKES ABOUT 2 CUPS

- ½ **cup sugar**
- ¼ **cup heavy cream**
- ¾ **cup water**
- ¾ **cup unsweetened cocoa powder, preferably Dutch process**
- 3½ **ounces extra-bittersweet chocolate, finely chopped**

In a medium saucepan, combine the sugar, cream and water and bring to boil over moderately high heat. Off the heat, whisk in the cocoa until smooth. Add the chocolate and stir until completely melted. Pour the mixture into a heatproof bowl and let cool to room temperature. Refrigerate until chilled. Transfer the mixture to an ice-cream maker; freeze according to the manufacturer's instructions.

CHOCOLATE SPAGHETTI

The leftover batter can be baked in whatever shape you like, such as ribbons or tuiles.

- 7 **tablespoons (3½ ounces) unsalted butter, softened**
- 1 **cup confectioners' sugar**
- ⅔ **cup all-purpose flour**
- ½ **cup unsweetened cocoa powder, preferably Dutch process**
- 3 **large egg whites**

1. In a large bowl, beat the butter with a wooden spoon until light and fluffy. Sift the confectioners' sugar, flour and cocoa over the butter. Add the egg whites and stir well to combine. Cover and refrigerate the batter for at least 30 minutes or up to 1 day.

2. Preheat the oven to 400°. Line a large baking sheet with parchment paper. Using a large metal spatula, spread ½ cup of the batter across the parchment paper as thinly as possible. Draw a large, clean, long-toothed comb along the length of the batter to make spaghetti-like strips. Bake for 3 to 4 minutes, or until the batter is just cooked through but still pliable.

3. Working quickly and beginning at one end of the strip, use a metal spatula to remove seven or eight of the spaghetti "strands." Wrap the warm strands around a 3-inch ramekin or other round dish and let them cool and crisp up. You will need to make a total of six bands of chocolate spaghetti to garnish the soufflés. Gently remove the strands of spaghetti once they have hardened. *—François Payard*

MAKE AHEAD The chocolate sorbet can be frozen in an airtight container for up to five days. The bands of chocolate-cookie spaghetti can be stored at room temperature in an airtight tin for up to two days.

WINE A Madeira, such as Leacock's 15 Year Old Bual or Blandy's 15 Year Old Malmsey

Chocolate Honey Caramels

MAKES 64

Bittersweet chocolate gives these caramels their deep chocolate taste.

- 1 tablespoon canola or other flavorless vegetable oil
- 1½ cups heavy cream
- 1¼ cups honey
- 8 ounces bittersweet chocolate, finely chopped
- ½ cup granulated sugar
- ½ cup firmly packed light brown sugar
- 2 tablespoons unsalted butter, softened
- 1 teaspoon pure vanilla extract

1. Line an 8-inch-square metal baking pan with aluminum foil, extending the foil over the sides of the pan. Thoroughly coat the foil with the canola oil.

2. In a heavy 3-quart saucepan, combine the cream, honey, chocolate, granulated sugar and brown sugar and bring to a boil over moderate heat. Using a pastry brush dipped in warm water, brush down the side of the pan a couple of times to prevent crystallization.

3. Raise the heat to moderately high and place a candy thermometer in the pan. Continue to cook the syrup, stirring constantly, until the temperature registers 254°, about 20 minutes.

4. Remove the saucepan from the heat and quickly stir in the butter and vanilla. Pour the caramel into the prepared pan and let cool to room temperature on a rack, at least 2 hours.

5. Use the ends of the foil to lift the caramel from the pan. Peel the foil off the back of the caramel. Coat the blade of a chef's knife with oil. Cut the caramel into eight equal strips, and then cut each strip into eight pieces. Arrange the caramels, without touching one another, between sheets of waxed paper, or wrap individually in waxed paper.   –*Carole Bloom*
MAKE AHEAD Store the caramels in an airtight container at room temperature for up to two weeks.

Creamy Caramels

MAKES 64

- 1 tablespoon canola or other flavorless vegetable oil
- 1½ cups heavy cream
- 1 cup light corn syrup
- ¾ cup sugar
- 3 tablespoons unsalted butter, softened
- 2 teaspoons pure vanilla extract

1. Line an 8-inch-square metal baking pan with aluminum foil, extending the foil over the sides of the pan. Thoroughly coat the aluminum foil with the canola oil.

2. In a heavy 3-quart saucepan, combine the cream, corn syrup and sugar. Stir continuously over moderate heat with a long-handled wooden spoon until the sugar is dissolved, about 5 minutes. Using a pastry brush dipped in warm water, brush down the side of the pan twice to prevent crystallization.

3. Raise the heat to moderately high and place a candy thermometer in the pan. Continue to cook the syrup, stirring constantly, until the temperature registers 250°, about 30 minutes.

4. Remove the saucepan from the heat and quickly stir in the softened butter and the vanilla. Pour the caramel into the prepared baking pan and let it cool to room temperature on a rack, at least 2 hours.

5. Use the ends of the foil to lift the caramel from the pan. Peel the foil off the back of the caramel. Coat the blade of a large chef's knife with oil. Cut the caramel into eight equal strips, and then cut each strip into eight pieces. Arrange the caramels, without touching one another, between sheets of waxed paper, or wrap the caramels individually in waxed paper.   –*Carole Bloom*
MAKE AHEAD Store the caramels in an airtight container at room temperature for up to two weeks.

Making Butterscotch Caramels, TOP; Chocolate Honey Caramels, RIGHT; and Nutty Caramels, LEFT.

Butterscotch Caramels

MAKES 117

These are my very favorite caramels. They're creamy and chewy with deep, long-lasting flavor.

- 2 sticks (½ pound) unsalted butter, cut into small pieces
- 1¼ cups light corn syrup
- 1 cup dark corn syrup
- 1 cup heavy cream
- ¾ cup firmly packed light brown sugar
- ½ cup granulated sugar
- 1 teaspoon pure vanilla extract

1. Generously butter a 13-by-9-inch metal baking pan. In a large heavy saucepan, combine the butter, light and dark corn syrups, cream, brown sugar and granulated sugar. Cook over moderate heat, stirring to dissolve the sugar. Using a pastry brush dipped in warm water, brush down the side of the pan twice to prevent crystallization. ➤

Assorted caramels

2. Raise the heat to moderately high and place a candy thermometer in the pan. Bring to a boil. Continue to cook, stirring constantly, until the temperature registers 248°, about 20 minutes.

3. Remove the pan from the heat; quickly stir in the vanilla. Pour the caramel into the prepared pan. Let cool to room temperature on a rack, at least 2 hours.

4. Remove the caramel from the pan. Oil the blade of a chef's knife. Cut the caramel crosswise into thirteen strips, then cut each strip into nine pieces. Arrange the caramels, without touching one another, between sheets of waxed paper, or wrap the caramels individually in waxed paper.   *–Carole Bloom*
MAKE AHEAD Store the caramels in an airtight container at room temperature for up to two weeks.

Lemon Orange Caramels

MAKES 64

Citrus adds a tangy flavor to these melt-in-your-mouth caramels. You could use the zest of two small limes to replace that from one of the lemons, or use all lemon or all orange zest. The differences will be subtle but noticeable.

- 1 tablespoon canola or other flavorless vegetable oil
- 1 cup granulated sugar
- ½ cup water
- Zest of 2 large well-washed oranges, minced
- Zest of 2 large well-washed lemons, minced
- 1½ cups heavy cream
- 1½ cups light corn syrup
- ½ cup firmly packed light brown sugar
- 2 tablespoons unsalted butter, softened

1. Line an 8-inch-square metal baking pan with aluminum foil, extending the foil over the sides of the pan. Thoroughly coat the foil with the canola oil.

2. In a small saucepan, combine ¾ cup of the granulated sugar with the water and citrus zest and bring to a boil over moderate heat. Remove from the heat, cover and set aside to infuse for at least 10 minutes.

3. In a heavy 3-quart saucepan, combine the remaining ¼ cup granulated sugar with the cream, corn syrup and brown sugar. Bring to a boil over moderate heat. Using a pastry brush dipped in warm water, brush down the sides of the pan twice to prevent crystallization.

4. Raise the heat to moderately high and place a candy thermometer in the pan. Continue to cook the mixture, stirring constantly, until the temperature registers 240°, about 18 minutes. Pour in the citrus syrup and cook, stirring constantly, until the temperature registers 254°, about 8 minutes longer.

5. Remove the saucepan from the heat and quickly stir in the butter. Pour the caramel into the prepared pan and let cool to room temperature on a rack, at least 2 hours.

6. Use the ends of the foil to lift the caramel from the pan. Peel the foil off the back of the caramel. Coat the blade of a large chef's knife with oil. Cut the caramel into eight equal strips, then cut each strip into eight pieces. Store the caramels, without touching one another, between sheets of waxed paper, or wrap the caramels individually in waxed paper.   *–Carole Bloom*
MAKE AHEAD Store the caramels in an airtight container at room temperature for up to two weeks.

Caramel Meringues

MAKES ABOUT 4 DOZEN

Make these treats on a dry day; humidity makes for sticky meringues.

- 4 large egg whites
- 2 cups sugar
- ½ teaspoon cream of tartar
- 1 teaspoon pure vanilla extract
- Pinch of salt
- ¼ cup water

caramel tips

Use a heavy-bottomed saucepan when making caramels to insulate the mixture from the heat and prevent scorching. Be sure it has a minimum capacity of three quarts so there's ample room to stir the bubbling mixture.

Remove any sugar crystals that may form when the syrupy mixture boils by washing down the side of the pan with a pastry brush dipped in warm water.

Cook caramels over moderate heat for maximum flavor and best color. Stir continuously with a long-handled wooden spoon. Each batch takes about twenty-five minutes.

Measure the temperature of the caramel as it cooks with an accurate thermometer, such as the Taylor candy thermometer, a long, slim, glass-and-mercury thermometer enclosed in a metal case with a footed base. The base rests on the bottom of the pan, allowing the bulb to be suspended in the caramel.

Remove the saucepan from the heat as soon as the caramel is ready and quickly blend in any remaining ingredients; don't stir too much or the caramels will be grainy.

Let the caramel cool completely before removing it from the baking pan. If it is cut too soon, the candy will be sticky and hard to cut cleanly.

Cut caramels with a sharp chef's knife rubbed with flavorless vegetable oil; use a sawing motion.

Store caramels at room temperature between layers of waxed paper in an airtight container for up to two weeks; leave space between them so they don't stick together. Or wrap individually in waxed paper or plastic and pack loosely in an airtight container. If you refrigerate caramels, they'll get soggy.

Harvest Crunch

1. Preheat the oven to 200°. Line four large baking sheets with parchment paper or aluminum foil. Bring a large skillet of water to a simmer over moderately high heat. Place the egg whites in a large stainless-steel or glass bowl and swirl over the hot water to warm the whites. Add 1 cup of the sugar and the cream of tartar. Beat with an electric mixer at medium speed for 30 seconds. Increase the speed to high and beat until the meringue is thick and glossy and holds a peak, 3 to 5 minutes. Beat in the vanilla and salt.

2. Fit a large pastry bag with a ½-inch plain tip and scoop the meringue into the bag. Pipe the meringue into tight, 3-inch-long S shapes. Bake the meringues for 1½ to 2 hours, or until they are firm to the touch and lift easily off the pan. Let cool on the baking sheets.

3. Have ready a bowl of ice water, a folded towel and a soup spoon. In a small heavy saucepan, combine the remaining 1 cup of sugar with the water. Cook over high heat, stirring, until the sugar dissolves. When the mixture boils, stop stirring and cook undisturbed until a deep gold-amber caramel forms. Set the bottom of the pan in the ice water for 30 to 60 seconds; stir the caramel as it cools.

4. When the caramel falls off the spoon in a thin, steady stream, lift the pan from the water and dry the bottom with the towel so that no water falls on the meringues. Hold the spoon high and drizzle the caramel over the meringues in abstract patterns; keep the spoon moving so you get pretty lines rather than blobs. Let the caramel set for 1 minute. —*Larry Hayden*

MAKE AHEAD Store in an airtight container for up to one day.

WINE Serving a sweetly floral-fragrant California Muscat, such as the 1995 Quady Essensia Orange Muscat or the 1996 Robert Pecota Moscato d'Andrea, with these caramel-topped treats recalls the classic pairing of orange and caramel.

Harvest Crunch

MAKES 2 CUPS

This instant praline can be made with any kind of seeds or nuts; it's terrific as a snack or as a dessert topping. Try flavoring the sugar with spices. Cinnamon and cayenne pepper, for example, are wonderful with pecans.

- 1 cup raw pumpkin seeds (about 5 ounces)
- 1 cup raw sunflower seeds (about 5 ounces)
- 1 large egg white, lightly beaten
- ½ cup sugar

Preheat the oven to 350°. Line a large rimmed baking sheet with parchment or waxed paper. Combine the pumpkin and sunflower seeds in a bowl and add just enough egg white to thoroughly moisten the seeds. Add the sugar and toss to coat. Spread the seeds on the prepared baking sheet and toast for 10 minutes. Stir to loosen the seeds and toast for 2 to 3 more minutes, or until light golden. Let the crunch cool and separate any clumps. —*Peggy Cullen*

MAKE AHEAD Keep in an airtight container for up to one week.

Crystal-Coated Walnuts

MAKES 5 CUPS

These addictive sweet and crisp walnuts were inspired by a trip to China.

- 1 pound walnut halves
- 1½ cups sugar
- ½ cup water
- 1 quart vegetable oil, for frying
- 3 tablespoons sesame seeds

1. In a large saucepan, cover the walnuts with water. Simmer over moderately low heat until soft, about 50 minutes; drain. Spread the nuts on a rack to dry.

2. In a medium saucepan, combine the sugar with the water. Bring to a boil and simmer over moderately high heat until the syrup reaches 230° on a candy thermometer, about 15 minutes. Add the walnuts and stir to coat them completely. Transfer the walnuts to a baking sheet in an even layer; let cool.

3. In a large saucepan, heat the oil until it reaches 350°. Fry the walnuts in four batches: for each batch, carefully lower the nuts into the hot oil and when it bubbles up, stir well. Fry the nuts until shiny and crisp, about 4 minutes. With a slotted spoon, transfer the walnuts to a rack set over a baking sheet and sprinkle with some of the sesame seeds. Repeat with the remaining walnuts, reducing the heat if the oil gets too hot. —*Susan Regis*

MAKE AHEAD The walnuts can be stored in an airtight container for up to one week.

Peanut Brittle

MAKES ABOUT 1 POUND

- ¼ cup water
- 1 cup sugar
- ⅛ teaspoon cream of tartar
- ½ cup light corn syrup
- 1½ cups roasted unsalted peanuts
- 1 tablespoon unsalted butter
- ½ teaspoon salt
- ½ teaspoon baking soda

Oil a large baking sheet. Bring the water to a boil in a saucepan. Add the sugar and cream of tartar and stir over moderate heat until the sugar is dissolved. Wipe the side of the pan down with a wet pastry brush. Stir in the corn syrup and cook over moderately high heat until the syrup is a light honey color and reaches 350° on a candy thermometer. Stir in the peanuts, butter and salt. Off the heat, stir in the baking soda. Immediately spread the mixture on the baking sheet with a wooden spoon. Let cool completely, then break into pieces. Store the candy in an airtight container for up to 1 week. *—Gale Gand*

Lark Creek Lollies

MAKES 4

These treats were inspired by chef Bradley Ogden's lollipops at the Lark Creek Inn.

- 4 **10-inch cinnamon sticks**
- ¼ **cup water**
- 2 **cups sugar**
- 1 **teaspoon vinegar**

I. Evenly space the cinnamon sticks on each of two lightly oiled baking sheets. In a saucepan, combine the water, sugar and vinegar and stir over moderately low heat until the sugar dissolves; wash down the crystals in the pan with a wet brush. Boil over moderate heat until the syrup is golden and reaches 320° on a candy thermometer, about 20 minutes. Cool the pan base in cold water for 10 seconds.

2. Working carefully, use a lightly oiled small ladle to pour 2 tablespoons of the caramel over the tip of each cinnamon stick. Let cool. *—Diana Sturgis*

CHAPTER 21 beverages

Homemade Eggnog (p. 415)

409   Crème de Framboise

409   Kir Normand

409   Blackberry Kir Royale

409   Sparkling Pineapple Punch

410   Red-Wine Passion

410   Fall Wine Punch

411   Rose-Hip Vodka

411   Cosmopolitan

411   Spicy Bloody Marys

412   Jamaican Gin and Gingers

412   Cafe Annie Margaritas

412   Pomegranate Margaritas

412   The Fernandito

412   Mango Rum Tango

413   Rum Punch

413   Papaya Ginger Sting

413   Christmas Coladas

413   Spiced Bourbon Lemon Twists

413   Starlights

415   Homemade Eggnog

415   Fresh Lemonade

415   Ginger Tea with Spices

Crème de Framboise and sparkling wine

Crème de Framboise

MAKES ABOUT 3 CUPS

A splash of this easy-to-make raspberry liqueur turns a glass of bubbly into a fabulous variation of the Kir Royale, or add sparkling cider for a Kir Normand (below).

1½ pounds fresh or thawed frozen raspberries
3 cups red wine
3 cups sugar
1 cup brandy

1. In a large bowl, mash the raspberries with a fork. Stir in the wine. Cover and set aside at room temperature for 2 days.
2. Pass the berries through a fine strainer into a medium saucepan, pressing to extract as much liquid as possible. Add the sugar and simmer over moderate heat until thick and syrupy, about 15 minutes. Pour the syrup into a heatproof bowl and cool to room temperature. Stir in the brandy. Pour the liqueur into clean jars or bottles and refrigerate for up to two months. *—Jane Sigal*

Kir Normand

10 SERVINGS

This fruity and effervescent drink recalls a Kir Royale but is made with sparkling cider instead of Champagne.

2 large Granny Smith apples (optional)
6⅔ cups cold dry sparkling hard cider, preferably French
6 tablespoons plus 2 teaspoons Crème de Framboise (above) or crème de cassis

1. Using a lemon zester or a channel knife, cut around the apples to make ten very thin, 6-inch-long strips of peel, allowing them to coil. The strips can be kept in ice water in the refrigerator for up to 2 hours.
2. Pour ⅔ cup of the hard cider into each of ten Champagne flutes. Add 2 teaspoons of the Crème de Framboise to each of the flutes and garnish with an apple strip. *—Marcia Kiesel*

Blackberry Kir Royale

8 SERVINGS

One 750-ml bottle Champagne or dry sparkling wine
About ¼ cup blackberry brandy
8 fresh blackberries, for garnish

Pour the Champagne into eight flutes. Add a dash or two of blackberry brandy to each glass and garnish each with a blackberry. *—John Fleer*

Sparkling Pineapple Punch

10 SERVINGS

A frozen pineapple-and-guava ring gives this punch drama.

1 cup guava nectar
One 3-pound ripe pineapple—peeled, cored and cut into 1-inch chunks
¼ cup honey
2 quarts cold unsweetened fresh pineapple juice (see "Making Juice," p. 412)
Two 750-ml bottles cold brut sparkling wine
¾ cup Calvados or cognac

1. Pour the guava nectar into an 8-inch metal ring mold or kugelhopf mold; the nectar should cover the bottom of the mold. Freeze the nectar until firm, about 25 minutes. Put the chunks of fresh pineapple and the honey in a blender and puree until smooth. Pour the pineapple puree over the frozen guava nectar, cover and freeze until solid, at least 2 hours.
2. In a large punch bowl, combine the pineapple juice, the sparkling wine and the Calvados. Warm the bottom of the ring mold under hot water to thoroughly loosen the pineapple guava ice. Invert the ring of ice onto a sheet pan, then carefully lower it into the punch with the guava-side up. Ladle the punch into glasses and serve. *—Marcia Kiesel*

MAKE AHEAD The pineapple guava ring can be made in advance and frozen for up to three days.

Blackberry Kir Royale

Red-Wine Passion

10 SERVINGS

This is a warm, very lightly spiced wine, spiked with flowery passion-fruit juice. Passion-fruit sorbet can stand in for the fresh juice here, if you prefer; use three quarters of a cup of melted sorbet and don't add any sugar.

Two 750-ml bottles red wine, such as
    Côtes du Rhône or Merlot
  6 star anise pods
One 3-inch cinnamon stick, broken
    in half
  1 teaspoon whole allspice berries
⅔ cup sugar
½ cup fresh passion-fruit juice
    (see "Making Juice," p. 412)
 10 half slices of orange

1. In a medium saucepan, combine the wine, star anise, cinnamon and allspice. Simmer over moderate heat for 5 minutes. Cover; remove from the heat. Let the wine steep, covered, for 20 minutes.
2. Whisk the sugar into the passion-fruit juice until dissolved.
3. Just before serving, reheat the wine mixture, but do not let it boil. Stir in the sweetened passion-fruit juice. Place an orange slice in each of ten brandy snifters. Ladle in the wine, leaving the spices behind, and serve.   —*Marcia Kiesel*

Fall Wine Punch

20 SERVINGS
SUGARED GRAPES
  2 pounds red and white seedless
    grapes, cut into 20 to 25
    clusters
  3 egg whites, lightly beaten
Sugar

PUNCH
 ¼ cup sugar
 ¼ cup cold water
Two 750-ml bottles red Zinfandel
One 750-ml bottle blush Zinfandel
 ½ cup (4 ounces) sweet vermouth
 ¼ cup (2 ounces) dry vermouth
  1 cup (8 ounces) peach brandy
  1 cup (8 ounces) Bacardi Limon
  1 cup (8 ounces) cranberry juice
GARNISH
  1 large block of ice
  4 cups thinly sliced fruit, such as
    peaches, pears and red apples
Seltzer, for serving (optional)

1. MAKE THE SUGARED GRAPES: Line a large baking sheet with waxed paper. Holding each grape cluster by its stem, dip it in the beaten egg whites and sprinkle with sugar. Arrange the clusters, without touching, on the baking sheet and freeze until solid (or up to 1 week).

LEFT: **Rose-Hip Vodka.** BELOW: **Fall Wine Punch.**

5 spirited tips

When mixing drinks, don't scrimp on the quality of the liquor. The better the alcohol, the gentler it is on your system. Here are some suggestions:

1. **Bourbon** Pick a smooth whiskey; my favorite is from Kentucky.

2. **Gin** Pour a pure British-made London Dry Gin.

3. **Hard cider** Try one of the dry, delicate ciders imported from France.

4. **Rum** Choose one that's been aged like cognac, preferably a 12-year-old from Jamaica.

5. **Tequila** This fiery spirit from Mexico should also be aged. Look for the word *añejo* on the label. *−Marcia Kiesel*

2. MAKE THE PUNCH: In a large bowl, combine the sugar, water, red and blush Zinfandel, sweet and dry vermouth, peach brandy, Bicardi Limon and cranberry juice and mix very well. Refrigerate overnight.

3. Pour the punch into a chilled punch bowl. Add the ice block and scatter the sliced fruit on top. Hang the sugared grapes around the edge of the bowl. Serve the punch in cups with a splash of seltzer and a grape cluster in each cup. *−Gary and Mardee Haidin Regan*

Rose-Hip Vodka

MAKES 1 LITER

Roses begin to produce hips around mid-July, after the petals fall. The tangy hips are ready to pick when they turn a fiery red-orange color. We gather them along the bluffs and beaches on Long Island. To make martinis, simply chill the vodka very well and serve it in martini glasses, garnished with fragrant wild or organic rose petals.

12 fresh rose hips, halved lengthwise

One 1-liter bottle vodka

A Spicy Bloody Mary

Add the rose hips to the bottle of vodka. Alternatively, pour the vodka in a large glass jar and add the rose hips. Seal the bottle or jar and store in a dark place for at least 3 weeks, or until the vodka becomes delicately flavored and colored by the rose hips. *−David Page*

Cosmopolitan

1 SERVING

1 ounce cranberry juice

1 ounce vodka

½ ounce Triple Sec

½ ounce fresh lime juice

Lemon twist, for garnish

Combine the cranberry juice, vodka, Triple Sec and lime juice in a shaker filled with cracked ice. Shake, then pour into a martini glass and garnish with the twist of lemon. *−Malachy Duffy*

Spicy Bloody Marys

8 SERVINGS

Here's a very potent version of the quintessential brunch drink.

5 cups tomato juice

3 cups vodka

⅓ cup fresh lemon juice

3 tablespoons Worcestershire sauce

2 tablespoons bottled horseradish

2 teaspoons Tabasco sauce

Freshly ground pepper

8 cucumber spears, for garnish

Lemon twists, for garnish

In a large chilled pitcher, combine the tomato juice, vodka, lemon juice, Worcestershire sauce, horseradish, Tabasco and pepper to taste. Refrigerate until chilled. Serve the Bloody Marys over ice, garnished with the cucumber spears and lemon twists. *−Jan Newberry*

Jamaican Gin and Gingers

10 SERVINGS

Forget ginger ale—ginger beer is a soft drink with a tangier bite that appeals to adults. Garnish with candied ginger.

½ cup sugar

¼ cup chopped candied ginger

Honey

2½ cups gin

6⅔ cups cold Jamaican ginger beer

1. In a mini-processor, combine the sugar and candied ginger; process to a coarse powder. Transfer to a shallow bowl. Lightly brush the rims of ten red-wine glasses or water goblets with honey. Dip the glasses into the ginger sugar and then, if you wish, freeze until ready to use; do not freeze your best crystal.

2. Fill each glass halfway with ice cubes; add ¼ cup gin. Pour ⅔ cup ginger beer in each glass and serve.   —*Marcia Kiesel*

---

making juice

To make fresh pomegranate juice, cut a pomegranate in half crosswise and use a citrus juicer, preferably a large one, to extract the juice. One large pomegranate yields one-third cup of juice, which can be frozen for up to six months.

To make fresh passion-fruit juice, cut the fruit in half crosswise. Working over a coarse strainer set over a bowl, use a small spoon to scrape the seeds and juice into the strainer; press firmly to extract as much juice as possible. Eight small passion fruit yield one-quarter cup of juice, which can be frozen for up to six months.

To make fresh pineapple juice, peel and core a pineapple, cut it into small chunks and puree in a blender. Work the puree through a fine-mesh strainer. Let the juice stand for about thirty minutes. Skim off any foam and use the clear juice. One pineapple yields about two cups of juice.

Cafe Annie Margaritas

16 SERVINGS

Making potent margaritas without sugar reduces the risk of hangovers.

Kosher salt

17 lime wedges

Ice

3 cups (1½ pints) top-quality silver tequila

1½ cups (12 ounces) Cointreau

1½ cups fresh lime juice

1. Pour a mound of salt on a plate. Run a lime wedge around the rim of each glass (preferably margarita glasses) and then dip the rim of the glass into the salt to coat. Put a lime wedge in each glass or on the rim.

2. Fill a large pitcher halfway with ice and add the tequila, Cointreau and lime juice. Stir well and pour the margaritas into the glasses, adding ice cubes to each glass if desired. Alternatively, fill a cocktail shaker with ice. Add ¼ cup plus 2 tablespoons of tequila, 3 tablespoons of Cointreau and 3 tablespoons of lime juice. Cover and shake vigorously for 1 minute. Pour the margaritas into two of the glasses and add ice if desired. Repeat with the remaining ingredients.   —*Robert Del Grande*

---

best sellers

Hot drinks from hot bars. Each recipe makes one drink.

Pear André Add two ounces cognac to three ounces warm pear syrup; garnish with a poached-pear quarter.—*Le Bar Lyonnais, Philadelphia*

Jerome Coffee Add one shot amaretto and one dash dark crème de cacao to one cup coffee; top with a dollop of whipped cream.—*The Hotel Jerome, Aspen*

The Frosty Add one shot Frangelico to five ounces steamed milk; garnish with chocolate shavings.—*Bistro 110, Chicago*

Pomegranate Margaritas

10 SERVINGS

1 cup sugar

½ cup water

2½ cups fresh pomegranate juice (see "Making Juice," left)

1 cup añejo tequila

¾ cup fresh lime juice

10 thin strips or slices of cucumber, for garnish

1. In a small saucepan, combine the sugar and water and simmer over high heat, stirring, until the sugar has dissolved; let cool completely.

2. In a tall pitcher, combine the sugar syrup with the pomegranate juice, tequila and lime juice. Stir well, fill the pitcher with ice and stir again. Pour into ten margarita, martini or cordial glasses. Garnish each margarita with a cucumber strip and serve.   —*Marcia Kiesel*

The Fernandito

1 SERVING

3 tablespoons chilled Bacardi Spice

1 tablespoon chilled cranberry juice

1 tablespoon chilled fresh orange juice

1 tablespoon chilled fresh lime juice

1 lime wedge

Pour the spiced rum, cranberry juice, orange juice and lime juice into a mixing glass half filled with ice cubes. Shake vigorously. Strain the drink into a martini glass and garnish with the lime wedge. —*Gary and Mardee Haidin Regan*

Mango Rum Tango

4 SERVINGS

4 large ripe mangoes, peeled and cut into large chunks

½ cup sugar

1 cup fresh orange juice

¼ cup fresh lime juice

¼ cup dark rum

Pinch of cinnamon

2 dashes of Angostura bitters

Pineapple wedges, for garnish

rum realities

A few myths and a couple of misunderstandings surround the making of rum. Herewith, some home truths to help set the (rum) record straight:

Great rums can be made with molasses as well as sugarcane.

An ounce of rum weighs in with the same number of calories (sixty-five in a one-ounce serving of 80-proof rum) as any other spirit of the same proof.

A dark-hued rum can be achieved not only by aging but also by the (legal!) addition of caramel coloring and flavoring.

No one island consistently produces better rum than another; it's the taste and ability of the rum maker that matters, not where he happens to set up shop.

In a blender, puree the mangoes and the sugar with the orange juice, lime juice, dark rum, cinnamon and Angostura bitters. Transfer to a pitcher and refrigerate until chilled. If the drink is too thick, thin it with a little water. Pour into large glasses and garnish with pineapple wedges. *—Tylun Pang*

Rum Punch

8 SERVINGS

Bambou restaurant in New York City makes a knockout version of this Jamaican drink.

2½ cups pineapple juice
2½ cups fresh orange juice
1 cup overproof white rum
½ cup dark rum
¼ cup coconut rum
¼ cup fresh lime juice
3 tablespoons grenadine

In a pitcher, combine the pineapple juice, orange juice, white rum, dark rum, coconut rum, lime juice and grenadine. Serve over ice. *—Herb Wilson*

Papaya Ginger Sting

4 SERVINGS

2 large papayas—peeled, seeded and cut into large pieces
½ cup honey
3 tablespoons fresh lime juice
2 teaspoons grated fresh ginger
2 dashes of Angostura bitters
2½ cups cold sparkling water
Crushed ice, for serving

In a blender, puree the papayas, honey, lime juice, ginger, bitters and ½ cup of the sparkling water. Transfer to a pitcher, stir in the remaining sparkling water and serve over ice. *—Tylun Pang*

Christmas Coladas

10 SERVINGS

If you can't find low-fat coconut milk, simply dilute three cups of full-fat unsweetened coconut milk with three cups of water.

6 cups unsweetened low-fat coconut milk
2½ cups fresh orange juice
1½ cups aged Jamaican rum
¾ cup pure maple syrup
1½ teaspoons pure vanilla extract

Combine all of the ingredients in a blender and blend until smooth. Pour into a tall pitcher, fill with ice and stir well. Pour the coladas into white-wine glasses and serve. *—Marcia Kiesel*

Spiced Bourbon Lemon Twists

10 SERVINGS

10 long strips of lemon zest, each studded with 3 whole cloves
1⅓ cups fresh lemon juice
1 cup superfine sugar
2 cups Kentucky bourbon
5 small ice cubes

Place one clove-studded strip of zest in each of ten Champagne flutes. In a bowl, whisk the lemon juice with the sugar until the sugar is dissolved. Add the bourbon and ice and whisk vigorously until cold, about 2 minutes. Using

a slotted spoon, skim the ice from the bowl and discard. Ladle the drink into the flutes and serve. *—Marcia Kiesel*

Starlights

This yummy formula for the sweet-bitter-sour Starlight comes from *New Classic Cocktails* (Macmillan).

4 SERVINGS

5 ounces Campari
1 ounce Cointreau
2 ounces fresh lemon juice
2 ounces fresh orange juice
2 ounces sugar syrup
Club soda
2 ounces of brandy
Lemon and lime slices, for garnish

Pour the Campari, Cointreau, the citrus juices and the sugar syrup over ice cubes. Shake until blended. Strain over ice cubes in a 1½ quart pitcher; add club soda almost to fill. Float the brandy on top and garnish with lemon and lime slices. *—Gary and Mardee Haidin Regan*

Starlights

Homemade Eggnog

Homemade Eggnog

10 SERVINGS

6 large eggs, separated
¾ cup sugar
3 cups milk
¼ cup bourbon
2 tablespoons dark rum
2 tablespoons brandy
1 cup heavy cream
½ teaspoon freshly grated nutmeg

1. Put the egg yolks in a medium bowl and set the bowl over a saucepan of simmering water. Add ¼ cup plus 2 tablespoons of the sugar and whisk over low heat until pale yellow and thick, about 5 minutes. Whisk in the milk, bourbon, rum and brandy and transfer to a large bowl.

2. In another large bowl, whisk the egg whites with the remaining ¼ cup plus 2 tablespoons of sugar until very soft peaks form. Stir the egg whites into the egg-yolk mixture. In a medium bowl, beat the heavy cream until it is lightly thickened. Fold the whipped cream and the nutmeg into the eggnog and chill thoroughly. Whisk to reblend before serving the eggnog. –George Mahaffey

MAKE AHEAD The eggnog can be refrigerated overnight. Stir before serving.

Fresh Lemonade

MAKES ABOUT 5 QUARTS

A summer picnic without lemonade is like Christmas without Santa. This recipe can be garnished with fresh fruit, such as raspberries.

3 cups fresh lemon juice (from 12 to 14 large lemons)
2 cups sugar
4 quarts water
Ice
Lemon wedges, for garnish

In a large glass bowl, combine the lemon juice, sugar and water. Stir to dissolve the sugar. Pour the lemonade into pitchers and serve over ice, garnished with lemon wedges.   –David Page

Ginger Tea with Spices

To develop the recipes in *Tonics* (Harper-Perennial), Robert Barnett consulted M.D.'s, Ph.D.'s, herbalists and cooks. Look for everything from chicken soup to therapeutic teas like this one.

MAKES 4 CUPS

One 1-inch piece of fresh ginger, peeled and grated
One ½-inch piece of Chinese cinnamon stick
4 cardamom pods, smashed open to release seeds
5 whole cloves
⅓ cup chopped mint
4 cups boiling water
Honey or sugar

Put all of the spices in a teapot. Add the water and let steep for 5 minutes. Strain into cups and sweeten. –Robert Barnett

index

Page numbers in **boldface** indicate photographs

A

Acorn Squash, Smoked, 324
Aioli, 145, **332**, **335**, 336
Alain Senderen's Syrup for Tropical Fruits, 337
Ale, Garlicky Steamer Clams in, 42-43, **43**
ALMONDS
    Almond Cake with Citrus Syrup, **343**, 344-46
    Almond and Carrot Cake, 346-47, **346**
    Almond and Strawberry Tart, 362-63, **363**
    Asparagus with Toasted Almonds and
      Garlic, 319
    Cognac Almond Truffles, **398**, 399
    Cold Poached Salmon with Beets and
      Skordalia, 154-55
    Fifteen-Minute Magic, 344, **344**
    Pear and Almond Tart, 364, **364**
    Skillet-Toasted Almonds, **12**, 13
    Spiced Lamb Shanks with Almonds and
      Dates, 253-54
    Wild Rice with Grapes and Toasted
      Almonds, 308, **308**
Amaranth and Hazelnuts, Pickled-Beet Salad
    with, 61-62
Anadama Bread and Fig Stuffing with Celery
    and Cracklings, 202
ANCHO CHILES. *See also* Chile peppers
    Chile Citrus Pork with Sautéed Pears,
      217, **217**
    Rio Rancho Steaks with Ancho Butter,
      240, **240**
ANCHOVIES, 102
    Christmas Spaghetti with Walnuts, 102
    Marinated Poached Fresh Tuna with Caper
      and Anchovy Sauce, 159-61, **160**
APPLES
    Apple Carrot Slaw, 56-57
    Apple Frisée Salad, 207
    Apple Pecan Crisp, 385
    Autumn Salad with Radicchio, Apples and
      Grapes, **50**, 51
    Baked Apples, 385
    Caramel Apple Tart, 365-66, **365**
    Cranberry Apple Butter, **330**, 331
    Granny-Smith-Apple Sorbet with Muscat
      and Grappa, **386**, 387
    Green Apple Slaw, 44
    Hot-Smoked Salmon with Apple Slaw, 43-44
    Maple-Glazed Sweet Potatoes and Apples,
      313
    Pumpkin and Apple Tart with Ginger,
      366-69, **367**
    Spinach-Stuffed Quail with Apple Frisée
      Salad, 207

APRICOTS
    Apricot Mustard, 210
    Apricot Soup, 380
    Turkey Sandwiches with Cranberry Apricot
      Relish, 297-298, **298**
Aromatic syrups, 337
ARTICHOKES. *See also* Vegetables
    Artichokes Simmered with Lemon and
      Honey, 317, **323**
    Nicola's Stuffed Artichokes, **316**, 317
    Sautéed Baby Artichokes with Lemon and
      Garlic, 317, **317**
    Savory Artichoke Bread Pudding, **52**, 275-76
    Shaved-Artichoke Salad, 62
    Stuffed Peppers with Couscous and
      Artichokes, **264**, 265
ARUGULA, 56
    B.O.A.T. Sandwiches, 301
    Braised Chicken in Arugula Cream, **176**, 177
    Creamy Low-Fat Arugula Pesto, **332**,
      335, **335**
    Roasted Beets with Arugula, 60, **61**
    Saucy Chicken and Arugula Meatballs,
      179-80, **180**
    Wilted Arugula and Prosciutto Frittata, **28**, 31
ASPARAGUS. *See also* Vegetables
    Asparagus with Toasted Almonds and
      Garlic, 319
    Caramelized-Onion and Asparagus Frittata,
      275
    Grilled-Asparagus Bruschetta, 15
    Spring Asparagus Salad with Quail-Egg
      Toasts, 62-63, **63**
Autumn Salad with Radicchio, Apples and
    Grapes, **50**, 51
AVOCADOS
    Avocado Grapefruit Salad with
      Pomegranate Dressing, 51-52, **51**
    Shrimp and Avocado in Mustard
      Vinaigrette, 31, **31**
    Shrimp-and-Avocado Pockets, 295
    Smoky Guacamole, 13

B

Baby-Green Salad with Chive Blossoms, 53
BACON
    B.O.A.T. Sandwiches, 301
    Linguine with Clams, Bacon and Hot Red
      Pepper, 100-101, **101**
    Oyster and Potato Stew with Crisp Bacon, 125
    Riesling-Marinated Chicken with
      Bacon-Wrapped Onions, 181-82, **181**
    Roasted Cod with Bacon-and-Spinach
      Stuffing, 139-40, **139**

Bahamian Grilled Fish, 143
Baked Apples, 385
Baked Pasta with Ragù and Ricotta, 106-108
Balsamic-Glazed Rack of Venison,
    259-60, **260**
Balsamic-Marinated Beef Tenderloin,
    237-38, **238**
Balsamic vinegar, 336
Bambou Crab Cakes, 39-40, **40**
BANANAS. *See also* Fruit
    Banana-Split Tart, 369-70
    Banana Tarts with Bittersweet Chocolate
      Sauce, 370-71
    Blueberry and Banana Brown Betty,
      376, 377
    Macadamia Shortbread with Fruit
      Compote and Banana Cream, 379-80,
      379
BARBECUE, 246
    Dimples' Barbecued Chicken, 172-73,
      172
    Easiest Barbecued Ribs, 224-25
    True Texas Barbecue Sauce, 172
Barbecued Baked Beans, 327
BARLEY
    Tabbouleh-Style Three-Grain Salad, 65
    Toasted Barley Mashed Potatoes,
      312, **312**
BASIL. *See also* Herbs; Pesto
    Basil and Cinnamon Syrup, 336-37
    Creamy Parmesan, Basil and Pine-Nut
      Dressing, 54
Basmati Rice, **306**, 307
BASS. *See also* Sea bass
    Black Bass with Burdock and Garlic
      Mustard, 134-35, **135**
    Grilled Wild Striped Bass, 134
    Sesame-Coated Striped Bass, 134, **326**
Bay Scallops with Sautéed Chanterelles,
    120, 121
Bay Scallops in Wood-Sorrel Butter Sauce,
    36, **37**
Beach-Plum Sauce, 261
Bean Curd, Steamed, with Scallions, 272
BEANS, CANNED OR DRIED. *See also*
    specific kinds
    Barbecued Baked Beans, 327
    Huevos Rancheros, 274-75, **274**
    Pan-Fried Bean Cakes, 272-73
Bean Salad with Fresh Salmon and Dill,
    278, 279
BEEF, 236-51
    salads, **66**, 67, 282
    for stews, 255
Beer. *See* Ale

BEETS. *See also* Vegetables
Cold Poached Salmon with Beets and
Skordalia, 154-55
Pickled-Beet Salad with Amaranth and
Hazelnuts, 61-62
Quails with Beet and Goat-Cheese Salad, 281
Roasted Beets with Arugula, 60, **61**
BELGIAN ENDIVE, 56
Endive and Roquefort Salad, 54, **54**
Parsley and Endive Salad, 52, **52**
BELL PEPPERS. *See also* Vegetables
Cod-and-Crab Cakes with Roasted-Pepper
Coulis, 141-43, **141**
Corn Chowder with Spicy Red-Pepper
Cream, 73-74
Olive-Oil and Pinot Blanc Squid with
Peppers, 123
Peperonata, **318**, 319
Pepper Steak, 246-48, **248**
Pickled-Pepper Relish, 58
Roasted Snapper with Peppers, Pine Nuts
and Tomatoes, 137-138, **137**
Roasted Sweet Peppers in Tomato Sauce,
258, 320
Spicy Red-Pepper Cream, 74
Stuffed Peppers with Couscous and
Artichokes, **264**, 265
Summer Squash, Sweet Pepper and
Polenta Casserole, 271-72, **272**
BERRIES. *See also* Fruit; *specific kinds*
Ginger Star Shortcakes with Summer
Berries, 383-85, **384**
Meringue Bowl with Sorbet and Fruit, 383, **383**
Sableuse and Wild-Berry Compote, 347
Wild-Berry Compote, 347
Beverages, 406-15
Biscotti, 356-57
Biscuit(s), 116, 289
topping, 204
Bittersweet Chocolate Bombes, 343, **343**
Bittersweet Chocolate Bread Pudding,
393-94, **393**
Bittersweet Chocolate Cream Sandwiches, 396
Black Bass with Burdock and Garlic Mustard,
134-35, **135**
BLACK BEANS
Black-Bean and Rice Salad with Fresh
Crab, 276-77
Black-Bean and Roasted-Vegetable
Burritos, 273, **273**
Chicken Chili, 192-93, **193**
Cuban Black Beans, 326
Fried Yuca Turnovers with Black Beans and
Chorizo, 30, **30**
Spicy Roast Beef with White-and-Black-
Bean Ragout, 238-39, **238**
Tortilla Salad, 279
Turkey Chili Potpie with Corn-Bread Crust,
204
BLACKBERRIES. *See also* Berries; Fruit
Blackberry Kir Royale, 409, **409**
Chocolate Buttermilk Cake with Blackberry
Meringue, 341-43, **342**
Nectarine and Blackberry Cobbler, 383

BLACK-EYED PEAS. *See also* Shell beans
Black-Eyed-Pea Salad, 65
Black-Eyed-Pea Salsa, 331
Black-Pepper Dressing, Mango, 56
Black Thai Sticky Rice, **306**, 307
Blanquette of Veal, Leeks and Peas, 232
BLUEBERRIES. *See also* Berries; Fruit
Blueberry and Banana Brown Betty,
376, 377
Peach and Blueberry Crisp, 382
Blue-Cornmeal Pancakes, 289-90, **289**
B.O.A.T. Sandwiches, 301
BOK CHOY
Jamaican Bok Choy, 323
Mirin-Glazed Sea Bass with Bok Choy,
133-34, **133**
BONIATO, 35, **35**
Crepas Cariocas, 34
BOURBON
Homemade Eggnog, **414**, 415
Spiced Bourbon Lemon Twists, 413
Bourride of Monkfish and Clams, 144-45, **145**
Braised Chicken in Arugula Cream, **176**, 177
Braised Chicken Pizzaiola, 177
Braised Lamb Shanks, **89**, 255-56, **256**
Braised Red Radishes, 320, **320**
Braised Short Ribs, 245
Braised Spring Vegetables, **185**, 318
BRANDY
Blackberry Kir Royale, 409, **409**
Crème de Framboise, **408**, 409
Homemade Eggnog, **414**, 415
Starlights, 413, **413**
Bread-and-Butter Pudding with Lemon Curd, 395
BREADS, 19, 202, 287-90. *See also*
Biscuits
recipes using
bruschetta, 14-17, **15**, **16**
crostini, 17, **17**
croutons, 71, 82
in desserts, 393-95
Ham and Cheese Strata, 276, **276**
Honeymoon French Toast, **286**, 287
in salads, 53, **54**, 62-63, **63**, 64-65
sandwiches, 294-301
Savory Artichoke Bread Pudding,
52, 275-76
in soups and stews, 71, 75-77, **76**, 114-
15, 117, 119-20, 123-25, 144-45, **145**
stuffings, 202
Sourdough Starter, 287
Brining chicken, 171
BROCCOLI
Broccoli Bread, 288
Mara's Pasta with Broccoli and Scallop
Sauce, 98-99
Broccoli Rabe with Polenta, Sausage and,
225-27, **226**
Broth, 269-71, 336. *See also* Stock
Brown-Bag Sushi, **304**, 305
Brownies, Chocolate Pumpkin, 351-52, **352**
Bruschetta, 14-17, 15, 16. *See also* Crostini
Brussels Sprouts with Walnuts, Balsamic
Vinegar and Mint, **200**, 324

BULGUR
Tabbouleh-Style Three-Grain Salad, 65
Bull's-Eyes with Mushrooms and Fontina, 294
Burdock and Garlic Mustard, Black Bass with,
134-35, **135**
Burritos, Black-Bean and Roasted-Vegetable,
273, **273**
BUTTER
Bay Scallops in Wood-Sorrel Butter Sauce,
36, **37**
clarified, 22
Farfalle with Crabmeat and Oregano
Butter, 99-100, **100**
Foil-Wrapped Halibut Fillets with Rosemary
Butter, 131
Molasses Butter, 385
Rio Rancho Steaks with Ancho Butter,
240, **240**
Butter Wafers, Clove and Lemon, 356
BUTTERNUT SQUASH. *See also* Winter
squash
Butternut-Squash Soup with Scallion
Cream, 77, **77**
Creamy Butternut Squash, Potato and
Tomato Gratin, 309-310
Riesling-Marinated Chicken with Bacon-
Wrapped Onions, 181-82, **181**
Butterscotch Caramels, 401-403, **401**, **402**

C

CABBAGE, 56
Apple Carrot Slaw, 56-57
Lobster-Stuffed Cabbage Rolls, 114-15
The Reubenesque, 298
Saigon Salad, **66**, 67
Spicy Coleslaw, 56
Stir-Fried Cabbage with Cashews, 324-25
Tuna Burgers with Sesame Slaw, 297, **297**
Cafe Annie Margaritas, 412
Cajun Salmon with Jicama-and-Melon Salad, 149
Cakes, 340-50
CAMPARI
Starlights, 413, **413**
Candies and confections, 356, **398**, 399-405
CANNELLINI BEANS. *See also* Beans,
canned or dried; White beans
Bean Salad with Fresh Salmon and Dill,
278, 279
Cannellini Beans with Sage, 326
Cannellini and Escarole Soup with Garlic
Oil, 81
Pasta with Cannellini Spinach Pesto, 94, **94**
CAPERS
Marinated Poached Fresh Tuna with Caper
and Anchovy Sauce, 159-61, **160**
Olive Caper Tapenade with Fresh Mint,
332, **332**, **335**
Roasted Veal Shoulder Stuffed with
Lemon, Capers and Parsley, 228, **229**
Sautéed Pork Scallops with Scallions and
Capers, 224, **224**
Veal Piccata with Orange, Capers and
Tarragon, 233

CARAMEL
candies, 400-403
tips for making, 403
Caramel Apple Tart, 365-66, **365**
Caramel Meringues, 403-404
Pumpkin Caramel Pudding Cakes,
349-50, **350**, **367**
Caramelized-Onion and Asparagus Frittata, 275
CARAWAY
Carrots with Coriander and Caraway,
323, **323**
Potato Bread with Dill and Caraway, 287-88
Sautéed Fall Greens with Caraway, 323
Caribbean-Spiced Grilled Pork Chops,
223, **223**
CARROTS. *See also* Vegetables
Almond and Carrot Cake, 346-47, **346**
Apple Carrot Slaw, 56-57
Carrots with Coriander and Caraway,
323, **323**
Chilled Carrot Ginger Soup, 71-72, **72**
Parsnip and Carrot Soup, 71
Roast Carrot Salad with Muscadine
Vinaigrette, 58, **58**
Smoky Escarole and Carrot Soup, **80**, 81
Winter-Squash and Carrot Puree, 324
Casablanca Salad, 66, **66**
Cashews, Stir-Fried Cabbage with, 324-25
Casserole Roast Chicken with Garlic Cream, 171
Casserole Roast Chicken with Peas and
Prosciutto, **170**, 171
Casserole Roast Chicken and Root
Vegetables, 169-71
Casserole-roasting chicken, 171
Catalan Tomato Bread, 14, **14**
CATFISH. *See also* Fish
Catfish Tacos with Tequila Cream Corn, 146
Pan-Fried Catfish with Salmoriglio Sauce,
145-46
Cauliflower and Potatoes, Curried, 324
CAVIAR
Chilled Leek Terrine with Caviar, 29, **29**
Potato-Chip Tower with Scallops and
Caviar, 36-38, **38**
CELERY. *See also* Vegetables
Anadama Bread and Fig Stuffing with
Celery and Cracklings, 202
Celery Root. *See* Vegetables
CHAMPAGNE, 409
Apricot Soup, 384, 384
Blackberry Kir Royale, 409, **409**
Oranges in Champagne Syrup, 389
CHANTERELLE MUSHROOMS. *See also*
Mushrooms
Bay Scallops with Sautéed Chanterelles,
120, 121
Pork Chops with Creamed Corn and
Chanterelles, 222
Chardonnay-Poached Salmon with Gamay
Noir Vinaigrette, 157-59, **158**
CHEDDAR. *See also* Cheese
Orwasher's Special, 300-301
Winter Vegetable Stew with a Cheddar
Crust, 269-71, **270**

CHEESE. *See also specific kinds*
Cheese Biscuits, 289
Grilled Eggplant and Cheese Pizzas,
291-93, **292**
Ham and Cheese Strata, 276, **276**
Individual Spinach-and-Cheese-Phyllo Pies,
21
Pasta Shells Stuffed with Grilled Radicchio,
94-97, **96**
Quesadillas, 298-99, **299**
Smoked Cheese, 25
Spinach-Filled Crespelle with Lemon
Sauce, 98, **98**
Three-Cheese-Stuffed Phyllo Triangles, 21-22
Wild-Mushroom and Cheese Pizza,
293-94, **294**
Cheesecake, Pumpkin, 371-72, **372**
Chelo, 307, **307**
CHERRIES. *See also* Fruit
Macadamia and Dried-Cherry Biscotti,
356-57, **357**
Polenta Cherry Cobbler, 378-79
Sour-Cherry Pancakes, 209
Chestnut Puree, Lobster with Nutmeg
Vinaigrette and, 42
CHICKEN, 162-193, 281-82, **281**
Chicken-Liver Crostini, 17, **17**
cooking techniques, 171, 175
Fusilli with Oven-Roasted Tomatoes and,
102-104, **104**
Saigon Wings, **46**, 47
salads, 187, 279-80, **280**
Smoked Chicken Breast, 24-25
soups and stocks, 80, 84-85, **84**, 85
trussing, 166
Chickpeas, Pasta and, 97-98
Chickweed Salad, 53
CHILE PEPPERS, 192, 222, 286. *See
also specific kinds*
Chile Citrus Pork with Sautéed Pears,
217, **217**
Chile Oil, 242
Chile Shrimp and Grits, 118
Dried-Chile Cream Sauce, 334
Green Chili, 249
Harissa, 268-69, 319
Hot and Tart Turkey, 204-206, **205**
Mediterranean Pepper Salad with
Sausages, 282
New-Potato Salad with Grilled Red Onions,
64, **240**
Quesadillas, 298-99, **299**
Salmon Steaks with Grilled Salsa,
149-50, **150**
Spicy Coleslaw, 56
Spicy Goan Shrimp, 116-17
Spicy Harissa, 319
Spicy Thai Beef Salad, 282
Spicy Tomato Relish, 191-92, **192**
Stuffed Rib-Eye Steaks with Chile Lime
Relish, 241
Chili, 192-93, **193**, 249
Chilled Carrot Ginger Soup, 71-72, **72**
Chilled Leek Terrine with Caviar, 29, **29**

Chilled Make-Ahead Summer Oatmeal, 283
Chimichurri Mixed Grill, 281-82, **281**
Chipotle Peanut Sauce, 335
CHIVES
Baby-Green Salad with Chive Blossoms, 53
Chive Oil, 40
Chive-Spiked Smoked Salmon on Chips,
14, **14**
Sweet Pea Soup with Chive Oil, 72-73, **73**
CHOCOLATE, 397
Banana Tarts with Bittersweet Chocolate
Sauce, 370-71
Bittersweet Chocolate Bombes, 343, **343**
Bittersweet Chocolate Bread Pudding,
393-94, **393**
Bittersweet Chocolate Cream Sandwiches,
396
Chocolate Buttermilk Cake with Blackberry
Meringue, 341-43, **342**
Chocolate Ganache Filling and Glaze, 341
Chocolate Ginger Crackles, 352-52, **352**
Chocolate Honey Caramels, 401, **401**,
402
Chocolate Pumpkin Brownies, 351-52, **352**
Chocolate Sorbet, 400
Chocolate Soufflé Symphony, 399-400,
399
Chocolate Spaghetti, 400
Cognac Almond Truffles, **398**, 399
Espresso Gelati Sundaes, 396, **396**
Fifteen-Minute Magic, 344, **344**
Mandarin Chocolate Cake, **340**, 341
Mocha Caramels, 400
Modeling Chocolate, 341
Nutty Chocolate Caramels, 400
St. Gallen Kloster Torte, 397-98, **397**
Spiced Chocolate Caramels, 400
Triple-Chocolate Candy-Cane Kisses, 399
The Ultimate Chocolate Pudding, **392**, 393
White-Chocolate Bread Pudding, 394-95
CHORIZO
Fried Yuca Turnovers with Black Beans and
Chorizo, 30, **30**
Shellfish Stew with Chorizo and Rouille,
119-20
Spanish Mussel and Chorizo Soup, 83
Christmas Coladas, 413
Christmas Eve Fish and Escarole Pie,
138-39, **138**
Christmas Spaghetti with Walnuts, 102
CIDER
Kir Normand, 409
Scallops with Cider, Gewürztraminer and
Sage, 121-23, **122**
Cilantro and Lime, Pan-Roasted Red Snapper
with, 135
CINNAMON
Basil and Cinnamon Syrup, 336-37
Red-Cooked Beef with Cinnamon,
239, **239**
Cioppino, 123-25, **124**
Citrus Custard Tarts with Caramelized Figs,
368, 369
Citrus Vinaigrette, 38-39

CLAMS
    Bourride of Monkfish and Clams,
      144-45, **145**
    Chimichurri Mixed Grill, 281-82, **281**
    Clams à la Marinière, 43
    Clams with Saffron, Tomato and Garlic,
      125, **125**
    Garlicky Steamer Clams in Ale, 42-43, **43**
    Grilled Chicken and Clam Paella, **182**, 183
    Linguine with Clams, Bacon and Hot Red
      Pepper, 100-101, **101**
Classic Greek Salad, 57, **57**
Clove and Lemon Butter Wafers, 356
Coal-Roasted Halibut, 131-33
COCONUT & COCONUT MILK
    Beef and Coconut Satays, 245
    Christmas Coladas, 413
    Coconut Shrimp with Tamarind
      Vinaigrette, 65
    Sweet Sticky Rice Treat, **394**, 395-96
    Swordfish Kebabs with Coconut Milk,
      148-49, **148**
    Thai Chicken and Coconut Soup, 85
    Thai Red Curry with Mussels, 127, **127**
COD. *See also* Fish
    Cod-and-Crab Cakes with Roasted-Pepper
      Coulis, 141-43, **141**
    Fried Christmas Cod, 140-41
    Roasted Cod with Bacon-and-Spinach
      Stuffing, 139-40, **139**
COFFEE
    Coffee Caramels, 400
    Espresso Gelati Sundaes, 396, **396**
    Jerome Coffee, 412
    Mocha Caramels, 400
COGNAC
    Cognac Almond Truffles, **398**, 399
    Pear André, 412
Cold Poached Salmon with Beets and
    Skordalia, 154-55
Compotes, 347, 379, **379**, 389
Concentrated Tomato Sauce, 105
CONDIMENTS, 331-32
    aioli, 145, **332**, **335**, 336
    Apricot Mustard, 210
    Green Tartare Sauce, 295
    Harissa, 268-69, 319
    Spicy Rémoulade Sauce, 24
Confections. *See* Candies and Confections
Cookies, 352-56. *See also* Biscotti;
    Brownies
Cool Cucumber Yogurt Dip, 332
Coriander and Caraway, Carrots with,
    323, **323**
CORN. *See also* Vegetables
    Catfish Tacos with Tequila Cream Corn, 146
    Corn Chowder with Spicy Red-Pepper
      Cream, 73-74
    Grilled Pork Chops with Succotash,
      220, 221
    Pork Chops with Creamed Corn and
      Chanterelles, 222
    Sam Hayward's Lobster and Sweet-Corn
      Soup, 82-83, **82**

    Sweet Corn Pancakes with Smoked
      Salmon, 44-45, **44**
    Tequila Cream Corn, 146
CORNISH HENS
    Cornish Hens with Nutty Brown-Rice
      Stuffing, **196**, 197
    Grilled Cornish Hens and Warm Potato-
      and-Portobello Salad, 197-98, **198**
CORNMEAL. *See also* Polenta
    Blue-Cornmeal Pancakes, 289-90, **289**
    Corn and Semolina Anadama Bread, 202
    Crispy Corn Bread, 288
    Jalapeño Corn Bread, 288-89
    Lemon Cornmeal Madeleines, 365, **365**
    Turkey Chili Potpie with Corn-Bread Crust,
      204
Coronation Chicken, **178**, 179
Cosmopolitan, 411
Country-Ham Croutons, 82
Country Loaf, 287
Court Bouillon, 153
COUSCOUS, **108**
    Chicken Couscous Salad, 187, **189**
    Italian Couscous with Parmesan and
      Herbs, 108, **186**
    Moroccan-Style Couscous, 108-109, **108**
    Stuffed Peppers with Couscous and
      Artichokes, **264**, 265
    Vegetable-Studded Couscous, 109
Cowboy Frittata, 275
CRAB
    Bambou Crab Cakes, 39-40, **40**
    Black-Bean and Rice Salad with Fresh
      Crab, 276-77
    Cod-and-Crab Cakes with Roasted-Pepper
      Coulis, 141-43, **141**
    Crab Ravioli with Shallot Cream, 40, **41**
    Farfalle with Crabmeat and Oregano
      Butter, 99-100, **100**
    Soft-Shell Crabs with Nasturtiums, 39, **39**
    Spicy Steamed Crabs, **112**, 113
    Spinach and Crabmeat Soup with
      Country-Ham Croutons, 81-82
CRANBERRIES
    Cranberry Apple Butter, **330**, 331
    Fennel and Watercress Salad with
      Cranberries and Pecans, 52
    Turkey Sandwiches with Cranberry Apricot
      Relish, 297-298, **298**
Creamy Butternut Squash, Potato and Tomato
    Gratin, 309-310
Creamy Caramels, 401, **402**
Creamy Garlic Tomato Sauce, 334
Creamy Low-Fat Arugula Pesto, **332**, 335,
    335
Creamy Parmesan, Basil and Pine-Nut
    Dressing, 54
Creamy Root-Vegetable Soup, 75
Crème de Framboise, **408**, 409
Crepas Cariocas, 34
Crespelle, Spinach-Filled, with Lemon Sauce,
    98, **98**
Crisp Shallots and Shallot Oil, 336
Crispy Corn Bread, 288

Crispy Salmon with Balsamic Glaze, 155-56, **156**
Crostini, 17, **17**. *See also* Bruschetta
Crumb-Crusted Ham with Orange Madeira
    Sauce, 227, **227**
Crystal-Coated Walnuts, 404, **404**
Cuban Black Beans, 326
CUCUMBERS
    Cool Cucumber Yogurt Dip, 332
    Nine-Spice Rack of Lamb with Cucumber
      Relish, 251, **250**
Cupcakes, Pumpkin-Seed, 350-51, **351**
Cured Salmon with Peppercorns, 45
Currants, Chicken with Fennel, Garlic and,
    175, **175**
CURRY
    Chicken and Red-Rice Curry, 182-83
    Coronation Chicken, **178**, 179
    Curried Cauliflower and Potatoes, 324
    Curried Chicken and Rice, 173-75
    Curried Pumpkin Soup with Spicy Lentil
      Crisps, 77-79, **78**
    Lobster Salad with Curried Vinaigrette,
      42, **42**
    New Delhi Curried Chicken, 190-92, **191**
    Pork Tenderloin with Grapefruit and Curry,
      219-221
    Salmon with Curried Spinach, 153-54, **155**
    Shrimp in Rich Curried Pea Broth,
      32-34, **32**
    Thai Chicken and Coconut Soup, 85
    Thai Red Curry with Mussels, 127, **127**

D

Dates, Spiced Lamb Shanks with Almonds
    and, 253-54
Dead-Simple Balsamic Vinaigrette, 54
Deep-in-the-Heart-of-Texas Chicken, 171-72
Desserts, 374-405. *See also* Cakes;
    Cookies; Pies, dessert; Tarts, dessert
DILL
    Bean Salad with Fresh Salmon and Dill,
      278, 279
    Dilled Shrimp Vol-au-Vents, 34-36, **36**
    Potato Bread with Dill and Caraway,
      287-88
    Savory Eggplant and Dill Frittata, 30-31
Dimples' Barbecued Chicken, 172-73, **172**
Dips & spreads, 13-14, 293, 332. *See also*
    Condiments
Double-Decker Pumpkin Chiffon Pie,
    372-73, **373**
Dried-Chile Cream Sauce, 334
Dried-Fruit Compote with Fresh Goat Cheese,
    389
DUCK
    Duck-Leg Stew with Lentils and Green
      Olives, 210-11
    Grilled Duck Breasts with Apricot Mustard,
      210
    Pinot-Noir-Braised Duck Legs, 210
    Smoked Molasses-Cured Duck
      Breasts, 25
Dutch-Oven Potatoes, 313

E

Easiest Barbecued Ribs, 224-25
Eel Canapés, Japanese, with Horseradish
    Crème Fraîche, 18-19, **18**
EGGPLANT. *See also* Vegetables
    Eggplant Caviar, 293
    Erica's Eggplant Parmesan, 266-67
    Grilled Eggplant and Cheese Pizzas,
        291-93, **292**
    Grilled Eggplant Parmesan, 266
    Lamb with Onion Juice and Grilled
        Eggplant, 251-52
    Pasta alla Norma, 91, **91**
    Roasted Tomato and Eggplant Tian, 321
    Savory Eggplant and Dill Frittata, 30-31
    Smoky Eggplant Dip, 13
    Steamed Eggplant with Garlic Sauce, 321
    Sweet-and-Sour Eggplant with Sautéed
        Pork, 223
EGGS, 274. *See also* Frittatas
    Bull's-Eyes with Mushrooms and Fontina,
        294
    Ham and Cheese Strata, 276, **276**
    Homemade Eggnog, **414**, 415
    Honeymoon French Toast, **286**, 287
    Huevos Rancheros, 274-75, **274**
    Poached Eggs Diavolo on Polenta, 273-74
Elizabeth's Potato Salad, 64
Endive and Roquefort Salad, 54, **54**
Erica's Eggplant Parmesan, 266-67
ESCAROLE
    Cannellini and Escarole Soup with Garlic
        Oil, 81
    Christmas Eve Fish and Escarole Pie,
        138-39, **138**
    Smoky Escarole and Carrot Soup, **80**, 81
Espresso Gelati Sundaes, 396, **396**

F

Fall Wine Punch, 410, **410**
Farfalle with Crabmeat and Oregano Butter,
    99-100, **100**
Farfalle with Morels and Fresh Pea Sauce,
    94, **95**
Fava Beans, Pasta with Rabbit and, 105-106, **107**
FENNEL
    Chicken with Fennel, Garlic and Currants,
        175, **175**
    Fennel and Watercress Salad with
        Cranberries and Pecans, 52
    Potato and Fennel Gratin, 310, **311**
The Fernandito, 412
Feta Dressing, Greek-Style, 55-56, **55**
Fifteen-Minute Magic, 344, **344**
FIGS. *See also* Fruit
    Anadama Bread and Fig Stuffing with
        Celery and Cracklings, 202
    Chicken Braised with Mission Figs,
        176, 177
    Citrus Custard Tarts with Caramelized
        Figs, **368**, 369

Figs Poached in Orange Muscat, 389
Roasted Turkey with Figs and Muscat
    Gravy, 198-203, **200**
Three-Citrus Custard with Fresh Figs,
    388, 389
FISH, 128-61. *See also specific kinds*
    Cioppino, 123-25, **124**
    Fish in Crazy Water, 137
    Smoked-Fish Chowder, 83-84, **83**
Focaccia with Black Olives, 289-90, **290**
Foil-Wrapped Halibut Fillets with Rosemary
    Butter, 131
FONTINA
    Bull's-Eyes with Mushrooms and Fontina,
        294
    Roasted-Vegetable and Fontina Tarts,
        19-21, **20**, **28**
Foraging for wild foods, 31
Frangipane Raspberry Squares, 354-55, **354**
Fresh Lemonade, 415
Fresh Tomato Sauce with Pecorino, 334, **334**,
    335
Fried-Chicken Salad, 279-80, **280**
Fried Christmas Cod, 140-41
Fried Yuca Turnovers with Black Beans and
    Chorizo, 30, **30**
Fried Zucchini Blossoms, 319
Frisée Salad, Apple and, 207
Frittatas, **28**, 30-31, 277-79
Fritters, Malanga 22
Frostings and fillings, 341, 354
The Frosty, 412
FRUIT. *See also specific kinds*
    Alain Senderen's Syrup for Tropical Fruits,
        337
    Chilled Make-Ahead Summer Oatmeal, 283
    desserts, 374-89
    dried
        Dried-Fruit Compote with Fresh Goat
            Cheese, 389
        Haroset, 331
    Fall Wine Punch, 410, **410**
    juice, 412
    Macadamia Shortbread with Fruit Compote
        and Banana Cream, 379-80, **379**
    Midsummer Fruit Tart, 361-62, **362**
    Tropical Fruit Soup, 380, **380**
Fusilli with Oven-Roasted Tomatoes and
    Chicken, 102-104, **104**

G

GAMAY NOIR
    Chardonnay-Poached Salmon with Gamay
        Noir Vinaigrette, 157-59, **158**
    Warm Potato Salad with Gamay Noir
        Vinaigrette, 157-59
GARLIC. *See also* Vegetables
    Asparagus with Toasted Almonds and
        Garlic, 319
    Cannellini and Escarole Soup with Garlic
        Oil, 81
    Casserole Roast Chicken with Garlic
        Cream, 171

Chicken with Fennel, Garlic and Currants,
    175, **175**
Clams with Saffron, Tomato and Garlic,
    125, **125**
Creamy Garlic Tomato Sauce, 334
Garlic Cheese Grits with Shrimp, 118-19
Garlic Oil, 242
Garlic Shrimp, 23
Garlicky Steamer Clams in Ale, 42-43, **43**
Parsley and Garlic Meatballs, 249, **258**
Pasta with Olive Oil, Garlic and Parsley,
    89, **89**, **256**
Potent Garlic Dip, 13
Roasted Chicken with Garlic, Rosemary
    and Potatoes, **164**, 165
Roasted-Garlic Mashed Potatoes,
    310-312, **310**
Roasted-Garlic Puree, 310-12
Sautéed Baby Artichokes with Lemon and
    Garlic, 317, **317**
Spice-Crusted Rib-Eye Roast with Garlic
    Jus, **236**, 237
Steamed Eggplant with Garlic Sauce, 321
Gaspergou Courtbouillon, 144, **144**
Gelato, 396, **396**
Georgian Lamb and Vegetable Stew, 256-57
Gewürztraminer, Scallops with Cider, and
    Sage, 121-23, **122**
Gin and Gingers, Jamaican, 412
GINGER
    Chilled Carrot Ginger Soup, 71-72, **72**
    Chocolate Ginger Crackles, 352-52, **352**
    Gingerbread, 19
    Gingerbread Cookies, 353-54, **353**
    Ginger Star Shortcakes with Summer
        Berries, 383-85, **384**
    Ginger Tea with Spices, 415
    Jamaican Gin and Gingers, 412
    No-Fat Ginger Soy Dressing, 55
    Papaya Ginger Sting, 413
    Plum and Ginger Crisp, 378, **378**
    Pumpkin and Apple Tart with Ginger,
        366-69, **367**
    Salmon with Ginger and Lime, **44**, 45
GOAT CHEESE. *See also* Cheese
    Dried-Fruit Compote with Fresh Goat
        Cheese, 389
    Garlic Cheese Grits with Shrimp, 118-19
    Goat Cheese with Piquillo Pepper Puree, 332
    Goat-Cheese, Tomato and Red-Onion
        Bruschetta, 16, **16**
    Quails with Beet and Goat-Cheese Salad,
        281
    Sweet Goat-Cheese and Walnut Tartlets,
        370, 371
    Toasted Goat Cheese with Mesclun,
        53-54, **54**
Golden Rice Pilaf with Spices, 308, **326**
Govindobhog Rice, **306**, 307
Granny-Smith-Apple Sorbet with Muscat and
    Grappa, **386**, 387
GRAPEFRUIT & GRAPEFRUIT JUICE
    Avocado Grapefruit Salad with
        Pomegranate Dressing, 51-52, **51**

Citrus Custard Tarts with Caramelized Figs, **368**, 369

Pork Tenderloin with Grapefruit and Curry, 219-221

Three-Citrus Custard with Fresh Figs, **388**, 389

GRAPES. *See also* Fruit

Autumn Salad with Radicchio, Apples and Grapes, **50**, 51

Wild Rice with Grapes and Toasted Almonds, 308, **308**

Grappa, Granny-Smith-Apple Sorbet with Muscat and, **386**, 387

Greek Salad, Classic, 57, **57**

Greek-Style Feta Dressing, 55-56, **55**

Green Apple Slaw, 44

GREEN BEANS

Bean Salad with Lime Vinaigrette, 60

Sesame-Dressed Haricots Verts in Roast Onions, 322

Summer Bean and Radish Salad, 58-60, **59**

Summer Bean Stew, 268

Green Chili, 249

Green-Olive Orange Dressing, 55, **55**

Green-Olive Tapenade, 13-14

Green Parsley Risotto with Sautéed Shrimp, 32, **33**

GREENS, 56. *See also* Salads; *specific kinds*

Baby-Green Salad with Chive Blossoms, 53

Minestra Maritata, 84-85, **84**

for salads, 56

Sautéed Fall Greens with Caraway, 323

Green Salad with Lemon Vinaigrette, 53

Green Tartare Sauce, 295

Grilled-Asparagus Bruschetta, 15

Grilled Beef Tenderloin with Merlot Sauce, 241-42, **241**

Grilled Chicken and Clam Paella, **182**, 183

Grilled Cornish Hens and Warm Potato-and-Portobello Salad, 197-98, **198**

Grilled Cured Chicken Breasts, 181

Grilled Duck Breasts with Apricot Mustard, 210

Grilled Eggplant and Cheese Pizzas, 291-93, **292**

Grilled Eggplant Parmesan, 266

Grilled Mahimahi and Green Tomatoes, **142**, 143

Grilled Pork Chops with Succotash, **220**, 221

Grilled Salmon with Sun-Dried-Tomato Sauce, 150-53, **151**

Grilled Stuffed Veal Chops, 228-30, **230**

Grilled Wild Striped Bass, 134

Grilling techniques, 131, 172, 173

GRITS

Chile Shrimp and Grits, 118

Garlic Cheese Grits with Shrimp, 118-19

Guinea Hen, Roasted, with Red-Wine Thyme Sauce, 198, **199**

H

HABANERO CHILES. *See also* Chiles; Scotch bonnet chiles

Sea-Bass Habanero, **132**, 133

HALIBUT

Coal-Roasted Halibut, 131-33

Foil-Wrapped Halibut Fillets with Rosemary Butter, 131

Shallot-Crusted Roast Halibut, **130**, 131

HAM

Country-Ham Croutons, 82

Crumb-Crusted Ham with Orange Madeira Sauce, 227, **227**

Ham and Cheese Strata, 276, **276**

Orwasher's Special, 300-301

Spinach and Crabmeat Soup with Country-Ham Croutons, 81-82

Haricots verts. *See* Green beans

HARISSA, 268-69, 319

Zucchini with Spicy Harissa, **189**, 319

Haroset, 331

Harvest Crunch, 404, **404**

HAZELNUTS

Hazelnut Praline, 356

Hazelnut Praline Balls, 356

Pear and Hazelnut Tart, 364-65, **367**

Pickled-Beet Salad with Amaranth and Hazelnuts, 61-62

Roast Quail with Hazelnuts and Port, 207-209, **208**

Wax-Bean Salad with Toasted Hazelnuts, 60

HERBS, 336. *See also specific kinds*

Coal-Roasted Halibut, 131-33

Herbed Rice Salad, 309

Italian Couscous with Parmesan and Herbs, 108, **186**

Penne Rigate with Fresh Herbs, **88**, 89

Roast Leg of Lamb with Orange and Herbs, 252-253, **311**

Sautéed Chicken with Herbs and Vermouth, 176

Sautéed Mushrooms with Walnuts and Herbs, 322, **323**

Sofrito, 332

White-Wine Herb Sauce, 333

Homemade Eggnog, **414**, 415

Home Spice Mix, 56-57

HONEY

Artichokes Simmered with Lemon and Honey, 317, **323**

Chocolate Honey Caramels, 401, **401**, **402**

Honey, Rosemary and Lavender Syrup, 336

Pork Rib Roast Glazed with Honey Mustard, 215-16, **216**

Romaine Leaves with Honey Mustard Dressing, 53

Honeymoon French Toast, **286**, 287

Hors d'oeuvres, 10-25

Horseradish Crème Fraîche, Japanese Eel Canapés with, 18-19, **18**

Hot Biscuits, 116

Hot-Smoked Salmon with Green-Apple Slaw, 43-44

Hot and Tart Turkey, 204-206, **205**

Huevos Rancheros, 274-75, **274**

I

ICE CREAM. *See also* Gelato

Banana Tarts with Bittersweet Chocolate Sauce, 370-71

Icing, Royal, **353**, 354

Individual Spinach-and-Cheese-Phyllo Pies, 21

Italian Couscous with Parmesan and Herbs, 108, **186**

J

JALAPEÑO CHILES. *See also* Chile peppers

Jalapeño Corn Bread, 288-89

Pickled Jalapeños, 331

Refried Beans with Pickled Jalapeños, 327

Shrimp with Tomato and Chile Pepper, 117, **117**

Jamaican Bok Choy, 323

Jamaican Gin and Gingers, 412

Jam, Sweet Onion, 331-32

Japanese Eel Canapés with Horseradish Crème Fraîche, 18-19, **18**

Japanese Rice, 305, **306**

Jerome Coffee, 412

JICAMA, **35**, 43

Cajun Salmon with Jicama-and-Melon Salad, 149

Jicama Cannelloni with Snapper Seviche, 43, **43**

Juice, 412

K

Kebabs, 148-49, **148**, 192, 245, **307**

Kir Normand, 409

L

LAMB, 251-59

Pasta with Abruzzi-Style Lamb Sauce, 106

for stews, 255

Lark Creek Lollies, 405

Lavender Syrup, Honey, Rosemary and, 336

LEEKS. *See also* Vegetables

Blanquette of Veal, Leeks and Peas, 232

Chilled Leek Terrine with Caviar, 29, **29**

Leeks with Miso Vinaigrette, 63

LEMONS, LEMON JUICE & ZEST

Almond Cake with Citrus Syrup, 344-46, **343**

Artichokes Simmered with Lemon and Honey, 317, **323**

Bread-and-Butter Pudding with Lemon Curd, 395

Chile Citrus Pork with Sautéed Pears, 217, **217**

Citrus Custard Tarts with Caramelized Figs, **368**, 369

Citrus Vinaigrette, 38-39
Clove and Lemon Butter Wafers, 356
Fresh Lemonade, 415
Green Salad with Lemon Vinaigrette, 53
Lemon Chicken with Golden Raisins,
190, **258**
Lemon Cornmeal Madeleines, 365, **365**
Lemon-Orange Caramels, 403
My Favorite Roast Chicken, 165-66, **165**
Roasted Chicken with Lemon and Parsley,
166, **167**
Roasted Veal Shoulder Stuffed with
Lemon, Capers and Parsley, 228, **229**
Sautéed Baby Artichokes with Lemon and
Garlic, 317, **317**
Sautéed Scallops with Rosemary and
Lemon, 120-21, **120**
Shrimp with Yarrow and Baked Lemon,
31-32, **32**
Spiced Bourbon Lemon Twists, 413
Spinach-Filled Crespelle with Lemon
Sauce, 98, **98**
Spinach and Parsley Soup with Lemon,
74-75, **74**
Stephanie's Poppy Cake, 347-49, **348**
Swordfish with Oregano and Lemon,
146, **147**
Three-Citrus Custard with Fresh Figs,
388, 389
LENTILS
Curried Pumpkin Soup with Spicy Lentil
Crisps, 77-79, **78**
Duck-Leg Stew with Lentils and Green
Olives, 210-11
Lentil Crisps, 79
Moroccan Spiced Salmon on Lentils, 159
Roasted Pork Tenderloin with Lentils and
Merlot Vinaigrette, 218-19, **219**
LETTUCE, 56. *See also* Salad
Sichuan Shrimp in Lettuce Leaves, 117-18
LIMA BEANS. *See also* Shell beans
Summer Bean Stew, 268
LIMES, LIME JUICE & ZEST
Bean Salad with Lime Vinaigrette, 60
Cafe Annie Margaritas, 412
Pan-Roasted Red Snapper with Cilantro
and Lime, 135
Papaya Ginger Sting, 413
Pomegranate Margaritas, 412
Salmon with Ginger and Lime, **44**, 45
Sea-Bass Habanero, **132**, 133
Stuffed Rib-Eye Steaks with Chile
Lime Relish, 241
Thai Lime Sauce, 334-35
Linguine with Clams, Bacon and Hot Red
Pepper, 100-101, **101**
LIQUEURS
Cafe Annie Margaritas, 412
Cosmopolitan, 411
The Frosty, 412
Jerome Coffee, 412
Kir Normand, 409
Starlights, 413, **413**
Liquor, 411. *See also specific kinds*

LOBSTER
Lobster Fisherman's Stew, 116
Lobster with Nutmeg Vinaigrette and
Chestnut Puree, 42
Lobster Pad Thai, 113-14, **114**
Lobster Salad with Curried Vinaigrette,
42, **42**
Lobster-Stuffed Cabbage Rolls, 114-15
Mediterranean Baked Lobster with Olive
Crumbs, 114
Sam Hayward's Lobster and Sweet-Corn
Soup, 82-83, **82**
Sara's Lobster and Mango Salad, 66-67
Sherry-Creamed Lobster with Biscuits,
115-16
Warm Green Salad with Lobster and
Oranges, 276
wine with, 115
Low-fat cooking techniques, 216, 232

M

MACADAMIA NUTS. *See also* Nuts
Macadamia and Dried-Cherry Biscotti,
356-57, **357**
Macadamia Shortbread with Fruit
Compote and Banana Cream,
379-80, **379**
Madeira Sauce, Orange, Crumb-Crusted Ham
with, 227, **227**
Mahimahi and Green Tomatoes, Grilled,
142, 143
MALANGA, 23
Malanga Fritters, 22, **23**
Mandarin Chocolate Cake, **340**, 341
MANGOES. *See also* Fruit
Mango Black-Pepper Dressing, 56
Mango Mignonette Sauce, 333
Mango Rum Tango, 412-13
Rhubarb Mango Crumble, 378
Sara's Lobster and Mango Salad, 66-67
MAPLE SYRUP
Christmas Coladas, 413
Honeymoon French Toast, **286**, 287
Maple Bread Pudding, 395
Maple-Glazed Sweet Potatoes and Apples,
313
Mara's Pasta with Broccoli and Scallop
Sauce, 98-99
Marinated Poached Fresh Tuna with Caper
and Anchovy Sauce, 159-61, **160**
Marmalade, Red-Onion, 17-18
MASCARPONE CHEESE
Bittersweet Chocolate Cream Sandwiches,
396
Ginger Star Shortcakes with Summer
Berries, 383-85, **384**
Pan-Roasted Chicken Breasts with
Mascarpone, 185, **185**
Warm Polenta Pancakes with Peaches and
Mascarpone, 381-82, **381**
Mashed Turnips and Potatoes, 312
Mashed Yukon Golds with Buttermilk,
244, 310

MEAT. *See also specific kinds*
cooking techniques, 259
frenching bones, 260
Meatballs, 179-80, **180**, 249, **258**
Mediterranean Baked Lobster with Olive
Crumbs, 114
Mediterranean Pepper Salad with Sausages, 282
Melon Salad, Jicama-and-, Cajun Salmon
with, 149
MENUS, 104, 113, 121, 133, 134, 141,
169, 173, 179, 183, 187, 190, 197,
201, 209, 215, 216, 218, 237, 240,
241, 244, 253, 256
meze table, 22
Passover, 189
MERINGUE(S)
Caramel Meringues, 403-404
Chocolate Buttermilk Cake with Blackberry
Meringue, 341-43, **342**
Meringue Bowl with Sorbet and Fruit,
383, **383**
MERLOT
Grilled Beef Tenderloin with Merlot Sauce,
241-42, **241**
Roasted Pork Tenderloin with Lentils and
Merlot Vinaigrette, 218-19, **219**
MESCLUN
Casablanca Salad, 66, **66**
Fried-Chicken Salad, 279-80, **280**
Toasted Goat Cheese with Mesclun, 53-54, **54**
Mexican Wedding Cookies, 355
Meze, 21, 22
Midsummer Fruit Tart, 361-62, **362**
Mid-Winter Soup, 80-81
Minestra Maritata, 84-85, **84**
Mini Poppy-Seed Pound Cakes, 349
MINT
Brussels Sprouts with Walnuts, Balsamic
Vinegar and Mint, **200**, 324
Minted Zucchini Patties, 19
Olive Caper Tapenade with Fresh Mint,
332, **332**, 335
Sugar Snap Peas with Mint Oil, 318
Mirin-Glazed Sea Bass with Bok Choy,
133-34, **133**
Miso Vinaigrette, Leeks with, 63
Modeling Chocolate, 341
MOLASSES
Molasses Butter, 385
Smoked Molasses-Cured Duck Breasts, 25
Monkfish and Clams, Bourride of, 144-45, **145**
Morels and Fresh Pea Sauce, Farfalle with, 94, **95**
Moroccan Spiced Salmon on Lentils, 159
Moroccan-Style Couscous, 108-109, **108**
MOZZARELLA. *See also* Cheese
Summer Pasta, 90, **90**
Muscadine Vinaigrette, Roast Carrot Salad
with, 58, **58**
MUSCAT
Figs Poached in Orange Muscat, 389
Granny-Smith-Apple Sorbet with Muscat
and Grappa, **386**, 387
Roasted Turkey with Figs and Muscat
Gravy, 198-203, **200**

MUSHROOMS. *See also specific kinds*
 Bull's-Eyes with Mushrooms and Fontina, 294
 Chicken Smothered in Cream with
  Mushrooms, 179
 Mushroom Broth, 269-71
 Mushroom Sauté, 89, **89**
 Red-Wine Mushroom Sauce, 333, **333**
 Sautéed Mushrooms with Walnuts and
  Herbs, 322, **323**
 Thai Mushroom Salad, 62, **62**
 Wild-Mushroom and Cheese Pizza,
  293-94, **294**
 Wild-Mushroom Fettuccine, 92, **93**
MUSSELS
 Mussel and Potato Stew, 126, **126**
 Spanish Mussel and Chorizo Soup, 83
 Thai Red Curry with Mussels, 127, **127**
MUSTARD
 Apricot Mustard, 210
 Chicken with Mustard-Seed and
  Onion Sauce, 187-189, **188**
 Grilled Duck Breasts with Apricot Mustard, 210
 Pork Rib Roast Glazed with Honey
  Mustard, 215-16, **216**
 Romaine Leaves with Honey Mustard
  Dressing, 53
MUSTARD GREENS. *See also* Greens
 Black Bass with Burdock and Garlic
  Mustard, 134-35, **135**
 My Favorite Roast Chicken, 165-66, **165**

N

Nasturtiums, Soft-Shell Crabs with, 39, **39**
Nectarine and Blackberry Cobbler, 383
New Delhi Curried Chicken, 190-92, **191**
New-Potato Salad with Grilled Red Onions, 64, **240**
New World Ciambotta, 267-68
Nicola's Stuffed Artichokes, **316**, 317
Nine-Spice Rack of Lamb with Cucumber
 Relish, 251, **250**
No-Fat Ginger Soy Dressing, 55
Nutmeg Vinaigrette and Chestnut Puree,
 Lobster with, 42
NUTS. *See also specific kinds*
 Cornish Hens with Nutty Brown-Rice
  Stuffing, **196**, 197
 Haroset, 331
 Nutty Butterscotch Caramels, 400
 Nutty Caramels, 400, **401**
 Nutty Chocolate Caramels, 400
 Pasta with Nut Pesto, 90

O

OATMEAL
 Chilled Make-Ahead Summer Oatmeal, 283
OILS, 336
 Chive Oil, 40
 Crisp Shallots and Shallot Oil, 336
 instant, 242
 Olive-Oil and Pinot Blanc Squid with
  Peppers, 123
 Sichuan Peppercorn Oil, 206

OKRA. *See also* Vegetables
 Summer Stew with Navy Beans and Okra,
  325-26, **326**
Olivata Croutons, 71
Olive-Oil and Pinot Blanc Squid with Peppers,
 123
OLIVES
 Chicken with Olives, Raisins and Onions,
  189-90, **189**
 Duck-Leg Stew with Lentils and Green
  Olives, 210-11
 Focaccia with Black Olives, 289-90, **290**
 Green-Olive Orange Dressing, 55, **55**
 Green-Olive Tapenade, 13-14
 Mediterranean Baked Lobster with Olive
  Crumbs, 114
 Olivata Croutons, 71
 Olive Caper Tapenade with Fresh Mint,
  332, **332**, **335**
 Pan-Seared Chicken and Green-Olive
  Rollatini, 185-87, **186**
 Tomato Sauce with Olives, Golden Raisins
  and Pine Nuts, 140-41
ONIONS. *See also* Vegetables
 Caramelized-Onion and Asparagus
  Frittata, 275
 Chicken with Mustard-Seed and
  Onion Sauce, 187-189, **188**
 Chicken with Olives, Raisins and
  Onions, 189-90, **189**
 Goat-Cheese, Tomato and Red-Onion
  Bruschetta, 16, **16**
 Lamb with Onion Juice and Grilled
  Eggplant, 251-52
 New-Potato Salad with Grilled Red Onions,
  64, **240**
 Pan-Seared Steaks with Vidalia Onions,
  244, **244**
 Pan-Seared Strip Steaks with Red-Wine
  Onion Sauce, 243, **244**
 Quick Onion Pullao, 271
 Red-Onion Marmalade, 17-18
 Riesling-Marinated Chicken with
  Bacon-Wrapped Onions, 181-82, **181**
 Roast Pork with Balsamic Onion
  Marmalade, **54**, 218
 Roasted Pork Loin with Sherry and
  Sautéed Red Onions, 218, **219**
 Sesame-Dressed Haricots Verts in Roast
  Onions, 322
 Sherry-Glazed Pork Chops with Fried
  Sweet Onion Rings, 222, **223**
 Sweet Onion Jam, 331-32
 Sweet Onion and Toasted-Walnut Rounds,
  18, **18**
ORANGES, ORANGE JUICE & ZEST
 Chile Citrus Pork with Sautéed Pears,
  217, **217**
 Christmas Coladas, 413
 Citrus Custard Tarts with Caramelized
  Figs, **368**, 369
 Crumb-Crusted Ham with Orange Madeira
  Sauce, 227, **227**
 Green-Olive Orange Dressing, 55, **55**

Lemon-Orange Caramels, 403
Oranges in Champagne Syrup, 389
Oven-Roasted Potatoes with Orange Zest,
 312
Pan-Roasted Salmon with Orange
 Vinaigrette, 277-79, **277**
Pistachio Ricotta Napoleons with Oranges,
 387-89, **387**
Roast Leg of Lamb with Orange and Herbs,
 252-253, **311**
Rum Punch, 413
Steamed Orange Beef, 248
Three-Citrus Custard with Fresh Figs,
 388, 389
Veal Piccata with Orange, Capers and
 Tarragon, 233
Warm Green Salad with Lobster and
 Oranges, 276
OREGANO. *See also* Herbs
 Farfalle with Crabmeat and Oregano
  Butter, 99-100, **100**
 Swordfish with Oregano and Lemon,
  146, **147**
Orwasher's Special, 300-301
Oven-Fried Chicken, 173
Oven-Roasted Potatoes with Orange Zest,
 312
Oxtail Stew with Pancetta, Slow-Roasted
 249-51
OYSTERS
 Oyster and Potato Stew with Crisp Bacon,
  125
 Turkey and Oyster Potpie with Biscuit
  Topping, 204

P

Pancakes, 23, 44-45, **44**, 209, 276, 289,
 289, 313
PANCETTA
 Perciatelli alla Gricia, 104
 Slow-Roasted Oxtail Stew with Pancetta,
  249-51
Pan-Flashed Ahi, 46
Panforte with Pears and Vanilla Cream,
 387
Pan-Fried Bean Cakes, 272-73
Pan-Fried Catfish with Salmoriglio Sauce,
 145-46
Pan-Roasted Chicken Breasts with
 Mascarpone, 185, **185**
Pan-Roasted Red Snapper with Cilantro and
 Lime, 135
Pan-Roasted Salmon with Orange Vinaigrette,
 277-79, **277**
Pan-Seared Chicken and Green-Olive
 Rollatini, 185-87, **186**
Pan-Seared Steaks with Vidalia Onions,
 244, **244**
Pan-Seared Strip Steaks with Red-Wine Onion
 Sauce, 243, **244**
Pantry essentials, 336
Panzanella, 64-65
Papaya Ginger Sting, 413

PARMESAN. *See also* Cheese
Creamy Parmesan, Basil and Pine-Nut
Dressing, 54
Erica's Eggplant Parmesan, 266-67
Grilled Eggplant Parmesan, 266
Italian Couscous with Parmesan and
Herbs, 108, **186**
Lamb Shanks on Polenta with a Parmesan
Crust, 254-55, **254**
Parmesan-Crusted Vegetarian
Sandwiches, 294-95, **294**
Shaved-Artichoke Salad, 62
Wild-Mushroom Fettuccine, 92, **93**
PARSLEY. *See also* Herbs
Green Parsley Risotto with Sautéed
Shrimp, 32, **33**
Parsley and Endive Salad, 52, **52**
Parsley and Garlic Meatballs, 249, **258**
Pasta with Olive Oil, Garlic and Parsley,
89, **89**, **256**
Pizza with Parsley Pesto and Potatoes,
290-91, **291**
Roasted Chicken with Lemon and Parsley,
166, **167**
Roasted Veal Shoulder Stuffed with
Lemon, Capers and Parsley, 228, **229**
Spinach and Parsley Soup with Lemon,
74-75, **74**
Tabbouleh-Style Three-Grain Salad, 65
PARSNIPS. *See also* Vegetables
Parsnip and Carrot Soup, 71
PASSION-FRUIT JUICE, 412
Red-Wine Passion, 410
PASTA, 86-109
in soups, 71, 79, **79**, 83
Pasta Shells Stuffed with Grilled Radicchio,
94-97, **96**
PASTRIES
dessert, 387-89, **387**
savory, 21-22, 30, **30**, 34-36, **36**
Pastry doughs, 364, 370
Pâte Brisée, 370-71
Pattypan squash. *See* Vegetables
PEACHES. *See also* Fruit
Peach and Blueberry Crisp, 382
Peach and Raspberry Crumble, 382
Summer Peach Clafoutis, 380, **380**
Sweet Peaches with Creamy Zabaglione,
381, **381**
Warm Polenta Pancakes with Peaches and
Mascarpone, 381-82, **381**
White Peaches with Crushed Raspberries, 382
PEANUTS & PEANUT BUTTER
Chipotle Peanut Sauce, 335
Peanut Brittle, 404-05
Sweet Peanut Dressing, 55
PEARS
Chile Citrus Pork with Sautéed Pears, 217, **217**
Panforte with Pears and Vanilla Cream, 387
Pear and Almond Tart, 364, **364**
Pear André, 412
Pear and Hazelnut Tart, 364-65, **367**
Pork Rib Roast with Pear Thyme Sauce,
214, 215

PEAS. *See also* Vegetables
Blanquette of Veal, Leeks and Peas, 232
Casserole Roast Chicken with Peas and
Prosciutto, **170**, 171
Farfalle with Morels and Fresh Pea Sauce,
94, **95**
Risi e Bisi, 79-80, **79**
Shrimp in Rich Curried Pea Broth,
32-34, **32**
Sugar Snap Peas with Mint Oil, 318
Sweet Pea Soup with Chive Oil, 72-73, **73**
PECANS. *See also* Nuts
Apple Pecan Crisp, 385
Fennel and Watercress Salad with
Cranberries and Pecans, 52
Pecorino, Fresh Tomato Sauce with, 334,
334, **335**
Penne with Ricotta and Tomato Sauce,
90-91, **91**
Penne Rigate with Fresh Herbs, **88**, 89
Penne with Sautéed Zucchini and Ricotta,
91-92, **92**
Peperonata, **318**, 319
PEPPERCORNS
Cured Salmon with Peppercorns, 45
Sichuan Peppercorn Oil, 206
Whiskey and White Peppercorn Syrup, 336
Pepper Steak, 246-48, **248**
Perciatelli alla Gricia, 104
PESTO. *See also* Basil
Creamy Low-Fat Arugula Pesto, **332**,
335, **335**
Pasta with Cannellini Spinach Pesto,
94, **94**
Pesto-Crusted Salmon, 149
Pizza with Parsley Pesto and Potatoes,
290-91, **291**
Roasted Chiappetti Leg of Lamb with
Pesto Stuffing, 252
Tomatoes with Pesto Oil, **28**, 29
PHYLLO
Individual Spinach-and-Cheese-Phyllo Pies,
21
Pistachio Ricotta Napoleons with Oranges,
387-89, **387**
Three-Cheese-Stuffed Phyllo Triangles,
21-22
Pickled-Beet Salad with Amaranth and
Hazelnuts, 61-62
Pickled Jalapeños, 331
Pickled-Pepper Relish, 58
PIES
dessert, 372-73, **373**
pastry, 373
savory, 138, **138**, 203-204, **203**, 257-59, **257**
PINEAPPLE. *See also* Fruit
juice, how to make, 412
Rum Punch, 413
Sparkling Pineapple Punch, 409
PINE NUTS
Creamy Parmesan, Basil and Pine-Nut
Dressing, 54
Roasted Snapper with Peppers, Pine Nuts
and Tomatoes, 137-138, **137**

Stuffed Tomatoes with Vegetables and
Pine Nuts, 320-21
Tomato Sauce with Olives, Golden Raisins
and Pine Nuts, 140-41
Pinot Blanc Squid with Peppers, Olive-Oil and, 123
PINOT NOIR
Pinot-Noir-Braised Duck Legs, 210
Pinot-Noir-Glazed Squabs with Roasted
Vegetables, 206-207
PINTO BEANS
Chicken Chili, 192-93, **193**
Refried Beans with Pickled Jalapeños, 327
Smoky Escarole and Carrot Soup, **80**, 81
Piquillo Pepper Puree, Goat Cheese with, 332
Piquillo peppers, 282
PISTACHIO NUTS. *See also* Nuts
Pistachio Biscotti, 357
Pistachio Ricotta Napoleons with Oranges,
387-89, **387**
PIZZA, 290-94
dough, 290-91
PLANTAINS
Crepas Cariocas, 34
PLUMS. *See also* Fruit
Beach-Plum Sauce, 261
Plum and Ginger Crisp, 378, **378**
Roasted Venison with Beach-Plum Sauce,
260-61, **261**
Poached Eggs Diavolo on Polenta, 273-74
Poached Salmon in Sorrel Sauce, **152**, 153
POBLANO CHILES. *See also* Chile peppers
Tall Tim's Texas Toasts, 17-18
POLENTA
Lamb Shanks on Polenta with a Parmesan
Crust, 254-55, **254**
Poached Eggs Diavolo on Polenta, 273-74
Polenta Cherry Cobbler, 378-79
Sausage and Broccoli Rabe with Polenta,
225-27, **226**
Summer Squash, Sweet Pepper and
Polenta Casserole, 271-72, **272**
Warm Polenta Pancakes with Peaches and
Mascarpone, 381-82, **381**
POMEGRANATES & POMEGRANATE
JUICE
Avocado Grapefruit Salad with
Pomegranate Dressing, 51-52, **51**
how to make juice, 412
Pomegranate Margaritas, 412
POPPY SEEDS
Mini Poppy-Seed Pound Cakes, 349
Stephanie's Poppy Cake, 347-49, **348**
Porcini Crostini, 17, **17**
PORK, 214-25
pasta with, 106-108
sandwiches, 299-300, **300**
soups, 84-85, **84**
for stews, 255
Port, Roast Quail with Hazelnuts and,
207-209, **208**
PORTOBELLO MUSHROOMS. *See also*
Mushrooms
Grilled Cornish Hens and Warm Potato-
and-Portobello Salad, 197-98, **198**

POTATOES. *See also* Vegetables
Chive-Spiked Smoked Salmon on Chips, 14, **14**
Cold Poached Salmon with Beets and Skordalia, 154-55
Creamy Butternut Squash, Potato and Tomato Gratin, 309-310
Curried Cauliflower and Potatoes, 324
Dutch-Oven Potatoes, 313
Elizabeth's Potato Salad, 64
Grilled Cornish Hens and Warm Potato-and-Portobello Salad, 197-98, **198**
Mashed Turnips and Potatoes, 312
Mashed Yukon Golds with Buttermilk, **244**, 310
Mussel and Potato Stew, 126, **126**
New-Potato Salad with Grilled Red Onions, 64, **240**
Oven-Roasted Potatoes with Orange Zest, 316
Oyster and Potato Stew with Crisp Bacon, 125
Pizza with Parsley Pesto and Potatoes, 290-91, **291**
Potato Bread with Dill and Caraway, 287-88
Potato-Chip Tower with Scallops and Caviar, 36-38, **38**
Potato and Fennel Gratin, 310, **311**
Roast Chicken with Warm Potato Salad, 168, **168**
Roast Farm Chicken with Potatoes, 183-85, **184**
Roasted Chicken with Garlic, Rosemary and Potatoes, **164**, 165
Roasted-Garlic Mashed Potatoes, 310-312, **310**
Rosemary Flank Steak with Roasted Potatoes, 245
Seared Salmon on Tartare Mashed Potatoes, 157
Sicilian Potato and Pasta Soup, 79, **79**
Toasted Barley Mashed Potatoes, 312, **312**
Tuna and Potato Salad, 67
Two-Potato Pancakes, **141**, 313
Warm Potato Salad with Gamay Noir Vinaigrette, 157-59
Potent Garlic Dip, 13
Potpies, 203-204, 257-59, **257**
Praline, Hazelnut, 356
Prebaked Pie Pastry, 373
Preserves, 17-18, **330**, 331
PROSCIUTTO
Casserole Roast Chicken with Peas and Prosciutto, **170**, 171
Grilled-Asparagus Bruschetta, 15
Puddings, **392**-95
PUMPKIN
Chocolate Pumpkin Brownies, 351-52, **352**
Curried Pumpkin Soup with Spicy Lentil Crisps, 77-79, **78**
Double-Decker Pumpkin Chiffon Pie, 372-73, **373**

Pumpkin and Apple Tart with Ginger, 366-69, **367**
Pumpkin Caramel Pudding Cakes, 349-50, **350**, 367
Pumpkin Cheesecake, 371-72, **372**
Pumpkin-Seed Cupcakes, 350-51, **351**
seeds
Harvest Crunch, 404, **404**
Pumpkin-Seed Cupcakes, 350-51, **351**
PUNCH
Fall Wine Punch, 410, **410**
Rum Punch, 413
Sparkling Pineapple Punch, 409

Q

QUAIL
Quails with Beet and Goat-Cheese Salad, 281
Roast Quail with Hazelnuts and Port, 207-209, **208**
Spinach-Stuffed Quail with Apple Frisée Salad, 207
White-Wing-Dove-Style Grilled Quail, 209
Quail-Egg Toasts, Spring Asparagus Salad with, 62-63, **63**
Quesadillas, 298-99, **299**
Quick Onion Pullao, 271

R

Rabbit and Fava Beans, Pasta with, 105-106, **107**
RADICCHIO
Autumn Salad with Radicchio, Apples and Grapes, 50, 51
Pasta Shells Stuffed with Grilled Radicchio, 94-97, **96**
RADISHES
Braised Red Radishes, 320, **320**
Summer Bean and Radish Salad, 58-60, **59**
RAISINS
Chicken with Olives, Raisins and Onions, 189-90, **189**
Lemon Chicken with Golden Raisins, 190, **258**
Tomato Sauce with Olives, Golden Raisins and Pine Nuts, 140-41
Ramp Gratin, Skillet, 318-19, **318**
RASPBERRIES. *See also* Berries; Fruit
Crème de Framboise, **408**, 409
Frangipane Raspberry Squares, 354-55, **354**
Peach and Raspberry Crumble, 382
Raspberry Fool, 382
White Peaches with Crushed Raspberries, 382
Ravioli, Crab, with Shallot Cream, 40, **41**
Red-Cooked Beef with Cinnamon, 239, **239**
RED SNAPPER. *See also* Fish
Fish in Crazy Water, 137
Jicama Cannelloni with Snapper Seviche, 43, **43**
Pan-Roasted Red Snapper with Cilantro and Lime, 135

Roasted Snapper with Peppers, Pine Nuts and Tomatoes, 137-138, **137**
Spicy Snapper, **136**, 137
RED WINE. *See also* Wine; *specific kinds*
Crème de Framboise, **408**, 409
Pan-Seared Strip Steaks with Red-Wine Onion Sauce, 243, **244**
Red-Wine Mushroom Sauce, 333, **333**
Red-Wine Passion, 410
Roasted Guinea Hen with Red-Wine Thyme Sauce, 198, **199**
Red and Yellow Tomato Salad, 57
Refried Beans with Pickled Jalapeños, 327
Relishes, 13-14, 17-18, 58, 191-92, **192**.
See also Condiments
The Reubenesque, 298
RHUBARB
Rhubarb Mango Crumble, 378
Strawberry and Rhubarb Pandowdy, 377, **377**
RICE, 309, 310
Basmati Rice, **306**, 307
Black-Bean and Rice Salad with Fresh Crab, 276-77
Black Thai Sticky Rice, **306**, 307
Brown-Bag Sushi, **304**, 305
Chelo, 307, **307**
Chicken and Red-Rice Curry, 182-83
Cornish Hens with Nutty Brown-Rice Stuffing, **196**, 197
Curried Chicken and Rice, 173-75
Golden Rice Pilaf with Spices, 308, **326**
Govindobhog Rice, **306**, 307
Green Parsley Risotto with Sautéed Shrimp, 32, **33**
Grilled Chicken and Clam Paella, **182**, 183
Herbed Rice Salad, 309
Japanese Rice, 305, **306**
Nicola's Stuffed Artichokes, **316**, 317
Quick Onion Pullao, 271
Risi e Bisi, 79-80, **79**
Salmon with Thai Rice Salad, 156, **157**
Squash- Blossom Rice, 308, **309**
Sushi Rice, 305-06
Sweet Sticky Rice Treat, **394**, 395-96
Tabbouleh-Style Three-Grain Salad, 65
Thai Jasmine Rice, 306, **306**
Thai Sticky Rice, 306, **306**
tips, 305
Torta di Riso, 349
Wehani Rice, 306, **306**
RICE NOODLES
Lobster Pad Thai, 113-14, **114**
Red-Cooked Beef with Cinnamon, 239, **239**
Rich Turkey Stock, 202-203
RICOTTA. *See also* Cheese
Baked Pasta with Ragù and Ricotta, 106-108
Penne with Ricotta and Tomato Sauce, 90-91, **91**
Penne with Sautéed Zucchini and Ricotta, 91-92, **92**
Pistachio Ricotta Napoleons with Oranges, 387-89, **387**
Torta di Riso, 349

Riesling-Marinated Chicken with Bacon-Wrapped Onions, 181-82, **181**
Rigatoni Timbale alla Gangivecchio, 105
Rio Rancho Steaks with Ancho Butter, 240, **240**
Risi e Bisi, 79-80, **79**
Risotto, Green Parsley, with Sautéed Shrimp, 32, **33**
Roast Carrot Salad with Muscadine Vinaigrette, 58, 58
Roast Chicken Stuffed with Tuscan Chard, 168-69, **169**
Roast Chicken with Warm Potato Salad, 168, **167**
Roast Farm Chicken with Potatoes, 183-85, **184**
Roast Leg of Lamb with Orange and Herbs, 252-253, **311**
Roast Pork with Balsamic Onion Marmalade, **54**, 218
Roast Quail with Hazelnuts and Port, 207-209, **208**
Roast Veal, 228
Roasted Beets with Arugula, 60, **61**
Roasted Chiappetti Leg of Lamb with Pesto Stuffing, 252
Roasted Chicken with Garlic, Rosemary and Potatoes, **164**, 165
Roasted Chicken with Lemon and Parsley, 166, **167**
Roasted Cod with Bacon-and-Spinach Stuffing, 139-40, **139**
Roasted-Garlic Mashed Potatoes, 310-312, **310**
Roasted-Garlic Puree, 310-12
Roasted Guinea Hen with Red-Wine Thyme Sauce, 198, **199**
Roasted Pork Loin with Sherry and Sautéed Red Onions, 218, **219**
Roasted Pork Tenderloin with Lentils and Merlot Vinaigrette, 218-19, **219**
Roasted Root Vegetables, 325, **325**
Roasted Snapper with Peppers, Pine Nuts and Tomatoes, 137-139, **137**
Roasted Sweet Peppers in Tomato Sauce, **258**, 320
Roasted Tomato and Eggplant Tian, 321
Roasted Turkey with Figs and Muscat Gravy, 198-203, **200**
Roasted Veal Shoulder Stuffed with Lemon, Capers and Parsley, 228, **229**
Roasted-Vegetable Bruschetta, 14-15, **15**
Roasted-Vegetable and Fontina Tarts, 19-21, **20**, **28**
Roasted-Vegetable Soup, 75-77, **76**
Roasted Venison with Beach-Plum Sauce, 260-61, **261**
Romaine Leaves with Honey Mustard Dressing, 53
Roquefort Salad, Endive and, 54, **54**
Rose-Hip Vodka, **410**, 411
ROSEMARY
    Foil-Wrapped Halibut Fillets with Rosemary Butter, 131
    Honey, Rosemary and Lavender Syrup, 336
    Lamb and Rosemary Potpies, 257-59, **257**

Roasted Chicken with Garlic, Rosemary and Potatoes, **164**, 165
Rosemary Flank Steak with Roasted Potatoes, 245
Rosemary Tuiles, 356
Sautéed Scallops with Rosemary and Lemon, 120-21, **120**
Steak with Rosemary Oil, 242, **243**
Rouille, Shellfish Stew with Chorizo and 119-20
Royal Icing, **353**, 354
RUM, 413
    Christmas Coladas, 413
    Homemade Eggnog, **414**, 415
    Mango Rum Tango, 412-13
    Rum Punch, 413
    Stephanie's Poppy Cake, 347-49, **348**

S

Sableuse and Wild-Berry Compote, 347
Saffron, Tomato and Garlic, Clams with, 125, **125**
SAGE
    Cannellini Beans with Sage, 326
    Sage Oil, 244
    Scallops with Cider, Gewürztraminer and Sage, 121-23, **122**
Saigon Salad, **66**, 67
Saigon Wings, **46**, 47
St. Gallen Kloster Torte, 397-98, **397**
Sake-Glazed Sea Bass, 22-23, **23**
Salad dressings, 54-56, 58. See also Salads; Vinaigrettes
SALADS, 48-67, 279
    chicken, 187, **189**, 279-80, **280**
    meat, 282
    quail, 281
    rice, 309
    seafood, 43, 276-77
    tips, 58
    vegetable, 44
SALMON, 154
    Bean Salad with Fresh Salmon and Dill, 282, 283
    Cajun Salmon with Jicama-and-Melon Salad, 149
    Chardonnay-Poached Salmon with Gamay Noir Vinaigrette, 157-59, **158**
    Cold Poached Salmon with Beets and Skordalia, 154-55
    Crispy Salmon with Balsamic Glaze, 155-56, **156**
    Cured Salmon with Peppercorns, 45
    Grilled Salmon with Sun-Dried-Tomato Sauce, 150-53, **151**
    Moroccan Spiced Salmon on Lentils, 159
    Pan-Roasted Salmon with Orange Vinaigrette, 277-79, **277**
    Pesto-Crusted Salmon, 149
    Poached Salmon in Sorrel Sauce, **152**, 153
    Salmon Burgers with Green Tartare Sauce, 295-97, **296**
    Salmon with Curried Spinach, 153-54, **155**

Salmon with Ginger and Lime, **44**, 45
Salmon Steaks with Grilled Salsa, 149-50, **150**
Salmon with Thai Rice Salad, 156, **157**
Seared Salmon on Tartare Mashed Potatoes, 157
smoked
    Chive-Spiked Smoked Salmon on Chips, 14, **14**
    Hot-Smoked Salmon with Green-Apple Slaw, 43-44
    Sweet Corn Pancakes with Smoked Salmon, 44-45, **44**
    wine with, 150
Salsa, Black-Eyed-Pea, 331
Sam Hayward's Lobster and Sweet-Corn Soup, 82-83, **82**
Sandwiches, 294-301
Sara's Lobster and Mango Salad, 66-67
SARDINES
    Pasta with Sardines, 102, **103**
    Spaghetti alla Siracusana, 101-102, **101**
SAUCES
    Beach-Plum Sauce, 261
    Chipotle Peanut Sauce, 335
    Creamy Garlic Tomato Sauce, 334
    Dried-Chile Cream Sauce, 334
    Fresh Tomato Sauce with Pecorino, 334, **334**, **335**
    Mango Mignonette Sauce, 333
    for pasta, 89-90, **89**, 105
    Red-Wine Mushroom Sauce, 333, **333**
    Thai Lime Sauce, 334-35
    True Texas Barbecue Sauce, 172
    White-Wine Herb Sauce, 333
Saucy Chicken and Arugula Meatballs, 179-80, **180**
SAUSAGES. See also Chorizo
    Chimichurri Mixed Grill, 281-82, **281**
    Mediterranean Pepper Salad with Sausages, 282
    Quesadillas, 298-99, **299**
    Rigatoni Timbale alla Gangivecchio, 105
    Sausage and Broccoli Rabe with Polenta, 225-27, **226**
    Smoked Italian Sausages, 25
Sauté of Chicken and Shallots, **174**, 175-76
Sautéed Baby Artichokes with Lemon and Garlic, 317, **317**
Sautéed Cherry Tomatoes with Shallots, **243**, 320
Sautéed Chicken with Herbs and Vermouth, 176
Sautéed Fall Greens with Caraway, 323
Sautéed Mushrooms with Walnuts and Herbs, 322, **323**
Sautéed Pork Scallops with Scallions and Capers, 224, **224**
Sautéed Scallops with Rosemary and Lemon, 120-21, **120**
Sautéing, 121, 171
Savory Artichoke Bread Pudding, **52**, 275-76
Savory Eggplant and Dill Frittata, 30-31
Savory Vegetable and Lamb Stew, **258**, 259

SCALLIONS
  Butternut-Squash Soup with Scallion
    Cream, 77, **77**
  Sautéed Pork Scallops with Scallions and
    Capers, 224, **224**
  Scallion Oil, 242
  Scallion Pancakes, 23
  Steamed Bean Curd with Scallions, 272
SCALLOPS
  Bay Scallops with Sautéed Chanterelles,
    120, 121
  Bay Scallops in Wood-Sorrel Butter Sauce,
    36, **37**
  Mara's Pasta with Broccoli and Scallop
    Sauce, 98-99
  Potato-Chip Tower with Scallops and
    Caviar, 36-38, **38**
  Sautéed Scallops with Rosemary and
    Lemon, 120-21, **120**
  Scallops with Cider, Gewürztraminer and
    Sage, 121-23, **122**
  Scallops in Zucchini Nests, 121
  Seared Sea Scallops, 38-39, **39**
SCOTCH BONNET CHILES. *See also*
Chiles
  Bahamian Grilled Fish, 143
SEA BASS
  Mirin-Glazed Sea Bass with Bok Choy,
    133-34, **133**
  Sake-Glazed Sea Bass, 22-23, **23**
  Sea-Bass Habanero, **132**, 133
Seared Lamb alla Romana, 256, **256**
Seared Salmon on Tartare Mashed Potatoes, 157
Seared Sea Scallops, 38-39, **39**
Seasoned Sliced Pan-Grilled Beef Steaks,
  242-43
Semolina, Corn and, Anadama Bread, 202
SESAME
  Sesame-Coated Striped Bass, 134, **326**
  Sesame-Dressed Haricots Verts in Roast
    Onions, 322
  Sesame Grilled Beef, 246, **247**
SHALLOTS
  Avocado Grapefruit Salad with
    Pomegranate Dressing, 51-52, **51**
  Crab Ravioli with Shallot Cream, 40, **41**
  Crisp Shallots and Shallot Oil, 336
  Sauté of Chicken and Shallots, **174**, 175-76
  Sautéed Cherry Tomatoes with Shallots,
    243, 320
  Shallot-Crusted Roast Halibut, **130**, 131
  Swiss Chard and Shallots, **311**, 323
Shaved-Artichoke Salad, 62
SHELL BEANS. *See also specific kinds*
  Grilled Pork Chops with Succotash,
    220, 221
Shellfish Stew with Chorizo and Rouille, 119-20
SHERRY
  Roasted Pork Loin with Sherry and
    Sautéed Red Onions, 218, **219**
  Sherry-Creamed Lobster with Biscuits,
    115-16
  Sherry-Glazed Pork Chops with Fried
    Sweet Onion Rings, 222, **223**

SHIITAKE MUSHROOMS. *See also*
Mushrooms
  Shiitake Mushroom Sauté with
    Watercress, 322
  Turkey and Mushroom Potpie, 203-204, **203**
SHRIMP
  Casablanca Salad, 66, **66**
  Chile Shrimp and Grits, 118
  Coconut Shrimp with Tamarind
    Vinaigrette, 65
  Crepas Cariocas, 34
  Dilled Shrimp Vol-au-Vents, 34-36, **36**
  Garlic Cheese Grits with Shrimp, 118-19
  Garlic Shrimp, 23
  Green Parsley Risotto with Sautéed
    Shrimp, 32, **33**
  Jicama Cannelloni with Snapper Seviche,
    43, **43**
  Shrimp and Avocado in Mustard
    Vinaigrette, 31, **31**
  Shrimp-and-Avocado Pockets, 295
  Shrimp Purses, 23-24, **24**
  Shrimp in Rich Curried Pea Broth,
    32-34, **32**
  Shrimp with Tomato and Chile Pepper,
    117, **117**
  Shrimp with Yarrow and Baked Lemon,
    31-32, **32**
  Sichuan Shrimp in Lettuce Leaves, 117-18
  Smoked Shrimp, 24, **24**
  Spicy Goan Shrimp, 116-17
  Tandoori Prawns, 119
Sichuan Peppercorn Oil, 206
Sichuan Shrimp in Lettuce Leaves, 117-18
Sicilian Potato and Pasta Soup, 79, **79**
Skillet Ramp Gratin, 318-19, **318**
Skillet-Toasted Almonds, **12**, 13
Slow-Roasted Oxtail Stew with Pancetta,
  249-51
Smoked Acorn Squash, 324
Smoked Cheese, 25
Smoked Chicken Breast, 24-25
Smoked-Fish Chowder, 83-84, **83**
Smoked Italian Sausages, 25
Smoked Molasses-Cured Duck Breasts, 25
Smoked Shrimp, 24, **24**
Smoked-Trout Spread, 14
Smoking, 25, **25**
Smoky Cubano Sandwiches, 299-300, **300**
Smoky Eggplant Dip, 13
Smoky Escarole and Carrot Soup, 80, 81
Smoky Guacamole, 13
Sofrito, 332
Soft-Shell Crabs with Nasturtiums, 39, **39**
SORBET
  Chocolate Sorbet, 400
  Chocolate Soufflé Symphony, 399-400, **399**
  Granny-Smith-Apple Sorbet with Muscat
    and Grappa, 386, 387
  Meringue Bowl with Sorbet and Fruit,
    383, **383**
  Tropical Fruit Soup, 380, **380**
Sorrel Sauce, Poached Salmon in, **152**, 153
Soufflé, Chocolate, Symphony, 399-400, **399**

SOUPS, 68-85
  Apricot Soup, 384, 384
  Bourride of Monkfish and Clams,
    144-45, **145**
  quick tips, 85
  Tropical Fruit Soup, 380, **380**
Sour-Cherry Pancakes, 209
Sourdough Starter, 287
SOY SAUCE
  No-Fat Ginger Soy Dressing, 55
  Red-Cooked Beef with Cinnamon, 239, **239**
  Soy-Sauce Chicken, 180-81
Spaghetti, Christmas, with Walnuts, 102
Spaghetti alla Siracusana, 101-102, **101**
Spanish Mussel and Chorizo Soup, 83
Sparkling Pineapple Punch, 409
Spiced Bourbon Lemon Twists, 413
Spiced Caramels, 400
Spiced Chocolate Caramels, 400
Spiced Lamb Shanks with Almonds and
  Dates, 253-54
SPICES, 336. *See also specific kinds*
  Ginger Tea with Spices, 415
  Golden Rice Pilaf with Spices, 308, **326**
  Home Spice Mix, 56-57
  Nine-Spice Rack of Lamb with Cucumber
    Relish, 251, **250**
  Spice-Crusted Rib-Eye Roast with Garlic
    Jus, **236**, 237
Spicy Bloody Marys, 411, **411**
Spicy Coleslaw, 56
Spicy Goan Shrimp, 116-17
Spicy Harissa, 319
Spicy Red-Pepper Cream, 74
Spicy Rémoulade Sauce, 24
Spicy Ribs, 225, **225**
Spicy Roast Beef with White-and-Black-Bean
  Ragout, 238-39, **238**
Spicy Snapper, **136**, 137
Spicy Steamed Crabs, **112**, 113
Spicy Thai Beef Salad, 282
Spicy Tomato Relish, 191-92, **192**
Spicy Tuna Tartare, 45-47
SPINACH
  Green Salad with Lemon Vinaigrette, 53
  Individual Spinach-and-Cheese-Phyllo Pies,
    21
  Pasta with Cannellini Spinach Pesto, 94, **94**
  Roasted Cod with Bacon-and-Spinach
    Stuffing, 139-40, **139**
  Salmon with Curried Spinach, 153-54, **155**
  Spinach and Crabmeat Soup with
    Country-Ham Croutons, 81-82
  Spinach-Filled Crespelle with Lemon
    Sauce, 98, **98**
  Spinach and Parsley Soup with Lemon,
    74-75, **74**
  Spinach-Stuffed Quail with Apple Frisée
    Salad, 207
SPREADS. *See also* Dips & spreads
Spring Asparagus Salad with Quail-Egg
  Toasts, 62-63, **63**
Squabs, Pinot-Noir-Glazed, with Roasted
  Vegetables, 206-207

SQUASH BLOSSOMS
  Fried Zucchini Blossoms, 319
  Squash-Blossom Rice, 308, **309**
SQUID
  Cioppino, 123-25, **124**
  Olive-Oil and Pinot Blanc Squid with
    Peppers, 123
Starlights, 413, **413**
Steak with Rosemary Oil, 242, **243**
Steamed Bean Curd with Scallions, 272
Steamed Eggplant with Garlic Sauce, 321
Steamed Orange Beef, 248
Stephanie's Poppy Cake, 347-49, **348**
STEWS
  chicken and poultry, 210-11
  fish and shellfish, 116, 119, 123-26
  meat, 241, 249-51, 256-57, **258**, 259
  vegetable, 269-71, **270**, 325, **326**
Stir-Fried Cabbage with Cashews, 324-25
Stock, 80, 153, 202-203, 312
STRAWBERRIES. *See also* Berries; Fruit
  Almond and Strawberry Tart, 362-63, **363**
  Strawberry and Rhubarb Pandowdy,
    376, 377
  Strawberry Tart, **360**, 361
Stuffed Peppers with Couscous and
  Artichokes, **264**, 265
Stuffed Rib-Eye Steaks with Chile Lime Relish,
  241
Stuffed Tomatoes with Vegetables and Pine
  Nuts, 320-21
Stuffed Zucchini Pesaro-Style, 265-66
Stuffing, Anadama Bread and Fig, with Celery
  and Cracklings, 202
Sugar Snap Peas with Mint Oil, 318
Summer Bean and Radish Salad, 58-60, **59**
Summer Bean Stew, 268
Summer Pasta, 90, **90**
Summer Peach Clafoutis, 380, **380**
Summer Squash, Sweet Pepper and Polenta
  Casserole, 271-72, **272**
Summer Stew with Navy Beans and Okra,
  325-26, **326**
SUN-DRIED TOMATOES
  Grilled Salmon with Sun-Dried-Tomato
    Sauce, 150-53, **151**
  Sun-Dried-Tomato Aioli, **332**,
    335, 336
  Vegetable and Sun-Dried-Tomato Tagine,
    268-69
SUNFLOWER SEEDS
  Harvest Crunch, 404, **404**
  Pumpkin-Seed Cupcakes, 350-51, **351**
Sushi Rice, 305-06
Sweet-and-Sour Eggplant with Sautéed Pork,
  223
Sweet-and-Sour Swordfish, 147-48, **148**
Sweet Corn Pancakes with Smoked Salmon,
  44-45, **44**
Sweet Goat-Cheese and Walnut Tartlets, **370**,
  371
Sweet Onion Jam, 331-32
Sweet Onion and Toasted-Walnut Rounds,
  18, **18**

Sweet Peaches with Creamy Zabaglione,
  381, **381**
Sweet Peanut Dressing, 55
Sweet Pea Soup with Chive Oil, 72-73, **73**
SWEET POTATOES. *See also* Vegetables
  Maple-Glazed Sweet Potatoes and Apples,
    313
  Two-Potato Pancakes, **141**, 313
Sweet Sticky Rice Treat, **394**, 395-96
Sweet-Tea-Cured Roast Pork, 216-17
SWISS CHARD
  Roast Chicken Stuffed with Tuscan Chard,
    168-69, **169**
  Swiss Chard and Shallots, **311**, 323
  White-Bean and Swiss-Chard Bruschetta,
    16-17
SWORDFISH
  Sweet-and-Sour Swordfish, 147-48, **148**
  Swordfish Kebabs with Coconut Milk,
    148-49, **148**
  Swordfish with Oregano and Lemon,
    146, **147**
Syrups, 336-37

T

Tabbouleh-Style Three-Grain Salad, 65
Tall Tim's Texas Toasts, 17-18
Tamarind Vinaigrette, Coconut Shrimp with, 65
Tandoori Prawns, 119
Tapenade, 13-14, 332, **332**, 335
Tarragon, Veal Piccata with Orange, Capers
  and, 233
TART(S)
  dessert, 360-371
  pastry, 364, 370
  savory, 19-21, **20**, **28**
TEA
  Ginger Tea with Spices, 415
  Sweet-Tea-Cured Roast Pork, 216-17
  Veal with Green Tea Leaves, 230-32, **231**
TEQUILA
  Cafe Annie Margaritas, 412
  Pomegranate Margaritas, 412
  Tequila Cream Corn, 146
Thai Chicken and Coconut Soup, 85
Thai Jasmine Rice, 306, **306**
Thai Lime Sauce, 334-35
Thai Mushroom Salad, 62, **62**
Thai Red Curry with Mussels, 127, **127**
Thai Sticky Rice, 306, **306**
Three-Cheese-Stuffed Phyllo Triangles,
  21-22
Three-Citrus Custard with Fresh Figs,
  388, 389
THYME
  Pork Rib Roast with Pear Thyme Sauce,
    214, 215
  Roasted Guinea Hen with Red-Wine Thyme
    Sauce, 198, **199**
Toasted Barley Mashed Potatoes, 312, **312**
Toasted Goat Cheese with Mesclun,
  53-54, **54**
Tofu. *See* Bean curd

TOMATILLOS
  Salmon Steaks with Grilled Salsa,
    149-50, **150**
TOMATOES, 336. *See also* Sun-dried
tomatoes; Vegetables
  B.O.A.T. Sandwiches, 301
  Braised Chicken Pizzaiola, 177
  Catalan Tomato Bread, 14, **14**
  Chicken and Red-Rice Curry, 182-83
  Clams with Saffron, Tomato and Garlic,
    125, **125**
  Concentrated Tomato Sauce, 105
  Creamy Butternut Squash, Potato
    and Tomato Gratin, 309-310
  Creamy Garlic Tomato Sauce, 334
  Erica's Eggplant Parmesan, 266-67
  Fresh Tomato Sauce with Pecorino,
    334, **334**, **335**
  Fusilli with Oven-Roasted Tomatoes and
    Chicken, 102-104, **104**
  Goat-Cheese, Tomato and Red-Onion
    Bruschetta, 16, **16**
  Grilled Mahimahi and Green Tomatoes,
    142, 143
  Pasta Shells Stuffed with Grilled Radicchio,
    94-97, **96**
  Penne with Ricotta and Tomato Sauce,
    90-91, **91**
  Red and Yellow Tomato Salad, 57
  Roasted Snapper with Peppers, Pine Nuts
    and Tomatoes, 137-138, **137**
  Roasted Sweet Peppers in Tomato Sauce,
    258, 320
  Roasted Tomato and Eggplant Tian, 321
  Saucy Chicken and Arugula Meatballs,
    179-80, **180**
  Sautéed Cherry Tomatoes with Shallots,
    243, 320
  Shrimp with Tomato and Chile Pepper,
    117, **117**
  Spicy Bloody Marys, 411, **411**
  Spicy Tomato Relish, 191-92, **192**
  Stuffed Tomatoes with Vegetables and
    Pine Nuts, 320-21
  Summer Pasta, 90, **90**
  Tomato Sauce, 89-90, **89**
  Tomato Sauce with Olives, Golden Raisins
    and Pine Nuts, 140-41
  Tomatoes with Pesto Oil, **28**, 29
  Yellow Tomato Gazpacho with Olivata
    Croutons, **70**, 71
Torta di Riso, 349
Torte, St. Gallen Kloster, 397-98, **397**
TORTILLAS, 299
  Black-Bean and Roasted-Vegetable
    Burritos, 273, **273**
  Catfish Tacos with Tequila Cream Corn,
    146
  Huevos Rancheros, 274-75, **274**
  Quesadillas, 298-99, **299**
  Tortilla Salad, 279
  Tortilla Soup, 85
Triple-Chocolate Candy-Cane Kisses, 399
Tropical Fruit Soup, 380, **380**

TROUT, SMOKED
    Smoked-Fish Chowder, 83-84, **83**
    Smoked-Trout Spread, 14
True Texas Barbecue Sauce, 172
Trussing chicken, 166
Tuiles, Rosemary, 356
TUNA
    Marinated Poached Fresh Tuna with Caper
      and Anchovy Sauce, 159-61, **160**
    Pan-Flashed Ahi, 46
    Spicy Tuna Tartare, 45-47
    Tuna Burgers with Sesame Slaw, 297, **297**
    Tuna and Potato Salad, 67
TURKEY, 198-206
    sandwiches, 297-98, **298**
    stock, 202-203
TURNIPS. *See also* Vegetables
    Mashed Turnips and Potatoes, 312
Two-Potato Pancakes, **141**, 313

U

The Ultimate Chocolate Pudding, **392**, 393

V

VANILLA, 336
    Panforte with Pears and Vanilla Cream,
      387
    Vanilla-Bean Syrup, 337
VEAL, 230-33
    with pasta, 105
    soups, 84-85, **84**
    for stews, 255
    Stuffed Zucchini Pesaro-Style, 265-66
VEGETABLES, 318-32. *See also specific
kinds*
    Black-Bean and Roasted-Vegetable
      Burritos, 273, **273**
    Braised Spring Vegetables, **185**, 318
    Casserole Roast Chicken and Root
      Vegetables, 169-71
    Creamy Root-Vegetable Soup, 75
    Georgian Lamb and Vegetable Stew, 256
    Mid-Winter Soup, 80-81
    New World Ciambotta, 267-68
    Parmesan-Crusted Vegetarian
      Sandwiches, 294-95, **294**
    Peperonata, **318**, 319
    picking tips, 321
    Pinot-Noir-Glazed Squabs with Roasted
      Vegetables, 206-207
    Roasted Root Vegetables, 325, **325**
    Roasted-Vegetable Bruschetta, 14-15, **15**
    Roasted-Vegetable and Fontina Tarts,
      19-21, **20**, **28**
    Roasted-Vegetable Soup, 75-77, **76**
    Savory Vegetable and Lamb Stew, **258**,
      259
    Tomato Sauce with Olives, Golden Raisins
      and Pine Nuts, 140-41
    Vegetable Mixed Grill, 267, **267**
    Vegetable Stock, 312
    Vegetable-Studded Couscous, 109

Vegetable and Sun-Dried-Tomato Tagine,
    268-69
Winter Vegetable Stew with a Cheddar
    Crust, 269-71, **270**
Venison, 259-61
VERMOUTH
    Sautéed Chicken with Herbs and
      Vermouth, 176
Vinaigrettes, 38-39, 53, 54, 58, **58**, 60, 63,
    65, 277-79, **277**. *See also* Salad
    dressings
VINEGAR. *See also* Vinaigrettes
    Balsamic-Glazed Rack of Venison,
      259-60, **260**
    Balsamic-Marinated Beef Tenderloin,
      237-38, **238**
    Brussels Sprouts with Walnuts, Balsamic
      Vinegar and Mint, **200**, 324
    Chicken Thighs with Malt Vinegar, 192
    Crispy Salmon with Balsamic Glaze,
      155-56, **156**
    Roast Pork with Balsamic Onion
      Marmalade, **54**, 218
VODKA
    Cosmopolitan, 415
    Rose-Hip Vodka, **410**, 411
    Spicy Bloody Marys, 411, **411**

W

Wafers, Clove and Lemon Butter, 356
WALNUTS. *See also* Nuts
    Brussels Sprouts with Walnuts,
      Balsamic Vinegar and Mint, **200**, 324
    Christmas Spaghetti with Walnuts, 102
    Crystal-Coated Walnuts, 404, **404**
    Sautéed Mushrooms with Walnuts and
      Herbs, 322, **323**
    Sweet Goat-Cheese and Walnut Tartlets,
      370, 371
    Sweet Onion and Toasted-Walnut Rounds,
      18, **18**
Warm Green Salad with Lobster and Oranges,
    276
Warm Polenta Pancakes with Peaches and
    Mascarpone, 381-82, **381**
Warm Potato Salad with Gamay Noir
    Vinaigrette, 157-59
WATERCRESS. *See also* Salads
    Fennel and Watercress Salad with
      Cranberries and Pecans, 52
    Shiitake Mushroom Sauté with
      Watercress, 322
    Watercress Salad, 52
WAX BEANS
    Summer Bean and Radish Salad,
      58-60, **59**
    Wax-Bean Salad with Toasted Hazelnuts, 60
Wehani Rice, 306, **306**
Whiskey and White Peppercorn Syrup, 336
WHITE BEANS. *See also* Beans, Canned
or Dried; Cannellini beans
    Spicy Roast Beef with White-and-
      Black-Bean Ragout, 238-39, **238**

Summer Stew with Navy Beans and Okra,
    325-26, **326**
White-Bean and Swiss-Chard Bruschetta,
    16-17
White-Chocolate Bread Pudding, 394-95
White Peaches with Crushed Raspberries,
    382
WHITE WINE. *See also* Wine; *specific
kinds*
    Veal Shanks Braised in White Wine, 230
    White-Wine Herb Sauce, 333
White-Wing-Dove-Style Grilled Quail, 209
Wild-Berry Compote, 347
Wild-Mushroom and Cheese Pizza, 293-94,
    294
Wild-Mushroom Fettuccine, 92, **93**
Wild Rice with Grapes and Toasted Almonds,
    308, **308**
Wilted Arugula and Prosciutto Frittata, **28**, 31
WINE. *See also* Red wine; White wine;
    specific kinds
    Fall Wine Punch, 410, **410**
    with seafood, 115, 150
    of Sicily, 97
WINTER SQUASH. *See also* Butternut
squash; Vegetables
    Smoked Acorn Squash, 324
    Winter-Squash and Carrot Puree, 324
Winter Vegetable Stew with a Cheddar Crust,
    269-71, **270**
Wok-smoking techniques, 25, **25**
Wood-Sorrel Butter Sauce, Bay Scallops in,
    36, **37**

Y

Yarrow and Baked Lemon, Shrimp with,
    31-32, **32**
YELLOW SUMMER SQUASH. *See also*
Vegetables
    Scallops in Zucchini Nests, 121
    Summer Squash, Sweet Pepper and
      Polenta Casserole, 271-72, **272**
Yellow Tomato Gazpacho with Olivata
    Croutons, **70**, 71
YOGURT
    Chilled Make-Ahead Summer Oatmeal, 283
    Cool Cucumber Yogurt Dip, 332
YUCA, 35, **35**
    Fried Yuca Turnovers with Black Beans and
      Chorizo, 30, **30**

Z

ZUCCHINI. *See also* Vegetables
    Fried Zucchini Blossoms, 319
    Minted Zucchini Patties, 19
    Penne with Sautéed Zucchini and Ricotta,
      91-92, **92**
    Scallops in Zucchini Nests, 121
    Stuffed Zucchini Pesaro-Style, 265-66
    Summer Squash, Sweet Pepper and
      Polenta Casserole, 271-72, **272**
    Zucchini with Spicy Harissa, **189**, 323

contributors

Joe Abuso is a chef and caterer based in Houston, Texas.

Jody Adams is chef and owner of the Rialto restaurant in Boston.

Jeffrey Alford and **Naomi Duguid** are cookbook authors, food writers and photographers. Their forthcoming book, *The Seductions of Rice* (Artisan), is due out in October of 1998.

Robert Barnett is the author of *Tonics* (Harper-Perennial).

Michel Benasra, the creator and owner of Baby Guess and Guess Home Collection, is an accomplished amateur chef.

Carole Bloom is a cookbook author, food writer, cooking teacher, pastry chef and confectioner. Her forthcoming book, *All About Chocolate* (Macmillan), is due out in October of 1998.

Charles Bowman is the chef at the Periyali restaurant in New York City.

Georgeanne Brennan is a cookbook author, food writer and cooking teacher. Her latest book is *The Food & Flavors of Haute Provence* (Chronicle).

George W. Brown, Jr., named one of America's Best New Chefs of 1997 by FOOD & WINE, is the chef at Seventeen Seventeen in Dallas.

Jocelyn Bulow is co-owner and occasional chef of Plouf in San Francisco.

Bob Chambers is the executive chef for Lancôme/L'Oreal in New York City.

Steven Chiappetti is chef/owner of Mango in Chicago.

Julia Child, well-known cookbook author, food writer and teacher, is the host of her own television series, *Baking With Julia.*

Josiah Citrin and **Raphael Lunetta**, named two of America's Best New Chefs of 1997 by FOOD & WINE, are chefs and owners of JiRaffe in Santa Monica, California.

Tony Clark, named one of America's Best New Chefs of 1997 by FOOD & WINE, is the chef/owner of the Philadelphia restaurant Tony Clark's.

John Cochran, named one of America's Best New Chefs of 1997 by FOOD & WINE, is the chef at Rupperts in Washington, D.C.

Jim Cohen is the executive chef at The Phoenecian Resort in Scottsdale, Arizona.

Michael Cordúa is a chef and owner of Churroscos and Américas restaurants in Houston. He was named one of FOOD & WINE's Best New Chefs in 1994.

Elaine Corn is a chef and cookbook author. Her most recent book is *Now You're Cooking for Company* (Harlow & Ratner).

Peggy Cullen is a New-York-City-based pastry chef, candymaker and food writer.

Amanda Cushman, a freelance food writer, is a member of the faculty of Peter Kump's New York Cooking School.

Gary Danko, one of FOOD & WINE's Best New Chefs of 1989, is the chef of Viognier in Draeger's in San Mateo, California.

Erica De Mane, a chef and cookbook author, is currently working on a cookbook to be published by Scribner.

Robert Del Grande is the chef/owner of Cafe Annie in Houston, Texas.

Malachy Duffy is a former senior editor at FOOD & WINE.

Joshua Eisen has worked as a chef in New York City. He currently writes and consults on both wine and food for *Fine Cooking*, *Wine & Spirits* and FOOD & WINE.

Jonathan Eismann is a chef and co-owner of the restaurants Pacific Time in Miami Beach and Pacific Heights in Coral Gables, Florida.

Todd English is chef and owner of two Boston restaurants, Olives and Figs. His most recent book, co-authored with Sally Sampson, is *The Olives Table* (Simon & Schuster).

Amy Farges is a food writer and owner of Aux Delices des Bois, a distributor of wild mushrooms. She is currently working on a cookbook due out from Workman in the spring of 1998.

Dean Fearing is the chef of The Mansion on Turtle Creek in Dallas.

Susan Feniger and **Mary Sue Milliken** are chefs and television co-hosts of *Too Hot Tamales* on the Food Network. Their latest cookbook is *Cooking with Too Hot Tamales* (William Morrow).

John Fleer is the chef of the Inn at Blackberry Farm in Tennessee.

Gale Gand is a chef and co-owner, with her husband, Rick Tramonto, of Brasserie T. in Boston. Their latest cookbook is *American Brasserie* (Macmillan).

Alex Garcia is chef/owner of Erizo Latino restaurant in New York City.

Darra Goldstein, the author of *The Vegetarian Hearth* (HarperCollins), teaches Russian in Williamstown, Massachusetts.

Dorie Greenspan is a cookbook author whose most recent cookbooks are *Baking With Julia* and *Pancakes from Morning to Midnight* (William Morrow).

Mireille Guiliano is the president of Clicquot, Inc., whose wines include Veuve Clicquot Champagnes.

Gordon Hamersley is the chef/owner of Hamersley's Bistro in Boston.

Larry Hayden is a pastry chef and teacher at Barefoot Contessa Fine Foods in East Hampton, New York. His forthcoming book, *Sweet Success!* (Scribner), is due out in the spring of 1998.

Marcella Hazan is a master chef and the author of *Essentials of Classic Italian Cooking* (Knopf). Her latest book is *Marcella Cucina* (HarperCollins).

Reed Hearon is chef/owner of Rose Pistola in San Francisco.

Maria Helm, the chef of PlumpJack Cafe in San Francisco, was named one of FOOD & WINE's Best New Chefs in 1996.

James Henahan is the executive chef for the restaurant in Simon Pierce's showroom in Quechee, Vermont.

David Hirsch, **Linda Dickinson** and **Susan Harville** are co-owners of the Moosewood Restaurant in Ithaca, New York, and co-authors of six cookbooks.

Peter Hoffman is chef/owner of Savoy restaurant in New York City.

John Hopkins, a food writer and cookbook author, is the camp chef for Don Donnelly's Cowboy Ride of Don Donnelly's Horseback Vacations.

Nancy Harmon Jenkins's latest cookbook is *Flavors of Puglia* (Broadway Books). She is working on a PBS series entitled *A Taste of the Mediterranean.*

Brian J. Karam is a pastry chef in Michigan.

Warren Katz is a teacher at Peter Kump's School of Culinary Arts in New York City.

Tim Keating is executive chef at the Four Seasons Hotel in Houston.

Kelsie Kerr is chef, with Marsha McBride, of Café Rouge in Berkeley, California. The two were named among America's Best New Chefs of 1997 by FOOD & WINE.

Marcia Kiesel is the associate director of FOOD & WINE's test kitchen and a co-author of *Simple Art of Vietnamese Cooking* (Simon & Schuster).

Sotohiro Kosugi, named one of America's Best New Chefs of 1997 by FOOD & WINE, is chef/owner of Soto Japanese Restaurant in Atlanta, Georgia.

Nicola Kotsoni is co-owner of the Periyali restaurant in New York City.

Emeril Lagasse, a chef and owner of Emeril's and NOLA restaurants in New Orleans and Emeril's New Orleans Fish House in Las Vegas, hosts two cooking shows on the Food Network. His latest cookbook is *Emeril's Creole Christmas* (William Morrow).

Anna Tasca Lanza is a chef and cookbook author. Her latest book is *The Heart of Sicily* (Clarkson Potter).

Seen Lippert is the chef at the restaurant Across the Street in New York City.

Keith Luce, named one of America's Best New Chefs of 1997 by FOOD & WINE, is chef at Spruce in Chicago.

Egi Maccioni is the wife and partner of Sirio Maccioni, the owner of Le Cirque 2000 in New York City. She is a partner, with her husband and sons, of Osteria del Circo, also in New York City.

George Mahaffey is a chef and cookbook author. His latest book is *Country Inn–The Best of Casual Country Cooking* (Sunset Books).

Nick Malgieri, a pastry chef and author of *How to Bake*, is the head of the baking program at Peter Kump's Cooking School in New York City.

Marsha McBride is chef, with Kelsie Kerr, of Café Rouge in Berkeley, California. The two were named among America's Best New Chefs of 1997 by FOOD & WINE.

Tim McKee, named one of America's Best New Chefs of 1997 by FOOD & WINE, is chef of D'Amico Cucina in Minneapolis.

Rick Moonen is chef and owner of Oceana Restaurant in New York City.

Tina Nicodemo is chef at La Cantina del Triunfo in Naples.

Cary Neff is chef at the Miraval Resort in Catalina, Arizona.

Jan Newberry, a cookbook editor, food writer and FOOD & WINE columnist, lives in Oakland, California.

Bradley Ogden, a chef and restaurateur, is the author of *Bradley Ogden's Breakfast, Lunch & Dinner* (Random House).

David Page is chef and co-owner, with his wife, Barbara Shinn, of Home Restaurant and Drovers Tap Room in New York City.

Charlie Palmer is chef and owner of the restaurant Aureole in New York City.

Tylun Pang is executive chef at Kea Kani Hotel in Maui, Hawaii.

Grace Parisi, a chef and food stylist, is the test kitchen associate for FOOD & WINE. She has written *Summer/Winter Pasta* (Quill).

François Payard is a pastry chef and co-owner, with Daniel Boulud, of Payard Pâtisserie & Bistro in New York City.

Jacques Pépin is a master chef, TV personality, food columnist, cookbook author and cooking teacher.

Colette Peters, an ace cake decorator, is the author of *Colette's Wedding Cakes*.

James Peterson is a chef and cookbook author. He is the author of *Fish and Shellfish* (William Morrow).

Steven Raichlen is a cookbook author and cooking instructor.

Gary and Mardee Haidin Regan are writers and consultants on wine and spirits.

Susan Regis is the chef at Biba restaurant in Boston.

Susan Lantzius Rich is associate editor and recipe developer/tester for FOOD & WINE Books.

Michael Roberts is a chef, food consultant, cookbook author and food writer. He is currently working on *Paris at Home* (William Morrow), due out in 1998.

Ruth Rogers and Rose Gray are the chef/owners of The River Café in London.

Michael Romano is chef/co-owner of Union Square Cafe in New York City.

Nira Rousso is a popular chef, cookbook author and food columnist in Israel.

Laura Byrne Russell is assistant editor and recipe developer/tester for FOOD & WINE Books.

Pilar Sanchez is chef of the Wine Center at Meadowood, a Napa Valley resort.

Chris Schlesinger is chef/owner of East Coast Grill & Raw Bar in Boston.

Sally Schneider is a chef, cookbook author, food writer and columnist for FOOD & WINE. Her forthcoming book, *A New Way To Cook* (Scribner), is due out at the end of 1998.

Cory Schreiber is chef/owner of Wildwood Restaurant & Bar in Portland, Oregon.

Lydia Shire is chef/owner of the restaurants Biba and Pignoli in Boston.

Jane Sigal is a senior editor at FOOD & WINE.

Dan Silverman, named one of America's Best New Chefs of 1997 by FOOD & WINE, is the chef at the restaurant Alison on Dominick in New York City.

Rori Spinelli is a professional cook and a freelance food stylist who is based in New York City.

Joachim Splichal, a cookbook author and food consultant, is chef/owner of Patina and Pinot Bistro in Los Angeles.

Heidi Steele is pastry chef of Moose's in San Francisco.

Sarah Stegner is chef at The Dining Room of The Ritz-Carlton hotel in Chicago.

Diana Sturgis is the test-kitchen director at FOOD & WINE.

Judith Sutton is a professional cook/pastry chef, food writer, cookbook editor and food consultant.

John Martin Taylor, owner of Hoppin' John's, a culinary bookstore and cooking school in Charleston, South Carolina, is a food writer and the author of *The Fearless Frying Cookbook* (Workman).

Katrin Theodoli is a cook and president/owner of Magnum Marine, a speedboat company in Miami.

Giovanna Tornabene is a chef and the author of *La Cucina Siciliana di Gangivecchio* (Knopf).

Antonio Visetti is chef and owner of the restaurant La Minose in Sicily.

Jean-Georges Vongerichten is chef/owner of the restaurants Jean Georges, Vong and Jo Jo in New York City.

Heather Watts and Jock Soto are New York City Ballet stars and the authors of *Our Meals* (Riverhead Books).

Jasper White is a consulting chef for Legal Sea Foods in Boston and various other restaurants and hotels in the United States, Canada and the Caribbean.

John Willoughby, a chef and co-author, with Chris Schlesinger, of *Lettuce in Your Kitchen* (William Morrow), is a frequent contributor to *The New York Times*.

Herb Wilson is chef at Bambou restaurant in New York City.

Victoria Wise is co-author of *The Well-Filled Tortilla* (Workman).

Marvin Woods is a Miami-based chef. His first cookbook, *Southern Exposure* (Random House), is due out in 1998.

Eileen Yin-Fei Lo is a cooking teacher, cookbook author and food writer. Her most recent cookbook is *The Chinese Way: Healthy Low-Fat Cooking from China's Regions* (Macmillan).

We would also like to thank the following individuals and restaurants for their contributions to this cookbook:

Apicius Culinary Consulting Co., New York City; Bistro 110, Chicago; The Hotel Jerome, Aspen; Le Bar Lyonnais, Philadelphia; Palace Café, New Orleans; the Frescobaldi and Mondavi wine families; and Connie Serrette and Allen Zeringue.

photo credits

William Abranowicz: 160, 224, 386; Melanie Acevedo: 6, 24, 25, 84, 104, 138, 147, 150, 157, 182, 193, 198, 226, 238, 284, 292, 297; Edward Addeo: 4, 398; Quentin Bacon: 7, 10, 18, 20, 29, 28, 66, 68, 78, 108, 139, 186, 258, 261, 330, 364, 367, 381, 408; Fernando Bengoechea: 54, 189, 326; Bill Bettencourt: 12, 18, 32, 39, 43, 48, 59, 63, 74, 79, 80, 92, 94, 96, 107, 109, 120, 156, 168, 185, 199, 212, 220, 273, 294, 300, 311, 357, 363, 370, 410; Anita Calero: 14, 38, 39, 46, 148, 172, 184, 208, 247, 267, 380, 410; Beatriz Da Costa: 41, 62, 73, 151, 152, 236, 276, 296, 304, 306, 307, 333, 340, 344, 387, 392, 394, 397, 399; Reed Davis: 14, 23, 29, 30, 33, 35, 43, 79, 83, 112, 200, 203, 227, 241, 281, 332, 334, 335; Miki Duisterhof: 51, 214, 353, 379, 383, 406, 413, 414; Mark Ferri: 91, 101, 103, 390, 401, 402; Timothy Greenfield-Sanders: 72, 178, 360; Gentl & Hyers: 36, 50, 86, 93, 169, 274, 365; Noelle Hoeppe: 17, 90, 318; Ruedi Hofmann: 42, 133, 144, 286, 298, 343; Matthew Hranek: 4, 23, 24, 31, 40, 44, 58, 66, 70, 120, 223, 338, 342, 352, 354, 355, 357, 409; Ken Kochey: 217, 260, 308, 312; Maura McEvoy: 189, 323, 345; Micheal McLaughlin: 26, 32, 37, 117, 135, 167, 230, 234, 240, 250, 291, 314, 325, 346, 384; Michael James O'Brien: 57, 316; Daniel Proctor: 52, 411; Maria Robledo: 290, 310; Jeremy Samuelson: 127, 132, 170, 174, 176, 191, 192; Zubin Shroff: 82, 114, 175; Evan Sklar: 244; Laurie Smith: 376, 377, 378; Ann Stratton: 2, 8, 15, 61, 76, 88, 95, 98, 101, 110, 122, 124, 125, 126, 128, 130, 136, 137, 142, 145, 148, 158, 164, 180, 181 194, 205, 216, 219, 223, 225, 229, 231, 238, 239, 243, 244, 254, 262, 264, 270, 278, 280, 299, 317, 318 351, 352, 368, 372 373, 374, 388, 404; Luca Trovato: 54, 77, 141, 257; Simon Watson: 55, 91, 100, 162, 188, 256, 277, 289; Jonelle Weaver: 16, 44, 89, 165, 166, 196, 256, 272, 294, 302, 309, 320, 348, 362, 364, 381, 393, 396.